STUDIES IN THE HISTORY OF ART · 82 ·

Center for Advanced Study in the Visual Arts

Symposium Papers LIX

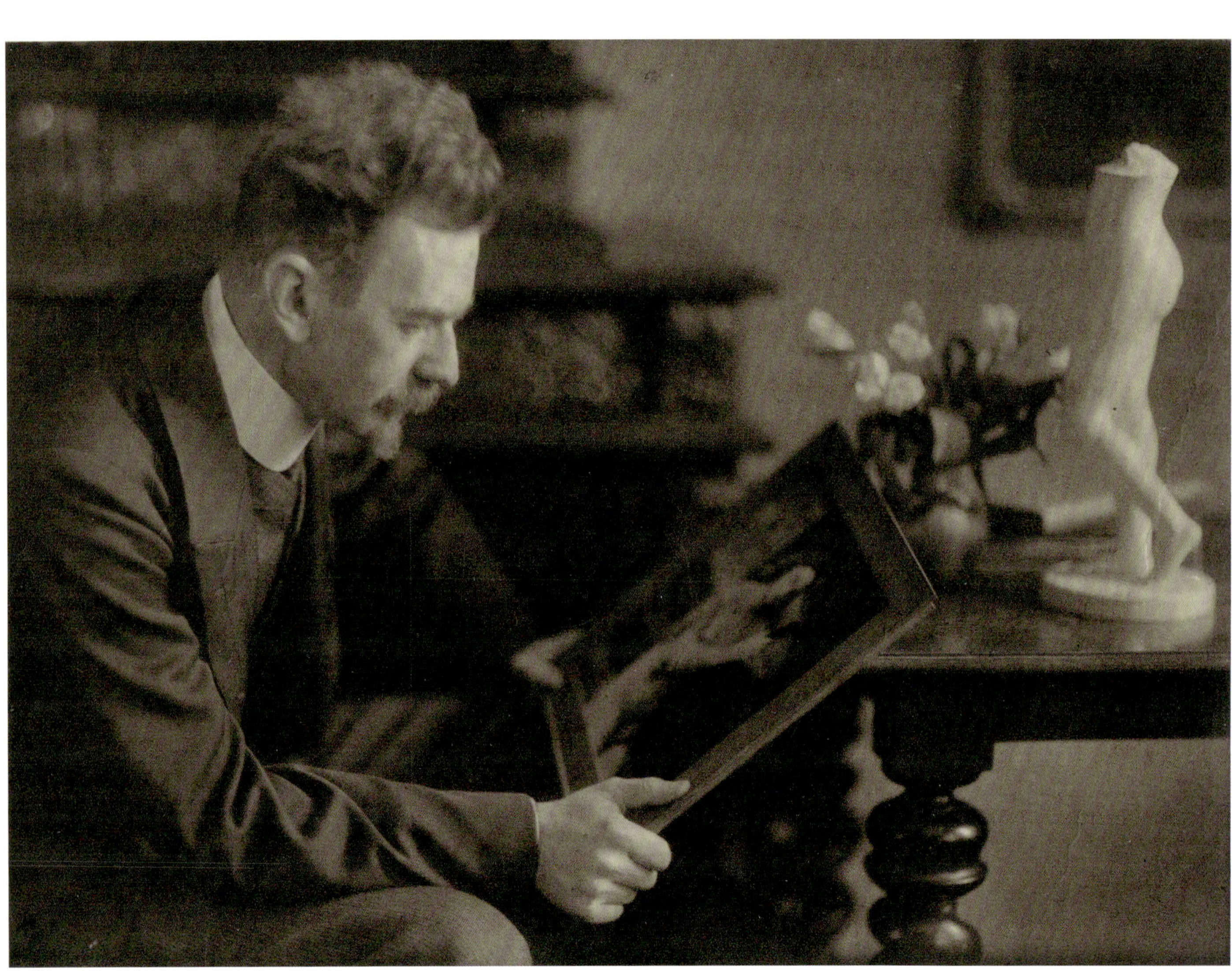

The Global Reception of Heinrich Wölfflin's
Principles of Art History

Edited by

EVONNE LEVY AND TRISTAN WEDDIGEN

National Gallery of Art, Washington

Distributed by Yale University Press
New Haven and London

This volume was produced by the Center for Advanced Study in the Visual Arts and the Publishing Office, National Gallery of Art, Washington
www.nga.gov

Editor in Chief
EMIKO K. USUI

Deputy Publisher and Production Manager
CHRIS VOGEL

Series Editor
THERESE O'MALLEY

Managing Editor
CYNTHIA WARE

Design Manager
WENDY SCHLEICHER

Program Assistants
ANNIE G. MILLER
JENNIFER ROKOSKI
CATHERINE SOUTHWICK

Typesetting and layout by Antje Kharchi
Typeset in Sabon and Whitney
Color separations by Altaimage, London and New York
Printed on Gardamatt by Conti Tipocolor in Italy

Distributed by Yale University Press
New Haven and London
www.yalebooks.com/art

Abstracted and indexed in BHA (Bibliography of the History of Art) and Art Index

Proceedings of the symposium "The Global Reception of Heinrich Wölfflin's *Principles of Art History* (1915–2015)," organized by the Center for Advanced Study in the Visual Arts, National Gallery of Art, and sponsored by the Arthur Vining Davis Foundations and the Social Sciences and Humanities Research Council of Canada. The symposium was held May 8–9, 2015, in Washington.

The Center for Advanced Study in the Visual Arts was founded in 1979 at the National Gallery of Art to foster the study of the history, theory, and criticism of art, architecture, urbanism, and photographic media, through programs of meetings, research, publication, and fellowships, and through the formation of a community of scholars.

Library of Congress Control Number: 2020930808

ISBN 978-0-300-25047-3
ISSN 0091-7338

Frontispiece: Heinrich Wölfflin, 1903, photograph by R. Dührkoop. © Universitätsbibliothek der Humboldt-Universität zu Berlin, Porträtsammlung

Contents

Preface

The publication of Heinrich Wölfflin's *Kunstgeschichtliche Grundbegriffe: Das Problem der Stilentwicklung in der Neueren Kunst* by F. Bruckmann in Munich in 1915 was inauspicious. The author's preface opens by saying that the book "ought to have been rather different." Constrained by the circumstances of World War 1, the Swiss art historian, then teaching in Munich, was determined to make his arguments as concise as possible, and he hoped to stimulate the reader to go beyond his text by including numerous black-and-white photographs, omitting for economy images that were well known.

At 260 pages, this was by no means a slender volume, but the 120 images were carefully laid out within running text and, by this placement, strengthened Wölfflin's arguments considerably. Where appropriate, such images as portraits by Albrecht Dürer and Frans Hals, or Magdalenes by Jan van Scorel and Guido Reni, appear on facing pages for easy comparison. This arrangement now seems ideal for the study of art history, but it was not then standard practice. Other wartime productions, such as Carl Neumann's *Aus der Werkstatt Rembrandts* (Heidelberg, 1918), followed the earlier model provided by the Kunstler-Monographien series, which, with the publication of Hermann Knackfuss's volume on Raphael (Bielefeld and Leipzig, 1898) inaugurated the layout of black-and-white images appropriately in sequence within the text. But these were monographs, illustrating works by single artists in chronological order, and the images did not challenge the reader to engage in visual dialogues between works by different masters from different traditions.

Wölfflin's innovation does not stand entirely alone, for this was a moment of creative thinking in the German art book world. A notable example is Carl Einstein's *Negerplastik*, also published in 1915, but in Leipzig. In this volume, just 27 pages of introductory text precede 108 carefully edited and manipulated original photographs of African sculptures. The author wanted to insist that these unfamiliar sculptures were truly works of art, and by publishing the photographs of them to such a high standard, as works of art in themselves, without text or even captions, he achieved his purpose. Einstein's definition of the painterly, or *malerisch*, in sculpture was influenced by hearing Wölfflin's lectures in Berlin even before the publication of *Principles*, but in 1915 his book took quite a different stance toward the relationship of text and image. Wölfflin's pairing of images in his slide lectures has often been identified as establishing a new paradigm in the teaching of art history; the visual argument of *Principles*, considered a publishing sensation, was equally ground-breaking. The book sold out immediately and was reissued in 1917, with only a few additions. Wartime strictures on space and paper, it would seem, contributed to the precision and accessibility of arguments that might otherwise have been clouded by detail.

The subsequent reputation of *Principles* has been extraordinary, if not always positive. The sixteen essays in this volume document the intense scrutiny to which the work has been subjected through the difficult process of translation, sometimes into languages for which no corresponding critical terms existed previously. As several authors point out, these terms, especially after the first translation of *Principles* into Spanish in 1924 and into English in 1932 (with an important reprint by Dover Publications in 1950) have become naturalized in the language of the history of art, a sort of practical theory that has cast aside many of its author's original precepts. This process has often glossed over aspects of *Principles* that, on closer examination, require a persistent reassessment of the text and its author. The history of the global publication, translation, and critical reception of Wölfflin's *Principles* as it enters the second century since its initial publication certainly presents an opportunity to consider the modern history of art as such, and several authors have taken that opportunity in their essays. On the positive side of the balance, Wölfflin's interests in theories of empathy have found new resonance, and the intense visual analysis he espoused has returned to respectability. His concept of the baroque, which had special critical resonance in Latin America, has stimulated renewed discussion, even as his failure to understand or define mannerism has passed the point of being interesting.

Several of these essays also call urgent attention to the question of race, which undergirds Wölfflin's theories of differences in national and geographical traditions. However useful *Principles* may turn out to be as a pedagogical tool, the question of its global reception, and indeed of a global art history, cannot ignore the extent to which art history in the first half of the twentieth century was infected by unfounded racial theories. Wölfflin's publisher, Hugo Bruckmann, and his wife, Elsa, were among the first supporters of Adolf Hitler in Munich and promoted National Socialism in the 1920s. By 1948 Bruckmann Verlag had published nine editions of *Principles*, seven of these by 1929, though Wölfflin had left Munich for Zurich in 1924. Several authors in this volume allude to the eventual rejection of Wölfflinian formalism in the 1960s and 1970s, with the arrival of structuralist and poststructuralist theory and the New Art History. Others, however, underline the ways in which Wölfflin's racial determinism (which was by no means unique to him) was found to be profoundly unacceptable long before that. The naturalizing, or "detheorizing," of *Principles* was at a certain point a "deracializing." That this could be accomplished so smoothly in the process of stripping the text down to its pedagogical essence is one indicator of just how contingent and prejudiced those theories were.

Evonne Levy and Tristan Weddigen, the scholarly editors of this volume, came to us several years ago with a proposition that the Center for Advanced Study in the Visual Arts organize a symposium in 2015 to celebrate the centenary of the publication of *Principles of Art History*. For both colleagues the event represented a culmination of their extensive international efforts to investigate the continuing importance of the volume and its past reception. Since 2012 Professor Levy has directed the Wölfflin Project at the University of Toronto through a series of seminars and meetings dedicated to the study of *Principles*. Professor Weddigen, formerly of the University of Zurich and now director of the Bibliotheca Hertziana, Max-Planck-Institut für Kunstgeschichte, in Rome, has had a longstanding interest in Wölfflin, and, together with Oskar Bätschmann, is engaged in publishing a new German edition and French translation of all of Wölfflin's writings. His related project "New Art Histories: Connecting Ideas, Objects, and Institutions in Latin

America," a collaboration between the University of Zurich and the Universidade Federal de São Paulo, Brazil, was supported by the Getty Foundation from 2011 to 2015, and his essay in this volume is one of its outcomes. Together, Levy and Weddigen edited a new English translation of *Principles* by Jonathan Blower, published by the Getty Research Institute in 2015. This elegant and affordable edition put *Principles*, together with editorial notes, Wölfflin's own prefaces, and critical introductions by the editors, in the hands of a new generation. Such intense focus on the text made the study of its reception and influence all the more pressing.

The symposium held at the National Gallery of Art on May 8–9, 2015, included all the speakers whose papers are published here, with the exception of Robert Born. Support for the symposium was provided by the Arthur Vining Davis Foundations, with further funding from the Social Sciences and Humanities Research Council of Canada. This publication was made possible by the Kress-Fontaine Fund for Scholarly Publications on European Works of Art in the Classical Tradition at the National Gallery of Art; the Social Sciences and Humanities Research Council of Canada; and a special endowment for scholarly publications at CASVA from the Andrew W. Mellon Foundation. As always, CASVA is indebted to Cynthia Ware in the publishing office of the National Gallery of Art. In this case, given the unusual difficulties presented by essays in multiple languages and by authors from different traditions, our debt is even greater. Chris Vogel and Wendy Schleicher of the publishing office managed production and design. Associate Dean Therese O'Malley has supervised and encouraged the project from the beginning. The appearance of this volume is a tribute to her and to her staff, especially Annie Miller, Jennifer Rokoski, and Catherine Southwick. Helen Tangires and Jeannette Shindell managed administration of the process throughout.

In conclusion, and looking back at the 2015 symposium, it is remarkable that most art historians working today continue to have some view of Wölfflin's importance and value. My own tripos examinations in Cambridge asked for discussion of Herbert Read's proposal that Wölfflin "had taken art history from chaos to scientific method." It was a loaded question, of course, but exactly what is wrong with Wölfflin's highly adaptive method demands continuing critical analysis. In 2015 David Summers regretted that he could not attend our conference but sent some thoughts. "I was much impressed," he wrote, "on my first youthful reading, but disappointed at the end when he could not explain how Delacroix and Ingres could be painting in the same place at the same time. Unraveling that problem as a theoretical problem has taken the rest of my life.…I very much hope your conference encourages thinking beyond Wölfflin's *Principles*, as opposed to encouraging their renewed uncritical use." These essays tell a series of remarkable stories about the power of a book and its readers to make a global impact that is as much about resistance as application, as much about productive challenges as considerable inadequacies.

ELIZABETH CROPPER
Dean, Center for Advanced Study in the Visual Arts

Vorwort

Eigentlich sollte der Text anders werden sollen. Nachdem ich über die Grundgedanken bereits vor einigen Jahren einmal vorläufig mich ausgesprochen hatte (Sitzungsbericht der Berliner Akademie der Wissenschaften 1912. XXXI), war es natürlich die einzelnen Begriffe nun in erhöhter Verdeutung festlicher durchzuführen.

Es muß endlich eine künstlerische Kontur, so wie Schritt auf Schritt die Entwicklung der modernen Kunst verfolgen kann, eine Kunstgeschichte, die nicht von einzelnen Künstlern erzählt, sondern in Rückenlage das Reich zeigt, wie aus einem lineareren Stil ein malerischer geworden ist, aus einem statuarischen ein architektonischer. Diese Entwicklung in ihrer Verzweigung, von Herauszeichnung, Verkürzzeichnung nachzuweisen, ist noch nicht die ganze Aufgabe, es müsste die einzelne Zielvorstellung im allgemeinen, die Kräfte der Zeit vorstellung überhaupt derselben werden, die Schwierung bezieht eine einzige d. d acksig, aber auch architektonisch geordnet. Zu den darstellenden Künsten Einzelnotizen Arbeiten.

An solche einstufigen Darlegungen aber ist jetzt mitten im Kriege, nicht zu denken. Kein Verleger, der auf die kostspielige Bildwerke sich einlassen. Die, die umständliche Forschung einer solchen künstgültigen Ihre Wemsen sein würden. Deshalb gebe ich meine Einzelnotizen auf einen möglichst kurzen und einfachen Ausdruck, so daß ich unter Verzicht auf alles Zeilenwerk nur die Hauptbegriffe der Entwicklung festzustellen

Introduction

J udging by academic book sales alone, Heinrich Wölfflin's *Kunstgeschichtliche Grundbegriffe: Das Problem der Stilentwicklung in der neueren Kunst (Principles of Art History: The Problem of the Development of Style in Early Modern Art,* hereafter referred to as *Principles)* has been a runaway success for over a century. The first two editions, issued in 1915 and 1917 in spite of wartime paper shortages—ten thousand copies of a richly illustrated art history book—sold out immediately while war was raging. By a conservative estimate, approximately seventy thousand copies have been sold in the original German language, half of those in the first ten years after publication.[1]

This volume explores the reach of *Principles* in and beyond the Germanophone world, beginning with a Spanish translation in 1924 that immediately elicited a highly consequential response halfway across the globe in Argentina. Since then, the book has appeared in twenty-two languages (Spanish, Russian, English, Japanese, French, Italian, Swedish, Serbo-Croatian, Dutch, Hebrew, Polish, Romanian, Hungarian, Turkish, Portuguese, Bulgarian, Chinese, Greek, Korean, Lithuanian, Croatian, and Slovenian, in that order), the last new translation having been undertaken in 2009.[2] Many of these have been repeatedly reprinted (approximately forty times in the United States since 1932, eleven in Korea since 1994), and there have

been several retranslations (five Chinese, two Japanese, two English, a second in French under way); in sustainable markets, the book remains in print.[3] Of course, translation is not the only indication that the book was being read outside the Germanophone world. Before World War II German was widely read, and every new translation opens the door to new readers who can reach to the language of translation; for instance, before the 1984 Portuguese translation, the book was read in French in Brazil, and Japanese art historians transmitted Wölfflin's ideas initially to Korean and Chinese scholars.[4] Besides complete translations, excerpts appeared in anthologies many times over and, even more significant, as a manifesto of formalism *Principles* continues to be kicked along by the innumerable secondhand summaries and discussions of it, in short, by its status as a modern classic.

The varied evidence of the diffusion of Wölfflin's *Principles,* of the uninterrupted reading of the text with pockets of vitality and of morbidity, must be reconciled with a century of often devastating critiques and a general sense across art history (in the United States especially) that the book is toxic. Wölfflin's *Principles* operates in some geographies of art history a lot like the Freudian father who must be repeatedly killed off; but it is, nonetheless, a defining work of the discipline that we cannot seem to live without.[5] The psychological explanation does not account for the trans-cultural adaptation of art-historical method the reception of Wölfflin's book exemplifies as well as the diversity of readers and readings it has so remarkably attracted: popular and academic, in the undergraduate classroom and at the highest levels of theoretical debate, as an active proposition and as a historical artifact. Shades of gray are many, and contradictions abound. The mechanisms that created a classic are worth examining. But to be clear: *Principles* would not have become a phenomenon in art history without the negative reception that continued to rearticulate its aims. Opposition is the oxygen that fuels the fire.

The focus of this volume is on a single publication, certainly Wölfflin's most important over the past century. As the essays published here make evident, into the reception of *Principles* is often folded a body of theory, descriptions, and attitudes that better characterize Wölfflin's other texts (empathy theory, national styles). And yet because *Principles* is his most resolved and most widely translated and read work with the most portentous totalizing title, it has become synonymous with Wölfflin himself. However imprecise, to speak of *Principles* is to speak of Wölfflin and vice versa. Wölfflin himself has achieved a kind of status as a concept.

Aims

This volume offers a variety of answers to a question the editors posed at the start of this project about what the history of Wölfflin's *Principles* can offer to a discipline asking about the prospects of a global art history. Could the reception of a singularly widely disseminated book, a recognized classic of a modern humanities discipline, offer a historical roadmap for this problem?[6]

The approach the editors have taken is first to follow along after the translations of *Principles*, concrete points of entry into institutional, commercial, intellectual, and political pathways of reception. We debated which languages (and therefore which countries in many cases) should be included. We based our decisions on the presence of significant histories of reception (a translation was key but not decisive), substantial activity in art history (including institutional infrastructure), and scholars who would take up the question. Not only did this project exceed our linguistic capacities, but it demanded a collective of scholars able to discern the social conditions Pierre Bourdieu called our attention to in the international circulation of ideas.[7] The gatekeepers of translations and their motivations, the authors of prefaces, the choice of publishing house, and the book covers themselves—all of these local codes needed decoders, as is exemplified by the essay in this volume by Wojciech Bałus on the Polish reception. Some countries, especially Holland, Russia, Australia, and Korea, could not be represented, much to our regret. Some of these lacunae are addressed here, drawing also on other symposia organized by the editors around the book's centennial.[8]

Aside from assessing the institutional role Wölfflin's book played—a pillar in the edifice of art history—this essay considers the book according to the tenet of reception studies that a literary work is brought into existence by its readers. In this regard we should take seriously the casting of *Principles* by its early readers as a classic, even a "world classic," with the implication (demonstrable in this case) that it is a universal text. The 1962 translation of Wölfflin's *Principles* into Hebrew, part of a library of standard works in literature and the humanities translated into Hebrew after the establishment of the state of Israel, implicitly acknowledged the book's status as such.[9] And the rapturous reception in neighboring disciplines, in spite of a difficult reception in art history, contributed to the book's stature.[10] Given the broad claims made for Wölfflin's book across the humanities, the full scope of the reception—in diverse disciplines, methodologically and geographically—is beyond the scope of any one study. In art history alone this reception history is almost congruent with that of the discipline itself. Our effort is to defamiliarize the historiography of this book by capturing the range of readings, with particular attention to the many dynamic acts of reading that entwined Wölfflin's formalism with the theories and methods of his contemporaries.

Institutional Paths of Diffusion

We have only to follow the trail left by Wölfflin's numerous students and the uncountable art historians who adopted his theories or method to grasp just how widely disseminated his way of seeing was in German universities.[11] Many international students also came to Germany (the acknowledged leader in art history before World War II) for advanced degrees in a discipline that was not offered in their own countries. We know that Wölfflin taught students from Sweden, the Netherlands, China, and Japan who returned to their countries with his method.

Most decisive for the global dissemination of Wölfflin's work were the German Jewish art historians forced to emigrate when their lives were imperiled by Hitler's Nuremberg laws: Wölfflin's direct students (and many more who engaged with his ideas, for or against) found refuge in England, the United States, Mexico, Brazil, and Canada.[12] The generation that helped to move the center of art history to the United States had an outsized influence on the discipline. To give one example, all but one among Germany's first generation of East Asian art specialists emigrated in the 1930s.[13] Of the three Wölfflin students in this group, Ludwig Bachhofer created a formalist school of East Asian studies at the University of Chicago that dominated the field for decades.[14] Wölfflin students in the United States, in sustaining one side of an enduring methodological confrontation between formalism and iconography, also helped to mark the battlefield on which the new art history would be fought, keeping Wölfflin's text very much in view. In Germany, by contrast, where much more ideological baggage accompanied the generation that carried on with Wölfflin's

formalism after the war, the book was much less in evidence.[15]

The century-long readership of *Principles* was above all a product of the expansion of university-level art history. It is striking the extent to which *Principles* appeared in curricula as new departments were founded. In Italy, Paolo d'Ancona, founder of art history at the University of Milan, translated the first excerpts into Italian in 1927, although a full translation was delayed until 1953.[16] Similarly, Wölfflin's ideas were very present in the writings about aesthetics by Chinese authors who brought European concepts to China in the 1930s, although the first complete translation did not appear until 1985 as art history's presence in the universities expanded.[17]

The robust reception of *Principles* in Central and Eastern European countries (accounting for nine of twenty-two translations) was often tied to the complementary and competing ideas of the Vienna School. For instance, in the newly formed sovereign First Czechoslovak Republic (1918–1938), the first art historian appointed to the university, Vojtěch Birnbaum, was trained in Vienna by Max Dvořák, but his work on the Czech baroque drew in equal measure on Wölfflin's *Principles*. In response to professional jealousies that led to accusations of Germanization or Austrianization, Birnbaum omitted the names of Wölfflin and Riegl in his published work.[18] So the foundational role of Wölfflin and the Vienna School for art history in Czechoslovakia was obscured at a moment of heightened national consciousness. The dual Strzygowskian and Wölfflinian foundations for the study of Georgian art were not, by contrast, initially hidden by Giorgi Chubinashvili, a native of Georgia who studied with Wölfflin in Munich (1913–1914) and was appointed in 1918 to one of the first art history chairs in the Democratic Republic of Georgia, three years before the republic was created.

The first full translation of *Principles* that can be definitively linked to a distinctive moment of institution building is the

English translation, issued in 1932, just as the Courtauld Institute of Art opened its doors in London.[19] Wölfflin's "conceptos" were also present around the founding of art history in Cuba (in 1936), with Luis de Soto y Sagarra's 1941 textbook, which conveyed the latest summary of Wölfflin's methods by Walter Passarge, as passed through the Argentinian Wölfflin whisperer, Ángel Guido.[20] The Hebrew translation also appeared around the establishment of the first department of art history at the Hebrew University of Jerusalem, with an introduction by its chair, Moshe Barasch.[21] And in Greece, art history expanded to post-Byzantine subjects in the 1960s, but it was only in 1992, during a major expansion of art history at Greek universities that a translation appeared.[22] There are certainly other motivations for translation, but it should be clear by now that *Principles* came to stand for the modern discipline of art history itself. In many places, without Wölfflin there was no art history.

Major Themes of Critique

Because *Principles* carried its critics with it, major themes of the early Germanophone reception are important to outline briefly.[23] The characterization of *Principles* as a formalist manifesto constitutes the irreducible core of the book's reception; Walter Passarge declared Wölfflin "der unerreichten Meister der formalin Interpretation," although Wölfflin himself may have coined the word "formalismus," all the while objecting to it.[24] The book was keenly read in 1919 and written about in 1925 by the Russian formalist Boris Eikhenbaum, who appreciated its possibilities for literature.[25] The first and only (unauthorized) Russian translation, dating to 1930, was produced in the circles of Mikhail Bakhtin.[26] Though Russian formalism was short lived, proponents of the New Criticism in literature picked up the formalist mantle in the United States after World War II. In art history, Kurt Zoege von Manteuffel (1881–1941) is credited with having first, and critically, isolated Wölfflin's exclusive attention to form.[27] August Schmarsow, Josef Strzygowksi, and Erwin Panofsky quickly joined in the skepticism of the one-sidedness of Wölfflin's substitution of form for *Geist*.[28]

Nearly inextricable from *Principles'* "formalism" was Wölfflin's view, shaped by the work of Konrad Fiedler and Adolf Hildebrand, of a double root of style in seeing and in expression. When Wölfflin proposed a shift between a classic-linear and a baroque-painterly sensibility as a matter of the eye *needing* something new, he formulated a history of perception that seemed immanent, inevitable, endowed with an evolutionary quality that divorced changing styles from historical circumstances. Benedetto Croce influentially termed this a theory of "pure visibility" and was critical of the implication that form was separate from rather than generating expression.[29] Formalism and pure visibility both alarmed Wölfflin's contemporaries for portending a kind of soulless view of the development of art. In Vienna and in the work of Max Dvořák, opposition to *Principles* broke out in the 1920s in an alternative methodology: *Geistesgeschichte*. Even within Wölfflin's workshop the understated references to *Geist* were addressed when Hans Rose added a book-length appendix on *Geistesgeschichte* to the fourth edition of Wölfflin's earlier work *Renaissance und Barock* and a festschrift dedicated to Wölfflin in 1924 folded him into *Geistesgeschichte* in its very title (*Beiträge zur Kunst- und Geistesgeschichte*).[30]

That these forms of seeing should occur in a lawful or predictable way became another topos of critique. This sense of the binding nature of Wölfflin's *Zeitstil* was challenged especially by Wilhelm Pinder, whose *Das Problem der Generation in der Kunstgeschichte Europas* (1926) argued that periods of artistic production do not unroll uncontested and one can find multiple expressions within a given generation.[31] Both the *Geistesgeschichte* generation and later empirically driven art historians invested in style bore down on the nuances of historical development Wölfflin's schema left out, especially mannerism.

Also problematic was the very structure of Wölfflin's account, those five pairs of antithetical formal qualities that endowed *Principles* with its dyadic structure. Wölfflin's "classic" (the term he preferred to Renaissance) is linear, planar, closed, multiple, and clear; his baroque is painterly, recessional, open, unified, and unclear. Panofsky objected to begin with to the claim that Wölfflin's pairs were "principles": *Grundbegriffen*, fundamental "concepts" (mistranslated "principles" from the start) are a priori formulations of artistic problems, not a posteriori characterizations of their solutions.[32] Was Panofsky's argument simply too philosophical to disrupt the widespread acceptance of Wölfflin's dyads? The novel design of the book itself, with its comparisons of classic and baroque works across page spreads, reinforced the comparative structure of the book (contractually required in most of the translations) and subsequently embedded in dual slide projection.[33] Although Wölfflin was not first here, *Principles* popularized the comparative procedure that shaped unconscious comparative thinking in generations of art historians, embedded as it was in our very technologies until digital projection and PowerPoint, a subject that has recently brought scholars back to Wölfflin's contribution to the discipline.[34]

Wölfflin also regretted his call in *Principles* for an "art history without names," by which he intended a history not only of artists but of seeing itself.[35] Wölfflin's opposition to the biographically driven art history of the reigning generation elicited Hermann Voss's vehement criticism of the deindividualization he found in Wölfflin's "philosophical" approach.[36] Voss may have isolated the term most visibly within art history, but he was not the only one to object: Bakhtin did so contemporaneously and much more influentially, and this would become the focus of a Marxist critique several decades later on the left as well as a conservative, humanist critique from the right.

Challenged by these major themes of critique (and there are others), *Principles* could have been demolished. But the opposite is true, for not only did the book survive; it became one of the most discussed works of art history.

Paths of Dissemination

Sustained critiques of Wölfflin's book were numerous, but a handful of authoritative readings—those of Benedetto Croce, Henri Focillon, E. H. Gombrich, and Arnold Hauser above all—had an impact beyond the contexts and linguistic zones in which they arose. The essays in this volume constitute a geography of art history in which criticism of Wölfflin's *Principles* crossed many borders. Every transmission is a transformation, and pathways soon tangle and lose contact with their sources. Though the complexity of transmission will quickly overwhelm us, it is a key task of this study to show how reception operates.

Benedetto Croce's critique of Wölfflin's "pure visibility" continued to reverberate in Italian aesthetics almost to today. But Croce's view, which Joseph Gantner unsuccessfully tried to reconcile with Wölfflin himself, found a translator and conduit to the Vienna School in Julius von Schlosser. As Gombrich put it in an obituary of Schlosser: "The result of his researches was a profound distrust in all easy-going aestheticism and formalism—a deep insight, that 'art' means a different thing to different times and societies."[37] Croce's response lived on in the work of members of the New Vienna School, including Hans Sedlmayr (who influenced a generation of German students at the University of Munich after the war) and émigrés who ended up in England, especially Otto Pächt, Johannes Wilde, and Gombrich. In Italy, Croce's view was also adopted, especially influentially by Lionello Venturi, who transmitted to Brazil a "tempered formalism," more ethical, more tied to its surroundings. There Venturi inspired a generation of art critics who embraced pictorial abstraction, led by Mario Pedrosa, who found in Venturi a less codified version of Wölfflin's formalism.[38]

Among an international group of formalists of the 1930s must be counted Henri Focillon, whose *La Vie des formes* (1934) was written in full awareness of Wölfflin's *Principles*.[39] In spite of general consonance and points of close agreement with *Principles*, Focillon saw Wölfflin as a nemesis, and much of *La Vie des formes* implicitly challenges *Principles*.[40] Focillon (who was instructor at Yale University from 1936 to 1943 and from 1940 was officially in the United States looking for allies in anti-German propaganda) undoubtedly contributed to the suspicion of German art history that one hears echoed among a new generation of American art historians after the war.[41] While it is difficult to measure the impact of his reaction to Wölfflin (who is never named in his writings), his student George Kubler concretized a critique of Wölfflin (mediated by Paul Frankl's revisions of Wölfflin's concept of style) with an alternative that has endured to today in *The Shape of Time*.[42] After translating *La Vie des formes* into English, Kubler developed a more radical version of Focillon's meditation on Wölfflin's *Zeitstil* in terms of "forms and time." Of the many ideas that Kubler put forward, one of the most disruptive to Wölfflin's progression of styles was that of a history of art composed of prime objects and replicas. In this context, style became synchronic rather than diachronic, and while Kubler recognized that styles changed, the determinism that many (including Focillon) criticized in Wölfflin was eliminated. Kubler's book became a vessel of further reflection on theory and method around formalism, though after this point it is nearly impossible to separate out the strands of Wölfflin and Focillon from Kubler.[43]

Late in life Gombrich admitted that although he had boasted of having skipped Wölfflin's lectures as a student, he was in fact under the thrall of formalism when he wrote his dissertation in 1933.[44] Gombrich was critical of Wölfflin on several points, including Croce's concern with pure visibility, though he later warned against the risk of atomization in Croce's thinking about the incommensurability of each and every work of art: one needed to try to classify. At the height of his influence, and inspired by Karl Popper, Gombrich sounded a warning cry that Wölfflin's *Principles* amounted to a lightly masked Hegelianism.[45] This critique was at the political end of Gombrich's spectrum, and it was key to his positioning of himself in the Cold War as a proponent of a humanist individualism. But it was his detection of a hidden classical norm in Wölfflin's opposing dyads that cut closest to the bone. Hans Sedlmayr had already rejected Wölfflin's dyads in his structural study of five singular church facades, which pointedly did not engage in comparison.[46]

Gombrich's views of Wölfflin were widely disseminated. Just to cite one example of their impact, the American scholar Svetlana Alpers, who did more to move the study of seventeenth-century Dutch art away from its iconographic investigation in *The Art of Describing: Dutch Art in the Seventeenth Century*, did so with the help of Gombrich's critique of Wölfflin's classical biases. Later, Marshall Brown's brilliant deconstruction of Wölfflin's text definitively exposed the flimsiness of the dyadic structure, though his conclusion was just the opposite of Gombrich's: the classic is baroque.[47] Ultimately it was neither Gombrich nor Brown but digital projection that definitively disrupted the habitus of dual projection.

Marxist readers may constitute the largest interpretive community of Wölfflin's text. In the early days of Stalinism Wölfflin's work was denounced as bourgeois formalism. Because the point of view was so strong, it would be difficult to identify a single critical text that served as a point of reference. The complicated and varied history of the book's reception after the formation of the Soviet Union indexes the extent to which bloc countries bowed to politico-intellectual orthodoxy. Institution building had, in both the Czech and Georgian cases, an openly political dimension that became increasingly problematic in the Soviet period. Chubinashvili was able to function in the first years of the Soviet absorption of Georgia until 1931, but by 1940 he had been dismissed from his position, in part because of his German training; in 1952 his work was publicly denounced in an article describing him as a "captive of Wölfflin's formalist schemes."[48] This would become a familiar refrain in the Soviet bloc: in the preface to the Romanian translation (1968), Wölfflin's work was denounced by a party official for the absence of a social history of art, but the book was otherwise treated as apolitical.[49] The situation was similar in Poland, where the thaw following the death of Stalin saw an opening for a translation, though, in order to pass through the censors, the translator's preface denounced the work, assessing it as nearly irrelevant.[50] The 1968 translation into Hungarian was also stimulated by a cultural thaw (1962–1969) that saw a push in the study of art and stronger relations with countries outside the bloc. Wölfflin's formalism was of interest, not because of the northern and southern European styles it outlined, but because it reinforced a national politics elsewhere.[51]

In Western Europe the reception of *Principles* on the left took an entirely different path. As Frederic J. Schwartz has shown, Frankfurt School cultural theorists had always shown an interest in art history and specifically in Wölfflin's theorization of style. Long before *Principles*, cultural theorists contrasted style (old, slow, integral to culture) to fashion (new, fast, integral to capitalism).[52] Hanna Levy, in the circle of Max Raphael in Paris in the mid 1930s, proposed a Marxist critique of Wölfflin's text already in 1936. But theirs were rather marginal voices in art history, and it would not be until the publication of Hungarian émigré Arnold Hauser's *Philosophy of Art* that an internationally received Marxist critique circulated widely outside the Soviet bloc.[53] Hauser decried Wölfflin's reduction of art to problems and successions of forms that do not value the individual artist and the historical circumstances that gave rise to their

work. In a sense, there is nothing new here: a critique of Wölfflin's "anonymous art history," with its immanent progression of style, its inner Hegelianism. And yet, the stakes of Hauser's critique are right on the surface: this "retrograde philosophy of history," which discredits revolution to reinstate tradition, of a kind of "group mind" that tends toward conformity and unconscious ideology. Hauser and Gombrich were both reacting to the Hegelian kernel, which was a new element in the postwar reception; *Geistesgeschichte* seemed far more vulnerable than formalism to this complaint. But rather than uniting against a common enemy, Gombrich also did battle with Hauser in this period, adding a layer of complexity to the reception of this work. The timing was also right, for Hauser's diluted Marxism would plant seeds for the "new art historians," who looked to his and to Gombrich's critiques of Wölfflin starting in the 1970s. Even more influential in Europe was the pedagogically clear and politically engaged work of Nicos Hadjinicolaou, *Art History and Class Struggle*, which rehearsed Wölfflin's *Principles* to a new generation, not unsympathetically but as the formalist extreme of style history.[54]

In West Germany, among politically engaged leftist art historians led by Martin Warnke and Horst Bredekamp, Wölfflin's *Principles* became the first victim in the opening salvo launched in the 1970s against unexamined patterns of thought of art historians who remained in universities after the war. Bredekamp thus views it as a paradox that shortly thereafter, Hubert Faensen's afterword to the first East German edition of *Principles* argued for the book's validity in establishing a scientifically grounded art history. It is no wonder that it took so long to excavate the Frankfurt School's productive engagement with Wölfflin's work.

Because the Marxist perspective on Wölfflin's *Principles* was so reductively clear, the revival of the text became highly symbolic in the post-Soviet era. With the Croatian translation in 1988, the point was made that following Croatian independence (declared in 1991; accepted in 1995 with the end of the four-year-long war of independence), the existing Serbo-Croatian translation would not suffice. And while a translation into the Georgian language has not yet materialized, it is a strong desideratum alongside efforts to commemorate the contributions of Giorgi Chubinashvili in establishing the discipline in Georgia.[55]

The Universality of *Principles*: European Art

When Leopold D. Ettlinger said in *Art History Today*, a lecture given in London and published in 1961, that the widespread application of Wölfflin's principles amounted to an overzealous application of their *Gesetzlichkeit* (lawfulness), there were many examples within the European tradition to demonstrate his point.[56] Immediately after the first edition appeared, art historians and other humanists tested Wölfflin's formalism and his dyads in particular on the arts of Europe and America from antiquity to the present, and Wölfflin himself opened up the prospect of ulterior applications.[57] Archaeologists were already implicated in this idea of transhistorical style, for the emergence of the Hellenistic baroque stood behind modern scholarship, including Wölfflin's on the baroque. In 1916 Gerhart Rodenwaldt, a Greek archaeologist, published a rigorous evaluation of the usefulness and pitfalls of working with concepts developed for early modern art.[58]

As Wölfflin himself commented several times in *Principles* on Gothic art, it is not surprising that medievalists took up his ideas as well.[59] Meyer Schapiro's dissertation (1929) viewed Moissac through Wölfflin's concept of the baroque; and in a letter of 1931 he spoke of plans for "a general work on Romanesque art" in which he would "distinguish it from Gothic in the same sense that Wölfflin studies Renaissance and Baroque in his *Kunstgeschichtliche Grundbegriffe*."[60] Joseph Gantner also turned to Wölfflin's concepts for his work on the Romanesque, though the greatest impact of Wölfflin's thinking in medieval art was felt through the work of his pupil Paul Frankl.[61]

The ancient and medieval subfields of art history are not the only ones that were written into Wölfflin's binaries. Wölfflin's own students sought to reconcile his system to modern art and architecture and photography.[62] Indeed, there is virtually no moment in the history of Western art that someone has not tried to test for conformity to Wölfflin's concepts.

The Cultural Mobility of Wölfflin's *Principles*

Many of the essays in this volume make evident just how often Wölfflin's concepts were tried out on the arts of South and East Asia and the Americas, on objects he never considered. Along pathways of diffusion of Wölfflin's book, our authors found transformative strategies of reading, of adaptation in local contexts and intellectual traditions. One case is the fierce promoter of *Américanidad*, the Argentinian architect Ángel Guido, who argued for a temporal inversion in colonial Latin American architecture that allowed him to make the point that a rational Eurindian classicism shone through the Spanish irrational.[63] When Wölfflin's categories were exposed as racially, biologically determined, and his classical canon was deemed incapable of discerning the mestizo American spirit in José Uriel García's *El nuevo indio* (1930), Guido revised his scheme to contest the racial basis.[64] This is but one instance of active appropriation, transformation, and recontextualization. Wölfflin's method rarely remains intact.

The inevitable revision of Wölfflin's key ideas points to another prevalent mode of reception, what Peter Krieger has called the "effect of synergy," in which Wölfflin's potential for art history is recognized only when harnessed to another thinker.[65] In Mexico that meant primarily Wilhelm Worringer; in Japan Wölfflin's ideas were combined with those of Riegl, Worringer, and others; and Ko Yu-seop, the founder of art history in Korea (who trained at Keio University in Tokyo), combined Wölfflin's style history with that of the Vienna School and a Marxist social art history.[66] The 1934 Japanese translation by Moriya Kenji of Walter Passarge's book on the state of the discipline, *Die Philosophie der Kunstgeschichte* (with a large section devoted to the reception of *Principles*), paved the way for this kind of methodological bricolage; the same may have been true in Mexico following the publication in 1932 of a Spanish translation of Passarge.[67]

While European scholars reacted very negatively to Wölfflin's "art history without names," outside Europe the idea was liberating. For instance, the first translator of *Principles* into Japanese, Sawaki Yomokichi (1886–1930), enthused in the 1920s over the prospect of moving the study of Japanese art away from the biographical, or more precisely, the personality-based art history that the editors of the progressive Shirakaba ("White Birch") group promoted.[68]

The indifference to authorship conveyed by an "art history without names" also created an opportunity to see without prejudice anonymous works outside of the European canon. José Moreno Villa set to work on the unattributed polychrome sculpture of colonial Mexico;[69] and Wölfflin's approach to style, alongside those of Riegl and Hildebrand, informed the new terms in which a decades-long debate over the undocumented Hakuhō and Tenpyō styles of Japanese Buddhist sculpture were reevaluated.[70] While Wölfflin's *Principles* cannot be held responsible for the absorption of the arts of Mesoamerica and India into histories of style that moved many artifacts out of ethnographic collections into art museums, the wide acceptance of his approach to style certainly helped to tear down preconceptions.

Both the transmediality of Wölfflin's concepts and their capacity to deal with anonymous artifacts contributed to claims for their universality. The potential of the transmedial, for instance, was seized upon by the Chinese scholar Teng Gu (student in Berlin of Wölfflin's student A. E. Brinckmann), who tested the limits of Wölfflin's concepts in characterizing Chinese painting of the Tang and Song dynasties as fundamentally linear, while admitting to a painterly trend

with the introduction of chiaroscuro from India. He also made a sweeping attempt to date a large cache of anonymous painted tiles from Yan, comparing them to works in bronze and in jade.[71] Here, as elsewhere, the step forward in cataloguing came up against limits that had to be articulated, ideas adapted to the Chinese context.

The extent to which *Principles* has been put to the service of characterizing regional and national styles of art production is also striking. Undeterred by the national or racial specificity of Wölfflin's text, Oskar Hagen applied Wölfflin's concepts to the art of the colonial United States and Luis de Soto y Sagarra employed them in characterizing the *cubanidad* of colonial art. Readers were willing to mobilize Wölfflin's methods, reconfiguring his European examples (as in the case of Hugo Kehrer arguing for a Spanish baroque eye), on new bodies of artifacts.[72]

While some were accused of having been colonized by Wölfflin's text, others successfully mobilized it for an anticolonial message. Although, in the absence of any social, political, or economic coordinates for style, Wölfflin's schema inevitably came up short as a totalizing system, it abundantly accomplished Wölfflin's primary goal: of teaching people to see—and to see many things other than European art. *Principles* was culturally mobile, and although there have been many mechanical readings of the text, there have also been many unpredictable encounters with it, many unruly readers who have felt limited by neither its subject nor its method.[73]

Teaching *Principles*

In 1930 Walter Passarge observed in his book on the state of Germanophone art history that *Principles* was marked by a strong pedagogical impulse.[74] Indeed, one of the very earliest stimuli for our reception project was an account of the evacuation of old master paintings from the Strossmayer Gallery in Zagreb in 1991, at the beginning of the Croatian War of Independence. In that case the curators, whose early training involved analyzing works in the collection, were particularly concerned to safeguard the works that had always been analyzed according to Wölfflin's *Principles*, for they felt that their own histories and identities as art historians were at stake.[75] The pedagogical life of the book in universities, art schools, and art museums helps us to grasp its tenacity in the face of so much criticism at the highest levels.

At times the teaching of Wölfflin's book and research went hand in hand, as was the case at Keio University, in Tokyo. Two Keio professors were behind translations of *Principles* with a clear shift in interest in the text: from Sawaki Yomokichi's intention to use the concepts in writing a history of Japanese art, to Kaizu Tadao's more historiographic interest, in 2000, in Wölfflin's language.[76] *Principles* has been upheld by the Keio school up to today as a guide for the analysis of Japanese sculpture dating from the eighth to the thirteenth century, though the idiosyncratic, self-referential formalism that has developed over decades makes it unclear if the book is still being read.

There are also cases of the opposite, when the teaching of the text was lost from view because it left no trace in scholarly research. Take the example of Willem Vogelsang, the first art historian appointed (in 1907) to a university professorship in Holland and a direct student of Wölfflin as well as of Riegl. In 1925, Vogelsang created gouache charts to illustrate formal ideas he taught in his course on the history of pictorial composition at the University of Utrecht.[77] Vogelsang drew from the work of Riegl, Schmarsow, and others, but among these are a few that illustrate Wölfflin's concepts, such as one that demonstrates recession. It is not surprising that Vogelsang saw the concepts as a useful tool, specifically for the teaching of Netherlandish art, which was central to *Principles*. Yet iconological and connoisseurial traditions so dominated Dutch art history through the 1970s that the existence of formalist instruction at the very beginnings of university-level art history in

Holland has gone unnoticed until recently.[78] Under the reign of iconography, the translation of *Principles* into Dutch in 1960 in an exceptional paperback pocket book with only half of the illustrations might be explained by the broad public for art history garnered by the popular television programs *Opeenbaar Kunstbezit* and *Kunstgrepen* (1959–1972), hosted by Pierre Janssen.[79] Wölfflin's *Principles* had a presence in Holland in the classroom that did not leave a perceptible legacy in the discipline.

The Dutch example helps to articulate a trenchant issue of this project: an often unacknowledged and unresolved contradiction between the ongoing teaching of Wölfflin in the classroom and its rejection or irrelevance in the realm of research. Leopold D. Ettlinger made the problem evident when, in his lecture *Art History Today*, he praised Wölfflin's books as "unsurpassed in training students to 'see.'" Yet he opened the same lecture in this spirit: "In this country, fortunately, we have so far been free from treatises with such ominous titles as 'Prolegomena to Art History,' or 'The Methods and Principles of Art Historical Study'—and long may it remain so."[80] The reference to Wölfflin's book is unmistakable. The fact is that concepts, methods, and theories in art history can be thoroughly criticized, even debunked, and also accepted as useful.

Whither *Principles*?

Wölfflin's *Principles* went out into the world, but, with few exceptions, the book itself has not undergone the metamorphosis the text underwent in the hands of its global readers. It has been subjected to limited genetic editing; comparison of the handwritten manuscript to the published text and careful study of the variants among the five editions issued during the author's lifetime have been undertaken only recently.[81] And *Principles* has been upended by a "queer light" reading and a sustained interpretation of the book's politics.[82] Over one hundred years the stability of the artifact itself has perhaps been unconsciously picked up even by scholars without direct knowledge of the text: *Principles* has long been emblematic of an "idea" or ideas of Wölfflin that have allowed it to be treated almost as an emblem of the discipline of art history itself.[83] This stability even in the face of critiques in every decade has enabled the book's operation on the entire discipline of art history: whether as type, antitype, or, increasingly, as an inextirpable founding chapter in the history of a discipline that has reached sufficient longevity that its own intellectual history is now a legitimate ongoing concern.

It is our goal to advocate not so much for a revival of Wölfflin as for an understanding of the book's peculiar powers of survival. The essays assembled here bring into view wildly diverse and dynamic readers of a world classic. They demonstrate with clarity that Wölfflin's polarizing *Principles* has long stood on a narrow strip of land that art historians worldwide can call common ground. There is more than one reason that *Principles* continues to be read, taught, translated, and reprinted. It would not have the global vitality that it does were it not for the transformation that takes place in the reading of a book that can be counted as a work of world literature.

NOTES

I express my gratitude to Tristan Weddigen for his collaboration on the Wölfflin Project for more than a decade and for his incisive comments at various stages of the composition of this text. My thanks also to Daniel Adler and to the directors, fellows, and staff of the Bibliotheca Hertziana, which generously hosted me in 2017–2018 when this text was written, and to Therese O'Malley, Cynthia Ware, and Elizabeth Cropper, without whose support and hard work this project could not have come to fruition.

1. This estimate is based on print runs of Bruckmann editions and sale records preserved by the Schwabe Verlag (Basel). My thanks to Liv Etienne of Schwabe for facilitating access to the archive.

2. For the editions see http://thewolfflinproject.uto-ronto.ca/editions-translations.

3. Serbo-Croatian, Dutch, Romanian, Bulgarian, and Swedish editions are out of print.

4. See the essays by Zhang Ping and Jens Baumgarten in this volume.

5. The apt analogy to Freud I owe to Adam Cohen, who appeared in the documentary film made by University of Toronto students, *Reading Wölfflin's Principles: Toronto Stories* (2015).

6. Few studies can serve as models. For a stimulating collection of essays see Rosa Bruno-Jofré and Jürgen Schriewer, eds., *The Global Reception of John Dewey's Thought: Multiple Refractions through Time and Space* (New York, 2012).

7. Pierre Bourdieu, "Les Conditions sociales de la circulation internationale des idées," *Actes de la recherche en sciences sociales* 5 (2005): 3–8.

8. "Grundlagen der Kunstgeschichte in der Schweiz: Von Rahn bis Wölfflin" (University of Zurich, 2012); "The Reception of Wölfflin's *Principles* in North America" (Clark Institute, 2012); "Reception of Wölfflin's *Principles of Art History*" (Tokyo, 2014), and three sessions on the global reception at the Renaissance Society of America meeting (Berlin, 2015). For summaries, see Evonne Levy and Tristan Weddigen, "The Global Reception of Wölfflin's *Principles*," in *Kunstgeschichten 1915: 100 Jahre Heinrich Wölfflin*, Kunstgeschichtliche Grundbegriffe, ed. Matteo Burioni, Burcu Dogramaci, and Ulrich Pfisterer (Zentralinstitut für Kunstgeschichte, Munich, 2015), 428–437. Jindřich Vybíral's paper "Birnbaum's 'Baroque Principle' and the Czech Reception of Heinrich Wölfflin" was published in *Journal of Art Historiography* 13 (December 2015); Regine Prange's Zurich paper was expanded in "Kunstgeschichte aus dem Geist der Gegenwart: Wölfflin und die Avantgarde," in *Das Problem der Form: Interferenzen zwischen modernen Kunst und Wissenschaft*, ed. Hans Aurenhammer and Regine Prange (Berlin, 2016), 87–108; Marshall Brown's Clark paper appears as "Undisciplined Reading: Heinrich Wölfflin's Passions," *Critical Inquiry* 44 (2018): 733–744. The Tokyo symposium has been published in Japanese: Mita Society for the Science of Arts, Keio University, "One Hundredth Anniversary of Heinrich Wölfflin's *Kunstgeschichtliche Grundbegriffe*," special issue, *Journal of the Science of Arts*, no. 19 (2015).

9. See the essay by Adi Efal Lautenschläger in this volume.

10. Meinhold Lurz, *Heinrich Wölfflin: Biographie einer Kunsttheorie* (Worms, 1981), 25–33. The extent to which Wölfflin's work bridged to other disciplines in the humanities is apparent in the list of authors in *Festschrift Heinrich Wölfflin: Beiträge zur Kunst- und Geistesgeschichte; zum 21. Juni 1924 überreicht von Freunden und Schülern* (Munich, 1924).

11. It is difficult to quantify Wölfflin's students, for the eighteen doctorates in Berlin (1901–1912) and sixty-nine in Munich (1912–1929) hardly capture the extent of his pedagogical reach. Vivien Trommer and Laura Windisch, "'…in den allgemeinen Verhältnissen wohl unterrichtet: Untersuchungen zur kunstgeschichtlichen Promotion um 1900," in *In der Mitte Berlins: 200 Jahre Kunstgeschichte an der Humboldt-Universität,*

ed. Horst Bredekamp and Adam S. Labauda (Berlin, 2010), 159–170; Liselotte Resch and Ladislaus Buzas. *Verzeichnis der Doktoren und Dissertationen der Universität Ingolstadt-Landshut-München 1472–1970,* vol. 7, *Philosophische Fakultät 1750–1950* (Munich, 1977).

12. See the essays by Evonne Levy, Peter Krieger, Jens Baumgarten, and Eric Michaud in this volume. On the Germanophone émigrés to the United States see, for orientation, Karen Michels, "Transfer and Transformation: The German Period in American Art History," in *Exiles and Émigrés: The Flight of European Artists from Hitler,* ed. Stephanie Barron with Sabine Eckmann (New York, 1997); Ulrike Wendland, *Biographisches Handbuch deutschsprachiger Kunsthistoriker im Exil: Leben und Werk der unter dem Nationalsozialismus verfolgten und vertriebenen Wissenschaftler,* 2 vols. (Munich, 1999).

13. William Cohn (1880–1961) built up the Museum of Eastern Art at Oxford; two others worked on European subjects under Wölfflin and only later became interested in Asian art: Curt Glaser (1879–1943) emigrated to the United States, where he did not find a position, and Otto Fischer moved to Basel in 1926 as director of the Kunstmuseum. Lothar Von Falkenhausen, "The Study of East Asian Art History in Europe: Some Observations on Its Early Stages," in *Bridging Times and Spaces: Papers in Ancient Near Eastern, Mediterranean and Armenian Studies Honouring Gregory E. Areschian on the Occasion of His Sixty-Fifth Birthday,* ed. Pavel S. Avetisyan and Yervand H. Grekyan (Oxford, 2017), 89–102. On William Cohn, see Alexander Cullen, "Bringing Asia to Oxford: Dr. William Cohn and the Museum of Eastern Art," in *Ark of Civilization: Refugee Scholars and Oxford University, 1930–1945,* ed. Sally Crawford, Katharina Ulmschneider, and Jaś Elsner (Oxford, 2017).

14. For the methodologically more varied history of Asian art studies at UCLA, see Lothar Von Falkenhausen, "East Asian Art History at UCLA: Its Development and Current Challenges," in *Global and World Art in the Practice of the University Museum,* ed. Jane Chin Davidson and Sandra Esslinger (London and New York, 2018).

15. See the essay by Horst Bredekamp in this volume and the proceedings of Deutscher Kunsthistorikertag 12, which marked an ideological break with the postwar generation: Martin Warnke, ed., *Das Kunstwerk zwischen Wissenschaft und Weltanschauung* (Gütersloh, 1970).

16. See the essay by Andrea Pinotti in this volume.

17. See the essay by Zhang Ping in this volume.

18. Vybíral, "Birnbaum's 'Baroque Principle.'"

19. See the essay by this author in this volume.

20. Walter Passarge, *Die Philosophie der Kunstgeschichte in der Gegenwart* (Berlin, 1930). See the essay by Tristan Weddigen in this volume.

21. See the essay by Adi Efal-Lautenschläger in this volume.

22. Areti Adamopolou, "Born of a 'Peripheral' Modernism: Art History in Greece and Cyprus," in *Art History and Visual Studies in Europe: Transnational Discourse and National Frameworks,* ed. Matthew Rampley et al. (Leiden and Boston, 2012), 379–391. Thanks to Nikolas Drosos for investigating the translation.

23. The first extensive outline of these themes is in Lurz, *Heinrich Wölfflin,* chapter 2.

24. Passarge, *Philosophie der Kunstgeschichte,* 18; Wölfflin, *Principles* (2015), 310; Joseph Gantner, ed., *Heinrich Wölfflin 1864–1945: Autobiographie, Tagebücher und Briefe,* 2nd enlarged edition (Basel and Stuttgart, 1984), 233.

25. Boris M. Eikhenbaum, *O literature* (On literature) (Moscow, 1987), 511, and Eikhenbaum, "Teorija formal'nogo metoda" (Theory of the formal method), in *O literature,* 377.

26. The translator was Adrian A. Frankovsky, philosopher and translator of English and German. Katerina Clark and Michael Holquist, *Mikhail Bakhtin* (Cambridge, MA, 1984), 101.

27. Kurt Nikolai Baron Zoege von Manteuffel, review of *Kunstgeschichtliche Grundbegriffe, Kunst für Alle* 32 (1916–1917): 160.

28. Lurz, *Heinrich Wölfflin,* 21–23.

29. See the essay by Andrea Pinotti in this volume.

30. Heinrich Wölfflin and Hans Rose, *Renaissance und Barock,* 4th enlarged ed. (Munich, 1926), 181–328; Hans Rose's appendix published in English as "Commentary to Heinrich Wölfflin, Renaissance and Baroque," trans. Arno Witte and Andrew Hopkins, *Journal of Art Historiography* 14 (2016). For the full citation of the festschrift see note 10 above.

31. Wilhelm Pinder, *Das Problem der Generation in der Kunstgeschichte Europas* (Frankfurt, 1926). See Passarge, *Philosophie der Kunstgeschichte,* 10.

32. Erwin Panofsky, "On the Relationship of Art History and Art Theory: Towards the Possibility of a Fundamental System of Concepts for a Science of Art [1924]," *Critical Inquiry* 35 (2008): 43–71.

33. Evonne Levy, "Wölfflin's *Principles of Art History* (1915–2015): A Prolegomenon for Its Second Century," in Wölfflin, *Principles* (2015), 4–9.

34. Matthias Bruhn, "Sortierungsprobleme: Vergleichendes Sehen in Kunst- und Bildwissenschaft seit Heinrich Wölfflin," in Burioni, Dogramaci, and Pfisterer, *Kunstgeschichten 1915,* 410–415; Lena Bader, "Bricolage mit Bildern: Motive und Motivationen vergleichenden Sehens," in *Vergleichendes Sehen,* ed. Lena Bader, Martin Gaier, and Falk Wolf (Munich, 2010), 18–42.

35. See Lurz, *Heinrich Wölfflin,* 18–21.

36. For the full exchange over several publications by both Voss and Wölfflin and the wider commentary and link to Wölfflin topoi, see Lurz, *Heinrich Wölfflin.*

37. E. H. Gombrich, "Obituary—Julius von Schlosser," *The Burlington Magazine* 74 (1939): 98–99.

38. Ana Cândida de Avelar, "'Our Thoughts on Lionello Venturi' and the 2nd National Art Critics Congress," published in the conference proceedings *Modernidade latina: Os Italianos e os Centros do Modernismo Latino-Americano* (São Paulo, 2013), http://www.mac.usp.br/mac/conteudo/academico/publicacoes/anais/modernidade/pdfs/ANA%20A_ING.pdf (last accessed February 2, 2019).

39. Henri Focillon, *The Problem of Form in Art*, trans. George Kubler (New York, 1948), 1.

40. Focillon, *The Problem of Form in Art*, 2. See Jacques Thuillier, "La 'Vie des formes,'" in *Relire Henri Focillon* (Musée du Louvre and École nationale supérieure des Beaux-Arts, Paris, 1998), 86–87 and 96n31.

41. Annamaria Ducci, "'Layer-Cake History': Kubler and Focillon at Yale, January 1940 (Starting from Some Manuscript Notes)," in *Im Maschenwerk der Kunstgeschichte: Eine Revision von George Kublers "The Shape of Time,"* ed. Sarah Maupeu, Kerstin Schankweiler, and Stefanie Stallhaus (Berlin, 2015), 71–91.

42. George Kubler, *The Shape of Time: Remarks on the History of Things* (New Haven, 1962). Wölfflin is mentioned here with Riegl and Focillon as among those who have tried to classify objects. Kubler chronicled critiques of Wölfflin, somewhat withholding his own judgment. See Ulrich Pfisterer, "George Kubler," in *Klassiker der Kunstgeschichte: Von Panofsky bis Greenberg*, ed. Ulrich Pfisterer (Munich, 1996), 208.

43. See George Kubler, "'The Shape of Time' Reconsidered," *Perspecta* 19 (1982): 112–121.

44. Gombrich's dissertation evaluated the conformity of Giulio Romano's architecture to the stylistic categories of Riegl, Wölfflin, Frankl, Sedlmayr, and Panofsky. E. H. Gombrich, "Giulio Romano als Architekt" (PhD diss, University of Vienna, 1933). For Wölfflin's lectures, see Gombrich, *Norm and Form: Studies in the Art of the Renaissance* (London, 1966), 92.

45. See the essay by Paul Binski in this volume. Claims of Wölfflin's Hegelianism are common in art historical works published in London in the 1960s.

46. Hans Sedlmayr, "Fünf römsiche Fassaden," *Epochen und Werke* 2 (1960): 57–93. The first version of this essay was written in the 1930s. See further Evonne Levy, *Baroque and the Political Language of Formalism (1845–1945): Burckhardt, Wölfflin, Gurlitt, Brinckmann, Sedlmayr* (Basel, 2016), 340–343.

47. Marshall Brown, "The Classic Is Baroque: On the Principle of Wölfflin's Art History," *Critical Inquiry* 9 (1982): 379–404.

48. Giorgi Natroshvili, "volflinis formalisturi sqemebis tyveobaSi" (Captive of the formalist schemes of Wölfflin), *literatura da xelovneba/Literature and Art* (April 11, 1952): 3–4. My thanks to Nino Simonishvili for translating and contextualizing this article for me.

49. "But that may have been its appeal, since Wölfflin offered the nearest thing to a logic of vision applicable independently of the politics that permeated Romanian life and letters." Andrei Pop, "The Unbearable Lightness of Seeing: Wölfflin in Bucharest, 1968," talk given at the Renaissance Society of America meeting, Berlin, 2015.

50. See the essay by Wojciech Bałus in this volume.

51. Robert Born, talk given at the Renaissance Society of America meeting, Berlin, 2015.

52. Frederic J. Schwartz, "Cathedrals and Shoes: Concepts of Style in Wölfflin and Adorno," *New German Critique* 76 (1999): 3–48.

53. Arnold Hauser, *Die Philosophie der Kunstgeschichte* (Munich, 1958; retitled *Methoden moderner Kunstbetrachtung*, 2nd ed., 1970); *The Philosophy of Art History* (London, 1958). Hauser addressed Wölfflin's *Principles* directly in a chapter of this work, but it must be understood as complementary to his widely read and translated *Social History of Art*, 2 vols. (London, 1951), which also addressed Wölfflin in the second volume, on the baroque.

54. Nicos Hadjinicolaou, *Art History and Class Struggle* (London, 1978). For the impact of this book in Holland, see Marga van Mechelen and Kitty Zijlmans, "Art History in the Netherlands," in *Art History and Visual Studies in Europe: Transnational Discourse and National Frameworks*, ed. Matthew Rampley (Leiden and Boston, 2012), 414.

55. A translation was in the works for the centenary but has not been completed. Nino Simonishvili is currently working on Wölfflin's legacy in Georgian art history.

56. Leopold D. Ettlinger, *Art History Today* (London, 1961), 10–11.

57. Wölfflin, *Principles* (2015), 79.

58. Gerhart Rodenwaldt, "Wölfflins Grundbegriffe und die Antike Kunst," *Zeitschrift für Ästhetik und allgemeine Kunstwissenschaft* 11 (1916): 432–441. Rodenwaldt likely studied with Wölfflin in Berlin.

59. Wölfflin, *Principles* (2015), 310.

60. Meyer Schapiro, *Romanesque Architectural Sculpture: The Charles Eliot Norton Lectures*, ed. and with an introduction by Linda Seidel (Chicago, 2006), xvii–xviii.

61. I owe these observations to Christopher Lakey, "The Photographic Mediation of Medieval Sculpture after Wölfflin," paper given at the Renaissance Society of America meeting, Berlin, 2015.

62. Prange, "Kunstgeschichte aus dem Geist der Gegenwart."

63. See the detailed analysis by Tristan Weddigen in this volume.

64. The French reception was also highly attentive to the racial kernel of *Principles*. See the essay by Eric Michaud in this volume.

65. See the essay by Peter Krieger in this volume.

66. Kim Youngna, "The Achievements and Limitations of Ko Yu-seop, a Luminary in Korean Art History," *Archives of Asian Art* 60 (2010): 79–87.

67. Walter Passarge, *Gendai bijutsushi riron* 現代美術史理論 (Tokyo, 1934), trans. Kenji Moriya; *La filosofia de la historia del arte en la actualidad*, trans. Emilio R. Sádia (Madrid, 1932).

68. Ichijo Kazuhiko, "Wölfflin in Yomokichi Sawaki: The Translation of Wölfflin's *Principles of Art History* and Its Reception in Japan," paper given at the conference at Keio University, Tokyo; published in Mita Society for the Science of Arts, Keio University, "One Hundredth Anniversary of Heinrich Wölfflin's *Kunstgeschichtliche Grundbegriffe*," special issue, *Journal of the Science of Arts*, no. 19 (2015).

69. José Moreno Villa, *La escultura colonial Mexicana* (Mexico City, 1941).

70. See the essay by Shirahara Yukiko in this volume.

71. Hui Guo, "Writing Chinese Art History in Early Twentieth-Century China" (PhD diss., Leiden University, 2011), chapter 2, "From Japan to Europe: Teng Gu's Internalization of Western Art Historical Ideas."

72. See the essay by Tristan Weddigen in this volume.

73. The complaint that *Principles* "mechanized" art history, first voiced in Passarge (*Philosophie der Kunstgeschichte*, 3), was repeated into the 1970s.

74. Passarge, *Philosophie der Kunstgeschichte*, 19.

75. I am grateful to Sanja Cvetnic (Zagreb) for refreshing my memory many years later and for providing photographs.

76. Ichijo, "Wölfflin in Yomokichi Sawaki."

77. Annemieke Hoogenboom, *De Evolutie van de Compositie: De kunsthistorische onderwijsplaten van Willem Vogelsang (1875–1954)* (Vianen, 2007). My thanks to the author for sharing her work on Vogelsang.

78. Marga van Mechelen and Kitty Zijlmans, "Art History in the Netherlands," in *Art History and Visual Studies in Europe: Transnational Discourses and National Frameworks*, ed. Matthew Rampley et al. (Leiden and Boston, 2012), 410–413.

79. Van Mechelen and Zijlmans, "Art History in the Netherlands," 413.

80. Ettlinger, *Art History Today*.

81. In spite of Joseph Gantner's command of Wölfflin's oeuvre and archive (which he assembled), he published little on the text. Jonathan Blower first compared the manuscript to the 1915 edition in his preface to the 2015 English translation. For remarks on significant changes as well as the differences among the seven editions published during Wölfflin's lifetime, see Editors' Notes, Wölfflin, *Principles* (2015). On Gantner, see Oskar Bätschmann's essay in this volume. On varieties of reception studies, including genetic editing and the "new philology," see André Lardinois, Sophie Levie, Hans Hoeken, and Christoph Lüthy, eds., *Texts, Transmissions, Receptions: Modern Approaches to Narratives* (Leiden, 2015).

82. Marshall Brown, "Undisciplined Reading: Heinrich Wölfflin's Passions," *Critical Inquiry* 44 (2018): 733–744, and Levy, *Baroque and the Political Language of Formalism*, 132–144, respectively.

83. For an analogous case of Thucydides, to whom people refer in the present (often in contradictory ways), see Katherine Harloe and Neville Morley, "Introduction: The Modern Reception of Thucydides," in *Thucydides in the Modern World: Reception, Reinterpretation, and Influence from the Renaissance to the Present*, ed. Katherine Harloe and Neville Morley (Cambridge, 2012), 1–24.

HORST BREDEKAMP

Wölfflin in Germany

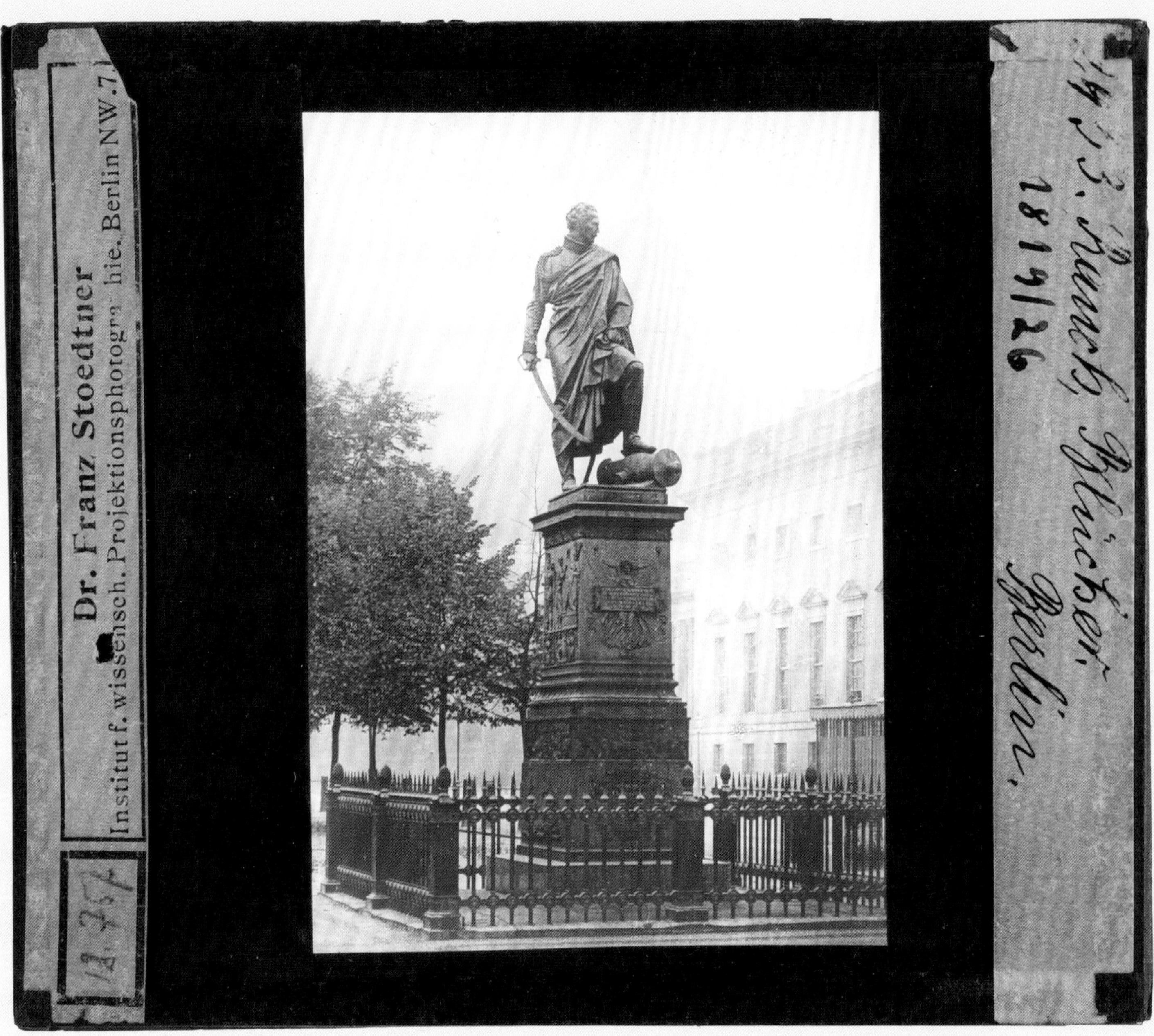
Dr. Franz Stoedtner
Institut f. wissensch. Projektionsphotographie. Berlin NW.7
14;13. Rauch, Blücher.
1819/26
Berlin.

In 1997 Stephan von Huene, a California artist of German descent, created an installation with two drums, tilted ninety degrees, on pedestals (fig. 1). On the drumheads, works of art were displayed as reversed images in a double projection. A viewer could hear interpretations in the form of short statements played on an audio device, emphasized or disregarded by the beats of attached drumsticks.[1]

The texts were based on a lecture Martin Warnke gave in 1970 at the Deutscher Kunsthistorikertag in Cologne that shook the German-speaking discipline. Using examples from popular art-historical publications, Warnke revealed how traditional thought patterns of submission had survived in our field: the subordination of details to the overall form, of reflection to movement, of the masses to the heroic individual, and of the exception to the general order.[2] Warnke sought to highlight the structural analysis of unconscious patterns of thought that had prevailed throughout time; these patterns in turn inspired von Huene to produce the work.

Von Huene also carried out research of his own, in the course of which he emphasized a passage in the 1932 English translation of Wölfflin's *Principles of Art History* that can be read as evidence of the very topoi that Warnke had classified as rhetorical "acts of enslaving" (*Knechtungsakte*): "The figures are developed as absolutely independent parts, and yet so work together that each seems governed by the whole.…[T]he individual part has lost its individual rights."[3]

Opposition to *Principles of Art History*

A large number of my generation read Wölfflin's formal analyses from this very perspective. My first essay, which I wrote with Franz-Joachim Verspohl shortly after the Cologne conference, explicitly argued against the Wölfflinian history of style, which, according to us, served only the ends of an "uncontradicted functioning of unproblematized, self-contained systems."[4] Wölfflin's approach to art history as a transhistorical history of vision, as was agreed at the time, had to be resisted in order to establish a historically oriented history of art in the present. The reasons for this antagonistic view lay in a chain of arguments that stemmed from the trauma of the National Socialist regime. Few disciplines in Germany lost as many Jewish scholars after 1933 as art history, among them the researchers connected to Aby Warburg's Kulturwissenschaftliche Bibliothek in Hamburg.[5]

Concurrent with the revival of the iconological methodology of the Warburg school in the 1960s, suspicion arose that Wölfflin's *Principles* had sterilized art history, making the discipline subservient to all those who, because of fear, collaborationism, or conviction, had stayed in Nazi-controlled Germany. From this perspective, Wölfflin's methods seemed to offer themselves to any and every form of authoritarian regime. In opposing Wölfflin's magnum opus, an old battle seemed to have been taken up again, but now with a more positive outcome.

The Retrieval of *Principles*

It could not have been more surprising, therefore, when *Principles* was reissued in the German Democratic Republic in 1983, accompanied by a comprehensive afterword by Hubert Faensen, which is among the best commentaries on this work ever written. In

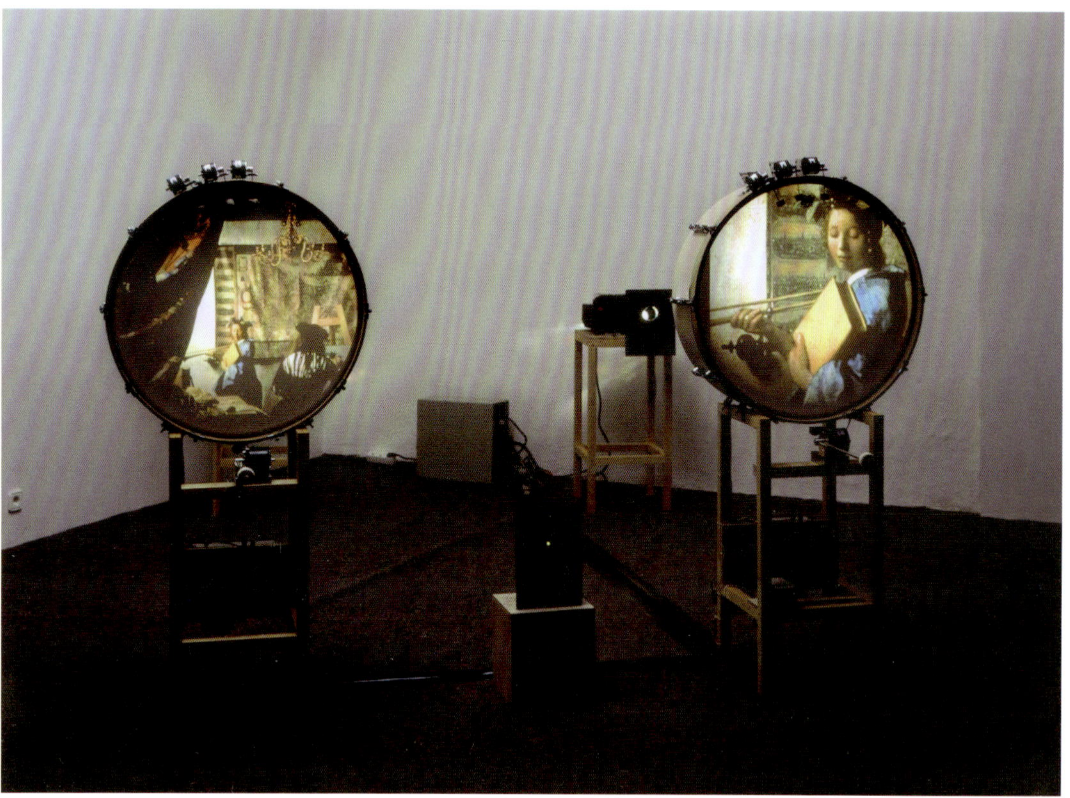

reading between the lines, its aim of giving the discipline a scientific foundation and thereby liberating it from the suspicion of belonging to a bourgeois tradition becomes evident.[6]

In West Germany, in turn, it was Martin Warnke himself who initiated the thaw of positions frozen in 1970. In 1989 he published an article in the journal *Representations* that tried to reconstruct a Wölfflin who was critical of his time and open-minded with respect to modernity.[7] The "icy pathos" of *Principles*, Warnke argued, was a kind of declaration of war against those who tried to use art as a sentimental tool of national self-elevation.[8] Similarly, the emancipation of art from historical pressures and the "bewildering alienation of the sign from the thing"[9] were, Warnke held, an immediate reaction prompted by Wölfflin's proximity to the art of his time and the dawn of abstraction.[10] And finally, the differences in folk psychology (*Völkerpsychologie*) that Wölfflin identified should be understood as elements of enrichment and not of conflict.[11]

The next year, in an article that had perhaps even greater impact, Warnke showed that the bipolarity of Wölfflin's *Principles*, being a structural element inherent to modernity itself, could equally be found in Warburg. Warnke concluded that the "techniques of polarization" common to both art historians had been applied to each of them individually by critics who portrayed "Wölfflin and Warburg as chiefs who commanded different schools."[12] As this treatment had harmed both, one should aim for a "polytheistic solution."[13] This premise was further nourished by the publication of Wölfflin's Berlin lectures on nineteenth-century art. Wölfflin appears as a contemporary, in touch and responsive to the modernists.[14]

His *Principles of Art History* took its final shape in Munich, after Wölfflin had accepted the call to the capital of Bavaria in 1912. This history has been analyzed in depth.[15] The remodernization of Wölfflin that finally raised the question concerning the universal validity of his methods, though, calls for a closer examination of his time in Berlin.[16] The capital of the German empire was the arena of deep-seated conflicts between defenders of tradition and partisans of the avant-garde, and it was in this city that *Principles of Art History* was conceived and compiled.

Wölfflin's Berlin: Personal, Social, and Art Historical

In his private sphere, in the social realm, and in his role as an art historian, Wölfflin's experience of Berlin was bifold. He longed for reclusion but often suffered from depression. Personally, he felt especially drawn to female company, but in that realm often raised expectations he was not willing or able to fulfill. His relationships with two women, Ricarda Huch and Lotte Warburg, may serve as examples. Most impressive is the correspondence with Huch, one of the most famous writers of her time, who had a close relationship to Wölfflin throughout her life. Her most apposite review of *Principles* shows an honesty that conveys her empathy.[17] In the Berlin years, a lifelong relationship began between Wölfflin and the art history student and later art historian and writer Lotte Warburg (fig. 2), the sister of Otto Warburg, who received the Nobel Prize in chemistry in 1931.[18] They were from the so-called Altona line of the Warburg family, whereas another well-known member of the family, Aby Warburg, belonged to one of the two branches in Hamburg. In Wölfflin's correspondence with Lotte Warburg, twenty years his junior, his driven and simultaneously reticent personality becomes obvious.[19]

In social terms, Berlin's mixture of opportunity and restraint both stimulated and daunted Wölfflin. With his appointment to the University of Berlin in 1901, he became part of the most famous academic institution of his time (fig. 3). In the same year, the Nobel Prize was founded. No other university received as many awards in the following decades until 1933.[20] In this environment, Wölfflin was one of the most respected scholars in the German Empire,

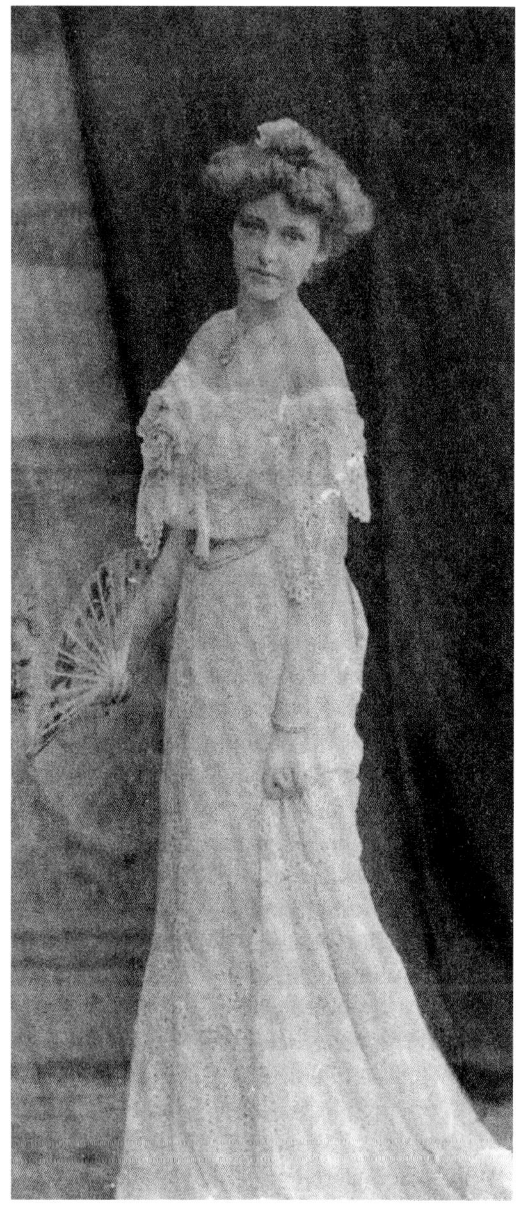

as demonstrated by his salary, which, in addition to the tuition fees for attending his lectures, was almost a third more than that of the world-famous physicist Max Planck. Furthermore, during his appointment negotiations, Wölfflin was given right of access to the imperial court. Without doubt, he belonged to the inner circle of the Berlin monarchy.[21]

Wölfflin's prestige was to no avail, however, in one of the most painful moments of his life, on May 20, 1904, the occasion of the kaiser's tour of the annual exhibition

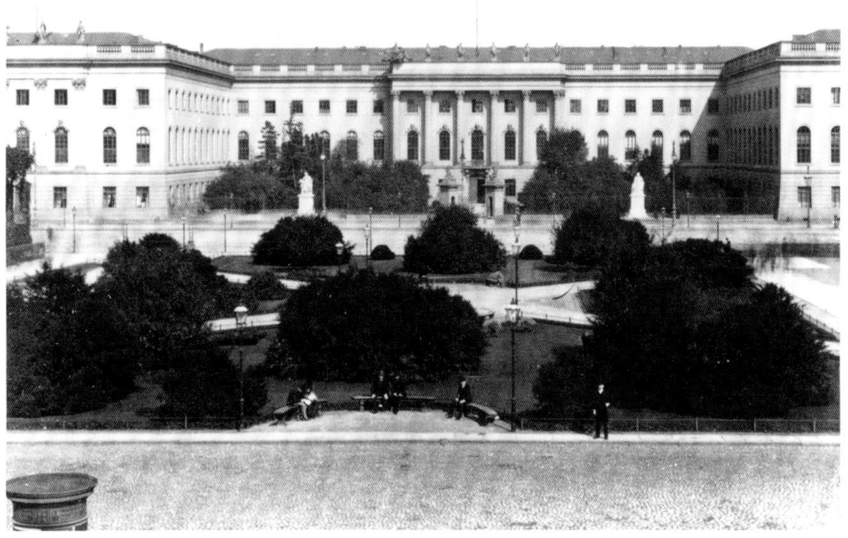

3. Friedrich-Wilhelms-Universität (today Humboldt-Universität), Berlin, photograph c. 1891
Stadtarchiv Berlin

4. Heinrich Wölfflin lecturing, 1920s, sketch by a student
Estate of Lotte Warburg

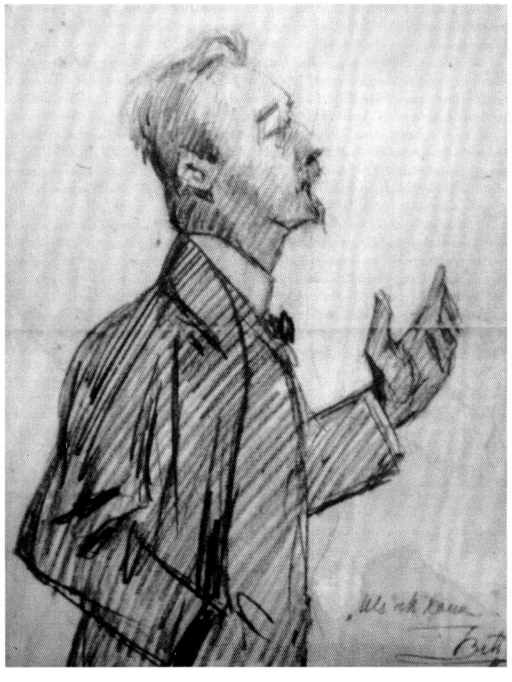

of the Königliche Akademie der Künste. Wölfflin was tasked with investing his extraordinary status in inspiring a sympathy with modern art in Kaiser Wilhelm, with the hope of influencing the selection of German art to be sent for display at the St. Louis World's Fair. The result was a complete failure; Wilhelm rejected Wölfflin in public in the most boorish manner.[22]

Wölfflin's conflicting personal and social experiences were consistent with his view of art history. Convinced that humanities lacked the verifiability that mechanics gives to physics, he had hopes, as he wrote in his dissertation (1886), for the empirical foundation of art history as it was ongoing in psychology.[23] Throughout his life, he was influenced by Wilhelm Wundt's *Vorlesungen über die Menschen- und Thierseele* (1863) and later writings like *Grundzüge der physiologischen Psychologie* (1874),[24] and presumably he had knowledge of Hermann Ebbinghaus's habilitation at the University of Berlin, *Über das Gedächtnis* (1885), which was one of the founding treatises of empirical psychology.[25]

Wölfflin's skepticism toward his own discipline was typical of his time; it also pertained to other fields like linguistics, which received an unforgettable critique in the work known as *The Lord Chandos Letter*, written by Wölfflin's Viennese friend Hugo von Hofmannsthal in 1902.[26] As the 1933 "Revision" to *Principles* demonstrates, Wölfflin was unable to harmonize these conflicts and remained fixated on the insufficiency of his own academic activities.[27]

Projecting and Drawing

In his lectures, Wölfflin transformed this sense of deficiency into the virtue of apodictic argumentation that created moments of a deep reflexivity. Many accounts testify to his superb elocution. He usually gave his lectures without a written text, using relatively short declarative statements that caused him recognizable struggles to formulate (fig. 4). His renown as a speaker was obviously the result of this manner, supported by the darkness of the lecture hall illuminated only by the projection of slides.[28]

For his regular lectures in Berlin, Wölfflin had inherited an enormous collection of large-format slides from his predecessor, Hermann Grimm, a pioneer of their use in teaching, whose reflection on the pluses and minuses of slide projection (1897) is a masterpiece of art-historical methodology.[29]

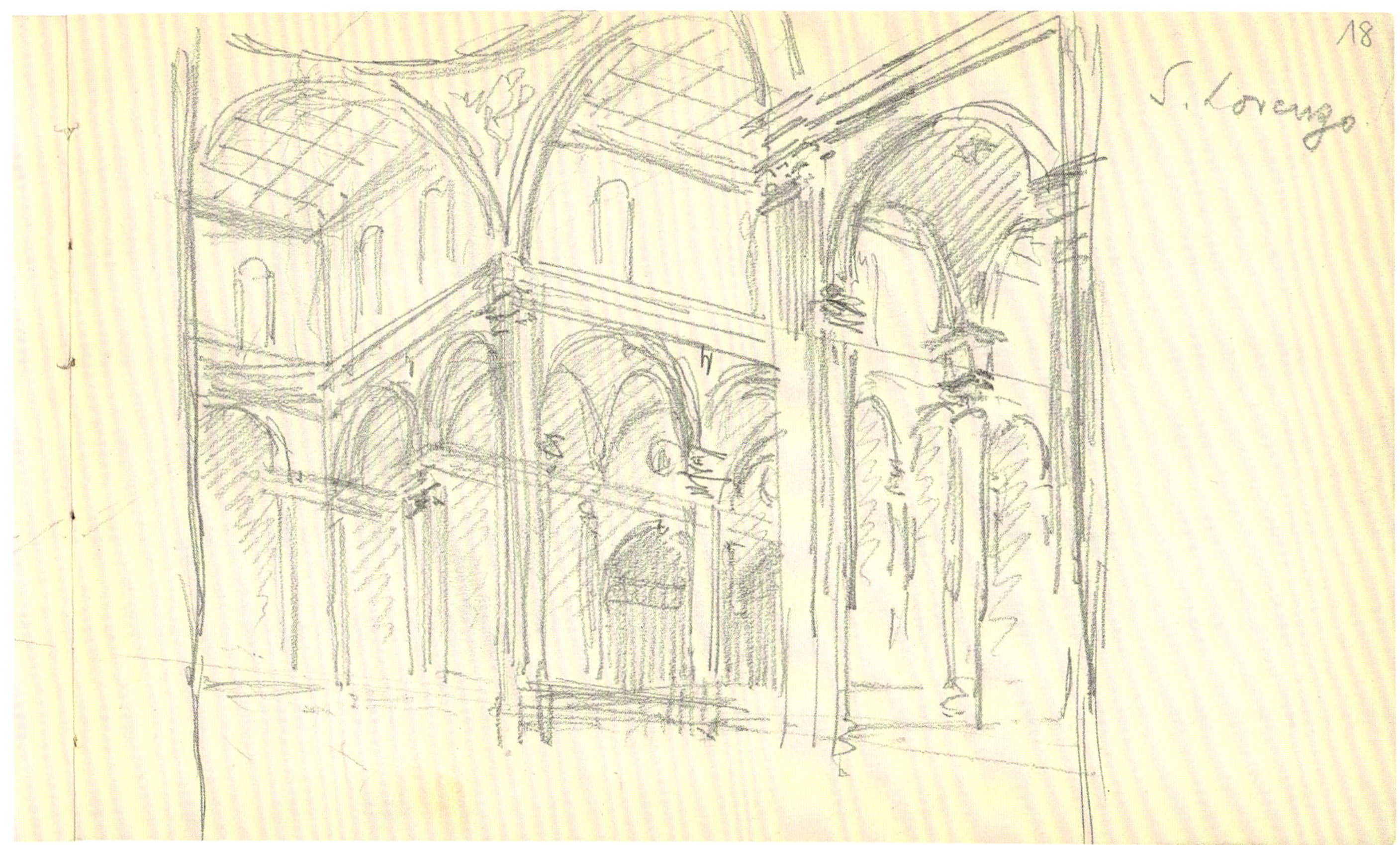

5. Heinrich Wölfflin, sketch of San
Lorenzo, Florence, 1888–1889,
pencil
*Universitätsbibliothek, Basel,
Nachlass Heinrich Wölfflin, NL95,
1973, II, 1b, Heft 10*

In Wölfflin's appointment negotiations, he
had been granted an enormous sum for the
development and expansion of this teaching medium. He used slides extensively,
and he took up Grimm's considerations on
their use in an essential essay on photography and art history.[30] Wölfflin brought
the technique of projection, which he
separately reflected upon in an essay for the
university's anniversary in 1910, to a new
high point.[31] Whether he invented double
projection is an open question. Not only in
Berlin but also, for example, in Halle, where
Wölfflin's successor Adolph Goldschmidt
worked, slide collections were established
and used in experimental ways; but in any
case Wölfflin used double projection already
in his years in Berlin, and in 1930 Ernst
Gombrich would be stunned by Wölfflin's
"magic of the two screens for the exercise of
comparisons."[32]

When he lectured, Wölfflin did not look
at his audience but faced the projection
wall instead (see fig. 4). His lectures on
nineteenth-century art, given in Berlin in
the summer of 1911, convey his presence
with peculiar immediacy. The stenographic
notation of these preserved lectures gives the
reader a strong understanding of the way in
which he used his virtuosic teaching method
of projection in the half-light of the lecture
hall to develop penetrating comparisons of
form.[33] The polarities that structure *Principles of Art History* are rooted in his celebra-
tion of the technical resources of his time for
comparing pictures in the most analytic and
intuitive way. One can speak of an interplay
out of which Wölfflin was able to meet the
spirit of his age, with its appreciation for the
formal exactitude of highly psychologically
charged opposites.

Wölfflin's lectures, which were understood
as a school of seeing, were accompanied by
the practice of drawing. Drawing was one of
the skills taught at the University of Berlin
in almost all fields: not only in archaeology and art history but also in sciences like
biology and—above all—medicine.[34] In

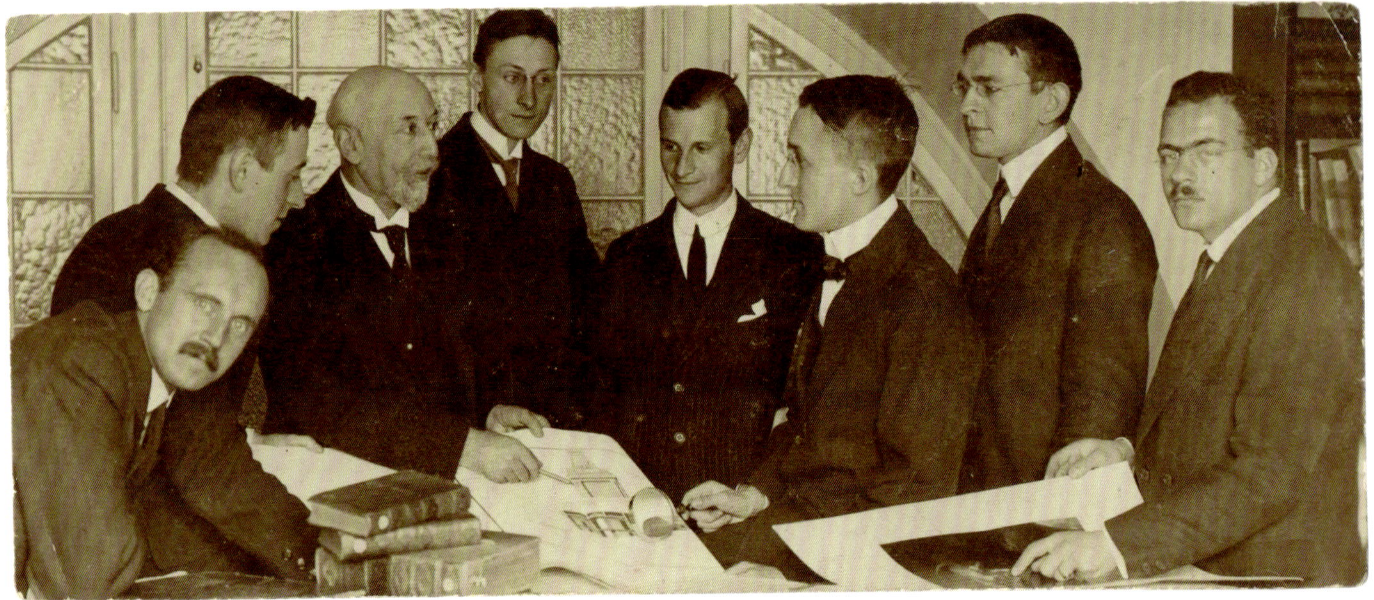

the motor skills of the hand Wölfflin saw
an unsurpassed instrument for extracting
the specific qualities of a composition and
the structural characteristics of styles. One
of his many architectural sketches analyzes
the structure of San Lorenzo in Florence
(fig. 5).[35] With his strong conviction that the
entire body and with it the drawing hand is
indispensable for perceiving the proper history of the visual, Wölfflin always remained
attached to his dissertation, "Prolegomena
to a Psychology of Architecture," and its
body-schematic perspective, which in the
field of the actual philosophy of embodiment
has made him an unexpected theoretical
precursor of current thoughts on this issue.[36]
Projection and drawing, machine and body:
the interdependent bipolarity of these fields
belonged to the essential possibilities that
Berlin's university offered to Wölfflin and
that he developed in an almost excessive way.

The Formulation of *Principles of Art History*

At the outset in Berlin, Wölfflin sensed the
need to formulate a methodological foundation for art history in the way of a clari-
fication of his thoughts and intuitions; this
seemed to be one of the expectations directed
at him.[37] In his lecture on *Principles of*

Art History during the winter semester of
1907/1908, he sketched out the book so fully
that the publishers wished already to "wrest
it from [his] hands."[38] In 1911 he was the
first art historian to be nominated as a member of the Preussische Akademie der Wissenschaften, and in his inaugural speech, "Das
Problem des Stils in der bildenden Kunst,"
he introduced the terminological concepts of
Principles of Art History.[39]

The book was polished into its final version in Munich and published in December
1915. Although it was almost immediately a
best seller, the first reaction among experts
was reserved or even oppositional. Aside
from the first spontaneous and thoroughly
positive responses,[40] critical voices, for
instance, those of Oskar Wulf and Rudolf
Kautzsch, prevailed.[41] The first truly positive
responses came from outside the discipline:
in 1917 from the literary scholar Oskar
Walzel and in 1919, after the war, from the
renowned and extremely influential philosopher Erich Rothacker.[42] By then, the book
was in its third printing, with ten thousand
copies sold and a broad discussion emerging
within the discipline. [43]

A prominent proponent was Erwin
Panofsky, who studied under Wölfflin's successor in Berlin, Adolf Goldschmidt (fig. 6).[44]

Having attended Wölfflin's lectures on Leonardo da Vinci in the winter semester of 1911/1912, Panofsky was among the first to take up Wölfflin's book for his own reflections on style.[45] This apparently inspired him to write his habilitation on problems of form in Michelangelo's work during his time in Berlin after World War I. In contrast to Wölfflin's structural "art history without names," Panofsky emphasized the autonomy of the style-shaping individual. Nevertheless, he used *Principles* as orientation, in order to develop and activate its categories.[46]

In 1930 *Principles* was so widely known that Walter Passarge dedicated an entire chapter of his *Die Philosophie der Kunstgeschichte in der Gegenwart* to its phenomenal success.[47] Wölfflin had become a classic during his lifetime, but he found his ideas cut and dried in their widespread, mostly misapprehended reception. It was in this spirit of critique and self-critique that he published the already cited "'Kunstgeschichtliche Grundbegriffe': Eine Revision" in 1933.[48] As much as he emphasized morphology and the material embeddedness of art in its time, he nevertheless held onto the relative independence of the history of vision, encapsulating his thoughts as he had in *Grundbegriffe* in the dictum "Not everything is possible at all times."[49]

This also applies to his own status. I began by trying to explain why Wölfflin's principles were themselves not always and unanimously appreciated in Germany, where he spent the greater part of his life. I have also tried to show that this varying degree of respect was not always objective or justified. A view from the outside could restore a more objective means of dealing with Wölfflin's theories and render his own doubts productive. In this process, the continual actualization of his school of seeing is indispensable for sharpening one's own eye.

NOTES

1. See Stephan von Huene, *What's Wrong with Culture?* (Neues Museum Weserburg Bremen, 1998), 57. See also *Stephan von Huene—Tune the World: Die Retrospektive*, ed. Christoph Brockhaus et al. (Ostfildern-Ruit, 2002), 203.

2. Martin Warnke, "Weltanschauliche Motive in der kunstgeschichtlichen Populärliteratur," in *Das Kunstwerk zwischen Wissenschaft und Weltanschauung*, Deutscher Kunsthistorikertag 12, ed. Martin Warnke (Gütersloh, 1970), 88–105.

3. Heinrich Wölfflin, *Principles of Art History: The Problem of the Development of Style in Later Art*, trans. M. D. Hottinger (London, 1932), 157; *Kunstgeschichtliche Grundbegriffe: Das Problem der Stilentwicklung in der neueren Kunst* (Munich, 1915), 169: "Hier hat man immer bewundert, wie die Figuren als lauter selbständige Stimmen ausgebildet sind und doch so ineinandergreifen, daß jede ihr Gesetz vom Ganzen aus zu empfangen scheint." See Yannis Hadjinicolaou, "Die Aktualität der 'Kritischen Kunstgeschichte' in Stephan von Huenes Blauen Büchern," *Kritische Berichte* 42, no. 4 (2014): 62–73, here 69. Von Huene's projection on the drum membranes refers to Wölfflin not only because it is double but because the two works of art are laterally reversed, to refer to Wölfflin's article "Über das Rechts und Links im Bilde," *Münchner Jahrbuch der bildenden Kunst*, n.s., 5 (1928): 213–224.

4. Horst Bredekamp and Franz-Joachim Verspohl, "Zur bürgerlichen Ideologie der Kunstgeschichte," *Tendenzen* 11, no. 65 (1970): 6–7, 10.

5. Ulrike Wendland, *Biographisches Handbuch deutschsprachiger Kunsthistoriker im Exil*, 2 vols. (Munich, 1999).

6. Hubert Faensen, afterword to Heinrich Wölfflin, *Kunstgeschichtliche Grundbegriffe: Das Problem der Stilentwicklung in der neueren Kunst* (Dresden, 1983), 379–433. Compare Hubert Faensen, "Wölfflins 'Kunstgeschichtliche Grundbegriffe,'" in *Künstlerisches und kunstwissenschaftliches Erbe als Gegenwartsaufgabe*, Humboldt-Universität zu Berlin, Sektion Ästhetik und Kunstwissenschaften, 2 vols. (Berlin, 1975), 1:71–85.

7. "I will investigate not whether Wölfflin was right or wrong, whether his *Principles of Art History* were right or wrong, but instead what they meant and what they achieved in *their day*" (Martin Warnke, "On Heinrich Wölfflin," *Representations* 27 [summer 1989]: 172–187, here 172. See Evonne Levy, "The Political Project of Wölfflin's Early Formalism," *October* 139 (winter 2012): 39–58.

8. Warnke, "On Heinrich Wölfflin," 173, 178. Wölfflin's restriction "to the boundaries of form represents a resistance to the political slogans of the time" (176; see also 174).

9. Wölfflin, *Principles of Art History* (1932), 21; see Warnke, "On Heinrich Wölfflin," 179.

10. From this point of view, Wölfflin's *Grundbegriffe* culminated in the observation that art had become a mere medium of viewing: "[D]as Tastbild ist zum Seebild geworden, die kapitalste Umorientierung, die die Kunstgeschichte kennnt." (The tactile picture has become the visual picture—the most decisive revolution which art history knows.) Wölfflin, *Kunstgeschichtliche Grundbegriffe* (1915), 24; *Principles of Art History* (1932), 21.

11. Warnke, "On Heinrich Wölfflin," 181. Compare Branko Mitrovic, *Rage and Denials: Collectivistic Philosophy, Politics, and Art Historiography, 1890–1947* (University Park, PA, 2015), 72–73.

12. Martin Warnke, "Warburg und Wölfflin," *Warburg: Akten des internationalen Symposions Hamburg 1990*, ed. Horst Bredekamp, Michael Diers, and Charlotte Schoell-Glass (Weinheim, 1991), 79–86, here 86.

13. Warnke, "Warburg und Wölfflin," 86.

14. Nobert M. Schmitz, "Heinrich Wölfflin—Ein Kunsthistoriker der Moderne," in Heinrich Wölfflin, *Kunstgeschichte des 19. Jahrhunderts: Akademische Vorlesung*, ed. Norbert M. Schmitz (Alfter, 1993), 129–156, here 131.

15. Matteo Burioni, Burcu Dogramaci, and Ulrich Pfisterer, eds., *Kunstgeschichten 1915: 100 Jahre Heinrich Wölfflin*, Kunstgeschichtliche Grundbegriffe (Zentralinstitut für Kunstgeschichte, Munich, 2015). See also, for the wider context of Wölfflin's *Grundbegriffe*, Evonne Levy, "Wölfflin's *Principles of Art History* (1915–2015): A Prolegomenon for Its Second Century," and Tristan Weddigen, "Approaching Wölfflin's Principles," in Heinrich Wölfflin, *Principles of Art History: The Problem of the Development of Style in Early Modern Art*, trans. Jonathan Blower, ed. Evonne Levy and Tristan Weddigen (Los Angeles, 2015), 1–46 and 47n68 respectively.

16. Joachim Rees, "Vergleichende Verfahren—verfahrene Vergleiche: Kunstgeschichte als komparative Kunstwissenschaft, eine Problemskizze," *Kritische Berichte* 40, no. 2 (2012): 32–47, here 47n45.

17. Ricarda Huch, "Kunst und Weltanschauung: Bemerkungen zu Wölfflins 'Kunsthistorischen Grundbegriffen,'" in *Mosaikbild einer Freundschaft: Ricarda Huchs Briefwechsel mit Elisabeth und Heinrich Wölfflin*, ed. Heidy Margrit Müller (Munich, 1994), 192–200.

18. See Cordula Koepcke, *Lotte Warburg: "Unglaublich! Daß ich gelebt habe!"; Eine Biographie* (Munich, 2000).

19. Lotte Warburg, *"Etwas für die Phantasie": Heinrich Wölfflins Briefwechsel mit "Züs Colonna"; Mit Erinnerungen und Erzählprosa von Lotte Warburg*, ed. Heidy Margrit Müller, with an essay by Peter G. Meyer-Viol (Munich, 1997).

20. For more detailed information see Horst Bredekamp and Adam Labuda, "Die institutionalisierte Kunstgeschichte, 1873–1945," in *Geschichte der Universität Unter den Linden, 1810–2010*, ed. Heinz-Elmar Tenorth, vol. 5, *Transformation der Wissensordnung* (Berlin, 2010), 435–458, here 443–447.

21. Information from Helmut Rausch, "Heinrich Wölfflin—eine überflüssige Spurensuche? Erste Anmerkungen und eine Dokumentation zu einer Vorlesung 'Kunstgeschichte des 19. Jahrhunderts' im Sommersemester 1911 an der Friedrich-Wilhelms-Universität zu Berlin" (master's thesis, Humboldt-Universität zu Berlin, 2006), 48.

22. Wölfflin reported the kaiser's words as "Sie machen mir gefälligst Front gegen diese moderne Richtung, in jeder Beziehung!" Heinrich Wölfflin to his parents, May 20, 1904, in *Heinrich Wölfflin, 1864–1945: Autobiographie, Tagebücher und Briefe*, ed. Joseph Gantner, 2nd ed., Basel, 1984), 206–208. The event was recounted even in the *New York Times* ("A Trap for the Kaiser, *New York Times*, July 31, 1904, 4). I thank Evonne Levy for this information.

23. "Man kann erst da exakt arbeiten, wo es möglich ist, den Strom der Erscheinungen in feste Formen aufzufangen. Diese festen Formen liefert der Physik zum Beispiel die Mechanik. Die Geisteswissenschaften entbehren noch dieser Grundlage; sie kann allein in der Psychologie gesucht werden" ("One can work exactly only when it is possible to capture the stream of phenomena in fixed forms. Mechanics, for instance, supplies physics with such fixed forms. The humanities still lack any such foundation; it is only in psychology that it can even be sought.") Heinrich Wölfflin, "Prolegomena zu Einer Psychologie der Architektur" (PhD diss., Universität München, 1886), in Heinrich Wölfflin, *Kleine Schriften*, ed. Joseph Gantner (Basel, 1946), 45–46. English translation from "Prolegomena to a Psychology of Architecture," in *Empathy, Form, and Space: Problems in German Aesthetics, 1873–1893*, ed. Robert Vischer et al., trans. and intro. Harry Francis Mallgrave and Eleftherios Ikonomou (Santa Monica, CA, 1994), 184.

24. Wölfflin, "Prolegomena," in *Kleine Schriften*, 14; see also 248. On the influence of Wilhelm Wundt, *Grundzüge der physiologischen Psychologie* (Leipzig, 1893), see Daniel Adler, "The Formalist's Compromise: Wölfflin and Psychology," in *German Art History and Scientific Thought: Beyond Formalism*, ed. Mitchell B. Frank and Daniel Adler (Burlington, VT, 2012), 73–95, here 85–87.

25. Hermann Ebbinghaus, *Über das Gedächtnis: Untersuchungen zur experimentellen Psychologie* (Leipzig, 1895). See Joan Goldhammer Hart, "Heuristic Constructs and Ideal Types: The Wölfflin/Weber Connection," in Frank and Adler, *German Art History and Scientific Thought*, 58–71, here 59.

26. Hugo von Hofmannsthal, *Ausgewählte Werke in zwei Bänden*, vol. 2, *Erzählungen und Aufsätze* (Frankfurt am Main, 1958), 337–348.

27. Heinrich Wölfflin, "'Kunstgeschichtliche Grund-begriffe': Eine Revision," *Logos: Internationale Zeitschrift für Philosophie der Kultur* 22 (1933): 210–218.

28. See Elke Schulze, "'Ich werde Mode!': Heinrich Wölfflin an der Berliner Universität," in *In der Mitte Berlins: 200 Jahre Kunstgeschichte an der Humboldt-Universität*, ed. Horst Bredekamp and Adam S. Labuda (Berlin, 2010), 91–101, here 94.

29. Hermann Grimm, "Das Universitätsstudium der neueren Kunstgeschichte," *Deutsche Rundschau*, no. 66 (1891): 390–413; Hermann Grimm, "Die Umgestaltung der Universitätsvorlesungen über neuere Kunst-geschichte durch die Anwendung des Skioptikons," in *Beiträge zur deutschen Culturgeschichte* (Berlin, 1897), 276–395. See Andreas Beyer, "Lichtbild und Essay: Kunstgeschichte als Versuch," in *Essayismus um 1900*, ed. Wolfgang Braungart and Kai Kauffmann (Heidel-berg 2006), 37–48, and Johannes Rößler, "Erlebnis-begriff und Skioptikon: Hermann Grimm und die Geisteswissenschaften an der Berliner Universität," in Bredekamp and Labuda, *In der Mitte Berlins*, 69–89.

30. Heinrich Wölfflin, "Wie man Skulpturen aufnehmen soll," *Zeitschrift für bildende Kunst*, n.s., 7 (1896): 224–228; n.s., 8 (1897): 294–297; reprinted in *Skulptur im Licht der Fotografie: Von Bayard bis Mapplethorpe*, ed. Erika Billeter (Bern, 1997): 409–413. Some of these magnificent slides have been restored and are in the slide library of the department of art and visual history, Humboldt-Universität zu Berlin. See Rausch, "Heinrich Wölfflin—eine überflüssige Spurensuche?," 10, 19–20, 25, and appendix 2.

31. Heinrich Wölfflin, "Der Apparat für Vorlesungen über neuere Kunstgeschichte," in Max Lenz, *Geschichte der Königlichen Friedrich-Wilhelms-Universität zu Berlin*, vol. 3 (Halle an der Saale, 1910), 265–266.

32. E. H. Gombrich, *Norm and Form: Studies in the Art of the Renaissance* (London, 1966), 92. On Wölfflin's use of double projection during his years in Berlin, Rausch, "Heinrich Wölfflin—eine überflüssige Spurensuche?," 10, 19, 33. The question of who invented double projection has been raised by Heinrich Dilly; see "Weder Grimm, noch Schmarsow, geschweige denn Wölfflin: Zur jüngsten Diskussion über die Diaprojektion um 1900," in *Fotografie als Instrument und Medium der Kunstgeschichte*, ed. Constanza Caraffa (Berlin, 2009), 91–116. Compare the vote for Goldschmidt: Dorothee Haffner, "'Die Kunstgeschichte ist ein technisches Fach': Bilder an der Wand, auf dem Schirm und im Netz," in *Bild/ Geschichte: Festschrift für Horst Bredekamp*, ed. Philine Helas et al. (Berlin, 2007), 119–129, here 121. See also Levy, "Wölfflin's *Principles of Art History*," 4, 37n.

33. Schmitz, "Heinrich Wölfflin —Ein Kunst-historiker der Moderne."

34. Elke Schulze, *Nulla dies sine linea: Universitärer Zeichenunterricht—eine problemgeschichtliche Studie* (Stuttgart, 2004); for Wölfflin, 158–163.

35. See Elke Schulze, "Il disegno: Strumento e linguaggio della visione scientifica," *Annali della Fondazione Europea del Disegno (Fondation Adami)* 3 (2007): 165–198.

36. Wölfflin, "Prolegomena," in *Kleine Schriften*; John Michael Krois, *Bildkörper und Körperschema: Schriften zur Verkörperungstheorie ikonischer Formen* (Berlin, 2011), 249–250. On the aspect of a body-related empathy based on the Pergamon Altar, see Alina Payne, "The Pergamon Altar, Heinrich Wölfflin, and German Art History at the Fin de Siècle," *RES* 53/54 (2008): 168–189.

37. "Berlin verlangt die universelle Bildung als Boden und die Behandlung der prinzipiellen Probleme. Va bene! Ich verlange nach nichts Anderem. Bisher habe ich das eigentlich künstlich zurückgedrängt." Journal entry of December 2, 1900, in Gantner, *Heinrich Wölfflin 1864–1945*, 150. See Meinhold Lurz, *Heinrich Wölfflin: Biographie einer Kunsttheorie* (Worms, 1981), 382.

38. Heinrich Wölfflin to his parents, August 1, 1907, in Gantner, *Heinrich Wölfflin 1864–1945*, 224.

39. Heinrich Wölfflin, "Das Problem des Stils in der bildenden Kunst," in *Sitzungsberichte der Königlich Preußischen Akademie der Wissenschaften* 31 (1912): 572–578.

40. Wilhelm Waetzold, "Besprechung von Heinrich Wölfflin, *Kunstgeschichtliche Grundbegriffe*, München 1915," *Kunst und Künstler* 14, no. 9 (1916): 468–471; Erwin Panofsky, "Das Problem des Stils in der bilden-den Kunst," *Zeitschrift für Ästhetik und allgemeine Kunstwissenschaft* 10 (1915): 460–467.

41. Oskar Wulff, "Kritische Erörterungen zur Prinzipienlehre der Kunstwissenschaft," *Zeitschrift für Ästhetik und allgemeine Kunstwissenschaft* 12 (1917): 1–34, here 7–10; Rudolf Kautzsch, "Der Begriff der Entwicklung in der Kunstgeschichte: Rede zur Kaiser-Geburtstagsfeier am 27. Januar 1917," *Frankfurter Universitätsreden* 7 (1917). See Warnke, "On Heinrich Wölfflin," 172–173.

42. Oskar Walzel, "Wölfflins Kunstgeschichtliche Grundbegriffe," *Internationale Monatsschrift für Wissenschaft, Kunst, und Technik* 11, no. 6 (1917): 699–726; Erich Rothacker, reviews of Heinrich Wölfflin, *Kunstgeschichtliche Grundbegriffe*; Hans Tietze, *Die Methode der Kunstgeschichte*; and Oskar Wulff, *Grundlinien und kritische Erörterungen zur Prinzipienlehre der bildenden Kunst*, *Repertorium für Kunstwissenschaft* 41 (1919): 168–176.

43. On sales of *Kunstgeschichtliche Grundbegriffe*: Warnke, "On Heinrich Wölfflin," 173.

44. On the photograph, see Gerda Panofsky, *Erwin Panofsky von zehn bis dreißig und seine jüdischen Wurzeln* (Passau, 2017), 148[145?]–149. On Wölfflin and Goldschmidt see Elizabeth Sears, "Eye Training: Goldschmidt/Wölfflin," in *Adolph Goldschmidt (1863–1944): Normal Art History im 20. Jahrhundert*, ed. Gunnar von Brands and Heinrich Dilly (Weimar, 2007), 275–294.

45. Panofsky, "Das Problem des Stils in der bildenden Kunst," 460–467.

46. Erwin Panofsky, *Die Gestaltungsprinzipien Michelangelos, besonders in ihrem Verhältnis zu denen Raffaels*, ed. Gerda Panofsky (Berlin and Boston, 2014).

47. Walter Passarge, *Die Philosophie der Kunstgeschichte in der Gegenwart* (Berlin, 1930), 16–36.

48. Wölfflin, "'Kunstgeschichtliche Grundbegriffe': Eine Revision."

49. "Nicht alles ist zu allen Zeiten möglich": Wölfflin, *Kunstgeschichtliche Grundbegriffe* (1915), 11.

OSKAR BÄTSCHMANN

Wölfflin's Swiss Legacy

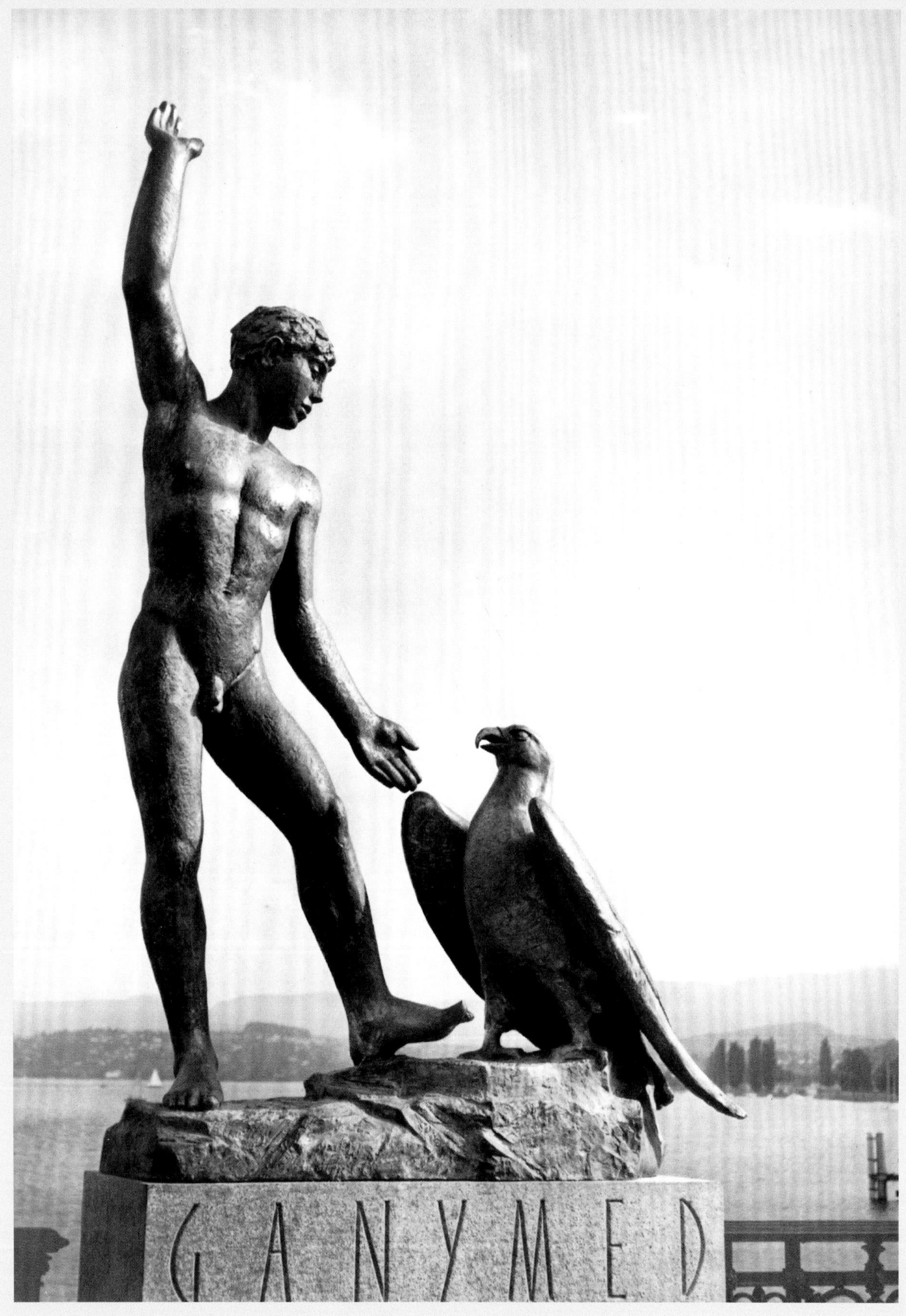
GANYMED

A t the start let me point out how difficult it is to determine how well a scholarly work is received. Art history has long since dealt with the reception of antiquities by artists, a part of reception. Production, distribution, and reception make up the three major research areas in art history. In general, "reception" is determined through similar repetitions of previously existing works or content. Reception mainly appears to be thought of as an active process of acceptance, in contrast to "influence," which assumes a passive recipient. Both notions about the reception of content and form suffer from an imprecise presumption of "historical context." In 1985 Michael Baxandall criticized "influence" as a hollow concept.[1] And for reception, criticism and systematic supplementation through historical explanation are largely lacking.

An investigation of processes of reception should include a search for indicators, criteria, and terms that make conclusions and qualifications possible.[2] In the case of *Kunstgeschichtliche Grundbegriffe (Principles of Art History)*, the reviews, the print runs, and the translations provide initial indications that then lead to chronology, geographical dissemination, and the names of people involved.[3] For example, it was only in 1952 that a literature professor in Geneva and his wife, Marcel and Claire Raymond, translated the work into French. The book was published in Paris by Plon, and three further editions would also appear in France.[4] Does it make sense to distinguish among national receptions given that Marcel Raymond was a professor of French literature at the University of Geneva and the translation of Wölfflin appeared in France? From its late appearance one must

not conclude that French art historians became aware of the book only in 1952.[5] A Wölfflin work was available in Paris as early as 1911 with the translation into French of his *Klassische Kunst* by Conrad von Mandach, then curator of Bern's Musée des Beaux-Arts.[6]

As for *Principles*, it has been widely noted that fields other than art history adopted its terms and method.[7] One example was provided by the Swiss archaeologist Arnold von Salis, who had studied under Wölfflin in Berlin, earned his doctorate there with a dissertation on Attic comedy, and was awarded a lecturership (*Privatdozentur*) in Bonn on the basis of a habilitation on the Pergamon Altar. In 1919 he published in Leipzig *Die Kunst der Griechen*.[8] In it he dispensed with notes, thinking that scholars would have no need of them and that laymen would find them an imposition. Accordingly, Wölfflin is not even mentioned. However, the archaeologist's demands that "the attempt at a systematic arrangement has to accompany an explanation of historical development" and that "the inner principles of development" need to be identified are close borrowings from Wölfflin.[9] There is also, as in the latter, a skepticism with regard to illustrations as inadequate substitutions for the original works.[10]

One of the transpositions of Wölfflin into another field was Fritz Strich's *Deutsche Klassik und Romantik*, first published in 1922.[11] Strich, who had earned his doctorate in Munich with a dissertation on Franz Grillparzer, had applied Wölfflin's terms to literary study as early as 1916, and on Wölfflin's recommendation assumed the chair in German literature at the University of Bern in 1929. For the first chapter

1. Edwin Scharff, *Heinrich Wölfflin*, 1923, bronze
University of Zurich, Institute of Art History; author photograph

2. Hermann Haller, *Heinrich Wölfflin*, 1924, bronze
University of Zurich, Institute of Art History; author photograph

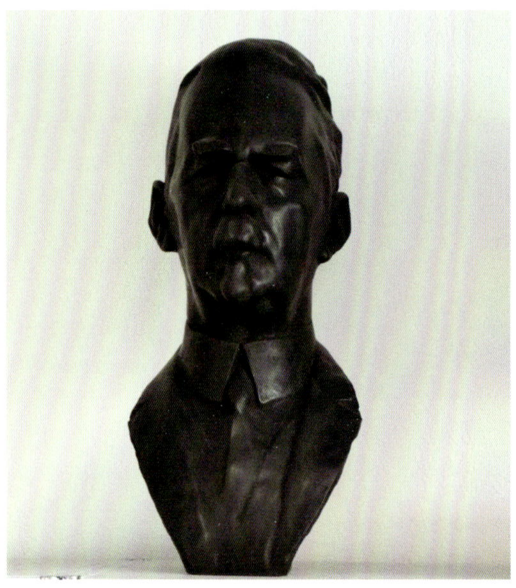

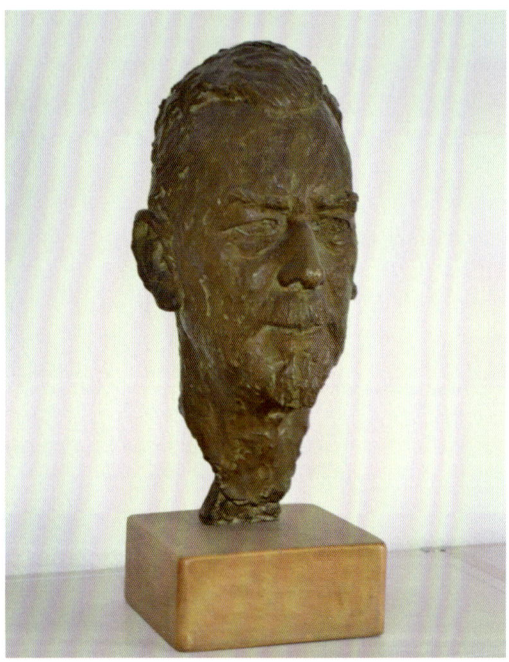

of *Deutsche Klassik und Romantik*, titled "Grundbegriffe," Strich wrote: "No one will have failed to note how greatly this book is indebted to the art-historical considerations of Heinrich Wölfflin and especially his *Principles*." The author argued for their validity in the humanities in general.[12] In his first chapter, to be sure, Strich undertook to oppose the "constantly repeated division of human thought into two directions," in Wölfflin into classic and baroque, with the thesis "eternity is…the highest principle of human culture."[13] Strich's admiration for Wölfflin was such that in 1956 he would call him, in somewhat high-flown terms, "my only teacher and master."[14] The book *Grundbegriffe der Poetik* by the Zurich Germanist Emil Staiger, published in 1946, could be considered an amendment to Wölfflin, whose lectures the author had attended as a student in 1927/1928.[15]

Friedrich Rintelen provides an example of a negative reception. In 1914 he succeeded Ernst Heidrich in the Basel chair that Wölfflin had held until 1901. After earning his doctorate in Munich with a work on Leibniz in 1902, Rintelen became an art historian and was promoted to lecturer at the University of Berlin in 1909, his qualifying work overseen by Wölfflin. His book *Giotto und die Giotto-Apokryphen* appeared in 1911.[16] Wölfflin is only mentioned in Rintelen's obituary for Ernst Heidrich: "It is clear how important the impact of Wölfflin's strict formality on Heidrich's essentially very flexible nature must have been, but it was no less certain from the beginning that Heidrich could not be completely absorbed in Wölfflin." According to Rintelen, in his dissertation on Dürer Heidrich had "applied only the theory of Wölfflin, not his way of thinking," since he was himself "above all totally Heidrich."[17] In the view of his own pupil Georg Schmidt, this problem common to all pupils had made Rintelen defensive: "Whereas Wölfflin generalized stylistic epochs using terms whose generality is ever in danger of no longer expressing anything essential, Rintelen not only atomized eras and within eras individual artists, but also in the individual artist every single work."[18] After that there cannot have been much left.

It would be nearly impossible to determine the degree to which Wölfflin's *Principles* was adopted in university teaching in Switzerland. Lists of courses at the universities of Basel, Bern, Freiburg, and Zurich up to 1945 do not include any course titles that could be related to Wölfflin.[19] Discussion of Wölfflin's work could of course be subsumed under titles like "Art-Historical Exercises," or under the numerous lectures on Italian painting, the Renaissance, or the baroque. Hanspeter Landolt, professor of art history at the University of Basel from 1965 to 1985, relates that he based his undergraduate seminar on Wölfflin's book every year.

Results of a brief survey of the public reception based only on Switzerland's most important newspaper, the *Neue Zürcher Zeitung*, are altogether disappointing. The name Heinrich Wölfflin was first mentioned in 1889 in connection with his little book on Salomon Gessner, then again in 1899 on the appearance of *Die klassische Kunst*. In 1901 his appointment to a professorship in Berlin was noted, in 1910 his elevation to privy councillor, and in 1911 there was one article on his maiden speech to the Preussische Akademie der Wissenschaften and another on his appointment in Munich. His numerous lectures in Switzerland were reported on, as well as his memorial speech for Heidrich in 1914. In 1921 Wölfflin's small book *Das Erklären von Kunstwerken* was advertised, and beginning in 1923 there were comments on his appointment in Zurich. Between 1888 and 1924 Wölfflin's name appeared fifty-five times in the *Neue Zürcher Zeitung*, but the first mention of *Principles* was on July 13, 1924, in a review of Franz Landsberger's monograph on Wölfflin by the editor T. (Hans Trog).[20] The conclusion: the *Neue Zürcher Zeitung* took no interest in *Principles* until 1924, when the book was in its sixth edition. An analogous search of the *Tribune de Genève* archive netted no results.

Zurich (1924–1945)

In 1924 Wölfflin left the University of Munich and took up the personal chair that was offered to him by the University of Zurich.[21] The universities of Basel and Bern had attempted to lure him back to Switzerland in 1919 and 1920,[22] and negotiations in 1923 had convinced him to pursue his teaching there. His appointment to the art history chair in Zurich, dated October 18, 1923, set the starting date as April 16, 1924, called for a teaching load of four to five hours a week, and guaranteed an annual salary of 10,000 francs.[23]

Writing that year in the *Preussische Jahrbücher*, Otto Grautoff sought to justify Wölfflin's departure from Munich, perceived as a kind of desertion.[24] Grautoff, who had received his doctorate at the University of Bern with a dissertation on Nicolas Poussin, became a mediator between Germany and France in the 1920s with his monthly journal *Deutsch-Französische Rundschau*. He reminded readers of the *Preussische Jahrbücher* that Wölfflin came from Switzerland, with its multiple languages, thanks to which the "Swiss mindset" was permeated with Latin notions. He suspected that Wölfflin had adopted from France the habit of introducing a work with a thesis and ending it with a conclusion, just as he had a style of writing that emulated "the short sentences of French thinkers with their even flow of syllables."[25]

From Munich Wölfflin took with him to Zurich the portrait bust by Edwin Scharff he had received as a parting gift from his students (fig. 1).[26] In Zurich the sculptor Hermann Haller also produced a portrait commissioned by friends and admirers (fig. 2). Needless to say, Wölfflin applied to the two his method of comparative analysis: "The Scharff bust…is a truly outstanding work.… [I]t is a daily admonition to improvement, for it exerts an authority that goes beyond nature. Pity that it now enters into competition with Haller: I fear that in the comparison the latter suffers."[27] The *Neue Zürcher Zeitung* compared Scharff's bust, with its "highly effective exaltation into the lordly, heroic," with Haller's, which presents "such an uncommonly humane, expressive figuration of the head."[28] The modest and somewhat softer Haller portrait appealed to the reviewer more than the archaistic, angular work by Scharff.

For his sixtieth birthday Wölfflin was presented with a festschrift by his friends and pupils, as well as an impressive encomium from Erwin Panofsky.[29] Sigfried Giedion discussed the festschrift in the *Neue Zürcher Zeitung* of July 13, 1924, and at the

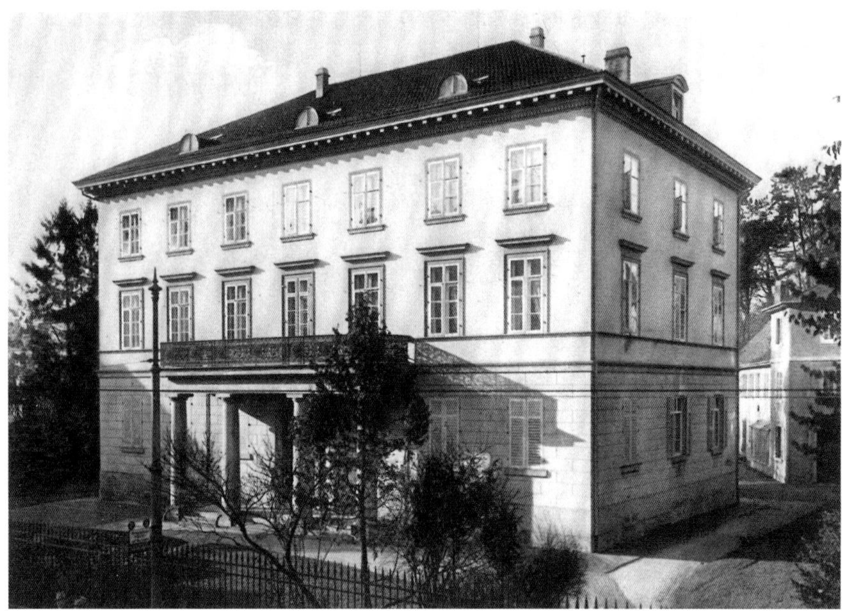

3. Haus zum Sihlgarten, Talacker 39, Zurich (1829)
Wikimedia Commons

4. Michael Stettler, c. 1935
Private collection

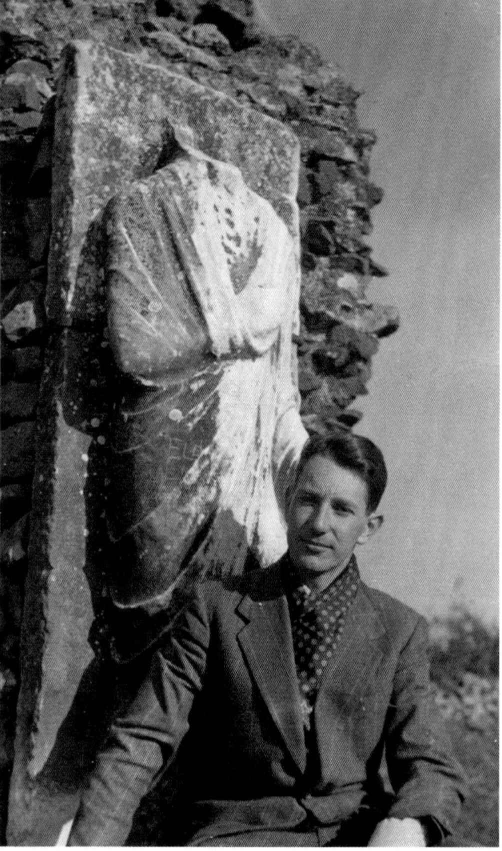

independent of the particular atmosphere of the time."[30]

This became Wölfflin's central focus in his Zurich years.[31] He gave lectures before large audiences, to be sure, but he had no pupils, for he oversaw only a single dissertation.[32] Only much later would Wölfflin confess that his teaching in Zurich was not very satisfying, despite its "numerical success": "I soon recognized that the connection to the students that had automatically been established at the various universities in Germany failed to develop."[33] In his inaugural lecture on June 14, 1924, "Die geschichtliche Betrachtung der Kunst" (The historical consideration of art), Wölfflin discussed the relationship between art history and other disciplines and literary texts. He called for a history of the eye, since this organ occupied "such an important place in the creation of a worldview as orientation in life."[34] He introduced the same theme once again in the essay "'Kunstgeschichtliche Grundbegriffe': Eine Revision," which appeared in the German journal *Logos* in 1933.[35] That essay begins with the thesis that any "historical consideration of art" gives rise to the danger of "allowing what is specific to art…to wither away." Placing the "specific" at the center of the discipline of art history, explaining it from its own presuppositions, and studying the inherent laws in its development as well as the way it is determined by "folk character" were Wölfflin's central concerns.

On Wölfflin's seventieth birthday the *Neue Zürcher Zeitung* published a two-page spread with congratulations from Ricarda Huch, Julius von Schlosser, Otto Grautoff, Ludwig Justi, Joseph Gantner, Willy Fries, and Gotthard Jedlicka.[36] The *Basler Zeitung* followed with encomiums from Walter Ueberwasser and Sigfried Giedion.[37] A few days later the *Neue Zürcher Zeitung* published a report on Wölfflin's retirement ceremony at the University of Zurich.[38] It particularly emphasized that the distinguished professor had asserted that his most urgent task was "to combat with all his energy the excessive tributes to him

same time the editor Hans Trog reported on the monograph by Landsberger and its support of Wölfflin's notion "that to the expressive component as one root of change in style a second has to be added that remains

5. Hermann Hubacher, *Heinrich Wölfflin*, 1944, bronze
University of Zurich, Institute of Art History; photograph by SIK-ISEA, *Zürich (Philipp Hitz)*

appearing in letters and publications." He denied being a "great art historian," for he had uncovered no new material and had held himself "deliberately aloof" from the history of ideas. All that he could claim was having worked out "specific laws in the development of fine art." His modesty was capricious, for the claim of having worked out art's developmental laws was the most one could have hoped for in the first decades of the twentieth century.

After withdrawing from teaching and to a great extent from public life, Wölfflin found himself somewhat isolated, despite continuing veneration and the many visitors who found their way to his apartment in the Haus Sihlgarten at Talacker 39 in Zurich (fig. 3). The house, built in 1826–1829 by Hans Conrad Stadler, was especially pleasing to Wölfflin, who considered it a model of "simple, precise, and comprehensible form"; in 1933 he described it as follows: "The house stands there, crystal hard and crystal clear as a sharp-edged white cube."[39] Years later one of his visitors, the young architect and art historian Michael Stettler (fig. 4), wrote of his impressions on meeting Wölfflin in the autumn of 1940 and from repeated visits up until 1944. Stettler stepped into the "urbane scholar's room with the Titian copy," where Wölfflin sat at a "sarcophagus-like writing table," and rose before the young visitor "to towering height" or to full "privy councillor, professorial" dignity.[40] Stettler also witnessed a visit to Wölfflin by Max Planck, from Berlin.

Wölfflin's eightieth birthday was marked by publication of the festschrift *Concinnitas: Beiträge zum Problem des Klassischen*, which alluded to Wölfflin's engagement with Leon Battista Alberti. Its contributions came from the most varied disciplines.[41] Former pupils commissioned a portrait bust from the sculptor Hermann Hubacher, but Wölfflin shied away from a third sculptural immortalization (fig. 5). Before sitting for it he quizzed the sculptor: "Aren't you too good for such work; and is it really rewarding to immortalize a head that exhibits the most obvious signs of decline?[42] In January

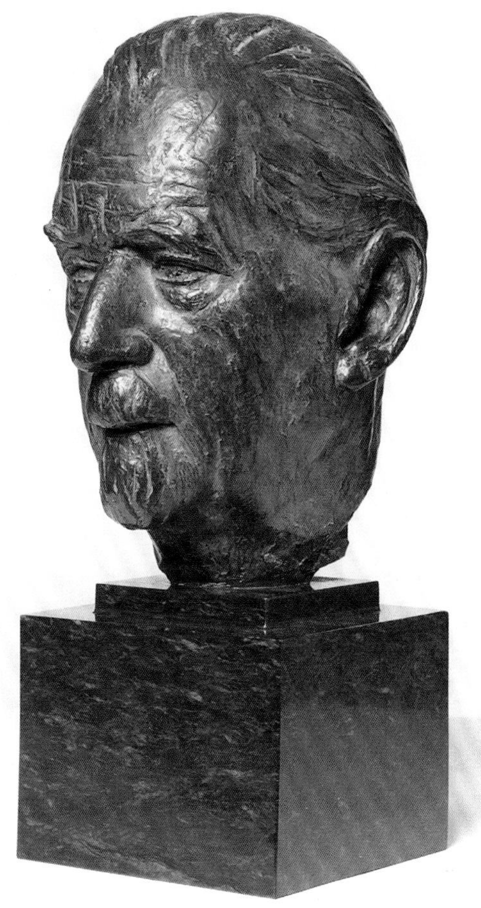

1944 Wölfflin appeared in the sculptor's atelier, and in 1964, on the occasion of the centennial of the art historian's birth, Hubacher published the entries in his diary about the portrait sittings.[43]

On January 30, 1942, Wölfflin asked the sculptor what the cost would be for a sculpture he was thinking of presenting to the city of Zurich: "It would have to be a *male* figure (Zurich already has a quantity of female ones) and indeed one of *strength*, so that the regularity of his physique comes through, disciplined beauty! The architectural setting would also have to be very severe."[44] In 1944 Wölfflin wrote a few lines to Hubacher: "I am still pleading for a freestanding figure next to the lake, to my mind a male figure would have to be placed there."[45] In 1952 the sculpture *Ganymede* (essay frontispiece) was installed on the shore of Lake Zurich.[46]

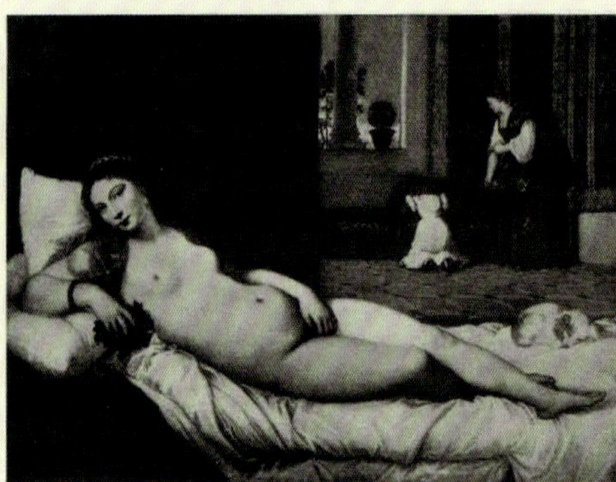

62. Tizian, Venus (Florenz)

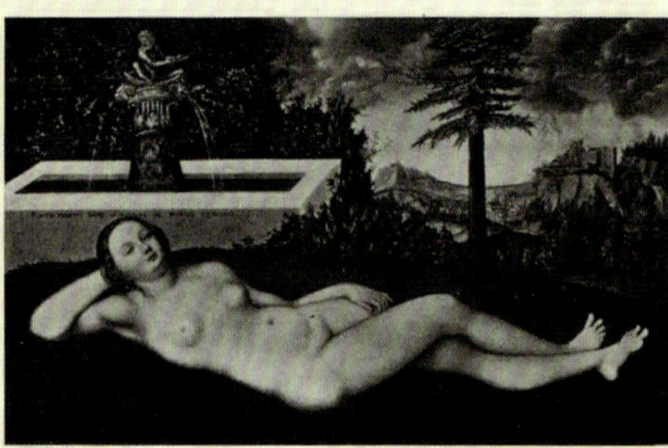

63. L. Cranach d. Ä., Quellennymphe, 1518 (Leipzig)

Wir greifen zunächst auf zwei Bilder des vorigen Kapitels zurück, die stehenden weiblichen Aktfiguren des Franciabigio und des Baldung Grien (Abb. 58 und 59). Die Verschiedenheit des Eindrucks im Sinne der stillen und der lauten Form wird von niemandem geleugnet werden, wesentlich aber ist nicht der andere Körperbau, etwa der auffällig hohe Bauch bei Baldung, sondern die Art wie der Deutsche die Funktion in der Form wirksam werden läßt. Man sieht das schon in der Wendung des Kopfes, im Achselgelenk, im durchgedrückten Knie, aber auch die scheinbar unbewegte Form ist hier durchweg mit Spannung geladen, so daß die Schenkel, ein herabhängender Arm ein ganz anderes Aussehn gewinnen. Auch bei dem Bauch ist es weniger die Rundung an sich als die Funktion des Vorspringens, die der deutschen Zeichnung ihren Nerv gibt. Wie still ist die Plastik des italienischen Körpers und wie einleuchtend ihr Zusammenhang mit der lässigen Bewegung! Und so das Bildganze: es ist der Unterschied des ruhig fließenden italienischen Ornaments und der drangvolleren deutschen Ranke.

Als neue Bilder bringen wir an dieser Stelle den liegenden Akt, wie ihn Giorgione und Tizian* gesehn haben, und als deutsche Parallele dazu ein Bild von Cranach*, das kaum ohne Zusammenhang mit solchen italienischen Vorbildern entstanden ist und darum für die Vergleichung um so instruktiver sein mag. Der individuelle Gegensatz zwischen Cranach und Baldung tritt vollkommen zurück vor der durchgehenden nationalen Gleichheit des Formgefühls. Kein Zweifel, erst das 16. Jahrhundert hat diese lange ruhige Linie bei Tizian (und Giorgione) reifen lassen, das Quattrocento ist kurzatmiger, aber die zappelnde Form Cranachs bedeutet für uns trotzdem eine „Hochrenaissance" und nicht eine bloße Vorstufe. Die Behandlung der gekreuzten Beine mit den gespreizten Zehen ist ungemein charakteristisch. Wir möchten dabei aber nicht nur auf den Unterschied des Bewegungsmotivs hingewiesen haben — die vornehm lässig gestreckten Beine dort und das Übereinanderschlagen der Beine hier, wo die Kreuzung oberhalb der Knie stattfindet —, der tiefere Gegensatz liegt in der Auffassung der Form als solcher, so daß der Leib in allen seinen Teilen von andern Spannungen erfüllt erscheint als bei Tizian. Und dieses andere Leben wird sich natürlich auch im Bildganzen widerspiegeln.

6. Heinrich Wölfflin, *Die Kunst der Renaissance: Italien und das deutsche Formgefühl* (Munich: Bruckmann, 1931), 144–145

Complementary Self-Reception

With the essay "Italien und das deutsche Formgefühl," reprinted in 1924 in the Swiss journal *Das Werk*, Wölfflin announced his renewed presence in art history in Switzerland.[47] Expanding this essay into a book was what mainly occupied him up until 1931.[48] The book, published as *Die Kunst der Renaissance: Italien und das deutsche Formgefühl* and subsequently in English as *The Sense of Form in Art* (fig. 6), was conceived as a counterpart to *Principles*. In 1921, in *Das Erklären von Kunstwerken*, Wölfflin had assigned to the historian the task of giving to the isolated work "context and atmosphere." He called the "artist's entire oeuvre" the "most fruitful" field of study, from which one obtains the notion of an artistic personality, the characterization of which has to be compared with contemporaries in order to discover how his individuality relates to the "typical genre of the generation."[49] Wölfflin proposed that artists of a given generation conform in their "essential features," and that these features constitute a "generational character." This was followed by the further assumption that for all the changes in styles there is something constant, "something enduring, a national way of creating form that adheres to the specific landscape, and that allows one to speak in general of a German or Italian type of construction."

In *Principles* Wölfflin wished to deal with "the internal history, the natural history of art so to speak, not with problems of the histories of artists."[50] To set his work apart from biographical studies, Wölfflin used the expression "art history without names," which was seen as a provocation.[51] When preparing the fourth edition in 1920, he felt the need to assure readers that he had never doubted the "value of the individual" but brought to his presentation only what lay "*beneath*" the individual."[52]

As in *Principles of Art History*, in *The Sense of Form in Art* Wölfflin had no desire to write about artists, or even expressly about art; his subject was "the basic sense of form," or the "premises of art."[53] Explaining these was his central concern: in *Principles* it was the shift from the Renaissance to the baroque, in *The Sense of Form in Art* it was the realities of ethnicity or race, defined territorially. In both cases it was a matter of the determination of artistic figures "beneath the individual"—on the one hand owing to the law of development and on the other "laws of race." Wölfflin worked all his life on this hypothesis of a matrix beneath the individual that determines the artistic activity of all individuals of a given time and a given "people." To this extent *Principles* and *The Sense of Form in Art* complement each other like time and space.

Wölfflin was perhaps only partially aware of the snares that came with any discussion of a "national" sense of form, for he considered only the difficulty of the approach, not the ideological problem. The issue of ethnic differences (the collective "nature" or character of a people) had become a veritable obsession in the last quarter of the nineteenth century and the beginning of the twentieth, most notably in the Deutsche Gesellschaft für Anthropologie, Ethnologie und Urgeschichte. Anthropology influenced German-language writing on art in two important ways: the inclusion of racial theories in the definition of national character and the adoption of "evolution" and "evolutionary history."[54]

Was Wölfflin hoping with his book from 1931 to retrieve the issue of German nationality from its ideological appropriation by ethnic psychology? Wilhelm Schlink has

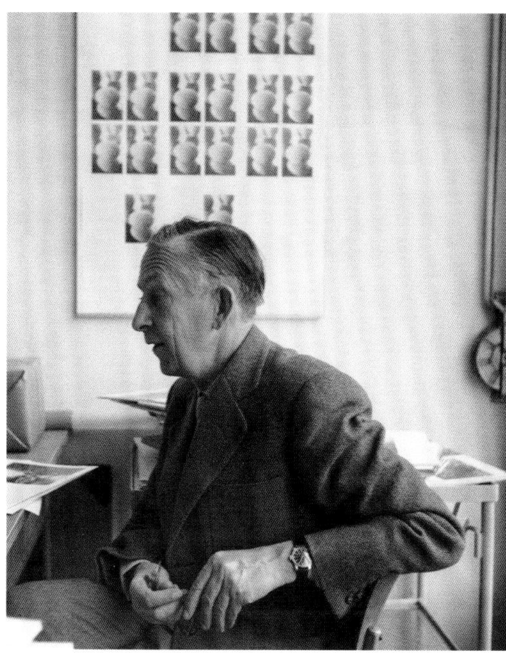

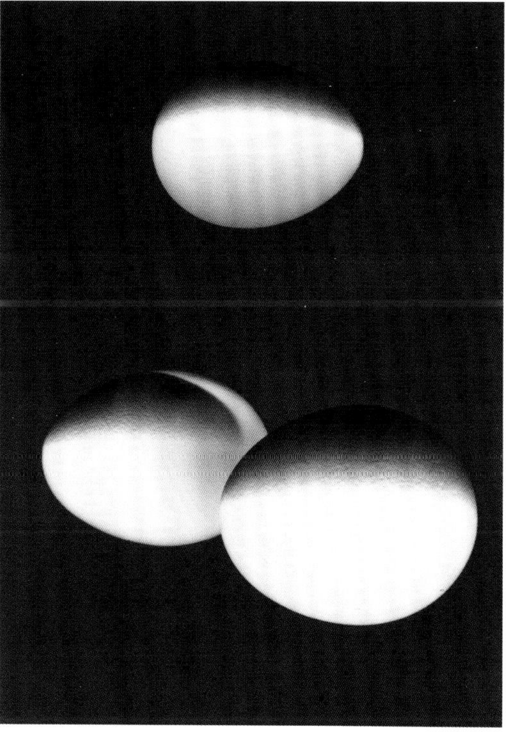

noted a "shying away from nationalistic tendencies on the part of the author": "Just as he rejected, beyond consideration of form, all approaches to the interpretation of art, art epochs, and changes in art based on cultural history, he also held himself aloof from any racial, nationalistic misuse of the

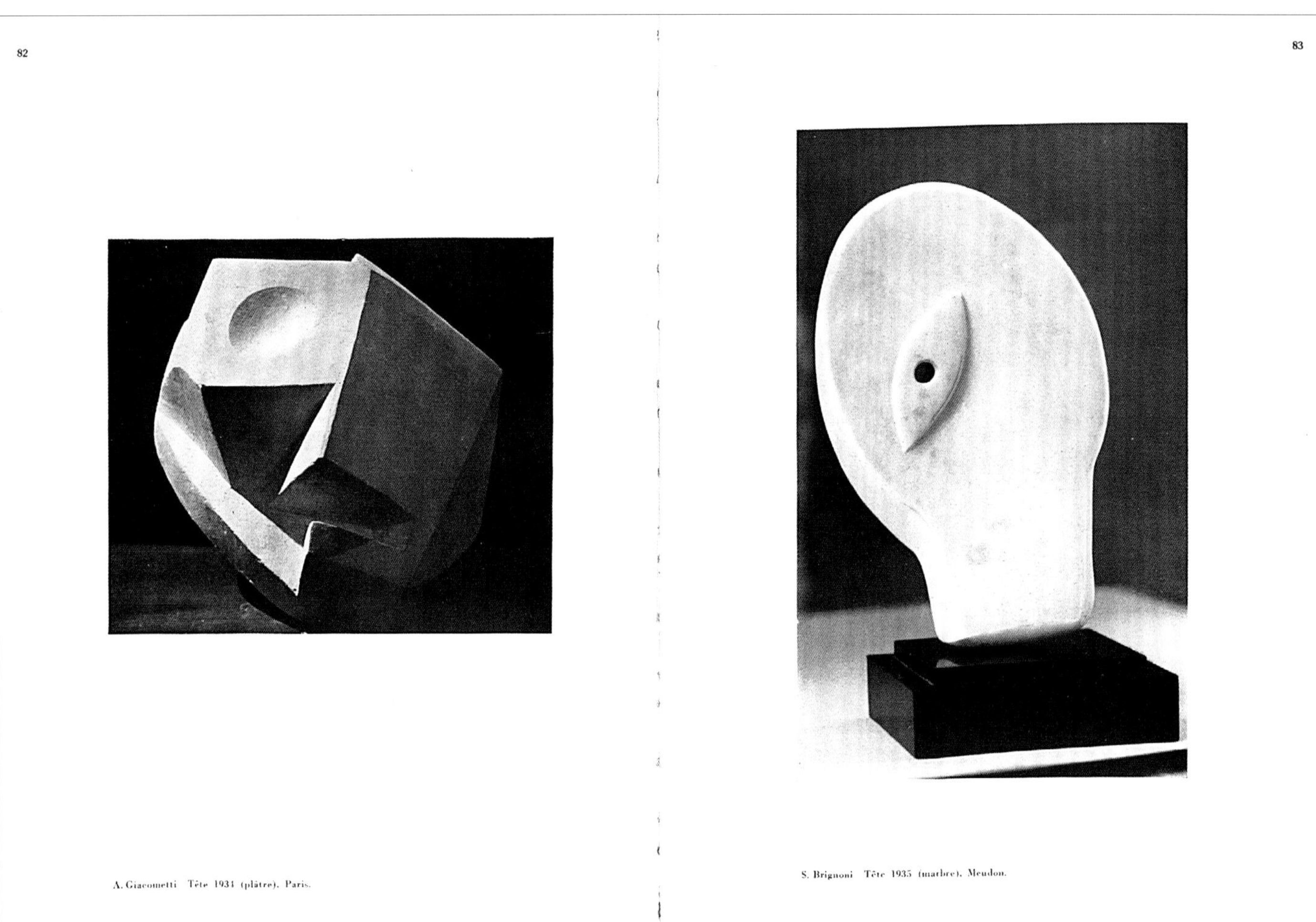

A. Giacometti   Tête 1931 (plâtre). Paris.

S. Brignoni   Tête 1935 (marbre). Meudon.

German sense of form."[55] Yet Wölfflin's theses were readily subject to misinterpretation. This is evident from the reaction of Julius von Schlosser in Vienna, who in 1934 situated Wölfflin's book between blood and veins, tribal history and race: "For it is about the engagement of the artistically sensitive German, beginning with Albrecht Dürer, and now here of a biracial Swiss, with the heritage of a southern, Romanic, specifically Italian essence that has lain in our blood since the beginning of our entire tribal history, now overly exalted, now maligned and denied."[56]

Swiss Pupils

Among Wölfflin's Munich pupils of Swiss nationality were Sigfried Giedion, Joseph Gantner, and Hans Finsler. Finsler became a famous photographer (figs. 7 and 8) and teacher at Zurich's Kunstgewerbeschule.[57] In the 1920s Giedion and Gantner turned to modernism, but without losing contact with their teacher.

In 1956, looking back at his unsuccessful application to the Eidgenössische Technische Hochschule in Zurich in 1934, Giedion wrote: "Had I stayed in Switzerland, constricted by the perennial battle with small power cliques, I feel that I would never have managed to produce the little I was perhaps destined to say. This is by no means the only reason why I am grateful to America and especially to Harvard University."[58] Giedion, born in Prague in 1888, completed his studies in mechanical engineering in Vienna in 1913, then took up the study of art history, and in 1922 earned his doctorate under Wölfflin at the University of Munich with his dissertation, "Spätbarocker und romantischer Klassizismus." In it Giedion confronted "baroque" and "romanticism" by way of the linking "classicism" and pursued the Wölfflinian question: "How is the romantic vision constructed?"[59] In Munich Giedion became acquainted with his future wife, Carola Welcker, from Cologne, who had transferred from the University of Bonn in 1915.[60] In the spring of 1925 the couple moved from Munich to Zurich, where they received all the important modern artists, architects, and writers in their welcoming home.[61] In 1937 Carola Giedion-Welcker published her book *Modern Sculpture* in German and English editions.[62] With its juxtaposed images (fig. 9), the layout, created by Herbert Bayer, adopts the way Wölfflin's *Principles* used illustrations.

In 1923 Giedion published a review of the Bauhaus exhibition in Weimar in the journal *Das Werk*.[63] It drew an objection to Bauhaus modernism from the Winterthur industrialist Richard Bühler, a cofounder of the Schweizerischer Werkbund. Giedion wrote a reply, but Joseph Gantner, the journal's editor beginning in January 1923, rejected it.[64] In it Giedion wrote that it was one of the tasks of the historian to attempt "to explain the often confusing ways of the present day."[65]

Joseph Gantner (fig. 10) took up this challenge. He had begun the study of art history under Wölfflin in Munich in 1915 and received his doctorate in 1920 with a dissertation on the nineteenth-century reception of Michelangelo.[66] In 1927, as a lecturer at the University of Zurich, Gantner gave his inaugural talk on the subject of Semper and Le Corbusier.[67] As editor of the journal *Das neue Frankfurt* from 1928 to 1932 and from his teaching at the Städtische Kunstschule in Frankfurt, Gantner acquired a profound knowledge of the new architecture and modern design.[68] In 1932 his booklet *Revision der Kunstgeschichte* (fig. 11) was published in Vienna, dealing "with the issue of a timely scholarly reform of art history."[69] Gantner postulated that "the most important task for younger art history researchers"

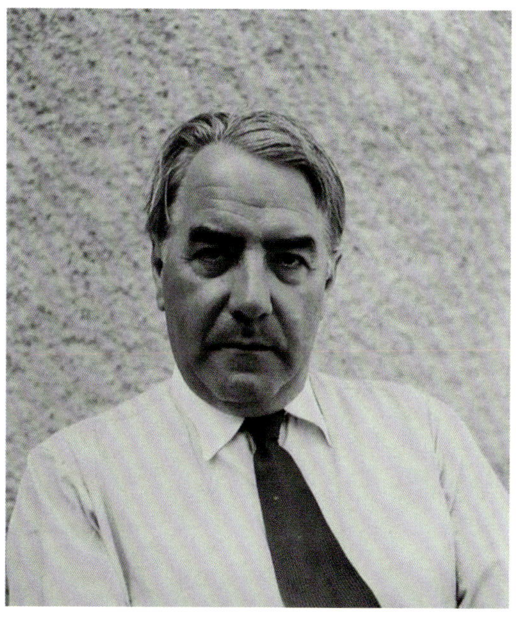

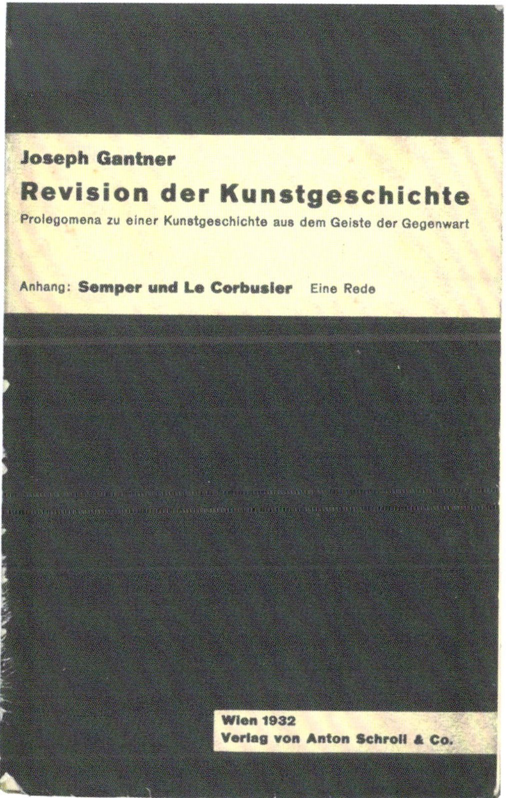

was "to reestablish the art-historical way of looking from today's point of view, thus the examination of the past from the present day."[70] The notion of working backward from the present instead of following a strict chronology had been repeatedly discussed in Munich circles formed around Hugo von

12. Wölfflin Medal of the City of
Zurich, c. 1987, 18-karat gold
*Treasury of the City of Zurich;
author photograph*

13. Sigfried Giedion
*gta Archiv, ETH Zurich, estate of
Sigfried Giedion*

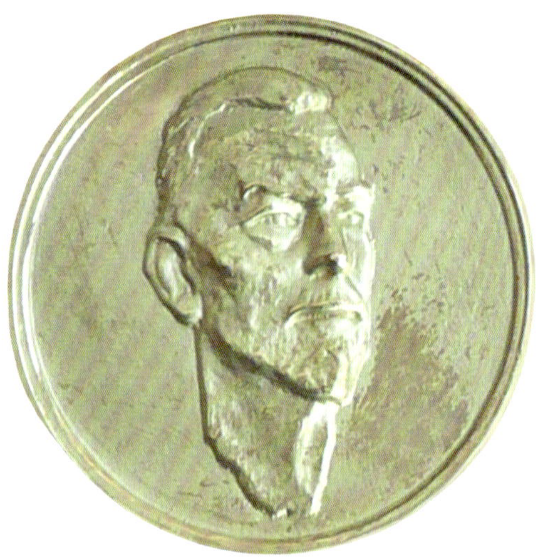

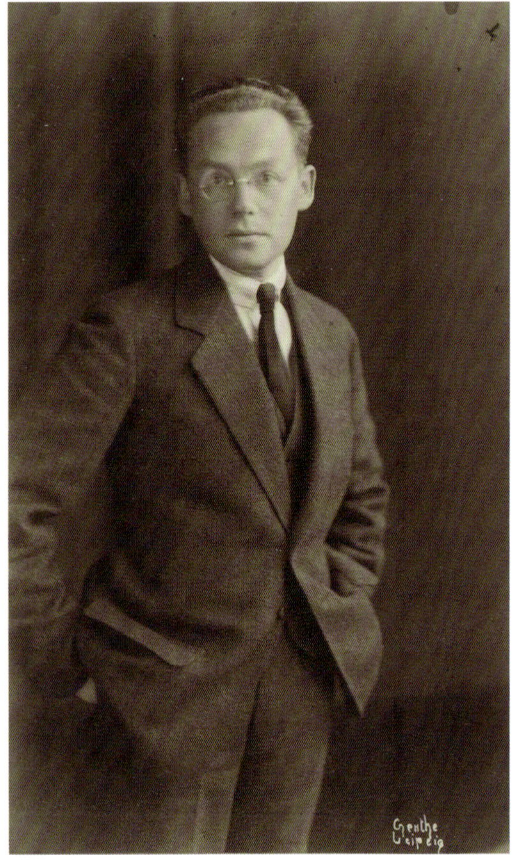

Tschudi.[71] Gantner abandoned such revi-
sionist ideas by 1938 at the latest, when on
Wölfflin's recommendation he was appointed
to the chair of art history at the University
of Basel.[72]

In Zurich Gotthard Jedlicka had also
realized that he would be unable to attain
a professorship without Wölfflin's approval.
When Jedlicka wrote his doctoral dissertation on Henri de Toulouse-Lautrec, Wölfflin
had asserted that he could stand neither the
candidate nor the painter.[73]

Gantner as pupil and holder of a chair in
Basel and Jedlicka with his chair in Zurich
after 1939 were in competition in their veneration of the master and for his legacy; in a
Solomonic division Wölfflin's papers would
go to Basel, his portrait busts, his library,
his photographs, and his writing table to
the University of Zurich.[74] Gantner became
a widely respected teacher to his numerous
students in Basel and tended to Wölfflin's
posthumous fame, publishing his writings,
diaries, and letters and giving commemorative addresses.[75] Today his increasing
preoccupation from the 1940s on with the
nebulous "prefiguration" of the work of art
seems problematic.[76]

On June 21, 1964, for the hundredth anniversary of Wölfflin's birth, the *Neue Zürcher
Zeitung* published several essays.[77] In 1965
Jedlicka published his memories of Wölfflin,
and proposed that a square in Zurich be
named after the famous art historian.[78] That
idea was rejected, but in 1987 the city of
Zurich began to award the Heinrich Wölfflin
Medal (fig. 12) for exemplary cultural merit,
and in 2013 Tristan Weddigen inaugurated
the Heinrich Wölfflin Lectures, presented by
prominent representatives of the discipline,
at the University of Zurich.

Giedion (fig. 13) probably realized most
productively the scholarly concerns of
Wölfflin, who followed his international
career attentively. In 1928 Giedion published
*Bauen in Frankreich, bauen in Eisen, bauen
in Eisenbeton* (fig. 14), for which Laszlo
Moholy-Nagy devised a way of using illustrations similar to that of *Principles*.[79] In the
introduction Giedion wrote that historians
should derive from the past elements for the
future.[80] Wölfflin responded: "Don't you
feel that there are covert lines leading from
'Renaissance and Baroque' to 'Building in
France'?"[81] On February 15, 1929, Walter
Benjamin sent a highly adulatory letter to
Giedion from Berlin-Grunewald: "I am

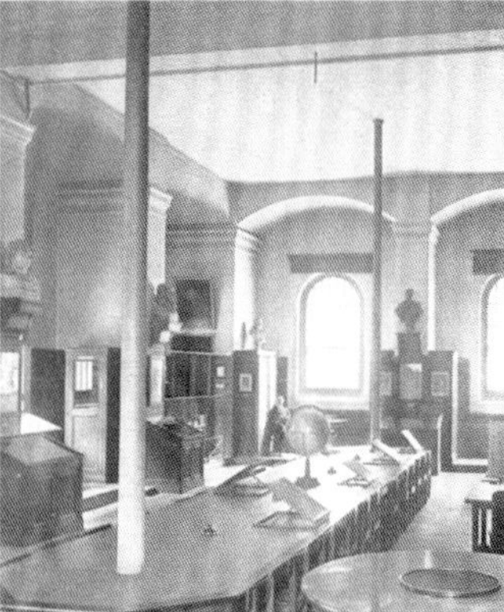

Abb. 10. Henri LABROUSTE:
LA RESERVE

(Erdgeschoß der Bibliothek Ste. Géneviève.) Gußeiserne Säulen gehen kühn, frei durch den Raum, als Teile des in den Bau versenkten eisernen Skeletts.

Er wies nach, daß die Schüler der Akademie zwar schöne Zeichnungen antiker Details lieferten, aber den innern Organismus der Bauten ganz übersahen. Er lernte einsehen, „daß die besten Bauten vom künstlerischen Standpunkt aus gerade jene seien, die nach einfachsten, wahrsten und rationellsten Methoden konstruiert waren"[1]).
Er drückte zum erstenmal den erweiterten SINN der KONSTRUKTION aus, wie er sich aus den neuen Möglichkeiten ergab[2]): Das Wesen der Konstruktion bestehe nicht im isolierten Studium handwerklicher Einzelheiten von Maurer- oder Schlosserarbeit, sondern in der Durchdringung aller Teile eines Baus.
Labrouste gehört zur Generation von 1830, von der in ganz anderm Zusammenhang gesagt wird, daß sie von einem großen Strom getragen werde, vom Verlangen nach Erneuerung des sozialen, moralischen und intellektuellen Lebens[3]).
Als man Labrouste die Bibliothek übertrug, galt er in den Augen von jedermann als die reinste Inkarnation des „esprit nouveau"[4]). Zwölf Jahre hatte man ihn in Paris herumlaufen lassen, ohne ihm auch nur einen Bau anzuvertrauen. Labrouste war über 40 Jahre alt, als man ihm die Bibliothek übergab.
Wissenschaft und Industrie gaben ihm nur sehr geringe Hilfsmittel. Trotzdem ver-

[1]) Eugène Millet: Heary Labrouste. Extrait du bulletin de la société centrale des architectes. (Exercice 1879—80. pag. 5.)
[2]) Es handelt sich um eine der wenigen persönlichen Äußerungen des Architekten H. Labrouste: „Travaux des élèves de l'école d'architecture de Paris pendant l'année 1839" in Revue gén. d'arch. 1840, pag. 59. „ . . . la construction consiste dans la combinaison de toutes les parties architecturales . . ."
[3]) Spühler, Der Saint-Simonismus, Zürich, 1926. pag. 22.
[4]) Delaborde. pag. 13.

22

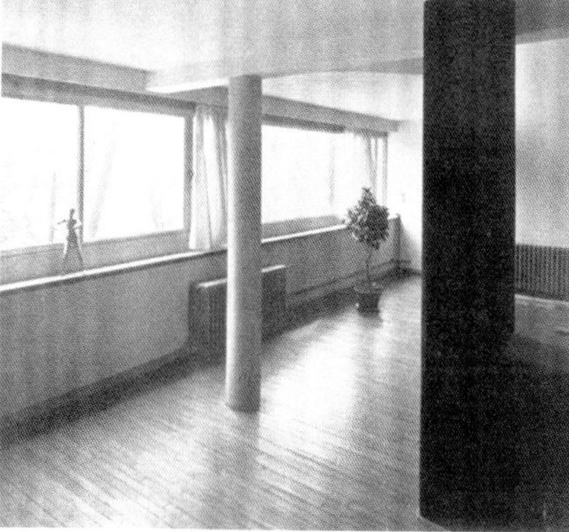

Abb. 11.
LE CORBUSIER:
HAUS COOK

Ungefähr 80 Jahre hat es gebraucht, bis man die Freiheit eines Labrouste: eine durchgehende Konstruktion (Säule) auch in einen Wohnraum ohne Hemmung zu zeigen wagte.

suchte er in der Bibliothek Ste. Géneviève zum ersten Mal einem Bau ein eisernes Skelett einzusetzen, vom Boden bis zum Dach. Ste. Géneviève ist gleichzeitig der erste reine Bibliotheksbau in Frankreich. Labrouste witterte im Eisen weitere Möglichkeiten als seine architektonischen Zeitgenossen. Das Material kam seinem Willen entgegen: „Condenser le sens de toutes choses"[1])!
Labrouste versenkt noch das eiserne Gerippe in den Bau, wie ein Werk in eine Uhr:
Der massive Mauerkern, der das Gebäude umschließt, bleibt noch unangetastet, aber in diesen Mauerkern ist vom Erdgeschoß bis zum First ein eisernes System gelegt: Säulen, Decken, Gewölbe, Träger, Dach-Konstruktion.
In einzelnen Räumen des Erdgeschosses (La Reserve) sind gußeiserne Säulen ohne sichtbares Gebälk mit dem Obergeschoß verkoppelt. Mitten durch den Raum gehen diese schlanken gußeisernen Rohre, die nur ein schmaler Flansch mit der Decke verbindet. Glatte Funktion, kein Gebälk mit der Andeutung von Stütze und Last, kein Ornament, kein Kapitäll. Das sind Dinge, die heute erst ein Corbusier oder Mart Stam wieder wagen. Abb. 11
Das Obergeschoß, zweischiffiger Lesesaal (84 m lang, 21 m breit), bildet mit dem Dach ein einziges konstruktives Skelett. Die halbkreisförmigen Binder stützen sich auf Gußsäulen und — längs den Wänden — auf Konsolen. Wenn die Pläne richtig Auskunft geben, so hat Labrouste diese halbkreisförmigen Binder bereits in drei Segmente zerlegt, um sie der Ausdehnung wegen nicht ganz starr zu machen. Bekanntlich Abb.13, 14

Abb. 10

[1]) Delaborde, pag. 13.

23

---

14. Sigfried Giedion, *Bauen in Frankreich, bauen in Eisen, bauen in Eisenbeton* (Berlin: Gebr. Mann, 2000; reprint of 1928 edition), 22–23

studying in your book (along with much else in which it touches me most directly) the heart-warming distinction between radical disposition and radical knowledge. You have the latter, and accordingly you are in a position to illuminate, or rather discover tradition from the point of view of the present."[82] (It was in this sense that in 1938 Giedion tried to arrange a meeting between Le Corbusier and Wölfflin. The latter avoided an encounter with the architect owing to their "generational differences," though he marveled at him "like a distant aurora borealis."[83])

In his autobiographical sketch Giedion refers to his first contact with Le Corbusier in 1925 and the founding of the Congrès international d'architecture moderne (CIAM) in 1928, which he served as secretary until 1956.[84] Walter Gropius arranged for Giedion to be invited to give the Charles Eliot Norton Lectures at Harvard University in 1938/1939. In 1941 they were published as *Space, Time and Architecture* (fig. 15). In his introduction Giedion wrote of Wölfflin: "In our personal contacts with him as well as through his distinguished lectures, we, his pupils, learned to grasp the spirit of an epoch." This was followed by a critical comment about Wölfflin's pupils: "Many of his pupils have tried to emulate [his] method of contrasting styles, but none have achieved the same depth and directness."[85]

Wölfflin forwarded his copy of *Space, Time and Architecture* to Gantner.[86] Gantner commissioned a doctoral student to

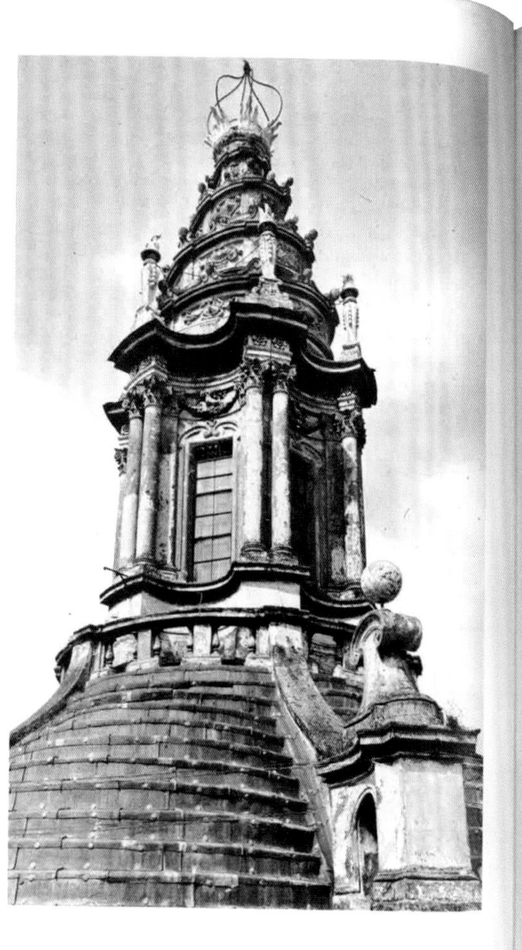

52. TATLIN. Project for a monument in Moscow, 1920. *This, like the Eiffel Tower and some other monuments of our time, is a contemporary realization of the urge toward the interpenetration of inner and outer space.*

←
51. FRANCESCO BORROMINI. Sant' Ivo, Rome. Lantern with coupled columns and spiral. *Culminating point for the movement that penetrates the whole design.*

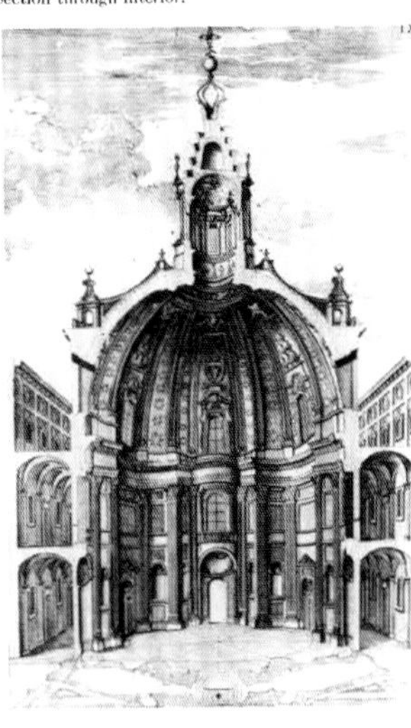

53. FRANCESCO BORROMINI. Sant' Ivo, Rome. Section through interior.

118

15. Sigfried Giedion, *Space, Time and Architecture* (Cambridge, Massachusetts: Harvard University Press, 1941), 118–119

write a review, but he failed to produce one. Gantner then sent the book back to Wölfflin, and wrote to Carola Giedion-Welcker: "Dear Frau Giedion, I truly felt I had done a good turn in urging the young Hugo Weber to review Giedion's book. But since you and Giedion would prefer that I write the review, nothing would be easier to accomplish."[87] It has proved impossible to discover any discussion of the book by Gantner either in the daily papers or in the professional journals. The incident would appear to speak for itself.

Giedion's next book, an excellent analysis of the industrial culture of the nineteenth century, appeared in 1948 under the title *Mechanization Takes Command.*[88] The subtitle, *A Contribution to Anonymous History,* is an obvious reference to Wölfflin's provocative expression "art history without names."[89] In his critique of this unusual book, Arnold Hauser reproved both Giedion and Wölfflin precisely for this doctrine of "anonymous history": "According to this view, individual artists are no more than the bearers and exponents of such impersonal tendencies, which follow their own autonomous and immanent laws, their own logic, and their own aims."[90] That was mean-spirited, for Giedion, naturally, was dealing not with artists but with craftsmen, inventors, engineers, and the industrial manufacturers of baths, kitchens, and all manner of machines who largely anonymously advanced the mechanization of various aspects of our lives.

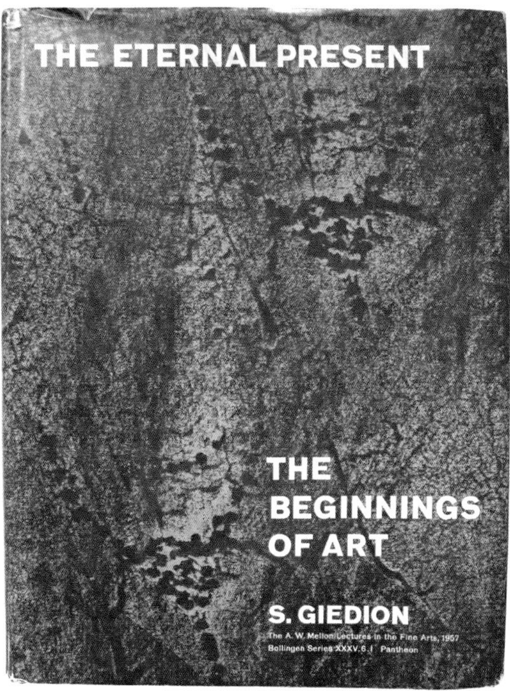

Giedion's last major publication was the two-volume *The Eternal Present* (fig. 16), developed from his A. W. Mellon Lectures in the Fine Arts.[91] With the invitation to deliver the 1957 Mellon Lectures at the National Gallery of Art in Washington, Wölfflin's most brilliant pupil had arrived at the Olympus of art history. Needless to say, Giedion's subtitle, *A Contribution on Constancy and Change*, took up Wölfflin's problem with the historiography of art. Giedion's examination of the beginnings of painting and architecture was an attempt to reintegrate into art history what Wölfflin's generation had lost to anthropology, ethnology, and prehistory.[92]

Critical Interest

In 1967 Eduard Hüttinger noted with regard to Wölfflin that his "central methodical theories" appeared to be lost in "an outdated realm of relevance only to the history of scholarship."[93] Despite its widescale reception after 1915, by 1967 Hüttinger ascertained a certain indifference to *Principles*, especially on the part of students. He also suggested that, "not to its advantage,"

present-day art history had broken off lively dialogue with Wölfflin's ideas. Interest in Wölfflin's work probably reached its nadir in the 1960s and 1970s. The younger generation adopted different approaches. In my case, as a "great-grandson" of Wölfflin and pupil of Joseph Gantner and Emil Maurer, who was Gantner's pupil, it was those of the Warburg school, especially Erwin Panofsky; the brilliant French rhetoricians; and the German philosophers. On the first day of my studies it was recommended that I read *Principles*—this came from a somewhat older fellow student, who was studying German literature under Emil Staiger. In 1986 a friend from my student days, Andreas Hauser, published an extraordinary analysis of Wölfflin's use of images that taught me to see.[94] Another friend of those years, Werner Oechslin, has focused intensively in the intervening decades on all aspects and problems of the baroque.[95] The next generation, now arrived at the zenith of its activity, is turning to the work of Wölfflin with new interest. Hubert Locher has shown the diachronic and synchronic context for this in his Bern habilitation.[96] Another sign of widespread interest is the project initiated at the University of Zurich by Tristan Weddigen, the publication of a new edition in German and translation into French of the collected works of Heinrich Wölfflin.[97]

NOTES

Translated from the German by Russell Stockman

My thanks to Barbara Basting, Therese and Tapan Bhattacharya-Stettler, Rainer Baum, Isabel and Toni Fuchs-Gantner, Evonne Levy, Stanislaus von Moos, Ulrich Pfisterer, Danièle Rinderknecht, Wilhelm Schlink (deceased), Filine Wagner, Tristan Weddigen, and Gerhard Wolf.

1. Michael Baxandall, *Patterns of Intention: On the Historical Explanation of Pictures* (New Haven, 1985), 58–62.

2. See Ingo Herklotz, "Rezeptionsgeschichte," in *Metzler Lexikon Kunstwissenschaft*, ed. Ulrich Pfisterer, 2nd ed. (Stuttgart, 2011), 391–394.

3. Heinrich Wölfflin, *Kunstgeschichtliche Grundbegriffe: Das Problem der Stilentwickelung in der neueren Kunst* (Munich, 1915); English translation: *Principles of Art History: The Problem of the Development of Style in Early Modern Art*, trans. Jonathan Blower, ed. Evonne Levy and Tristan Weddigen (Los Angeles, 2015). On editions and translations, see Matteo Burioni, Burcu Dogramaci, and Ulrich Pfisterer, eds., *Kunstgeschichten 1915: 100 Jahre Heinrich Wölfflin, Kunstgeschichtliche Grundbegriffe* (Zentralinstitut für Kunstgeschichte, Munich, 2015), 303–349.

4. Heinrich Wölfflin, *Principes fondamentaux de l'histoire de l'art: Le problème de l'évolution du style dans l'art moderne*, trans. Claire and Marcel Raymond (Paris, 1952). The book was published without introduction or afterword.

5. See Joan Goldhammer Hart, Roland Recht, and Martin Warnke, eds., *Relire Wölfflin* (Paris, 1995).

6. Heinrich Wölfflin, *L'Art classique: Initiation au génie de la Renaissance italienne*, trans. and intro. by Conrad de Mandach (Paris, 1911). See Zita Caviezel-Rüegg, "Mandach, Conrad von," in *Historisches Lexikon der Schweiz*, http://www.hls-dhs-dss.ch/textes/d/D27742.php (accessed January 22, 2019). Von Mandach was promoted to professor at the University of Bern on the basis of this translation and a few essays and taught there until 1940, from 1936 on as honorary professor.

7. See Claudia Steinhardt-Hirsch, "Die Rezeption der Grundbegriffe," chapter 9 in Burioni, Dogramaci, and Pfisterer, *Kunstgeschichten 1915*, 351–353.

8. Arnold von Salis, *Die Kunst der Griechen* (Leipzig, 1919).

9. Von Salis, *Die Kunst der Griechen*, v–vi.

10. Von Salis, *Die Kunst der Griechen*, vii.

11. Fritz Strich, *Deutsche Klassik und Romantik oder Vollendung und Unendlichkeit: Ein Vergleich* (Munich, 1928).

12. Strich, *Deutsche Klassik und Romantik*, 415.

13. Strich, *Deutsche Klassik und Romantik*, 5.

14. Fritz Strich, *Zu Heinrich Wölfflins Gedächtnis* (Bern, 1956); see Heinrich Dilly, "Heinrich Wölfflin und Fritz Strich," in *Literaturwissenschaft und Geistesgeschichte 1910 bis 1925*, ed. Christoph König and Eberhard Lämmert (Frankfurt am Main, 1993), 256–286.

15. Emil Staiger, *Grundbegriffe der Poetik* (Zürich, 1946); Nanni Baltzer et al., "'…dass die Luft hier mit Kunst nicht so geschwängert ist wie in Berlin oder München, ist mir sympathisch': Heinrich Wölfflin an der Universität Zürich, 1924–1934," *Georges-Bloch-Jahrbuch des Kunsthistorischen Instituts der Universität Zürich* 5 (1998): 182–183 (cited subsequently as Baltzer et al., "Heinrich Wölfflin an der Universität Zürich").

16. Friedrich Rintelen, *Giotto und die Giotto-Apokryphen* (Munich, 1911; 2nd ed., Basel, 1923); for Rintelen, see Joseph Gantner, "Der Unterricht in Kunstgeschichte an der Universität Basel 1924–1938," in *Kunstwissenschaft an Schweizer Hochschulen*, vol. 1, *Die Lehrstühle der Universitäten in Basel, Bern, Freiburg und Zürich von den Anfängen bis 1940* (Schweizerisches Institut für Kunstwissenschaft, Jahrbuch 1972/1973) (Zürich, 1976), 22–23.

17. Friedrich Rintelen, *Reden und Aufsätze* (Basel, 1927), 195; for Heidrich, see Nikolaus Meier, "Ernst Heidrich (1880–1914): Zur Grundlegung der Kunstwissenschaft," *Zeitschrift für Ästhetik und allgemeine Kunstwissenschaft* 28 (1980): 19–50.

18. Georg Schmidt, "Friedrich Rintelen 1881 bis 1926," *Das Werk* 13 (1926): 198–204; for Georg Schmidt, see Roger Fayet, "Georg Schmidt und die Frage der künstlerischen Werte," *RIHA Journal*, 0097 (September 26, 2014): 1–32, https://www.riha-journal.org/articles/2014/2014-jul-sep/fayet-georg-schmidt.

19. *Kunstwissenschaft an Schweizer Hochschulen*, 1:89–133. The course lists are not complete; the universities of Geneva, Lausanne, and Neuenburg are not included.

20. T. [Hans Trog], "Charakteristikon," *Neue Zürcher Zeitung*, July 13, 1924, 3; for the mentions, see "Heinrich Wölfflin," *nzz Archiv* 1780, http://zeitungsarchiv.nzz.ch/search/result/?SEARCH_query=Heinrich+Wölfflin (accessed May 31, 2016), review of Franz Landsberger, Heinrich Wölfflin (Berlin, 1924).

21. Adolf Reinle, "Der Lehrstuhl für Kunstgeschichte an der Universität Zürich bis 1939," in *Kunstwissenschaft an Schweizer Hochschulen*, 1:84–86. For Wölfflin's appointment and teaching activity in Zürich, see the carefully documented study by Nanni Baltzer et al. (note 15, above), 170–199.

22. Joseph Gantner, ed., *Heinrich Wölfflin 1864–1945: Autobiographie, Tagebücher und Briefe* (Basel, 1982), 324, 332; Gantner, "Der Unterricht in Kunstgeschichte," 22–23. Heinrich Wölfflin to Anna Bühler-Koller, November 21, 1920, in Gantner, *Heinrich Wölfflin 1864–1945*, 332, 344. Wölfflin had applied for the professorship in art history at the University of Bern on November 22, 1889; see Walther Rehm, *Heinrich Wölfflin als Literarhistoriker* (Munich, 1960), 133–134 (original of the application letter in the Staatsarchiv des Kantons Bern).

23. *Aus dem Protokoll des Regierungsrates 1923, Sitzung vom 18. Oktober 1923*, Universität Zürich, Archiv.

24. Otto Grautoff, "Heinrich Wölfflin zum sechzigsten Geburtstag," *Preussische Jahrbücher* 3 (1924): 242–252; for Grautoff, see Evonne Levy, "The German Art Historians of World War I: Grautoff, Wichert, Weisbach and Brinckmann and the Activities of the Zentralstelle für Auslandsdienst," *Zeitschrift für Kunstgeschichte* 74 (2011): 373–400; Nikolaus Meier, "Heinrich Wölfflin in München: Kunstwissenschaft und Wissenschaftstopographie," in *200 Jahre Kunstgeschichte in München*, ed. Christian Drude and Hubertus Kohle, Münchener Universitätsschriften des Instituts für Kunstgeschichte, vol. 2 (Munich, 2003), 94–111.

25. Grautoff, "Heinrich Wölfflin zum sechzigsten Geburtstag," 243–244.

26. Gantner, *Heinrich Wölfflin 1864–1945*, 367, 368, 371. Edwin Scharff was a founding member of Munich's New Secession in 1913 and became a professor at the Hochschule für Bildende Künste in Berlin in 1923, but in 1937 he was vilified as a "degenerate artist"; see Helga Jörgens Lendrum, *Der Bildhauer Edwin Scharff (1887–1955): Untersuchungen zu Leben und Werk, mit einem Katalog der figürlichen Plastik* (diss., University of Göttingen, 1989; Göttingen, 1994), 11–50. In addition to the portrait bust of Wölfflin in bronze from 1923/1924, he executed a head in black granite in an Egyptian style that is now at the University of Munich.

27. Gantner, *Heinrich Wölfflin 1864–1945*, 370–371; see also Wölfflin to Hermann Hubacher, September 10, 1943, 481–482.

28. [g.], *Neue Zürcher Zeitung*, June 21, 1924, 2.

29. *Festschrift Heinrich Wölfflin: Beiträge zur Kunst- und Geistesgeschichte, zum 21. Juni 1924 überreicht von Freunden und Schülern*, ed. Paul Wolters, Ernst Beling, and Karl Vossler (Munich, 1924); Erwin Panofsky, "Heinrich Wölfflin: Zu seinem 60. Geburtstage am 21. Juni 1924," *Hamburger Fremdenblatt*, June 21, 1924; reprinted in Erwin Panofsky, *Deutschsprachige Aufsätze*, ed. Karen Michels and Martin Warnke, 2 vols. (Berlin, 1998), 2:1105–1108.

30. Sigfried Giedion, "Schriften zu H. Wölfflins 60. Geburtstag," and T. [Hans Trog], "Charakteristikon," 3.

31. For Wölfflin's multifaceted impact, see Meinhold Lurz, *Heinrich Wölfflin: Biographie einer Kunsttheorie* (Worms, 1981), 11–52.

32. Gotthard Jedlicka, *Heinrich Wölfflin: Erinnerungen an seine Jahre in Zürich (1924–1945)*, Neujahrsblatt der Zürcher Kunstgesellschaft (Zurich, 1965); Thea and Peter Vignau-Wilberg, "Bibliographie der kunsthistorischen Dissertationen in der Schweiz 1866–1970," in *Kunstwissenschaft an Schweizer Hochschulen*, 1:186, no. Zü 35.

33. Quoted from Gotthard Jedlicka, "Heinrich Wölfflin: Zum hundertsten Geburtstag, 21. Juni 1964," *Neue Zürcher Zeitung*, Sunday, June 21, 1964, insert "Literatur und Kunst." For his "numerical success," see the statistics in Baltzer et al., "Heinrich Wölfflin an der Universität Zürich" (see note 15 above), 175–182.

34. See the reports in *Neue Zürcher Zeitung*, Tuesday, June 17, 1924, 1–2, and Saturday, June 21, 1924, 1; also Reinle, "Der Lehrstuhl für Kunstgeschichte an der Universität Zürich," 86.

35. Heinrich Wölfflin, "Kunstgeschichtliche Grundbegriffe: Eine Revision," *Logos: Internationale Zeitschrift für Philosophie der Kultur* 22 (1933): 210–218.

36. *Neue Zürcher Zeitung*, Sunday, June 17, 1934, 5–6.

37. Sigfried Giedion and Walter Ueberwasser, "Heinrich Wölfflin: Zu seinem 70. Geburtstag," *Basler Zeitung*, June 20, 1934.

38. G. Heider-Hartog, "Festvorlesung Heinrich Wölfflins," *Neue Zürcher Zeitung*, Tuesday, June 26, 1934, Abendausgabe no. 1153, 6, 1.

39. Heinrich Wölfflin, "Die alte Stadt," in *Zürich: Geschichte, Kultur, Wirtschaft*, published with the collaboration of the City Council (Zurich, 1933), 19–48: "Kristallhart und kristallklar steht das Haus als scharfbegrenzter weisser Kubus da."

40. Michael Stettler, "Heinrich Wölfflin," in Michael Stettler, *Rat der Alten: Begegnungen und Besuche*, 3rd enlarged ed. (Bern, 1980), 121–134.

41. *Concinnitas: Beiträge zum Problem des Klassischen; Heinrich Wölfflin zum achtzigsten Geburtstag am 21. Juni 1944 zugeeignet* (Basel, [1944]).

42. Heinrich Wölfflin to Hermann Hubacher, September 10, 1943, in Gantner, *Heinrich Wölfflin 1864–1945*, 481–482.

43. Hermann Hubacher, "Begegnung und Gespräch: Tagebuchnotizen aus dem Jahre 1944," *Neue Zürcher Zeitung*, Sunday, June 21, 1964, insert "Literatur und Kunst."

44. Heinrich Wölfflin to Herman Hubacher, January 30, 1942, in Gantner, *Heinrich Wölfflin 1864–1945*, 477.

45. Hubacher, "Begegnung und Gespräch."

46. Wti., "Ganymed am Bürkliplatz," *Neue Zürcher Zeitung*, June 21, 1952, 13; Jedlicka, *Heinrich Wölfflin*, 32.

47. Heinrich Wölfflin, "Italien und das deutsche Formgefühl," *Logos: Internationale Zeitschrift für Philosophie der Kultur* 10 (1922): 251–260; reprinted in *Das Werk* 11, no. 6 (1924): 145–153, and in Heinrich Wölfflin, *Gedanken zur Kunstgeschichte: Gedrucktes und Ungedrucktes* (Basel, 1940), 119–126.

48. It was followed by the publication of shorter essays and a switch from Verlag Bruckmann to Verlag Schwabe in Basel.

49. Heinrich Wölfflin, *Das Erklären von Kunstwerken* (Leipzig, 1921), 7–8.

50. Wölfflin, *Kunstgeschichtliche Grundbegriffe* (1915), viii; *Principles* (2015), 75.

51. Wölfflin, *Kunstgeschichtliche Grundbegriffe* (1915), v; *Principles* (2015), 72.

52. In defending his notion of "Kunstgeschichte ohne Namen" (art history without names) Wölfflin wrote: "Es bezeichnet aber jedenfalls deutlich die Absicht, etwas zur Darstellung zu bringen, das *unter* dem Individuellen liegt." See "In eigener Sache," *Kunstchronik und Kunstmarkt*, n.s. 31 (1920): 397–399; reprinted in Wölfflin, *Gedanken zur Kunstgeschichte*, 15–18; see also the discussion of "Wölfflin-Topoi" in Lurz, *Heinrich Wölfflin*, 13–24.

53. Heinrich Wölfflin, *Die Kunst der Renaissance: Italien und das deutsche Formgefühl* (Munich, 1931), 8; English translation, *The Sense of Form in Art: A Comparative Psychological Study*, trans. Alice Muehsam and Norma A. Shatan (New York, [1958]), 19.

54. See Eric Michaud, *Les Invasions barbares: Une généalogie de l'histoire de l'art* (Paris, 2015), 174–224; Evonne Levy, *Baroque and the Political Language of Formalism (1845–1945): Burckhardt, Wölfflin, Gurlitt, Brinckmann, Sedlmayr* (Basel, 2015), 144–156; Oskar Bätschmann, "Heinrich Wölfflin: Italien und das deutsche Formgefühl," in *Vivace von espressione: Gefühl, Charakter, Temperament in der italienischen Kunst; Kunsthistorische Studien zu Ehren von Sybille Ebert-Schifferer*, ed. Marieke von Bernstorff, Susanne Kubersky, and Maurizia Cicconi, Veröffentlichungen der Bibliotheca Hertziana Max-Planck-Institut für Kunstgeschichte (Munich, 2018), 299–319.

55. Wilhelm Schlink, "'Ein Volk, eine Zeit, eine Kunst': Heinrich Wölfflin über das nationale Formgefühl," in *L'Idée du style dans l'historiographie artistique: Variantes nationales et transmissions*, ed. Sabine Frommel and Antonio Brucculeri (Rome, 2012), 169. See Martin Warnke, "Warburg und Wölfflin," in *Aby Warburg: Akten des internationalen Symposiums Hamburg, 1990*, ed. Horst Bredekamp et al. (Weinheim, 1991), 79–86.

56. Julius von Schlosser, "Von Heinrich Wölfflins Sendung," *Neue Zürcher Zeitung*, June 17, 1934, first Sunday edition, 4. See Evonne Levy, *Baroque and the Political Language of Formalism*, 144–156. For Julius von Schlosser, see Thomas Lersch, "Schlossers Hakenkreuz: Eine Replik," *Kritische Berichte* 18, no. 4 (1990): 113–117.

57. Dorothee Huber, ed., *Sigfried Giedion: Wege in die Öffentlichkiet; Aufsätze und unveröffentlichte Schriften aus den Jahren 1926–1956* (Institut für Geschichte und Theorie der Architektur, ETH, Zürich, 1987), 14–18; Thilo Koenig and Martin Gasser, eds., *Hans Finsler und die Schweizer Fotokultur: Werk, Fotoklasse, moderne Gestaltung 1932–1960* (Zürich, 2006).

58. Giedon, "Autobiographische Skizze, [1956]," in Huber, *Sigfried Giedion*, 9; see Sokratis Georgiadis, *Sigfried Giedion: Eine intellektuelle Biografie* (Institut für Geschichte und Theorie der Architektur, ETH, Zürich, 1989).

59. Sigfried Giedion, "Spätbarocker und romantischer Klassizismus" (diss., Universität München, 1922); see Stanisalus von Moos, "Die Schriften von Sigfried Giedion," in *Hommage à Giedion: Profile seiner Persönlichkeit*, ed. Paul Hofer and Ulrich Stucky (Basel and Stuttgart, 1971), 187–198.

60. Iris Bruderer-Oswald, *Das Neue Sehen: Carola Giedion-Welcker und die Sprache der Moderne* (Bern, 2007), 28–55.

61. Bruderer-Oswald, *Das Neue Sehen*, 50–55.

62. Carola Giedion-Welcker, *Moderne Plastik: Elemente der Wirklichkeit; Masse und Auflockerung* (Zürich, 1937).

63. Sigfried Giedion, "Bauhaus und Bauhauswoche zu Weimar," *Das Werk* 10 (1923): 232–234.

64. See the discussion, the objection, and Gantner's response, following Giedion, "Bauhaus und Bauhauswoche," 308–309; and Giedion's unpublished reply in Hofer and Stucky, *Hommage à Giedion*, 22–24. For E. Richard Bühler, see *Gestaltung, Werk, Gesellschaft: 100 Jahre Schweizerischer Werkbund SWB*, ed. Thomas Gnägi, Berndt Nicolai, and Jasmine Wohlwend Piai (Zürich, 2013), 423–424.

65. Hofer and Stucky, *Hommage à Giedion*, 22.

66. See "Gantner, Joseph," *Dictionary of Art Historians*, https://dictionaryofarthistorians.org/gantnerj.htm (accessed August 29, 2015); Joseph Gantner, *Michelangelo: Die Beurteilung seiner Kunst von Lionardo bis Goethe; Beiträge zu einer Ideengeschichte der Kunsthistoriographie* (n.p., n.d. [1922]).

67. See Joseph Gantner, *Revision der Kunstgeschichte: Prolegomena zu einer Kunstgeschichte aus dem Geiste der Gegenwart* (Vienna, 1932), 62–89.

68. *Das neue Frankfurt: Internationale Monatsschrift für die Probleme kultureller Neugestaltung*, published 1926/1927 to 1931, with the subtitle was *Monatsschrift für die Probleme moderner Gestaltung* beginning in 1928: http://digi.ub.uni-heidelberg.de/diglit/neue_frankfurt (accessed September 22, 2015).

69. *Das neue Frankfurt* 5 (November–December 1931): 215.

70. Gantner, *Revision der Kunstgeschichte*, 44–61; see the critique by Herbert von Einem, "Aufgaben der Kunstgeschichte in der Zukunft," *Zeitschrift für Kunstgeschichte* 5 (1936): 1–7.

71. Wassily Kandinsky and Franz Marc, eds., *Der Blaue Reiter* [1912], Neuausgabe von Klaus Lankheit (Munich and Zürich, 1979), 23.

72. Wölfflin always recommended his own pupils for Basel; see Christine Verzar, "After Burckhardt and Wölfflin: Was There a Basel School of Art History?," *Journal of Art Historiography* 11 (December 2014): 1–31; Gantner, "Der Unterricht in Kunstgeschichte," 22–23.

73. Jedlicka, *Heinrich Wölfflin*, 7.

74. *Auszug aus dem Protokoll des Erziehungsrates des Kantons Zürich vom 24. Juli 1941*, Universität Zürich, Rektoratsarchiv 141 A/2.

75. Heinrich Wölfflin, *Kleine Schriften (1886–1933)*, ed. Joseph Gantner (Basel, 1946); Gantner, *Heinrich Wölfflin 1864–1945*; see also Joseph Gantner, "Erinnerungen," in *Kunsthistoriker in eigener Sache*, ed. Martina Sitt (Berlin, 1990), 133–166.

76. See, for example, Joseph Gantner, *Rodin und Michelangelo* (Vienna, 1953).

77. *Neue Zürcher Zeitung*, Sunday, June 21, 1964, supplement "Literatur und Kunst," with contributions by Gotthard Jedlicka, Hermann Hubacher, and Eduard Hüttinger, and Wölfflin's address to the PEN Club from 1944.

78. Jedlicka, *Heinrich Wölfflin*, 32.

79. Sigfried Giedion, *Bauen in Frankreich, bauen in Eisen, bauen in Eisenbeton* (Leipzig and Berlin, 1928), published in English as *Building in France, Building in Iron, Building in Ferroconcrete*, trans. J. Duncan Berry (Santa Monica, CA, 1995); *Sigfried Giedion und die Fotografie: Bildinszenierungen der Moderne*, ed. Werner Oechslin and Gregor Harbusch (Zürich, 2010).

80. Giedion, *Bauen in Frankreich*, 1.

81. Giedion, "Autobiographische Skizze, [1956]," in Huber, *Sigfried Giedion*, 9.

82. Walter Benjamin to Sigfried Giedion, February 15, 1929, Sigfried Giedion Papers, gta Archiv, eth Zürich, 43B-K-1929-02-15.

83. Heinrich Wölfflin to Sigfried Giedion, January 20, 1938, in Gantner, *Heinrich Wölfflin 1864–1945*, 457.

84. Giedion, "Autobiographische Skizze, [1956]," in Huber, *Sigfried Giedion*, 9.

85. Sigfried Giedion, *Space, Time and Architecture: The Growth of a New Tradition* (Cambridge, MA., 1941), 2; see Alina Payne, "Architecture, Objects and Ornament: Heinrich Wölfflin and the Problem of *Stilwandlung*," in Frommel and Brucculeri, *L'Idée du style*, 137, and, by the same author, *From Ornament to Object: Genealogies of Architectural Modernism* (New Haven and London, 2012), passim.

86. Heinrich Wölfflin to Sigfried Giedion, June 15, 1942: "Dear Herr Giedion, . . . immediately after receipt, I forwarded it [*Space, Time and Architecture*] to Gantner (Basel), who promised to produce a public review."

87. Joseph Gantner to Carola Giedion-Welcker, June 28, 1942, Sigfried Giedion Papers, Archiv gta, eth Zürich, 43B-K-1942-06-28.

88. Sigfried Giedion, *Mechanization Takes Command, a Contribution to Anonymous History* (New York, 1948).

89. See Stanislaus von Moos, "'Nachwort' zu Sigfried Giedion," in *Die Herrschaft der Mechanisierung: Ein Beitrag zur anonymen Geschichte* (Frankfurt am Main, 1982), 781–816.

90. Arnold Hauser, review of Sigfried Giedion, *Mechanization Takes Command*, *The Art Bulletin* 34 (1952): 251–253.

91. Sigfried Giedion, *The Eternal Present: A Contribution on Constancy and Change*, 2 vols., The A. W. Mellon Lectures in the Fine Arts, National Gallery of Art, Washington (New York, 1962–1963).

92. For the loss of Altamira through neglect, see Ulrich Pfisterer, "Altamira—oder: Die Anfänge von Kunst und Kunstwissenschaft," *Vorträge aus dem Warburg-Haus* 10 (2007): 13–80.

93. Eduard Hüttinger, "Wölfflins Werk—heute," *Zeitschrift für Ästhetik und allgemeine Kunstwissenschaft* 12 (1967): 104–116.

94. Andreas Hauser, "Grundbegriffliches zu Wölfflins 'Kunstgeschichtlichen Grundbegriffen,'" in *Beiträge zu Kunst und Kunstgeschichte um 1900* (Jahrbuch des Schweizerischen Instituts für Kunstwissenschaft 1984–1986) (Zürich, 1986), 39–53.

95. As indications of his unending engagement, see Werner Oechslin, "Barock: Zu den negativen Kriterien der Begriffsbestimmung in klassizistischer und späterer Zeit," in *Europäische Barock-Rezeption*, ed. Klaus Garber, 2 vols. (Wiesbaden, 1991), 2:1225–1254 and "Das Wort 'klassisch' hat für uns etwas Erkältendes (Heinrich Wölfflin)," in *Welche Antike? Konkurrierende Rezeptionen des Altertums im Barock*, Wolfenbütteler Arbeiten zur Barockforschung, vol. 47, ed. Ulrich Heinen (Wiesbaden, 2011), 1:183–206.

96. Hubert Locher, *Kunstgeschichte als historische Theorie der Kunst*, 2nd ed. (Munich, 2010).

97. The first two volumes, *Die Jugendwerke des Michelangelo* and *Salomon Gessner*, ed. Tristan Weddigen and Oskar Bätschmann, will be published in 2020 by Schwabe in Basel.

HANS AURENHAMMER

Formalist Dissent: Why Did the Vienna School Ignore Wölfflin's Principles?

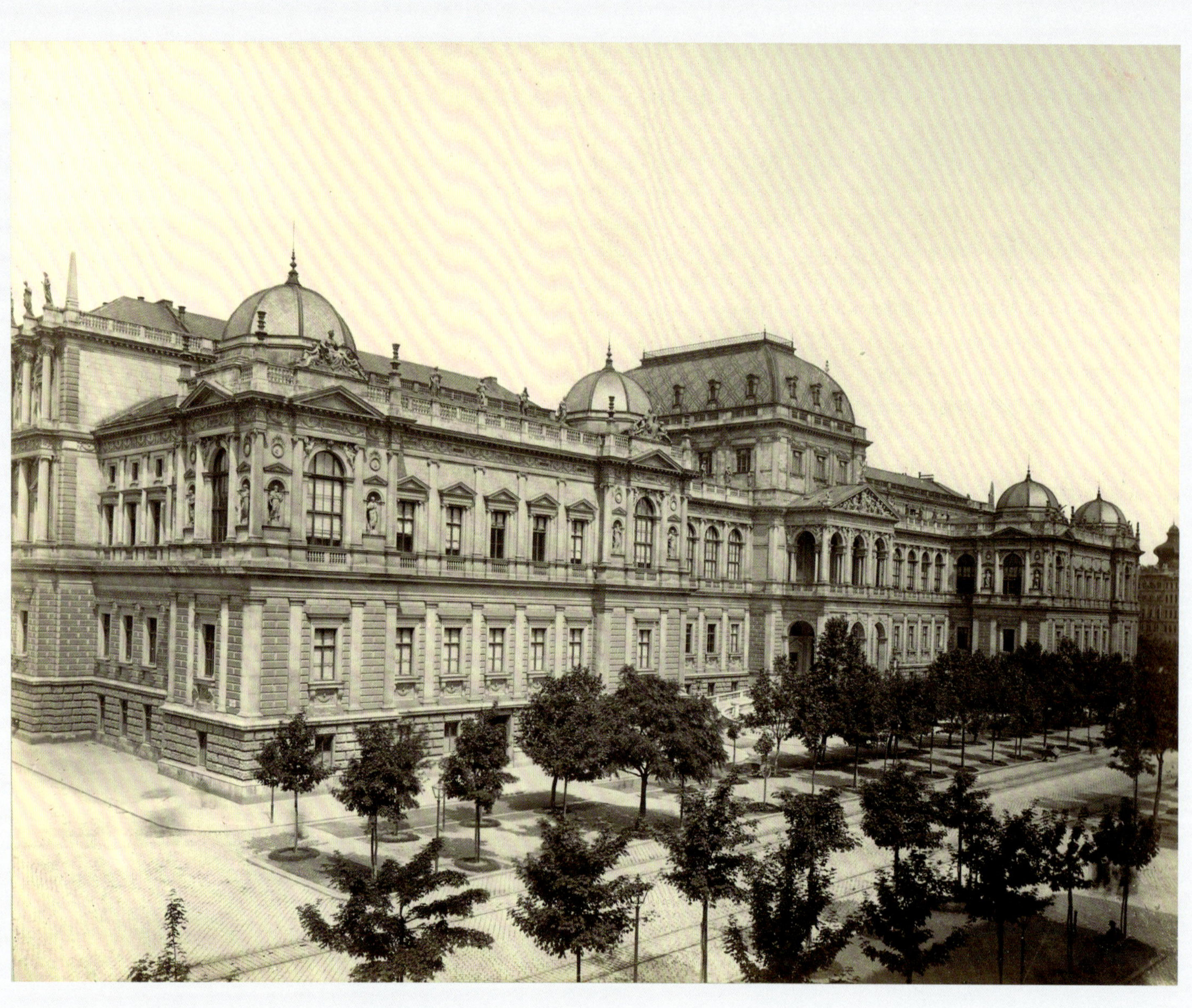

Heinrich Wölfflin and the exponents of the so-called Vienna School are usually referred to in a single breath as the protagonists of the formalist method around 1900. Some thirty years ago, the American specialist Joan Goldhammer Hart gave a lecture entitled "Some Reflections on Wölfflin and the Vienna School." In it, she emphasized "the similarity of their approaches," adding that Wölfflin and the Viennese professors Franz Wickhoff and Alois Riegl had formed a "network" and an "invisible college," even if they had only rarely met in person.[1] The analogies, of course, are obvious: in the work of both Wölfflin and his Viennese contemporaries, a general history of style took the place of individual artists' biographies, the analysis of form took precedence over the cultural-historical context, and previously repudiated styles such as the baroque were rehabilitated, now from the perspective of a sensibility influenced by modern art. If we reconstruct the specific reception of Wölfflin's writings by Viennese art historians from about 1890 to 1950, however, we get a less harmonious picture—in fact, we detect in their outlooks a surprising dissociation from Wölfflin's views. Riegl read his early works, above all *Renaissance und Barock* (*Renaissance and Baroque*; 1888), relatively soon after their publication (and Josef Strzygowski read them even earlier). The intensity that characterized this initial phase of productive encounter, however, soon diminished. That was already true of *Die klassische Kunst* (*Classic Art*; 1899). And a famous work like *Kunstgeschichtliche Grundbegriffe* (*Principles of Art History*; 1915) was met with astonishing reticence in Vienna. The reason for this indifference is partly chronological.

Wölfflin had outlived all his famous Viennese colleagues. When *Principles* was published in 1915, Riegl and Wickhoff had been dead for many years. And Hans Tietze's book *Die Methode der Kunstgeschichte*—in a sense an initial stock-taking of the Viennese positions (dedicated, significantly, to his teachers Riegl and Wickhoff)—came out in 1913, that is, two years too early to respond to *Principles*.[2] Above all, however, the neglect of *Principles* is a reflection of more fundamental methodological differences between the Vienna School and Wölfflin, which became evident quite early on, as we will see in the following.

Josef Strzygowski and Wölfflin's Early Writings

It may come as a surprise that the first scholar in the Viennese context to read Wölfflin's writings was Josef Strzygowski, who would later become a bitter opponent of the Vienna School and, in view of his enthusiasm for "the Orient" and Asia, shared few of Wölfflin's interests, which were concentrated primarily on European art. Strzygowski reacted to Wölfflin's book *Die Jugendwerke des Michelangelo* as early as 1891, the year of its publication.[3] Of the various art historians discussed below, Strzygowski is probably the only one whose criticism Wölfflin responded to in person. In May 1891 Wölfflin was in Vienna to visit museums and collections and met with Strzygowski, whom he knew from the years when they were both at the Deutsches Archäologisches Institut in Rome (1886–1888).[4] The conversation between the two young associate professors of almost the same age evidently revolved around

Strzygowski's essay, published the same year, about the development of the young Michelangelo. There he had made critical observations on the book by Wölfflin, whom he referred to as "my friend."[5] Afterward, Wölfflin noted in his diary how much he admired Strzygowski's work ethic: "The same disposition led him to good observations of M[ichel]A[ngelo]." And Wölfflin was compelled to admit: "I barely touched on the Battle of the Centaurs." [6]

Strzygowski, who was appointed professor in Graz in 1892, reacted to his Swiss colleague not only on these specialized matters. His book *Das Werden des Barock bei Raphael und Correggio*, which came out in 1898, is a response to Wölfflin's first major work, *Renaissance und Barock* (1888).[7] Here, like his colleague August Schmarsow, Strzygowski was participating in the contemporary debate on the artistic category of the painterly and its role in the development of modern art. [8] In his discussion, he proceeded on the assumption of a "turnaround" (*Umschwung*) from a more rigorous to a "painterly style" (*malerischer Stil*), consummated by Raphael in his dramatic mass compositions in the Stanza d'Eliodoro in the Vatican, which he animated with the use of chiaroscuro effects.[9] Strzygowski recognized this stylistic change not only in the late work of Raphael, but also earlier, in that of Leonardo da Vinci and Michelangelo.[10] He thus regarded the painters of the High Renaissance as the true founders of the baroque. Here Strzygowski was reacting to an inconsistency in how Wölfflin had periodized the sixteenth century, vacillating, as he had, between the conception of a continual artistic development and the belief in a generally valid aesthetic norm. (And, as the section on Max Dvořák below will show, Strzygowski was not alone in this observation.) In *Renaissance and Baroque*, Wölfflin had distinguished clearly between the High Renaissance and the baroque, while pointing out the precarious nature of the dividing line between them: "the peak is a very fine ridge" ("die Höhe ist nur ein ganz schmaler Grat").[11] By the time *Classic Art* came out in 1899—one year after Strzygowski's book on the baroque—Wölfflin had turned the High Renaissance into an absolute artistic ideal that also integrated the "painterly" traits of the late work of Raphael.[12]

In *Werden des Barock*, however, Strzygowski was not seeking to emphasize historical continuity, even if that is how it might look at first sight. On the contrary, he broke this continuity, in keeping with his racial ideology, and subordinated it to an entirely different system of coordinates. For example, he rejected what he considered the typical Italian "baroque in the bad sense of the word" ("Barock im schlechten Sinn des Wortes"), which had begun with Correggio's "modern" art—an art that, in his view, was merely playing for effect.[13] This he contrasted to the baroque of the ingenious outsider Michelangelo, whose creativity had sprung from a Gothic and Germanic "feeling for life" (*Lebensgefühl*), and from whom he traced a hidden link to the "German" Rembrandt.[14] Strzygowski ultimately saw the origins of the baroque in the "migration and [the] pervasion of Christian ideology by the Germanic peoples" ("Völkerwanderung und [der] Durchdringung des christlichen Ideenkreises durch die germanischen Völker").[15] The book's frontispiece accordingly presents the Christ of *The Transfiguration* as "Raphael's bequest to Germanic Christendom" ("Vermächtnis Raphaels an die germanische Christenheit").[16] Let us refrain, however, from further pursuing these absurd aberrations of an Aryan "Nordic viewpoint." In any case, Wölfflin ignored Strzygowski's emphasis on the protobaroque and Germanic character of the High Renaissance—a reaction the latter still held against him years later, as we will see[17]—although in 1909 Wölfflin did recommend him for a professorship in Basel, citing what he called the "universality of [Strzygowski's] historical interrogation."[18]

Alois Riegl

When we recapitulate the process by which the baroque was reevaluated in the late nineteenth and early twentieth centuries, we naturally do not think of Strzygowski's long-forgotten book.[19] Rather, the first scholar who comes to mind after Wölfflin is Alois Riegl, who, after serving as curator at the Österreichisches Museum für Kunst und Industrie, was a professor in Vienna from 1894 until his death in 1905.[20] Yet Riegl initially developed his research on the baroque entirely independently of Wölfflin, a circumstance hitherto overlooked. His *Entstehung der Barockkunst in Rom* (*Origins of Baroque Art in Rome*)—in which Wölfflin, as is well known, figures quite prominently—seems to contradict this surprising discovery. That is because the book, which was published posthumously in 1908, incorporates two late Riegl lecture courses given in the winter semesters of 1898/1899[21] and 1901/1902.[22] Yet Riegl had already given an extensive series of lectures on the art history of the baroque era ("Kunstgeschichte des Barockzeitalters") in the winter semester of 1894/1895—the first ever on this subject at the University of Vienna, as he himself pointed out.[23] At the time, he was evidently not familiar with Wölfflin's book on the baroque, which is quite astonishing in view of Strzygowski's work of the same period.[24] Nor did Riegl take any notice of Wölfflin's essay on Roman triumphal arches,[25] published a year earlier, when in these lectures he enthusiastically raised the question of baroque qualities in the architecture of the Roman imperial period, a subject that had also preoccupied Wölfflin.[26] Riegl's overall concept of the baroque—which in the posthumous book publication is limited to the development in Rome up to Bernini—must be reconstructed on the basis of the early lecture manuscripts. They are more comprehensive than Wölfflin's observations and more ambitious than the book version, encompassing the period from the sixteenth to the eighteenth century and addressing both painting and sculpture—not just Italian, but also (and in this respect he followed Cornelius Gurlitt above all)[27]—developments in Germany and Austria.[28]

It wasn't until 1898 that Riegl finally read Wölfflin's *Renaissance and Baroque*. Now he praised the latter's "serious, in-depth discussion of the essence of the baroque style" ("ernstes tieferes Eingehen auf das Wesen des Barockstils"). At the same time, however, he noticed that he could nevertheless not emancipate himself from an "aversion to the [baroque] style as such" ("Abneigung gegen den Stil als solchen"), reminiscent of Burckhardt.[29] Finally, in 1901, in a passage also included in the later published version, Riegl stated that Wölfflin's book "is at present the best written on the Italian baroque" but also voiced some criticism.[30] Without attempting to carry out an exact comparison, let us take a brief look at how Wölfflin inspired Riegl to change his conception of the baroque, but also—an equally revealing aspect—the extent to which Riegl could or would not follow his colleague.

"It would…be pointless to start by establishing a fixed date for the beginning of the baroque age and baroque art in general," Riegl had written. "We must reserve the right to determine the date of inception for each country and each art form separately."[31] In the periodization of the Italian baroque, Riegl had initially still vacillated, sometimes dating its commencement at around 1550 and sometimes as late as 1563, the year marking the conclusion of the Council of Trent.[32] On the other hand, he viewed the baroque inclination toward monumentality as a mere continuation of the High Renaissance.[33] Now, however, he adopted Wölfflin's clear dividing line around 1520, leading him to regard Correggio as a baroque painter, but—in contrast to Strzygowski—not Raphael.[34] In the first lecture of 1894/1895, Riegl had discussed all artistic media but failed to show how they related to one another chronologically. Baroque architecture began, in his view, with Michelangelo, baroque painting with the Carracci, and baroque sculpture only with Bernini. In keeping with Riegl's evolved idea of the late 1890s of a uniform *Kunstwollen* (a term that defies translation; roughly "will to art") governing all artistic media, however, he now strove to gain a better understanding of "the interaction between the various arts in the Italian baroque style" ("das Zusammenwirken der verschiedenen Künste im italienischen Barockstil"). In this he considered himself validated by Wölfflin: "In this direction—of pointing out the relationship especially between painting and architecture—Wölfflin at least made the first attempts." ("Nach dieser Richtung, den Zusammenhang, speziell zwischen Mal[erei] und Archit[ektur] aufzuzeigen, hat Wölfflin wenigstens die ersten Versuche gemacht.")[35]

For Riegl it was above all Wölfflin's architectural analyses, which in some cases he even adopted verbatim, that were exemplary.[36] In particular the still very brief passages on Italian architecture from Michelangelo to Carlo Maderno in his 1894/1895 lectures profited from this influence.[37] In his early baroque lectures, Riegl concentrated primarily on analyzing the relationship between monumental structure and the decoration of surfaces, which he described in great detail. This was an approach that betrayed his roots in the critique of nineteenth-century historicism. Now he took orientation from Wölfflin's interpretation of the architectonic whole as the manifestation of a dramatic struggle and dichotomy between oppressive mass and aspiring form, between horizontal and vertical elements. At the same time, however, clear methodological differences are evident. In Riegl's opinion, "[Wölfflin's] definition of the baroque style as 'massiveness and movement' is not profound enough."[38] And he was critical of the contradictory categories of painterly and plastic (*malerisch, plastisch*)—which were central to Wölfflin as well as to Schmarsow.[39] Riegl's analyses investigate not only form but also the specific conception of content and emotional expression. To this end, he developed a system of concepts far more differentiated than Wölfflin's, limited not merely to well-known polarities such

as optic/haptic[40] or objective/subjective (*optisch/taktisch, objektivistisch/subjektivistisch*), but also—as in his voluminous essay *Das holländische Gruppenporträt*—will and sensation (*Willen, Empfindung*) as well as coordination and subordination (*Koordination, Subordination*). From Adolf von Hildebrand's *Das Problem der Form in der bildenden Kunst* (1893) he adopted the terms "proximate view" and "distant view" (*Nahsicht, Fernsicht*)—independently of Wölfflin, it seems, whose engagement with the sculptor's theories were first made public in *Classic Art* of 1899.[41]

In 1901 Riegl wrote: "Wölfflin's baroque…appears to be an aberration and a decline, but it is never made clear to the reader why this was required for the purposes of a further progression."[42] It is here, on the matter of the role of the baroque within the framework of universal art history, that Riegl's core criticism of Wölfflin sets in. While on the one hand Wölfflin recognized the affinities between the baroque and modern art—he associated the elements of ecstasy and intoxication, for example, with Richard Wagner's *Tristan and Isolde*—he viewed the baroque above all retrospectively, as the antithesis to the Renaissance norm.[43] "In his aesthetic-historical evaluation of the baroque style, Wölfflin did not offer much more than Burckhardt," was Riegl's charge.[44] For Riegl, on the other hand, the baroque was the beginning of modern art, a development that had led to the impressionism of his own time: "What separates the modern artistic view from the antique began with Michelangelo and Correggio in a definitively self-conscious phase."[45] In the bold panorama of a global history of art set forth by Riegl in this very period in the manuscript for his book *Historische Grammatik der bildenden Künste* (written in 1897–1898 but not published until 1966), 1520—the year of Raphael's death and the commencement of the religious schism—meant more than just the beginning of the baroque.[46] It marked no less than the historical upheaval from the medieval Christian era to the most recent period in the development of humankind, specific to a natural-scientific worldview and the Germanic peoples and lasting into Riegl's own day. In this teleological perspective, the baroque, as a "precursor of modern art" ("eine Vorstufe der modernen Kunst"), took on the status of historical necessity that was denied to it—according to Riegl—by Wölfflin (but also Schmarsow).[47]

It is not surprising that Riegl accordingly rejected Wölfflin's explanation of stylistic change as an expression of a new sense of life and the body.[48] In the summer semester of 1899, speaking on the unexpected subject of the "law of frontality" (*Frontalitäts-gesetz*) so essential to ancient Egyptian art, he stated: "This is a point much cherished by recent scholars. Among well-known art historians, Wölfflin was the person to elevate this to a major factor in his explanation of artistic progress, even recently; man wants to see himself in art as he behaves, as he composes himself, in society."[49] Here Riegl was presumably thinking not only of the famous comparison between the pointed Gothic crakow and the wide, comfortable Renaissance shoe as a manifestation of the differing feeling of form but also of Wölfflin's *Classic Art*, which was not published until 1899, and thus indeed "recently."[50] There Wölfflin associates the stylistic "physiognomy" of the High Renaissance with the codes of courtly behavior described by Baldassarc Castiglione in *Il libro del cortegiano*.[51] In Riegl's view, sociopsychological explanations of this kind were fallacies. The social and habitual patterns "merely parallel the phenomenon of frontality.... Although this observation is certainly correct, it offers no substantive explanation."[52]

Even though delayed, Riegl's critical reading undoubtedly represented the most productive reception Wölfflin encountered in Vienna. It came to his notice only in 1908, when *Origins of Baroque Art in Rome* was published posthumously. Wölfflin's review of the book praises Riegl's gift of formal analysis but cannot conceal a certain irritation. He stressed that the concepts "haptic" and "optic" were "nothing fundamentally new" ("keine prinzipiell neuen") but were identical with his own, and he ignored Riegl's far more complex system of categories entirely. The limitations to any mutual understanding between the two are also evident in his conclusion: "the 'why' of the entire phenomenon [that is, baroque art] naturally goes unanswered."[53] Riegl would have said much the same—and in much the same terms—about Wölfflin. In his foreword to *Principles*, Wölfflin would then refer to Riegl, with his terms "optic" and "haptic," as an important pioneer in the development of "principles" (*Grundbegriffe*). He described Riegl as "probably the most prominent example of a scholar who, with a complete mastery of his material, gave serious methodological consideration to the reasons for the formation of style and consistently sought to refine his conceptual tools."[54] However, he evaded a more in-depth critical response to Riegl (and August Schmarsow) with the courtly comment: "I should have to write another book altogether if I were to discuss all these authors thoroughly."[55]

Max Dvořák

After Riegl's death in 1905, Wölfflin was no longer one of the fundamental points of reference in Vienna. "At the time, there were a lot of reservations about Wölfflin in Vienna," recalled Dagobert Frey, who had studied with Max Dvořák, the successor of Wickhoff and Riegl, in 1913–1914.[56] A memo by Wölfflin on the meeting of the International Congress of Historical Sciences in Berlin in August 1908, to which he had invited Dvořák, provides some insights into the tensions within the academic world: "But there are also differences of schools and individuals that should be settled. Exchange friendly handshakes. People have a different effect from afar. Close up, the evil Viennese, in their representative (Dvořák), look completely harmless."[57]

By "the evil Viennese" Wölfflin was presumably referring not so much to personal animosities as in general to the stinging, often injurious reviews in the journal *Kunst-geschichtliche Anzeigen*, edited by Wickhoff (and continued by Dvořák after Wickhoff's death). In principle, Wölfflin was in all regards respected in Vienna. This is evident, for instance, in Hans Tietze's *Methode der Kunstgeschichte*, which refers to Wölfflin's formal analyses as "classic examples."[58] On the other hand, Dvořák's unpublished lectures, the manuscripts of which have come down to us in their entirety, provide evidence that Wölfflin was nevertheless viewed with a certain amount of skepticism. From his first course on baroque art in Italy, held in 1905/1906, to his last, interrupted by his death in 1921, Dvořák explored the art of the sixteenth and seventeenth centuries in depth, revising his interpretations again and again with a view to the latest developments in contemporary art.[59] He initially adhered closely to Riegl, whose baroque lectures of 1894/1895 he would have heard as a student and whose *Origins of Baroque Art in Rome* was edited for publication on his initiative.[60] As is well known, Dvořák's ongoing revision of the baroque concept (which will not be elaborated on here) ultimately arrived, around 1920, at the "invention" of mannerism as an epoch in its own right between the High Renaissance and the baroque.[61] In all of those lectures, Dvořák "most warmly" recommended Wölfflin's writings to his listeners, but he was not sparing with criticism.[62] That this criticism did not change throughout the various phases of Dvořák's methodology—from the formalism of his beginnings to the emphatic *Geistesgeschichte* of his late years—is a telling symptom: Wölfflin no longer had a stimulating effect on Vienna.

In 1911 Dvořák observed:

Wölfflin's views are based on Burckhardt, and his notion of Renaissance art is accordingly dogmatic. Even more succinctly than Burckhardt, Wölfflin construes the concept of a consummately developed, classical art…, followed by dissolution and decline, which he apparently endeavors to prove in a factual and objective manner, an approach that naturally amounts to a vicious circle since the supposed criteria for the decline are measured by the yardstick of the supposedly absolutely valid Renaissance art and not by aspects of further development.[63]

Here Dvořák combined precisely the same antinormative and anticlassical points of criticism already introduced by Riegl. And like Riegl he made Wölfflin out to be the heir of Burckhardt, who is considered responsible for defining the Renaissance as an aesthetic norm. As early as 1905, Dvořák pointed out (not without reason) that Wölfflin had rehabilitated the baroque but ultimately continued to make his assessments from a classicist standpoint.[64] (Dvořák's younger friend Tietze came to a similar conclusion in 1913.[65]) And, he continued, "If one wants to see what was progressive in baroque art, one must not only look backward."[66] Wölfflin's sharp distinction between Renaissance and baroque thus denied the continuity of development that, in Dvořák's eyes, connected the two epochs uninterruptedly and ultimately led from antiquity to modernity. Dvořák had read Wölfflin's *Classic Art*. He did not see the High Renaissance as a "culmination," however, but only as one of the "beginnings" of the baroque (and in this respect he came astonishingly close to Strzygowski, who had been his fierce rival since 1909).[67] As late as 1921, Dvořák made reference to Wölfflin's well-known dictum "The peak is a very fine ridge" if only to use it against Wölfflin himself: the High Renaissance, he observed, was "not an abiding norm" ("keine bleibende Norm"), but merely "a transitional stage in the general current of development that, hardly attained, was already overcome" ("ein Durchgangs-stadium in dem allgemeinen Fluss der Entwicklung, das, kaum erreicht, auch schon wieder überwunden wurde").[68]

It is conspicuous that nowhere in Dvořák's completely extant lectures, which often responded very promptly to current developments, is there an explicit reference to Wölfflin's *Principles*. Dvořák apparently took no notice of Wölfflin's most successful book. It is not difficult to understand the reason for this. When *Principles* came out in 1915, Dvořák was giving his lecture course on idealism and realism in early modern art, in which he finalized his turn to *Geistesgeschichte*.[69] Dvořák now regarded art history as a process kept in dialectic motion through the dichotomy of the material and the spiritual.[70] Wölfflin's formal analytical concepts and his cyclical conception of history were no longer much help here. Characteristically, in 1913 Wölfflin himself had, only briefly, considered drawing a connection between his basic pairs of concepts, for example, painterly and linear, and idealism and naturalism—in other words, precisely the categories of *Weltanschauung* used by Dvořák at the time.[71] However, Wölfflin abandoned the idea again, undoubtedly because it would have compromised his concept of an expressionless level of depiction if the forms of seeing were now understood as the expression of certain intellectual attitudes. As we know, Wölfflin had reservations about his colleague's *Geistesgeschichte*. This is evident in his disappointed review of the posthumously published compilation of Dvořák's essays, *Kunstgeschichte als Geistesgeschichte* of 1924.[72]

Was there really no response to *Principles* in Vienna? At first sight, Dvořák seems to have made direct (though not explicit) reference to the work on one occasion. In the autumn of 1915, he added an angry "extempore" to his lecture on idealism and realism, in which he expressed his discomfort with systematic concepts. "Often I think to myself, excuse the drastic word, let the devil take art history."[73] That discipline tended to forget that the conception of art was not a constant, but differed from one epoch to the next:

For the majority of human beings, a work of art remains a work of art, regardless of the period from which it originates, a fact from which we can construe attributes of the artistic and classify them in random systems. In the process, we commit a cardinal error: not only the outward attributes of art, but also the concept of the work of art, of the artistic, was not constant, but different in different periods, and the result of the general evolution of humanity.… [T]o whatever extent a continuity of development prevails, to that extent it is also necessary to consider, in all matters, the dissimilarity of principles that results from this development.[74]

For that reason, Dvořák continued, *Grundbegriffe* (that is, Wölfflin's *Principles*) should also be historically differentiated. A "science" ("Wissenschaft") that derived "general aesthetic principles" from the "comparison of works of art of different periods" ("Vergleich von Kunstwerken aus verschiedenen Perioden…ästhetische allgemeine Prinzipien") only caused "confusion" ("Verwirrung") because it built on "false historical assumptions" ("falsche geschichtliche Voraussetzungen").[75]

Naturally, it does not seem far fetched to understand this appeal for the historicization of "principles" as a criticism of Wölfflin's book, which had just been published. But I'm not quite sure that that was the case. It is also possible that Dvořák was referring here to the writings of a former pupil of Wölfflin's: Wilhelm Worringer's *Abstraktion und Einfühlung* (1907) and *Formprobleme der Gotik* (1911).[76] In repudiation of Worringer's bold speculations, which were influenced more by Riegl than by Wölfflin and ultimately aimed for an ahistorical and implicitly racial psychology of the nations, Dvořák (incidentally, here again seconded by Tietze) frequently cited very similar arguments.[77]

Josef Strzygowski and *Principles*

As is well known, the methodological problems of *Principles* were discussed extensively in Germany in the 1920s.[78] In Vienna, however, no comparable debate was carried out. The only exception there was Josef Strzygowski, who, as noted above, had been the first of that scholarly community to read Wölfflin. Let us touch on Strzygowski's extremely polemical criticism at least briefly. After 1918 he obsessively propagated his project of an antihumanist world art history transcending the boundaries of Europe, to be written anew from an Aryan "northern standpoint." His attacks on established scholarship were leveled above all at his predecessors at the University of Vienna, Wickhoff and Riegl, but also against his former friend Wölfflin, who, he felt, failed to show due regard for his scholarly accomplishments.[79] In the essay "Norden und Renaissance" (1920) and in *Die Krisis der Geisteswissenschaften* (1923), Strzygowski accused Wölfflin of preferring the ancient Mediterranean culture over the north and of methodological one-sidedness.[80] The bullet points of his criticism are art history without names; reduction of art to the laws of form; and a disregard for elementary factors such as "soil" (*Boden*), the "people" (*Volk*) or the "ingenious creator" (*genialer Schöpfer*), which Strzygowski considers the sole vehicles of a vibrant artistic development that was usurped and swallowed up by European "power art" (*Machtkunst).* Strzygowski regarded Wölfflin's *Principles* as a "patchwork" (*Stückwerk*) that led to "intellectual atrophy" (*geistige Verödung*).[81] He therefore set about replacing the five pairs of concepts by a single one that differed from Wölfflin's in that it encompassed the level of meaning, not just that of form. As might be expected, what Strzygowski meant by that was the contrast between the Aryan north and the antique, humanist south.[82] Let it be mentioned briefly here that Strzygowski's racialist invective represents an early example of criticism of "abstract" formalism, which in the 1920s and 1930s was not limited to the Warburg school and—this was long overlooked—could also be politically rightist in sentiment.[83] Another Viennese art historian, Dagobert Frey, would later reject Wölfflin's *Principles* in comparable manner from a vitalistic, holistic standpoint.[84] It must not be forgotten, however, that the differentiation between the Romanic south and the Germanic north had already played a fundamental role in Riegl's construction of history.[85] And in 1922, in his lecture "Italien und das deutsche Formgefühl," even Wölfflin discussed the issue of national stylistic constants and the contrast between north and south.[86] As we know, his last book was published in 1931, bearing the same title as the lecture.[87]

Hans Sedlmayr and the New Vienna School

For Strzygowski, Wölfflin and the Vienna School belonged to the same group of scholars, whom he considered his enemies: the "likeminded humanists" ("humanistische Gesinnungsgenossen").[88] The 1920s debate over *Principles*, however, emphasized precisely the differences between Wölfflin and Riegl. In 1924, for example, in his methodological discussion of the possibility of "art-theoretical principles" ("kunstwissenschaftliche Grundbegriffe"), Erwin Panofsky gave preference to Riegl's system.[89] And Edgar Wind likewise referred to the latter in his only recently published dissertation of 1922, which Panofsky approved and studied in depth.[90] As late as 1930, Hans Jantzen voiced his conviction that "the limitations of the Wölfflinian terminology" could be overcome "only with Riegl's help" in order to arrive at positive categories—as opposed to Wölfflin's normative categories, derived from a classical ideal.[91] You would expect this debate to have found an echo in those of the young Viennese art historians who, in the late twenties, counted not least of all on recourse to Riegl to yield a new level of rigor in art-theoretical methods. But even in this so-called New Vienna School—whose spokesperson was Hans Sedlmayr, professor in Vienna from 1934 to 1945—Wölfflin's *Principles* did not play a central role.[92] In fact, one could almost say that, for Sedlmayr, the historian of baroque architecture, *Renaissance and Baroque* was still Wölfflin's most influential work, just as it had been for Riegl and Dvořák. Sedlmayr's deliberations on the fictional materiality of Roman baroque architecture,[93] for instance, are reminiscent of Wölfflin's description of the "soft, full lushness" ("weiche, volle Saftigkeit") of baroque buildings, "the ideal materiality whose inner vitality and poise are expressed in the architectural members" ("idealen Materie, deren inneres Leben und Sich-Haben die Bauglieder zum Ausdruck bringen").[94]

In "Die Quintessenz der Lehren Riegls" of 1929 (the methodological introduction to

Riegl's collected essays), Sedlmayr did discuss Riegl's theory of the "ultimately possible basic types, within which any empirically observable *Kunstwollen* can subsist" ("letzten wesensmöglichen Grundtypen, innerhalb welcher sich alles empirisch konstatierbare Kunstwollen bewegt").[95] He was referring to the a priori aesthetic principles of Riegl that Panofsky had attempted to systematize in his important 1924 essay.[96] There is no mention here, however, of Wölfflin's *Principles*,[97] any more than there is in Sedlmayr's programmatic text *Zu einer strengen Kunstwissenschaft* of 1931.[98] And the same applies to the essay entitled "Probleme der Interpretation," which was begun around 1940 but published only in 1956, virtually unchanged, with the title "Kunstwerk und Kunstgeschichte."[99] Here Sedlmayr—who from 1951 onward was able to portray himself as Wölfflin's Munich successor—sang his intellectual father's praises but mentioned only the latter's essay "Über das Erklären von Kunstwerken," the "hitherto most complete and most concise exposition of the problems under discussion here" ("bisher vollständigste und knappste Darstellung der hier erörterten Probleme").[100] Sedlmayr saw the decisive difference between his approach and Wölfflin's in the evaluation of the "isolated work of art" ("isoliertes Kunstwerk"), of which Wölfflin is known to have written that it "always has something unsettling about it for the art historian" ("für den Historiker immer etwas Beunruhigendes [hat]"),[101] while for Sedlmayr it formed the actual core of the analysis. In a remark not included in the printed version, he was more forthright: Wölfflin, "to whom art history owes so much" ("dem die Kunstgeschichte außerordentlich viel verdankt"), was an example of how you could "arrive at results using the wrong methods" ("mit falschen Methoden Ergebnisse erzielen").[102] It is precisely this concentration on the individual work and its structure that surely explains why, in their theoretical discussions, the early Sedlmayr and the New Vienna School as a whole paid virtually no attention either to Wölfflin's principles, or, ultimately, to Riegl's.[103] Both

of them, Sedlmayr mentioned in a memo, had applied "preconceived (speculatively derived) categories to the artworks" ("vorgefasste [spekulativ abgeleitete] Kategorien an die Kunstwerke") from the outside.[104] In 1934 Dvořák's pupil Karl Maria Swoboda wrote in comparable manner of the "arbitrarily snatched-up Wölfflinian categories" ("willkürlich aufgerafften Wölfflinschen Kategorien") that were of no use for gaining an understanding of the work of art as an "entity of its own kind" ("Gebilde eigener Art").[105] In 1929 the Austrian archaeologist Guido von Kaschnitz-Weinberg, who in many ways shared Sedlmayr's point of view and that of structural analysis, likewise pointed out the "questionable value of pairs of terms that always had to be applied to the artistic development from the outside" ("fragwürdige[n] Wert von Begriffspaaren, die immer erst von außen an die Kunstentwicklung herangebracht werden müssen"). In his opinion, new, flexible terms could be developed only if you took the "given artwork itself" ("[das] gegebene Kunstwerk selbst") as your starting point.[106]

Julius von Schlosser

In 1940, in the introduction to his *Gedanken zur Kunstgeschichte*, which he had originally intended to dedicate to Julius von Schlosser (who died in 1938), Wölfflin wrote: "The recognition, expressed repeatedly in public, from a man like Schlosser was of great value to me precisely because it came from Vienna, that is, from a place where people actually held a different point of view." ("Die öffentlich wiederholt ausgesprochene Anerkennung eines Mannes wie Schlosser ist mir von großem Wert gewesen, gerade weil sie von Wien kam, von einer Seite also, wo man eigentlich anders eingestellt war.")[107] Any survey of the problematic Viennese reception of Wölfflin's work must naturally include Julius von Schlosser, to whom the final section of this essay is accordingly devoted. After many years of employment with the imperial collections (now the Kunsthistorisches Museum),

Schlosser was a professor in Vienna from 1922 to 1936 (and the teacher and predecessor of Hans Sedlmayr). He attached particularly great importance to his "intellectual friendship" (*Geistesfreundschaft*) with Wölfflin,[108] in his words the "greatest living communicator of more recent art history" ("größter lebender Darsteller der neueren Kunstgeschichte"),[109] even though the two had met only on a few rare occasions and Schlosser's letters barely go beyond the exchange of primly expressed courtesies.[110] The reasons for this ostentatious reference are not entirely clear. They could hardly have been substantive in nature. After all, Benedetto Croce, whom Schlosser revered as the one who had freed him from his intellectual crisis, had criticized Wölfflin's theory of the "double root of style," the dualism of form and content. It was none other than Schlosser himself who had translated this review by the Italian philosopher—which was a source of distress to Wölfflin for the rest of his life—into German.[111] And Schlosser also took a dim view of Adolf von Hildebrand's sculpture theory, which was of key importance to Wölfflin.[112] Wölfflin and Schlosser, who were nearly the same age, presumably shared above all a self-conception as supposed "outsiders" (*Außenseiter*) to the academic world, and—following the deaths of so many of their colleagues—an awareness of being among the last remaining representatives of an earlier generation.[113]

On Wölfflin's seventieth birthday, on June 21, 1934, Schlosser opened the congratulatory addresses in *Neue Zürcher Zeitung* with a strangely emphatic contribution entitled "Von Heinrich Wölfflins Sendung" (On Heinrich Wölfflin's mission), which he also published in the Viennese magazine *Belvedere*, and which ultimately reveals more about the author himself than about the jubilarian.[114] The text revolves primarily around Wölfflin's last book, *Italien und das deutsche Formgefühl*. It refers to the work as a "book of confession" (*Bekenntnisbuch*), which he, Schlosser, had read "with a sense of inner shock" ("mit innerer Erschütterung"). The personal connection

is obvious—Schlosser cites the "Hessian and Lombardic" blood that he felt "in his veins." And the reference to the contemporary political situation is also unmistakable. One year after Hitler's accession to power in the German Reich and the establishment of the Austrofascist dictatorship in Austria, Schlosser speaks darkly and solemnly of the "gravest hour of fate of the German people as a whole" ("schwerste[n] Schicksalsstunde des deutschen Gesamtvolkes"). The right-wing conservative Viennese academics of German nationality—a category to which Schlosser undoubtedly also belonged—would certainly have understood the code word *Gesamtvolk* (the German people as a whole).[115] Schlosser links this sentiment to, of all things, his praise of the "German-Swiss" (*Deutschschweizer*) Wölfflin, who held a place "between the races" ("zwischen den Rassen"), and whose true mission was to mediate between the German and the Italian cultures.

Conspicuously, Schlosser did not mention a single other work by the jubilarian, including—yet again, one would like to say—*Principles*.[116] In conclusion, however, he observed that scholars were indebted to Wölfflin for "what he…endeavored to teach us about the original phenomenon of art and the history of its language" ("was er…uns über das Urphänomen der Kunst und die Geschichte ihrer Sprache zu lehren unternommen hat"). As we know, the late Schlosser had adopted from Karl Vossler—a Romance philologist of Munich and friend of Benedetto Croce—the conviction that art history must not be a mere "*linguistic* history" (*Sprachgeschichte*) of art but can do justice to the pure expression of the great works only as "*stylistic* history" (*Stilgeschichte*). Style is conceived of here not in the sense of formalist art history but in the Goethean sense—that is, as an absolute value rather than the designation of a historical epoch. Thus it cannot be overlooked that Schlosser here portrays Wölfflin in somewhat compromised form as a historian solely of the supraindividual language of art. And this seems particularly odd in view of the fact that, at the beginning of his article, he had referred to Croce and Vossler, of all scholars, along with Wölfflin, as his "intellectual friends" (*Geistesfreunde*). A year later, in his essay "'Stilgeschichte' und 'Sprachgeschichte' der bildenden Kunst," Schlosser again spoke very highly of Wölfflin, and especially of his book *Die Kunst Albrecht Dürers*, in which he even saw "'the stylistic-historical' aspect, in the highest sense" ("das im höchsten Sinn 'Stilgeschichtliche'") prominently featured.[117] Significantly, however, Schlosser's assessment of *Principles of Art History* was in a different vein. Now he mentioned the book explicitly but cited Croce's criticism: here Wölfflin had departed from actual stylistic history and taken his place "on the grounds of linguistic history" ("auf dem Boden der Sprachgeschichte"). As Wölfflin's friendly letters of thanks show, these differences in matters of content should not be overrated.[118] It should nevertheless be pointed out, by way of conclusion, that the relatively aloof attitude of the Vienna School toward Heinrich Wölfflin, and particularly his *Principles*—encountered consistently from Alois Riegl to Hans Sedlmayr—even applied to his "intellectual friend" Julius von Schlosser.

We can cite several reasons why, by 1945 at the latest, the "Vienna School of art history" had come to an end as a living tradition. Of all the art historians expelled by the Nazis after 1938 for "racial" and "political" reasons, very few returned to Austria after World War II. Productive new approaches of the 1920s and 1930s, for example the integration of the psychoanalytical and iconological perspectives, were no longer pursued in Vienna. What is more, the fascist tendencies that had taken root in the Vienna School under Sedlmayr were hardly questioned: in view of the latter's dismissal as professor in 1945, a serious discussion of the political dimension of art history seemed superfluous. In the climate that prevailed in Viennese art history of the postwar period—characterized, as it was, by stylistic history and positivist research but hardly

by theoretical reflection[119]—critical reflection on Wölfflin's *Principles* barely played a role, even if the book continued to be recommended to students as a classic formal-analytical text. This is true in the teaching of the abovementioned Karl Maria Swoboda, who, after his years at the German University in Prague (1934–1945), was a professor in Vienna from 1946 to 1960. Yet it also holds for the very theoretical-minded Otto Pächt, who, around 1930, along with Sedlmayr, had been among the protagonists of the New Vienna School and who returned to Vienna from exile in England to serve as a professor from 1963 to 1971. (The appointment of Sedlmayr by the government and the university against the wishes of the Kunstgeschichtliches Institut had come to naught on account of fierce protests against the former Nazi.) In his 1970/1971 lecture "Methodisches zur kunsthistorischen Praxis," Pächt made reference to Wölfflin's text "Das Erklären von Kunstwerken" (just like his former colleague Sedlmayr, whom he frequently quoted), but made no mention whatsoever of *Principles*.[120] There was evidently nothing relevant about Wölfflin's book for Pächt's methodological deliberations, which linked his theoretical concepts of the period around 1930 with fierce polemics against iconology, the school of thought predominant in the 1960s.

NOTES

Translated from the German by Judith Rosenthal

1. Joan Goldhammer Hart, "Some Reflections on Wölfflin and the Vienna School," in *Akten des XXV. Internationalen Kongresses für Kunstgeschichte*, ed. Hermann Fillitz and Martina Pippal, vol. 1, *Wien und die Entwicklung der kunsthistorischen Methode* (Vienna, 1984), 53.

2. Hans Tietze, *Die Methode der Kunstgeschichte: Ein Versuch* (Leipzig, 1913).

3. Heinrich Wölfflin, *Die Jugendwerke des Michelangelo* (Munich, 1891). The foreword is dated October 1890 (IV). See Joan Goldhammer Hart, "Heinrich Wölfflin: An Intellectual Biography" (PhD diss., University of California, Berkeley, 1981), 236–241.

4. On their joint time in Rome, see Hart, "Some Reflections," 53.

5. Josef Strzygowski, "Studien zu Michelangelo's Jugendentwicklung," *Jahrbuch der Königlich Preussischen Kunstsammlungen* 12 (1891): 207–219, here 216n1. Here Strzygowski discussed Michelangelo's *Battle of the Centaurs* in far greater detail than Wölfflin and strove to clarify the iconography as well as to identify references to texts by classical authors, something Wölfflin—who was solely interested in formal composition—had neglected. Strzygowski also went further than Wölfflin as regards the *Madonna della Scala*. Wölfflin considered the Virgin's pose in classical profile a splendid new invention by Michelangelo (*Jugendwerke*, 13). Strzygowski, on the other hand, attributed the motif to an older relief of the Madonna credited to Desiderio da Settignano.

6. "Die gleiche Sinnesart hat ihn bei MA zu guten Beobachtungen geführt." Heinrich Wölfflin diary, October 1890–June 1891, notebook 25, 120r, Universitätsbibliothek Basel, Nachlass Heinrich Wölfflin. Thanks to Evonne Levy for pointing out this entry to me.

7. Josef Strzygowski, *Das Werden des Barock bei Raphael und Correggio nebst einem Anhang über Rembrandt* (Strasbourg, 1898). See also Josef Strzygowski, "Der malerische Stil," *Zeitschrift für bildende Kunst* 30 (1895): 305–309; Josef Strzygowski, "Studien zu Leonardos Entwicklung als Maler," *Jahrbuch der Königlich Preussischen Kunstsammlungen* 16 (1895): 159–175. Heinrich Wölfflin, *Renaissance und Barock: Eine Untersuchung über Wesen und Entstehung des Barockstils in Italien* (Munich, 1888); English translation: *Renaissance and Baroque*, trans. Kathrin Simon (London, 1964, 1984; Ithaca, 1966). See Hart, "Heinrich Wölfflin," 139–211; Meinhold Lurz, *Heinrich Wölfflin: Biographie einer Kunsttheorie* (Worms, 1981), 100–123; Evonne Levy, "The Political Project of Wölfflin's Early Formalism," *October* 139 (2012): 39–58; Evonne Levy, *Baroque and the Political Language of Formalism (1845–1945): Burckhardt, Wölfflin, Gurlitt, Brinckmann, Sedlmayr* (Basel, 2015), 101–116.

8. August Schmarsow, *Zur Frage nach dem Malerischen: Sein Grundbegriff und seine Entwicklung*, vol. 1 of *Beiträge zur Ästhetik der bildenden Künste* (Leipzig, 1896).

9. This change had already been described in Anton Springer, *Raffael und Michelangelo* (Leipzig, 1878), 279–283. On the nineteenth-century conception of the "painterly" Raphael: Christoph Wagner, *Farbe und Metapher: Die Entstehung einer neuzeitlichen Bildmetaphorik in der vorrömischen Malerei Raphaels* (Berlin, 1999), 102–121 (with quotations from Carl Friedrich von Rumohr and Johann David Passavant).

10. Already Strzygowski ("Studien," 219) saw in the *Doni Tondo* the "individual quality" that made Michelangelo "the originator of the baroque."

11. Wölfflin, *Renaissance und Barock*, 3 (editors' translation).

12. Works that contradicted this ideal, such as Raphael's *Fire in the Borgo* in the Stanza dell'Incendio, were dismissed as workshop products. Heinrich Wölfflin, *Die klassische Kunst: Eine Einführung in die italienische Renaissance* (Munich, 1899), 105; English translation: Heinrich Wölfflin, *Classic Art: An Introduction to the Italian Renaissance*, trans. Peter and Linda Murray (New York, 1952), 108.

13. Strzygowski, *Werden des Barock*, 98.

14. Strzygowski, *Werden des Barock*, 78, 113. On the nineteenth- and twentieth-century conception of Michelangelo in general, see Joseph Imorde, *Michelangelo Deutsch!* (Berlin, 2009). Without making explicit reference to him, Strzygowski's views on Rembrandt were naturally indebted to Justus Langbehn, *Rembrandt als Erzieher* (Leipzig, 1890).

15. Strzygowski, *Werden des Barock*, 79.

16. Strzygowski, *Werden des Barock*, frontispiece caption. Thus—contrary to a frequently voiced opinion—it was not only in Strzygowski's late period but from the very beginning that his outlook was dominated by such ideologies. On the other hand (*Werden des Barock*, 79), he at least saw "the danger of not being taken seriously" when he made such statements ("die Gefahr, [mit solchen Aussagen] nicht ernst genommen zu warden").

17. See Josef Strzygowski, *Die Krisis der Geisteswissenschaften: Vorgeführt am Beispiele der Forschung über bildende Kunst; ein grundsätzlicher Rahmenversuch* (Vienna, 1923), 322.

18. Joseph Gantner, "Der Unterricht in Kunstgeschichte an der Universität Basel 1844–1938," in *Die Lehrstühle der Universitäten in Basel, Bern, Freiburg und Zürich von den Anfängen bis 1940*, yearbook, Schweizerisches Institut für Kunstwissenschaft (1972/1973), 19. The same year, however, Strzygowski accepted an offer from the University of Vienna, where he remained a professor until his retirement in 1933. As late as February 1902, he visited Wölfflin in Berlin. See Joseph Gantner, ed., *Heinrich Wölfflin 1864–1945: Autobiographie, Tagebücher und Briefe* (Basel, 1982), 164.

19. On the history of research on the baroque, see the following surveys: Ute Engel, *Stil und Nation: Barockforschung und deutsche Kunstgeschichte (ca. 1830 bis 1933)* (Munich, 2015); Levy, *Baroque and the Political Language of Formalism*. Also: Andrew Leach, John Macarthur, and Maarten Delbeke, eds., *The Baroque in Architectural Culture, 1880–1980* (Farnham, 2015).

20. To cite just a few important works on Riegl: Margaret Olin, *Forms of Representation in Alois Riegl's Theory of Art* (University Park, PA, 1992); Richard Woodfield, ed., *Framing Formalism: Riegl's Work* (Amsterdam, 2001); Peter Noever, Artur Rosenauer, and Georg Vasold, eds., *Alois Riegl Revisited: Beiträge zu Werk und Rezeption* (Vienna, 2010); Diana Reynolds Cordileone, *Alois Riegl in Vienna: An Institutional Biography, 1875–1905* (London, 2014).

21. Alois Riegl, "Italienische Kunstgeschichte von 1550 bis 1800," lectures, winter semester 1898/1899, manuscript, Universität Wien, Institut für Kunstgeschichte, Archiv. Contrary to the title, the timespan discussed in the manuscript goes only as far as Maderno, i.e., the early seventeenth century.

22. Alois Riegl, "Italienische Kunstgeschichte von 1520 bis 1700," lectures, winter semester 1901/1902, Universität Wien, manuscript, Institut für Kunstgeschichte, Archiv.

23. Alois Riegl, "Kunstgeschichte des Barockzeitalters," lectures, winter semester 1894/1895, manuscript, Universität Wien, Institut für Kunstgeschichte, Archiv, 1. On the confusing state in which the manuscripts of Riegl's baroque lectures have come down to us (with revisions, corrections, repeated sections) and the history of their posthumous publication, see Arnold Witte, "Reconstructing Riegl's 'Entstehung der Barockkunst in Rom,'" in Riegl, *The Origins of Baroque Art in Rome*, ed. and trans. Andrew Hopkins and Arnold Witte (Los Angeles, 2010), 34–59, esp. 38–42. (However, I find it difficult to follow Witte's argument according to which Riegl had himself already revised his manuscript for a planned printed edition.)

24. Riegl, 1894/1895, 34, cites only Jacob Burckhardt and Cornelius Gurlitt as sources. The fact that he had not yet read Wölfflin has hitherto been overlooked. Not even Margaret Olin recognized this circumstance in her outstanding deliberations on the antiquity chapter of the first lecture series (*Forms of Representation*, 30–38). This oversight probably came about because, in the manuscripts in the archive in Vienna, the introduction to the lectures of 1898/1899 (1–7), in which Wölfflin already receives mention, is right before the introduction to the lectures of 1894/1895 (with different pagination, 1–30), in which there is no reference to Wölfflin. Evonne Levy, "Riegl and Wölfflin in Dialogue on the Baroque," in *The Baroque in Architectural Culture*, 87–96, takes my reevaluation of Riegl's first baroque lectures into account.

25. Heinrich Wölfflin, "Die antiken Triumphbogen in Italien: Eine Studie zur Entwicklungsgeschichte der römischen Architektur und ihr Verhältnis zur Renaissance (1893)," in Heinrich Wölfflin, *Kleine Schriften (1886–1933)*, ed. Joseph Gantner (Basel, 1946), 51–71. Wölfflin, *Renaissance und Barock*, x, discusses the original plan of a "parallel account of the antique Baroque" ("parallele Darstellung des antiken Barocks").

26. Riegl, 1894/1895, 31–46. The architecture of the Roman imperial period is discussed later in Alois Riegl, *Die spätrömische Kunstindustrie* (Vienna, 1927), 23–81 (first edition 1901, preparatory work starting 1898). In English, Alois Riegl, *Late Roman Art Industry*, ed. and trans. Rolf Winkes (Rome, 1985), 19–50.

27. Cornelius Gurlitt, *Geschichte des Barockstiles und des Rococo in Deutschland* (Stuttgart, 1889). As in Riegl's later lecture, Gurlitt here continued on from a discussion of the Italian baroque: Cornelius Gurlitt, *Die Geschichte des Barockstiles in Italien* (Stuttgart, 1887).

28. See Riegl, 1894/1895, 59–238: "Barockarchitektur in Italien (16.–18. Jahrhundert)"; 1–89 with new pagination: "Barockmalerei in Italien"; 1–112, again with new pagination: "Deutsche Kunst im Barockzeitalter." On this section, Witte ("Reconstructing Riegl's 'Entstehung,'" 39) merely remarks in misleading manner: "The last part discussed German baroque art, especially painting with, for example, Rembrandt and Albrecht Dürer as its main subjects." Actually, Riegl here expounded on German (and Austrian) architecture (9–78), sculpture (78–89), and painting (90–112). The last of these sections begins with Adam Elsheimer and then discusses the painters of the seventeenth and eighteenth centuries by genre (landscape, animal depiction and still life, history painting), quite summarily toward the end, presumably for reasons of time. As a result, important painters of eighteenth-century Austria, such as Johann Michael Rottmayr, Daniel Gran, Paul Troger, and Franz Anton Maulbertsch are mentioned on page 112 in just a few sentences. According to Riegl's introduction of 1894/1895, he originally planned to go into Dutch and Spanish painting (Einleitung, 12–16). He finally addressed himself to these two subjects in 1896, in lectures devoted specifically to them. See the list of Riegl's lectures in Riegl, *Late Roman Art Industry*, xxix. On Riegl's lectures on Spanish painting: Hans Aurenhammer, "La Escuela de Viena y Velázquez: Recepción crítica de la monografía de Justi por Alois Riegl y Max Dvořák," in *Carl Justi y el arte español* (Madrid, 2016), 201–218; Hans Aurenhammer, "'Wozu also ein Kolleg, würde es da nicht genügen,…das Buch von Justi zu lesen?'—Riegls und Dvořáks kritische Rezeption von Justis 'Velázquez' in Ihren Vorlesungen (1896–1908)," in *Carl Justi und die Kunstgeschichte*, ed. Bettina Marten and Roland Kanz, Ars Iberica et Americana, vol. 20, Kunsthistorische Studien der Carl Justi-Vereinigung (Frankfurt am Main, 2016), 93–102.

29. See Riegl, 1898/1899, "Einleitung," 4. On Riegl's reception of Wölfflin, also see the discerning analysis in Levy, "Riegl and Wölfflin."

30. Riegl, *Origins*, 101 (*Entstehung*, 13). Here Gurlitt, Schmarsow, and Strzygowski come off less well.

31. "Ein festes Datum für den Beginn des Barockzeitalters und der Barockkunst im Allgemeinen festzusetzen wäre somit ein müßiges Beginnen. Wir müssen uns vorbehalten, den Anfangstermin jeweilig im einzelnen nach Ländern und Künsten festzustellen." Riegl, 1894/1895, 22.

32. Riegl, 1894/1895, 17–22, on periodization. Like Jacob Burckhardt before him, Riegl regarded Michelangelo's designs for the stairway of the Biblioteca Laurenziana in Florence "the starting point of baroque architecture" ("den Ausgangspunkt der Barockbaukunst"); however, it took the Counter-Reformation, after the mid-sixteenth century, to provide the actual "impetus" (*Anstoss*) for the development of the baroque.

33. See Riegl, 1894/1895, 26: "But from the beginning of the sixteenth to the beginning of the eighteenth century, the aim of architecture was directed toward the sensualization of the great, mighty, and grandiose in both church and secular architecture. Baroque architecture had already received all these fundamental features of its essence as the legacy of the High Renaissance. In that respect, there is no difference between the two styles. In that respect, the High Renaissance transitions directly into the baroque, leaving no development gap between the two." ("Aber vom Anfang des 16. bis in den Anfang des 18. Jh. ist das Ziel der Baukunst auf die Versinnlichung des Großen, Gewaltigen, Grandiosen gerichtet gewesen, sowohl in der Kirchen- als in der Profanarchitektur. Alle diese Grundzüge ihres Wesens hat die Barockarchitektur bereits als Erbe der Hochrenaissance empfangen, Darin ist zwischen beiden Stilen kein Unterschied. Darin geht die Hochrenaissance unmittelbar in das Barock über, lässt keine Kluft der Entwicklung zwischen ihnen beiden.")

34. Riegl, *Origins*, 97 (*Entstehung*, 7). See Wölfflin, *Renaissance and Baroque*, 17.

35. Riegl 1901/1902, 12 (crossed out in the text and therefore not included in Riegl, *Origins*).

36. See, for example, Riegl, *Origins*, 102 (*Entstehung*, 81).

37. Riegl, 1894/1895, 59–106.

38. "Seine Definition des Barockstiles als 'Massigkeit und Bewegung' ist nicht tief genug." Riegl, *Origins*, 101 (*Entstehung*, 13).

39. Riegl, *Origins*, 102 (*Entstehung*, 14) corrects Wölfflin's and Schmarsow's dual terms "plastic" and "painterly" (in keeping with the terminology he had developed in *Historical Grammar of the Visual Arts* and *Late Roman Art Industry*): "It might have been better to describe it as an opposition between the tactile and the optical—tactile delineation and visible coloredness" ("…besser taktisch-optisch—tastbare Begrenztheit und sichtbare Farbigkeit)." (Translation slightly changed.)

40. See Mechthild Fend, "Sehen und Tasten: Zur Raumwahrnehmung bei Alois Riegl und in der Sinnesphysiologie des 19. Jahrhunderts," in *Visualisierte Körperkonzepte: Strategien in der Kunst der Moderne*, ed. Barbara Lange (Berlin, 2007), 15–38.

41. On this subject, see Olin, *Forms of Representation*, 134–135. Strzygowski, *Werden des Barock*, 39n2, also discusses the perusal of *Das Problem der Form*. On Wölfflin's reception of Hildebrand's work: Lurz, *Heinrich Wölfflin*, 156–157; Hart, "Heinrich Wölfflin," 226–227, 232–235, 242–252. English translation: *The Problem of Form in Painting and Sculpture*, rev. and trans. Max F. Meyer and Robert Morris Ogden (New York, 1907).

42. "Auch bei Wölfflin erscheint er als Verirrung und Verfall, ohne daß wir sähen, daß es um höherer Fortschritte willen so kommen mußte." Riegl, *Origins*, 101 (*Entstehung*, 13).

43. On Wagner, see Wölfflin, *Renaissance and Baroque*, 87.

44. "In seiner ästhetisch-historischen Schätzung des Barockstiles hat sich Wölfflin noch nicht weit von Burckhardt entfernt." Riegl, *Origins*, 101 (*Entstehung*, 13).

45. "Mit Michelangelo und Correggio ist dasjenige, was die moderne Kunstanschauung von der antiken trennt, zuerst in eine entschiedene selbstbewußte Phase getreten." Riegl, *Origins*, 130 (*Entstehung*, 47). On Riegl's modernity, see, in general, Regine Prange, "Konjunkturen des Optischen—Riegls Grundbegriffe und die Kanonisierung der künstlerischen Moderne," in *Alois Riegl Revisited*, 109–128.

46. See Alois Riegl, *Historische Grammatik der bildenden Künste* (Graz, 1966); English translation, *Historical Grammar of the Visual Arts*, foreword by Benjamin Binstock, trans. Jacqueline E. Jung (New York, 2004), 95–105, 167–185.

47. Riegl, *Origins*, 93, 102 (*Entstehung*, 1, 15).

48. See Wölfflin, *Renaissance and Baroque*, 71–88 ("The Causes of the Change in Style").

49. "Das ist ein Moment, das bei neueren Forschern sehr beliebt ist. Von namhaften Kunsthistorikern hat es Wölfflin zu einem Hauptfaktor seiner Erklärung für die Kunstentwicklung erhoben, auch neuerlich: wie der Mensch sich gesellschaftlich benimmt und wie er sich kostümiert, das will er auch in der Kunst sehen." Riegl, *Historical Grammar*, 358 (*Historische Grammatik*, 258; here "even recently" omitted). Here Riegl takes as his point of departure the viewpoint that explains the formal principle of frontality by citing the "ceremonious spirit" ("zeremoniösem Geiste") of the ancient Egyptians, which can also still be recognized in the dignified bearing of the "modern Orientals" ("modernen Orientalen").

50. Heinrich Wölfflin, "Prolegomena zu einer Psychologie der Architektur," in Wölfflin, *Kleine Schriften*, 44–45; Wölfflin, *Renaissance and Baroque*, 58. On this matter, see Frederic J. Schwartz, *Blind Spots: Critical Theory and the History of Art in Twentieth-Century Germany* (New Haven, 2005), 2–7.

51. Wölfflin, *Classic Art*, "Die neue Gesinnung", 207–230.

52. "Sie sind nur Parallelerscheinungen zur Frontalität.…Die Wahrnehmung ist richtig, aber sie gibt noch keine Erklärung." Riegl, *Historical Grammar*, 358 (*Historische Grammatik*, 259). From Riegl's point of view, the common root of all phenomena is the striving for harmony that, in keeping with the Egyptian worldview, tends toward crystallinism. For a general discussion of this subject: Regine Prange, *Das Kristalline als Kunstsymbol—Bruno Taut und Paul Klee: Zur Reflexion des Abstrakten in Kunst und Kunsttheorie der Moderne* (Hildesheim, 1991), 26–29.

53. "Das 'Warum' der ganzen Erscheinung bleibt freilich unbeantwortet." Heinrich Wölfflin, review, "Alois Riegl, Die Entstehung der Barockkunst in Rom (Vienna, 1908)," *Repertorium für Kunstwissenschaft* 31 (1908): 356–357.

54. "…so ist Alois Riegl wohl der auffallendste Typus eines Gelehrten, der über die Gründe der Stilbildung methodisch nachgedacht und in der Arbeit am vollkommen beherrschten Material die begrifflichen Werkzeuge beständig zu verfeinern versucht hat." Heinrich Wölfflin, *Kunstgeschichtliche Grundbegriffe: Das Problem der Stilentwicklung in der neueren Kunst* (Munich, 1915), VIII; English translation, *Principles of Art History: The Problem of the Development of Style in Early Modern Art*, trans. Jonathan Blower, ed. Evonne Levy and Tristan Weddigen (Los Angeles, 2015), 73. In a note, however, Wölfflin makes reference to "the inherent blind spots and dangers of the Rieglian perspective" ("die Einseitigkeiten und Gefahren, die in der Rieglschen Betrachtungsweise liegen") and to Ernst Heidrich's well-known critique. See Ernst Heidrich, *Beiträge zur Geschichte und Methode der Kunstgeschichte* (Basel, 1917), 82–109. For a thorough analysis of the importance of Riegl for Wölfflin's *Principles* (a matter not to be discussed in greater depth in the present context), see Levy, "Riegl and Wölfflin"; Evonne Levy, "Wölfflin's *Principles of Art History* (1915–2015): A Prolegomenon for Its Second Century," in Wölfflin, *Principles* (2015), 11–13; Levy, *Baroque and the Political Language of Formalism*, 132–144.

55. Wölfflin, *Principles* (2015), 74. Also see Lurz, *Wölfflin*, 34–36.

56. "Wölfflin stand man damals in Wien zurückhaltend gegenüber." Dagobert Frey, in *Österreichische Geschichtswissenschaft der Gegenwart in Selbstdarstellungen*, ed. Nikolaus Grass, vol. 2 (Innsbruck, 1951), 54. Frey attributed the "rejection of a systematic art-theoretical notion" ("Ablehnung einer kunstwissenschaftlich systematischen Auffassung") to the Viennese emphasis on the "artwork as a historical phenomenon" ("Kunstwerk als historisches Phänomen"). (In that case, though, the rejection would also apply to Riegl.) Frey wrote similarly in "Probleme einer Geschichte der Kunstwissenschaft (1958)," in *Bausteine zu einer Philosophie der Kunst* (Darmstadt, 1976), 63. Dvořák had received support from Wölfflin in developing his career. In 1909, the latter's positive assessment led to Dvořák's being offered a professorship in Basel, which he turned down, however, because the same year he became a full professor in Vienna. Gantner, *Unterricht*, 20.

57. "Aber es gibt auch Differenzen von Schulen und Individuen, die überbrückt werden sollen. Austausch freundschaftlichen Händedrucks. Die Menschen wirken von fern anders. Die bösen Wiener sehn in ihrem Vertreter (Dvořák) von nahem ganz harmlos aus." Diary, August 13, 1908, notebook 49, 21r, quoted and translated in Hart, *Wölfflin*, 484. Thanks to Evonne Levy for pointing out this entry to me. In section VIIb of the conference — "Medieval and Modern Art History," overseen by Wölfflin—Dvořák gave a paper on the medieval mosaics in the Basilica of St. Mark in Venice ("Die mittelalterlichen Mosaiken der Markuskirche in Venedig"). The manuscript has survived in the archive of the Institut für Kunstgeschichte at the University of Vienna. See Hans Aurenhammer, "L'arte medievale a Venezia: Riflessioni viennesi intorno al 1900," *Ateneo Veneto* 200 (2013): 193–211, here 202–205.

58. Tietze, *Methode*, 240.

59. Max Dvořák, "Geschichte der venezianischen Malerei des 16. Jahrhunderts (= Geschichte der barocken Kunst in Italien)," lectures, winter semester 1905/1906, manuscript, Universität Wien, Institut für Kunstgeschichte, Archiv; Max Dvořák, "Die Entwicklung der Barockkunst," lectures, winter semester 1920/1921, reprinted in Max Dvořák, *Geschichte der italienischen Kunst im Zeitalter der Renaissance: Akademische Vorlesungen*, vol. 2 (Munich, 1928), 93–210.

60. See Riegl, *Origins*, 90 (*Entstehung*, v–vi). Dvořák and Arthur Burda jointly published Riegl's manuscript.

61. On Dvořák's development, particularly with regard to the baroque and mannerism: Hans Aurenhammer, "Max Dvořák, Tintoretto und die Moderne: Kunstgeschichte 'vom Standpunkt unserer Kunstentwicklung' betrachtet," *Wiener Jahrbuch für Kunstgeschichte* 49 (1996): 9–39; Hans Aurenhammer, "Max Dvořák (1874–1921): Von der historischen Quellenkritik zur Kunstgeschichte als Geistesgeschichte," in *Österreichische Historiker: Lebensläufe und Karrieren, 1900–1945*, vol. 2, ed. Karel Hruza (Vienna, 2012), 169–200; Hans Aurenhammer, "Inventing 'Mannerist Expressionism': Max Dvořák and the History of Art as History of the Spirit," in *The Expressionist Turn in Art History: A Critical Anthology*, ed. Kimberly A. Smith (Farnham, UK, 2014), 187–208. On the broader historical context: Hans Aurenhammer, "Manner, Mannerism, 'Maniera': On the History of a Controversial Term," in *Maniera: Pontormo, Bronzino and Medici Florence*, ed. Bastian Eclercy (Munich, 2016), 14–23.

62. Max Dvořák, "Geschichte der italienischen Skulptur und Malerei im Zeitalter der Renaissance," 1, lectures, winter semester 1911/1912, manuscript, Universität Wien, Institut für Kunstgeschichte, Archiv, 18.

63. "Wölfflin beruht in seinen Anschauungen auf Burckhardt und demgemäß ist seine Auffassung der Renaissancekunst eine dogmatische. Noch prägnanter als Burckhardt konstruiert er den Begriff einer höchstentwickelten, klassischen Kunst…, der Auflösung und Verfall folgte, den Wölfflin anscheinend sachlich und objektiv zu belegen versuchte, wobei es sich freilich um einen circulus vitiosus handelt, da die angeblichen Verfallskriterien nach dem Maßstabe der vermeintlich absolut gültigen Renaissancekunst und nicht nach Momenten des Fortschrittes und der Weiterentwicklung bemessen sind." Dvořák, 1911/1912, 17–18. (Dvořák continued by commenting: "The advantage of the books [Wölfflin's *Classic Art* and *Renaissance and Baroque*] lies in their clear analysis of the artworks of the Renaissance, which may survive the conclusions the author drew from it, and which caused him to be unjust towards other periods in art." ("Der Vorzug der Bücher liegt in der klaren Analyse der Kunstwerke der Renaissance, die die Konsequenzen überleben dürfte, welche der Autor aus ihr gezogen hat und die ihn gegen andere Kunstperioden ungerecht gemacht haben.")

64. This criticism from Vienna takes on a further dimension in view of the political subtext of Wölfflin's interpretation of the baroque as pointed out in Levy, "Political Project" (regardless of whether it was conscious or unconscious on Wölfflin's part). There Wölfflin is shown to have represented not only a classicist aesthetic ideal vis-à-vis the baroque but also a bourgeois-individualist political stance ultimately associated with an antimodern attitude.

65. Tietze, *Methode*, 86: "[F]or him, the Renaissance and its art of beautiful, calm existence remains the chief yardstick against which the subsequent period is measured.…Wölfflin measures the baroque against the Renaissance." ("[D]ie Renaissance mit ihrer Kunst des schönen, ruhigen Seins bleibt für ihn das Zentrale, an dem die Folgezeit gemessen wird.…Wölfflin misst das Barock an der Renaissance.")

66. "Wenn man sehen will, was in der barocken Kunst fortschrittlich gewesen ist, darf man nicht immer nur nach rückwärts blicken." Dvořák, 1905/1906, 25. Here also see 134 and 487 for the critique of Wölfflin's endeavor to attribute the baroque to a new "mental disposition" ("psychische Disposition").

67. Max Dvořák, "Geschichte der italienischen Skulptur und Malerei im Zeitalter der Renaissance," II, lectures, summer semester 1912, manuscript, Universität Wien, Institut für Kunstgeschichte, Archiv, 4 (aimed explicitly against Wölfflin's *Classic Art*).

68. Dvořák, *Geschichte der italienischen Kunst*, 2:191.

69. Max Dvořák, "Idealismus und Realismus in der Kunst der Neuzeit," lectures, winter semester 1915/1916, manuscript, Universität Wien, Institut für Kunstgeschichte, Archiv.

70. Dvořák, 1915/1916, 18.

71. See Hart, *Wölfflin*, 434, with reference to Wölfflin's entry of September 29, 1913.

72. Heinrich Wölfflin, "Rezension von Max Dvořák, *Kunstgeschichte als Geistesgeschichte: Studien zur abendländischen Kunstentwicklung* (Munich, 1924)," *Deutsche Literaturzeitung* 11 (1924): 908–910.

73. "Oft denke ich mir, verzeihen Sie das drastische Wort, der Teufel möge die Kunstgeschichte holen." Dvořák, 1915/1916, 96*.

74. "Für die Mehrzahl der Menschen bleibt das Kunstwerk ein Kunstwerk, aus welcher Zeit es auch stammen mag, eine Tatsache, [aus] der man Kennzeichen des Künstlerischen ablesen und in willkürliche Systeme ordnen kann. Man begeht dabei einen Kardinalirrtum: nicht nur die äußeren Kennzeichen der Kunst, sondern auch der Begriff des Kunstwerkes, des Künstlerischen war nicht konstant, sondern in verschiedenen Perioden verschieden und das Ergebnis der allgemeinen Evolution der Menschheit.…[S]o sehr auch eine Kontinuität der Entwicklung herrscht, so sehr ist es auch notwendig, die Verschiedenheit der Grundbegriffe, die das Ergebnis dieser Entwicklung bedeutet, in allen Fragen in Betracht zu ziehen." Dvořák, 1915/1916, 99*–101*.

75. Max Dvořák, "Idealismus und Realismus," typescript by Carola Bielohlawek of the lecture of the winter semester of 1915/1916, Universität Wien, Institut für Kunstgeschichte, Archiv, 26. (The transcript reproduces Dvořák's oral presentation of the text, which always differed slightly from the manuscripts of his lectures.)

76. In English, Wilhelm Worringer, *Abstraction and Empathy: A Contribution to the Psychology of Style*, trans. Michael Bullock (New York, 1953); Wilhelm Worringer, *Form Problems of the Gothic* (New York, 1920). See Hannes Böhringer and Beate Söntgen, eds., *Wilhelm Worringers Kunstgeschichte* (Munich, 2002); Claudia Öhlschläger, *Abstraktionsdrang: Wilhelm Worringer und der Geist der Moderne* (Paderborn, 2005); Norberto Gramaccini and Johannes Rössler, eds., *Hundert Jahre "Abstraktion und Einfühlung": Konstellationen um Wilhelm Worringer* (Munich, 2012).

77. Tietze, *Methode*, 98, 396–397. See, for example, Dvořák, 1915/1916, 19–20, where Dvořák distinguishes his historical categories of idealism and realism from those of Worringer: "These are not fixed fundamental aesthetic categories of the kind that, like Worringer's, exhaust the concept of the artistic, which must be regarded as a completely arbitrary and doctrinaire qualification of the concept of the artistic.…" ("Es handelt sich dabei nicht um feststehende ästhetische Grundkategorien, die wie Worringers Abstraktion und Einfühlung den Begriff des Künstlerischen erschöpfen würden, was als eine ganz und gar willkürliche und doktrinäre Einschränkung des Begriffes des Künstlerischen angesehen werden muss.…")

78. On this subject, see Lurz, *Wölfflin*, 226–239.

79. See Strzygowski, *Krisis*, 322: Here the author stated that in *Classic Art* Wölfflin had made no reference to his—that is, Strzygowski's—*Werden des Barock*, and that in the introduction to *Principles* Wölfflin had ignored his "insights" ("Einsichten").

80. Josef Strzygowski, "Norden und Renaissance," *Zeitschrift für bildende Kunst* 55 (1920): 98–103; Strzygowski, *Krisis*, esp. 55–56, but also 109, 125, 172, 187, 241, 243.

81. Strzygowski, *Krisis*, 187.

82. See, for example, Strzygowski, *Krisis*, 194–195; Josef Strzygowski, *Kunde, Wesen, Entwicklung* (Vienna, 1922), 195.

83. See Daniela Bohde, "Kulturhistorische und ikonographische Ansätze in der Kunstgeschichte im Nationalsozialismus," in *Kunstgeschichte im "Dritten Reich"—Theorien, Methoden, Praktiken*, ed. Ruth Heftrig et al. (Berlin, 2008), 189–204; Daniela Bohde, *Kunstgeschichte als physiognomische Wissenschaft: Kritik einer Denkfigur der 1920er bis 1940er Jahre* (Berlin, 2012).

84. Dagobert Frey, "Zur wissenschaftlichen Lage der Kunstgeschichte: Probleme und Aufgaben," in *Kunstwissenschaftliche Grundfragen: Prolegomena zu einer Kunstphilosophie* (Vienna, 1946), 23–79, esp. 28–49. Much earlier, in *Gotik und Renaissance als Grundlagen der modernen Weltanschauung* (Augsburg, 1929), XXI–XXX, Frey had undertaken a critical analysis of the applicability of Wölfflin's principles to other arts, a topic much discussed in the 1920s.

85. On this figure of thought in general, see Eric Michaud, "Nord–Sud," in *Histoire de l'art: Une discipline à ses frontières* (Paris, 2005), 76–84; and, more recently, Eric Michaud, *Les Invasions barbares: Une généalogie de l'histoire de l'art* (Paris, 2015), on Riegl esp. 134–140, 179–183.

86. Heinrich Wölfflin, "Italien und das deutsche Formgefühl," *Logos: Internationale Zeitschrift für Philosophie der Kultur* 10 (1922): 251–260.

87. Heinrich Wölfflin, *Die Kunst der Renaissance: Italien und das deutsche Formgefühl* (Munich, 1931); English translation, *The Sense of Form in Art: A Comparative Psychological Study*, trans. Alice Muehsam and Norma A. Shatan (New York, [1958]). On this subject, see Nikolaus Meier, "Italien und das deutsche Formgefühl," in *Kunstliteratur als Italienerfahrung*, ed. Helmut Pfotenhauer (Tübingen, 1991), 306–327; Hans Christian Hönes, *Wölfflins Bild-Körper: Ideal und Scheitern kunsthistorischer Anschauung* (Zürich, 2011), 151–204; Bohde, *Physiognomie*, 102–103.

88. Strzygowski, *Krisis*, 241.

89. Erwin Panofsky, "Über das Verhältnis der Kunstgeschichte zur Kunsttheorie: Ein Beitrag zu der Erörterung über die Möglichkeit 'kunstwissenschaftlicher Grundbegriffe' (1924)," in Erwin Panofsky, *Deutschsprachige Aufsätze*, vol 2, ed. Karen Michels and Martin Warnke (Berlin, 1998), 1035–1063, and earlier, "Der Begriff des Kunstwollens (1920)," in *Deutschsprachige Aufsätze*, 2:1019–1034, here 1029–1030.

90. Edgar Wind, *Ästhetischer und kunstwissenschaftlicher Gegenstand: Ein Beitrag zur Methodologie der Kunstgeschichte*, ed. Pablo Schneider (Hamburg, 2011), esp. 230–287. Also see Edgar Wind, "Zur Systematik der künstlerischen Probleme," *Zeitschrift für Ästhetik und allgemeine Kunstwissenschaft* 18 (1925): 438–486, esp. 480–486.

91. Hans Jantzen, "Besprechung von Alois Riegl, Gesammelte Aufsätze (1929)," *Kritische Berichte zur kunstgeschichtlichen Literatur* 3 (1930–1931): 65–74.

92. On this subject in general, see Christopher Wood, "Introduction," in *The Vienna School Reader: Politics and Art Historical Method in the 1930s* (New York, 2000), 1–81.

93. Hans Sedlmayr, *Die Architektur Borrominis* (Vienna, 1930), 42; Hans Sedlmayr, "Fünf römische Fassaden (1937)," in *Epochen und Werke: Gesammelte Schriften zur Kunstgeschichte* (Vienna, 1960), 2:57–79. Levy, in *Baroque and the Political Language of Formalism*, 341–343, pointing out, among other things, the hitherto unknown, longer manuscript version of "Fünf römische Fassaden" convincingly shows how Sedlmayr criticizes Riegl's and Wölfflin's interpretations of the baroque in analyses of individual works and seeks to surpass them.

94. Wölfflin, *Renaissance und Barock*, 32 (editors' translation). Ernst Gombrich's brilliant Viennese dissertation on Giulio Romano, approbated in 1933, likewise links approaches relatively new at the time, for example structural analysis, physiognomy, and psychoanalysis, but remains indebted to Wölfflin's analysis of the baroque on the core concept of the architectonic struggle between mass and form. On this subject, see Hans Aurenhammer, "'Gestörte Form': Gombrich, Giulio Romano und die Neue Wiener Schule der Kunstgeschichte," in *Das Problem der Form—Interferenzen zwischen moderner Kunst und Kunstwissenschaft*, ed. Hans Aurenhammer and Regine Prange (Berlin, 2016), 135–162. Gombrich had heard Wölfflin lecture in Berlin in 1930, when the latter served there as an interim professor. E. H. Gombrich, *Die Krise der Kulturgeschichte: Gedanken zum Wertproblem in den Geisteswissenschaften* (Stuttgart, 1983), 125. On Gombrich's later criticism of Wölfflin, see Levy, "Wölfflin's Principles," 29–30.

95. Hans Sedlmayr, "Die Quintessenz der Lehren Riegls (1929)," in *Kunst und Wahrheit: Zur Theorie und Methode der Kunstgeschichte* (Hamburg, 1958), 31 and esp. 22–25.

96. Panofsky, "Über das Verhältnis." Sedlmayr did not mention this essay (although he had obviously read it), but only Panofsky, "Begriff des Kunstwollens" and Wind, "Zur Systematik der künstlerischen Probleme."

97. In "Quintessenz," 32–33, Sedlmayr discussed only the "two roots of style according to Wölfflin" ("zwei Wurzeln des Stils bei Wölfflin"). He equated them with the alternative concepts of "naturalism and idealism" ("Naturalismus und Idealismus"), thus misunderstanding Wölfflin, who sought to distinguish between an expressionless form of depiction and the "mood of the times" ("Zeitstimmung"). Here Sedlmayr was presumably thinking more of the ideas on the "double root of all art" ("doppelten Wurzel aller Kunst") developed in Tietze, *Methode*, for instance, 89.

98. Hans Sedlmayr, "Zu einer strengen Kunstwissenschaft (1931)," in *Kunst und Wahrheit*, 35–70.

99. Hans Sedlmayr, "Kunstwerk und Kunstgeschichte," in *Kunst und Wahrheit*, 87–127. First published as Hans Sedlmayr, *Kunstwerk und Kunstgeschichte* (= *Hefte des Kunsthistorischen Seminars der Universität München* 1 [1956]).

100. Sedlmayr, "Kunstwerk," 123–125. Here Sedlmayr tried to claim Wölfflin's deliberations on the "unexchangeability of right and left in the picture" ("Unvertauschbarkeit von Rechts und Links im Bilde") as virtually experimental proof of his theory that the essence of the artwork is to be sought not in its formal aspects but in its "visual character" ("anschaulichen Charakter"). This is not convincing because the exchange of the sides is indeed of relevance to the form. See Heinrich Wölfflin, "Über das Rechts und Links im Bilde," in *Gedanken zur Kunstgeschichte: Gedrucktes und Ungedrucktes* (Basel, 1941), 82–89.

101. Heinrich Wölfflin, "Das Erklären von Kunstwerken," in Wölfflin, *Kleine Schriften*, 165–177, here 167. In preliminary studies for his interpretive essay, Sedlmayr noted: "But to truly understand the work of art, one cannot be first and foremost a historian." ("Aber um das Kunstwerk wirklich zu verstehen, darf man nicht in erster Linie Historiker sein.") Landesbibliothek Salzburg, estate of Hans Sedlmayr, Teil 2 B, Schachtel 5, Nr. 20. Here I would once again like to thank Evonne Levy for placing these materials at my disposal.

102. Landesbibliothek Salzburg, Nachlass Hans Sedlmayr, Teil 2 B, Schachtel 5, Nr. 20.

103. Otto Pächt, "Gestaltungsprinzipien der westlichen Malerei des 15. Jahrhunderts," in *Methodisches zur kunsthistorischen Praxis: Ausgewählte Schriften*, ed. Jörg Oberhaidacher, Artur Rosenauer, and Gertraut Schikola (Munich, 1977), 17–58, here 301n9, represents a certain exception. Pächt examines Wölfflin's paired "closed form and open form" as a way of lending sharper contours to his own notion of the "detail of reality" (*Wirklichkeitsausschnitt*) reproduced in the painting as "form-entirety" (*Formganzes*).

104. Landesbibliothek Salzburg, Nachlass Hans Sedlmayr, Teil 2 B, Schachtel 5, Nr. 20.

105. Karl Maria Swoboda, *Neue Aufgaben der Kunstgeschichte* (Brno, 1934), 20.

106. Guido von Kaschnitz-Weinberg, "Riegl, Spätrömische Kunst (Rezension) (1929)," in *Kleine Schriften zur Struktur* (Berlin, 1965), 1–14, here 6, 10.

107. Wölfflin, *Gedanken*, 3. On the dedication to Schlosser, see Heinrich Wölfflin, to his sister, Zurich, March 9, 1936, in Gantner, *Heinrich Wölfflin 1864–1945*, 451; Schlosser to Wölfflin, March 5, 1936, Universitätsbibliothek Basel, Nachlass Heinrich Wölfflin.

108. Julius von Schlosser, "Von Heinrich Wölfflins Sendung," *Neue Zürcher Zeitung*, no. 1088 (Sunday, June 17, 1934), 4.

109. Julius von Schlosser, *Materialien zur Quellenkunde der Kunstgeschichte*, VII. Heft: *Die Geschichtsschreibung des Barock und des Klassizismus* (Vienna, 1920), 75; adopted in Julius von Schlosser, *Die Kunstliteratur: Ein Handbuch zur Quellenkunde der neueren Kunstgeschichte* (Vienna, 1924), 461. Wölfflin was flattered: see Wölfflin, diary entry end of February 1920, in Gantner, *Heinrich Wölfflin 1864–1945*, 336.

110. Gombrich, a pupil of Schlosser's at the time, recalled a visit from Wölfflin to the seminar in Vienna. See Gombrich, *Die Krise der Kulturgeschichte*, 125.

111. Benedetto Croce, "La teoria dell'arte come pura visibilità: Nota: Un tentativo eclettico nella storia delle arti figurative (1911)," in *Nuovi saggi di estetica* (Bari, 1948), 251–257. Translated by Julius von Schlosser in Benedetto Croce, "Zur Theorie und Kritik der Geschichte der bildenden Kunst," *Wiener Jahrbuch für Kunstgeschichte* 4 (1926): 1–51, here 36–47. Later republished as Benedetto Croce, "Die Theorie der Kunst als reiner Sichtbarkeit (1911), Anhang: Ein eklektischer Versuch in der Geschichtsschreibung der bildenden Künste," in *Kleine Schriften zur Ästhetik*, trans. Julius von Schlosser (Tübingen, 1929), 2:206–212. On Croce's criticism of Wölfflin: Lurz, *Wölfflin*, 14–15. As late as 1936, Wölfflin inquired with Schlosser as to where he could find Croce's essays on the "theory of visibility": Schlosser to Wölfflin, September 10, 1936, Universitätsbibliothek Basel, Nachlass Heinrich Wölfflin. Thanks to Evonne Levy for pointing out this and other unpublished letters of Schlosser's to me.

112. Julius von Schlosser, "Ein Lebenskommentar," in *Die Kunstwissenschaft in Selbstdarstellungen*, ed. Johannes Jahn (Leipzig, 1924), 95–134, here 110.

113. See Schlosser to Wölfflin, October 13, 1936: "For decades, I have regarded you as a figure in a realm high above the 'viri eruditissimi,' (to quote Burckhardt for my part as well), the university guild, in which I was also an 'outsider'—naturally by far more modest standards. I believe I am in a position to say that I had the opportunity to get closer to you on a personal level as well, sadly only in a few brief hours that, for all their brevity, were all the more precious, even if I always—again, in the sense of Master Burckhardt—remained an 'eminus' in his shell (and the same presumably also applies somewhat to you?)." ("[S]eit Jahrzehnten schwebt mir Ihre Gestalt hoch über den 'viri eruditissimi,' [um auch meinerseits ein Wort Burckhardts zu gebrauchen], der Universitätszunft, in der ich ja auch, freilich in viel bescheidenerer Art, ein 'Außenseiter' gewesen bin. Ich glaube sagen zu dürfen, daß ich Ihnen auch menschlich, leider nur in wenigen, dafür aber desto kostbareren Stunden, nähertreten durfte, wenn ich auch immer [und etwas davon trifft wol (sic) auch bei Ihnen zu?] wieder im Sinne Meister Burckhardts, ein 'Eminus' im Schneckenhaus geblieben bin.") Universitätsbibliothek Basel, Nachlass Heinrich Wölfflin.

114. Julius von Schlosser, "Von Heinrich Wölfflins Sendung: Zum 70. Geburtstag," *Belvedere* 12 (1934): 1–3.

115. See Hans Aurenhammer, "Zäsur oder Kontinuität? Das Wiener Kunsthistorisches Institut im Ständestaat und im Nationalsozialismus," in *Wiener Schule: Erinnerung und Perspektiven* (= *Wiener Jahrbuch für Kunstgeschichte* 53 [2004]): 11–54, here 17–25 (with further reading).

116. Schlosser, "Ein Lebenskommentar," 120–121, also regarded Schmarsow, Wölfflin, and Tietze's search for "principles of art theory" (*Grundbegriffen der Kunstwissenschaft*) as symptoms of the same intellectual crisis to which he himself had fallen prey in the years preceding World War I.

117. Julius von Schlosser, "'Stilgeschichte' und 'Sprachgeschichte' der bildenden Kunst: Ein Rückblick," *Sitzungsberichte der Bayerischen Akademie der Wissenschaften: Philosophisch-historische Abteilung* (1935): 3–39, here 22. See Heinrich Wölfflin, *Die Kunst Albrecht Dürers* (Munich, 1905).

118. Wölfflin to Schlosser, July 21, 1934, and March 11, 1935, in Gantner, *Heinrich Wölfflin 1864–1945*, 441 and 444–445.

119. See Aurenhammer, "Zäsur oder Kontinuität"; Hans Aurenhammer, "Das Wiener Kunsthistorische Institut nach 1945," in *Zukunft mit Altlasten: Die Universität Wien 1945 bis 1955*, ed. Margarete Grandner, Gernot Heiss, and Oliver Rathkolb (Innsbruck, 2005), 174–188.

120. Pächt, *Methodisches zur kunsthistorischen Praxis*, 194, 225.

TRISTAN WEDDIGEN

Wölfflin in the Hispanic World

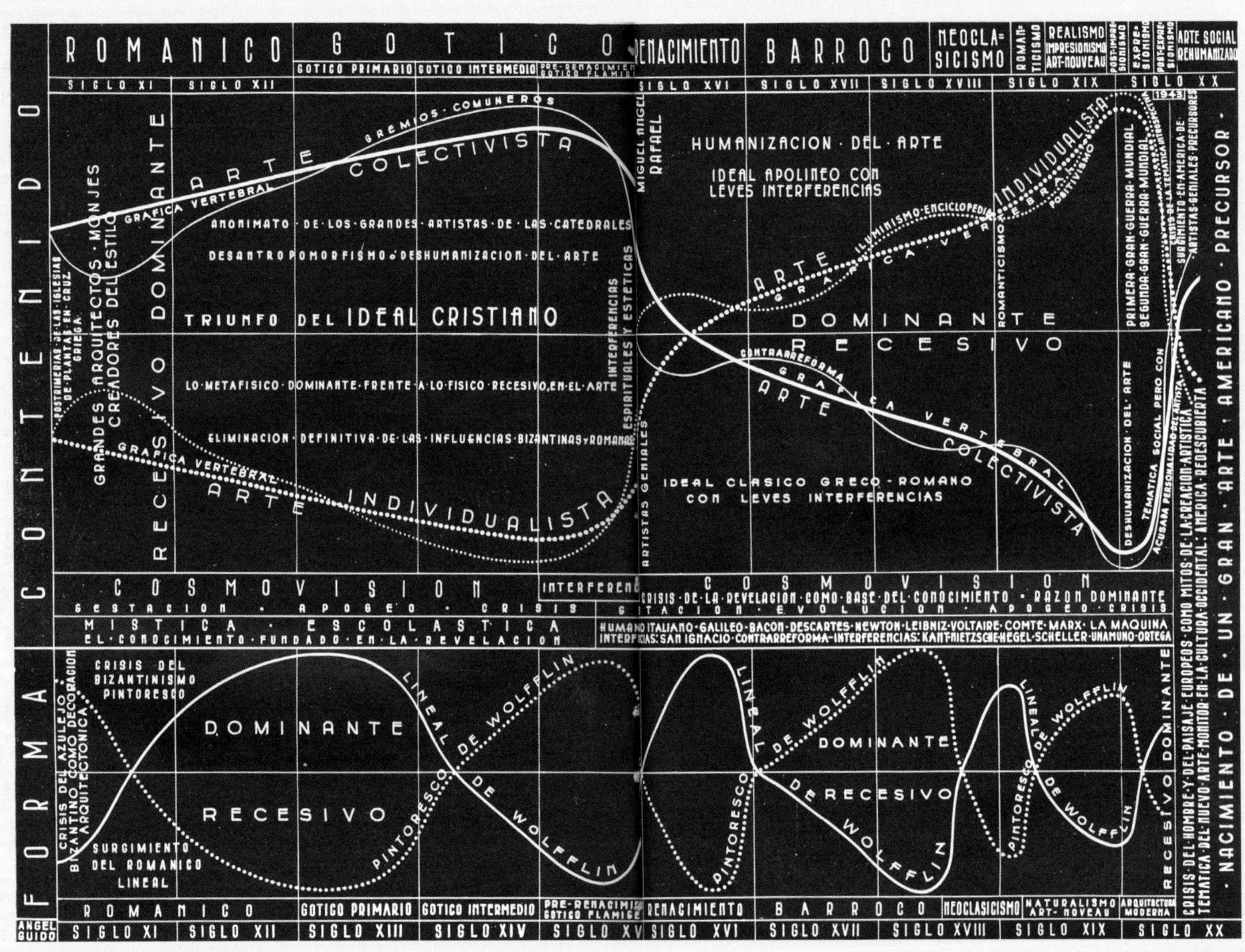
ROMANICO
GOTICO
RENACIMIENTO
BARROCO
NEOCLA-SICISMO
ROMAN-TICISMO
REALISMO IMPRESIONISMO ART-NOUVEAU
POST-IMPRE-SIONISMO
EXPRE-SIONISMO
ARTE SOCIAL REHUMANIZADO
GOTICO PRIMARIO
GOTICO INTERMEDIO
PRE-RENACIMIEN GOTICO FLAMIG
SIGLO XI
SIGLO XII
SIGLO XVI
SIGLO XVII
SIGLO XVIII
SIGLO XIX
SIGLO XX
[1943]
CONTENIDO
GRANDES ARQUITECTOS MONJES CREADORES DEL ESTILO
POSTRIMERIAS DE LAS IGLESIAS DE PLANTA EN CRUZ GRIEGA
ARTE DOMINANTE
GRAFICA VERTEBRAL
GREMIOS · COMUNEROS
COLECTIVISTA
MIGUEL ANGEL RAFAEL
HUMANIZACION · DEL · ARTE
IDEAL APOLINEO CON LEVES INTERFERENCIAS
ANONIMATO · DE · LOS · GRANDES · ARTISTAS · DE · LAS · CATEDRALES
DESANTROPOMORFISMO o DESHUMANIZACION · DEL · ARTE
TRIUNFO DEL IDEAL CRISTIANO
LO · METAFISICO · DOMINANTE · FRENTE · A · LO · FISICO · RECESIVO, EN · EL · ARTE
ELIMINACION · DEFINITIVA · DE · LAS · INFLUENCIAS · BIZANTINAS y ROMANAS
RECESIVO DOMINANTE
GRAFICA VERTEBRAL
ARTE INDIVIDUALISTA
INTERFERENCIAS ESPIRITUALES Y ESTETICAS
ARTISTAS GENIALES
ARTE
GRAFICA VERTEBRAL
ILUMINISMO · ENCICLOPEDIA
INDIVIDUALISTA
ROMANTICISMO
POSITIVISMO
DOMINANTE
RECESIVO
CONTRARREFORMA
GRAFICA VERTEBRAL
ARTE COLECTIVISTA
IDEAL CLASICO GRECO · ROMANO CON LEVES INTERFERENCIAS
PRIMERA · GRAN · GUERRA · MUNDIAL
SEGUNDA · GRAN · GUERRA · MUNDIAL
DESHUMANIZACION · DEL · ARTE
TEMATICA SOCIAL PERO CON
ACUSADA PERSONALIDAD ARTISTICA
SURGIMIENTO EN AMERICA DE ARTISTAS GENIALES PRECURSOR
NACIMIENTO · DE · UN · GRAN · ARTE · AMERICANO · PRECURSOR
COSMOVISION
GESTACION · APOGEO · CRISIS
MISTICA · ESCOLASTICA
EL · CONOCIMIENTO · FUNDADO · EN · LA · REVELACION
INTERFEREN
COSMOVISION
CRISIS · DE · LA · REVELACION · COMO · BASE · DEL · CONOCIMIENTO · RAZON DOMINANTE
GESTACION EVOLUCION APOGEO CRISIS
HUMANO ITALIANO · GALILEO · BACON · DESCARTES · NEWTON · LEIBNIZ · VOLTAIRE · COMTE · MARX · LA MAQUINA
INTERFIAS: SAN IGNACIO · CONTRARREFORMA · INTERFERENCIAS: KANT-NIETZSCHE-HEGEL-SCHELLER-UNAMUNO-ORTEGA
FORMA
CRISIS DEL AZULEJO BIZANTINO COMO DECORACION ARQUITECTONICA
SURGIMIENTO DEL ROMANICO LINEAL
CRISIS DEL BIZANTINISMO PINTORESCO
DOMINANTE
RECESIVO
LINEAL DE WOLFFLIN
PINTORESCO · DE · WOLFFLIN
LINEAL DE WOLFFLIN
PINTORESCO DE WOLFFLIN
DOMINANTE
RECESIVO
LINEAL DE WOLFFLIN
PINTORESCO DE WOLFFLIN
RECESIVO DOMINANTE
CRISIS · DEL · HOMBRE · Y · DEL · PAISAJE · EUROPEOS · COMO MITOS · DE · LA · CREACION · ARTISTICA
TEMATICA · DEL · NUEVO · ARTE · MONTOR · EN · LA · CULTURA · OCCIDENTAL · AMERICA · REDESCUBIERTA
ROMANICO
GOTICO PRIMARIO
GOTICO INTERMEDIO
PRE-RENACIMI GOTICO FLAMIG
RENACIMIENTO
BARROCO
NEOCLASICISMO
NATURALISMO ART-NOVEAU
ARQUITECTURA MODERNA
ANGEL GUIDO
SIGLO XI
SIGLO XII
SIGLO XIII
SIGLO XIV
SIGLO XV
SIGLO XVI
SIGLO XVII
SIGLO XVIII
SIGLO XIX
SIGLO XX

Journals, local and international, durable and short-lived, indisputably innumerable, were the strategic instruments of the modernist discourse. Correspondingly, the Hispanic reception of Heinrich Wölfflin's writings, especially of *Kunstgeschichtliche Grundbegriffe*, starts in *Revista de occidente*, which the Germanophile philosopher José Ortega y Gasset had founded in Madrid in 1923 in an effort to Europeanize the Spanish-speaking intelligentsia. The November 1924 issue carried a review of Wölfflin's oeuvre by the Spanish writer and art critic Ángel Sánchez Rivero.[1] The article celebrated Wölfflin's sixtieth birthday and promoted the first translation of Wölfflin's *Grundbegriffe* into Castilian, by the Spanish painter, poet, and critic José Moreno Villa.[2] Published that year in Madrid as *Conceptos fundamentales en la historia del arte* in Ortega's series Biblioteca de ideas del siglo XX, it has been reprinted a dozen times since. Together with the Biblioteca de la Revista de occidente, the collection disseminated contemporary theory in translation, proposing new scientific models for the humanities and the arts and publishing the work of authors such as the Neo-Kantian Heinrich Rickert, the quantum theorist Max Born, the biologist Jakob von Uexküll, the philosopher of history Oswald Spengler, and the historian of mathematics Roberto Bonola. This scientific context framed Wölfflin's psychological "natural history of art" as *Kunstwissenschaft*, that is, as a hard science of art.[3]

Sánchez's intellectual portrait of Wölfflin, so substantial that it was reviewed in Switzerland in the *Neue Zürcher Zeitung*, pronounced *Grundbegriffe* the culmination of Wölfflin's work, including *Renaissance und Barock* and *Die klassische Kunst*, which were not yet available in Spanish.[4] The article also established Wölfflin as the vanquisher of nineteenth-century positivism, which had advanced to become the modernists' concept of the enemy, embodied in the so-called milieu theory developed by Hippolyte Taine in his canonical *Philosophie de l'art* (1865), published in Castilian in 1922.[5] Taine conceived of art as a passive result of influences and external factors that include the physical, such as landscape, climate, and soil, and the social, such as habits, history, and race. Milieu theory was antithetical to the idea of an ontological essence and political agency of art, as advocated by avant-garde thinkers such as Ortega or the Argentinian Ricardo Rojas.[6] Sánchez emphasized, however, the art-critical potential of Wölfflin's concepts, as they offered exact, abstracted descriptions of pure and basic "aesthetic emotions."[7] He singled out Wölfflin's disputed notion of an "art history without names," shaped by the rhythmic recurrence of metahistorical styles, stressing the advantages of Wölfflin's empirical and comparative method over that of his contemporaries, namely Alois Riegl, whose works were not yet translated; Wilhelm Worringer, whose *Formprobleme der Gotik* appeared in Catalan in 1925; and Oswald Spengler, whose *Der Untergang des Abendlandes* was translated in 1923/1927 for the Biblioteca de ideas del siglo XX.[8] Thus, with Ortega's initiative, German aesthetics in the 1920s expanded into the Hispanic world with Wölfflin's *Grundbegriffe* at the forefront, resulting in methodological discussions in Spain and then in Latin America.[9]

Across the Atlantic, Sánchez's review had an immediate and lasting impact on

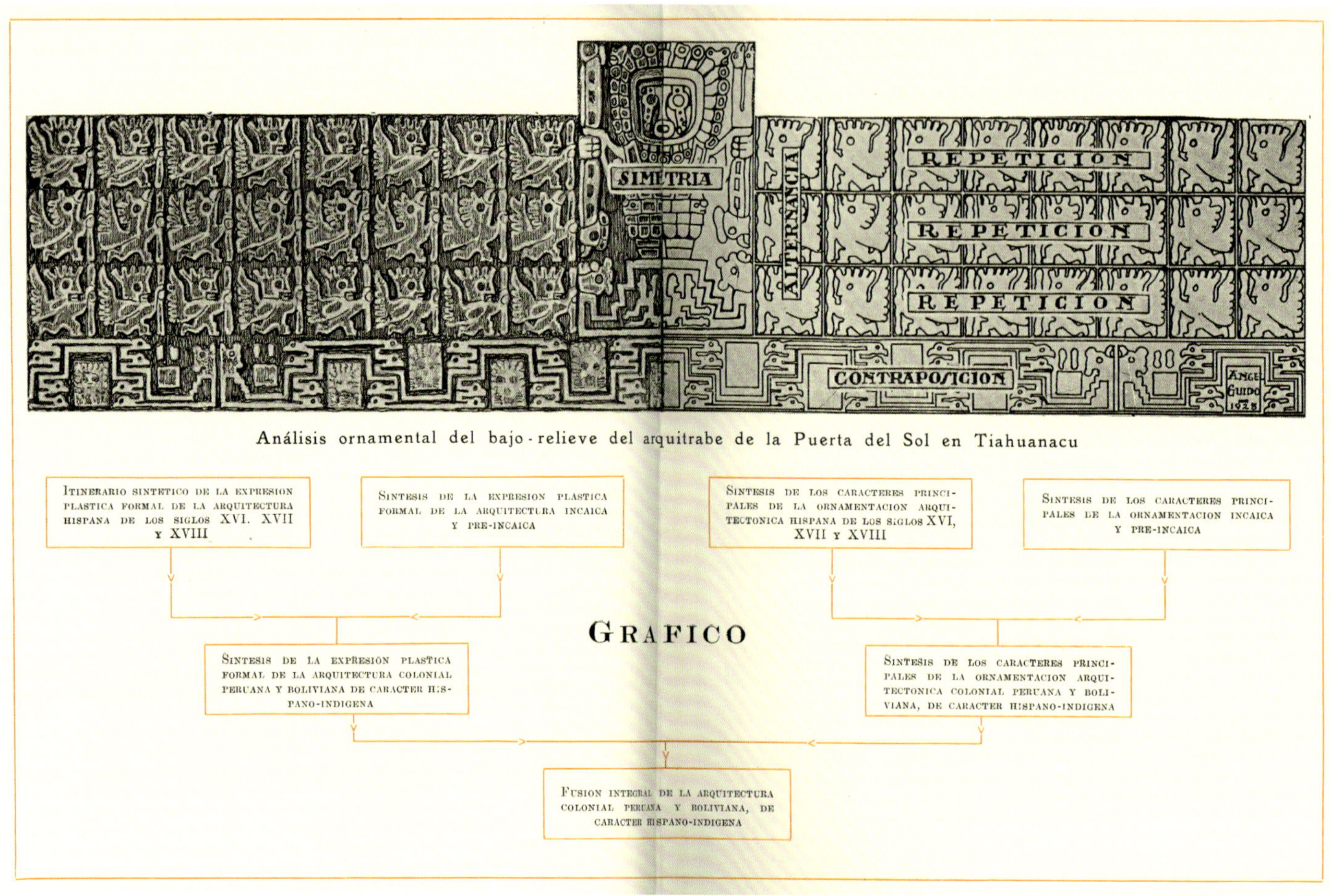

1. Formal analysis of the Gate of the Sun, Tiwanaku, Bolivia, from Ángel Guido, *Fusión hispano-indígena en la arquitectura colonial* (Rosario, 1925)

the Argentinian architect and art theorist Ángel Guido (1896–1960) from Rosario, who became possibly the most influential and least studied early transmitter of German aesthetics to Latin America, especially of Wölfflin's formalism. Recent scholarship on the literary poetics of the baroque and neobaroque, especially that of Arabella Pauly and Monika Kaup, emphasizes that he was one of the pioneers of a hybrid, or mestizo, aesthetics.[10] Guido's first major work, *Fusión hispano-indígena en la arquitectura colonial* (published in May 1925, within months of the appearance of the Castilian translation of *Grundbegriffe*), introduced and popularized the notion that Latin American colonial architecture emerged from a Hispanic and Indian racial and artistic fusion.[11] The book, including papers given and published since 1923, testifies to Guido's pre-Wölfflinian aesthetics, which

need to be sketched out here to show the impact of *Conceptos*. Guido's approach was based on what could be called a geometric formalism.[12] Although Wölfflin himself moved away from this kind of methodology after his book *Renaissance und Barock*, it was now propagating in Western modernist art-historical and artistic research. Guido's geometrical formal analysis of style, though, was based on Rafael Doménech's pattern book *Tratado de técnica ornamental* (1920) and its classification of structural rhythms of ornament. It was probably also inspired by August Thiersch's studies on composition and proportion of 1883 and even by the *tracés régulateurs* in Le Corbusier's *Vers une architecture* (1923).[13] Guido, however, drew his objects of study also from his own explorations of Bolivia and Peru and from authors such as Charles Wiener and André Michel.[14]

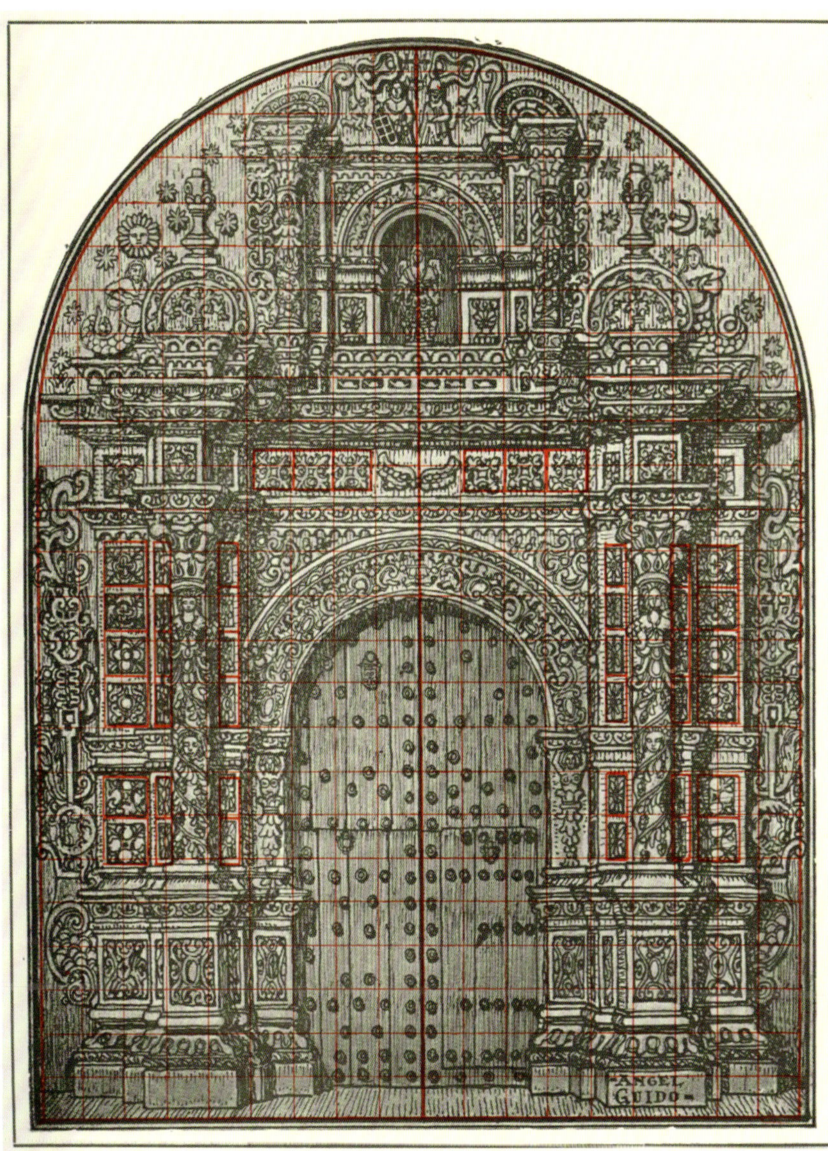

2. Formal analysis of the portal of the church of San Lorenzo, Potosí, from Ángel Guido, *Fusión hispano-indígena en la arquitectura colonial* (Rosario, 1925)

treatise *Eurindia* (1924), which mentions Guido's poetry and his brother Alberto's painting, became Guido's ideological compass.[16] According to Rojas, Latin America, primarily Argentina, is the heir of the Eurasian transmission of civilization from East to West, destined to become the mythical "Eurindia." Its landscape as well as its Inca and Aztec cultures modify the European historical cycles of opposite concepts, forming a new "aesthetic rhythm" and a unity of land and race, both understood not as physical but as spiritual forces.[17]

Using "modern methods" of formal analysis, Guido derived pre-Columbian abstract "ornamental laws" from archaeological artifacts, such as textiles, but, most important, from an architectural monument, the Gate of the Sun at Tiwanaku in Bolivia, published by the archaeologist Arthur Posnansky (fig. 1).[18] The laws consist of six "spatial rhythms:" symmetry, repetition, alternation, contraposition, interchange, and series. Guido then identifies such aboriginal rhythms in the ornamentation of baroque colonial art, supposedly executed by Amerindians and mestizos: for instance, in the reliefs of the portal of the church of San Lorenzo in Potosí, the "objective" indigenous influence consists of autochthonous iconographic elements, such as Indian-looking caryatids, while the "subjective" one surfaces in the symmetrical patterns, which he shows on a red grid (fig. 2).

While Guido's geometric formalism was original, as it abstained from Posnansky's iconographic approach, he received the idea of a Hispano-indigenous fusion, a synthesis of "Orientalism and Occidentalism," from the architect and architectural historian Martín S. Noel of Buenos Aires. Guido considered Noel his comrade in arms in an "artistic crusade" for a new Americanism in the arts. Since the early 1920s, Noel had affirmed that colonial Latin America, under the influence of pre-Columbian craft and iconography, had developed its own idiom of Andalusian-Mudéjar baroque.[19] For instance, in 1926, he introduced the concept of *arquitectura hispano-americana*,

The prologue of his *Fusión*, a regionalist credo that bears the anti-Corbusian title "Hacia una arquitectura nuestra" (Towards an architecture of our own), contributed to a first wave of Pan-Americanism in the arts. Guido propagandized a synthesis of pre-Columbian and colonial architecture as a new unitary model for America's "aesthetic emancipation" from European eclecticism and "hybridity."[15] Here, Guido refers to Ricardo Rojas, his lifelong intellectual mentor, for whom he built a programmatic villa in the criollo style in Buenos Aires in 1927 and later designed theater settings. Rojas's racialist and nationalist aesthetic

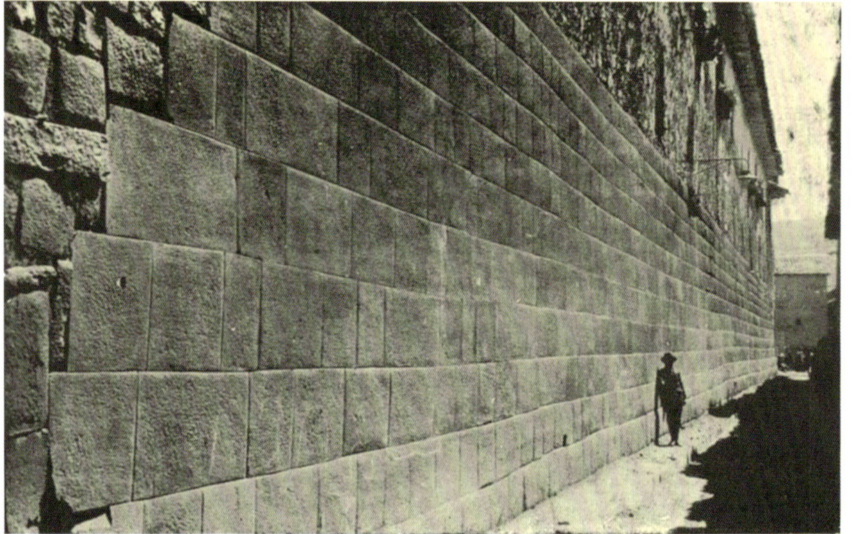

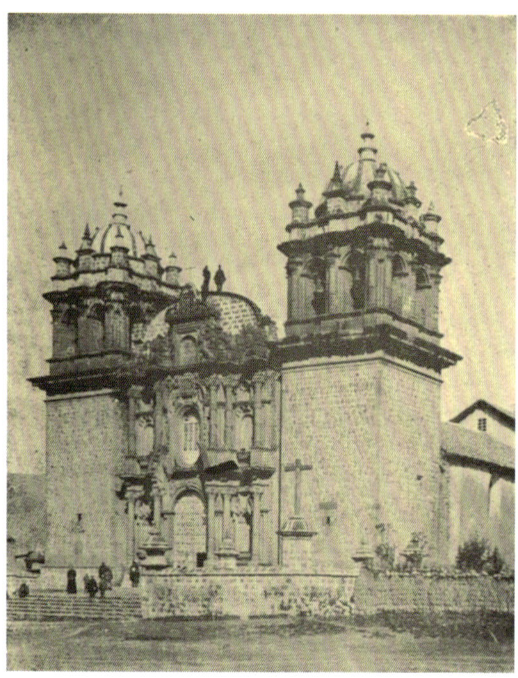

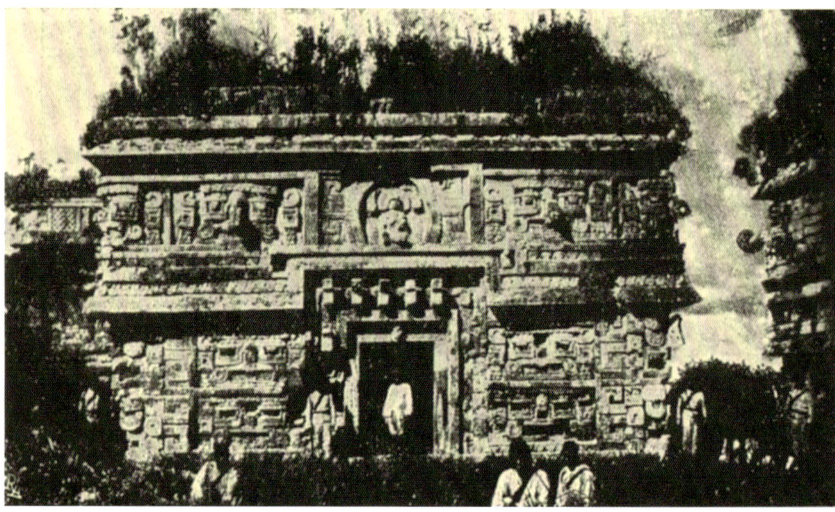

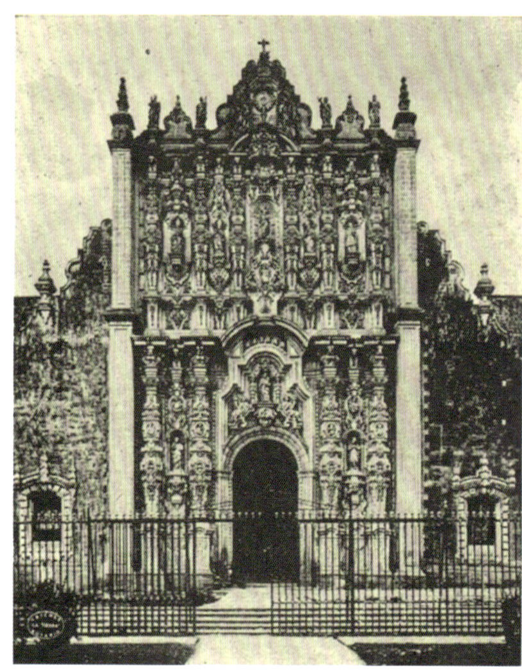

3. Inca wall, Cuzco, from Ángel Guido, *La arquitectura hispano-americana a través de Wölfflin* (Rosario, 1927), 35

4. Church of San Sebastián, Cuzco, from Ángel Guido, *La arquitectura hispanoamericana a través de Wölfflin* (Rosario, 1927), 20

5. Palacio de las Monjas, Uxmal, from Ángel Guido, *La arquitectura hispanoamericana a través de Wölfflin* (Rosario, 1927), 38

6. Sagrario, Catedral Metropolitana, Mexico City, from Ángel Guido, *La arquitectura hispanoamericana a través de Wölfflin* (Rosario, 1927), 42

a fusion of archaic indigenous techniques and forms with Spanish colonial architecture, itself mixed with Arab elements, designating *americanismo* as a model for a new culture and race.[20] Similarly, in 1924, under the impact of Rojas's *Eurindia*, the Argentinian architect Héctor Greslebin had identified "arquitectura eurocolonial o europrecolombiana" as a style of its own, neither "a foreign exoticism" nor "our Indianism," but the result of a fusion of Spanish and indigenous, or creole, sources.[21] Despite immediate criticism, Guido's and Noel's concept of fusion was widely adopted and survived in scholarship until the 1950s, for instance, in Henry-Russell Hitchcock's *Latin American Architecture since 1945.*[22]

Then the translation of Wölfflin's *Grundbegriffe*, publicized by Sánchez, instantly shifted Guido's methodological basis from an "archaeological" to a "scientific" approach, inspiring him to innumerable politico-methodological lectures and articles. Perhaps as early as 1924, he replaced his geometrical with a psychological formalism, to explain Hispano-American fusion and to promote an indigenist, regionalist, and neocolonial modern architecture, which supported the project of inventing an Argentinian tradition.[23] Guido's methodological shift was a radical one, because the earlier geometrical analysis might still have been compatible with the new psychological notion of stylistic development, as Moreno proved in his compositional studies of Rubens's works published in the *Revista* one year after the translation of Wölfflin's work appeared.[24]

Guido published "La arquitectura hispanoamericana a través de Wölfflin," one of his lectures from the third Congreso Panamericano de Arquitectos, held in Buenos Aires in July 1927, several times and in different formats.[25] He also had it printed as an independent pamphlet, in two parts, that begins by establishing the concept of a Hispano-Incaic baroque (*barroquismo hispanoincaico*) through Wölfflin's methodology. Following a short exposition of Wölfflinian aesthetics, which were supposed to dismiss Taine's materialism, Guido applied the idea of linear, "bioaesthetic" progress toward Riegl's "optical" and Wölfflin's "atectonic," first to Spanish architecture of the seventeenth and eighteenth centuries, the source of the Hispanic American baroque.[26] Relying on Otto Schubert's standard *Geschichte des Barock in Spanien* (1908), which had just appeared in a Spanish edition (1924), Guido identified three characteristics of Spanish baroque architecture: its aesthetic idiosyncrasy and autonomy in relation to Italian classicism; the anticlassical influence of the Mudéjar style, which had been integrated into the Hispanic history of style since the mid-nineteenth century; and the baroque instability of the picaresque novel, an observation that announces the literary outburst of Gongorism in 1927.[27] The history of Iberian art and architecture already seemed to prove that, both under the universal laws of stylistic development and in accepting local influences, a peripheral style could achieve autonomy from the cultural center.

Reassessing post-Conquest architecture, Guido saw Hispanic American baroque as a "bioaesthetic," morphological development, parallel to and independent from the mother country's own.[28] While the two shared a stylistic "destiny," a distinct Latin American "physiognomy" arose, Guido stated, using influential Spenglerian and Wölfflinian terms while deriving the notions of aesthetic "emotion" and "rhythm" from Sánchez and Rojas.[29] Guido observed that New World baroque inverted the Spanish and European development according to Wölfflin, as it subordinated ornament to structure and gained "haptic" and "linear" qualities, such as clarity, continence, planarity, stillness, and relative unity, which are reminiscent of the Quattrocento but actually did not originate from Europe, where, with the transition to the baroque, these qualities had long since fallen into oblivion. The Latin American reversal of the Wölfflinian process arose, according to Guido, in the fusion of the imported Spanish baroque with local Inca art, achieved through the craftsmanship of Quechua and Aymara workmen forced by the secular and ecclesiastic authorities. It established itself in the former Inca highlands of Peru and Bolivia in the seventeenth and eighteenth centuries as a true Hispano-Incaic school. In their works, the artisans not only represented native fauna and flora, that is, indigenous iconographic motifs, but expressed a linear "pathos" in all forms of art. Following Ernst Kretschmer's physiognomics, publicized in 1923 in the *Revista*, artistic styles could become the subject of a psychoarchaeology of past cultures and races, and as Manuel G. Morente, the translator of Worringer, commented on Spengler a year later: "The method of history is the 'physiognomic method,' and its tool is 'intuition.'"[30]

The second part of Guido's pamphlet is dedicated to establishing the *diversidad barroca* (baroque diversity) between the north and the south of Latin America following the model of *Kunstgeografie*, which, according to Wölfflin, sought both aesthetic unity and diversity in northern and southern European peoples and, according to Worringer, drew transhistorical

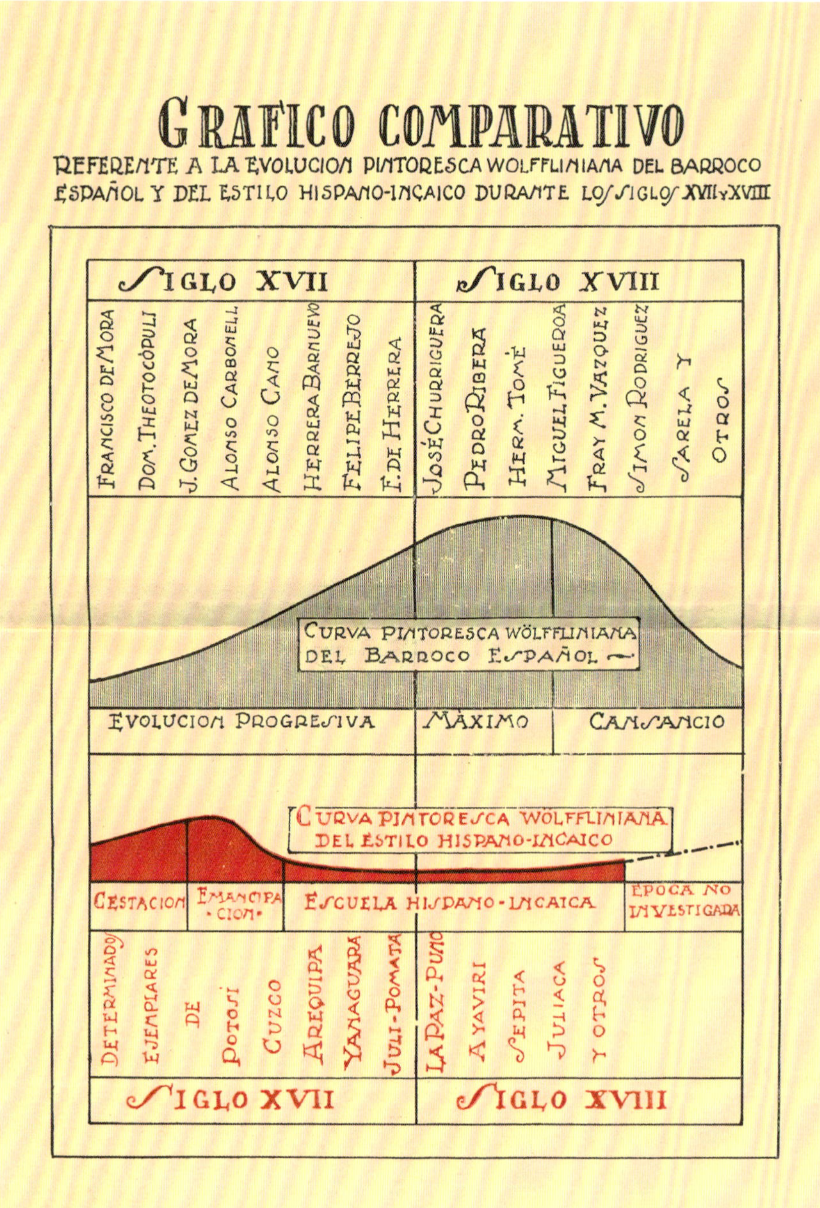

7. Wölfflinian painterly development of the Spanish baroque and the Hispano-Incaic style during the seventeenth and eighteenth centuries, from Ángel Guido, *La arquitectura hispanoamericana a través de Wölfflin* (Rosario, 1927)

continuities between the Middle Ages and the baroque.[31] Guido faithfully applied Wölfflin's "psychophysiological formula" to his own "historic-aesthetic research" and the Wölfflinian baroque categories—painterliness, recession, open form, unity, and relative clarity—to photographic material from opposite regions: first to Inca (fig. 3) and to Peruvian-Bolivian southern colonial monuments (fig. 4), then to Aztec (fig. 5) and to Mexican northern baroque monuments (fig. 6). The conclusion was that, in Mexico, the baroque grew "pseudopainterly"

under the impact of moderately linear Aztec aesthetics, whereas, in the south, the Hispano-Incaic became strictly "nonpainterly" under the influence of the stern linearity of Inca art. By this stratagem, Guido managed to transfer the paradigmatic European art-historical north-south divide to Latin America, characterizing the north as medieval-baroque and the south as classical. At the same time, he insisted on American independence from the colonial baroque diktat, expressed in a shift toward the linear in respect to the European history of style, thus also suggesting that America, before Europe, generated a new, Eurindian classicism. Guido's Latin American history of art used indigenism for nationalist purposes to defeat European art-historical dominance with its own methods. Yet his idea that the New World resembled a social experiment or Arendtian "laboratory" where it was possible to observe the impact of a uniform European style on a variety of virgin indigenous peoples who reacted with different forms of mestization seemed to prove the racialist roots of style much more clearly than the rather intricate European case did.

In addition to reproductions of his own etchings of baroque facades, inspired by Juan Kronfuss's sketches of Argentinian colonial architecture and displayed at the Congreso, Guido presented a "comparative graph of the Wölfflinian painterly development of the Spanish baroque and the Hispano-Incaic style during the seventeenth and eighteenth centuries" (fig. 7). This transformed Wölfflin's psycho-physiological principles into "measuring units" and complied with Ortega's interdisciplinary notion of the human sciences.[32] By avoiding the genealogical-tree model, which would have represented the New World baroque as a gnarled branch hanging from the vigorous European trunk, Guido aimed at suggesting universal forces and their specifically Latin American dynamics, here reduced to a "curva pintoresca," that is, to a certain degree of baroqueness, aptly manifesting itself in curves.[33] The upper part of the linear scheme shows the "Wölfflinian painterly

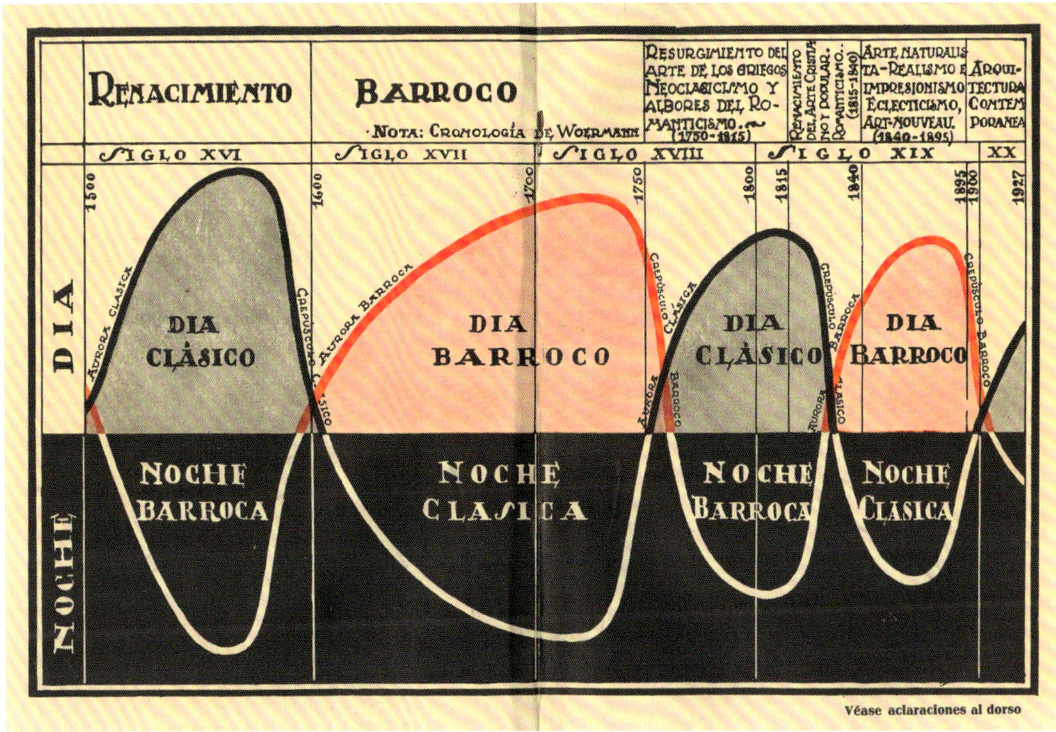

curve of the Spanish baroque," its stylistic evolution in art and architecture from the early seventeenth century to its classicist "exhaustion" in the late eighteenth century. The lower part depicts the contemporaneous "Wölfflinian painterly curve of the Hispano-Incaic style," from its "gestation" to its sudden "emancipation" from Spanish models under indigenous influence. The resulting "Hispano-Incaic School" is based instead on exemplary buildings from Potosí, Cuzco, and other Andean locales, showing how convenient a Wölfflinian "art history without names" could be in the face of material without secure attribution or dating. The further progress of the painterly curve into neoclassicism and historicism remains, however, "unresearched" ("no ivestigada"), as it probably challenged Guido's scheme.

In parallel with his explicitly Wölfflinian essay, Guido published *Orientación espiritual de la arquitectura en América*, a paper in which he elaborated on the very theme of the Congreso Panamericano.[34] In this essay, Guido used Wölfflinian formalism as a tool for criticizing contemporary developments, especially Corbusian modernism, and for

projecting "a genuinely American future architecture."[35] As this regionalist endeavor relied on factors such as tradition, landscape, and nation, Guido here needed to merge the old theories of Taine with the modern ones of Riegl and Wölfflin.[36] Following Wölfflin's bioaesthetic law of development, Guido could predict that a new linearism would arise and overcome decaying painterliness. In France, however, the rejection of historicism and eclecticism in favor of Germanic modernism was so violent as to call on a figure like Le Corbusier, in whose mechanization and standardization Guido saw the decadence and the end of architecture as an art.[37] Indeed, he would attack Le Corbusier in the pamphlet *Machinolâtrie de Le Corbusier*, apparently written in 1929, immediately after the Swiss architect lectured in Buenos Aires, thus clashing with the modernists grouped around Victoria Ocampo and the journal *Martín Fierro*.[38] Nevertheless, Guido's *retour à l'ordre*, consisting of a "lección de la masa, el plano y la línea" (lesson of mass, plan, and line), which defined the formal elements of plastic creativity expressed in ferroconcrete, was

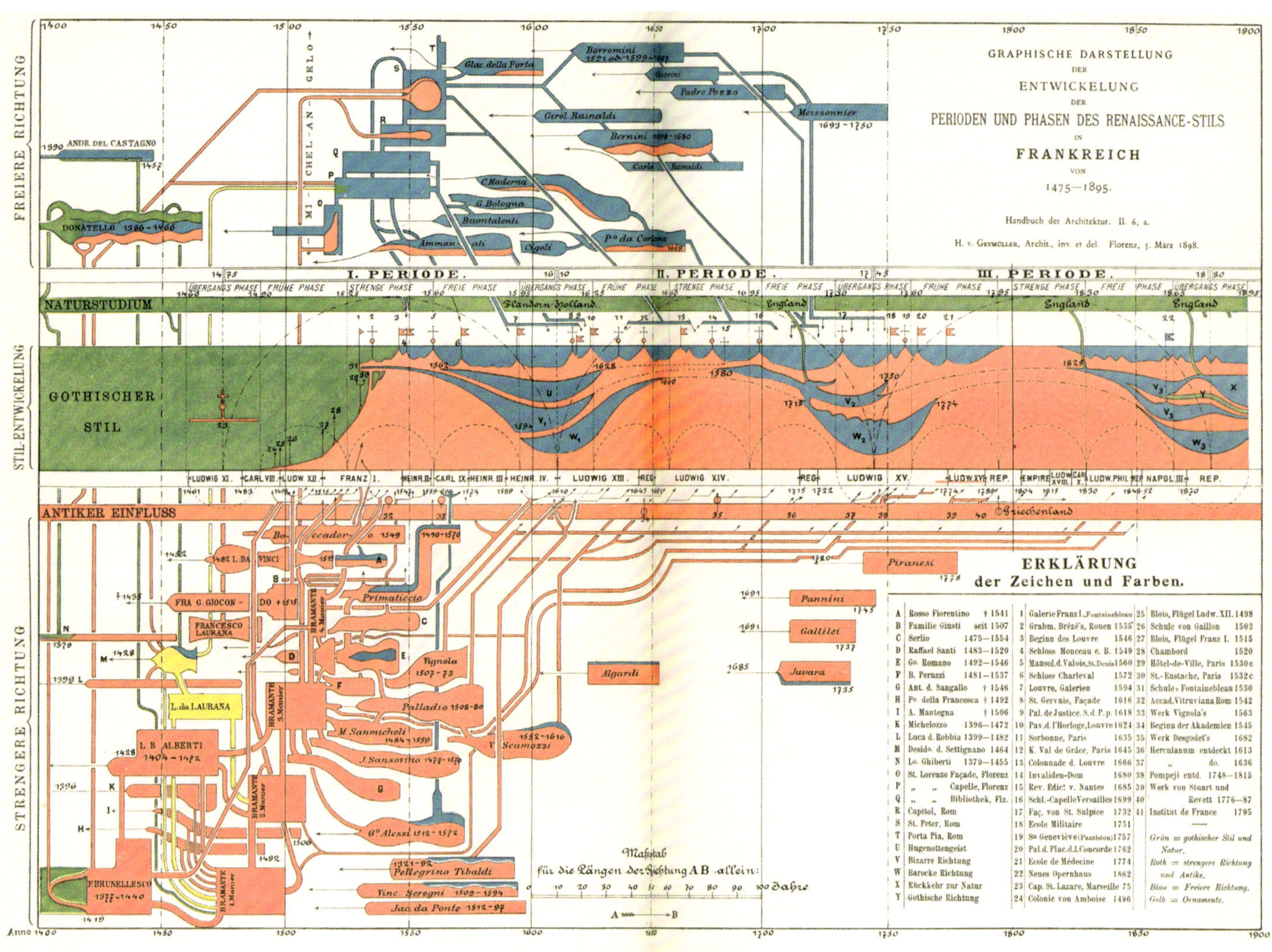

9. Development of the Renaissance style in France, from Heinrich von Geymüller et al., *Die Baustile: Historische und technische Entwickelung; Des Handbuches der Architektur, zweiter Theil, 6. Band: Die Baukunst der Renaissance in Frankreich, Erstes Heft* (Stuttgart, 1898)

clearly inspired by Le Corbusier's "Leçon de Rome."[39] In reference to Wölfflin's conclusion to *Grundbegriffe*, in which he acknowledged the force of national character in the history of styles, Guido proposed to Americanize that lesson of modernism by following the model of colonial fusion.[40] In order to establish a "living Eurindia," first, eclectic cosmopolitan architecture needed to be abolished; second, precolonial, Hispano-American, and folkloristic forms must be adopted and modernized; third, the American landscape had to be studied; fourth, the best European spiritual and aesthetic orientation, that is, the *lección*, must be accepted, but regionalized.[41]

In *Orientación espiritual de la arquitectura en América*, Guido included another

diagram, a morphological history of European modern art strictly following Wölfflin's *Grundbegriffe* (fig. 8) and extending the rhythm of the two transhistorical styles, the classical and the baroque, to the revival of the classical in modern architecture.[42] Guido admitted that his boundary lines represented an average of many that vary according to peoples and artists. Guido's chronology referred to Karl Woermann's *Geschichte der Kunst aller Zeiten und Völker* (1904–1911), which had just appeared in a Spanish edition (1923–1924).[43] Guido illustrated the cyclical recurrence of the two opposed styles by twin heavenly bodies: they become active in daylight, overlap at dawn and dusk, and then disappear below the horizon of cultural consciousness, into a zone of darkness, in

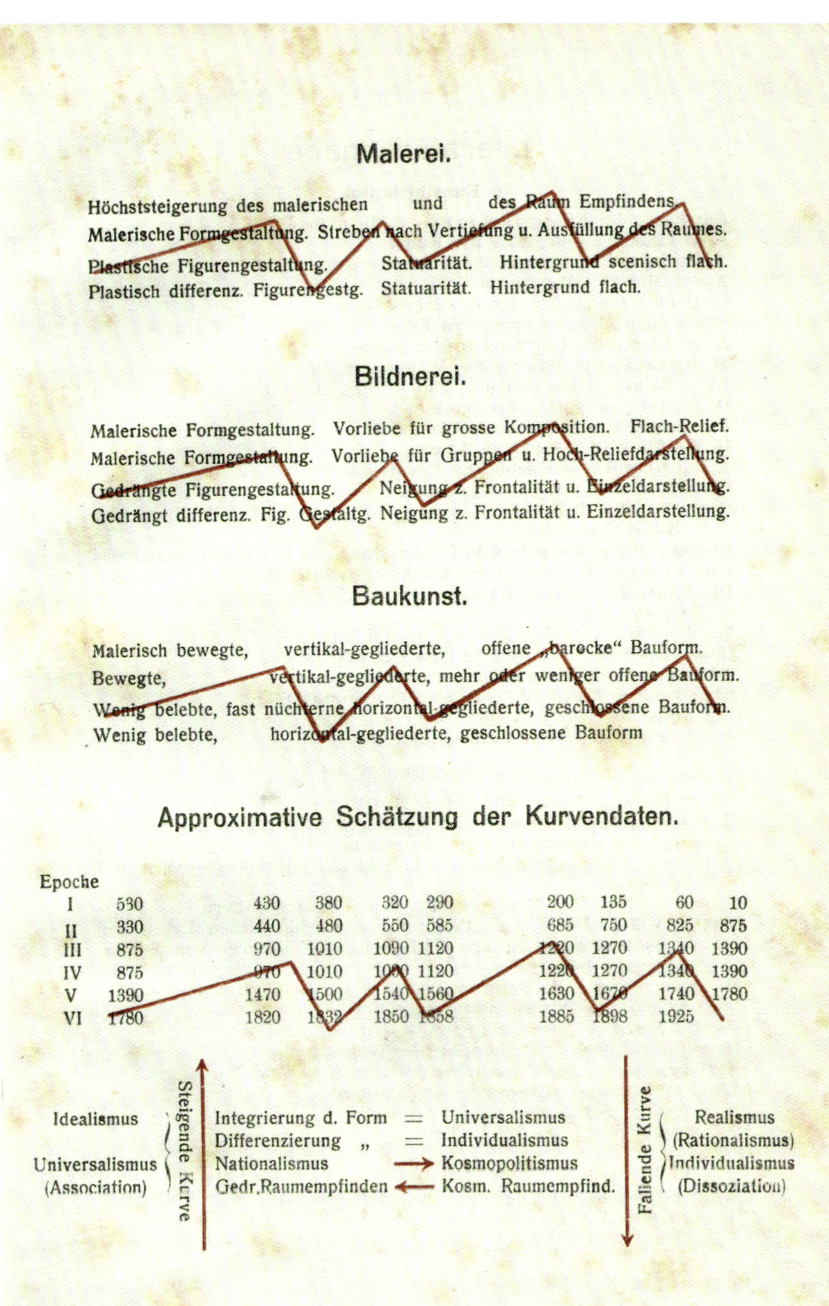

Epoche										
I	530		430	380	320	290		200	135	60	10
II	330		440	480	550	585		685	750	825	875
III	875		970	1010	1090	1120		1220	1270	1340	1390
IV	875		970	1010	1090	1120		1220	1270	1340	1390
V	1390		1470	1500	1540	1560		1630	1670	1740	1780
VI	1780		1820	1832	1850	1858		1885	1898	1925	

10. Waves of art-historical development, from Herbert Krauss, *Das Wellengesetz in der Geschichte: Kunsthistorische Studie zur Festlegung der geschichtlichen Periodizität* (Bern, 1929)

by the aura of hard science, were in vogue in the humanities as visualizations of the hidden natural, social, and psychic laws of culture. While Wölfflin refrained from diagrams, Guido's own could have been inspired by Heinrich von Geymüller's synopsis of French Renaissance architecture from 1475 to 1895, published in *Die Baukunst der Renaissance in Frankreich* (1898), which illustrates the sources, currents, and channels of stylistic influences and the waves of the classical and the Gothic across the long Renaissance (fig. 9).[44] Guido's oscillating history of style can be compared to Herbert Krauss's *Das Wellengesetz in der Geschichte* (1929), which refers to Spengler, Worringer, and Paul Frankl and whose diagram illustrates the historical peaks and lows of Wölfflinian categories, such as painterly and plastic, receding and flat, open and closed, in the course of the history of European art (fig. 10).[45] Similarly, László Moholy-Nagy's sinuous illustration (fig. 11) of Georg Gustav Wieszner's *Pulsschlag deutscher Stilgeschichte* (1930) popularized Wölfflinian formalism, imagining a stylistic pulse swinging between collectivist and individualist tendencies every three centuries.[46] Pál Ligeti's *Der Weg aus dem Chaos* (1931) saw a way out of a deep crisis of civilization, if humanity felt the pulse of world art history (fig. 12): the curve always starts with the architectural, leads to the sculptural, and ends with the pictorial, which varies Wölfflin's rhythm of the linear and the painterly and unfolds the potential pacifism of art history as a prognostic and prophetic method.[47]

Noel, however, in his *Teoría histórica de la arquitectura virreinal* (1932), which looked back at the question of heteronomy and autonomy of the New World baroque and at Rojas's impact on Americanism, appeared to offer the first critique of Wölfflin's decontextualized formalism. He argued that the German "biological method," when limited to a "crude analysis of forms," a "psychology of architecture," and "morphological processes," lacked the necessary critical analysis of historical

which styles survive in hibernation, as it were, waiting to be resuscitated. Indeed, in cyclical theories of art such as Guido's, the survival of styles, such as the suppressed indigenous culture reemerging in the colonial mestizo baroque, surfaced as an inherent problem and was answered with notions of cosmic pulses, psychic archetypes, and racialist genetics.

Indeed, from 1900, eternal returns, rhythms, curves, and waves, consecrated

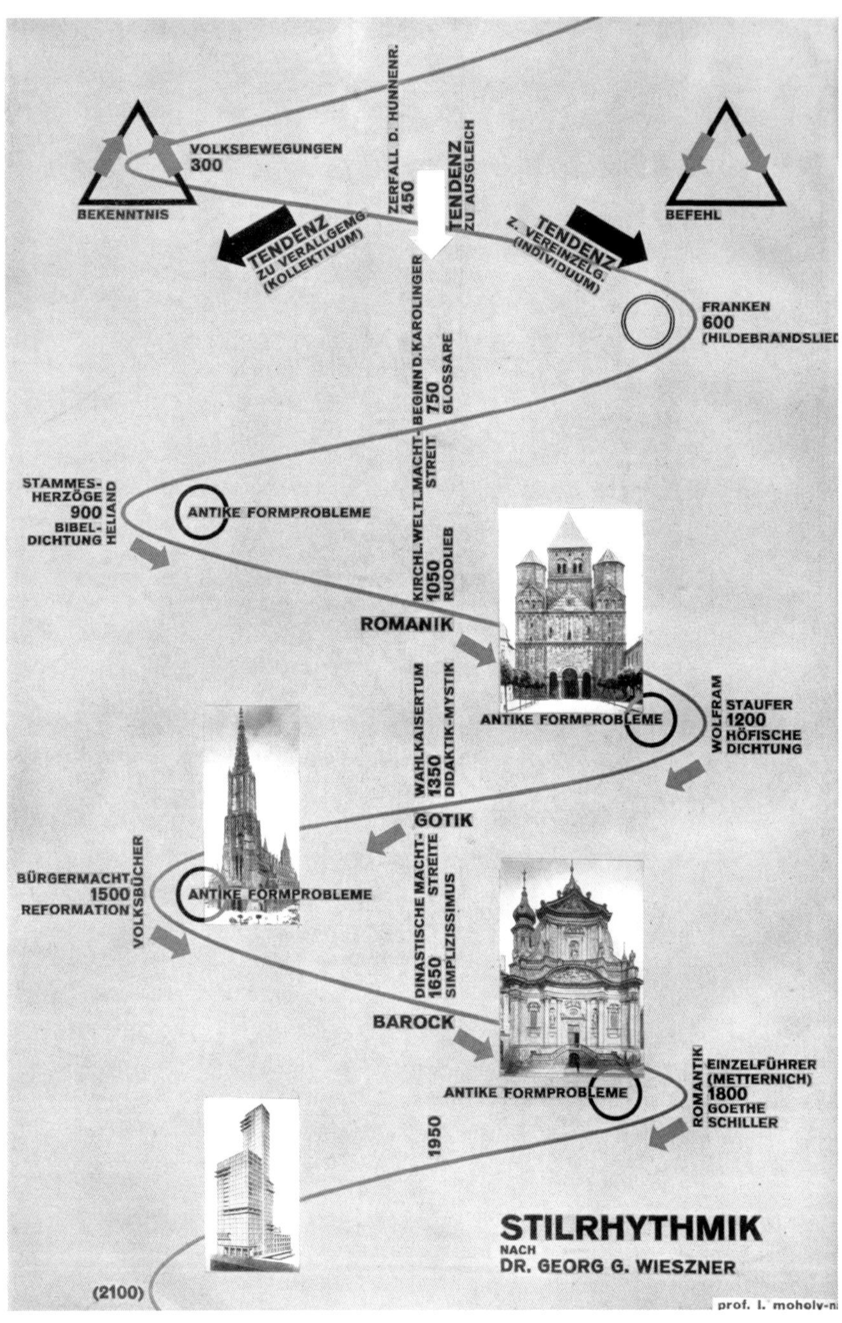

11. László Moholy-Nagy, diagram of the rhythm of style, from Georg Gustav Wieszner, *Der Pulsschlag deutscher Stilgeschichte, 1. Teil: Von den Anfängen bis ins 16. Jahrhundert* (Stuttgart, 1930)

facts.[48] By insisting on the term "Hispano-American," which he claimed to have coined in 1922, he revised Guido's racialism and Wölfflinian formalism in favor of a Latin American *Kunstgeografie* and the mapping of a "historical-aesthetic process" by which conquerors and indigenous peoples clashed, mixed, and reacted: in this perspective, his cartographic representation of the trajectories of architectural currents, leading to specific Hispano-American fusions

(fig. 13), clearly was meant as an alternative to Guido's abstract Wölfflinian "painterly curves."[49]

The specific notion of race, for the most part shared by the aforementioned authors, is summed up in José Uriel García's influential *El nuevo indio* (1930), which explicitly refers to Guido's Wölfflinian theories. For Uriel García, in the post-Conquest mestizo American, spirit ruled over race and blood, the latter meaning "tradition"; and "the new Indian is really an ethnic group, if not, above all, a moral entity," which cannot be defined on the basis of physiognomy.[50] He further revised Guido by stressing that the Indian will to form, an expression of a spiritual or psychological, and not a biological, mestization, so drastically departed from the classical canon that its art escaped Wölfflinian aesthetic analysis, which, for example, cannot distinguish a highland from a lowland style of architecture. Thus, Wölfflin's "open form" and "closed form" should be applied objectively to the respective formative types of landscape, not just subjectively to works of art.[51]

Guido himself must have then recognized the gap between his own psychological and racialist Wölfflinian formalism and his contemporaries' more geographic and anthropological approach, as he further tried both to schematize and exemplify his methodology.[52] His *Arqueología y estética de la arquitectura criolla*, published in 1932, sustained a "historical-aesthetic" method against the previous "aesthetic-anecdotal" and "biographical-aesthetic" study of "Indo-Spanish" art.[53] His goal was to reduce the history of style to the formula "arte español + arte indígena americano = arte criollo o mestizo."[54] Guido paired Wölfflin's "aesthetic-objective" theory with Worringer's subjective theory of will to form while partly admitting the value of Taine's milieu theory, now approximated to Uexküll's biological notion of *Umwelt* and Spengler's of landscape.[55] Guido, first, based his scientific procedure on "antagonisms," that is, Wölfflin's five pairs of principles, in order to define the Indian contribution as the "difference" between the Spanish and

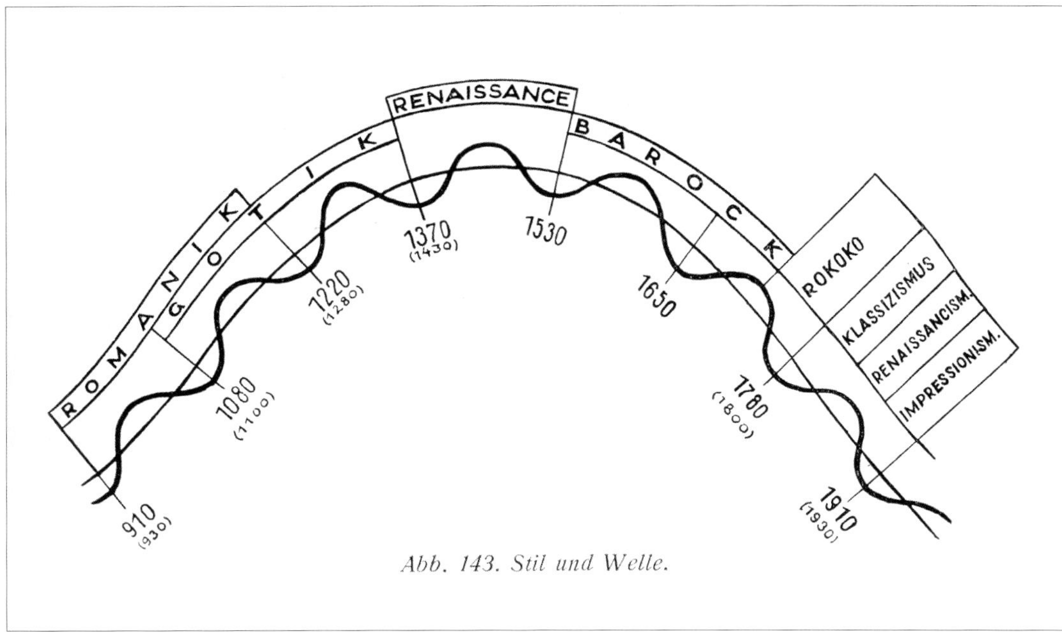

Abb. 143. Stil und Welle.

12. Formal waves and stylistic periods of art, from Paul (Pál) Ligeti, *Der Weg aus dem Chaos: Eine Deutung des Weltgeschehens aus dem Rhythmus der Kunstentwicklung* (Munich, 1931)

the creole styles that results from the comparison of two respective buildings.[56] The characteristic American "aclasicamiento" (classicizing) thus developed not from the classical tradition but from indigenous influence, which thus represented America's antiquity.[57] Second, Guido referred to Worringer's will to form and *Einfühlung*, that "symbolic sympathy" or "inductive self-suggestion," in order to show that the creole aesthetic would differ from its Hispanic counterpart; for "vernacular" and "circumstantial" reasons, it expressed an indigenous spirit of rebellion against the dictatorship of the sword and the cross.[58] In the late 1920s Guido was one of the first to theorize an aesthetics of mestization, which would be a much-debated concept up to today. However, he seems here, as the ambiguity of his equation betrays, to have subsumed the mestizo in the creole, or the indigenous in the colonial.[59] In so doing, he appropriated the indigenous for his own Hispanic elite and contributed to an aesthetization of colonial history. Although he seems to have opened his mind to new contexts of colonial and neocolonial architecture in California on a Guggenheim grant in 1932, only much later in his oeuvre would he start to differentiate criollo and mestizo.[60]

In 1935 Guido systematized his methodological credo in *Concepto moderno de la historia del arte: Influencia de la 'Einfühlung' en la moderna historiografía de arte*, whose title itself subordinates Wölfflin's principles to the concept of empathy.[61] This programmatic history of art history heavily and openly relied on the recent Spanish translation (1932) of Walter Passarge's *Die Philosophie der Kunstgeschichte in der Gegenwart* (1930) rather than on the rarely accessible texts of Henri Bergson, Wilhelm Dilthey, Conrad Fiedler, and others.[62] Guido's small book backed a scientific revolution, which overturned the nineteenth-century positivist and materialist order by privileging "forma" over "medio," that is, form over context or environment. For Guido, form, in postclassicist times, was created by the will. Thus "psychohistory," *Weltanschauung*, and the "psychospiritual orientation" of cultural production stepped into the focus of scholarship. While previously art history was understood as a "natural history of form," modern art history aimed at becoming a "history of the spirit of form."[63] Guido distinguished three currents of thought: first, a "technogenetic," mechanistic, and Marxist materialism from Gottfried Semper to Le Corbusier

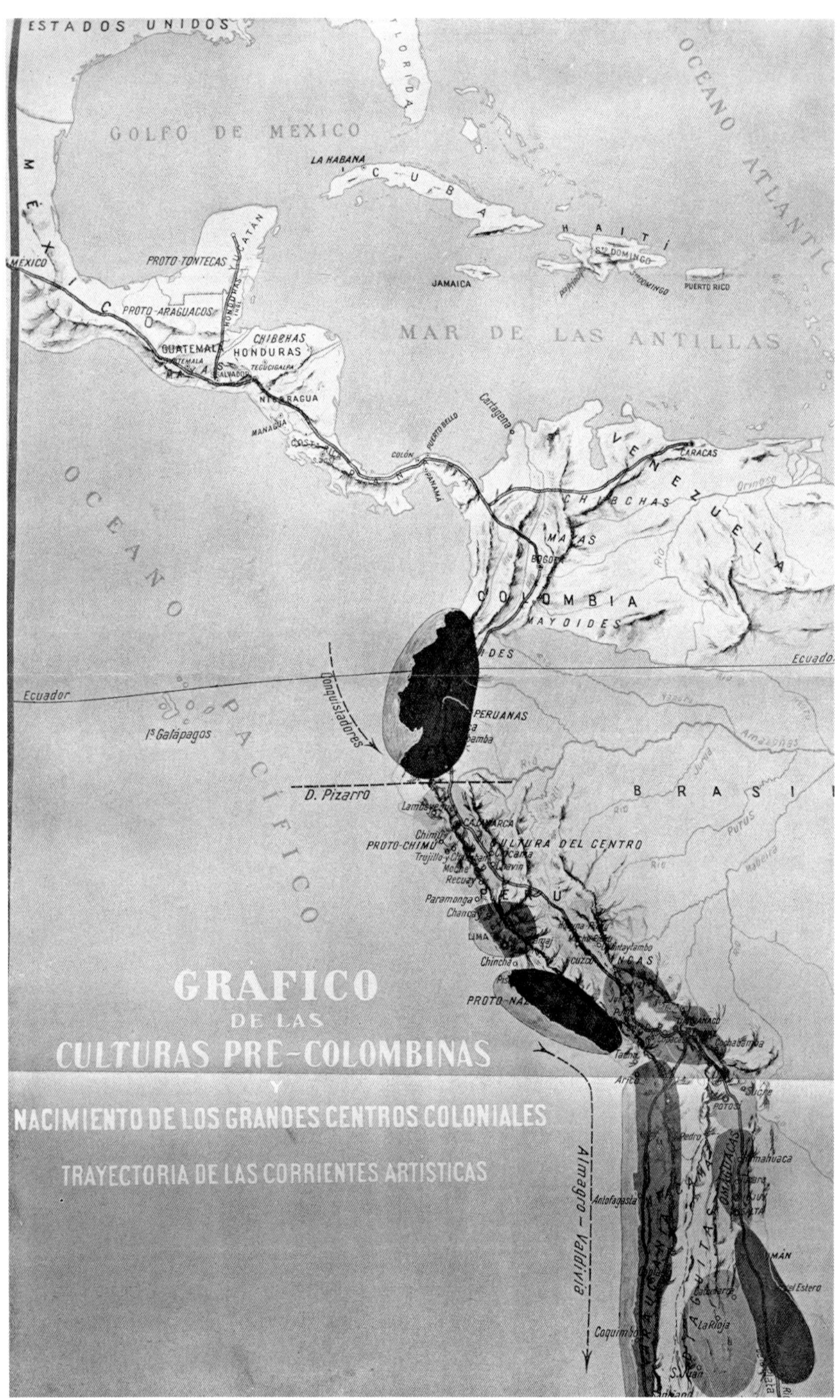

13. Artistic currents in Latin America, from Martín S. Noel, *Teoría histórica de la arquitectura virreinal, Prima parte: La arquitectura proto-virreinal* (Buenos Aires, 1932)

"endopathy," "introjection," or "symbolic sympathy," by which the art historian, like a spiritualist medium, empathizes with the historical work of art, actualizing and enlivening it, and identifies with the "historical man," whose "pathos" shaped aesthetic form.[65] While Guido offered a lengthy chapter on Wölfflinian formalism, which he claimed to have been the first to apply to the history of American art, he now clearly admitted the need to extend it by the means of the will to form. Wölfflin allegedly recognized this himself, and his followers, such as Frankl, put it into effect.[66] Consequently, Guido's essay gives most space to the *Formwille*, from Riegl and August Schmarsow to Worringer's "ethnopsychology" and, finally, to the spiritual "psychohistory" of Max Dvořák.[67] The latter appealed to Guido because Dvořák studied Spanish art and overcame Worringer's racialist notion of will, as religious and philosophical ideas transcend such categories. By these means, Guido wished to open art-historical investigation to a "geopsychology" of popular art and folklore, including the aesthetic phenomena of America, which eluded the European canon.[68]

In the 1930s Guido further extended his engagement with Wölfflin's concepts in the direction of Wilhelm Pinder's theory of generations. He published an article about the influence of the landscape on the South American baroque in the journal of the Ibero-Amerikanisches Institut in Berlin, which Guido joined and visited in 1938, under National Socialist rule.[69] Apparently, Guido's indigenist and nationalist aesthetics was just compatible enough with *Blut und Boden* ideology. Another case for Guido's new tripartite methodology is his *Catedrales y rascacielos* (1936), an Americanist reinterpretation of the skyscraper inspired by Francisco Mujica's *History of the Skyscraper* (1929), Hugh Ferriss's *The Metropolis of Tomorrow* (1929), and Joaquín E. Weiss's *El rascacielos* (1934). Here, to analyze the "horizontalism" and "verticalism" of the skyscraper, he attributed the "polarized concepts" of classicism and anticlassicism

and Walter Gropius; second, a "scientist" Taineian positivism, although it ultimately failed to explain living works of art merely on the basis of their contextual factors; and, third, modern "German" idealism, mostly based on Wölfflinian formalism and Rieglian will to form.[64] The synthesis of the two is *Einfühlung*, a "sentimental projection,"

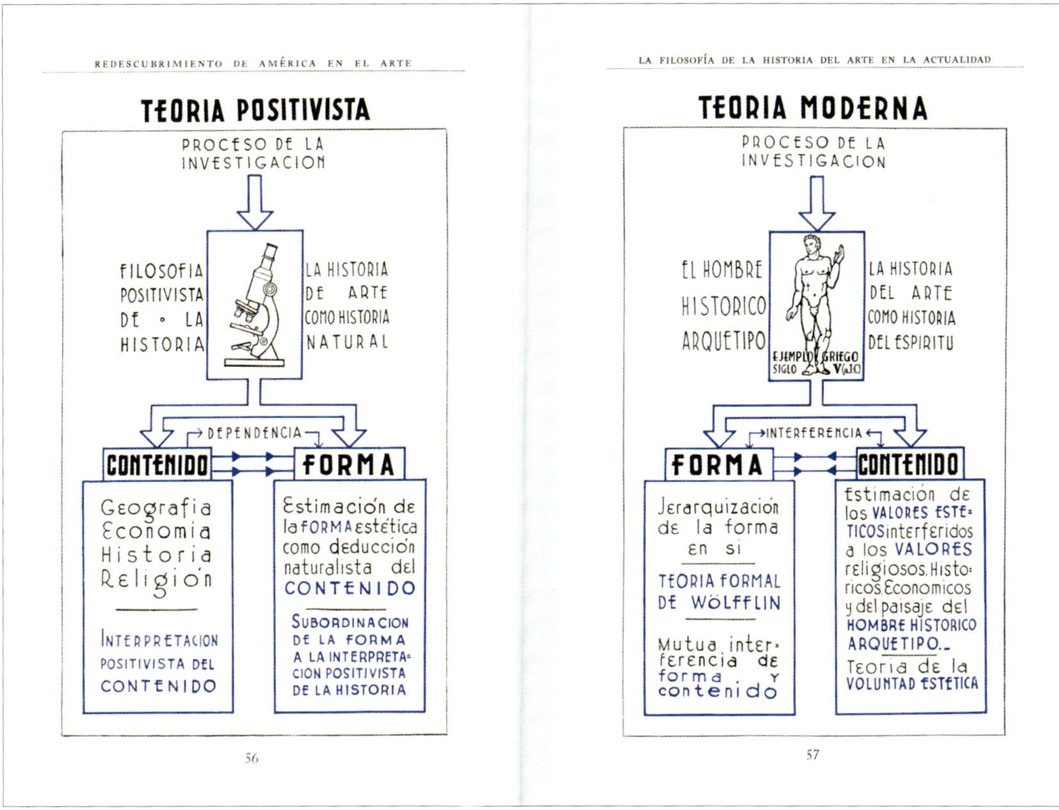

to Wölfflin, of anthropomorphism and deanthropomorphism to Worringer, and of naturalism and idealism as well as immanence and transcendence to Dvořák.[70] The Worringerian shift also became evident when in 1941 he discussed colonial painting, which he tried to establish as worthy of collecting, as Pablo Montini has shown.[71] Guido also defined "mestizo medievalism" as "a sort of Hegelian synthesis of a Hispanic thesis and an Indian antithesis," which again subverted Wölfflin's classical and baroque.[72]

This phase of Guido's continual methodological self-fashioning is summarized in yet another diagram, probably of the kind he used in his lectures, in the first edition of his collected papers (1940). It contrasted "positivist theory" with "modern theory" (fig. 14).[73] While the former understands art history as natural history and deduces aesthetic form from geographic, economic, historical, and religious "content," which is Taine's milieu, the latter puts historical archetypes of man at the center: art history

as *Geistesgeschichte* admits an interaction between form and content, aesthetic and archetypal values, Wölfflinian formalism and Worringerian voluntarism.[74]

The third edition of Guido's collected essays, titled *Redescubrimiento de América en el arte* (1944), presents the sum of his historiographic thought in a blackboard-like diagram: the "cardiogram of the pulse of art history from the eleventh to the twentieth centuries" (see essay frontispiece).[75] The timeline, divided into centuries and stretching from the Romanesque to 1943, deals in the lower part with the history of "form" and in the upper part with the history of "content." The history of form relies on the second diagram of 1927 (see fig. 8), but with a longer time span and a more apparent precision in the modulation of chiastic waves. While the two mirrored lines now bear the more abstract terms "the linear of Wölfflin" and "the painterly of Wölfflin," so as to avoid confusion with the period term "baroque," their disappearance and resurgence through time are now designated with

SIGLO XIX	ARTE HUMANIZADO	PROGRESIVO ACERCA-MIENTO A LA VIDA Y A LA NATURALEZA	NEOCLASICISMO		ALEJAMIENTO DE LA VIDA Y REALIDAD CIRCUNDANTES
			ROMANTICISMO		TEMATICA ANTICLASICISTA Y SENTIMENTAL. PROGRESIVA VINCU-LACION ENTRE VIDA Y PINTURA
			REALISMO Y NATURALISMO		
			IMPRESIONISMO		TRANSICION IMPRESIONISMO DIVISIONISMO PUNTILLISMO
SIGLO XX	ARTE DESHUMANIZADO	EVASION DE LA REALIDAD	POST-IMPRESIONISMO	SENDEROS DE EVASION	INTELECTUAL INSTINTIVO IMAGINATIVO SENTIMENTAL
		EXACERBADA EVASION DE LA REALIDAD	EXPRESIONISMO		CUBISMO EXPRESIONISMO SUBJETIVISMO VALORI PLASTICI ROMANTICISCO PLASTICO PUERILISMO CONSTRUCTIVISMO FAUVISMO VERISMO DADAISMO SURREALISMO
	REHUMANIZA-CION DEL ARTE		POST-EXPRESIONISMO		A. CORRIENTE INDIVIDUALISTA
					B. CORRIENTE COLECTIVISTA

15. History of modern European art, from Ángel Guido, *Redescubrimiento de América en el arte*, 3rd ed. (Buenos Aires, 1944), 522

"dominant" and "recessive," terms from evolutionary biology. As these two properties are attributed to both categories, a genetic notion of style seems to cede to the Spenglerian idea of style as a returning battleground of peoples and cultures. The history of content, instead, inspired by Wieszner's 1930 diagram of the "heartbeat" of the history of art (see fig. 11), describes the development of yet two other forces, collectivism and individualism, which undulate independently of the classical and the baroque. From the eleventh to the fifteenth century, under the influence of Christianization, scholastic mysticism, and revelatory knowledge, corporate collectivism increasingly dominated individualism, as the metaphysical did the physical. This development is expressed by "desantropomorfismo ó deshumanización," stylization versus abstraction, which Ortega introduced as a modern aesthetic problem.[76] Indeed,

inspired by Worringer, Guido conceived "humanización" and "deshumanización," or figuration and abstraction, as Wölfflinian opposites that shape the history of Western art.[77] However, this progression experienced a crisis in the sixteenth century, caused by "spiritual and aesthetic interferences," the fading of the idea of truth through revelation, the entry onto the stage of artistic geniuses Raphael and Michelangelo, and the transformation of the *Weltanschauung* under the rule of reason, leading from Italian humanism to the machine. From then on, individualism won out over collectivism, resulting in an "Apollonian" and classical "humanización del arte," only temporarily influenced by factors such as the individualist Enlightenment, the collectivist Counter-Reformation, and positivism, and by thinkers from Saint Ignatius to Ortega. Finally, with postimpressionism, expressionism, and two world wars, this development was inverted again, as modernism fell into a deep crisis and collectivism once more prevailed over individualism. While personal introspection declined, social topics arose. According to Guido, the near future promised the instauration of "un arte social rehumanizado," a kind of socialist realism.[78] While European man and landscape now failed to work as myths of artistic creativity, a new form of art surfaced to guide Occidental culture: "America rediscovered," Guido's own credo. The answer to the modern crisis of the West was the "birth of a great avant-garde American art," which he called, following Franz Roh, an American collectivist postexpressionism (fig. 15) that, in particular, included the Mexican muralists David Alfaro Siqueiros, Diego Rivera, and José Clemente Orozco, to whom Guido had devoted several publications from as early as 1933.[79] In sum, Guido's last diagram uses Wölfflinian and other contemporary aesthetic and scientific paradigms to visualize the history of art as part of a spiritual and political development leading to a crisis of Western modernism, which was, according to him, overcome by the Americanist revolution he propagated and the subsequent establishment of a Eurindian culture.

Until the end of his intellectual career, Guido remained faithful to his prewar Wölfflinian and Worringerian aesthetics. In 1956, in reference to Wölfflin's student Sigfried Giedion, he still saw in formalism and *Einfühlung* the basis for the language of modern architecture.[80]Also that year, in his volume on hybrid architecture in Peru, *La arquitectura mestiza en las riberas del Titikaca*, he stated that only the Spanish baroque could embrace Latin American folkloristic and indigenous influences and adapt to landscape and human settlement in order to mold, first, the metropolitan "creole baroque," and then the rural "hybrid baroque."[81] The latter, he wrote, revealed a rebellious "hybrid will of shape" and was generated from a spiritual, not biological, "Indo-European symbiosis."[82] The application of Wölfflin's categories led to the updated formula "Spanish baroque + Indian art = hybrid baroque."[83] As Guido's volume was part of Noel's series Documentos de arte coloniál sudamericano, founded in 1943 and including French and English translations, it thus must be noted that the influential term "hybrid baroque" most probably originates from this series dedicated to the mestizo style.[84] Up to and beyond World War II, Guido's influence remained tangible. For instance, his theory of miscegenation constitutes an unacknowledged source for Leopoldo Castedo's *A History of Latin American Art from Pre-Columbian Times to the Present* (1969).[85] However, postwar scholars such as Robert C. Smith, who rejected Guido's political agenda to embrace the Good Neighbor Policy, counted Guido and Noel among the "interpreters rather than historians."[86]

The Iberian Baroque Aeon

While Guido applied Wölfflin's *Grundbegriffe* to Latin American art, others projected modern racialist aesthetics onto Spanish art. In 1924 Hugo Kehrer, a student of Wölfflin's and later National Socialist and Francoist, sketched out the necessity for a Spanish *Formgefühl*, independent of the Italian eye, suited to the essential baroqueness of the Iberian spirit.[87] In this vein, Doménech's *El nacionalismo en arte* (1928) put the *Kunstwissenschaft* of Wölfflin and others in the service of a Spanish national "will to creation."[88] And the racialist *Patterns and Principles of Spanish Art*, first set out in 1931 and published in 1936 by Wölfflin's student Oskar Hagen, applied the categories of planarity and recession.[89]

However, a main moment of the Spanish reception of *Grundbegriffe* occurred in interwar France, where there was a gradual reception of Wölfflinian aesthetics and a reevaluation of the notion of the baroque, even though, as an art-historical period term, the latter remained subordinated to the classical.[90] Between 1910 and 1939, at the former Abbey of Pontigny in Burgundy, the philosopher Paul Desjardins organized the so-called Décades, usually three ten-day-long humanistic summer academies devoted to key contemporary topics and attended by major European intellectuals and artists. The first Décade, of August 1931, was dedicated to "the baroque and the irreducible difference in taste according to peoples."[91] The topic suggested that the baroque was an issue as important for Europe as colonialism and religious conversion, themes subsequently discussed that summer. Desjardins delegated the Décade's organization to his son-in-law, the classicist Jacques Heurgon, who involved a group of German art historians from the Roman circle of the archaeologist Ludwig Curtius, but Erwin Panofsky declined. On the Francophone side, Jean Cassou, Georges de Traz, Paul Alfassa, and Henri Focillon were invited but ultimately did not join the meeting, the curators and critics perhaps feeling uncomfortable about an encounter with the German *Kunstwissenschafter.*[92]

Finally, the intrepid Cuban-Catalan writer and art critic Eugenio d'Ors was assigned to lead the summer academy. He was an eminent intellectual, to whom Cassou had dedicated a portrait in de Traz's

Europeanist *Revue de Genève* two years earlier.[93] The interlocutors were, apart from Heurgon and other scholars, artists, and interested auditors, most prominently the art historians Walter Friedlaender, Hans Tietze, Heinrich Brauer, Rudolf Wittkower and his wife, Margot Holzmann, and Hugo Buchtal from Germany; Timon Henricus Fokker from the Netherlands; and Paul Fierens from Belgium—who at the time happened to be studying the work of Hermann Hubacher, the Swiss sculptor who would receive commissions for a bust of Wölfflin's (1944) and the Zurich *Ganymede* in his memory (1952).[94]

Another of the guests, Werner Hager, who had studied one semester under Wölfflin in Munich, recalled in 1995 that the Décade's motto demonstrated a willingness to rehabilitate the baroque from traditional classicist deprecation. For this purpose, he recalled, Desjardins had invited d'Ors as the conference "matador," whose diffuse, all-embracing, and dramatic conception of the baroque was put up as a "target" to be shot at with sharper, art-historical definitions; Hager's task was to represent the German viewpoint, "firmly based on Wölfflinian concepts."[95] After an interruption during World War I, the Décades resumed, promoting a Franco-German understanding and pacifism at large, taking place, it must be noted, only two years before Adolf Hitler's seizure of power, after which most of the German art historians just named lost their positions and fled.[96] Apart from a short newspaper report by Fierens and a retrospective one by d'Ors, no testimony survives, for German troops looted the abbey's archives.[97] However, it can be assumed that Desjardins understood the baroque as a Pan-European, if not transnational and transhistorical, style, capable of tempering the "irreducible difference" among peoples—a task for which d'Ors, dreaming of a new Holy Roman Empire, believed it to be suited.

D'Ors, who had studied in Germany, was active in Paris for several years, and whose reception is overshadowed by his Falangist beliefs, is probably the most important Spanish yet Gallophile transmitter of German aesthetics and reader and popularizer of Wölfflin's work, which he was able to read in German.[98] D'Ors's report on the Décade was first published in 1936 (copyright 1935) as *Du baroque* (in a French translation by Agathe Rouart-Valéry, daughter of Paul Valéry), received immediate sympathetic reviews by Fierens and others, and was reprinted many times thereafter.[99] The publication was timely, as it was competing with Focillon's *Vie des formes* of 1934 and with thoughts on the baroque by Max Raphael, rejected as Wölfflin's student, whose 1933 article in *Minotaure* conceived the term as a "union of the spiritual and the sexual," a "synthesis of the Romanic and the Gothic," an expression of social realities, and, most importantly, a phenomenon disjoined from the classical.[100] As *Du baroque* appeared the year the Spanish Civil War broke out, it was published in Castilian only in 1944, now with illustrations and the title *Lo barroco*, probably in order to back Francoist politics that identified the baroque as the physiognomy of *hispanidad*.[101] However, one year later, at the opposite end of the political spectrum, an Italian edition of d'Ors's book gave Luciano Anceschi the opportunity to promote a post-Crocean and postwar reception of Wölfflin and a powerful, post-*razionalismo* reappraisal of the baroque.[102]

D'Ors's essay is a "chronicle" of the "tournament" and "quarrel" over the idea and origin of the baroque—a battle over a stylistic term, which not only referred to the *querelle* of the classical *anciens* and the baroque *modernes*, but also implicitly addressed the vexed question of the past and future civilizing supremacy of nations and races, which d'Ors answered with a fervent antinationalism and Europeanism that advocated for a baroque transcending the notorious divide between Protestantism and Catholicism, north and south.[103] By beginning his book with published and unpublished specimens of his famous *glosas* related to the baroque, starting in 1908 and ending with ones written after the summer academy, d'Ors actually appropriated Desjardins's Décade and painted a personal Iberian destiny in and a love for the baroque, despite his own vigorous classicist beliefs. Yet d'Ors's narrative becomes politically shifty: his essay starts with an anecdote of 1911 about his fascination with the Germanic iconography of the Wild Man, in which he parallels the baroque with primitivism; then the book ends with a last-minute note that Hitler's Germany, in the face of a contemporary classicism ending postwar romanticism, is devoted to a pagan, that is, baroque cult of the savage. Tellingly enough, d'Ors omitted this last note from the Spanish edition of 1944, the moment the Franco regime declared its "neutrality" in the face of Germany's imminent defeat.[104]

For d'Ors, Wölfflin's work, following Jacob Burckhardt's, rehabilitated and expanded the notion of the baroque—as a noun and not an adjective—and thus provided the foundation of his own theory, which remained essentially classicist.[105] Wölfflin's two opposed styles, the classical and the baroque, were first adopted by d'Ors in terms of the classical and the romantic and now reappeared as universal morphological principles of civilization: by his "formula," "forms that weigh" are classical, "forms that fly" are baroque, paraphrasing Wölfflin's *fest* and *schwebend*.[106] On the basis of precisely these Orsian concepts, Cassou published his *Apologie de l'art baroque* (1927), which explained the baroque as a German and especially Iberian phenomenon that oscillated with the classical and affected all aesthetic aspects of life. Referring explicitly to both the Wölfflinian modern recurrence of the baroque and José Moreno Villa's morphological analysis, Cassou managed to sketch a dynamic constant, leading, for example, from Spanish polychrome sculpture to El Greco, to Bartolomé Esteban Murillo, to Pablo Picasso.[107] Wölfflin's idea of the superhistorical recurrence of styles, for instance, of the resurgence of the baroque in impressionism, was already foundational for d'Ors, who emphasized that it was a "cosmic rhythm"

but not a fixed historical cycle as conceived by Friedrich Nietzsche, whose notes *Vom Barockstile* of 1879 were influential for d'Ors and were discussed in Pontigny.[108] Even the second of the three topics that structured the Décade—the "philosophy," "natural history," and "geography" of the baroque—refers to Wölfflin's idea of a natural history of seeing.[109] Throughout his writings, d'Ors shared Wölfflin's and his contemporaries' criticism of Taine's positivist milieu theory and, furthermore, objected to Werner Weisbach's restrictive definition of the baroque as an expression of the Catholic Reformation.[110]

Apart from a divulgation of Wölfflinian aesthetics, d'Ors's main contribution to the baroque discourse consisted in the radical emancipation of the term from both chronology and geography and a conception of it as a "system" or supertemporal "constant" with a "relative invariability" that channeled and shaped the course of historical time.[111] D'Ors clearly relied on Worringer's idea of a hidden kinship between the Gothic and the baroque, an idea reiterated by Wölfflin himself, but inverted the genealogy: he declared the Gothic merely a "historical style" that could return only as pastiche or plagiarism, whereas the baroque was a "style of culture" that revived in new shapes, a distinction exemplified by Eugène Emmanuel Viollet-le-Duc's churches versus Hector Guimard's Métro stations. Indeed, the Gothic was merely a primitive form of the baroque.[112] Another aspect of d'Ors's reception of Worringer, which countered Wölfflin's didactic comparative method, became evident in the illustrated Spanish edition of *Du baroque*. Worringer provocatively used images in his *Formprobleme der Gotik* not as "exact scientific proofs for textual statements" but to "strike some chords of mood accompanying the text" and to inspire a "wholly different understanding"; similarly, d'Ors interspersed his essay with diverse images, ranging from the Altamira cave paintings, to Mexican baroque churches, to contemporary popular fiestas.[113]

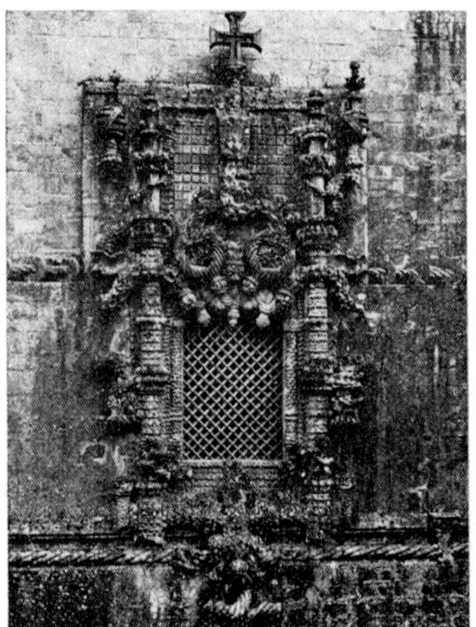
Ventana del Convento de Tomar *(Portugal)*.

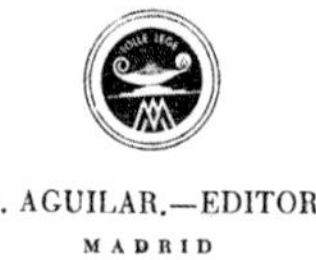

EUGENIO D'ORS
DE LAS RR. ACADEMIAS ESPAÑOLA Y DE S. FERNANDO

LO BARROCO
CON 54 ILUSTRACIONES

M. AGUILAR.—EDITOR
MADRID

Chief for d'Ors were Spengler's notions of a morphology of history, of formal simultaneity, and of recurring destinies and forms of civilization.[114] Starting from there, d'Ors conceived human constants not as a deterministic law of history, but as "types," which he called aeons, a metaphysical category that had "a history."[115] The recurring "idée-événement" might comprise, for instance, the idea of empire, Goethe's "eternal feminine," races as cultural entities, Rome versus Babel, and the baroque versus the classical, which, similar to Jungian archetypes, reveal themselves in "polymorphic manifestations."[116] To explain how aeons receded and reemerged in time and space, a crucial issue for Guido too, d'Ors adopted a biological metaphor. While Darwinian evolutionary biology had relativized and dissolved the notion of genus, contemporary genetics based on Gregor Mendel's laws of inheritance, rediscovered in 1900, and August Weismann's "germ plasm theory" offered a model for discontinuous inheritance, assuming fixed elements or types within change and "dominant" and "recessive" factors in human history.[117] It must be noted that in 1928 Guido had already imagined Mendelian laws of Eurindian fusion for a "biología estética," declaring the Hispanic to be recessive and the Indian to be dominant, corresponding to the respective powers of the baroque and the classical.[118] In this, he was borrowing from a Spenglerian article on colonial Cuzco by José Uriel García of 1924, which explained the "superposition" and shifting relations of domination of the two cultures as resulting from the "biological catastrophe" of the Conquest.[119] With the subterfuge of biological metaphors, d'Ors was able to conceive a developmental history of artistic styles and of human culture at large that did not dissolve into a continuous and amorphous historical mutation growing out of positivist accumulation but that could be understood as the interplay of a few specific, unchanging, universal forces. Thus, d'Ors's taxonomic approach to the baroque, as it were, remained classicist, while he expressed his classicism in a baroque prose.

17. The species of the baroque genus, from Eugenio d'Ors, *Du baroque* (Paris, 1936)

In Pontigny, d'Ors's theses were at first greeted with skepticism. Then, against the Germans' defenses, both Panofskyan and Wölfflinian, which tried to limit the baroque to church facades from Giacomo della Porta to Francesco Borromini, d'Ors brought on, in his words, a "weapon of war," a "battering ram": a photograph of the early sixteenth-century window of the Convent of the Order of Christ in Tomar, Portugal, attributed to Diego Arruda (fig. 16).[120] By fully conforming to Wölfflinian characteristics of the baroque—painterliness, depth, and "dynamism" (d'Ors's term)—this example of Manueline baroque, for d'Ors, not only outshone later rococo architecture but also demonstrated the nonchronological, superhistorical essence of the baroque.[121] This stratagem caused, d'Ors asserted, the sudden "conversion" of Friedlaender to the idea of the baroque aeon: indeed, the latter himself then presented another, apparently even more compelling photograph, that of the antique yet fully Borrominesque Late Hellenistic Temple of Venus of Baalbek—a comparison, however, that had been standard since Franz Kugler's *Handbuch der Kunstgeschichte* (1842) and reproposed by

several authors, such as Matila C. Ghyka (1927) and Ligeti (1931).[122] D'Ors's visual argument, which opens the Spanish edition, was so influential that, for instance, the window at Tomar reappeared prominently in Victor Lucien Tapié's *Baroque et classicisme* (1957), which refers to the Décade and to Wölfflin's *Grundbegriffe* as opening a global view on the baroque as a period style.[123]

Now the path was cleared for a universal, "cosmic," "pantheistic," Dionysian, vitalistic, and libertine concept of the baroque that opposed an intellectualist, normative, and authoritarian classicism.[124] In this view, inspired by Bergson, whose lectures d'Ors had attended, in the baroque, culture imitates nature, whereas in the classical, culture imitates itself.[125] Thus the baroque is as "absurd" as nature, is a "humiliation of reason," and has an affinity to folklore, landscape, rusticism, and other forms of primitivism.[126] Indeed, the baroque has its own source: "as *antiquity* is the precursor of the classical, so is *prehistory* that of the baroque."[127] Then, to contribute to a "modern science of culture" and to stress the naturalness of the baroque, d'Ors adopted Carl Linnaeus's binomial nomenclature for a taxonomy that runs through twenty-two species, from the primitive, prehistorical, and foundational *Barocchus pristinus* to the regionalist and nationalist *Barocchus officinalis* (fig. 17).[128] His table subsumes different species of epochal and geographical styles under the genus of the universal baroque.[129] For instance, he declares mannerism a species of the baroque (*Barocchus Maniera*), explicitly against German, especially Panofskyan, attempts to relativize the autonomy of the Wölfflinian baroque by introducing the concept of mannerism.[130] Ultimately, d'Ors cannibalized Wölfflin's baroque: "the Wölfflinian baroque is nothing but *one of the infinite possible Orsian baroques.*"[131]

D'Ors and Guido probably knew each other's work.[132] D'Ors developed a theory similar to Guido's biological universalization and Hispanic adaptation of Wölfflin's dualistic natural history of style and

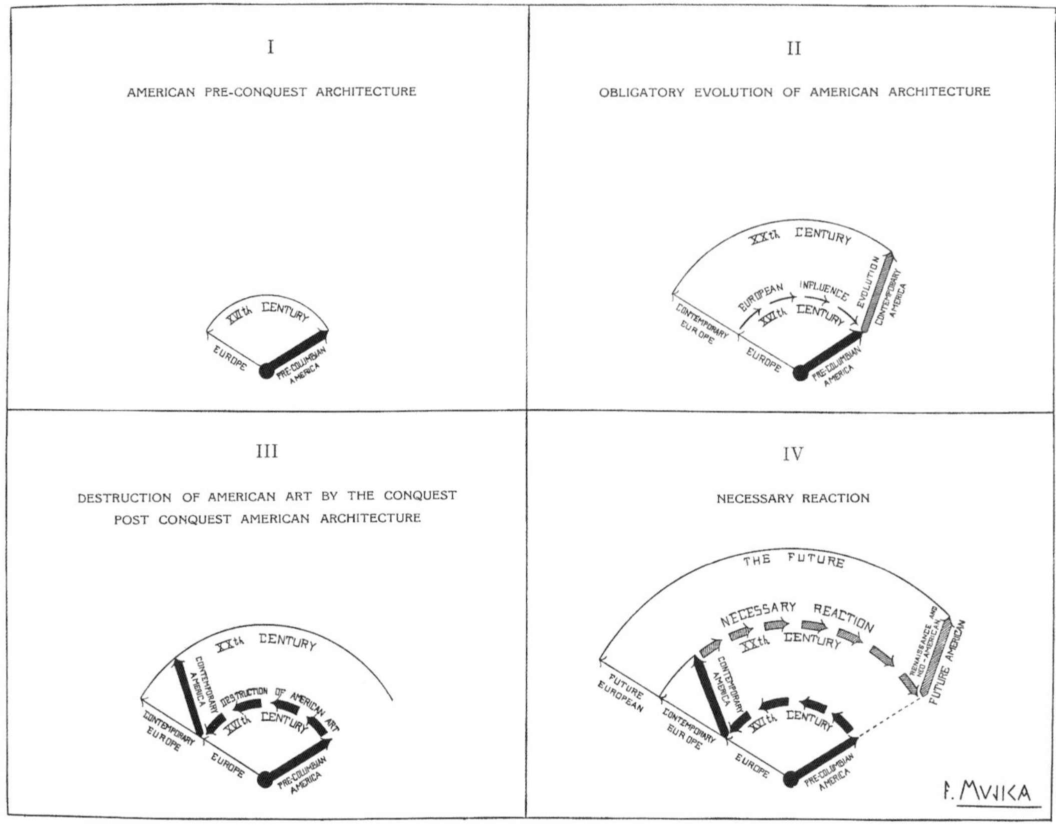

acknowledged that the recently labeled "colonial style," that "ultramarine derivation of the Jesuit style," inspired contemporary architects—as it did Guido—across the Americas from California to Argentina. However, he opposed its nationalist misuse, probably meaning Guido's.[133] Similarly, d'Ors noted, American archaeologists discovered interesting echoes of primitive and archaic baroque in autochthonous art and architecture but too often adopted unacceptable nationalist prejudices.[134] And those in the Americas who claimed to continue Inca and Aztec traditions today contributed only to the artificial *Barocchus officinalis*.[135] In general, the contentious question of national character remained, for d'Ors, in the hands of propagandists of every hue.[136] While Guido held the criollo view that colonial baroque was a European import blended with indigenous forms, d'Ors, thanks to a universalist stance, asserted that the European baroque itself began with the first contact with America, when the Old World was affected and infected by the

new one's irrationality, as the window of Tomar is meant to prove.[137] This swing back to the Iberian Peninsula had already been a subject of conjecture for Otto Schubert and especially for Noel, who, in *España vista otra vez* of 1929, imagined artisans of Quechua and Aztec origin employed in Spain, preparing a modern transcontinental national identity.[138] While d'Ors rejected the nationalist and regionalist appropriations of the baroque characteristic for Guido, he still firmly maintained that Portugal was the true homeland of the baroque and that the *Barocchus manuelinus* was its archetype, as in the case of Nuno Gonçalves, the Portuguese *primitif*, whose work even anticipated the "baroque *Sehnsucht*"in modern art.[139] His interest in early modern Portugal was most probably elicited in 1929 by a suggestive article authored by Myron Malkiel-Jirmounsky, who, in 1932, also published the first general appreciation of Wölfflin's work in France. Malkiel-Jirmounsky described Manueline architecture as an autochthonous product of the encounter with India and America, as a fusion of "national, antique, and exotic" forms; he evoked the poetic tournaments at court fought with *glosas* on preestablished questions, which prefigured d'Ors's staging of the Décade at Pontigny; and, most important, he reproduced a photograph of the window at Tomar.[140] D'Ors's focus on Portugal not only substantiated the idea of an Iberian origin of the baroque; it may also have indicated his fascination for António de Oliveira Salazar's rising Estado Novo.

But by the 1940s Wölfflin's eminence was fading. Seemingly to counter the rumor of his passing, d'Ors published a two-part tribute in the Falangist *Arriba España* that hardly conceals that it was probably a rash and recycled obituary in which he recalled a lecture he gave on Spanish polychrome sculpture at the University of Zurich, perhaps in 1933, on Wölfflin's recommendation.[141] For d'Ors, Wölfflin, in his struggle against nineteenth-century evolutionist relativism, had ultimately failed to transform art history into a history or science of culture because he did not recognize those constants that structure history. In reviving him, if briefly, d'Ors buried him twice.

Postwar Mexican and Cuban *Nachleben*

Wölfflin's idea of the baroque endured after World War II through its appropriation by Guido and d'Ors, and it reappeared prominently when the New World hybrid baroque became a historiographic and utopian means of reversing the colonial relationship and constructing alternative modernities.[142] This was the case in postrevolutionary Mexico, which Peter Krieger discusses in this volume. Guido himself acknowledged the idiosyncrasy of Mexico's colonial fusion, which was set apart from that of South America by the impact of Aztec culture.[143] Before Guido, however, Sylvester Baxter had observed in his *Spanish-Colonial Architecture in Mexico* (1901) that Mexican colonial architecture was "the Spanish Renaissance carried out by Indian artisans" and thus developed its own individuality and charm

and a spirit of workmanship comparable to that of medieval Europe.[144] Similarly, Sacheverell Sitwell's influential, although not scholarly, *Southern Baroque Art* (1924) identified two sources of influence unique to Mexican colonial art and architecture: the Moorish and the Aztec, the latter stemming from the Ameridians enslaved by the Catholic Church.[145] The recovery of the pre-Columbian past was key to postrevolutionary modernism and its construction of a Mexican national identity and thus became foundational to the narrative of modern Mexican art and architecture.[146] In 1929 the Mexican architect Francisco Mujica explained the American "mixed style" as a combination of "the European idea of construction with the American sense of ornamentation" and saw the model for the modern skyscraper in Mayan temples; for him, the colonial "destruction of American art" had interrupted its natural evolution, an outcome that now called for a "necessary reaction" against the dominance of European styles in contemporary American architecture to create a future "Renaissance and neo-American" architecture (fig. 18).[147] From 1930 onward, Guido, too, developed an interest in the morphology of the skyscraper and then saw postwar Mexican muralism, and architecture such as the Ciudad Universitaria, as models for a new synthesis with the pre-Columbian, guided by Wölfflinian *Einfühlung*.[148]

The immigration of Wölfflinian ideas came also, for instance, via José Moreno Villa, the Spanish translator of *Grundbegriffe*, who fled to Mexico from Spain in 1937. He stressed the poetic aspects of Wölfflin's language in his own study of Mexican colonial sculpture (1942), which similarly tried to deduce stylistic developments empirically from anonymous works.[149] Here he proposed to replace previous stylistic terms such as "hybrid" with "tequitqui," meaning "tributary" in Nahuatl and denoting the "Mexican Mudéjar."[150] In his subsequent study (1948), dedicated to the Mexicanness of Mexican art, he asserted that "all tequitqui is anachronic," as it encompassed the Romanesque, the Gothic,

the Renaissance, and the baroque.[151] He
resolved this challenge to Wölfflinian history of art by observing that, on the one
hand, European models from different times
reached the Americas, and that, on the other
hand, indigenous artisans, starting from
the most primitive practices, could progress
quickly in learning ever more advanced techniques, so that an artist could evolve from
a medieval to an early modern style in his
lifetime, an ontogenetic idea that Wölfflin
himself had considered.[152] Concerning the
temporality of stylistic development, according to Moreno, Mexicanness manifested
itself in "bicentennial rhythmic explosions,"
first in anachronic tequitqui sculpture, then
in unconsciously mestizo ultrabaroque
architecture, and finally in consciously
mestizo modern painting, proving that the
New World followed aesthetic laws different
from Europe's.[153] Another import of prewar
Kunstwissenschaft, Paul Westheim's *Arte
antiguo de México* (1950), showed that the
Mexican reception of Wölfflin was focused
on precolonial art and architecture, which
held an importance in the construction of a
national aesthetic identity similar to that of
the baroque in Argentina and Brazil.[154]

In Cuba, however, an even more powerful
reception of Wölfflin's thought, especially of
his *Grundbegriffe,* can be observed. To start,
Alberto Camacho endorsed colonial architecture against European eclecticism and
functionalism and diffused Guido's
ideas at the University of Havana.[155] A few
years later, the Puerto Rican émigré to Cuba
Luis de Soto y Sagarra, historian of art and
aesthetics and founder of the University
of Havana art history department in 1936,
was in close contact with Guido and based
his teaching on the latter's Wölfflinian
methods.[156] His *Filosofía de la historia
del arte* (1941) is a textbook of historical
aesthetics.[157] The recommended readings
consist of the Spanish translation of Passarge's *Philosophie der Kunstgeschichte in
der Gegenwart,* the source of a substantial
part of de Soto's secondhand methodological readings, and of Guido's *Concepto
moderno de la historia del arte,* which he

summarized, stressing the notion of *Einfühlung.*[158] De Soto also followed Passarge's
identification of three recent art-historical
methods: the *histórico-formal,* the *psico-
histórico* (*geistesgeschichtlich*), which he
assessed as surpassing the first, and *the
personal,* referring to the artist. His own
approach, however, was meant to be a mixture of the three, in order to determine style
as a formal development, an expression, and
a product of physical and spiritual factors,
that is, an index of civilization, because art
history is "historia visible."[159] Most of de
Soto's book is dedicated to the explication
of Wölfflin's principles and to the consideration, based on Passarge, of their critical
reception since Panofsky, as the Spanish
edition of *Grundbegriffe* did not include
Wölfflin's "Revision" of 1933.[160] However,
he added his own view on the matter: for
him, form and content could not be separated, and the Wölfflinian principles could
be simplified to *lineal* versus *pictórico* in
painting, *superficial* versus *profundo* in
sculpture, and *forma* versus *espacio* in
architecture, a reduction that rescinded the
universalism of Wölfflin's categories.[161] As
heirs of Wölfflinian formalism, apart from
his friend Guido, he mentioned in particular Frankl, the former student of Wölfflin
and then Jewish émigré to the United States,
whom Guido had already identified as an
intermediary between Wölfflin and Riegl.
Frankl had visited Cuba in 1938/1939, and
De Soto quoted some thoughts of Frankl
on a new set of classical and baroque principles from their correspondence.[162] Taking
Guido's political agenda as a template, de
Soto added Worringerian "voluntarism" to
Wölfflinian formalism to reach the goal of
conceiving style as a result of "national factors," that is, geography, society, and race,
or ethnos, and to address the *cubanidad* of
Cuban art, defined by insularity, tropicality, and environmental homogeneity.[163] The
other factors were temporality, for which
Wilhelm Pinder's generational theory was
instrumental, and individuality.[164] This
led, finally, following Passarge, to that
persistent question of the times concerning

the "rhythm in art-historical development," which fell into two distinct classes: the periodicity and continuity of artistic evolution.[165] It is notable that de Soto ended his textbook by remarking that the value of theories of stylistic rhythm is relative and thus merely of methodological and heuristic nature, as their principles and laws cannot be established scientifically a priori. Instead, he argued, innumerable and changing spiritual and material factors shaped the aesthetic will to form as human expression.[166] From this, again, it becomes clear that abstracted natural laws of art history associated with Wölfflin could not satisfy the needs of regionalist, nationalist, and ethnicist art histories of former European colonies. This is why modern art theory in Latin America supplemented Worringerian voluntarism and expressionism so as to construct a collective aesthetic identity around hybrid and peripheral phenomena.

De Soto handed the Wölfflinian torch over to his student Martha de Castro, who received her degrees from the University of Havana and Columbia University with theses on John Dewey and on Cuban baroque architecture.[167] Her writings, such as *Un ensayo de aplicacíon de la teoría de Wölfflin a la arquitectura colonial cubana* (1942), follow closely the path of Guido, with whom she was in contact.[168] Her master's thesis, "La arquitectura barroca del virreinato del Perú," published in 1943, cleaves to Guido's early geometrical formalism but adds that linear "pseudo-Plateresque" decoration derives most probably from silverwork and represents an indigenous contribution to a Berninesque viceregal baroque.[169] Moreover, she explicitly complements Wölfflin's principles with Riegl's and Worringer's concepts of will to form, *Einfühlung*, and race, mediated through Guido, to explain how Andean peoples absorbed the stylistic shock of the conquest.[170] In the late eighteenth and early nineteenth centuries, lacking suitable stone and an indigenous aesthetic spirit, Cuba developed a modest and sober baroque with a restrained Churrigueresque decoration of Herrerian volumes. By applying the five

Wölfflinian principles, de Castro identifies, nevertheless, *movimiento borrominesco* as a characteristic of the Cuban baroque, embodied in the facade of Havana cathedral. De Castro's aim was to situate Cuban architecture in the genealogy and geography of the Latin American baroque as defined by Guido's Wölfflinian paradigm. However, without significant examples of precolonial architecture, she had to renounce Guido's fusionism and reinstate Taine's positivism. She stressed the latter in her subsequent publications and declared that styles are the product of national, temporal, and individual factors.[171] Since national influence includes geographic, social, and racial aspects, Cuban colonial baroque was a Spanish import altered by uniform Caribbean tropicality and by a racist definition of African influences, expressing a creole will to form that lacked Guido's indigenist postcolonialism while accepting his evolutionary terms "dominant" and recessive."[172] Still, through de Castro, Guido's Wölfflinian and Worringerian and Rojas's Eurindian ideas survived in Cuba up to the 1950s.[173]

This was the context in which the Cuban writer Alejo Carpentier, who lived in Paris at the same time as d'Ors and who returned to his homeland in 1939, developed the line of thought leading to his "Lo barroco y lo real-maravilloso" (1976).[174] Carpentier's influential surrealist concept of the "marvelous real," introduced in 1949, refers to the *magischer Realismus* coined by Wölfflin's student Franz Roh, whose *Nach-Expressionismus* (1925) had been translated in 1927 for the *Revista de Occidente* as *Realismo mágico*, a term Noel and Guido quickly appropriated.[175] Carpentier, who inverted the term's original meaning, denoting a new, postexpressionist classicism, explicitly adhered to d'Ors's Spenglerian idea of the baroque as a human constant and cyclic creative pulsation opposed, in a Wölfflinian manner, to classicism.[176] On the one hand, he implicitly followed Guido by stating that the baroque was engendered by fusion, symbiosis, mestization, and creolization, making America its adopted land of origin.[177] On the other hand, he extended the semantic field of the baroque, starting from pre-Columbian, especially Aztec, art, in order to merge it with the primitivist notion of an authentic and quotidian *real maravilloso*.[178] In consequence, Carpentier freed the baroque from de Castro's nationalist and racist connotations.

Last but more important is José Lezama Lima's "La curiosidad barroca," a chapter from his *Expresión americana* (1957), a founding text of the postwar Latin American baroque discourse in the literary and visual arts that imagines the "American baroque gentleman," a male personification of the continent.[179] In the first paragraph, the Cuban writer gave a short history of the term "baroque" from its negative and restrictive sense to its recent expansive signification.[180] Obliquely referring to d'Ors as "some critic," Lezama ridiculed his overly expanded definition of the *barroco*, characterizing his approach as Spanish neocolonial. D'Ors was a convinced Eurocentric, but Lezama nevertheless overlooked d'Ors's more complex approach to the exotic origins of the Iberian baroque. Lezama's goal was to postulate an American baroque, independent from and superior to its European pendant, which lacked the tension or disruptive synthetic force he called Plutonism.[181] Moreover, so as to reclaim the baroque for Latin America, Lezama stated that Europe, in contrast, regarded the baroque as decadent, a notion he attributed, *pars pro toto*, to Worringer. However, while the latter did see the baroque as a resurgence of the Gothic, he did not, as Lezama states, describe it as a degenerate final stage.[182]

From this point on, Lezama's essay reveals, as scholarship has noted, some familiarity with Guido's writings.[183] More precisely, Lezama's reception of the third edition of Guido's collected essays, *Redescubrimiento de América en el arte* (1944), whose title honors Waldo Frank's *The Re-Discovery of America* (1929), verged on plagiarism.[184] When Lezama stated that the American baroque was the "art of counter-conquest," he was less reversing Weisbach's

argument in *Der Barock als Kunst der Gegenreformation*, as he claimed, than inspired by the "reconquista americana" or "reconquista criolla," which Guido coined in *América frente a Europa en el arte* (1936).[185] For Lezama, hybrid colonial baroque was a seventeenth- and eighteenth-century "first American reconquest," a silent opposition to the "first European conquest," which devastated pre-Columbian cultures in the sixteenth century. At the same time, it was a model for a twentieth-century "second American reconquest," which would follow the classicist, then eclecticist "second European conquest" of the nineteenth century.[186]

For Lezama, baroque architecture and its decoration absorbed and channeled natural, indigenous, and colonial forces toward a new and tense unity that led the baroque as such to its zenith of expression. While he took his instances of Cuzco painting directly from the third issue of the journal *Sur*, he followed Guido's main examples when mentioning the churches of Juli and Puno as manifestations of a Hispano-American will to form. And this was even more the case when he illustrated the Plutonic power of mestization with the indigenous iconography of the portal of San Lorenzo in Potosí, whose author, assumed to be the Quechua architect and sculptor José Condori (or Kondori), designed its hybrid caryatids, renamed Indiatids, parading like feathered Inca princesses against the background of colonial repression.[187] As early as 1923, and then in his *Fusión* of 1925 (see fig. 2), Guido had seen an epitome of hybrid aesthetics in this portal and Latin American baroque as a kind of subversive mimicry.[188] For Guido, its ornamental system revealed a subjective, that is, formal, Indian influence on colonial architecture. Its exotic caryatids were a case for an objective, that is, iconographic, influence that he interpreted as a subversive and even heretical expression of an aboriginal culture devastated by colonial Catholicism and slavery. While Sitwell had noted already in 1924 that, in the case of the church and monastery of San Augustín in Querétaro, Aztec and Maya influenced stone carvings included Indian-looking caryatids, Guido seems to have introduced the neologism *Indiátide* in 1927 for a hybrid type of American column that signified the painful neo-Indian revolt, chiseled in stone, against the colonial *mita* system of forced labor. *Indiátide* was then adopted as an art-historical term from the 1930s onward by Uriel García, Noel, Géo-Charles, and others until today, adding, as it were, an American order in the theory and history of Western architecture.[189]

The same is true for Lezama's attribution of the portal to the Quechua architect and sculptor Condori, which Guido first proposed in 1932, following a hint from Luis Subieta Sagárnaga, although Guido's archival research in early 1931 proved unsuccessful. Nonetheless, the imaginary artist soon entered the Latin American pantheon, to stay there until today, as a role model for a neobaroque rebellion.[190] However, as early as 1945 Robert C. Smith, and in 1951 Pál Kelemen, who had studied under Wölfflin in Munich, expressed doubts about the documentary evidence of Guido's attribution, which was, a few years after the publication of Lezama's essay, exposed by Mario J. Buschiazzo as a local legend.[191] Political Americanism had blinded prewar scholarship to the fact that there was no documentary, formal, iconographic, technical, or any possible racial evidence to support the activity of an indigenous artist. Especially after Thomas DaCosta Kaufmann's recent critical rereading of the portal of San Lorenzo as a product of miscegenation, scholars are now aware of essentialist approaches, although the question remains whether we dare to ask why things look different rather than the same.[192]

For Lezama, just as Condori personified Inca rebellion and a new Inca-Hispanic racial and cultural equality, so the half-legendary sculptor and architect Antônio Francisco Lisboa, called Aleijadinho, the "little cripple," born of a Portuguese architect and an African slave, personified a new African-Portuguese-American syncretistic identity voicing a superior Latin American

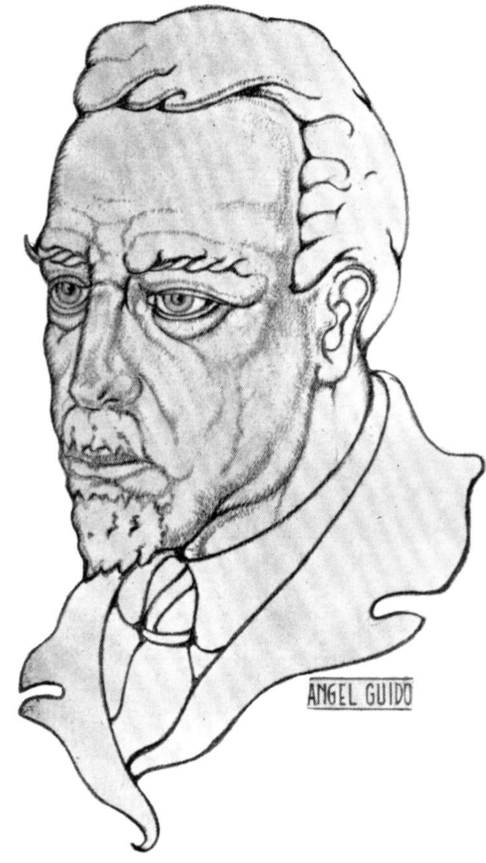

baroque in Ouro Preto.[193] Again, the idea of a pairing of two heroic baroque artists, Condori and Aleijadinho, who embraced Hispanic and Lusitanian miscegenation goes back to Guido, who caught up in 1931 with the rediscovery of Aleijadinho orchestrated in 1929 – 1930 by Brazilian modernists such as Carlos Drummond de Andrade, Lúcio Costa, Manuel Bandeira, Mário de Andrade, and especially José Marianno Filho, on the occasion of the artist's assumed bicentenary.[194] Photographs of works by Condori and Aleijadinho also open Guido's volume of collected writings (1944), which was accessible to Lezama, illustrating "arte mestizo hispano-americano" and "arte lusitano-americano" respectively, a new version of Wölfflinian national idioms.[195]

Guido's appraisal of Aleijadinho, which was a model for Lezama's and which he also published in English and based on Marianno's studies, sees him as a counterpart of the Peruvian revolutionary José Gabriel Túpac Amaru and as an exponent of a telluric rebellion, a reconquest of America, a countercrusade, and iconoclasm against European dominion.[196] As a tragic figure and grotesque outcast in every respect, Aleijadinho personified the aesthetic revolt and expressed his will to form in sculptural work that transgressed Western canons of beauty and thus was presented by Guido as a model for neocreole art.[197] Here, Guido clearly leaves behind the Wölfflinian history of style, which could not account for the supposed Afro-Portuguese idiosyncrasy of Aleijadinho, as his work could not have originated as a blend of Portuguese baroque with a nonexistent indigenous preconquest monumental architecture, either American or African. Instead, Guido opted for Wölfflin's later notion of national *Formgefühl*, as personified by an individual artist such as Albrecht Dürer, or rather for Worringerian voluntarism, more apt for an Americanist political program, but in terms of a heroic and Christological self-victimization. In this way, Aleijadinho's art became an expressionistic exteriorization of the tormented mulatto self, in effect dispossessing the American people of their colonial holocaust.[198] In later publications, Guido even saw in Aleijadinho's personal "pathological-aesthetic process" a development from the baroque to the Gothic; and by pairing him with Francisco de Goya, whom he pictured as a rebellious, anti-Bourbon, folklorist genius, Guido merged the two artists in an "aesthetics of the tortured" that proved the "supremacy of the spirit" in American and Hispanic art and thus obliquely transferred Americanist models to support Francoist constructions of *hispanidad*.[199]

Lezama somehow marks the end of the history of the Latin American reception of Wölfflin's thought, which dissolved into a larger stream of both a scholarly and a poetic history of style, after undergoing many translations and adaptations, which go back mostly to Guido. Indeed, Guido's likeness of the Swiss art historian (fig. 19), probably based on a portrait of 1914 by the society photographer Ernst Sandau, embodied his appropriation of Wölfflin's thought,

as he rendered his physiognomy in a fashionable formalizing, vernacular neocreole style. However, from the mid-1930s, in Latin America Worringer's transhistorical racialist and expressionist voluntarism and other reconceptualizations of the baroque, such as d'Ors's, overshadowed Wölfflin's analytical approach to meet the needs of a Latin American political aesthetics in the service of nationalist and postcolonial identity-building.[200] The Spanish and Latin American reception of Wölfflinian aesthetics was led by the early translations of *Principles* and of Passarge's book, and, lacking substantial colonial Renaissance heritage, it focused on the baroque. While in Europe the debate on the baroque was intimately linked with modern and avant-garde aesthetics, in Latin America it filled an eminently political function, which explains why Wölfflin's core idea of a psychological "history of the eye" was mostly ignored. After the war, the French and especially US archaeological and iconological scholarship, such as that of George Kubler, Kelemen, or Germain Bazin, while not oblivious to Wölfflin, definitively shifted the paradigm. Nevertheless, the postwar discourse on style and on the baroque inherited some problems of *Kunstwissenschaft* around 1900, including racialist essentialism, the cult of both the genius and the people, the decontextualization of works of art in favor of their recontextualization in photographic narratives, and more, which still need to be uncovered by means of a reconstruction of dynamic transcultural networks of art-historical ideas. While tracing the interrelations among a few authors and texts and their mediums and translations may give at least a sketchy picture of an aspect of the intellectual history of the early twentieth century, the history of our global and digital scholarship will be a challenge for future self-reflection and will call for new methods.

NOTES

This essay issues from the project New Art Histories: Connecting Ideas, Objects, and Institutions in Latin America, supported by the Getty Foundation from 2011 to 2016 and carried out in collaboration with Jens Baumgarten of the Universidade Federal de São Paulo, to whom I am deeply obliged. First results of this project were published in Tristan Weddigen, "Hispano-Incaic Fusions: Ángel Guido and Latin American Modernity," ed. Mita Society for the Science of Arts, *Journal of the Science of Art*, no. 19 (2015): 44–58; Weddigen, "Wölfflin in Lateinamerika: Ángel Guidos Entwurf eines mestizischen Barock," in *Weltgeschichten der Architektur: Ursprünge, Narrative, Bilder, 1700–2016*, Veröffentlichungen des Zentralinstituts für Kunstgeschichte in München, vol. 40, ed. Matteo Burioni (Munich, 2016), 174–177; and Weddigen, "Hispano-Incaic Fusions: Ángel Guido and the Latin American Reception of Heinrich Wölfflin," *Art in Translation*, vol. 9, no. S1 (2017): 92–120. This essay also ensues from a project on Wölfflin's *Grundbegriffe*, headed by Evonne Levy, to whom I am equally grateful. Moreover, I thank Pablo Montini, Gabriela Siracusano, and Julia Gelshorn for their precious time and support and Chantal Dornonville de la Cour for her help, and express special thanks to Mara Freiberg Simmen for editing the references. This essay has greatly profited from the expertise of many colleagues and friends. Research has been supported by the Bibliotheca Hertziana–Max Planck Institute for Art History (project number BH-P-19-32).

1. Ángel Sánchez Rivero, "Enrique Wölfflin: Una manera de considerar la historia del arte," *Revista de occidente* 2, no. 17 (November 1924): 256–273. See also Enrique Lafuente Ferrari, "Palabras liminares," in Heinrich Wölfflin, *Conceptos fundamentales en la historia del arte* (Madrid, 1985), Biblioteca de ideas del siglo XX [Madrid, 1924]. On Sánchez see José de Nordenflycht Conha, *Historiografía de la arquitectura durante el período virreinal en América del Sur: Discursos, textos y contextos* (Universidad de Granada, 2013), 105; Enrique Selva, "La meditación interrumpida de Ángel Sánchez Rivero," in *Ondulaciones: El ensayo literario en la España del siglo XX*, ed. Jordi Gracia and Domingo Ródenas de Moya, Casa de la riqueza: Estudios de cultura de España, vol. 29 (Madrid and Frankfurt am Main, 2015), 173–194, here 182–185.

2. Heinrich Wölfflin, *Conceptos fundamentales en la historia del arte*, trans. José Moreno Villa, Biblioteca de ideas del siglo XX, vol. 7 (Madrid, 1924) [Heinrich Wölfflin, *Kunstgeschichtliche Grundbegriffe: Das Problem der Stilentwicklung in der neueren Kunst*, 4th ed. (Munich, 1920)]; reissued in 1985 with a foreword by Enrique Lafuente Ferrari. See also José Moreno Villa, *Vida en claro: Autobiografía* (Mexico City, 1944), 114.

3. Wölfflin, *Conceptos* (1924), XII–XIII, 23.

4. Heinrich Wölfflin, *Renacimiento y barroco*, foreword by Bernard Teyssèdre, Comunicación (Madrid, 1977) [Heinrich Wölfflin, *Renaissance und Barock: Eine Untersuchung über Wesen und Entstehung des Barockstils in Italien* (Munich, 1888)]; Heinrich Wölfflin, *El arte clásico: Iniciación al conocimiento del Renacimiento italiano*, trans. Amelia I. Bertarini, foreword by José R. Destéfano (Buenos Aires, 1955) [Heinrich Wölfflin, *Die klassische Kunst: Eine Einführung in die italienische Renaissance* (Munich, 1899)]. See "Ein spanische Würdigung Heinrich Wölfflins," *Neue Zürcher Zeitung*, December 17, 1925.

5. Sánchez Rivero, "Enrique Wölfflin," 266–267; Hippolyte Taine, *Filosofía del arte*, trans. Cebrián Ambrosio, Colección universal Calpe (Madrid, 1922) [Hippolyte Taine, *Philosophie de l'art: Leçons professées à l'École des beaux-arts* (Paris, 1865)]. See also Marcelino Menéndez Pelayo, *Historia de las ideas estéticas en España*, 9 vols. (Madrid, 1883–1891), 5:133–148.

6. Ricardo Rojas, *Eurindia: Ensayo de estética fundado en la experiencia histórica de las culturas americanas*, Obras de Ricardo Rojas, vol. 5 (Buenos Aires, 1924), 127, 264, 333.

7. Sánchez Rivero, "Enrique Wölfflin," 257.

8. Wilhelm Worringer, "El espíritu del arte gótico," *Revista de occidente* 2, no. 11 (May 1924): 178–211; Wilhelm Worringer, *La esencia del estilo gótico*, trans. Manuel G. Morente, Biblioteca de la Revista de occidente (Madrid, 1925) [Wilhelm Worringer, *Formprobleme der Gotik* (Munich, 1911)]. Oswald Spengler, "Pueblos y razas," *Revista de occidente* 2, no. 15 (September 1924): 351–374; Oswald Spengler, *La decadencia de occidente: Bosquejo de una morfología de la historia universal*, 4 vols., Biblioteca de ideas del siglo XX, vols. 4, 6, 8, 9 (Madrid, 1923–1927).

9. Federico Kuntze (Friedrich Kuntze), "El nuevo estilo en los métodos científicos: Dificultades de su comprensión," *Revista de occidente* 4, no. 39 (September 1926): 317–352; José Jordán de Urries y Azara, *Comentarios de estéticos alemanes a la doctrina artística de Wölfflin*, Conferencias dadas en el Centro de Intercambio Intelectual Germano-Español, vol. 20 (Madrid, 1928). See also Menéndez Pelayo, *Historia de las ideas estéticas en España*, 4:1.

10. On Guido see Pedro Martínez Inclán, "Últimas obras del profesor Ángel Guido," *Arquitectura y urbanismo (Havana)* 5, no. 45 (April 1939): 10–16; Robert C. Smith and Elizabeth Wilder, eds., *A Guide to the Art of Latin America*, Latin American Series, vol. 21 (Washington, 1948); Julián Garcés, "Ángel Guido (1896–1960)," *Revista de historia de América*, no. 50 (December 1960): 504–505; Alberto Nicolini, "Ángel Guido: Dibujante, periodista, crítico, urbanista, arquitecto," *Summa: Revista de arquitectura, tecnología y diseño*, nos. 215–216 (1985): 34–38; Arabella Pauly, *Neobarroco. Zur Wesensbestimmung Lateinamerikas und seiner Literatur*, Bonner romanistische Arbeiten, vol. 46 (Frankfurt am Main, 1993), esp. 13–36; Alberto Nicolini, "Ángel Guido y las teorías estéticas de la fusión hispano-indígena," in

Arquitectura neocolonial: América Latina, Caribe, Estados Unidos, ed. Aracy Amaral, Arte universal (São Paulo, 1994), 207–214; Noemí Adagio, "'¡Hay que salvar a la arquitectura que se hizo atea!': Ángel Guido y su apuesta a la dimensión artística de la disciplina," *Block*, no. 1 (August 1997): 34–42; Bibiana Cicutti and Alberto Nicolini, "Ángel Guido, arquitecto de una época de transición," *Cuadernos de historia* 9 (June 1998): 7–59; Ana María Telesca, Laura Malosetti, and Gabriela Siracusano, "Impacto de la 'moderna' historiografía europea en la construcción de los primeros relatos de la historia del arte argentino," in *(In)disciplinas: Estética e historia del arte en el cruce de los discursos; XII coloquio internacional de historia del arte*, ed. Lucero Enríquez, Estudios de arte y estética, vol. 50 (Mexico City, 1999), 395–425; Thomas DaCosta Kaufmann, *Toward a Geography of Art* (Chicago, 2004), 278–282; Fernando Valenzuela, "Painting as a Form of Communication in Colonial Central Andes: Variations on the Form of Ornamental Art in Early World Society" (PhD diss., Universität Luzern, 2009), 143–148; Elizabeth Kuon Arce et al., *Cuzco–Buenos Aires: Ruta de intelectualidad americana (1900–1950)* (Cuzco, 2009); Gauvin Alexander Bailey, Carla Rahn Phillips, and Lisa Voigt, "Spain and Spanish America in the Early Modern Atlantic World: Current Trends in Scholarship," *Renaissance Quarterly* 62, no. 1 (2009): 1–60, 7–9; Gauvin Alexander Bailey, *The Andean Hybrid Baroque: Convergent Cultures in the Churches of Colonial Peru*, History, Languages, and Cultures of the Spanish and Portuguese Worlds (Notre Dame, IN, 2010), 16–19; Lois Parkinson Zamora and Monika Kaup, eds., *Baroque New Worlds: Representation, Transculturation, Counterconquest* (Durham, NC, 2010), 178–82; Ana María Rigotti, "Monumento a la Bandera de Rosario: Síntesis de búsquedas excéntricas en la modernidad argentina," CURDIUR, *Laboratorio de Historia Urbana. Comunicaciones congresos* (2011); Pablo Montini and Gabriela Siracusano, *Anales del Museo Histórico Provincial de Rosario. 1: Ángel Guido* (Rosario, 2011); Monika Kaup, *Neobaroque in the Americas: Alternative Modernities in Literature, Visual Art, and Film*, New World Studies (Charlottesville, 2012), 261–265; Bibiana Cicutti and Bibiana Ponzini, "En busca de la identidad americana: Ideas y enseñanza en la Escuela de Arquitectura de Rosario," in *Facultad de Arquitectura, planeamiento y diseño: 90 años*, ed. Bibiana Cicutti and Bibiana Ponzini (Rosario, 2013), 27–39; Nordenflycht Conha, *Historiografía de la arquitectura durante el período virreinal en América del Sur*, 41, 105–112.

11. Ángel Guido, *Fusión hispano-indígena en la arquitectura colonial*, preface by Martín S. Noel (Rosario, 1925). See also Felipe Cossio del Pomar, *Pintura colonial (escuela cuzqueña): Nueva edición ilustrada, corregida y aumentada* (Cuzco, 1928).

12. Ángel Guido, "Arequipa colonial," *Riel y fomento* (1923): 13–16; Guido, "Patios paceños—Bolivia," *Riel y fomento* (1923); and Guido, "La influencia aborigen en la arquitectura colonial: San Lorenzo de Potosí," *Riel y fomento* (December 1923): 31–35.

13. Heinrich Wölfflin, *Renaissance und Barock: Eine Untersuchung über Wesen und Entstehung des Barockstils in Italien* (Munich, 1888), 54, fig. 12; Rafael Doménech, Gregorio Muñoz Dueñas, and Francisco Pérez Dolz, *Tratado de técnica ornamental* (Barcelona, 1920), 21–59; August Thiersch, *Handbuch der Architektur, Vierter Teil: Entwerfen, Anlage und Einrichtung, 1. Halbband: Architektonische Komposition, Proportion in der Architektur*, 3rd ed. (Stuttgart, 1904) [Darmstadt, 1883]; Le Corbusier (Charles-Édouard Jeanneret), *Vers une architecture* (Paris, 1923), 49–64. See also Erwin Panofsky, "Die Entwicklung der Proportionslehre als Abbild der Stilentwicklung," *Monatshefte für Kunstwissenschaft* 14 (1921): 188–219; Miloutine Borissavliévitch, *Les Théories de l'architecture: Essai critique sur les principales doctrines relatives à l'esthétique de l'architecture* (Paris, 1926); Hubert Locher, "Diagrammatische Abstraktion als Grundlage der Stilbestimmung: Erwin Panofsky und Rudolf Wittkower," in *Stil-Linien diagrammatischer Kunstgeschichte*, ed. Wolfgang Cortjaens and Karsten Heck (Munich, 2014), 212–231.

14. Charles Wiener, *Pérou et Bolivie: Récit de voyage; suivi d'études archéologiques et ethnographiques et de notes sur l'écriture et les langues des populations indiennes* (Paris, 1880), esp. 636–639; André Michel, ed., *Histoire de l'art depuis les premiers temps chrétiens jusqu'à nos jours* (Paris, 1905–1929).

15. Guido, *Fusión hispano-indígena*, 21–26, 133.

16. Rojas, *Eurindia*; Ricardo Rojas, *Ollantay: Tragedia de los Andes* (Buenos Aires, 1939); Ángel Guido, "Cristianización de las formas," *La revista de "El circulo"* (spring 1923): 34–36; Ángel Guido, "En defensa de Eurindia," *Revista de "El Círculo"* (autumn–winter 1924): 37; Ángel Guido, "Ricardo Rojas, místico de la argentinidad (homenaje al doctor Ricardo Rojas en el segundo aniversario de su muerte)," *Boletín de la Academia Nacional de la Historia* 36, no. 30 (1959): 165–179. See also Manuel Pedro González, "El *Ollantay* de Ricardo Rojas," *Revista hispánica moderna: Boletín del Instituto de las Españas* 10, nos. 1–2 (January–April 1944): 34–36; Margarita V. Gutman, "Casa Ricardo Rojas o la construcción de un paradigma," DANA: *Documentos de arquitectura nacional y americana*, no. 21 (September 1986): 47–60, 48–56; Virginia Bonicatto, "La materialización de una estética nacional: Ricardo Rojas en la arquitectura argentina," foreword by Rose Marie San Juan, *Boletín de estética*, no. 15 (2010–2011): 5–29; Amanda Salvioni, "De lo inmaterial literario al monumento arquitectónico: La casa-museo de Ricardo Rojas," in *Patrimonio culturale e cittadinanza / Patrimonio cultural y ciudadanía: Italia/Argentina*, Il capitale culturale / Studies on the Value of Cultural Heritage, Supplementi, vol. 2 (Macerata, 2015), 127–152.

17. Another, comparable Americanist point of reference, although not mentioned explicitly by Guido, is the Mexican philosopher José Vasconcelos's essay *La raza cósmica* (1925), which imagines a future, universal mestizo race rising from Hispanic-American soil. See José Vasconcelos, *La raza cósmica: Misión de la raza iberoamericana; notas de viajes a la América del Sur* (Paris, 1925).

18. Arthur Posnansky, *Eine prähistorische Metropole in Südamerika: Band 1 / Una metrópoli prehistórica en la América del Sud: Tomo 1* (Berlin, 1914), 118–184; See also Guido, *Fusión hispano-indígena*, 159–173. Michel, *Histoire de l'art*, for example, 514, 636, 637. Cf. Guido, *Fusión hispano-indígena*, 77–79, figs. 2–5.

19. Martín S. Noel, "Prefacio," in Guido, *Fusión hispano-indígena en la arquitectura colonial* (Rosario, 1925), 11–18, 14, 17; see also 24, 44, 161. Martín S. Noel, *Contribución a la historia de la arquitectura hispano-americana*, 2nd ed. (Buenos Aires, 1923) [Buenos Aires, 1921]; Martín S. Noel, "El barroco andaluz y al arquitectura de la colónia," *Raza española: Revista de España y América* 4, no. 37 (1922): 52–76; Martín S. Noel, *Fundamentos para una estética nacional: Contribución a la história de la arquitectura hispano-americana* (Buenos Aires, 1926), esp. 151–216; Margarita V. Gutman, "Martín Noel: Discurso único, obras diversas," *Cuadernos de historia* 9 (June 1998): 61–115.

20. Noel, *Fundamentos para una estética nacional*, 153. See also Martín S. Noel, *Teoría histórica de la arquitectura virreinal, Prima parte: La arquitectura proto-virreinal* (Buenos Aires, 1932), 21.

21. Héctor Greslebin, "El estilo renacimiento colonial: Conferencia realizada el 27 de Octubre de 1923 en el Salón de Actos de la Facultad de Ciencias Exactas, Fisicas y Naturales, bajo el patrocinio del Centro Estudiantes de Arquitectura," *Revista de arquitectura: Órgano del Centro de Estudiantes de arquitectura (Buenos Aires)* 10, nos. 38–39 (February–March 1924): 2–3.

22. "'Fusión hispano-indígena en la arquitectura colonial' por Ángel Guido," *Caras y caretas*, August 22, 1925, 131; Henry-Russell Hitchcock, *Latin American Architecture since 1945* (New York, 1955), 13. See also Enrique Finot, *La cultura colonial española en el Alto Perú* (New York, 1935); Enrique Finot, "La cultura colonial española en el Alto Perú (Apuntes para una historia del arte colonial en Bolivia)," *Revista hispánica moderna: Boletín del Instituto de las Españas* 1, no. 3 (April 1935): 161–173; Alfredo Benavides Rodriguez, *La arquitectura en el Virreinato del Perú y en la Capitanía General de Chile* (Santiago de Chile, 1941), 43, 91; Martha de Castro, "La arquitectura barroca del virreinato del Perú," *Universidad de la Habana* 9, nos. 52–54 (January–June (1944): 188–213; Mario J. Buschiazzo, *Historia de la arquitectura colonial en Iberoamérica* (Buenos Aires, 1961).

23. See Ángel Guido, *Concepto moderno de la historia del arte: Influencia de la 'Einfühlung' en la moderna historiografía de arte*, preface by José Léon Pagano, 2nd ed. (Santa Fc, Argentina, 1936 [1935]), 92; Ofelia Funes, "La *Kunstwille* y la segunda emancipación americana," in *Europa y Latinoamérica: Artes visuales y música*, III: *Jornadas de estudios e investigaciones* (Buenos Aires, 1999); Mauro F. Guillén, "Modernism without Modernity: The Rise of Modernist Architecture in Mexico, Brazil, and Argentina, 1890–1940," *Latin American Research Review* 39, no. 2 (2004): 6–34; Nordenflycht Conha, *Historiografía de la arquitectura durante el período virreinal en América del Sur*, 105–112.

24. José Moreno Villa, "Tras la morfología de Rubens," *Revista de occidente*, year 3, vol. 8, no. 21 (January–March 1925): 333–350.

25. Ángel Guido, *La arquitectura hispanoamericana a través de Wölfflin [La arquitectura hispanoincaica a través de Wölfflin]* (Rosario, 1927), 12–14, 15–16 (the title on the cover differs from the one inside) See also Ángel Guido, "Diversidad barroca en el arte hispanoamericano," *La prensa*, January 1, 1927; Ángel Guido, "El barroquismo hispano-incáico a través de la teoría de Wölfflin: Trabajo aprobado por el Tercer Congreso Panamericano de Arquitectos," *Arquitectura: Órgano oficial de la Sociedad de Arquitectos (Montevideo)* 13, no. 118 (September 1927): 279–283; Ángel Guido, "Diversidad barroca en el arte hispano-americano," *Arquitectura: Órgano oficial de la Sociedad de Arquitectos (Montevideo)* 13, no. 120 (November 1927): 319–322; Ángel Guido, "El Cuzco, problema de arte," *Arquitectura: Revista de la Sociedad de Arquitectos (Rosario)* 1, no. 12 (1928): 33–44. See also "Wölfflin y Ángel Guido," *Revista de las Españas*, April 1–May 31, 1928, 67; "Ingeniero Ángel Guido, que pronunció en la Facultad de Ingeniería su conferencia 'La arquitectura hispanoamericana de acuerdo con la teoría de Wolfflin,'" *Caras y caretas*, September 29, 1929, 60.

26. Guido, *La arquitectura hispanoamericana a través de Wölfflin*, 12–14, 15–16.

27. Otto Schubert, *Historia del barroco en España*, trans. Manuel Hernández Alcalde (Madrid, 1924) [Otto Schubert, *Geschichte des Barock in Spanien* (Esslingen, 1908)]. See also, for example, José Amador de los Rios, *El estilo mudéjar en arquitectura: Discurso leído en junta pública de 19 de junio de 1859* (Madrid, 1872).

28. Guido, *La arquitectura hispanoamericana a través de Wölfflin*, 17–26.

29. Ángel Guido, "Fisonomía setecentista de La Paz: Templo de San Francisco," *La prensa*, January 1, 1928. See also Oswald Spengler, *Der Untergang des Abendlandes: Umrisse einer Morphologie der Weltgeschichte, Erster Band: Gestalt und Wirklichkeit*, 7th ed. (Munich, 1920) [Vienna, 1918], 144–5, 276; Wölfflin 1924, 316; Rojas, *Eurindia*, 11–3, 18–20; Martín S. Noel, *España vista otra vez* (Madrid, 1929), 67, 153–154, 210, 230; Martín S. Noel, *El arte en la América española* (Buenos Aires, 1942), 87–95; Pauly, *Neobarroco*, 22–24; Daniela Bohde, *Kunstgeschichte als physiognomische Wissenschaft: Kritik einer Denkfigur der 1920er bis 1940er Jahre*, Schriften zur modernen Kunsthistoriographie, vol. 3 (Berlin, 2012).

30. Manuel G. Morente, "Una nueva filosofía de la historia: ¿Europa en decadencia?," *Revista de occidente* 1, no. 2 (August 1923): 175–182. See also Ernesto Kretschmer (Ernst Kretschmer), "El individuo y el medio (nuevas ideas biológicas)," *Revista de occidente* 1, no. 2 (August 1923): 161–174; Noel, *España vista otra vez*, 186, 210; Vicente Romero Espinoza, "Le latino-américanisme à la lumière du 'Déclin de l'Occident,' 1919–1939," 3 vols. (PhD diss., Université de Paris VII-Denis Diderot), 1994–1995.

31. Guido, *La arquitectura hispanoamericana a través de Wölfflin*, 43–60. See also Worringer, *La esencia del estilo gótico*, 11, esp. 129.

32. See Juan Kronfuss, *Arquitectura colonial en la Argentina* (Buenos Aires, [1920]); John T. Graham, *The Social Thought of Ortega y Gasset: A Systematic Synthesis in Postmodernism and Interdisciplinarity* (Columbia, MO, 2001).

33. See Astrit Schmidt-Burkhardt, *Stammbäume der Kunst: Zur Genealogie der Avantgarde* (Berlin, 2005); *Stil-Linien diagrammatischer Kunstgeschichte*, ed. Wolfgang Cortjaens and Karsten Heck (Munich, 2014).

34. Ángel Guido, *Orientación espiritual de la arquitectura en América* (Rosario, 1927). See also Ángel Guido, "Orientación espiritual de la arquitectura en América: Fragmento de un trabajo correspondiente al tema oficial IV, del III Congreso panamericano de arquitectos," *Arquitectura: Revista de la Sociedad de Arquitectos (Rosario)* 1, no. 9 (1928): 33–40.

35. Guido, *Orientación espiritual* (1927), 7.

36. Guido, *Orientación espiritual* (1927), 12, 41. See also Cossio del Pomar, *Pintura colonial*, 13–14.

37. Guido, *Orientación espiritual* (1927), 25–30. See also Ángel Guido, "Decadencia de la arquitectura moderna francesa: Capítulo del trabajo 'Orientación espiritual de la arquitectura en América' presentado al III Congreso panamericano de arquitectos,'" *Arquitectura: Revista de la Sociedad de Arquitectos (Rosario)* 1, no. 9 (1928): 19–21.

38. Ángel Guido, *La Machinolâtrie de Le Corbusier* (Rosario, 1930). See also Le Corbusier-Saugnier (Charles-Édouard Jeanneret), "Arquitectura: Estética del ingeniero," *Martín Fierro: Periódico quincenal de arte y crítica libre* 4, no. 41 (May 28, 1927): 9–10; Le Corbusier (Charles-Édouard Jeanneret), "Arquitectura de época maquinista," *Revista de occidente* 6, no. 59 (May 1928): 157–193; Le Corbusier, *Précisions sur un état présent de l'architecture et de l'urbanisme avec un prologue américain, un corolaire brésilien, suivi d'une température parisienne et d'une atmosphère moscovite*, Collection de "L'Esprit nouveau" (Paris, 1930); Peter Meyer, "La Machinolâtrie de Le Corbusier," *Das Werk* 17 (1930): XLVII. See also Jorge Francisco Liernur and Pablo Pschepiurca, *La red austral: Obras y proyectos de Le Corbusier y sus discípulos en la Argentina (1924–1965)*, Las ciudades y las ideas (Bernal, 2008), 92–94; Adriana Collado, "La difusión de la arquitectura moderna en el interior de Argentina: Revistas de Rosario, 1926–1933," *De arquitectura*, no. 23 (2001): 26–30; Verónica Capasso, "En la búsqueda de una estética nacional: Un análisis desde la arquitectura," *ASRI: Arte y sociedad: Revista de investigación*, no. 5 (October 2013).

39. Guido, *Orientación espiritual* (1927), 38–39. See Le Corbusier, *Vers une architecture*, 119–140.

40. Guido, *Orientación espiritual* (1927), 63–64. See Wölfflin 1924, 315–317.

41. Guido, *Orientación espiritual* (1927), 76–77.

42. Reprinted in Ángel Guido, "Arquitectura moderna," *Arquitectura: Revista de la Sociedad de Arquitectos (Rosario)* 1, no. 12 (1928): 45–54, fig. p. 52.

43. Karl Woermann, *Historia del arte en todos los tiempos y pueblos*, 6 vols. (Madrid, 1923–1924) [Karl Woermann, *Geschichte der Kunst aller Zeiten und Völker*, 6 vols. (2nd ed., Leipzig, 1920–1922)].

44. Heinrich von Geymüller et al., *Die Baustile: Historische und technische Entwickelung; Des Handbuches der Architektur, zweiter Theil, 6. Band: Die Baukunst der Renaissance in Frankreich, Erstes Heft* (Stuttgart, 1898), fig. p. 28.

45. Herbert Krauss, *Das Wellengesetz in der Geschichte: Kunsthistorische Studie zur Festlegung der geschichtlichen Periodizität* (Bern, 1929), fig. p. 115. See also Friedrich Cornelius, *Die Weltgeschichte und ihr Rhythmus* (Munich, 1925).

46. Georg Gustav Wieszner, *Der Pulsschlag deutscher Stilgeschichte, 1. Teil: Von den Anfängen bis ins 16. Jahrhundert* (Stuttgart, [1930]), 5. See also Schmidt-Burkhardt, *Stammbäume der Kunst*, 276–281.

47. Paul Ligeti (Pál Ligeti), *Der Weg aus dem Chaos: Eine Deutung des Weltgeschehens aus dem Rhythmus der Kunstentwicklung* (Munich, 1931) [Paul Ligeti, *Új Pantheon felé. A kultúrák élete a művészet tükrében* (Budapest, 1926)].

48. Noel, *Teoría histórica de la arquitectura virreinal*, 25–26.

49. Noel, *Teoría histórica de la arquitectura virreinal*, 27, 30, 34. See also Noel, "Prefacio," 18n; Guido, *Fusión hispano-indígena*, 44; Martín S. Noel and José Torre Revello, *Arquitectura virreinal*, foreword by Emilio Ravignani, Estudios y documentos para la historia del arte colonial, vol. 1 (Buenos Aires, 1934), 78.

50. José Uriel García, *El nuevo indio*, prologue by Mario Vargas Llosa, Clásicos peruanos (2nd ed., Lima, 2011) [Cuzco, 1930], 25–27.

51. Uriel García, *El nuevo indio*, 169–171, 183.

52. Ángel Guido, *Eurindia en la arquitectura americana: Conferencia pronunciada en Santa Fe, bajo el auspicio del Departamento de extensión universitaria*, ed. Departamento de extensión universitaria, vol. 6 (Santa Fe, 1930), 1929.

53. Ángel Guido, *Arqueología y estética de la arquitectura criolla*, ed. Superiores, Colegio Libre de Estudios (Buenos Aires, 1932), 3–4. See also Ángel Guido, "El espíritu de la emancipación americana en un artista indio de Potosí," *La prensa*, January 1, 1932.

54. Guido, *Arqueología y estética de la arquitectura criolla*, 3.

55. Guido *Arqueología y estética de la arquitectura criolla*, 13. See also Jakob von Uexküll, *Ideas para una concepción biológica del mundo*, trans. Ramón María Tenreiro (Madrid, 1922); Biblioteca de ideas del siglo XX, vol. 3 [Jakob von Uexküll, *Umwelt und Innenwelt der Tiere* (Berlin, 1909)]; Fernando Vela, "El individuo y el medio (nuevas ideas biológicas)," *Revista de occidente* 1, no. 1 (July 1923): 95–105; Spengler 1924, 364.

56. Guido, *Arqueología y estética de la arquitectura criolla*, 14.

57. Guido, *Arqueología y estética de la arquitectura criolla*, 25.

58. Guido, *Arqueología y estética de la arquitectura criolla*, 32.

59. Ángel Guido, "La influencia india en la arquitectura colonial," *La prensa*, October 20, 1929. See also Harold E. Wethey, *Colonial Architecture and Sculpture in Peru* (Cambridge, MA, 1949), 8; George Kubler and Martin Soria, *Art and Architecture in Spain and Portugal and Their American Dominions 1500 to 1800*, The Pelican History of Art (London, 1959), 91–92; Leopoldo Castedo, *A History of Latin American Art from Pre-Columbian Times to the Present*, trans. Phyllis Freeman (London, 1969), 11–12; Santiago Sebastián López, José de Mesa Figueroa, and Teresa Gisbert de Mesa, *Arte iberoamericano desde la colonización a la independencia (segunda parte)*, Summa artis, Historia general del arte, vol. 19 (Madrid, 1985), 473; Gutman, "Casa Ricardo Rojas," 56; Romero Espinoza, *Le latino-américanisme*, 576; Antonio San Cristóbal, "La interpretación europeocéntrica de la arquitectura planiforme surperuana," *Histórica* 22, no. 2 (December 1998): 309–342; Valenzuela, "Painting as a Form of Communication in Colonial Central Andes," 93, 143–148.

60. *Exposición de arte religioso retrospectivo: V.º Congreso Eucarístico Nacional*, ed. Ángel Guido (Rosario, 1950), 32–34. See also Ana María Rigotti and Noemí Adagio, "Guido, Ángel Francisco," in *Diccionario de arquitectura en la Argentina: Estilos, obras, biografías, instituciones, ciudades*, ed. Jorge Francisco Liernur and Fernando Aliata, 5 vols. (Buenos Aires, 2004), vol. E–H, 130–137; Rigotti; "Monumento a la Bandera de Rosario"; Montini and Siracusano, *Anales del Museo Histórico Provincial de Rosario*, 67–68.

61. Guido, *Concepto moderno de la historia del arte*.

62. Walter Passarge, *Die Philosophie der Kunstgeschichte in der Gegenwart*, Philosophische Forschungsberichte, vol. 1 (Berlin, 1930).

63. Guido, *Concepto moderno de la historia del arte*, 24–26.

64. Guido, *Concepto moderno de la historia del arte*, 35–72.

65. Guido, *Concepto moderno de la historia del arte*, 75–85.

66. Guido, *Concepto moderno de la historia del arte*, 91–118.

67. Guido, *Concepto moderno de la historia del arte*, 143–164. See also Luis de Soto y Sagarra, *Filosofía de la historia del arte*, vol. 1 (Havana, 1943), 40–41.

68. Guido, *Concepto moderno de la historia del arte*, 167–171.

69. Ángel Guido, "Einfluss der Landschaft auf das südamerikanische Barock," *Ibero-Amerikanisches Archiv* 13, no. 2 (1939–1940): 148–157; Ángel Guido, "El estilo mestizo o criollo en el arte de la Colonia," in *IIº Congreso internacional de historia de América reunido en Buenos Aires en los días 5 a 14 de julio de 1937: Conmemoración del IV centenario de la fundación de la ciudad de Buenos Aires*, vol. 3, ed. Academia Nacional de la Historia and Junta de Historia y Numismática Americana (Buenos Aires, 1938), 474–494; Juan Giuria, "Arqto. Ángel Guido: Su visita y sus conferencias," *Arquitectura: Órgano oficial de la Sociedad de Arquitectos (Montevideo)* 25, no. 201 (1939): 4–16; Ángel Guido, "La arquitectura hispano-americana," in *Primer congreso de la cultura hispano-americana: Acto inaugural (Salta)*, vol. 1, ed. Daniel García-Mansilla (Buenos Aires, 1942), 137–164. See also Hedda Oehlke, "Nationalismus in der Baukunst Südamerikas," *Ibero-Amerikanisches Archiv* 8, no. 4 (1934–1935): 350–360; "Aus dem Arbeitsgebiet des Ibero-Amerikanischen Instituts," *Ibero-Amerikanisches Archiv* 12, no. 4 (January 1939): 488–490; Ronaldo Vainfas and Ronald Raminelli, "Los americanistas del III *Reich*: La *Ibero-Amerikanisches Archiv* en los tiempos del nazismo," *Historia y sociedad* 6 (1999): 69–84.

70. Ángel Guido, *Catedrales y rascacielos* (Buenos Aires, 1936), 26. See also Ángel Guido, "Génesis, apogeo y crisis del rascacielo, III: Espíritu del rascacielo," *Cursos y conferencias: Revista del Colegio Libre de Estudios Superiores* 4, no. 7 (1934): 697–706; Ángel Guido, "Radiografía del rascacielo," in *Redescubrimiento de América en el arte* (Buenos Aires, 1944), 719–746; Ángel Guido, "Evolución de la arquitectura durante el siglo XX," *Cuadernos del Congreso por la Libertad de la Cultura* 19 (1956): 225–238. See also Francisco Mujica, *History of the Skyscraper* (Paris, 1929); Hugh Ferriss, *The Metropolis of Tomorrow* (New York, 1929); Joaquín E. Weiss, *El rascacielos: Su génesis, evolución y significación en la arquitectura contemporánea* (Havana, 1934).

71. Montini and Siracusano, *Anales del Museo Histórico Provincial de Rosario*.

72. See Ángel Guido, "Estudio histórico y estético," in *Exposición de arte religioso retrospectivo: Coronación de la Virgen del Rosario*, ed. Ángel Guido, foreword by Julio Marc (Rosario, 1941), 21–58, 46.

73. See also Ángel Guido, "La pintura desde David a Picasso," *Nun: Critica, artes, letras* 1, no. 1 (1941), unpaginated.

74. See Ángel Guido, "Rehumanización del arte," *La prensa*, December 27, 1936.

75. Ángel Guido, *Redescubrimiento de América en el arte*, 3rd ed. (Buenos Aires, 1944) [Rosario, 1940], 536–537. Cf. See also Adriana Beatriz Armando, "Ángel Guido: Conquistas europeas y reconquistas americanas," in *Territorio, memoria y relato en la construcción de identidades colectivas*, ed. Beatriz Dávilo et al., 3 vols. (Rosario, 2004), 1:259–265.

76. See José Ortega y Gasset, *La deshumanización del arte: Ideas sobre la novela*, Biblioteca de la Revista de occidente (Madrid, 1925).

77. Guido, "Rehumanización del arte" (1936); Guido, "Rehumanización del arte. Artículo publicado en 'La prensa' de Buenos Aires del 27 de diciembre de 1936," in *Redescubrimiento de América en el arte*, Conferencias y textos, vol. 16 (Rosario, 1940), 165–186; figures on pages 181–186 illustrating figuration versus abstraction.

78. See Guido, "Rehumanización del arte" (1936 and 1940).

79. See Franz Roh, *Realismo mágico: Post expresionismo; problemas de la pintura europea más reciente*, trans. Fernando Vela, Biblioteca de la Revista de occidente (Madrid, 1927); [Franz Roh, *Nach-Expressionismus: Magischer Realismus; Probleme der neuesten europäischen Malerei* (Leipzig, 1925)]. See Ángel Guido, "David Alfaro Siqueiros: Un gran pintor mexicano," *La prensa*, March 26, 1933; also published in Guido, *Redescubrimiento de América en el arte* (Buenos Aires, 1944), 581–596. Ángel Guido, "Diego Rivera," *La prensa*, March 10, 1935; Ángel Guido, "América frente a Europa en el arte," *Universidad: Publicación de la Universidad Nacional del Litoral*, no. 2 (July 1936): 7–23, here 12–13; Ángel Guido, "Diego Rivera: Los dos Diegos; Conferencia pronunciada en el paraninfo de la Universidad de Montevideo, el día 17 de mayo 1940, con los auspicios de la Comisión Municipal de Cultura," in *Redescubrimiento de América en el arte* (Buenos Aires, 1944), 665–718. Ángel Guido, "José Clemente Orozco: Estética de lo torturado," in *Redescubrimiento de América en el arte* (Buenos Aires, 1944), 597–616 [Ángel Guido, "José Clemente Orozco: Estética de lo torturado," *La prensa*, February 27, 1944]. Guido, "Evolución de la arquitectura durante el siglo XX," 238.

80. Guido, "Evolución de la arquitectura durante el siglo XX," 228.

81. Ángel Guido, *La arquitectura mestiza en las riberas del Titikaca: Secunda parte*, Documentos de arte colonial sudamericano, vol. 9 (Buenos Aires, 1956), XXX–XLVIII, esp. XXXV.

82. Guido, *La arquitectura mestiza*, XXXI, XLVII.

83. Guido, *La arquitectura mestiza*, XLIV.

84. On the term, see also Guido, *Fusión hispano-indígena*, 24. See also Bailey, *The Andean Hybrid Baroque*, 15–43; Carolyn S. Dean and Dana Leibsohn, "Hybridity and Its Discontents: Considering Visual Culture in Colonial Spanish America," *Colonial Latin American Review* 12, no. 1 (2003): 5–35.

85. See also Miguel Solà, *Historia del arte hispano-americano: Arquitectura, escultura, pintura y artes menores en la América española durante los siglos XVI, XVII y XVIII*, Biblioteca de iniciación cultural, Colección Labor, Sección IV, Artes plásticas, vols. 371–372 (Barcelona, 1935), 182–184; Alfred Neumeyer, "The Indian Contribution to Architectural Decoration in Spanish Colonial America," *The Art Bulletin*, 30, no. 2 (1948): 104–121, 105n11.

86. Smith and Wilder, *A Guide to the Art of Latin America*, 2.

87. Hugo Kehrer, "Spanischer Barock: Eine Skizze," in *Festschrift Heinrich Wölfflin: Beiträge zur Kunst- und Geistesgeschichte, Zum 21. Juni überreicht von Freunden und Schülern*, ed. Paul Wolters, Ernst Beling, and Karl Vossler (Munich, 1924), 233–243; Christian Fuhrmeister, "Kontinuität und Blockade," in *Kunstgeschichte nach 1945: Kontinuität und Neubeginn in Deutschland*, ed. Nikola Doll et al., Atlas, Bonner Beiträge zur Renaissanceforschung, vol. 3 (Cologne, 2006), 21–38, here 24–31.

88. Rafael Doménech, *El nacionalismo en arte: Notas sobre la vida artística contemporánea*, Biblioteca de ensayos, vol. 5 (Madrid, 1928), 149, 189; Soto y Sagarra, *Filosofía de la historia del arte*, 59.

89. Oskar Frank Leonard Hagen, *Patterns and Principles of Spanish Art*, University of Wisconsin Studies in Language and Literature, vol. 38 (Madison, 1936). Wölfflin's private library included a copy, bequeathed in 1945 to the Kunsthistorisches Institut, Universität Zürich, L82, probably unread. On Hagen see Levy's contribution to the present volume.

90. On the history of the terms see Georges Bataille, "Le Cheval académique," *Documents: Doctrines, archéologie, beaux-arts, ethnographie* 1, no. 1 (April 1929): 27–31. Victor-Lucien Tapié, *Baroque et classicisme*, Civilisations d'hier et d'aujourd'hui (Paris, 1957). Michela Passini, "L'Historien face à l'histoire de l'art: Outillage et horizon intellectuel de Victor-Lucien Tapié," in *Victor-Lucien Tapié: Relire "Baroque et classicisme*," ed. Claire Mazel and Hélène Rousteau-Chambon, Collection "Art et société" (Rennes, 2014), 19–28. Jacques Thuillier, "Wölfflin et la France," in *Relire Wölfflin*, ed. Joan Goldhammer Hart, Roland Recht, and Martin Warnke, introduction by Jacques Thuillier, Louvre, conférence et colloques (Paris, 1995), 11–29, here 20–21. Eugenio d'Ors, *Du baroque*, trans. Agathe Rouart-Valéry (Paris, 1936), 120, 174. Subsequent citations of the French title are to this first edition. On Louis Hautecœur and d'Ors see Antonio Brucculeri, "Classico e barocco, categorie oltre gli stili: Eugenio d'Ors e Louis Hautecoeur, interpretazioni a confronto nel contesto francese," in *L'Idée du style dans l'historiographie artistique: Varianti nationales et transmissions*, ed. Antonio Brucculeri and Sabine Frommel, Hautes études, Histoire de l'art (Rome, 2012), 321–336. For the French reception of Wölfflin see Eric Michaud's contribution to this volume.

91. Eugenio d'Ors, "Nuevos ensayos / Pontigny / Montpellier," *ABC*, October 4, 1929, 3–5; Anne Huergon-Desjardins, ed., *Paul Desjardins et les Décades de Pontigny: Études, témoignages et documents inédits*, preface by André Maurois (Paris, 1964), 406.

92. François Chaubet, *Paul Desjardins et les Décades de Pontigny* (Villeneuve-d'Ascq, 2000), 139–140, photograph of Desjardins, Friedlaender, and d'Ors in Pontigny.

93. Jean Cassou, "La Pensée d'Eugenio d'Ors," *La revue de Genève*, July–December 1929, 385–390; Jean Cassou, "Eugenio d'Ors, écrivain espagnol," *Mercure de France*, year 35, vol. 176, no. 635 (December 1, 1924), 541–543. See also Pauly, *Neobarroco*, 24–27.

94. Other participants according to d'Ors, *Du baroque*: a Pierre Denis (musician), a Seleix (Belgian literary scholar), and Louis Jacques Goudman (Dutch painter); other participants according to d'Ors, *Novísimo glosario*, 733–736: José Antonio de Artigas Sanz (Spanish engineer); his daughter Adelia (librarian); Fierens's wife, Odette; Marie Madeleine Machet (teacher); and Isabel Dato (Spanish duchess). D'Ors met Fierens and Tietze again, in 1934; see Eugenio d'Ors, *Nuevo glosario*, 3 vols., Glosario completo (Madrid, 1947–1949), vol. 3, 284–286; Paul Fierens, *Hermann Hubacher*, Les Artistes suisses (Paris, 1932).

95. Werner Hager, "Ein Weg zur Kunstgeschichte am Beginn des Jahrhunderts," *Wiener Jahrbuch für Kunstgeschichte* 48, no. 1 (1995): 223–238, here 238.

96. See also Manfred Bock, *Versöhnung oder Subversion? Deutsch-französische Verständigungs-Organisationen und -Netzwerke der Zwischenkriegs-zeit*, Edition Lendemains, vol. 30 (Tübingen, 2014), 88–110.

97. Paul Fierens, "À Pontigny: Entretiens sur le baroque," *Les Nouvelles littéraires, artistiques et scientifiques: Hebdomadaire d'information, de critique et de bibliographie*, August 29, 1931, 6; Eugenio d'Ors, "Revisión del barroco," *Arriba España*, November 7, 1943. See also Diana Vlasie, "Invention du surréalisme et découverte critique du baroque" (PhD diss., Université de Paris VII–Diderot, 2013), 47n76.

98. Antonino González, "L'estètica d'Eugeni d'Ors, nucli de la seva filosofia," in *El pensament d'Eugeni d'Ors*, ed. Josep-Maria Terricabras, Noms de la filosofia catalana, vol. 6 (Girona, 2010), 297–334, here 312–334, 262–275.

99. Eugenio d'Ors, "Le Baroque, constante historique," *Revue des questions historiques* year 63, 122, no. 1 (January 1935): 11–18, summary of the Décade; d'Ors, *Du baroque*. Ángel Zarraga, "Le baroque mexicain," *Renaissance* 19, nos. 10–12 (October–December 1936): 11–14; Paul Fierens, "Du baroque," *Journal des débats politiques et littéraires*, April 21, 1937, 4; Émile Henriot, "Controverse autour du baroque," *Le Temps*, January 18, 1937; Jean Babelon, "Eugenio d'Ors—Du baroque," *Gazette des beaux-arts*, year 79, ser. 6, vol. 17, no. 1 (January 1937): 189; Lucien Colombelle, "Du baroque, par Eugénio d'Ors," *Art et idées: Revue bimestrielle*, year 2, vol. 6, no. 9 (June 1937): 31; Georges Charensol, "L'Art baroque," *Le Matin*, October 30, 1938, 4, reference to the Tomar window as in Reynaldo dos Santos, *L'Art portugais: Architecture, sculpture, peinture* (Paris, 1938). See also Pilar Sáenz, *The Life and Works of Eugenio d'Ors*, Studies in Language and Literature (Troy, MI, 1983), 65–67; Pauly, *Neobarroco*, 25–27; Zamora and Kaup, *Baroque New Worlds*, 75–92; Antonino González González, *Eugenio d'Ors: Es arte y la vida* (Madrid, 2010), 102–165; Brucculeri, "Classico e barocco"; Kaup, *Neobaroque in the Americas*, 48–49; Vlasie, "Invention du surréalisme," 46–55.

100. Henri Focillon, *Vie des formes*, Forme et style, Essais et mémoires d'art et d'archéologie (Paris, 1934). Max Raphael, "Remarque su le baroque," *Minotaure: Revue artistique et littéraire* 1, no. 1 (1933): 48–52.

101. Eugenio d'Ors, *Lo barroco* (Madrid, 1944). Eugenio d'Ors, *Lo barroco*, ed. Ángel d'Ors and García Navarro de d'Ors, foreword by Alfonso E. Pérez Sánchez, 2nd ed., Metrópolis (Madrid, 2002) [Eugenio d'Ors, *Lo barroco*, ed. Alfonso E. Pérez Sánchez (Madrid, 1993)]. Julián Gállego, "Eugenio d'Ors, *Lo barroco*," *Revista de ideas estéticas*, no. 8 (1944): 105–106. See also d'Ors, *Nuevo glosario*, vol. 3, 382–383 (1934), 1030–1035 (1942/1943). Johannes Großmann, "'Baroque Spain' as Metaphor: Hispanidad, Europeanism and Cold War Anti-Communism in Francoist Spain," *Bulletin of Spanish Studies: Hispanic Studies and Researches on Spain, Portugal and Latin America* 91, no. 5 (2014): 755–771. On the history of the editions see Ángel d'Ors and García Navarro de d'Ors, "Nota a la presente edición," in Eugenio d'Ors, *Lo barroco* (2002), 17–19.

102. Eugenio d'Ors, *Del barocco*, ed. Luciano Anceschi, Collezione Il pensiero (Milan, 1945) [Paris, 1936].

103. Ors, *Du baroque*, 12, 81, 107.

104. Ors, *Du baroque*, 23–24, 155, 157, 180, 240–242. Addendum in French only, in Ors, *Lo barroco* (2002).

105. D'Ors, *Du baroque*, 100–102, 106, 115, 170. See also Pedro Muro Romero, "La teoría de la 'forma' de Eugenio D'Ors," *Archivo hispalense: Revista histórica, literaria y artística* 55, no. 169 (1972): 63–78; Helmuth Rothert, *Eugenio d'Ors: Gestalt und Werk*, 1978, 160–188, 227–233.

106. D'Ors, *Du baroque*, 138; Heinrich Wölfflin, *Principles of Art History: The Problem of the Development of Style in Early Modern Art*, ed. Evonne Levy and Tristan Weddigen, trans. Jonathan Blower, Texts and Documents (Los Angeles, 2015) [Heinrich Wölfflin, *Kunstgeschichtliche Grundbegriffe: Das Problem der Stilentwicklung in der neueren Kunst* (Munich, 1915)], [15] 96.

107. Jean Cassou, "Apologie de l'art baroque," *L'Amour de l'art* 8, nos. 10–11 (October–November 1927): 349–354, 417–423; Moreno Villa, "Tras la morfología de Rubens."

108. D'Ors, *Du baroque*, 14, 105, 146. Friedrich Wilhelm Nietzsche, *Menschliches, Allzumenschliches I und II: Kritische Studienausgabe*, ed. Giorgio Colli and Mazzino Montinari, Sämtliche Werke, vol. 2 (Munich, 1988) [Berlin/New York, 1967], 437–439, no. 144. See also Gonzalo Sobejano, *Nietzsche en España (1890–1970)*, 2nd ed. (Madison, WI, 2004) [Madrid, 1967], 565–581.

109. D'Ors, *Du baroque*, 107.

110. D'Ors, *Du baroque*, 100, 117; d'Ors, *Nuevo glosario*, vol. 2, 319–321 (1928), 322–323 (1928). See also Enrique Lafuente Ferrari, "La interpretación del barroco y sus valores españoles," in Werner Weisbach, *El barroco, arte de la contrarreforma*, ed. Enrique Lafuente Ferrari (Madrid, 1942), 9–47, 11, 16, presenting the book as post-Wölfflinian.

111. D'Ors, *Du baroque*, 84–86, 88.

112. D'Ors, *Du baroque*, 118. See also Heinrich Wölfflin, *Die Kunst der Renaissance: Italien und das deutsche Formgefühl* (Munich, 1931).

113. Worringer, *La esencia del estilo gótico*, 11.

114. D'Ors, *Du baroque*, 103, 109.

115. D'Ors, *Du baroque*, 90, 94. Sáenz, *Life and Works*, 89. Gregg Lambert, *The Return of the Baroque in Modern Culture* (London/New York, 2004), 39–48.

116. D'Ors, *Du baroque*, 90–92, 95–96.

117. D'Ors, *Du baroque*, 88, 91–93. See also Zamora and Kaup, *Baroque New Worlds*, 9.

118. Ángel Guido, "Eurindia arqueológica," *La prensa*, June 3, 1928; Guido, *Eurindia en la arquitectura americana*, 27; Guido, "Río de Janeiro: Análisis estético-espectral du su paisaje," *La prensa*, January 15, 1934.

119. José Uriel García, "El Cuzco de la colonia. Ensayo de interpretación histórica," *Revista universitaria* 8, nos. 44–45 (1924): 30–42, esp. 34–35. See also Uriel García, *El nuevo indio*, 167.

120. D'Ors, *Du baroque*, 110–111, 190, 115. See also Eugenio d'Ors, *L'Art de Goya: Goya, peintre baroque; Goya, peintre européen; Goya, peintre des regards* (Paris, 1928), 18–25; Eugenio d'Ors, *Ferdinand et Isabelle: Rois catholiques d'Espagne*, trans. Paul-Henri Michel, Vies des hommes illustres, vol. 72 (Paris, 1932), 74–81.

121. D'Ors, *Du baroque*, 111.

122. D'Ors, *Du baroque*, 113–114. See also Ors, *Nuevo glosario*, vol. 2, 324–325 (1928); vol. 3, 229 (1934). Matila C. Ghyka, *Esthétique des proportions dans la nature et dans les arts* (Paris, 1927), 400n1, pl. 88, figs. 1, 2; Ligeti, *Der Weg aus dem Chaos*, 9, fig. 3. Franz Kugler, *Handbuch der Kunstgeschichte* (Stuttgart, 1842), 304. See also Kubler and Soria, *Art and Architecture in Spain and Portugal*, 103; George Kubler, *The Shape of Time: Remarks on the History of Things* (New Haven 2008) [New Haven, 1962], 51.

123. Tapié, *Baroque et classicism*, 21–23.

124. D'Ors, *Du baroque*, 130–132.

125. D'Ors, *Du baroque*, 132, 134, 147. Sergio Rojas, *Escritura neobarroca: Temporalidad y cuerpo significante*, Colección Contratiempo (Santiago de Chile, 2010), 157–173.

126. D'Ors *Du baroque*, 131–132, 135–136.

127. D'Ors, *Du baroque*, 154.

128. D'Ors, *Du baroque*, 117, 157, 162.

129. D'Ors, *Du baroque*, 158.

130. D'Ors, *Du baroque*, 167.

131. D'Ors, *Du baroque*, 158, 161.

132. Maximiliano Fuentes Codera, "La encrucijada de posguerra y la primera estancia de Eugenio d'Ors en Argentina," *Historia y política*, no. 28 (July–December 2012): 245–272: Guido may have attended the conference d'Ors gave at the Círculo de la Biblioteca in Rosario in 1921. See also Noel, *España vista otra vez*, 285. Benjamín Jarnés, "La arquitectura en América," *La gaceta literaria: Ibérica, americana, internacional; letras, artes, ciencia (Madrid)*, April 15, 1928, 4, and, in the same issue, Eugenio d' Ors, "Cúpula y monarquía," 5. Guido's writings were reviewed in this same special architectural issue of *La gaceta literaria*, in which d'Ors also published a *glosa* on the political meaning of baroque architecture.

133. D'Ors, *Du baroque*, 102, 169.

134. D'Ors, *Du baroque*, 169.

135. D'Ors, *Du baroque*, 172–173.

136. D'Ors, *Du baroque*, 186.

137. D'Ors, *Du baroque*, 238–240.

138. Schubert, *Historia del barroco en España*, 147–148, 212, 217, 245; Noel, *Contribución*, 86; Noel, *España vista otra vez*, 170–171; Noel, *Teoría histórica de la arquitectura virreinal*, 252. See also Guido, *Fusión hispano-indígena*, 62; Guido, *La arquitectura mestiza en las riberas del Titikaca*, XLVIII, reviewed in Julián Garcés, "Ángel Guido: *La arquitectura mestiza en las riberas del Titikaca*," *Revista de historia de América*, no. 44 (December 1957): 481–482; Mario J. Buschiazzo, "El problema del arte mestizo," *Anales del Instituto de Arte Americano e Investigaciones Estéticas* 22 (1969): 84–102, 100; Carla Guillermina García and Carla Maranguello, "Metodologías de análisis sobre arte colonial en la historiografía artística argentina: Aportes, cambios y permanencias," *Épocas: Revista de historia*, no. 6 (2012): 137–155.

139. D'Ors, *Du baroque*, 13–14, 121, 164, 186, 191. See also Noel, *España vista otra vez*, 39; José de Figueiredo, ed., *L'Art portugais de l'époque des grandes découvertes au XXe siècle* (Paris, 1931).

140. Myron Malkiel-Jirmounsky, "L'art manuélin au Portugal," *L'Amour de l'art* 8 (1927): 309–316, fig. p. 313; Myron Malkiel-Jirmounsky, "Un grand théoricien d'art: Heinrich Wölfflin," *Gazette des beaux-arts*, ser. 6, 8 (1932): 233–244. See also Brucculeri, "Classico e barocco," 325n. 34.

141. Eugenio d' Ors, "Novísimo glosario," *Arriba España*, June 28, 1944, 3, and June 29, 3, 238–240; d'Ors, *Novísimo glosario*, Glosario completo (Madrid, 1946), 238–240.

142. On the neobaroque see Françoise Moulin-Civil, "Le Néo-baroque en question: Baroque, vous avez dit baroque?," *América: Cahiers du CRICCAL*, no. 20 (1998): 23–49; César Augusto Salgado, "Hybridity in New World Baroque Theory," *The Journal of American Folklore* 112, no. 445 (1999): 316–331; Irlemar Chiampi, *Barroco y modernidad*, Sección de obras de lengua y estudios literarios (Mexico City, 2000); Monika Kaup, "Becoming Baroque: Folding European Forms into the New World Baroque with Alejo Carpentier," *The New Centennial Review* 5, no. 2 (2005): 107–149; Monika Kaup, "Neobaroque: Latin America's Alternative Modernity," *Comparative Literature* 58, no. 2 (2006): 128–152; Lois Parkinson Zamora, *The Inordinate Eye: New World Baroque and Latin American Fiction* (Chicago, 2006), 115–166; Monika Kaup, "'The Future Is Entirely Fabulous': The Baroque Genealogy of Latin America's Modernity," *Modern Language Quarterly* 68, no. 2 (2007): 221–241; Walter Moser, "The Concept of Baroque," *Revista canadiense de estudios hispánicos* 33, no. 1 (2008): 11–37; Raúl Antelo, "Postautonomía: Pasajes," *Pasajes*, no. 28 (2008–2009): 10–21; Marie-Pierrette Malcuzynski and Wendy B. Faris, "The (Neo) Baroque Effect: A Critical Inquiry into the Transformation and Application of a Conceptual Field to Comparative American Studies," *Comparative Literature* 61, no. 3 (2009); 295–315; Kaup, *Neobaroque in the Americas*; Allen Young, "How the Baroque Learned to Speak Spanish," *Revista canadiense de estudios hispánicos* 38, no. 2 (2014): 351–377.

143. See also Francisco de la Maza, "Ángel Guido, *Redescubrimiento de América en el Arte*, Rosario, Argentina, 1941," *Anales del Instituto de Investigaciones Estéticas* 3, no. 10 (1943): 138–139.

144. Sylvester Baxter, *Spanish-Colonial Architecture in Mexico* (Boston, 1901), 18; Spanish translation, *La arquitectura hispano colonial en México*, introduction by Manuel Toussaint (Mexico City, 1934), 19.

145. Sacheverell Sitwell, *Southern Baroque Art: A Study of Painting, Architecture and Music in Italy and Spain of the 17th & 18th Centuries* (New York, 1924), 223. Sacheverell Sitwell, *Spanish Baroque Art with Buildings in Portugal, Mexico, and Other Colonies* (London, 1931), 67.

146. See also Hitchcock, *Latin American Architecture since 1945*, 27; Johanna Lozoya, *Las manos indígenas de la raza española: El mestizaje como argumento arquitectónico* (Mexico City, 2010).

147. Mujica, *History of the Skyscraper*, 16. Daniel Schávelzon and Jorge Tomasi, eds., *La imagen de América: Los dibujos de arqueología americana de Francisco Mujica Díez de Bonilla* (Buenos Aires, 2005). See also Ángel Guido, "Influencia indígena en el arte colonial mexicano," *La Prensa*, April 8, 1934).

148. Guido, "Génesis, apogeo y crisis del rascacielo"; Guido, *Catedrales y rascacielos*; Guido, "Radiografía del rascacielo"; and Guido, "Evolución de la arquitectura durante el siglo XX," 237–238.

149. José Moreno Villa, *La escultura colonial mexicana* (Mexico City, 1942), 65–66.

150. Moreno Villa, *La escultura colonial mexicana*, 16–17.

151. José Moreno Villa, *Lo mexicano en las artes plásticas*, Ensayos críticos sobre arte mexicano, vol. 2 (Mexico City, 1948), 14, 19.

152. Moreno Villa, *Lo mexicano en las artes plásticas*, 20–22. See also Wölfflin, *Principles of Art History* (2015), 75, from the preface to the first edition, omitted from Moreno's translation.

153. Moreno Villa, *Lo mexicano en las artes plásticas*, 30–31, 59.

154. Paul Westheim, *Arte antiguo de México* (Mexico City, 1950); Franz Roh, *Nach-Expressionismus: Magischer Realismus; Probleme der neuesten europäischen Malerei* (Leipzig, 1925); Paul Westheim, *Ideas fundamentales del arte prehispánico en México*, trans. Mariana Frenk (Mexico City, 1957). Westheim adapted Roh's *magischer Realismus* to "realismo mítico" in a book with the Wölfflinian title *Ideas fundamentales del arte prehispánico en México*. See also Walter Lehmann, *Altmexikanische Kunstgeschichte: Ein Entwurf in Umrissen*, Orbis pictus / Weltkunst-Bücherei, vol. 8 (Berlin, 1921); Dúrdica Ségota, "Paul Westheim (1886–1963): Expresionismo, un potencial universal," in *El arte en México: Autores, temas, problemas*, ed. Rita Eder (Mexico City, 2001), 321–341; and Peter Chametzky, "Paul Westheim in Mexico: A Cosmopolitan Man Contemplating the Heavens," *Oxford Art Journal* 24, no. 1 (2001): 25–43.

155. Alberto Camacho, "Ángel Guido," *Colegio de arquitectos de La Habana* 12, no. 7 (August 1928): 24–29; Alberto Camacho, "Algunos juicios en el extranjero sobre la obra del autor," in Ángel Guido, *La Machinolâtrie de Le Corbusier* (Rosario, 1930). See also Martínez Inclán,"Últimas obras del profesor Ángel Guido"; Guido, "Evolución de la arquitectura durante el siglo XX," 232; Roberto Segre, "Tango habanero," *Casa de las Américas*, no. 203 (1996): 51–60, 56.

156. See also Ángel Guido, "Presentación de Luis de Soto," in *Palabras de un rector: Discursos y conferencias; primer año de función rectoral, 1948, 3 mayo, 1949*, ed. Ministerio de Educación de la Nación/Universidad Nacional del Litoral (Santa Fe, 1949), 115–121; Guido, "Evolución de la arquitectura durante el siglo XX," 232; Guido, *La arquitectura mestiza*, XII.

157. Luis de Soto y Sagarra, *Filosofía de la historia del arte: 1* (Havana, 1943; copy in the collection of the author, inscribed "To Mr. Alfred H. Barr Jr. Sincerely Luis de Soto Havana, Jan. 1944," left unopened).

158. Soto y Sagarra, *Filosofía de la historia del arte*, 25. See also Walter Passarge, *La filosofía de la historia del arte en la actualidad*, trans. Emilio R. Sádia (Madrid, 1932) [Walter Passarge, *Die Philosophie der Kunstgeschichte in der Gegenwart* (Berlin, 1930)]; Guido, *Concepto moderno de la historia del arte*.

159. Soto y Sagarra, *Filosofía de la historia del arte*, 37–44, 45. See also Passarge, *La filosofía de la historia del arte en la actualidad*, 179.

160. Soto y Sagarra, *Filosofía de la historia del arte*, 63–140, 141–158.

161. Soto y Sagarra, *Filosofía de la historia del arte*, 151.

162. Soto y Sagarra, *Filosofía de la historia del arte*, 160–165. See also Guido, *Concepto moderno de la historia del arte*, 111–113.

163. Soto y Sagarra, *Filosofía de la historia del arte*, 177–191, 193–218.

164. Soto y Sagarra, *Filosofía de la historia del arte*, 219–250.

165. Soto y Sagarra, *Filosofía de la historia del arte*, 251–258. Passarge, *La filosofía de la historia del arte en la actualidad*, 180.

166. Soto y Sagarra, *Filosofía de la historia del arte*, 256–258.

167. Martha de Castro, *Estudio critico de las ideas pedagógicas de John Dewey* (Havana, 1939); *Contribución al estudio de la arquitectura cubana: Algunas ideas acerca de nuestro barroco colonial* (Havana, 1940); *The Baroque Architecture of the Vice-Royalty of Peru* (Havana, 1942). See also John Dewey, *Art as Experience* (New York, 1934); Soto y Sagarra, *Filosofía de la historia del arte*, 151.

168. Martha de Castro, "Un ensayo de aplicación de la teoría de Wölfflin a la arquitectura colonial cubana," *Revista bimestre cubana*, January–February 1942, 99–114.

169. Martha de Castro, "La arquitectura barroca del virreinato del Perú," published in three parts: *Universidad de la Habana* 8, nos. 50–51 (September–December 1943): 145–445; 9, nos. 52–54 (January–June 1944): 188–213; and 9, nos. 55–57 (1944): 118–144, here 125–126. See also Martha de Castro, "Influencia indígena en el barroco español del virreinato del Perú," typescript, October 1942, University of Texas at Austin, University of Texas Libraries, Benson Latin American Collection, NA 913 C378, 14 pages.

170. Castro, "La arquitectura barroca del virreinato del Perú," part 3, 130–131.

171. Martha de Castro, "Arte cubano colonial," *Universidad de la Habana* 13, nos. 76–81 (January–December 1948): 257–276; Martha de Castro, "Arte cubano colonial," *Universidad de la Habana* 14, nos. 82–87 (January–December 1949): 49–86.

172. Castro, *The Baroque Architecture of the Vice-Royalty of Peru*, 5.

173. Martha de Castro, "De lo lineal a lo pintoresco según Enrique Wölffin, en sus *Conceptos fundamentales de la historia del arte*," *Arquitectura (Havana)*, no. 265 (August 1955): 391–395.

174. Alejo Carpentier, "Lo barroco y lo real-maravilloso," in *Razon de ser (conferencias)* (Caracas, 1976), 51–72. See also Steve Wakefield, *Carpentier's Baroque Fiction: Returning Medusa's Gaze*, Colección Támesis, Serie A, Monografías (Rochester, NY, 2004), 33–38; Kaup,"Becoming Baroque."

175. Alejo Carpentier, *El reino de este mundo (Relato)* (Mexico City, 1949), 7–17; Alejo Carpentier, "De lo real maravillosamente americano," in *Tientos y diferencias (ensayos)*, Colección Poemas y ensayos (Mexico City, 1964), 115–135, here 129–135. See also Franz Roh, "Realismo mágico: Problemas de la pintura europea más reciente," *Revista de occidente* 5, no. 48 (June 1927): 274–301; Roh, *Realismo mágico: Post expresionismo; problemas de la pintura europea más reciente*, trans. Fernando Vela (Madrid, 1927). See also Noel, *España vista otra vez*, 268, 274, 284; Guido, "Rio de Janeiro"; Martín S. Noel, *En la Arequipa indohispanica*, Documentos de arte colonial sudamericano, vol. 10 (Buenos Aires, 1957), XX; Pauly, *Neobarroco*, 66–78.

176. Alejo Carpentier, *Razon de ser (conferencias)* (Caracas, 1976), 53. See also Severo Sarduy, *Barroco*, Colección perspectivas (Buenos Aires, 1974), 16.

177. Carpentier, *Razon de ser*, 64.

178. Carpentier, *Razon de ser*, 62.

179. José Lezama Lima, *La expresión americana* (Havana, 1957), 31–54; German translation, *Die amerikanische Ausdruckswelt*, trans. Gerhard Poppenberg, foreword by Carlos Fuentes, afterword by José Prats Sariol (Frankfurt am Main, 1992; reissues and republications, José Lezama Lima, *La expresión americana*, ed. Irlemar Chiampi (Mexico City, 1993), 79–106; José Lezama Lima, "Baroque Curiosity: Chapter 2 from *La expresión americana*," in *Baroque New Worlds: Representation, Transculturation, Counterconquest*, ed. Lois Parkinson Zamora and Monika Kaup (Durham, NC, 2010), 212–240; José Lezama Lima, *La expresión americana*, ed. Leonor A. Ulloa, Justo C. Ulloa, and Irlemar Chiampi, Ensayos completos, vol. 3 (Almería, 2011), 129–165. Edgardo Dobry, "Barroco y modernidad: De Maravall a Lezama Lima," *Orbis tertius* 14, no. 15 (2009); Sergio Ugalde Quintana, "Barock, afrokubanische Kultur und Zusammenlebenswissen bei José Lezama Lima," in *Wissensformen und Wissensnormen des ZusammenLebens: Literatur— Kultur—Geschichte—Medien*, ed. Ottmar Ette, Linguae & litterae, vol. 14 (Berlin, 2012), 206–219.

180. Lezama Lima, *La expresión americana* (1957), 31.

181. Lezama Lima, *La expjresión americana* (1957), 31–32.

182. See Worringer, *La esencia del estilo gótico*; Chiampi, *Barroco y modernidad*, 21.

183. Ester Gimbernat de González, "La curiosidad barroca," in *Coloquio internacional sobre la obra de José Lezama Lima*, ed. Cristina Vizcaino, 2 vols. (Madrid, 1984), vol. 1, 59–65, 61; Raúl Antelo, "O arquivo e o presente," *Gragoatá*, no. 22 (2007): 43–62; Zamora and Kaup, *Baroque New Worlds*, 210.

184. Julio E. Payró, "Ángel Guido: Redescubrimiento de América en el arte," *Sur*, August 1942, 81–83. Waldo Frank, *Redescubrimiento de América*, trans. Julia Héctor de Zaballa (Madrid, 1929); Biblioteca de la Revista de occidente [Waldo Frank, *The Re-Discovery of America: An Introduction to a Philosophy of American Life* (New York, 1929)]. See also Pauly, *Neobarroco*, 94–99.

185. Werner Weisbach, *El barroco, arte de la contrarreforma*, trans. Enrique Lafuente Ferrari (Madrid, 1942) [Werner Weisbach, *Der Barock als Kunst der Gegenreformation* (Berlin, 1921)]. For Guido's influential concept see Ángel Guido, "América frente a Europa en el arte," *Mensual de cultura popular*, no. 12 (January 1937): 16. Ángel Guido, "América frente a Europa en el arte," in *Redescubrimiento de América en el arte* (Rosario, 1940), 15–36, Conferencias y textos, vol. 16. Ángel Guido, "América frente a Europa nel arte," in *Redescubrimiento de América en el arte* (Buenos Aires, 1944), 26–42. Ángel Guido, "América frente a Europa en el arte/L'America di fronte all'Europa nell'arte," in *Palabras de un rector. Discursos y conferencias. Primer año de función rectoral. 1948–3 mayo–1949*, ed. Ministerio de Educación de la Nación/Universidad Nacional del Litoral (Santa Fe, 1949), 125–139. *La gran aventura del barroco en América / La grande aventure du baroque en l'Amérique*, ed. Ángel Guido (Santa Fe, 1949). Ángel Guido, "America's Relation to Europe in the Arts: Chapter 1 from *Redescubrimiento de América en el arte*," in *Baroque New Worlds: Representation, Transculturation, Counterconquest*, ed. Lois Parkinson Zamora and Monika Kaup (Durham, NC, 2010), 183–197.

186. On the important concepts see Guido, "América frente a Europa nel arte" (1944), 30. See also Ángel Guido, "El espíritu de la emancipación en dos artistas americanos: El indio Condori y el mulato Aleijadinho; conferencia pronunciada en la Sala Magna de la Universidad del Litoral, en Santa Fe (rep. Argentina), el 19 de noviembre de 1931, con los auspicios del Instituto Social de dicha Universidad," in *Redescubrimiento de América en el arte*, 3rd ed. (Buenos Aires, 1944), 157–224, 161. See also Lafuente Ferrari, "La interpretación del barroco y sus valores españoles" (1942); Enrique Lafuente Ferrari, "La interpretación del barroco y sus valores españoles," *Boletín del Seminario de Estudios de Arte y Arqueología* 7 (1940–1941): 13–66. On other sources see Lezama Lima, *La expresión americana* (2011), 129n1.

187. Mariano Picon Salas, "El medievalismo en la pintura medieval," *Sur* 1 (winter 1931): 162–166, fig. p. 24/25. Lezama Lima, *La expresión americana* (1957), 34. Vitruvius, *De architectura libri decem*, 1.1.5. See also Pauly, *Neobarroco*, 94–99.

188. Guido, "La influencia aborigen en la arquitectura colonial"; Guido, *Fusión hispano-indígena*, 103–111; and Guido, "Eurindia arqueológica." See also Oehlke, "Nationalismus in der Baukunst Südamerikas"; Castro, "La arquitectura barroca del virreinato del Perú" (1943), 168–169, fig. XIV; Salgado, "Hybridity in New World Baroque Theory"; Wakefield, *Carpentier's Baroque Fiction*, 41; Zamora, *The Inordinate Eye*, 288–292. While in 1922 Vicente Lampérez y Romea acknowledged Aztec, Maya, and Inca traditions emerging in a more or less painterly *estilo criollo*, he saw in the portal of San Lorenzo the most horrifying manifestation of creolism. See Vicente Lampérez y Romea, "La arquitectura hispanoamericana en las épocas de la colonización y de los virreinatos: Conferencia de la serie organizada en el Museo del Prado, el 17 de marzo de 1922," *Raza española: Revista de España y América*, no. 40 (April 1922): 58–59.

189. Sitwell, *Southern Baroque Art*, 232–234, and *Spanish Baroque Art*, 75; Guido, "Fisonomía setecentista de La Paz"; Guido, "El Cuzco, problema de arte," 35; Guido, "La influencia india en la arquitectura colonial"; Guido, *Eurindia en la arquitectura americana*, 37; Guido, "El espíritu de la emancipación en dos artistas americanos," 172–173; and Guido, "América frente a Europa nel arte," 33. Uriel García, *El nuevo indio*, 171–175; Noel, *El arte en la América española*, 55; Géo-Charles (Charles Louis Prosper Guyot), *Art Baroque en Amérique Latine*, Collection Psyché (Paris, 1954), 8, 20; Castedo, *A History of Latin American Art*, 173; Ramón Gutiérrez, *Arquitectura y urbanismo en Iberoamérica*, 3rd ed. (Madrid, 1997), 182.

190. Guido, "El espíritu de la emancipación americana"; Guido, *Arqueología y estética de la arquitectura criolla*, 10–11; Guido, "El estilo mestizo o criollo en el arte de la Colonia," 482; Guido, "El espíritu de la emancipación en dos artistas americanos," 168. Kuon Arce et al., *Cuzco–Buenos Aires: Ruta de intelectualidad americana (1900–1950)*, 346: letter of November 25, 1931, from Ángel Guido to Ricardo Rojas, to whom Guido sent photographs of Condori's works. See also Castro, *The Baroque Architecture of the Viceroyalty of Peru*, 5, 9, and "Un ensayo de aplacíon de la teoría de Wölfflin," 110; Pedro-Juan Vignale, "El maestro anónimo de la portada de San Lorenzo de Potosí," *Revista de arquitectura: Sociedad Central de Arquitectos, Buenos Aires* 29, no. 280 (April 1944): 156–162; Pedro-Juan Vignale, "El maestro anónimo de la portada de San Lorenzo de Potosí," *El arquitecto peruano* 10, no. 102 (January, 1946), 9–13; Martín S. Noel, *Las iglesias de Potosí*, Documentos de arte colonial sudamericano, Bolivia, vol. 3 (Buenos Aires, 1945), XXVII. See also Gimbernat de González, "La curiosidad barroca," 61; Nike Bätzner, "Engel mit indianischem Antlitz," in *Die Aktualität des Barock*, ed. Nike Bätzner (Zurich, 2014), 80–90.

191. Robert C. Smith, *The Colonial Art of Latin America: A Collection of Slides & Photographs* (Washington, DC, 1945), 25; Pál Kelemen, *Baroque and Rococo in Latin America* (New York, 1951), 190–191; Mario J. Buschiazzo, "El problema del arte mestizo: Contribución a su esclarecimiento," in *XXXVI Congreso internacional de americanistas: Actas y memorias*, ed. Alfredo Jiménez Núñez, 4 vols. (Seville, 1966), 4:229–244; Buschiazzo, "El problema del arte mestizo."

192. Thomas DaCosta Kaufmann, "Maîtrise ou métissage? Vers une interprétation de la façade de San Lorenzo de Potosi," *Revue de l'art*, no. 121 (1998): 11–18; Kaufmann, *Toward a Geography of Art*, 276–299.

193. Lezama Lima, *La expresión americana* (1957), 51–54. See also Géo-Charles, *Art baroque en Amérique latine*, 16.

194. Ángel Guido, "El Aleijadinho," *La prensa*, January 11, 1931; Guido, "O Aleijadinho: The Little Cripple of Minas Geraes," *Bulletin of the Pan American Union* 65, no. 8 (1931): 813–822; Guido, "El estilo mestizo o criollo en el arte de la Colonia," 495–504; Guido, *El Aleijadinho: El gran escultor leproso del siglo XVIII en el Brasil* (Santa Fe, 1938); Guido, "El 'Aleijadinho': El gran escultor leproso del siglo XVIII en América," in *IIº Congreso internacional de historia de América reunido en Buenos Aires en los días 5 a 14 de julio de 1937: Conmemoración del IV centenario de la fundación de la ciudad de Buenos Aires.* vol. 3 (Buenos Aires, 1938), 495–504; and Guido, "El espíritu de la emancipación en dos artistas americanos." See also José Marianno Filho, "Mestre Aleijadinho e sua obra: Conferência pronunciada do púlpito da Igreja de São Francisco de Assis, de Ouro Preto, em 29 de agosto de 1930," *O cruzeiro*, August 30, 1930, 15–30. Bibliography: Judite Martins, "Apontamentos para a bibliografia de Antônio Francisco Lisboa," *Revista do Serviço do patrimônio histórico e artístico nacional*, no. 3 (1939): 179–206; José Marianno Filho, *Antônio Francisco Lisboa* (Rio de Janeiro, 1945); Smith and Wilder, *A Guide to the Art of Latin America*, 164–168; James E. Hogan, "'O Aleijadinho': An Annotated Bibliography," *Latin American Research Review* 9, no. 2 (1974): 83–94; Elizabeth Wilder Weisman, "The History of Art in Latin America 1500–1800: Some Trends and Challenges in the Last Decade," *Latin American Research Review* 10, no. 1 (1975): 7–50; Jens Baumgarten and André Tavares, "Le baroque colonisateur: Principales orientations théoriques dans la production historiographique," *Perspective: La Revue de l'INHA*, no. 2 (2013): 288–307, 416–421.

195. Guido, *Redescubrimiento de América en el arte* (1944), 8, 10.

196. Guido, *Redescubrimiento de América en el arte* (1944), 159–160.

197. Oswaldo de Andrade, "Manifesto antropófago," *Revista de antropofagia* 1, no. 1 (May 1928): 3, 7. See also Guido, "Evolución de la arquitectura durante el siglo XX."

198. See also Guido, "El espíritu de la emancipación en dos artistas americanos," 170.

199. Ángel Guido, *Supremacía del espíritu en el arte (Goya y el Aleijadinho)*, Extensión unversitaria, vol. 60 (Santa Fe, 1949); Ángel Guido, "Supremacía del espíritu en el arte: Goya y el Aleijadinho," *Universidad: Publicación de la Universidad Nacional del Litoral*, no. 21 (autumn 1949): 145–163. See also Ángel Guido, "El dolor en el arte de América y de Europa: Goya y el Aleijadinho / Goya e l'Aleijadinho; il dolore nell'arte di America e di Europa," in *Palabras de un rector: Discursos y conferencias; primer año de función rectoral. 1948, 3 mayo, 1949*, ed. Ministerio de Educación de la Nación / Universidad Nacional del Litoral (Santa Fe, 1949), 167–189.

200. See Pauly, *Neobarroco*, 19–22.

PETER KRIEGER

Baroque and Neobaroque: Long-Term Effects of Kunstgeschichtliche Grundbegriffe *in Mexico and the Globalization of an Idea*

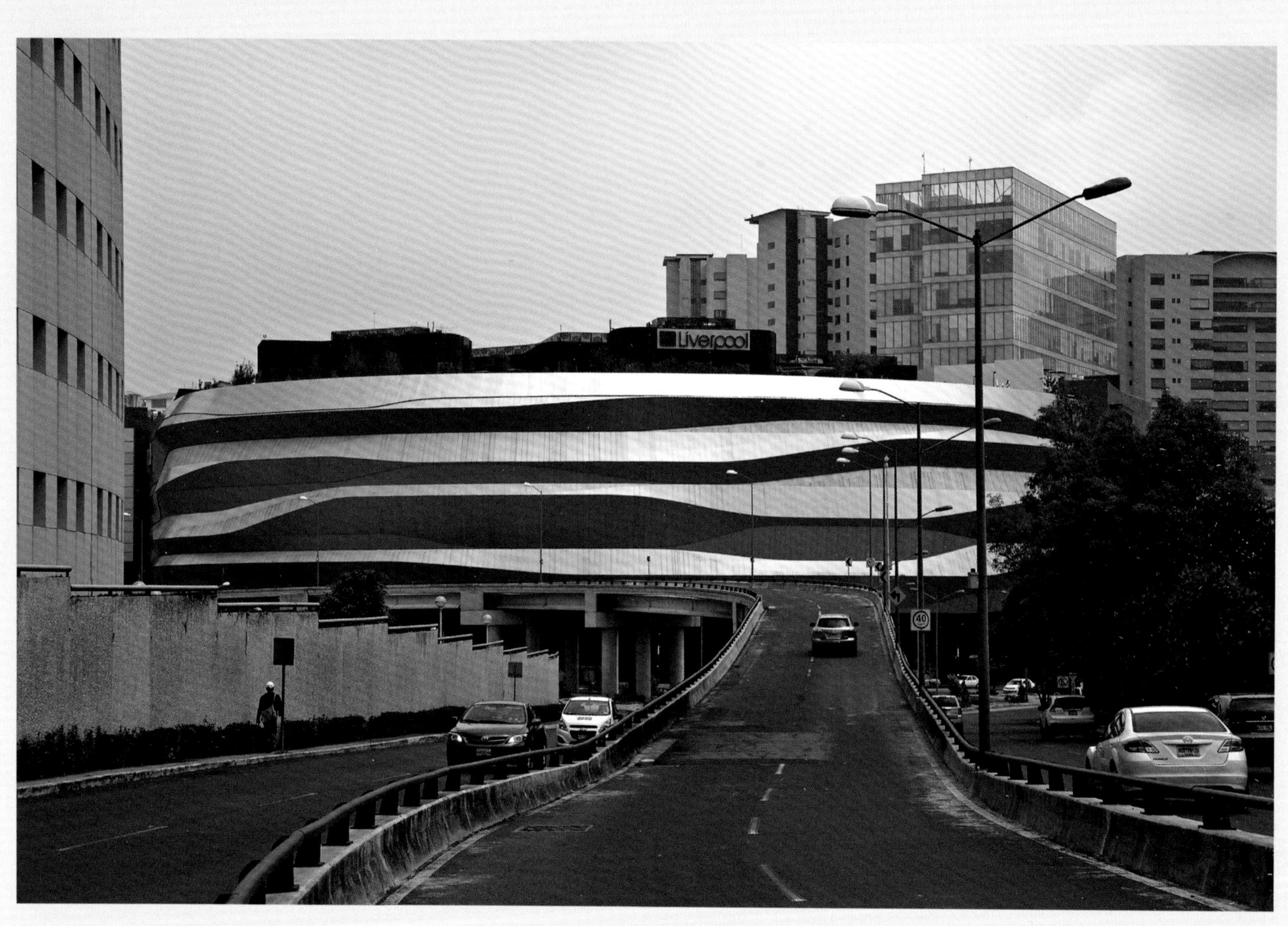

Four aspects structure my overview of the reception of Heinrich Wölfflin's *Kunstgeschichtliche Grundbegriffe* (*Principles of Art History*) in Mexico: the history of editions in Spanish; the intellectual obstacles to their reception; the tracing of implicit influences in research on baroque art in Mexico; and the contemporary potential of Wölfflin for transdisciplinary debates on the neobaroque in the twenty-first century.

Editions of the Spanish Translation

The Castilian translation of Wölfflin's work, *Conceptos fundamentales de la historia del arte*, is still a best seller in the Spanish-speaking discipline of art history. The first Spanish edition came out in 1924 in a series published by Espasa Calpe. By 1952 a third edition circulated among Mexican and other Latin American readers. Subsequent editions appeared in 1985 and 2007, and another publisher reprinted the book in 2002. The translator, José Moreno Villa, was a Spanish-born chemist, historian, and poet who studied in Germany, then emigrated to Mexico in 1937 to escape Franco's government. He lived and worked in Mexico until his death in 1955.[1] So there is a bio-bibliographical connection between the original book and its introduction to Iberian art historians and then to readers in Mexican universities, mainly at the Universidad Nacional Autónoma de México (UNAM), where the Laboratorio de Arte was founded in 1935 and renamed and extended in 1936 as the Instituto de Investigaciones Estéticas.

While other key texts of art historiography, such as Panofsky's writings, were translated and imported from Argentina during the second half of the twentieth century, Wölfflin's reception in Mexico was a product of postcolonial cultural relations between Mexico and Spain.[2] Moreno's translation became the standard edition for Spanish-speaking Latin America. Yet, despite these favorable conditions, the content of the book had a limited impact on humanities in Mexico. Only recently has *Grundbegriffe* become required reading for graduate students of art history at UNAM. There is, then, potential for the centenarian work.

Obstacles

There were four major obstacles to Wölfflin's reception in Mexico. First, his analytical and later depersonalized approach to artistic phenomena countered a Latin American tradition of poetic, almost emotional, art criticism and history, in which the artist's personality and mentality were often seen as catalysts to creative processes and their visual communication.[3] This is similar to nineteenth-century biographical art writing, a branch of belles lettres.

In his foreword to the 1985 Spanish edition of *Grundbegriffe*, Enrique Lafuente Ferrari complained about the "arid, aseptic ideal" of Wölfflin's art history without names. He discredited it as a "dehumanization" of the discipline, referring to a notion of Spanish philosopher Juan Ortega y Gasset, who equated abstraction with dehumanization.[4] However, Lafuente's rejection lacked a profound understanding of the original text, where Wölfflin clearly stated that there is no "objective seeing," only cultural and psychic determination of perception.[5] Lafuente's statement implicitly describes a racist stereotype: that Latin

3. Rojkind Arquitectos, Liverpool Interlomas, Mexico City, 2011
Photograph by Onnis Luque; courtesy of Daniel Escotto Editores

American art historians substitute emotional, literary descriptions for precise observation and verbalization of visual information. Nevertheless, there is an implicit tendency for philosophical imagination to overshadow the direct perception of the image itself. That is the second reason for Wölfflin's limited reception in Mexico. Yet one of the few Mexican philosophers who read and processed Wölfflin's ideas, Bolívar Echeverría, recognized in one of his books on the Latin American baroque that, while *Grundbegriffe* might be outmoded, it still offered "the most systematic description" of, and was thus "the indispensable theoretical reference for[,] all understanding of the baroque in the visual arts."[6]

The third obstacle was generated by the influence of historiography in aesthetic research. Innumerable Mexican art-historical publications still reduce the understanding of artistic phenomena to a reconstruction of historical facts. For example, the main art-historical institute, the Instituto de Investigaciones Estéticas, was named in parallel to the earlier historical institute, Instituto de Investigaciones Históricas. Art history was called aesthetic research, but the first generations of Mexican art historians all based their studies in historiographical thinking. Until recently, undergraduate students at UNAM interested in art history first had to study history and then specialize in the graduate program. Within this dominating conceptual framework, Wölfflin's abstract art-historical concept, focused on visual constructions and ways of seeing, was more or less neglected. For many Mexican authors writing on art, historiographical facts seemed to be more trustworthy than exposure to visual information and structural principles.

The extreme rejection of Wölfflinian formal analysis occurred when the social history of art was established in Mexico in the 1970s, for example, in the writings of Nicos Hadjinicolaou.[7] In the view of a left-wing, strictly determined social history of art, Wölfflin's concept was unjustly discredited as a boring, conservative, and

superseded history of style. We find a similar limitation in criticism of contemporary art. The approach to the complex conceptual messages of contemporary Mexican art is often reduced to the renarration of artists' myths and biographies, or to basic historical, political, social, or cultural knowledge of the subject matter of works of art.[8] The description of the visual communication of a contemporary art installation would be discarded as an unnecessary, backward-looking, conservative intellectual operation.

The fourth reason *Grundbegriffe* has not had a productive heritage in Mexico is a fixation on written sources for understanding art, that is, on iconography and iconology. Wölfflin's conceptual and most influential counterpart was Erwin Panofsky, who was introduced in Mexico via George Kubler's writings, published in 1939 and 1960.[9] However, the Panofskyan intellectual boom was based in a simplification of his complex thinking, focusing on his famous three-level interpretive scheme of iconography and iconology. In a similar instance of reduced complexity, Wölfflin's *Grundbegriffe* was not received as an integral concept of interpretation but rather used as a repository of isolated terms.

Reception

In spite of these obstacles, *Principles* did have a partial, fragmentary reception in Mexico, mainly in the research areas of pre-Hispanic and colonial baroque art and to a lesser degree in modern art. In the study of pre-Columbian art, Wölfflin's work was closely related to Wilhelm Worringer's *Abstraktion und Einfühlung* through the writings of the German émigré Paul Westheim, art critic of the expressionist period and editor of the journal *Kunstblatt*, who arrived in Mexico in 1941.[10] Research on Mesoamerican art faces the problem that there are no written sources other than the few surviving Maya codices. Therefore, formal analysis such as that of Wölfflin's *Grundbegriffe* did have a certain impact on this field. When Westheim came to Mexico, he began to study Mesoamerican artifacts as art, not as anthropological documents, as had been done until then. Influenced by his expressionist formation, he introduced into this area of study Worringer's ideas of *Abstraktion* and *Einfühlung* and, as a collateral effect, also Wölfflin's. Westheim's book on ancient Mexican art of 1950 and even more his *Ideas fundamentales del arte prehispánico en México* of 1957 promoted *Grundbegriffe* via Worringer.[11] The title "fundamental ideas" is an obvious allusion to Wölfflin, but in conceptual terms, the reception and actualization of Worringer dominates.

Eulalia Guzmán, in an article titled "Carácteres fundamentales del arte (indígena)," published in 1946, also alluded to *Grundbegriffe*.[12] Wölfflin's influence can be seen as well in Salvador Toscano's book *Arte precolombino de México y de la América Central* of 1944, reissued three times,[13] and Justino Fernández's *Coatlicue: Estética del arte indígena antiguo* of 1954.[14] While Toscano only "[took] advantage of Wölfflin…in general terms,"[15] Férnandez, who became the director of the Instituto de Investigaciones Estéticas in 1957, presented a detailed, 110-page bibliographical review of studies on Mesoamerican art, which confirmed the synergetic reception of Wölfflin, conditioned by Worringer. In the foreword, Samuel Ramos quoted Fernández, who stated that both German-speaking art historians had had a remarkable reception in Mexico, fusing "the naturalist formalism of Wölfflin" with the "psychologism of Worringer," applied mainly by Toscano and Westheim.[16] Fernández characterized the latter as a "man well trained in the ideas of Wölfflin and Worringer" whose interpretations of art depended on the "will to form."[17]

In the remainder of this essay I will not go into the details and conceptual roots of absurd terms like "naturalist formalism," the expressionist "psychologism" of art, or even Riegl's "will to form" but will concentrate on the limited reception of Wölfflin in Mexico. Indeed, as the expert in Mesoamerican art Durdica Segota writes,

the "will to form" became an attractive but almost empty formula of interpretation for Mexican researchers.[18] And of Wölfflin's antagonist key terms, only "closed form" and "open form" are frequently used—a general observation based on my teaching experience in Mexico. But basically, experts on Mesoamerican art no longer read Wölfflin; in some cases they quote this important book second hand. And in the 1970s, the intellectual fashion of semiotics overshadowed Wölfflin's method of visual analysis, which then was devalued as empty "formalism."

Research on baroque art in Mexico reveals similar problems with the reception of *Grundbegriffe*, mainly because of the Worringer-Wölfflin nexus, which indeed represents a misunderstanding of the latter's position. Yet, in this field of research these two figures also legitimized the nationalist encoding of the baroque in the former Spanish viceroyalty. Fernández, who wrote extensively on baroque and modern as well as indigenous art, stated that "Wölfflin's formalism and Worringer's 'will to form'" were antecedents of the nationalist understanding of Mexican baroque art by Manuel Toussaint, director of the Instituto from 1939 until his death in 1955.[19] As a witness to the Mexican Revolution, Toussaint developed an interest in redefining the cultural heritage of his country in terms of a normative national and revolutionary identity, which he found in the baroque art of New Spain. So, explicitly, Wölfflin was used to support an ideological construction of post-revolutionary Mexican art historiography. Although his Eurocentric *Grundbegriffe* did not address the different baroque expressions of the Americas, his analytical apparatus would have been useful for describing the New World mestizo baroque, in which decorative elements dominated the structural expression of buildings and hybrids of imported ornaments and indigenous applied arts traditions created an almost anarchic, subversive, antimonarchic style.[20] This "barroco de Indias," manifested in architecture, visual arts, theater, and literature, became fundamental material on which to base cultural identities in the Americas.[21]

The Italian Emilio Cecchi was the first European art historian to recognize this potential, in a book on Mexican art published in 1948. Cecchi was surprised by the "richness of the ultrabaroque"; but, limited by his Eurocentric view, based on Wölfflin and Nietzsche, he also rejected this art as an "expression of the instinct," using the cliché of the irrational Latin American.[22] Beyond these stereotyped, implicitly racist evaluations, Cecchi created an interesting conceptual synergy of two different but conceptually related ways of thinking about the viceregal baroque: Wölfflin's and Friedrich Nietzsche's understandings of the baroque style. In his short but influential text "Vom Barockstile" of 1878, Nietzsche had claimed the baroque as an antidote of heterogeneity against the homogeneous Hegelian concept of linear, rational progress.[23] His "preference for unconformity and contradiction," even the recognition of the "dramatic tensions," "the strong passions and gestures, of the ugly-sublime," coined the terms of an alternative understanding of the New World baroque.[24] Nietzsche's ideas on the baroque affected Walter Benjamin's critique of progress, Eugenio d'Ors's transhistorical concept of plural baroque expressions in different cultures—and Wölfflin's focus on the differentiation between seemingly rational Renaissance and apparently irrational baroque forms.[25] This complexity is inherent in the Mexican debates on the mestizo baroque as an expression of national identity. Again, Wölfflin cannot be profiled as a key figure, as we have seen in the Wölfflin-Worringer relationship. In this case Wölfflin's conceptual potential is perceived through the discursive power of another philosopher or art historian.[26]

The Mexican nationalist encoding of the viceregal baroque was also promoted by the artist Gerardo Murillo, known as Dr. Atl. In the six-volume work he wrote and edited on Mexican baroque churches, published in 1924–1927, the term "*ultra*baroque" expresses the difference of the Mexican

from the European monarchic-Catholic baroque.[27] This altered use of a nineteenth-century stylistic term serves not analytical but ideological purposes—and indeed has almost no reference to Wölfflin's concept. However, even Dr. Atl's rehabilitation of the Latin American baroque implicitly recalls Wölfflin's own change from disdain for the baroque in *Renaissance und Barock* of 1888 to the more rational evaluation of this style in *Kunstgeschichtliche Grundbegriffe* almost thirty years later.[28] In one of his books, Atl captured the "morbidity" and "flourishing monstrous" spirit of a baroque altarpiece in Santa Clara in Querétaro as a "sense of *bello pittorico*"[29] (figs. 1 and 2).

The modern vanguard artist's rediscovery of the complex, contradictory, and picturesque beauty of baroque art recalls Jakob von Falke's *Geschichte des modernen Geschmacks*, published in 1866, where he depicts baroque as irregularity, attractive even for the vanguard art of his time.[30] Later, *Grundbegriffe* reanimated this notion. Wölfflin's book must be also revisited in the context of European vanguard art of its time. And there we find its considerable impact on debates about Mexican baroque and neobaroque. Although the reception of *Grundbegriffe* as a methodological handbook was indeed very limited in the field of Mexican baroque studies, the inherent conceptual energy that anarchic baroque form represents for contemporary art and for ideological constructions of national identity have persisted right up to the present. The seemingly decadent, irregular, and irrational visual language of the mestizo baroque fed the artistic and ideological imagination of later generations.[31]

Potential

Recent interdisciplinary research on the topicality of the baroque in the twenty-first century, such as a research project on the neobaroque at the University of Western Ontario, signals a revival of Wölfflin's *Grundbegriffe* after a hundred years.[32] The book's persisting impact lies in the fact

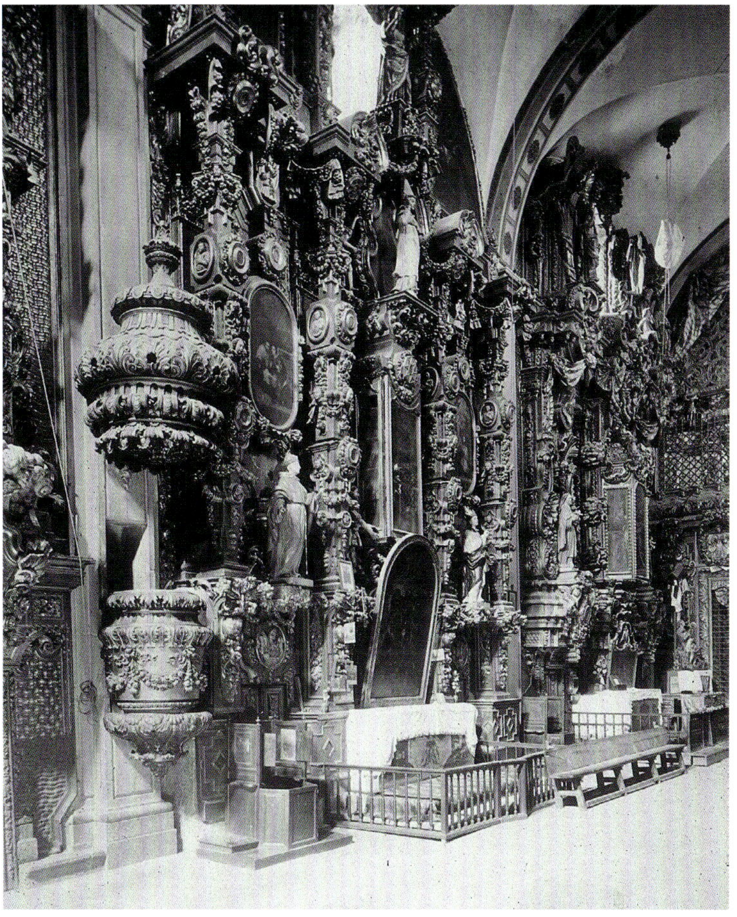

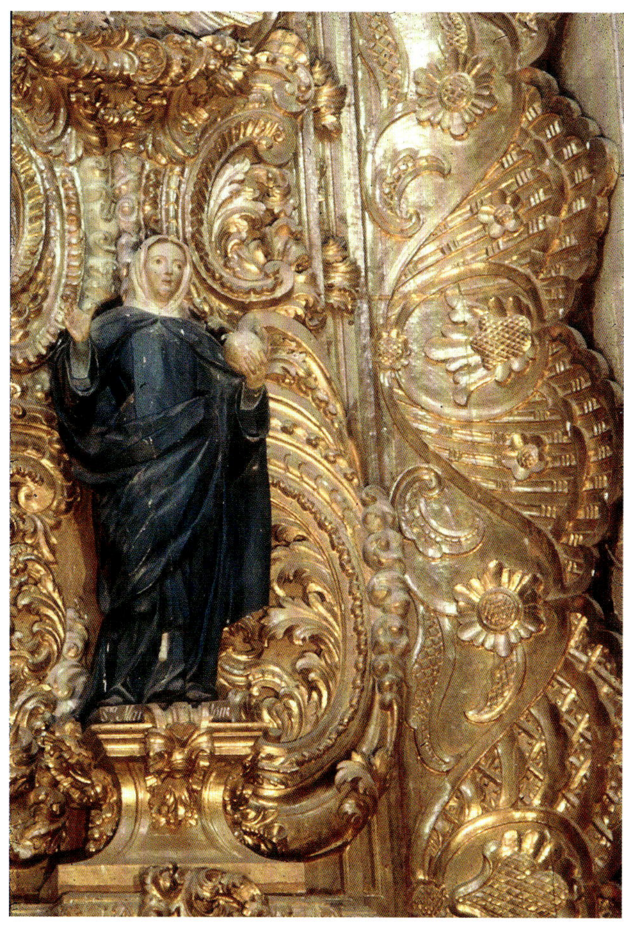

that traditional stylistic and iconographic research on the baroque has been sustained by a complex understanding of the patterns of visual communication, the paradigms of seeing.[33] Yet contemporary studies may focus less on Wölfflin's concepts of art-historical interpretation than on terminology. This perspective often leads to an arbitrary, vague understanding of the transhistorical and transcultural phenomena of the so-called neobaroque. The binomial terminology of *Grundbegriffe*, but also many other terminological inventions in the book, serve to describe the architectural "reemergence of baroque traditions and forms of expression" in the late twentieth and early twenty-first centuries.[34]

I have analyzed elsewhere how postmodern and neobaroque production of architecture through images and "views" (*Ansichten* in German) coincide with baroque principles captured in *Grundbegriffe*.[35] The dissolution of tectonic forms, generating a complex order, oscillating between light effects and aleatory design patterns on facades—these and other characteristics of Wölfflin's reading of historical baroque architecture apply to spectacular contemporary neobaroque architecture (fig. 3 and essay frontispiece).[36] Moreover, the "transformation of fixed form into flowing form," which he detected in Roman baroque architecture, anticipated the visual ideology of early twenty-first-century blob architecture.[37]

Thus, the content and research methodology of Wölfflin's writing on the Roman baroque are apt for updating in another, related field of recent art and architectural history: the Latin American neobaroque, contextualized in the aesthetically and socially degenerate megalopolis.[38] Here we can trace an unexpected and even contradictory transcultural and transhistorical effect of Wölfflin's description of excessive

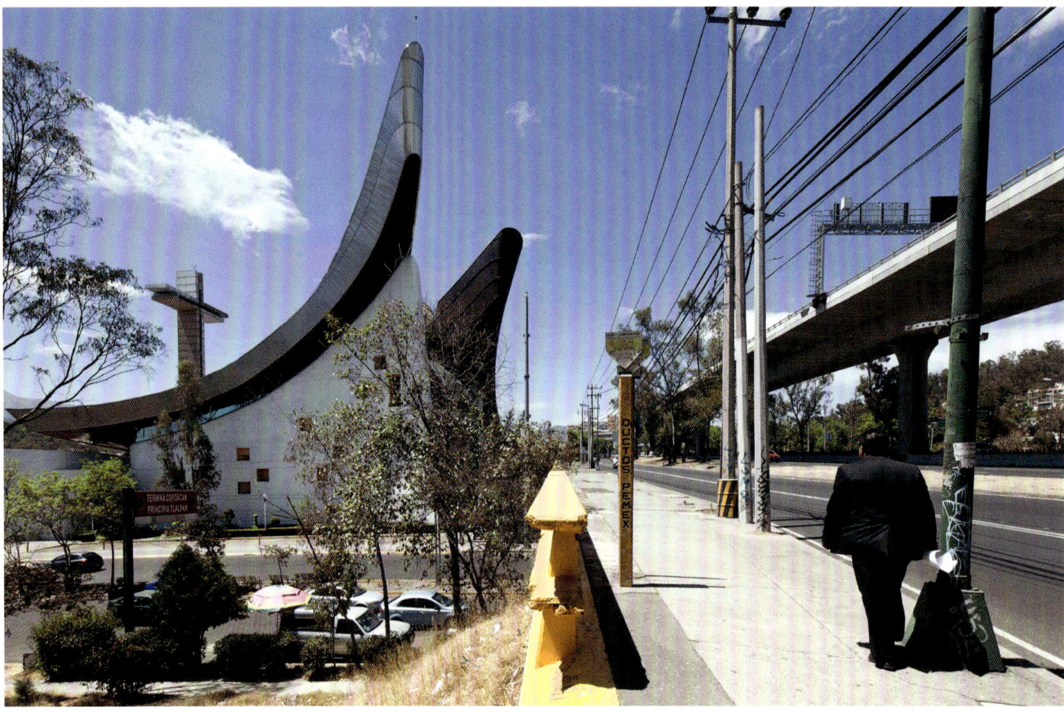

and impressive baroque forms. European baroque, with the characteristic elements analyzed in *Grundbegriffe*, becomes "the ideal medium for transculturation."[39] And many of the terms that Wölfflin established subsequently in art historiography are suitable for explaining phenomena of contemporary cultural crisis, as expressed in the unstable and often spectacular imagery of the neobaroque megalopolis. Wölfflin's sustainable terminology, valid even after a century and adaptable to contemporary understanding, allows a monarchic and Catholic form (the historic baroque) to be related to the anarchic, excessive imagery of the twenty-first-century neobaroque. Contemporary scholars can even widen the limited scope of genre in *Grundbegriffe* (painting, sculpture, and architecture) toward a complex analysis of hyperurban imaginaries in the twenty-first century.[40]

These potential transhistorical transfers recall Wölfflin's own relation to the vanguard art and culture of his time. Whereas his view was clearly Eurocentric, today's world art history should include Latin American (and other world arts') expressions of baroque and neobaroque. Here the established terminology of *Grundbegriffe* can provide useful tools for understanding the visual constructions of the "ex-centric" Latin American modernity of the twentieth century, inspired by subversive adaptation of colonial baroque formulas to alternative "cultural revision and renewal."[41] It is clearly beyond the scope of *Grundbegriffe* to provide an understanding of how European colonial baroque was altered into the Latin American "anti-institutional baroques,"[42] but a creative and anarchic reading of Wölfflin's work after one hundred years, from a Mexican perspective, may provide insight.

Spanish and Latin American baroque were blind spots in Wölfflin's academic work, and Euro- and US-centered art historiography do not compensate for this lack. This problematic situation can be corrected even within the framework of an hommage to one of the most influential books in art history, distributed globally from its Swiss-German point of origin. Reactivating *Grundbegriffe* in the process of including Latin American art history in the US and European canon with equal recognition would prevent the petrification of an established academic "classic."

Wölfflin's art historiography conceived the "history of seeing," and this conceptual heritage unfolds inspiration for the complex knowledge production of not only Mexican but global neobaroque cultures. His formal typology can be converted into an epistemological instrument for interpreting the visual symptoms of the reality crisis of the present.[43] In this sense, rereading *Grundbegriffe* helps us to understand and criticize contemporary baroque symptoms and phenomena such as ontological instability, complex hybridity, irritating metamorphosis, polycentered expressivity, and ephemeral spectacle—all modes of "visual delusion" in postutopian cultures and societies.[44]

NOTES

1. José Moreno Villa, *Vida en claro: Autobiographia* (Mexico City, 1944; reprinted 1976); *José Moreno Villa (1887–1955)*, ed. Juan Pérez de Ayala (Madrid, 1987).

2. For example, Erwin Panofsky, *El significado en las artes visuales* (*Meaning in the Visual Arts*), Biblioteca de diseño y artes visuales, vol. 7 (Buenos Aires, 1970). The term "postcolonial" refers here not to postcolonial theory but to the autonomous intellectual construction of Mexico after independence from Spain beginning in the early nineteenth century.

3. On Wölfflin's approach to artistic phenomena see Gabriele Wimböck, "Im Bilde: Heinrich Wölfflin (1864–1945)," in *Ideengeschichte der Bildwissenschaft*, ed. Jörg Probst and Jost Philipp Klenner (Frankfurt am Main, 2009), 97–98.

4. Enrique Lafuente Ferrari, "Palabras liminares," in Heinrich Wölfflin, *Conceptos fundamentales de la historia del arte*, foreword by Enrique Lafuente Ferrari, trans. José Moreno Villa (Madrid, 2007, earlier editions 1924, 1997), 13. José Ortega y Gassett, *La deshumanización del arte: Ideas sobre la novela* (Madrid, 1925; republished as *La deshumanización del arte y otros ensayos de estética*, foreword by Valeriano Bozal (Madrid, 1987). Heinrich Wölfflin, *Kunstgeschichtliche Grundbegriffe: Das Problem der Stilentwicklung in der neueren Kunst* (5th ed., Munich, 1921), IX.

5. Wölfflin, *Kunstgeschtliche Grundbegriffe* (1921), XI ("In jeder neuen Sehform kristallisiert sich ein neuer Inhalt der Welt") and 1.

6. Bolívar Echeverría, *La modernidad de lo barroco* (Mexico City, 2013; 1st ed., 1998), 108n8.

7. Nicos Hadjinicolaou, *Historia del arte y lucha de clases* (Mexico City, 1975). Peter Krieger, "Words Don't Come Easy: Comentarios a la crítica y exposición de las artes plásticas actuales," *Universidad de México*, nos. 597–598 (October–November 2000): 25–29.

8. Krieger, "Words Don't Come Easy."

9. George Kubler, *The Shape of Time: Remarks on the History of Things* (New Haven, 1962), and *Studies in Ancient American and European Art: The Collected Essays of George Kubler* (New Haven, 1960).

10. By Paul Westheim: *Obras maestras del México antiguo* (Mexico City, 1985); *Arte antiguo de México* (Madrid, 1988). About Paul Westheim: Bernd Fechner and York-Egbert König, *Paul Westheim: Kunstkritiker—Publizist—Sammler* (Berlin, 2015); Ines Rotermund-Reynard, "'Dieses ist ein Land, in dem ein Kunstmensch leben kann': Der Kunstkritiker Paul Westheim im Prozess der Akkulturation während der französischen und mexikanischen Emigration, 1933–1963" (diss., Freie Universität Berlin, 2007). On Westheim's wife, Mariana Frenk-Westheim, who translated Westheim's and Worringer's writings into Spanish, see Peter Krieger, "In memoriam Mariana Frenk Westheim," *Anales del Instituto de Investigaciones Estéticas* 86 (2005): 219–225.

11. Paul Westheim, *Arte antiguo de México*, trans. Mariana Frenk-Westheim (Mexico City and Buenos Aires, 1950), and *Ideas fundamentales del arte prehispánico en México*, trans. Mariana Frenk-Westheim (Mexico City and Buenos Aires, 1957).

12. Eulalia Guzmán, "Carácteres fundamentales del arte (indígena): México prehispánico," in *México prehispánico: Culturas; deidades; monumentos; antología de "Esta Semana, This Week" 1935–1946*, ed. Emma Hurtado (Mexico City, 1946).

13. Salvador Toscano, *Arte precolombino de México y de la América Central* (Mexico City, 1952; 3rd ed., 1970).

14. Justino Fernández, *Coatlicue: Estética del arte indígena antiguo* (Mexico City, 1954). A second edition was published in 1959 and a third as *Estética del arte mexicano: Coatlicue, El Retablo de los Reyes, El Hombre* (Mexico City, 1990). Subsequent citations are to the first edition.

15. Fernández, *Coatlicue*, 68 and 102.

16. Samuel Ramos, foreword to Fernández, *Coatlique*, 29 (quotation from Fernández's text, 109).

17. Fernández, *Coatlicue*, 108.

18. Interview with Durdica Segota, research professor (*investigadora*), Instituto de Investigaciones Estéticas, UNAM, March 2015.

19. Fernández, *Coatlicue*, 273.

20. Monika Kaup, *Neobaroque in the Americas: Alternative Modernities in Literature, Visual Art, and Film*, New World Series, ed. J. Michael Dash (Charlottesville, VA, 2012), 249–272.

21. Walter Moser, "The Concept of Baroque," in "La constitución del barroco hispánico: Problemas y acercamientos," special issue, *Revista canadiense de estudios hispánicos*, 33, no. 1 (fall 2008): 19.

22. Emilio Cecchi, *Messico* (Florence, 1948); Fernández, *Coatlicue*, chapter entitled "Críticos e historiadores extranjeros del siglo XX," 323.

23. Friedrich Nietzsche, "Vom Barockstile," in *Sämtliche Werke: Kritische Studienausgabe in fünfzehn Bänden*, vol. 2, *Menschliches-Allzumenschliches I und II*, ed. Giorgio Colli and Mazzino Montinaria (Berlin, 1980), 437–439.

24. Lois Parkinson Zamora and Monika Kaup, eds., *Baroque New Worlds: Representation, Transculturation, Counterconquest* (Durham, NC, 2010), 5, 44 (translation by Monika Kaup).

25. Zamora and Kaup, *Baroque New Worlds*, 42.

26. Wölfflin was transferred to Mexico also by the Spanish professor Diego Angulo Íñiguez, head of the Laboratorio de Arte in Seville in the mid-1920s; however, he represented a backward-oriented, one-dimensional, and nationalist Spanish art historiography of his time. Later, in the 1980s, Clara Bargellini, research professor (*investigadora*) at the Instituto de Investigaciones Estéticas, UNAM, trained in the United States (PhD, Harvard University), introduced Wölfflin in her seminars on Mexican baroque, as an alternative to iconography.

27. Gerardo Murillo, ed., *Iglesias de México*, 6 vols. (Mexico City, 1924–1927), vol. 3, *Tipos ultrabarrocos, Valle de México*. Murillo's intention was to recodify the Mexican Catholic baroque heritage as an autonomous cultural creation, worthy of preservation in the antimonarchic, antireligious postrevolutionary system of the 1920s. Justino Fernández (*Coatlicue*, 258), regarded this publication as an important advance in art-historical research on the specific configuration of the baroque in New Spain (Mexico).

28. Martin Warnke, "Die Entstehung des Barockbegriffes in der Kunstgeschichte," in *Europäische Barock-Rezeption*, ed. Klaus Garber, Wolfenbütteler Arbeiten zur Barockforschung, vol. 20 (Wiesbaden, 1994), 1222.

29. Gerardo Murillo (Dr. Atl), quoted in Fernández, *Coatlicue*, 261.

30. Warnke, "Die Entstehung des Barockbegriffes," 1221–1222, referring to von Falke's notion of baroque as breaking the rules, liberating the "energy of the particular form" beyond normative aesthetics.

31. Warnke ("Die Entstehung des Barockbegriffes," 1223), states that the encounter of late nineteenth-century vanguard and baroque art would not have been productive in the twentieth century. Yet the debates on the Latin American neobaroque confirm that this synergy created revitalized forms of cultural identity.

32 See *Neo-Baroques: From Latin America to the Hollywood Blockbuster*, ed. Walter Moser, Angela Ndalianis, and Peter Krieger (Leiden and Boston, 2017).

33. Wölfflin provided a basis for thematizing the paradigms of seeing in neobaroque cultures in Christine Buci-Glucksmann's *Baroque Reason* (London, 1994; originally published in French, 1984) and *Madness of Vision: On Baroque Aesthetics* (Athens, OH, 2013). See also Moser, "The Concept of Baroque," 15.

34. Zamora and Kaup, *Baroque New Worlds*, 1–2.

35. Peter Krieger, "Notre Dame du Périphérique: Identidad visual de la iglesia católica en la mega-Ciudad de México," in *La imagen sagrada y sacralizada*, ed. Peter Krieger, XXVIII coloquio internacional de historia del arte (Mexico City, 2011), 345–373; "Arquitectura contemporánea para el culto católico en México: Estrategias de investigación e interpretación" and introduction, in *Sacralización, culto y religiosidad en la nueva arquitectura latinoamericana: 1960–2010*, ed. Peter Krieger and Iván San Martín (Mexico City, 2009), 12–25; "Form Follows Effect: Principles of Baroque Impression Management in Contemporary Mexican Catholic Church Architecture (an Implicit Homage to Wölfflin)," in *The Invention of Baroque: Visualized Paradoxes of a Corporate Identity*, ed. Jens Baumgarten (São Paulo, forthcoming).

36. Wölfflin, *Kunstgeschichtliche Grundbegriffe* (1921), 69, 71, 76, 78, 127, 129, and 169; Peter Krieger, *Epidemias visuales: El Neobarroco de Las Vegas en la Ciudad de México / Visual Epidemics: Las Vegas Neo-Baroque in Mexico City* (Mexico City, 2017).

37. Wölfflin, *Kunstgeschichtliche Grundbegriffe* (1921), 162: "Umbildung der starren Form in die flüssige Form."

38. Krieger, *Epidemias visuales*.

39. Kaup, *Neobaroque in the Americas*, 255.

40. Peter Krieger, "Aesthetics and Anthropology of Megacities—A New Field of Art Historical Research," in *Cannibalisme disciplinaire: Histoire de l'art et anthropologie*, ed. Thierry Dufrêne (Paris, 2009), 197–211; "L'Image de la mégalopole: Comprendre la complexité visuelle de Mexico," *Diogène: Revue internationale des sciences humaines* (UNESCO), no. 231 (July–September 2010): 74–89; "Spiel-Regeln der Megastadt und der Gegenwartskunst in Mexiko," in *Künste und Regelwerk*, ed. Hans Rudolf Reust, Peter J. Schneemann, and Anselm Stalder (Munich, 2013), 131–142; "Megalópolis México—perspectivas críticas," in *Megalópolis: La modernización de la ciudad de México en el siglo XX*, ed. Peter Krieger (Mexico City, 2006), 27–54.

41. Kaup, *Neobaroque in the Americas*, 270, 271, 260; Zamora and Kaup, *Baroque New Worlds*, 7, 8, 9, 10.

42. Kaup, *Neobaroque in the Americas*, 253.

43. Moser, Ndalianis, and Krieger, *Neo-Baroques: From Latin America to the Hollywood Blockbuster*.

44. Moser, Ndalianis, and Krieger, *Neo-Baroques*, 25; "visual delusion": Niklas Luhmann, *Die Kunst der Gesellschaft* (Frankfurt am Main, 1997), 383.

PAUL BINSKI

The Reception of Principles of Art History
in England

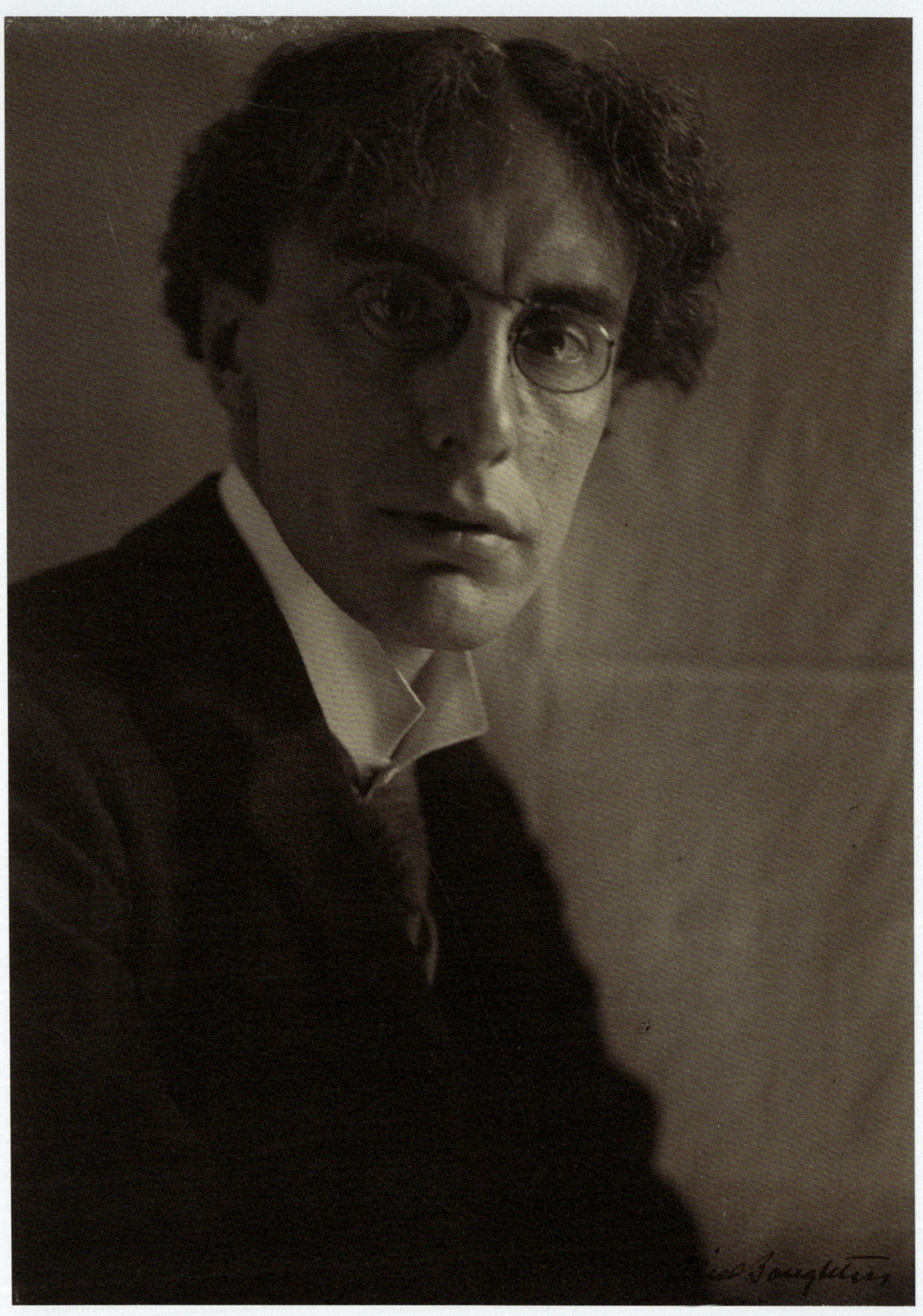

According to Michael Podro, Heinrich Wölfflin was "explicitly concerned with the construction of critical systems."[1] His reception in England, however, was anything but systematic and, as I shall suggest, was a response far more of individual historians and critics and of small groups than of institutions.

Early Reception: Fry, Clark, and Read

The coterie, the "invisible college," has always mattered in the English intellectual and critical tradition and with it the conversation of friends and allies. Indeed, English reception of Heinrich Wölfflin's work started in earnest with a member of one such coterie, the Bloomsbury group: the critic, artist, and art guru Roger Fry (1866–1934) (fig. 1). In the December 1903 number of *The Athenaeum*, Fry had reviewed Wölfflin's *Die klassische Kunst* (1899), there retitled for English readers as *The Art of the Italian Renaissance* and more generally known by the title *Classic Art*.[2] Fry's main concern in this review was more the canon than method: to him, Wölfflin was rehabilitating the art of the Seicento, lost from sight in accounts of the Renaissance since Jacob Burckhardt's *Die Kultur der Renaissance in Italien* (1860). The Quattrocento had abandoned the grand style, the sublime, for the sweet, rational middle style; but then Leonardo, Raphael, and Michelangelo restored "greatness," religious idealism, the power of "condensation" or concentration of effect. From an English perspective, Fry spotted in Wölfflin a rehabilitation of the grand manner of Sir Joshua Reynolds.

Canonicity of period style remained an issue for Fry when he returned in 1921 to review *Principles* itself, in *The Burlington Magazine* under "The Baroque."[3] From the point of view of its dissemination outside Germany, *Principles* had had the serious misfortune to appear just after the outbreak of war in 1914, so Fry was reviewing the fourth edition (1920), the first available to him. (He remarked that a book that had already sold twenty thousand copies in Germany might stretch to only two thousand in sales in England.) By this time Fry considered Wölfflin "the only writer I get ideas from."[4] He was interested in Wölfflin's method, his philosophy, which he duly set out in the review. Not only was Wölfflin post-Burckhardtian: it was *Principles* that "first made evident the general principles involved" in understanding the formal differences between Renaissance and baroque art. What mattered even more for Fry was "[u]nderstanding of the problems of the creator," knowing "what mental conditions in the artist's mind are implied by [a] configuration."[5] By now Fry himself wrote with great certainty as a formalist, one who held the conviction, in Michael Fried's words, that "all persons capable of experiencing aesthetic emotion in front of painting…are responding when they do so to relations of pure form."[6] In discussing *Principles* Fry took issue with Wölfflin's insistence that baroque "principles" were fundamentally northern or Germanic; he agreed with Wölfflin's method of seeing the same visual principles as operative in the sister arts; and he underlined the importance of the transition from tactile to optical values whose roots went back at least to Georg Wilhelm Friedrich Hegel's lectures on aesthetics, and in which Alois Riegl, Bernard Berenson, and others also showed

1. Alice Boughton, *Roger Fry*, c. 1900, platinum print
© *National Portrait Gallery, London*

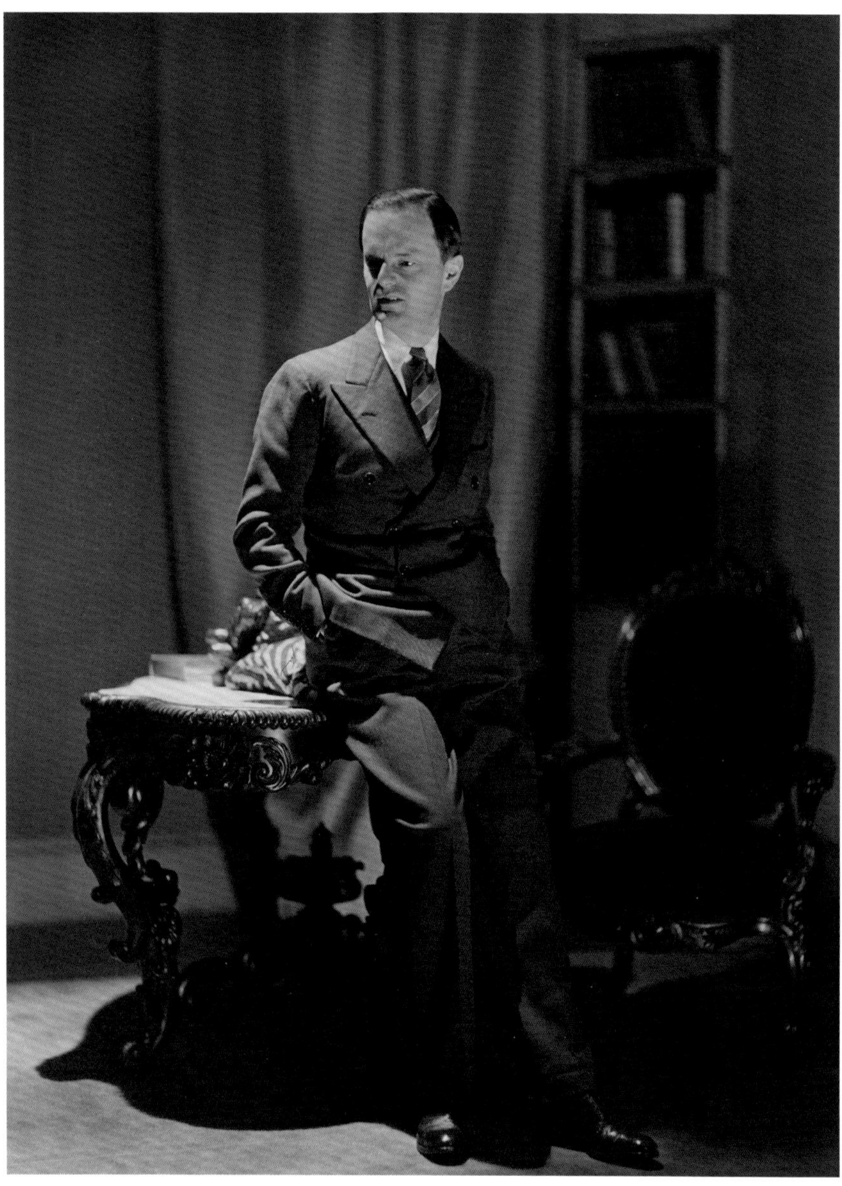

2. Howard Coster, *Kenneth Clark, Baron Clark*, 1934, film negative
© National Portrait Gallery, London

formalist art criticism, for instance, Jacqueline Falkenheim suggests that it is hard to trace direct influence on Fry of such writers as Konrad Fiedler and Adolf von Hildebrand and claims too that Fry struggled to read German.[9] Yet clearly there was some affinity. And it is clear that in some of his last writing Fry specifically followed the authority of Wölfflin, for example, in his Slade Lectures, given in Cambridge in 1933–1934:

But in the Hellenistic period which follows after the conquests of Alexander there occur definite changes in style, some of which are of interest to us.… The result of this was, I think, a heightening of the plastic sensibility in these later artists, a clearer understanding of what are the possibilities of plastic expression. The poses become freer, with a greater sense of the balance of opposing inclinations of planes, and at times the sculptors became aware of the possibilities of chiaroscuro — they discovered the baroque.[10]

In Wölfflin, Fry had found encouragement or authorization for beliefs about form and psychology rather than scope for the wholesale transfer of a system. Such pre-1920 essays by Fry as "The Artist's Vision" and "An Essay in Aesthetics," writes Falkenheim, "deal with problems of perception and the attempt to find concrete structural principles to equal the aesthetic experience, which must have been conditioned, or at least encouraged, by contemporary German aesthetic speculation": one instance is Fry's writings on Cézanne, in which he notes the "utmost parallelism of the objects to the picture plane."[11] "An Essay in Aesthetics" illustrates this type of affinity and discusses the "emotional elements of designs" in terms of rhythm, line, mass, space, light and shade, color, and the inclination of the eye to a plane — only the last adumbrating *Principles*.[12] Yet such ideas were not solely derived from Wölfflin. Some of them could also have developed from Berenson's widely consulted *Italian Painters of the Renaissance* (1896), in which Berenson finds "life enhancement" in tactile values, movement, spatial composition, and color, or so-called ideated sensations.[13]

much interest.[7] But he was not entirely wedded to Wölfflin's general views of historical development as a history of polarities or of Renaissance and baroque expression as clearly opposed. For Fry, history was a process of gathering, of enrichment, as well as of cyclical abandonment and return; to him the relationship of a work of art to its context was never clear.[8]

There was clearly a distinction between providing an exposition of Wölfflin's ideas or sympathizing with some of them, and actually deploying his method systematically. In her study of Fry and the beginnings of

In regard to intellectual lineage, Wölfflin as read after 1920 was clearly one part of a complex mix, and this remained true of his reception in England down to the end of the twentieth century. What had been at stake for Fry above all was Wölfflin's setting aside of the old empiricism of art history and his new emphasis on mind, form, and empathy. Wölfflin showed why form and psychology are serious and also historical issues and why art history itself might be taken seriously. Even so, between 1921 and the early 1930s and the establishment of the Courtauld and Warburg Institutes in London in 1932–1933, critical reception of *Principles* was not broadly based. For example, in 1970 the critic Adrian Stokes (1902–1972) wrote to Richard Wollheim: "You were asking about influences. I have been thinking whether I can help more. Of Hildebrand I didn't know at the relevant times nor, shamefully, many of the Germans, nor even of Wölfflin till the late thirties."[14]

Reception was certainly furthered by the publication, with Fry's encouragement, of Marie Hottinger's 1932 English translation, which coincided, significantly, with the opening of the Courtauld Institute at Portman Square in October 1932, the first reading lists of which demonstrate immediate dissemination of Wölfflin's work.[15] We find it energized at the same time by a young, patrician figure whose stance was defiantly "Continental," namely Kenneth Clark (1903–1983), made director of the National Gallery in London at the age of thirty in 1933 (fig. 2). Three years earlier Clark had been invited by Tancred Borenius to deliver two lectures at University College London, and his topics were the German art historian Alois Riegl, and Wölfflin.[16] The invitation came about partly because of Clark's contacts with Roger Fry, whom Clark regarded highly. In a distinctly double-edged remark, Clark described *Principles* as "much the best choice because Wölfflin is what is rare in German speculative writers—perfectly sane and level headed."[17] Clark, as his early interest in the Gothic Revival shows, was basically Ruskinian in outlook, though it

was exactly John Ruskin's moralism that twentieth-century formalists were repudiating. Ruskin himself, once the most influential critic of his time, generally disavowed German theory, but not so Clark, who was perhaps closer to Walter Pater, who had certainly read Hegel. Clark read German and began as an undergraduate with the works of Alois Riegl, going to Germany in 1926. Though by his own admission Germany was very much not his "spiritual home," Clark said: "Realising that almost all writers on philosophy and the history of art who had influenced me deeply—Hegel, Schopenhauer, Jacob Burckhardt, Wölfflin, Riegl, Dvořák—had all been German or German-trained…[I] later made a determined effort to soak myself in German culture, and spent almost the whole of one long vacation in Dresden and Munich."[18] In his lecture on *Principles*, Clark wasted no time in calling Wölfflin "by common consent, the best living writer on art."[19] Yet he did not endorse the writer entirely. He noted that Wölfflin's claim about the formal coherence of the arts in any visual epoch was not supported by his own tendency to take examples of painting from northern Europe and examples of sculpture and architecture from Italy—so raising the suspicion that his theory was not as coherent or universal as it claimed.

What mattered in this early assimilation of *Principles* was the larger claim about the standing and practice of art history more generally: that patrician, humanist, and value-driven art history and the "aesthetic" upper-class tendency to effeteness or "sensitive reading" in English art appreciation needed to be replaced by something more ambitious and rigorous, something less like criticism and more like a value-free science. Matthew Potter remarks: "Clark's lectures on Riegl and Wölfflin from 1930 represent the first attempt at self-reflective engagement with the middle years of the tradition of German critical historians of art by a British scholar."[20] Indeed, as Sam Rose has observed, what matters in Clark's lectures is that they mark an early point in the identification of *both* Riegl and Wölfflin as

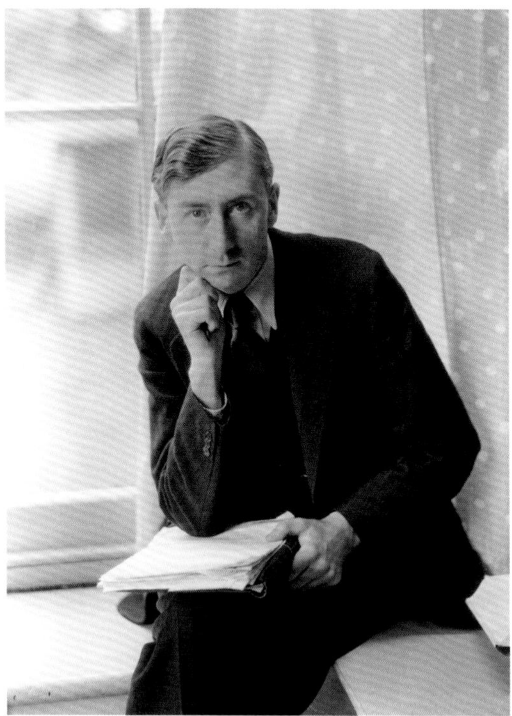

"canonical" authorities. Riegl's works were not to be translated into English until later in the century.[21] The point is that *Principles* remained part of a critical mix that also included Riegl, and that, for all its idealism, appealed strongly to English empiricism.

Clark's general view was endorsed in a 1933 review of the new English translation of *Principles* in *The Burlington Magazine* by the critic Hubert D. Waley (1892–1968).[22] According to Waley, Wölfflin had replaced a hierarchism of value by a sort of pendulum of style; he had substituted "analysis and definition" for "arrogance and declamation"; the aesthetician or critic was no longer a high priest or prophet but a scientist, for reading Wölfflin was like watching a chemistry experiment. As Waley concluded, "The first problem which meets us is why certain arrangements of form have the power of producing certain states of mind."[23] Further acclaim is found in a review article on Wölfflin by the art historian and keeper at the British Museum, Roger Hinks (1903–1966). Hinks saw Wölfflin's work as part of "a revolt of scientific history" against a "Procrustean scale of classic values." *Principles* was an "epoch-making" contribution to the "campaign against criticism" immediately recognized as "a masterpiece and a model of historical method," he wrote. "Wölfflin immediately disclaimed any interest in value: which is as much as to say that he dissociated himself from criticism."[24]

The same high regard for Wölfflin's impact and scientific seriousness is apparent in Herbert Read's introduction to a new edition of *Die klassische Kunst* published in 1952, seven years after Wölfflin's death: according to Read, Wölfflin "had found art criticism a subjective chaos and left it a science."[25] Read (1893–1968; fig. 3), an influential aesthetician and critic and a more incisive thinker than Clark, had familiarized himself with the writings of Wölfflin, Riegl, Max Dvořák, Wilhelm Worringer, and Benedetto Croce for his study *Education through Art* (1943), researched when he was a Leon Fellow at the University of London in 1940–1942. Designed for schoolteachers, its purpose was to place art at the center of education in such a way that their art could afford psychological insight into children as "types." For Read, Wölfflin's "objective contrasts" "have their origin in subjective factors that correspond to distinctive psychological types," which Read explored with reference to such theorists as Carl Jung, Sigmund Freud, and especially Ernst Kretschmer.[26] Read was an important figure in the reception of Wölfflin because he had started to use both his and Riegl's ideas in such works as *The Meaning of Art* (1931) and in his articles in the widely read periodicals *The Times Literary Supplement* and *The Listener*. In the latter in 1930, for instance, he had remarked that the character of art was due to the "will to form which is a reflection of the artist's personality," a formula manifestly borrowed from Riegl, in whom Read may have been interested from his own days as a curator at the Victoria and Albert Museum.[27] Read was only the first general popularizer of Wölfflin and Riegl: the true period of dissemination awaited the postwar years and the regalvanizing of public culture, particularly through the medium of broadcasting.

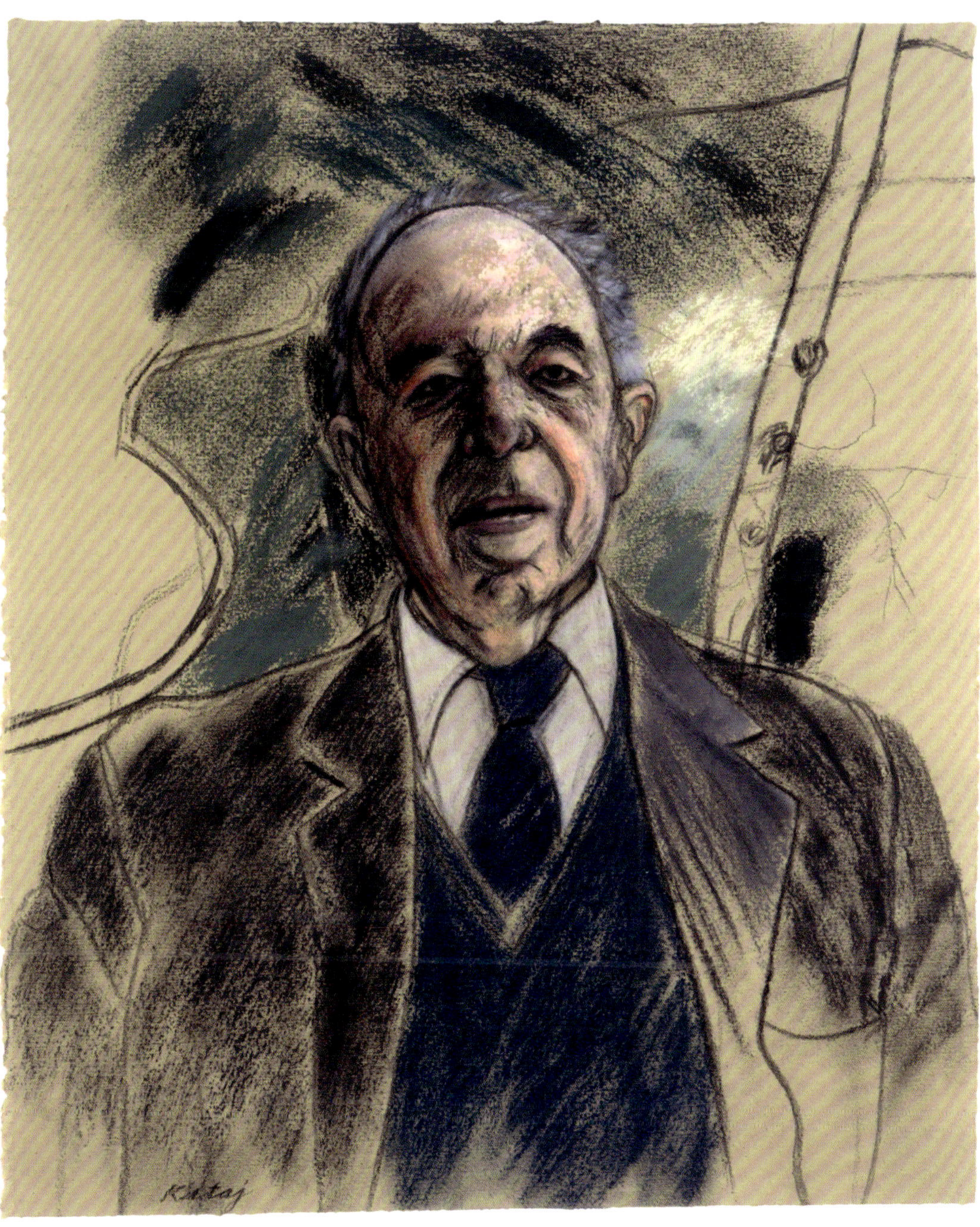

4. R.B. Kitaj, *Sir Ernst Hans
Josef Gombrich*, 1986, pastel and
charcoal
© *National Portrait Gallery, London*

Postwar Critiques and Practices: Gombrich and Pevsner

Publication in 1932 of the English translation of *Principles* coincided with a period of institutionalization of the curriculum of history of art as a higher-education subject in England. By 1939 Wölfflin's writings had gained not only attention but also a measure of acceptance in tandem with those of Riegl and Worringer. So far, *Principles* specifically had been seen as subverting the classical canon of art; renewing interest in the grand manner of the Seicento; penetrating the workings of mind; undermining the old class-based, patrician art history; ejecting Ruskinian moralism; and allowing, in effect, a more contextual, relativist critique of art history. Not uncharacteristically, the English were recasting Wölfflin in terms of the larger debates of English culture and society itself, in particular, given the massive social

Art history, a clumsy but useful term, does not hold
in this country the position that has been given to
Kunstgeschichte on the Continent, and an academic
discipline that in Europe and America is fully recognized
has here few professional chairs or university departments assigned to it. Our tradition of connoisseurship,
the detailed study of works of art and objects of antiquity in order to decide their date and provenance, is, it
is true, well established.... This resolute objectivity
has been the complete antithesis of the exuberance
of *Stilkritik*. We still suspect the wider speculations
by which analysis of styles provides not only a precise
instrument of attribution but also an indication of
phases of emotional temperament.[28]

It is as if Fry, Read, and Clark had written
in vain. Anti-Germanism may itself have
been a factor after the war.[29] Nevertheless,
expatriated German or German-trained
academics were now undoubtedly influencing opinion, which was in turn to become
more divergent and more politically colored.
Kunstwissenschaft was now alive and well
on English soil. As art history started to
rise in the universities, its tone and practices were professionalized, as Fry, Read,
and Clark doubtless had wished. Whatever
the reception now accorded to Wölfflin's
work in Germany, in England his critical
fortunes divided more or less along political-
disciplinary lines, and that divergence is
mapped by two figures in particular: Ernst
Gombrich (1909–2001), eventually director of the Warburg Institute (fig. 4), and
Nikolaus Pevsner (1902–1983) of Birkbeck
College, University of London (fig. 5), one
Austrian, the other German, one humanist, the other liberal, both victims of Nazi
persecution.

One very important divide in the English-
speaking world that influenced academic
opinion about Wölfflin at this time was

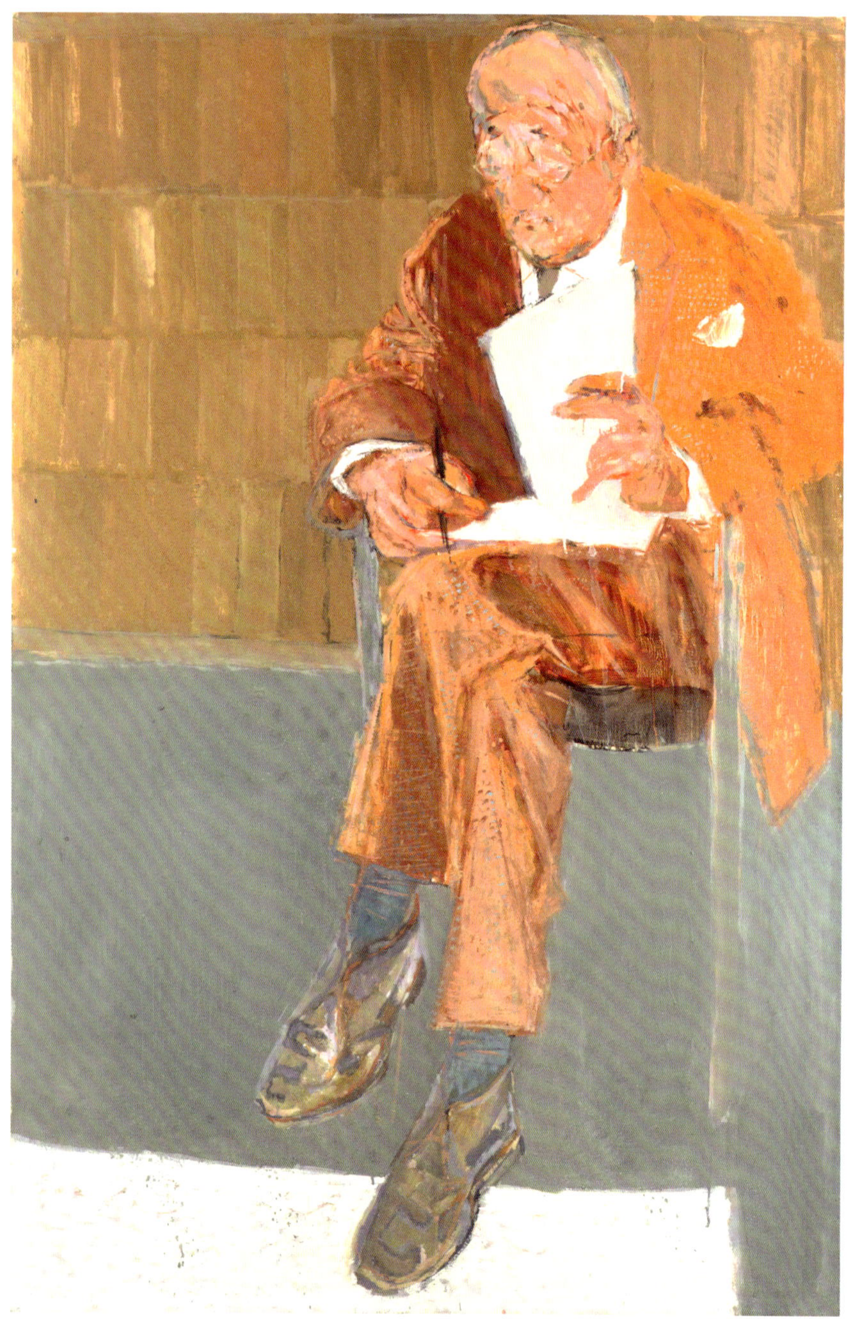

5. Hans Schwarz, *Nikolaus
Pevsner*, c. 1969, oil on board
© *National Portrait Gallery, London*

change that followed World War II, the idea
of art history as a discipline that could be
practiced not by a social elite but rather by
a scientifically informed educational elite of
professional art historians with the sort of
method that distinguished a discipline from
a subject.

The debate changed direction after World
War II also at least in part because new
internationalist forces were at work, and the

that between logically and scientifically oriented "analytic" philosophy as it developed in the first half of the twentieth century, the main exponents of which were Bertrand Russell, Ludwig Wittgenstein, and Gottlob Frege, and the so-called Continental school, which derived many of its premises from German idealism. In 1946 Bertrand Russell had defined this split as one between "British" and "Continental" philosophy.[30] For aestheticians sympathetic to Continental philosophy of the idealist type, Wölfflin was unavoidable because he provided one of the few statements of method and terminology that could properly be said to have emerged from within the discipline of art history, a statement that was also coming to define it. Gombrich's particular orientation, inspired not least by Karl Popper, was more generally toward the analytic school. Like Popper, Gombrich persistently highlighted the dangers implicit in the historical and philosophical traditions that had produced Wölfflin, Riegl, and Worringer.[31] Read had hailed Wölfflin as creating a "science" of art history. Not so for Gombrich, for whom Wölfflin's suspect idealism placed him firmly on the wrong side of the religion-science divide. The interesting point, however, is that Gombrich formulated this ultimately political stance within the particular professional context of the Warburg Institute, whose traditions belonged far more within the so-called Continental philosophical tradition.[32] His own intellectual origins within the circle of Julius von Schlosser (1866–1938) and the Viennese school of *Bildung* also carried with them a disposition toward cultural, not formal, analysis, which necessarily affected his estimate of Wölfflin's work.

In addition there seems to have been an element of iconoclasm in Gombrich's personal attitude to Wölfflin. In 1930, just when Clark was lecturing on Wölfflin in London, Gombrich was attending his lectures in Berlin and was not enthralled:

I remember the high hopes with which I went to Berlin University and the impression Wölfflin's personality made on me, the tall Swiss with beautiful blue eyes and a firm and self-assured manner of delivery that held the *auditorium maximum* spellbound. I confess that the spell did not work on me for very long. Soon heretical doubts spoilt some of my pleasure, though I was still unable to formulate the reason for my increasing disappointment.[33]

By the time of the publication of Gombrich's volume of essays *Norm and Form: Studies in the Art of the Renaissance* (1966), he had indeed formulated the reasons for his disappointment. He expressed these in a section titled "Critical Polarities in Wölfflin."[34] Wölfflin had given "art history the fateful tool of systematic comparison." His so-called critical polarities, however, were not polarities at all, but points on a sliding scale, the hidden norm or axis of which was classicism, Vasari's idea of perfection. Roger Fry had seen in Wölfflin the possibility of a post-Burckhardtian anticlassicism; for Gombrich, Wölfflin actually, though subliminally, reinforced exactly that classical model or stance through a form of sleight of hand that concealed a normative classicist standpoint. In this regard Gombrich's thinking, at this point at least, had points in common with the restrained reception accorded by the Vienna School to Wölfflin's work.[35]

Clearly much more than this was at stake for Gombrich, and his essay *In Search of Cultural History* (first delivered as a lecture in 1967) shows why: by this account, Wölfflin was the inheritor of German romanticism and idealism, which had produced not just Hegel but also Burckhardt and Marx.[36] Gombrich recognized that neither Burckhardt nor Wölfflin was straightforwardly Hegelian but suggested that "it is precisely those people who want to discard all 'preconceived' theories who are most likely unconsciously to succumb to their power."[37] As Burckhardt's successor at Basel, Wölfflin was now dragged in passing by Gombrich into the debate on the back of slightly tendentious thinking about what Hegelian metaphysics was deemed to be, as a branch of nonfalsifiable religion and so precisely not science. Politically, Gombrich in retrospect reads very like a Cold Warrior, situated not just within the history of neo-Kantian epistemology and perceptualism but also within postwar political and social discourse as a Popperian, Hayekian free marketeer, friend of the so-called Open Society and scourge of Platonism, Hegelianism, Marxism, and all bases for totalitarianism as he saw it. Yet, paradoxically, it is an open question whether Gombrich's own entirely relativistic "history of vision," namely *Art and Illusion* (which opens with Wölfflin's formulation that "not everything is possible in every period") and his later book *The Sense of Order*, necessarily sympathetic to the notion of empathy, are so very alien to the very tradition he condemns.[38] Indeed, the passages on Wölfflin and the psychology of style in *The Sense of Order* are among the warmest and least qualified he wrote on the subject.[39] The suspicion is that Gombrich, in repudiating much of this tradition, also (to use his own formula) unconsciously succumbed to its power.

Nikolaus Pevsner in contrast was a mild-mannered social progressive and evangelist of the modern movement and a devotee of visual analysis. Whereas Gombrich wrote almost exclusively about figurative arts, Pevsner's domain was architecture.[40] Pevsner was the most important writer in England to have studied under Wölfflin for any length of time in a university context (Gombrich quickly abandoned his lectures) and to have demonstrably assimilated his ideas into practice. Indeed, he had read *Principles* while still at school.[41] Like Gombrich, he was not impressed by Wölfflin in person. In the early 1920s, in Munich, Pevsner attended Wölfflin's lectures: "The professor was nearing sixty…tall, quietly and rather formally dressed (blue pinstripe, double breasted) and frighteningly aloof"; he talked a good deal about himself, but the lectures contained nothing that wasn't in his books and were "to the exacting freshman, rather a bore."[42] Recent work on Pevsner has not shied away from another issue in his early formation and sympathies: although he was forced to flee to England in 1933 he may have had an

attraction to Nazi doctrines.[43] His doctoral training at Leipzig under Wilhelm Pinder (1878–1947), soon to be a Nazi sympathizer, proved crucial. In the 1920s Pinder encouraged Pevsner to undertake a study of the geography of art, specifically the baroque of his hometown of Leipzig. This *Kunstgeographie* owed a great deal to Wölfflin's belief that regional differences underlay the dialectic of art. In this regard *Principles* was absolutely primary in Pevsner's formation because his intellectual interest in the geography of art persisted.[44] Pevsner's early training with Pinder and the influence upon both of a critic of Wölfflin, August Schmarsow (1853–1936), reminds us again that, as with earlier English writers, Wölfflin's influence seldom worked alone or without resistance.[45]

That Pevsner was a Wölfflinian in many important respects is indisputable.[46] He was a confirmed "two-projector man" and found many English lecture theaters technically wanting in this quite basic Wölfflinian technology.[47] Pevsner was always a practical critic and tended not to bandy around theory—he was not an especially distinctive or assertive theorist. So his language is permeated, in a way already familiar to the prewar English critical tradition, by a subliminal rather than by a systematic "Wölfflinianism." A key text for this is Pevsner's influential *An Outline of European Architecture* (1942), in which he says at the outset, "The Gothic style was not created because someone invented rib vaulting; the Modern Movement did not come into being because steel frame and reinforced concrete construction had been worked out—they were worked out because a new spirit required them."[48] Pevsner carried Wölfflinian ideas into such domains as medieval art and architecture, about which he wrote very tellingly; in regard to English medieval architecture, he dramatized formal change by means of Wölfflin's familiar polarities. Thus for all its illogicalities (by French standards), thirteenth-century English Gothic architecture is marked by "the clarity and erectness of the English lancet window" and by "a precision of surface to be compared only

with the classic Greek art of the Parthenon": in effect a Gothic classicism. Indeed,
because "the Classic is only a moment in
the history of a civilization," it quickly gives
way to the baroque.[49] Thus the classicism of
the thirteenth century was to be displaced
in England by the brilliant baroque of the
fourteenth, "decades in England which liked
to mix their media and play from one into
the other just as they liked in their carved
foliage to glide from one form into the other
instead of isolating part from part, as had
been the rule in the carving of the Leaves of
Southwell. Now all one sees is an incessant
ripple and flow, lights and shadows whisk-
ing over bossy surfaces, fascinating but far
removed from the clarity of a hundred years
before." His discussion of the extraordinary
undulating wall arcading of the Lady Chapel
at Ely Cathedral of the 1320s is really a
deft study of Gothic *Unklarheit*.[50] Pevsner
frequently uses Wölfflin's language and
thought patterns, as when, in the passage
just quoted, he attributes agency to decades,
not artists, or when he uses the language of
stylistic polarity and empathy.[51] But because
his work always had a strongly positivistic
inclination, his reception of Wölfflin was
quite unlike that of, say, the art critic Adrian
Stokes (1902–1972), who explored the psychology of form and the empathetic relation
of mass to surface in architecture in ways
indebted to Wölfflin's writings and their
interest in the connection between the perception of architecture and the perception of
the human body.[52]

Both Gombrich and Pevsner were best-
selling writers, but Pevsner also particularly
adopted the medium of radio. As Stephen
Games points out in his edition of Pevsner's
later radio broadcasts, "Over a period of
32 years [he] gave more talks for the British
Broadcasting Corporation than any other art
historian before or since."[53] Pevsner's teacher
Pinder had himself been a popularizer.[54]
Pevsner matters because his public broadcasting presented Wölfflinian thought in an
accessible, nonelitist way to a huge public,
far larger than that for the writings of Fry
or Read. It is worth recalling that in the

1930s Kenneth Clark's London lectures on
German art historians had, in fact, reached
remarkably few. He later recounted,

I…wrote two serious lectures on Wölfflin and Riegl
which I gave, at the instigation of Tancred Borenius, in
an enormous hall in London University. When I mounted
the rostrum there were about fifteen pupils in the hall.
"Wait," said Tancred, "the students will come in their
thousands." In fact no one else came. This sobering
experience cured me temporarily of my itch to lecture.[55]

Intelligent, well-paced radio broadcasting was another matter: now, truly, people
began to hear about Wölfflin, possibly in
numbers undreamed of even in Europe
and the United States. In one such radio
broadcast on the BBC Third Programme
in 1952, "Reflections on Not Teaching Art
History," Pevsner even offered a succinct
and accessible history of the discipline
and the emergence, with Burckhardt and
Wölfflin, of what he called "history of art
proper."[56] In Wölfflin, "the history of art
finally discovered itself"—and central to
that discovery was the analysis of style.
According to Pevsner, Wölfflin teaches us
that the history of art is the history of the
eye, of seeing; that style consists of certain
common formal characteristics within any
period. Formal analysis is fundamental, yet
it also leads to rigid overemphasis on form-
style. To Pevsner, the "artificiality of isolating" form from subject matter was a key
snag, which he identified also in the writing
of Fry. Pevsner did not appear to concur
with Gombrich's assessment that Wölfflin
was, by virtue of his metaphysics, a cultural
historian. For Pevsner, iconography, or what
he cozily calls "subjectology," was a reaction
to "the aestheticism of the Wölfflin–Roger
Fry approach."

Quite clearly, for Pevsner anti-aestheticism
mattered because of his own social and
modernist agenda, his belief in political
responsibility rather than aesthetic sensibility. This commitment created a tension
with English romantics influenced by the
aesthetic movement, such as the poet John
Betjeman (1906–1984). Even better known

than Pevsner, Betjeman fought the same fights as Pevsner to preserve, and educate the public about, English architecture. Yet he dismissed Germanic professionalism and system, which he regarded as the hallmark of "Herr Professor Doktor" Pevsner (to use Betjeman's sardonic phrase).[57]

Undoubtedly the central and most problematic text for an assessment of Wölfflin's role in Pevsner's thought was that of the 1955 Reith Lectures, broadcast on Sunday evenings—prime time—on the BBC Home Service.[58] In these lectures, issued under the title *The Geography of Art* and subsequently published as *The Englishness of English Art* (1956), Pevsner took on the much more sensitive issue of national identity.[59] His agenda was to identify national traits that might be either receptive to or helpful in the formulation of, a postwar British modernism, and in this regard the Reith Lectures must be read alongside Pevsner's more persuasive, if less widely read, *Pioneers of Modern Design* (1936), which traced the roots of Continental modernism in part to nineteenth-century insular ideas.

Pevsner's writing is, on the face of it, so lucid, so sensible and winning for a general public, that it is easy to discount its evasions. *The Englishness of English Art* is throughout marred by soft, empathetic thinking: fundamental national differences, such as those between low-pitched English medieval wooden roofs and their "majestic counterparts in Late Gothic Germany," are "felt" rather than simply observed.[60] Pevsner shows a willingness to tolerate the most absurd contradictions in the pursuit of "Englishness": in the chapter "Perpendicular England," the English emerge by turns as illogical and reasonable.[61] Then there was the question of race. As Games points out, the Reith Lectures identified "two distinct racial types" in England: one "tall with long head and long features, little facial display and little gesticulation, the other round-faced, more agile, and more active."[62] (Pevsner's mentor Pinder had discussed *Volk*, *Rasse*, and *Stamm*.)[63] Particularly difficult was Pevsner's tribute, in the foreword

to *The Englishness of English Art*, to the art historian Dagobert Frey, like Pinder implicated in Nazism, who in 1942 had published *Englisches Wesen in der bildenden Kunst*.[64] Not all this can be laid at the feet of Wölfflin, for race had been a dimension of much English critical writing of the previous generation or two; yet the fact remains that *Principles* had authorized, though not disciplined, further thought about what, in the introduction, Wölfflin called "the style of the school, the country, the race." Pevsner ends *The Englishness of English Art* precisely with reflections on race, nation, and climate.[65] Just how habitual and widespread this mindset was at the time is made apparent by "The Ideological Antecedents of the Rolls-Royce Radiator," a paper Erwin Panofsky delivered in 1962 to the American Philosophical Society, a text vaguely wedded to racial theory (the English are irrational partly because of their "Celtic" legacy), but fully committed to the notion, apparent in Pevsner, of a medieval English romantic and sublime imaginary.[66]

Above all it was Wölfflin's habitual thinking in binaries or polarities that provided Pevsner with one of his main expository tools, the "seemingly opposed forms and principles" that energized English art, showing "how useful the notion of polarities, or contraries, proves in action": Decorated and Perpendicular Gothic; Vanbrugh and Burlington; Hogarth and Reynolds; Constable and Turner—both "concerned with an atmospheric view of the world, not with the firm physical objects in it"—in contrast to the formal English house and landscaped garden.[67] Characteristically, Pevsner's 1969 Walter Neurath Memorial Lecture set Ruskin against Eugène-Emmanuel Viollet-le-Duc in another such binary, discussing "Englishness and Frenchness in the Appreciation of Gothic Architecture."[68] Gombrich was a brilliant essayist, Pevsner a subtle tactician of the image; and his lectures, aimed at a general public and a receptive audience of undergraduates (including the author of this contribution), were from a visual point of view a revelation of the enduring powers of Wölfflin's dual-projector method, at least until the fateful days when the binary method fell victim to the pluralities of PowerPoint.

Wölfflin, Podro, and Baxandall

Pevsner produced few pupils by the standards of university teachers at that time, and in that sense he did not found a "school": his influence was mostly through publication and broadcasting, and especially through his extraordinary county-by-county survey, *The Buildings of England*, first formulated in 1938, the greatest national by-product of *Kunstgeographie*.[69] At large, however, English architectural writing was guided, and continues to be guided, quite as much by a form of archaeological empiricism deriving from such nineteenth-century writers as Robert Willis and absolutely unconcerned with psychology or agency.[70] Even so, significant Courtauld Institute projects, such as Paul Crossley's re-edition of Paul Frankl's *Gothic Architecture* (1962), a text originally influenced by Wölfflin, indicated the continuing vitality of the German critical tradition for English commentators toward the year 2000.[71]

At large, the new university program, driven by the government's Robbins Report of 1963, which advocated an expansion in the numbers receiving a university education in Britain, coincided with the establishment of new universities, soon to gain art history departments, at Sussex, Essex, Warwick, York, and Norwich (East Anglia), while art history as a subject started to grow at undergraduate level at older universities such as Cambridge, Leeds, and Manchester. Inevitably the social composition of undergraduates broadened in terms of class identity. The program lasted until the 1990s, when further educational reform brought many other institutions, typically the polytechnics, closer to the model of universities, thus homogenizing the corporate provision of higher education and in effect hugely expanding it. Despite this there were continuities in terms of the established literature of the history of art. The works of Heinrich Wölfflin were read and examined at undergraduate level when the subject was introduced at Cambridge in the early 1960s and were taught and examined throughout the era of the new art history. Of that period Elizabeth Cropper notes in a personal memoir, "History and Tradition," that at Cambridge "the history of art history, which has become such a focus in recent years, was a fundamental course, and we all read Wölfflin, Berenson, Fry, Riegl, Worringer, and many others."[72] Yet when Francis Haskell (1928–2000), a Cambridge graduate and professor of the history of art at Oxford from 1967, came to survey the relation of history and its images, Wölfflin did not figure at all in his account.[73] His predecessor at Oxford, the Warburgian Edgar Wind (1900–1971), was a critic of Wölfflin.[74]

The institutional position in the 1960s was rather more fluid and complex, and, indeed, interesting, than just the matter of expanding universities or the singularity of particular institutional outlooks. Other stakeholders included the art schools, which had "general studies" courses that encouraged an entirely different kind of intellectual traffic. In a transcribed recorded memoir, Michael Baxandall (1933–2008) laid particular emphasis on this porosity between institutions: "I suppose the main shift in the character of art history was the development of general studies departments in art schools, which was mandated in this period, and a lot of the more interesting younger art historians went into these general studies departments.... Michael Podro did that, and T. J. Clark...for a time."[75] What Baxandall understood, in a thoroughly liberal and anti-elitist spirit, was that there was no purely "institutional" reception of Wölfflin in England, because people switched institutions more freely than now.

The relative diversity and fluidity of institutional provision and interinstitutional experience at this time is well measured by the close personal and intellectual interaction of Gombrich's students and editors at the Warburg Institute, Michael

Podro (1931–2008) and Baxandall himself. Podro, a philosopher and art historian, represents an example of the mobile career type of the period. He began his career at the Slade School of Art before studying with both Gombrich and Richard Wollheim (1923–2003), going on to teach at Camberwell School of Arts and then working at the Warburg Institute and eventually Essex University, where he became professor in an important new department. Mixed careers of this type deserve emphasis because their salient feature—the liberal and dynamic interaction of art practice and aesthetic theory—was soon to be set aside as the tide increasingly favored the styles of professionalized systematic theoretical engagement typical of the new art history. Podro's work was founded in the study of art theory from Kant to the late nineteenth century.[76] Without doubt his most celebrated historical study was *The Critical Historians of Art*, published in 1982, a work devoted solely to the German tradition of engagement that had developed since the eighteenth century, "critical" because, in his words, it "made a serious attempt to say things about the visual arts that would register the energy and complexity of the arts themselves." Its literature "continued to exert an influence largely through shadowy reminiscences," he wrote, "the texts themselves having slipped from view."[77] Podro devoted two chapters to the works of Wölfflin, the first on *Classic Art*, the second on *Principles*, or, more exactly, "The *Principles* and Its Problems."[78] These are by far the longest and most searching passages of English-language criticism devoted to Wölfflin since Roger Fry and Gombrich's *Norm and Form*, appearing just at the time when Wölfflin's own methods had passed out of common currency. Podro's rigor and independence of mind as a thinker are evident throughout his work, and it may be worth recalling that his PhD supervisor, the philosopher Richard Wollheim, also admired Wölfflin's "justly famous" account of Raphael's Stanze in *Classic Art* despite the fact that, according to him, Wölfflin, Henri Focillon, and Riegl,

the "philosophical" art historians, so to speak, "were confused about the status of their investigation" because they could not separate, or for that matter properly connect, the general transformative powers of art from or to the specific instances of that transformation.[79]

Podro's subtle account is equally mixed, and Wölfflin does not emerge unscathed. In setting out his account of the "critical art historians," Podro uses Wölfflin as a bridge between Semper, Göller, and Riegl and interpreters such as Warburg and Panofsky. Podro opens his chapter "Wölfflin and Classic Art" with the view that "[f]or many of us, whatever our reservations, it would be hard to find a replacement for *The Principles of Art History* as a model for the analysis of painting."[80] But it quickly becomes evident that Podro is unsatisfied with Wölfflin's fundamental project of establishing the "double root" of style (broadly speaking, extrinsic and intrinsic causes, or the cultural ethos and the visual tradition itself), and so with the problem that engaged Erwin Panofsky, the relation of form to content. Thus, according to Podro, "when an artist draws upon earlier work he derives from it not simply visual forms but dramatic dispositions, not only ways of defining forms but sensitivity towards the character of what is depicted."[81] Indeed, he continues, "We have no way of determining in principle what an artist may take over from earlier artists, as opposed to what he takes over from other sources within his culture."[82] In setting out and not resolving these inherent problems in Wölfflin's method, Podro notes the critiques of Schmarsow and Frankl, observing that, while the descriptive skill of Wölfflin's schemata has never been in doubt, "[w]hat has been challenged is the theoretical force or status of his concepts, the importance or significance which he gives to them."[83]

What also needs emphasizing is the way in which leading commentators working in English art schools or universities assimilated Wölfflin's writing to developed or developing practices within other disciplines. The history of quite small yet influential coteries was vital to this. One such coterie was formed around the éminence grise of English literary criticism in the time of the expansion of the universities, F. R. Leavis (1895–1978), who taught for most of his career at Cambridge.[84] Both Podro and Baxandall began their intellectual lives studying not art history or philosophy, but English literature at Cambridge with Leavis. Leavis was the doyen of a notion of intellectual seriousness in critical practice, as opposed to literary dilettantism. In this he stood in an analogous relation to the perception that Wölfflin had placed English art history on a serious footing. Leavis was not a relativist like Wölfflin: value was central to him. He was, however, interested in form and close reading, and it may have been the analogous sensitivity of Wölfflinian visual analysis that attracted the Leavisite art historians.

Baxandall was, by his own admission, stimulated by Wölfflin's formal analyses. Like Podro, he was versed in an approach to literary criticism inaugurated at Cambridge by I. A. Richards (1893–1979), locally called "prac-crit" (practical criticism), in which students were asked to examine texts without knowing who wrote them or when, and so read them without presupposition. This decontextualization was a basis of the so-called new criticism, an insular form of literary engagement *ohne namen*, "without names."[85] Close and sensitive reading mattered to students in such courses. Baxandall recorded: "The first two art history books I remember liking were Wölfflin's *Classic Art*, and Erwin Panofsky's *Meaning in the Visual Arts*," noting also that Wölfflin "was doing close observation, which I liked, partly because that fitted the literary critical training I'd had."[86] Indeed, in retrospect Baxandall's notion of cognitive style, of the "period eye," of the cultural relativism of seeing, manifestly resembles Wölfflin's "history of seeing" and belief that "not everything is possible in every period."[87] It was precisely the Leavisite aspect of Baxandall's early mental preparation, its emphasis ultimately on value, tradition, and context,

that colored his understanding of Wölfflin. Value was the one aspect of criticism that Roger Hinks had seen as repudiated by Wölfflin, along with criticism itself. At one point in his *Limewood Sculptors of Renaissance Germany* (1980), Baxandall remarks in defense of his method of singling out the really great carvers: "[O]nly very good works of art, the performances of exceptionally organized men, are complex and coordinated enough to register in their forms the kinds of cultural circumstances sought here; second-rate art will be little use to us."[88] This is not exactly the view of Wölfflin, but it is a version of a covert belief within Hegelian criticism that only successful works reveal the zeitgeist; failed works of art are inexpressive of it.

Canon and Curriculum

For critics working in England, whether those sympathetic to Continental philosophy of the idealist type, those attempting to professionalize the discipline of the history of art, or those establishing curricula for expanding postwar universities, Wölfflin's *Principles* as an exemplification of method (the *idea* of a method, that is) was unavoidable. Inevitably Wölfflin was read and understood in the light not of some overall systematic project but rather of specific critical inclinations and traditions. Fry recognized in Wölfflin an account of form and psychology that chimed in with his own thinking, as did Read and to a lesser extent Clark. None of these men worked in universities or institutes. Wölfflin finally enabled the ties with the great tradition of moral criticism exemplified by John Ruskin—indeed, the English tradition of criticism itself—to be severed in favor of science. The disaster of World War II created a much more politically divided climate in which Wölfflin's works were conscripted either to the case against idealism (Gombrich) or to the case of general art education and social improvement (Pevsner). Podro's and Baxandall's accounts of Wölfflin, susceptible to his thought yet recognizing a certain distance from it as Wölfflin's entire method fell into disuse, also need to be understood in terms of the prevailing critical and political climate outside art history. By the later 1970s some of the warmest reception of Wölfflin's work came not from the English political left, broadly understood, but from the conservative new right as conservatives and conservative aestheticians retraced their origins back to Kantian and Hegelian thought.[89] That the climate was turning against the German tradition understood broadly is clear. "Heaven knows, one is tired of the old stories of the great generation—beautiful Wölfflin, Riegl and his carpets, etc.," said T. J. Clark in 1974, in a spirited defense of the inner purpose of idealist art history, and of its understanding of ideology; but it was Clark who, no less tired of recent trends in art history ("for diversification, read disintegration"), still recognized that such writers belonged to a heroic phase of the subject.[90]

Running through all this was another persistent strand, less easy to articulate but important to address nevertheless: the agon of English and European thought. One of the strengths of Wölfflin in the early years of his reception was precisely his status as an authoritative outsider—a status shared by Gombrich and Pevsner—even though anti-German sentiment was always in the background. This outsider status, coupled with at least one strand of ideological doubt about his work, created a kind of intellectual distancing. So the question was always to what, exactly, his ideas would be assimilated, given the unsystematic character of the professional practice of art history in England. Baxandall captures the problem, the sense of unease:

[T]his is complicated, because in England there was the old-established and rather good English tradition of sensitive art criticism, maybe too sensitive.…It wasn't a homogeneous art-historical tradition or art-critical tradition, but there were individual streams which were good and which I was fond of and still like. I still like the tradition of Ruskin for all sorts of reasons. This didn't adapt very gracefully, I feel, to the arrival of German

and Austrian practices, which were obviously so much more advanced and came from a different general culture. What one had for a stage in England was a sort of German, Kantian art history without the Kantian background, which was an impoverished thing. I don't know many people of my generation who've managed, apart from Michael Podro, because it's a very difficult thing for someone who is not of that culture to grasp the general context and frame of German art history. We haven't had that sort of education. Even though we'd been taught the same things, Plato, say, we've been taught it in a different way. So I was worried in those years in London about what was happening both to the English traditions and to the German-Austrian traditions in England. I still am, rather. I think the hybrid is not altogether graceful, and a lot of the strengths of both sides have been lost.[91]

Wölfflin's writings fell out of curricular use with the rise of the new art history and the French-inspired "linguistic turn" in England, as in the English-speaking world: no longer regarded as living theory, they became instead "historiography" and, as such, a legitimate object of suspicion or outright repudiation.[92] But two final points need to be made about the curricular demotion of Wölfflin. The first is that it may very well have been short lived, since Wölfflin's theories of form, seeing, and above all empathy (*Einfühlung*) are garnering renewed attention in the wake of the "new aesthetics" of current practice, not least within the history of the emotions and neuroaesthetics. As David Freedberg has recently remarked, "there is much that is pertinent not only in [Maurice] Merleau-Ponty (most obviously of all), but also in the great nineteenth-century empathy theorists, Robert Vischer and Theodore Lipps, and even that eventually most reactionary of art historians, Heinrich Wölfflin. I speak not of the oldness of the past, but its newness, its topicality, its always prophetic possibilities."[93] The intellectual power and durability of the works of the "critical art historians" of the later nineteenth century is again evident as critics and art historians try to crystallize in their own minds what the agency of art truly is, or might be.[94]

The second (related) point concerns a more fundamental truth about the durability of *Principles* even at the lowest point of its *fortuna critica*. This is that the discourse of art history has become irreversibly permeated by its language. Canon has triumphed over curriculum. Wölfflin's writings, and particularly *Principles* in view of its clarity and memorability, have entered the mindset of art history at a level defined by that most cosmopolitan of critics, George Steiner, as the "individually internalized cluster or crystallization of remembered, exegetically re-enacted texts or text fragments" that defines not a curriculum but a canon in its most dignified, and useful, sense: it "enters into the reader … by a process of penetration, of luminous insinuation."[95] In England in the period covered by this essay, Wölfflin both penetrated and insinuated, and it was the ability of his text to be revisited and assimilated to national or local concerns by critics and historians of widely differing interests and inclinations that ensured its longer-term success.

NOTES

This essay owes its origin to a conversation in Cambridge with Elizabeth Cropper. I am greatly indebted to Sam Rose for reading a draft, making insightful suggestions, and drawing my attention to literature, most of which I incorporate with thanks. I also thank the editors for setting me straight on a number of points.

1. Michael Podro, *The Critical Historians of Art* (New Haven, 1982), 152.

2. Roger Fry, review, *The Athenaeum* 3974 (December 26, 1903): 862–863. For the English translation by Peter and Linda Murray, see *Classic Art: An Introduction to the Italian Renaissance* (Oxford and New York, 1952). For Fry's role in the propagation of Wölfflin's thought in Britain see Evonne Levy, "Wölfflin's *Principles of Art History* (1915–2015): A Prolegomenon for Its Second Century," in Heinrich Wölfflin, *Principles of Art History: The Problem of the Development of Style in Early Modern Art*, trans. Jonathan Blower, ed. Evonne Levy and Tristan Weddigen (Los Angeles, 2015).

3. Roger Fry, "The Baroque," *The Burlington Magazine* 39 (September 1921): 145–148. Fry republished much of this review verbatim in "The Seicento," in *Transformations: Critical and Speculative Essays on Art* (London, 1926), 95–124.

4. Roger Fry to Vanessa Bell, April 10, 1920, Tate Archive, Charleston Trust, 8010.5.812. He writes, "Goodbye my dear please write to me soon. I'm reading a German book on art by Wölflin [*sic*] the only writer I get ideas from. I must tell you about it in another letter. Yrs Roger." The author thanks the editors for passing on this reference, acknowledging Alison Syme.

5. Fry, "The Baroque," 146.

6. Michael Fried, *Roger Fry's Formalism*, The Tanner Lectures on Human Values, delivered at the University of Michigan, November 2 and 3, 2001, https://tannerlectures.utah.edu/_documents/a-to-z/f/fried_2001.pdf, 6.

7. Podro, *Critical Historians of Art*.

8. According to Jacqueline V. Falkenheim, *Roger Fry and the Beginnings of Formalist Art Criticism* (Ann Arbor, 1973), 82.

9. Falkenheim, *Roger Fry*, 52.

10. Roger Fry, *Last Lectures*, introduction by Kenneth Clark (Cambridge, 1939), 203–204. I am grateful to Sam Rose for this reference.

11 Falkenheim, *Roger Fry*, 52, 97.

12. Roger Fry, "An Essay in Aesthetics," in *Vision and Design*, ed. J. B. Bullen (1920; reprinted Oxford and New York, 1981), 23–24.

13. Bernard Berenson, *The Italian Painters of the Renaissance* (London, 1972), 244.

14. Janet Sayers, *Art, Psychoanalysis, and Adrian Stokes: A Biography* (London, 2015), 265.

15. For the circumstances of the translation and Fry's role in it see Evonne Levy, "Wölfflin's *Principles of Art History* (1915–2015)," 30–31. I am grateful to the editors for the information about the Courtauld reading lists.

16. Matthew C. Potter, "Breaking the Shell of the Humanist Egg: Kenneth Clark's University of London Lectures on German Art Historians," *Journal of Art Historiography* 11 (December 2014): 1–34.

17. Potter, "Breaking the Shell," 5.

18. Potter, "Breaking the Shell," 8.

19. Potter, "Breaking the Shell," 18–30.

20. Potter, "Breaking the Shell," 34.

21 Alois Riegl, *Late Roman Art Industry*, trans. Rolf Winkes (Rome, 1985); Alois Riegl, *Problems of Style: Foundations for a History of Ornament*, trans. Evelyn Kain (Princeton, 1992); Alois Riegl, *Historical Grammar of the Visual Arts*, trans. Jacqueline E. Jung (New York, 2004).

22. Hubert D. Waley, "The Swing of the Pendulum," *The Burlington Magazine* 62 (May 1933): 246–247.

23 Waley "Swing of the Pendulum," 247.

24. Roger Hinks, "Thoughts on Reading Woelfflin," *The Criterion* 11/45 (1932): 690–697, here 692.

25. Herbert Read, introduction to *Heinrich Wölfflin, Classic Art: An Introduction to the Italian Renaissance* (1952; 4th ed., Oxford, 1980), v.

26. Herbert Read, *Education through Art* (London, 1943), 94, 100.

27. Herbert Read, "Aesthetics and the Science of Art," *Times Literary Supplement*, April 18, 1929, 320, and "The History of Art," *The Listener*, July 2, 1930, 24. For the Victoria and Albert, see Lee Beard, "Pottery as Precedent: Herbert Read and the Sculptural Form," in *Re-Reading Read*, ed. Michael Paraskos (London, 2007), 122–133. I owe these references to Sam Rose.

28. Thomas Sherrar Ross Boase, preface to Joan Evans, *English Art, 1307–1461* (Oxford, 1949), v.

29. I am grateful to the editors for pointing out this possibility in regard to the period of T.S.R. Boase's directorship.

30. Bertrand Russell, *A History of Western Philosophy* (London, 1946), 668–672.

31. Explored in Podro, *Critical Historians of Art.*

32. See the collection of essays "The Warburg Institute," *Common Knowledge* 18, no. 1 (2012), and, for Warburg, E.H. Gombrich, *Aby Warburg: An Intellectual Biography* (Chicago, 1970).

33. E. H. Gombrich, *Norm and Form: Studies in the Art of the Renaissance* (London, 1966), 92.

34. Gombrich, *Norm and Form*, 89–98; see Levy, in Wölfflin, *Principles of Art History* (2015), 1–46, quotation on 29–30.

35. See the essay by Hans Aurenhammer in this volume.

36. E. H. Gombrich, *In Search of Cultural History* (Oxford, 1969).

37. Gombrich, *In Search of Cultural History*, 14.

38. E. H. Gombrich, *Art and Illusion: A Study in the Psychology of Pictorial Representation* (London, 1960), 4; *The Sense of Order: A Study in the Psychology of Decorative Art* (London, 1979).

39. Gombrich, *The Sense of Order*, 201–204.

40. Susie Harries, *Nikolaus Pevsner: The Life* (London, 2011), and for a useful set of essays, Peter Draper, ed., *Reassessing Nikolaus Pevsner* (Aldershot, UK, 2004).

41. Ute Engel, "The Formation of Pevsner's Art History: Nikolaus Pevsner in Germany, 1902–1935," in Draper, *Reassessing Nikolaus Pevsner*, 29–50, here 32.

42. Harries, *Nikolaus Pevsner*, 52–53.

43. Harries, *Nikolaus Pevsner*, 110–111, 116–119.

44. Mathew Aitchison, "Wölfflin, Pinder and Pevsner: *Kunstgeographie* from the Baroque to Modernism," in *Audience: The 28th Society of Architectural Historians, Australia and New Zealand (SAHANZ) Annual Conference*, ed. Antony Moulis and Deborah van der Plaat (Brisbane 2011), 1–13. In general, see Thomas DaCosta Kaufmann, *Toward a Geography of Art* (Chicago, 2004).

45. See Paul Crossley, introduction, Draper, *Reassessing Nikolaus Pevsner*, 5, and Engel , "The Formation of Pevsner's Art History," 29–50, here 30–34. For Schmarsow and Wölfflin, see Podro, *Critical Historians of Art*, 143–149.

46. Stephen Games, ed., *Pevsner: The Complete Broadcast Talks; Architecture and Art on Radio and Television, 1945–1977* (Farnham, UK, and Burlington, VT, 2014), 244, 257.

47. Harries, *Nikolaus Pevsner*, 619.

48. Nikolaus Pevsner, introduction to *An Outline of European Architecture* (Harmondsworth, 1942); numerous editions often giving the first as 1943 though some copies bear the date 1942, here quoted from the 1970 edition, 17.

49. Pevsner, *Outline of European Architecture*, 127, 128. On Pevsner and the Middle Ages see Richard Marks, "The Englishness of English Gothic Art?," in *Gothic Art and Thought in the Later Medieval Period*, ed. Colum Hourihane, Index of Christian Art, Occasional Papers, 12 (Princeton, 2011), 64–89.

50. Pevsner, *Outline of European Architecture*, 140.

51. See Paul Crossley, introduction, in Draper, *Reassessing Nikolaus Pevser*, 4.

52. Stephen Kite, *Adrian Stokes: An Architectonic Eye; Critical Writings on Art and Architecture* (London, 2008), 132.

53. Games, *Pevsner: The Complete Broadcast Talks*, xi.

54. See Crossley in Draper, *Reassessing Nikolaus Pevsner*, quotation on 6.

55. Potter, "Breaking the Shell," 4.

56. Games, *Pevsner: The Complete Broadcast Talks*, 201–202.

57. For this see Tim Mowl, *Stylistic Cold Wars: Betjeman versus Pevsner* (London, 2000).

58. Games, *Pevsner: The Complete Broadcast Talks*, 241–315. The recorded lectures are available from the BBC at http://www.bbc.co.uk/programmes/poohg2wt#play.

59. Nikolaus Pevsner, *The Englishness of English Art* (Harmondsworth, 1956), here cited in the 1976 reprint. The literature is extensive: for context see David Peters Corbett, Ysanne Holt, and Fiona Russell, eds., *The Geography of Englishness: Landscape and the National Past, 1880–1940*, Studies in British Art, 10 (New Haven and London, 2002). For a discussion of Pevsner in this connection, see Andrew Causey, "Pevsner and Englishness," in Draper, *Reassessing Nikolaus Pevsner*, 161–174.

60. Pevsner, *The Englishness of English Art*, 95.

61. Pevsner, *The Englishness of English Art*, 90–127, and see Games, *Pevsner: The Complete Broadcast Talks*, 242–243.

62. Games, *Pevsner: The Complete Broadcast Talks*, 244.

63. Harries, *Nikolaus Pevsner*, 56–58, 170, 258–259, 486; Games, *Pevsner: The Complete Broadcast Talks*, 244.

64. Games, *Pevsner: The Complete Broadcast Talks*, 249–252.

65. Pevsner, *The Englishness of English Art*, 193.

66. Erwin Panofsky, "The Ideological Antecedents of the Rolls-Royce Radiator," *Proceedings of the American Philosophical Society* 107, no. 4 (1963): 273–288. Panofsky does not mention Pevsner's work.

67. Pevsner, *The Englishness of English Art*, 16, 24.

68. Nikolaus Pevsner, *Ruskin and Viollet-le-Duc: Englishness and Frenchness in the Appreciation of Gothic Architecture* (London, 1969).

69. Harries, *Nikolaus Pevsner*, 237–238.

70. Alexandrina Buchanan, *Robert Willis and the Foundation of Architectural History* (Cambridge, 2013).

71. Paul Frankl, *Gothic Architecture*, revised and expanded by Paul Crossley (New Haven and London, 2000).

72. Elizabeth Cropper, "History and Tradition: A Personal Memoir," Villa I Tatti, September 14, 2011. I am grateful to Professor Cropper for allowing me to read her memoir.

73. Francis Haskell, *History and Its Images: Art and the Interpretation of the Past* (New Haven and London, 1993).

74. Michael Ann Holly, *Panofsky and the Foundations of Art History* (Ithaca and London, 1984), 99–100.

75. Richard Cándida Smith, interview (transcript of tape recordings), "Michael Baxandall, Substance, Sensation, and Perception," Getty Research Institute, Art History Oral Documentation Project, J. Paul Getty Trust, 1998, 90.

76. Michael Podro, *The Manifold in Perception: Theories of Art from Kant to Hildebrand* (Oxford, 1972).

77 Podro, *Critical Historians of Art*, preface.

78 Podro, *Critical Historians of Art*, 98–151.

79. Richard Wollheim, *Art and Its Objects* (New York, 1968), 12–14, 145. See also Richard Wollheim, "Pictorial Style: Two Views," in *The Concept of Style*, ed. Berel Lang (Ithaca, 1987), 183–202; for a considered discussion of the relationship of Wollheim to Wölfflin see Jason Gaiger, "The Analysis of Pictorial Style," *British Journal of Aesthetics* 42, no. 1 (2002): 20–36.

80. Podro, *Critical Historians of Art*, 98.

81. Podro, *Critical Historians of Art*, 129. For Panofsky and Wölfflin, see Holly, *Panofsky and the Foundations of Art History*.

82. Podro, *Critical Historians of Art*, 131.

83. Podro, *Critical Historians of Art*, 129.

84. I. D. MacKillop, *F. R. Leavis: A Life in Criticism* (New York, 1997).

85. I. A. Richards, *Practical Criticism: A Study of Literary Judgment* (London, 1929).

86. Smith, "Michael Baxandall, Substance, Sensation, and Perception," 21 and 37. See Jules Lubbock, "'To Do a Leavis' on Visual Art: The Place of F. R. Leavis in Michael Baxandall's Intellectual Formation," in *Michael Baxandall, Vision and the Work of Words*, ed. Peter Mack and Robert Williams (Farnham, UK, and Burlington, VT, 2015), 25–47, quotation on 33 and note 69 and on 57.

87. Michael Baxandall, *Painting and Experience in Fifteenth-Century Italy: A Primer in the Social History of Pictorial Style* (Oxford, 1972). See also Hal Foster, *Design and Crime (and Other Diatribes)* (London and New York, 2002), 88.

88. Michael Baxandall, *The Limewood Sculptors of Renaissance Germany* (New Haven and London, 1980), 10.

89. For example, Roger Scruton, *The Aesthetics of Architecture* (London, 1979), in which Wölfflin's work is repeatedly cited with admiration.

90. Both quotations from T. J. Clark, "The Conditions of Artistic Creation," *The Times Literary Supplement*, May 24, 1974, 561–562.

91. Smith, "Michael Baxandall, Substance, Sensation, and Perception," 111.

92. I cite, for instance, Donald Preziosi, *Rethinking Art History: Meditations on a Coy Science* (New Haven and London, 1989), 7.

93. David Freedberg, "Movement, Embodiment, Emotion," in *Les Actes de colloques en ligne du musée du quai Branly*, Histoire de l'art et anthropologie, INHA/Musée du quai Branly, Paris, 2009, http://actes-branly.revues.org/330.

94. For a recent overview of this issue, including remarks on the genealogy of the study of *Einfühlung*, see Caroline Van Eck, *Art, Agency and Living Presence: From the Animated Image to the Excessive Object* (Leiden, 2015), 23.

95. George Steiner, "Critic/Reader," in *George Steiner: A Reader* (Oxford, 1984), 91.

EVONNE LEVY

Wölfflin's Principles *in the United States:*
A Love-Hate Relationship

PRINCIPLES OF ART HISTORY

HEINRICH WÖLFFLIN

the problem of the development of style in later art

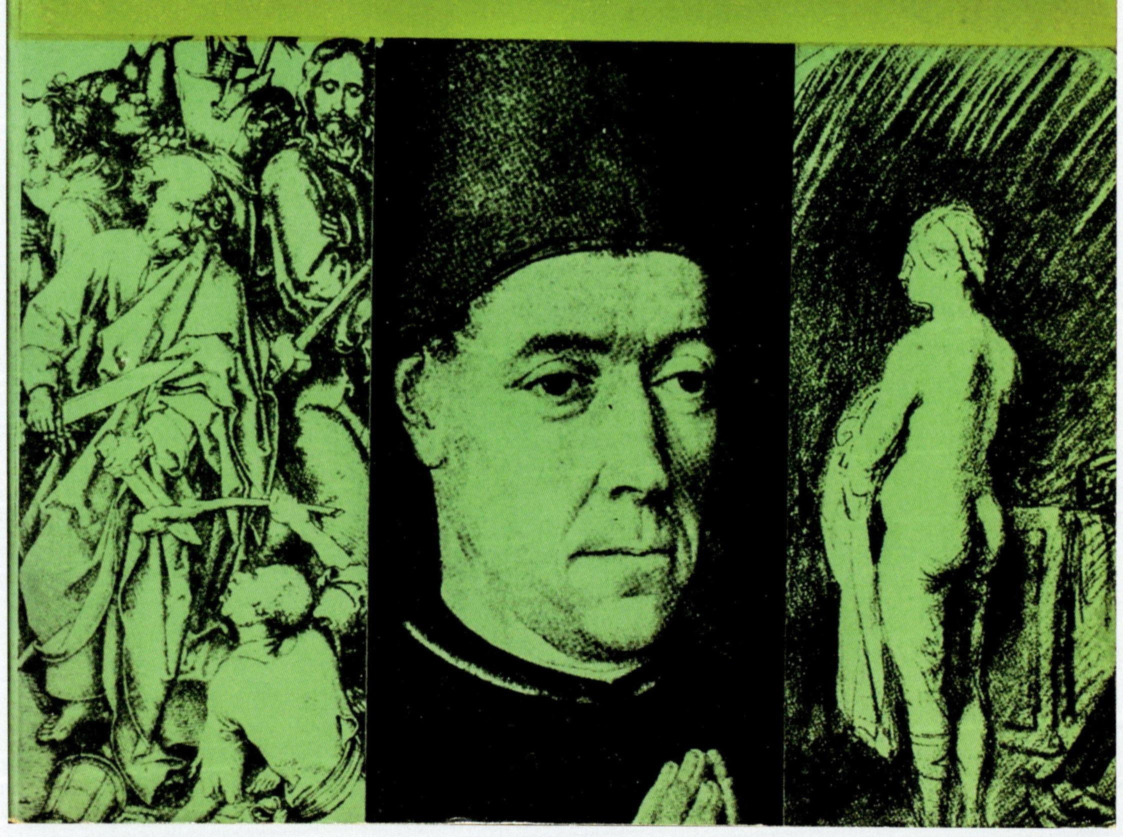

The reception of Wölfflin's *Principles* was arguably more robust in the United States than anywhere else in the world. This is partly a function of scale: after 1933, with a major injection of art-historical talent from Germanophone countries, art history as a discipline grew exponentially. But the coincidence of that growth with a newly available translation of a European classic of a modern discipline helped to implant *Principles* as a foundation for the teaching of art history by a newly Europeanized professorate. The Dover edition of *Principles* that has circulated in the United States since 1950 has gone through dozens of printings, testifying to the continual use of the book in university classrooms for many decades (fig. 1). What is unique about the US reception, though, is the great extent to which various waves of methodological renewal, from the late 1960s to today, were positioned explicitly against Wölfflinian formalism. Unlike Germany, where the text simply became irrelevant, in the United States there was a greater, perhaps unconscious attachment to it that kept it in view, even as it was repeatedly killed off. This essay traces the surprisingly numerous byways of transmission in many subfields of the discipline, the peculiar American themes of the reception, and the unique tenacity of opposition to it.

Before 1932

Anglophone readers had their first taste of Wölfflinian formalism with the 1903 translation of *Die klassische Kunst*.[1] Wölfflin's work fully reached an English-speaking audience on both sides of the ocean, however, only after the appearance in 1932

of the English translation of *Principles*, copublished by London and New York presses.[2] (There has never been a Canadian edition of any of Wölfflin's publications.) Wölfflin himself never traveled to North America. He declined an invitation to speak at the opening of *Exhibition of Contemporary German Art*, organized by Roger Fry, at the Metropolitan Museum of Art in 1909.[3] When his student Kurt Gerstenberg asked if he had considered seeing the art collections in America, he replied, "What is the point? It is nothing but an accelerated version of Europe."[4]

There is no question that the appearance of *Kunstgeschichtliche Grundbegriffe* in the middle of World War I had a negative impact on US reception, not least because of the precipitous decline of German-language learning.[5] German had been the most widely spoken second language in the United States before the war.[6] Upon US entry into the conflict in 1917, German-language instruction in primary and secondary education collapsed. Nonetheless, because reading knowledge of German continued to be expected of many university-level students and German titles appeared on undergraduate and graduate reading lists, an early readership of *Grundbegriffe* in the United States was not out of the question. The title appeared for the first time on the College Art Association's list of "Books for the College Art Library" in 1929, having been passed over in 1920.[7] The demand for English translations of German-language works rose as the exchange of art historians between Germany and the United States intensified. In the 1920s German art historians already occupied permanent teaching positions or came as guest professors to the

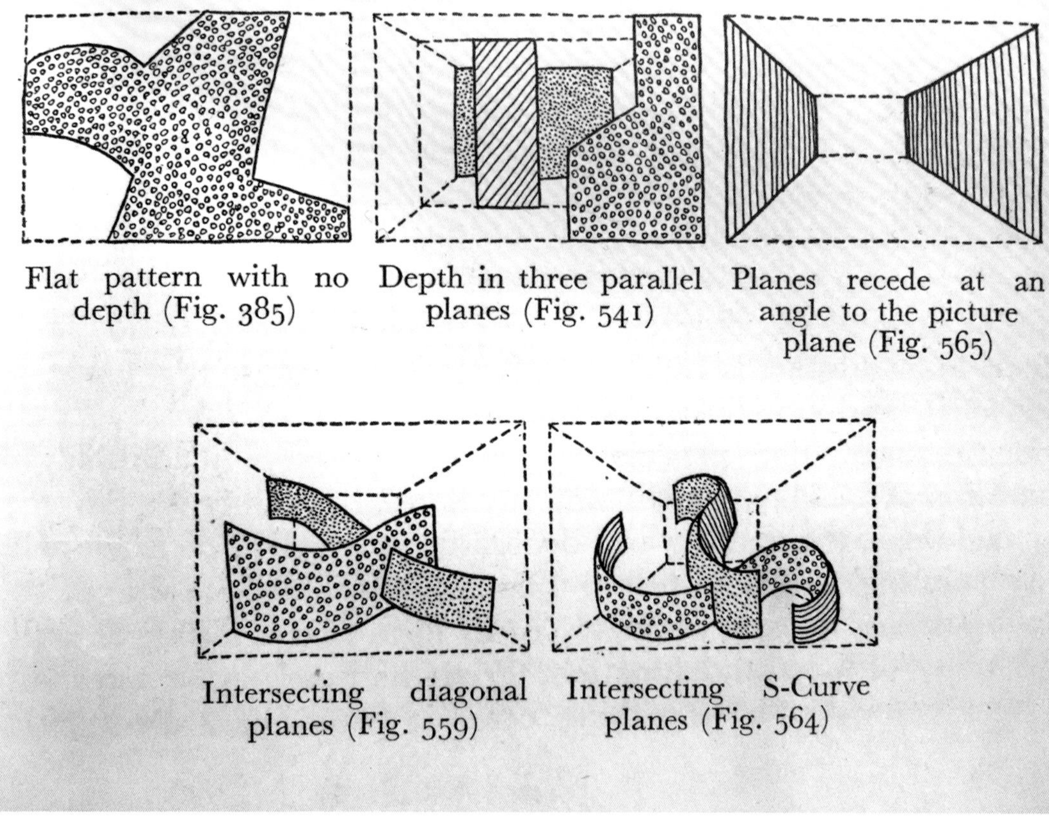

2. Helen Gardner, *Art through
the Ages: An Introduction to Its
History and Significance*, rev. ed.
(New York: Harcourt, Brace and
Company, 1936)

United States, and many American scholars traveled to Europe.

Robust interest in the late 1920s in an English translation of *Grundbegriffe* demonstrates diffuse knowledge of Wölfflin's text before 1932. In 1930, when the publisher George Bell and Sons in London approached F. Bruckmann Verlag, Wölfflin's publisher in Munich, about translating the text, Bell's representative learned that Bruckmann had received inquiries about the English-language rights from three scholars in the United States: Ernst Diez, Paul Green, and Walter Heil. As Bruckmann put it, "the interest for the book especially among American scholars and students seems to be very great." Although none of these three was engaged as translator (Bell would eventually contract with Marie D. Hottinger, a Scottish translator living in Zurich), their backgrounds give a sense of the work's scholarly public in the United States. [8]

Ernst Diez, a pupil in Vienna of both Alois Riegl and Josef Strzygowski, taught at Bryn Mawr College from 1926 to 1938, when he returned to Vienna.[9] Trained in Islamic art but active in many areas of Asian art, Diez engaged with questions of style in his scholarship of the 1930s. His collaboration with his colleague Otto Demus in Vienna, on the book *Byzantine Mosaics in Greece, Hosios Lucas and Daphni* (1931) was the first analysis of the style of these monuments.[10] Diez's interest in Wölfflin's book was oppositional, carrying on the Vienna school coolness to Wölfflin's formalism.[11] Diez was clearly interested in the early modern material treated in *Grundbegriffe*, for in 1930–1931 he was to teach a course titled "The Origin of Baroque Art in Italy and Other Countries." After the English translation appeared, Diez introduced a new course, "Philosophy of Art," that undoubtedly took up *Principles of Art History*.[12]

Having studied in Munich, where he worked at the Alte Pinakothek and the Graphische Sammlung, Walter Heil was the only one of the three prospective translators with a direct relationship to Wölfflin. The new curator of European art at the Detroit Institute of Arts, Heil joined the German-trained William (born Wilhelm) Valentiner (director, 1924–1945).[13] Arriving in Detroit just before the opening of Paul Cret's new building, Heil encountered a museum in which the audience was being built from the ground up. The new building aroused an interest in illustrated lectures on the history of art, and series were prepared for European travelers. Heil's plan to translate *Grundbegriffe* was likely motivated by a pedagogical need in the museum context alongside an interest in Wölfflin's work shared by Valentiner.

The North Carolina playwright Paul Green learned about *Grundbegriffe* from the German literary scholar Gustav Plessnov and from the psychiatrist and art historian Hans Prinzhorn while on a Guggenheim Fellowship year in Germany, 1928–1929. It was presented to him as a book that was being discussed widely at the time: "Professor Prinzhorn of the University of Frankfurt recently said to me in conversation:

Heinrich Wölfflin is a man who only comes once in a generation. He equals any of the other art-critics of Germany in his learning, but he surpasses them all in his capacity to put it in the language that everybody uses. He is 'popular' without sacrificing scholarship.[14]

Green returned from Germany convinced of the applicability of Wölfflin's understanding of epochal *Sehformen* to historicist drama, encouraging him to move away from classical drama, as well as to collect the folkloric stories to use in his plays.[15] Green endorsed the title to the Henry Holt Company for the US edition of Bell's publication.[16]

When Marie Hottinger's *Principles of Art History* came out in 1932, the belatedness of the translation of a book already in its seventh German edition was noted by more than one American reviewer.[17] Not everyone was satisfied by the translation, with its Teutonic character and unfamiliar vocabulary. One reviewer preferred "tonal" to Hottinger's "painterly," "lighting" to "illumination," "cycles" to "periodicity," and "equilibrium" to "equipoise."[18] In the mid-1930s William Valentiner habitually translated *malerisch* in Wölfflin's sense as "painteresque" (a term in circulation in the field of photography), and in 1936 Ernst Scheyer, a pupil of Wölfflin lineage newly arrived from Germany, endorsed the term.[19] Even Erwin Panofsky took a swipe at the neologism "painterly" as a prime example of the German émigré art historians' difficulties in translating their specialized lexicon into English.[20] But Philip McMahon, who taught the course "Principles and History of Criticism" at the Institute of Fine Arts for many years, welcomed the opportunity to take the book, whose vocabulary had already entered art history in the United States unattributed to Wölfflin, on its own terms.[21]

Hottinger's translation was rapidly disseminated to colleges and universities in the United States and Commonwealth countries in the Carnegie Corporation's art book set, and it appeared quickly in college and university courses.[22] The book was promoted also to a wider public on the "White List" of books approved by the Catholic Church.[23] And in 1937 *Principles* ("an extremely provocative analysis") was included on a list of art history publications compiled by Metropolitan Museum of Art staff for the American Library Association.[24]

Wölfflin's concepts were immediately, if selectively, injected into the most widely used survey textbook, Helen Gardner's *Art through the Ages*.[25] In the second revised edition, published in 1936, *Principles* had a palpable presence in a new section on form accompanied by spatial diagrams illustrating Wölfflin's paired concepts of plane and recession (fig. 2). And a new section on the baroque seems to have been, if not inspired, then supported, by Wölfflin's book. In subsequent editions reference to *Principles* would be limited to the section on the baroque, though general discussions of style based on Wölfflin's thinking increasingly dominated the introduction. Wölfflin's *Principles* quickly entered the art-historical

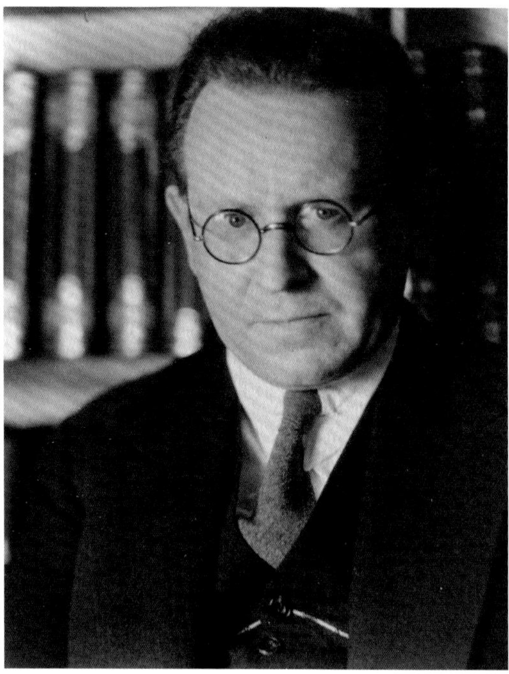

groundwater, not always with attribution and usually alongside other approaches to the work of art.

The Myth of the Triumph of Iconology

In many accounts of art history in the United States, 1933 marks a turning point with the arrival of approximately one hundred thirty German and Austrian art historians fleeing Nazi Europe. In this by now mythic tale, Erwin Panofsky is the hero, and the iconology that he and his colleagues watered down into a workable iconography for positivist and pragmatic American students triumphs over formalism.[26] In some versions of this story, iconography, with a strong focus on imagery that supported the values of Renaissance humanism, replaced the theoretical debates that dominated German art history of the 1920s and 1930s in which Wölfflin's text was embedded. In other accounts iconography represented an apolitical alternative to style history, with its nationalist and racial implications.[27] Aspects of this narrative are hard to refute. But even the American Panofsky described his work as combining the iconological and stylistic approaches; iconology was as disputed as

a German import as was formalism;[28] and while the European debates were not pursued quite in the same terms in the United States, the texts under debate, including *Principles*, were not cast aside.[29] On the contrary, formalism and its sibling, style analysis, would harden into the methodological antipode of iconography. For decades art history was presented to students as an either-or proposition, the "twin pillars of the discipline," as one scholar put it when assessing the crisis of art history in the 1980s.[30]

In this unbalanced account it has not been sufficiently appreciated just how many Wölfflin *Schuler* (those who either wrote dissertations under him or considered his work key for theirs) and grand-*Schuler* ended up in the United States in the 1930s. That such a block of formalist-trained historians could pass under the radar is owing to the strength of the inherited narrative; the diversity of their areas of expertise, spread over many subfields; the positions (professorial or curatorial) they took; and the level of prominence they achieved.[31] While not all will occupy us here, the group of direct pupils includes Oskar Hagen, Ulrich Middeldorf, Walter Friedlaender, Franz Landsberger, Martin Weinberger, Alfred Neumeyer, Paul Frankl, Ludwig Bachhofer, Jakob Rosenberg, Wolfgang Born, and Justus Bier. There were also those who took his courses or studied his method, heavily imprinted on Wölfflin pupils like A. E. Brinckmann.[32] Sigfried Giedion, a Wölfflin student who spent several years at universities in the United States as a visiting scholar starting in 1939, exerted an enormous influence on the history of modern architecture. Many other Germanophone art historians who cannot be considered Wölfflin's direct students nonetheless taught and engaged actively with his work, among them Paul Zucker; Richard Krautheimer (who attended lectures by Wölfflin and Wölfflin's student Paul Frankl); and, later, Rudolf Wittkower (Columbia University, 1956–1969).

There is no better example of how Wölfflin's thought was transmitted by his students in the United States than Oskar Hagen (fig. 3), the first pupil to arrive (and not because he was forced out by the racial policies of the Hitler regime). Son of a German father who became a naturalized American and a British mother, Hagen founded the University of Wisconsin's department of history and criticism of art in 1925.[33] He quickly overcame the anti-German sentiment experienced by a previous German professor (Arnold Sommerfeld) when his first lecture course on Renaissance into baroque art attracted five times more students than predicted.[34] Just how Wölfflin's work served Hagen in his assimilation to the United States, which he recounted in a memoir of his emigration, reads like an academic fairy tale. Arriving in New York by ship, Hagen went with his family to Ithaca, where he was hosted by German relatives. Frustrated that he was unable to practice his English surrounded by German-speaking friends and family, he went to the library, found the English translation of Wölfflin's *Classic Art*, and worked through it systematically, mastering a vocabulary that at the very least would help his teaching in English.[35] Wölfflin's words and ideas permeated his teaching, as he put it, "in the manner of Wölfflin on the basis of his *Principles*," though he was frustrated by his students' need to master the names of artists and the geography of art.[36]

Hagen brought Wölfflin's method to teaching and scholarship alike. His early work, *Deutsches Sehen*, written just after World War I in Germany, and his first major English-language publication, *Patterns and Principles of Spanish Art* of 1936, extracted the national forms of seeing that are present in Wölfflin's *Principles*.[37] Many of Hagen's students took up precisely the question of national and racial psychologies of style, a question pressed upon them also by their emigration. In Hagen's latter title, revised in 1943, he combined Wölfflin's *Sehformen*, which he called "visual patterns," with "emotional predispositions," or underlying psychological traits, using examples from literature and art in the more up-to-date

approach of *Geistesgeschichte* (cultural history). Another Wölfflin student in the United States, Alfred Neumeyer, reviewed the revised second edition of *Patterns and Principles of Spanish Art*, noting the Wölfflinian genealogy and the problems associated with it: namely, that the link between basic patterns and psychological constituents is infrequently drawn. "There are rare examples in art-historical literature of the interpenetration of the psychological with the formal strata," he wrote.[38] The critique of an attempt to synthesize formalism with cultural history was being discussed among Wölfflin students in Europe and in the United States too.[39]

One of the more important ways in which Wölfflin's *Principles* had an early and enduring impact on art history in the United States was his students' study of American painting.[40] Layers of immigration challenged attempts to locate a cultural essence or unity independent of European models. Hagen's *The Birth of the American Tradition* (1940) is thoroughly Wölfflinian in its thinking, from the intention to concentrate on problems of form in the work of leading artists, to the lament that he had to cover so much basic biographical material (a wish for an art history without names). Hagen sets up an American current and a European (mostly British) countercurrent in constant battle. The best American painters expressed their independence in an archaic art that was "direct," "instinctive," and "deeply felt."[41] In the assimilation of European traditions, a distinctly American art was born. Wolfgang Born attended Wölfflin's lectures in 1914 when *Grundbegriffe* was being written, as he recalled in his obituary of Wölfflin for the *Art Journal*. He later fled Nazi Europe for the United States, where he taught at several institutions. He turned his attention to American art in studies of still life and landscape painting. Born understood American art through Wölfflin's notion of the organic development of styles. And while the balance of his text leans as much to the historical and biographical as to descriptive formalism, an American art on Wölfflinian

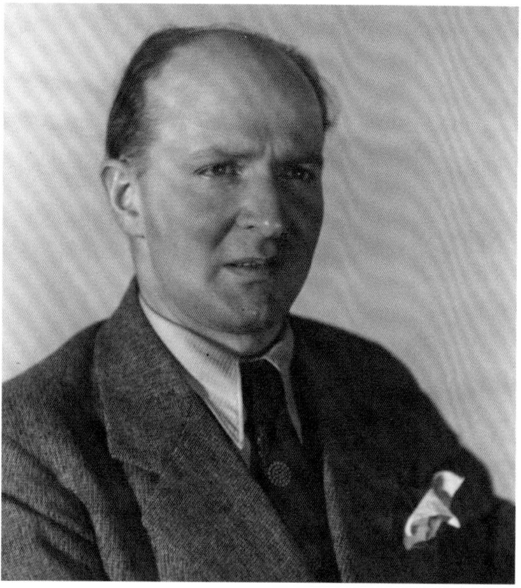

4. Ludwig Bachhofer, c. 1936
University of Chicago Library, Special Collections Research Center

grounds emerges in the chapter on the panoramic style, governed by a distinctive American "space-feeling" that demands a moving spectator.[42]

The histories of Hagen and Born set the terms for decades—so much so that as late as 1969, in *American Painting of the Nineteenth Century*, Barbara Novak (a student of the formalist-trained Julius Held) divided American painting into two dominant strains: one linear, measured, conceptual; the other, tied to Europe, painterly and atmospheric.[43] A few years later, Alfred Neumeyer put the capstone on the formalist-driven émigré accounts of American painting with his *Geschichte der amerikanischen Malerei*, a work described as mirroring German science but with a difference.[44] In an assessment of American art studies in 1988, Wanda Corn observed that the emergence of American art from the shadow of European art was impeded by formalism's dominance.[45] Given how many of Wölfflin's students took up the subject, the pervasive influence of Wölfflin's *Principles* clearly contributed to the problem.

The history of Chinese art was another subdiscipline established early in the United States along formalist lines by a Wölfflin student.[46] Ludwig Bachhofer (fig. 4), who studied with Wölfflin in Munich, left Germany in 1935 for the University of Chicago, where he held the first chair of East Asian art history.[47] Bachhofer applied Wölfflin's concepts first to Japanese woodcuts in his dissertation (1921), written under Wölfflin, and subsequently to Chinese art and to early Indian sculpture.[48] Bachhofer's discipleship to Wölfflinian formalism was announced in his introduction to *A Short History of Chinese Art*:

No explanation should be necessary for the great emphasis laid upon problems of form. Form is the only means of expression an artist has at his disposal, whatever considerations may have determined his subject matter. It is form alone that makes a vessel, a statue, or a painting a work of art. But form never remains the same. It changes continually and I saw my main task in describing these changes. They revealed themselves as so many phases of a logical, orderly, and organic evolution.[49]

Bachhofer's students and theirs sustained the method. Chief among the former was Max Loehr, pupil of Bachhofer in Munich in the 1930s, who was appointed to the University of Michigan in 1951, then to Harvard in 1960. Like Bachhofer, who found equivalents for Wölfflin's archaic, classic, and baroque in Chinese art, Loehr classified Chinese bronzes as archaic, classic, and decadent (the last being the moment when the organic unity of style began to break down). Wölfflin's core idea of development helped to counter arguments that Chinese bronzes did not change over time but continually copied established types.[50] Loehr defended his exclusion of questions of function and meaning by saying that in these works meaning was not independent of form. In a paraphrase of Wölfflin's famous statement—"One ought to be able to recognize the essential elements of individual style from nothing more than the delineation of a nostril"—Loehr claimed that "once a style has been recognized, even a fragment or detail (as part of an organized whole) should be sufficient to reveal its place."[51]

Bachhofer's strictly Wölfflinian method was hotly debated in the late 1940s by scholars of Chinese art in the United States in the pages of *The Art Bulletin*. Otto Maenchen-Helfen, at the time Neumeyer's colleague at Mills College, disputed Bachhofer's dating of works and the a priori assumption of absolute unities of styles.[52] Bachhofer replied, in the spirit of Wölfflin, that such unities were never absolute and his own statement to that effect had been overlooked.[53] Benjamin Rowland carried on the dispute more explicitly on methodological grounds, putting his finger on the inappropriate application of Wölfflin's concepts to Chinese art. Rowland viewed style in Bachhofer's work as a "sinister autonomous force," an "authoritarian," a priori system to which the evidence was "coerced" to bend, a widespread complaint about Wölfflin's *Principles*.[54]

Yet Max Loehr's work shows that this type of formalism most certainly continued; and once the chronological proposals of Bachhofer and Loehr held up against new archaeological evidence, the method was vindicated. But, as would often be the case, the Wölfflinian legacy quickly disappeared from sight for many, since Bachhofer ceased to cite the origins of the system within which he so obviously worked. Loehr, in turn, engaged intensely with Bachhofer's publications, though there can be no doubt that he knew Wölfflin's *Principles* as well.[55] The Wölfflinian origin was recognized during the disciplinary debates of the 1980s and viewed as an unfortunate obstacle to the pursuit of style analysis in Chinese art.[56] As late as 2001 and 2003, Jerome Silbergeld and Wen C. Fong mounted impassioned defenses of style history as the still crucial work of the historian of Chinese art. Fong's Wölfflin-inspired diagram of the changing representation of space in Chinese painting (fig. 5), though distinguished from Western construction and practices of seeing, proves the point.[57] By contrast, Wölfflinian formalism did not have a grip on the history of Japanese art in the United States, the conservatism of which derived from other sources.[58]

Bachhofer was not Wölfflin's sole pupil to study art outside Europe, but most of Wölfflin's students who emigrated to the United States were trained in early modern European art. Among them was one of *Principles'* greatest critics: Walter Friedlaender. A pupil of Wölfflin in Berlin, Friedlaender had an enduring impact on the reception of *Principles* with his 1925 essay on the anticlassical, or mannerism. This work, translated and transmitted to a generation of students at New York University's Institute of Fine Arts, opened up an alternative formalist account of sixteenth-century painting that explicitly questioned Wölfflin's succession of styles.[59] Leo Steinberg, who first read *Principles* in London at age seventeen or eighteen, recalled how Friedlaender's outline of mannerism disrupted Wölfflin's ideas:

Friedlaender's point was that proto-Baroque artists such as the Carracci in Bologna, Cerano in Lombardy, Cigoli in Florence, were not reacting to the Renaissance; they were reacting to the preceding phase of Mannerism, and in important respects they were linking up with the ideals of the Renaissance. So everything had to be redone, and Wölfflin was cited as the man who had been so woefully wrong. Wölfflin was very much there, but as a deceiver, and we felt happy to have superseded him.[60]

Perhaps troubled by the mannerist problem, Renaissance scholars have tended to read *Classic Art*, while *Principles* effectively became Wölfflin's baroque book.[61]

While formalism, often linked to connoisseurship, was a dominant strain in the post-1933 art history carried across by the German émigrés, those same historians were aware of the prominence of the Warburg school and were part of a process of methodological "amalgamation."[62] In an article of 1941, Wolfgang Stechow saw an opportunity to reconcile formalism and the study of meaning in the current revival of figurative art in the work of Picasso, the surrealists, and the WPA artists. In his account of the interaction between contemporary art and art history as the cleaving of form from subject matter, Wölfflin's *Principles* earns an admiring description, even though Stechow notes both the controversies around it and the purely formal analyses it inspired. The figurative turn augured not only a reconciliation with art of a public alienated by

5. Wen C. Fong et al., *Images of the Mind: Selections from the Edward L. Elliott Family and John B. Elliott Collections of Chinese Calligraphy and Painting at the Art Museum, Princeton University* (Princeton: The Art Museum, Princeton University, 1984), 21

National Gallery of Art Library, Washington

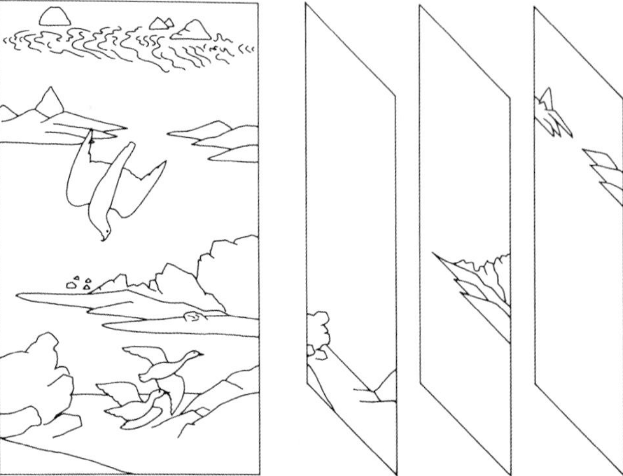

Figs. 13a, b. Diagrams of *Hawk and Ducks*, fig. 18, showing additive mountain motifs receding in three separate stages

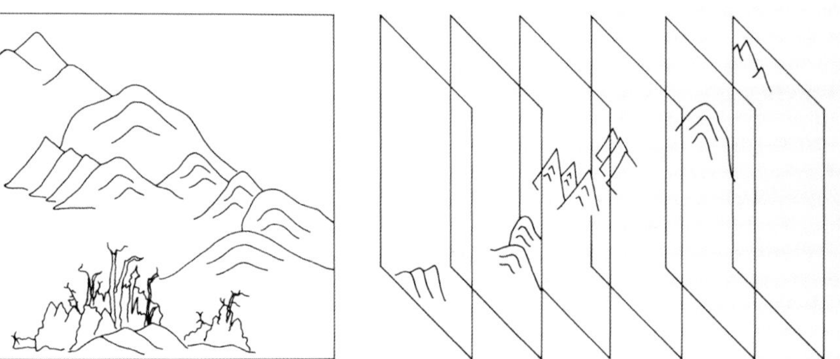

Figs. 14a, b. Diagrams of Li-sheng, *Dream Journey through the Hsiao and Hsiang Rivers*, fig. 53, showing overlapping mountain motifs receding in a continuous sequence

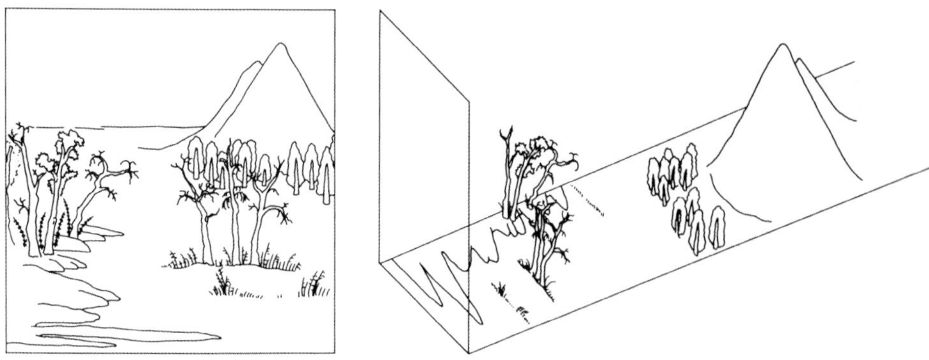

Figs. 15a, b. Diagrams of Chao Meng-fu, *Autumn Colors on the Ch'iao and Hua Mountains*, fig. 66, showing landscape elements arranged along a continuously receding ground plane

abstraction but also a return in art history to a concern with "subject matter transmuted into content through form."[63]

Others absorbed with reluctance the synthesis of formalism and iconology acknowledged by many as a normal way of proceeding. Julius Held, who described himself as trained in style and connoisseurship, became aware of iconology during his early studies in Vienna but became versed in it only once he was teaching in New York, even then considering himself a "fringe iconographer." The work of Rudolf Wittkower, who joined the Warburg Institute in 1934 and emigrated to the United States in 1956, is a good example of the endurance of a Germanophone formalism alongside iconology. According to an unpublished lecture he gave in 1933, just before leaving Germany for England, Wittkower considered formalism—meaning Wölfflin's *Principles*, which he read in the third edition (fig. 6)—the most important direction in baroque studies, followed by Riegl's psychological approach, and, as third, a sociology of art. Iconology was not yet at the table.[64] When he returned to art history's methods more generally, in a lecture given in Delaware in 1959, Wittkower (now identified as a Warburgian) repositioned style history amid the surge in postwar "symbolic studies." He was critical of Wölfflin's *Principles* as a work of system-building based on personal experience but maintained the necessity of a terminology of style, "as long as we recognize its heuristic and pragmatic value." Nonetheless, he continued to place formalism before iconology:

The various stylistic methods to which I have referred have pride of place in Europe as well as in America. There are relatively few art historians to whom the question of the WHAT appears more vital than that of the HOW. The WHAT takes us to iconography.... Although nowadays the importance of iconographical studies need hardly be emphasized, the widespread reluctance to embark on them may be due to the fact that over the *what*, the *how* is often forgotten, and this indicates one of the limitations of the iconographical approach.[65]

While acknowledging the contribution of iconology to methodological renewal in the discipline, Wittkower still insisted on the primacy of formal analysis *and* situated style history as the *conscience* of iconology, a reminder of what it overlooks.

In the postwar period the two methodological lines brought in by the German émigrés — formalism, especially Wölfflin's, and Panofsky's iconography and iconology — hardened into opposing camps. This was especially evident in Italian

Renaissance studies, which sustained a discourse of Western humanism and could easily be contrasted to the mechanistic, anti-individualist "art history without names" that Wölfflin came to represent. Nonetheless, the presence in the United States of many Wölfflin-trained formalists complicates considerably the myth of the triumph of iconology. Formalism, not just in its connoisseurial guise (art history with names), remained central to art history in the United States into the 1960s and even beyond.

Theory De-Theorized

Whatever the reasons those German émigrés who had engaged in the 1920s in theoretical debates (and not all did) felt the need to downplay or abandon them altogether, the turn away from them was reinforced by a democratizing ethos of American aesthetics.[66] The pragmatist philosopher John Dewey's *Art and Experience* of 1934, a signal text of that ethos, held that art was to be experienced directly as a living thing, without the need for other forms of knowledge, without theory divorced from experience. While his vitalist themes are quite consonant with many of Wölfflin's ideas (and Dewey was likely familiar with them, as he thanks Meyer Schapiro in his preface), Dewey's pragmatism, and the positivism of Sidney Hook and others, set up a book like *Principles* as abstract thinking and moored it to the German debates.

From the 1930s, *Principles* already had a dual existence among the professoriate. On the one hand its theoretical propositions, for better or worse, were recognized as marking the arrival of advanced art history in the United States. Symptomatic was the lament by Fiske Kimball: "I was too old when I came to understand Wölfflin. I could no longer change."[67] On the other hand, among the Wölfflin-trained émigrés were scholars who were oriented toward museum work and connoisseurship, for whom Wölfflin's formalism was key, primarily to the stylistic judgments that informed the many monographic studies of artists that *Principles*

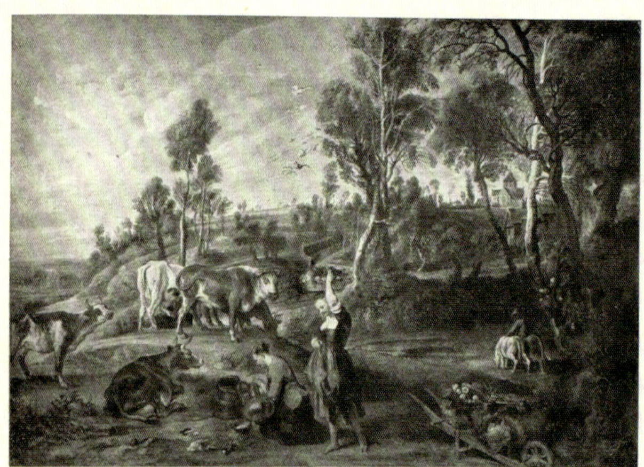

strömung, die Empfindung des romanischen Barock bedingt stark seinen
Stil und so empfangen wir von ihm mehr als von den „zeitlosen" Holländern
die Aufforderung, uns von dem, was man als Z e i t s t i l bezeichnen muß,
eine Vorstellung zu machen.

Man gewinnt diese Vorstellung am besten in Italien, weil hier die Entwicklung unabhängig von außen sich vollzogen hat und das Durchgehende
des italienischen Charakters in allem Wechsel sehr wohl erkennbar bleibt.
Der Stilwandel von der Renaissance zum Barock ist ein rechtes Schulbei-
spiel, wie ein neuer Zeitgeist sich eine neue Form erzwingt.

Hier kommen wir auf vielbegangene Wege. Nichts liegt der Kunst-
historie näher als Stil- mit Kulturepochen parallel zu setzen. Die Säulen
und Bogen der Hochrenaissance reden so vernehmlich von dem Geist der
Zeit wie die Figuren Raffaels und eine Barockarchitektur gibt die Vorstellung von dem Wandel der Ideale nicht minder deutlich, als wenn man die
breit ausladende Gebärde Guido Renis mit der edlen Getragenheit und Größe
der Sixtinischen Madonna vergleicht.

Es sei erlaubt, diesmal ausschließlich auf architektonischem Boden zu
bleiben. Der Zentralbegriff der italienischen Renaissance ist der Begriff der
vollkommenen Proportion. Wie in der Figur, so hat diese Zeit im Bauwerk
versucht, das Bild der in sich ruhenden Vollkommenheit zu gewinnen. Jede

9

KUNSTGESCHICHTLICHE GRUNDBEGRIFFE

Form zu abgeschlossenem Dasein herausgebildet, frei in den Gelenken;
lauter selbständig atmende Teile. Die Säule, der Flächenausschnitt an der
Wand, das Volumen eines einzelnen Raumgliedes wie des Raumganzen, die
Massen des Aufbaues insgesamt — es sind lauter Gestaltungen, die den
Menschen ein in sich befriedigtes Dasein finden lassen, über menschliches
Maß hinausgehend, aber der Phantasie noch immer zugänglich. Mit unend-
lichem Wohlgefühl empfindet der Sinn diese Kunst als Bild eines erhöhten
freien Daseins, an dem ihm teilzunehmen vergönnt ist.

Der Barock bedient sich desselben Formensystems, aber er gibt nicht mehr
das Vollkommene und Vollendete, sondern das Bewegte und Werdende,
nicht das Begrenzte und Faßbare, sondern das Unbegrenzte und Kolossale.
Das Ideal der schönen Proportion verschwindet, das Interesse hängt sich
nicht an das Sein, sondern an das Geschehen. Die Massen kommen in Bewegung, schwere, dumpf-gegliederte Massen. Die Architektur hört auf — was
sie in der Renaissance im höchsten Grade gewesen ist — eine Gelenkkunst
zu sein und die einst zum Eindruck höchster Freiheit getriebene Durch-
gliederung des Baukörpers weicht einer Zusammenballung von Teilen ohne
eigentliche Selbständigkeit.

Diese Analyse ist gewiß nicht erschöpfend, aber sie kann genügen, um zu
zeigen, in welcher Weise Stile Zeitausdruck sind. Es ist deutlich ein neues
Lebensideal, das aus der Kunst des italienischen Barock spricht und wenn
wir die Architektur vorangestellt haben, weil sie die eindrücklichste Ver-
körperung dieses Ideals gibt, so sagen die zeitgenössischen Maler und Bildhauer in ihrer Sprache doch dasselbe und wer die psychischen Grundlagen
des Stilwandels auf Begriffe bringen will, wird hier wahrscheinlich rascher
das entscheidende Wort erfahren als bei den Architekten. Das Verhältnis
des Individuums zur Welt hat sich verändert, ein neues Gefühlsreich hat sich
aufgetan, die Seele drängt nach Auflösung in der Erhabenheit des Über-
großen und Unendlichen. „Affekt und Bewegung um jeden Preis", so gibt
der Cicerone in kürzester Formel die Charakteristik dieser Kunst. —

Wir haben mit der Skizzierung der drei Beispiele von individuellem Stil,
von Volksstil und von Zeitstil die Ziele einer Kunstgeschichte illustriert, die
den Stil in erster Linie als Ausdruck faßt, als Ausdruck einer Zeit- und
Volksstimmung wie als Ausdruck eines persönlichen Temperaments. Es ist
offenbar, daß damit die künstlerische Qualität der Hervorbringung nicht an-
gerührt ist: das Temperament macht wohl kein Kunstwerk, aber es ist das,
was man den stofflichen Teil der Stile nennen kann, in dem weiten Sinne,

10

6. Heinrich Wölfflin, *Kunst-geschichtliche Grundbegriffe*, 3rd edition (Munich: Bruckmann, 1918), 9 and 10, copy with annotations by Rudolf Wittkower

National Gallery of Art Library, Washington

had eschewed.[68] Consider Jakob Rosenberg, scholar of seventeenth-century northern European art and author of a monograph on Rembrandt, who said that Wölfflin's impact was decisive in his orientation to the visual over the literary, to "the phenomenon of style." And although he "later rejected some of his professor's oversimplified concepts, he often stressed his fundamental debt to this giant among the founders of modern art history."[69] The style historians, including the connoisseurs, could be counted among the "antiphilosophical" "masters of empiricism," as James Ackerman later characterized some members of this generation of German émigré art historians.[70] Julius Held later recalled: "Maybe one can say — and I would admit that — that I'm too much of a traditionalist to really consider more the theoretical foundations of what I'm doing.... Maybe I should have thought more about the philosophical basis for what we were doing...."[71] On the other hand, Panofsky noted as a "blessing" the contact and occasional conflict of the German art historian with "Anglo-Saxon positivism, which is, in principle, distrustful of abstract speculation."[72]

We can hear this intersection of the German avoidance of an open debate on historical theory and the Deweyan ethos in

Irving Lavin's recollections of the Institute of Fine Arts in the early 1950s.[73] Amid a general suspicion of theory, the ideas of Wölfflin and Riegl were considered racially tainted and contrary to an ethos of individualism; these authors were read, but not in courses. Shunning theory, Lavin's generation sought insights gained from direct engagement with works of art, which Wölfflin would have endorsed.[74] In 1955 Ackerman, a frequent spokesperson in the discipline, noted the determination of émigré German scholars to overcome Wölfflin's psychologically based formalism and Riegl's *Kunstwollen* with more objective historical approaches. He observed in 1958 that "most of us have enough respect for theory to guide students to, say, Wölfflin, Focillon, or Geoffrey Scott," but "we have been bullied by our materialistic surroundings into a suspicion of theory, into an unwillingness to examine the principles and values by which we work."[75]

Again, this does not mean that *Principles* disappeared entirely; but, absorbed rather than studied and openly debated, it was drained of its theoretical premises. In various essays on the state of art history written in the late 1950s and early 1960s, Ackerman assessed the implications of a general suspicion of theory. One result was a kind of "mechanical" application of Wölfflinian formalism and other theories in the absence of debate on their premises. Related is the enduring place that Wölfflin's principles found in the undergraduate classroom as "effective supports" to introductory art history: "In almost every case, this course was not oriented to teaching historical method but rather *how to see* works of art."[76] As Wölfflin's own motto was "sehen lernen," he would not have objected to the use of *Principles* for students to learn to see: that was the point. The problem is that the debate about what it means to see, one of the most complex theoretical issues in *Principles*, dropped out. Ackerman saw the danger in having "allowed the systems that give meaning to these terms to slip into the unconscious," where they "operate without the

benefit of our control, as a barrier against new perceptions."[77]

The theoretical propositions of *Principles* did come under scrutiny in the 1950s and early 1960s, when there was an interest in a new theorization of style. The first major statement was Meyer Schapiro's 1953 essay "Style." Wölfflin is a central figure, praised for a general construction that "simplifies and organizes the field." At the same time Schapiro stressed the problematically internal nature of Wölfflin's system, calling for an external history of style along Marxist lines (a project with little resonance in the McCarthy era).[78] The far more devastating critique soon came from Arnold Hauser, who was teaching at Brandeis University (1957–1959) when *The Philosophy of Art History* was published.[79] Hauser also fell on the strictly internal nature of Wölfflin's idea of development, pointing explicitly to the troubling Hegelianism of *Principles*, but his primary complaint was the passive group-think implicit in Wölfflin's art history without names. He countered that styles are consensual and emerge from social conditions, strongly criticizing the reactionary idea that any external pressure is but an interruption of the course of development. (Bachhofer clung to this idea with particular tenacity.) Hauser's invective against group-think echoed ideas widely diffused in Hannah Arendt's *The Origins of Totalitarianism* (1951).

These critiques of Wölfflin's *Principles*, written when style was still considered central to art history, created strong ripples across the discipline and stimulated others. Ackerman referred again to the atmosphere of "suspicion of philosophical speculation" in an essay of 1962, in which he openly called for a new theory of style, to which, until recently, no American scholar had made a contribution. Stimulated by the writings of Schapiro and Hauser, and obviously with Wölfflin in mind, Ackerman made a series of proposals to preserve style as a key structure in art history: to assert the individual artist over deterministic historical forces while finding a new way to explain

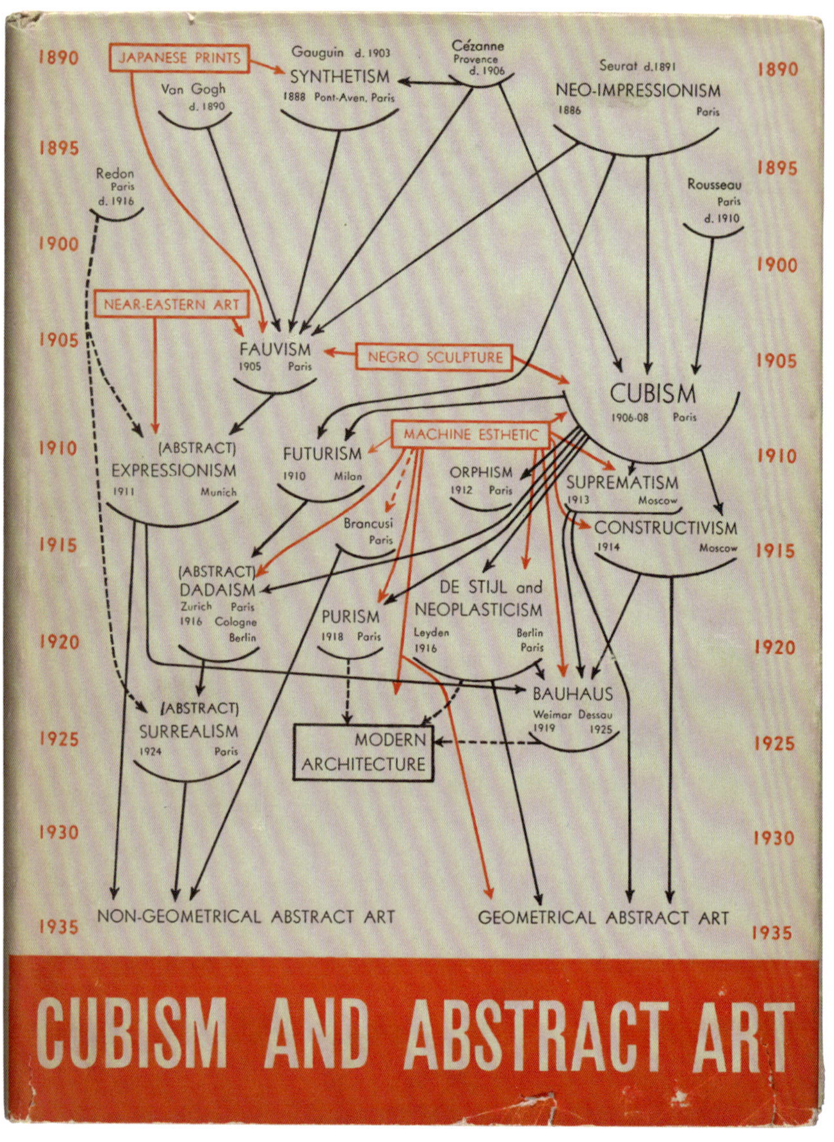

7. Alfred H. Barr, *Cubism and Abstract Art* (Museum of Modern Art, New York, 1936)

© 1936 The Museum of Modern Art, New York

recurrent patterns. The first new major theory was George Kubler's *The Shape of Time* (1962), which explicitly overturned the use of biological analogies in accounts of stylistic change, valuing series over development and putting the perception of difference and thus agency into the hands of artists.[80] And in 1964 Max Loehr explicitly responded to Hauser's critique of immanence in Wölfflin's "art history without names" while continuing to sustain Wölfflin's internal history of art, though not in his name.[81]

One cannot discount the anti-Wölfflinian impact on art historians in the US (many trained in England) of E. H. Gombrich's *Norm and Form*, published in London in

1966. There he maintained that Wölfflin merely reiterated Vasari's classical ideal.[82] Even more devastating, he pointed to the false sense of polarities on which *Principles* was based. On both points Gombrich was highly influential, but it was only with the advent of PowerPoint that art historians were compelled to dismantle what Gombrich referred to as the "fateful tool of systematic comparison" that Wölfflin gave to art history.

The diffused knowledge of Wölfflin's *Principles* in the United States gave it a privileged place in the late 1950s, when, as mentioned earlier, some art historians awakened to the absence of a theoretical basis for art history, and in the 1960s, which saw a renewed call for a self-aware practice, with a rising interest in social art history. One of the products of this call was the publication in 1971 by Eugene Kleinbauer of *Modern Perspectives in Western Art History*, the first anthology of classic texts, including *Principles*. The extremely well-informed introduction to that volume confirmed that the primarily empirical basis of contemporary art history had produced "cautiousness, skepticism and indeed theoretical paralysis."[83]

Principles and Modernism: From Plane to Flatness

Wölfflin's *Principles* may have had its most profound impact in the United States as the foundation for Alfred Barr's and Clement Greenberg's highly influential accounts of modernism. Once their views were disseminated, the history of formalism in the United States became one of the crossing of different tracks as the Wölfflinian foundation was lost and recuperated.

When Alfred Barr devised his *Principles*-inspired chart of the modern movements for the 1936 exhibition *Cubism and Abstract Art* at MOMA (fig. 7), the English translation of *Principles* had been out for four years. Between Barr's Ivy League education, his extensive travels in Germany, and his entire circle of acquaintance (including Meyer Schapiro and Philip McMahon), we can be certain he knew the text.[84] With the chart,

Barr brought order to the multiplying modern movements, arranging over a dozen of them into a binary scheme: "geometrical abstract art," characterized by abstraction, pure design, and organization, and "nongeometrical abstract art," characterized by pure spontaneity, distortion, and deformation — Mondrian's linearity on one side, the surrealists' sumptuous painterliness on the other. Although the vocabulary of Wölfflin's ten principles is not especially present, his binaries, with the psychological spirit of a rational classicism on the one side and an emotional baroque on the other, provide the underlying structure for Barr's historical scheme.[85] If we had any doubt of the origin of the binary, the charts Barr created in 1939 for an exhibition of Italian art, 1500 – 1800 (fig. 8), show stylistic binaries of early modern art mapping onto those of the modern (displayed alongside the Italian art exhibition as proof of ancestry).[86] In addition to being enduringly influential, Barr's charts show the susceptibility of Wölfflin's binaries to a diagrammatic, scientific logic.

If Barr's modernism was structured by the rational historical ordering made possible by Wölfflin's antitheses, Clement Greenberg both absorbed Barr's genealogy and dug into the intuitive possibilities of Wölfflin's formalism. Educated in art history (and fluent in German), Greenberg read and cited Wölfflin's *Principles.* He noted Wölfflin's death in his first review of the work of David Smith (1946). From Wölfflin's planar and recessional, Greenberg became attuned to the vibrations of forms between surface and recession, helping him to arrive at one of his central contentions: that the great achievement of abstract painting was its total adherence to the picture plane, that is, its flatness. Greenberg did not mechanically transfer Wölfflin's terms but worked through Wölfflin's formalism as it applied to the present: his notions of unity ("Crisis of the Easel Picture," 1948), of the apparent chaos or loss of order in the baroque ("Jackson Pollock: Inspiration, Vision, Intuitive Decision," 1967), and of the sensibility Daniel Adler has identified with the painterly.[87]

Because Greenberg's formalism was so specific and consistent (baroque unity "devolved" into the all-over painting), it was easy to lose sight of the obvious debt to Wölfflin that subtended his long-standing preoccupation with the emergence of modern painting out of Renaissance and baroque art.[88] But the terms of Wölfflin's *Principles* resurface explicitly in his 1962 essay "After Abstract Expressionism":

If the label "Abstract Expressionism" means anything, it means painterliness: loose, rapid handling, or the look of it; masses that blotted and fused instead of shapes that stayed distinct; large and conspicuous rhythms; broken color; uneven saturations or densities of paint; exhibited brush, knife, or finger marks — in short, a constellation of qualities like those defined by Wölfflin when he extracted his notion of the *Malerische* [*sic*] from Baroque art. As we can now see, the displacing of the quasi-geometrical as the dominant mode in New York abstract art after 1943 offers another instance of that cyclical alternation of painterly and non-painterly which has marked the evolution of Western art (at progressively shorter intervals after Manet) since the 16th century.[89]

Greenberg initially fixed on the opticality of Wölfflin's painterly baroque to promote a specific direction of modern painting and sculpture, but he remained tied to Wölfflin's cyclical historical scheme (very likely mediated by Barr's chart of the modern movements).

One of the reasons that art critics like Roger Fry and Greenberg as well as the curator Alfred Barr were so taken by *Principles* was that it provided a historical genealogy for impressionism (the most recent art Wölfflin addressed), and they picked up the narrative where Wölfflin left off. Arnold Hauser's account of impressionism in *The Social History of Art* (1951), while overwhelmingly rejecting Wölfflin's formalism, still owed much to Wölfflin's view of impressionism as the final fulfillment of the subjective, fragmentary, dynamic sense of becoming he identified with the baroque.[90] But from the 1960s, Wölfflinian and Greenbergian formalisms most definitely crossed in US impressionism studies. Greenberg (very

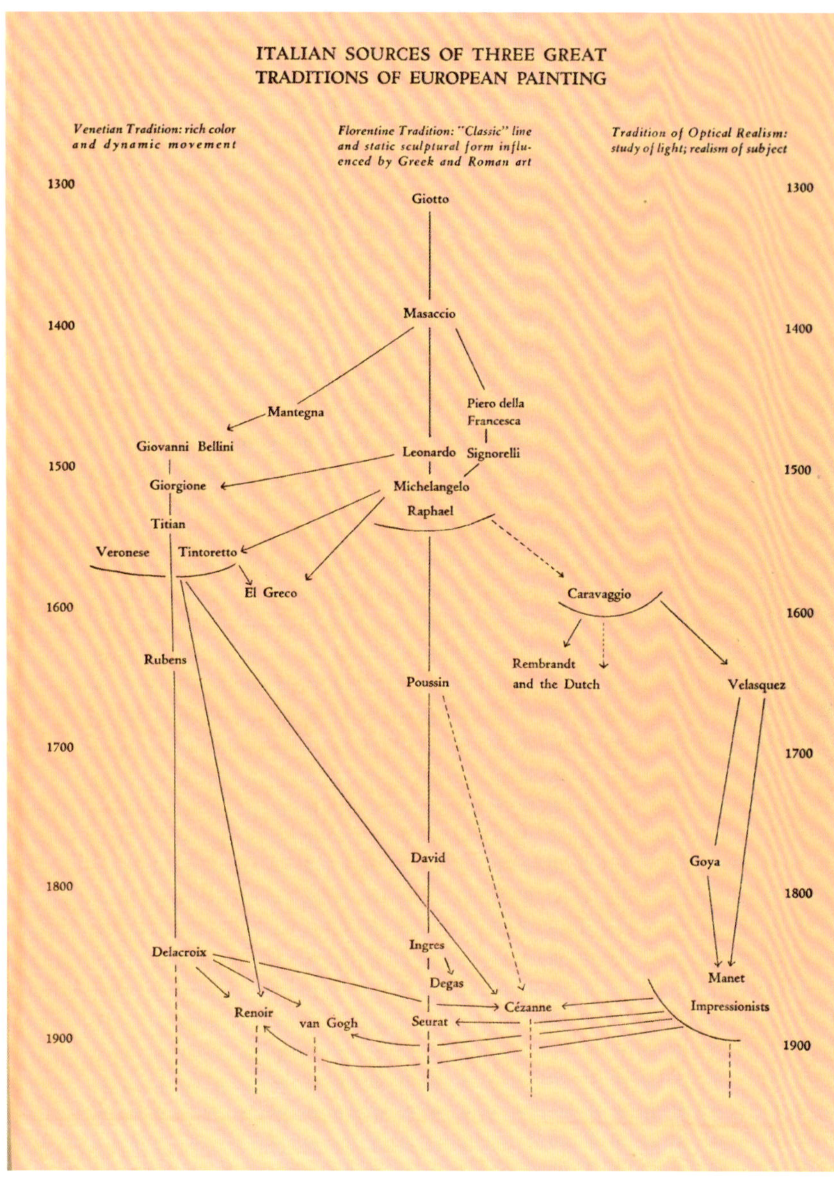

8. "Italian Sources of Three Great Traditions of European Painting," in *Italian Masters Lent by the Royal Italian Government* (Museum of Modern Art, New York, 1940), end page, chart by Alfred H. Barr

National Gallery of Art Library, Washington

much following Barr) took impressionism as both the conclusion of the early modern and the point of origin of the modern. His highly persuasive genealogy of the pursuit of flatness—starting with Manet, with impressionism marking the point of origin of abstraction—became authoritative, the biggest disruption to Wölfflin's categories to date. Meyer Schapiro attempted to synthesize the two formalisms in his lectures on impressionism, first given in the 1960s and revised in his later years.[91] Kermit Champa (fig. 9) would be more taken up by Greenberg's narrative than by Wölfflin's. His *Studies in Early Impressionism*, which acknowledges Greenberg's inspiration, is a formalist manifesto, against the positivism of John Rewald's documentary account of the movement.[92]

It was not just in studies of impressionism that Wölfflinian and Greenbergian formalisms crossed. Americanists also saw in Greenberg's narrative an opportunity for a new genealogy of American painting as a striving toward flatness.[93]And in Chinese studies, even the devoted Wölfflinian Max Loehr took over part of the Greenbergian genealogy of style in a paper on Chinese painting (1970), in a new periodization in which style changed from representational, to subjective representation, to styles as subject matter (art about art).[94] Wen Fong would subsequently find Leo Steinberg's revision of Greenberg's notion of the flat in his reading of Robert Rauschenberg's *Bed* useful to an exploration of the materiality of the picture surface in Yuan literati painting of around 1300.[95]

For a new generation of modernist art historians who came of age when Greenberg's formalism was far more important than Wölfflin's, it was the father rather than the grandfather who had to be killed off first. Thus it is no surprise that the American art historians Rosalind Krauss and Michael Fried, whose formalisms grew out of Greenberg's work, are not usually connected to Wölfflin's. And when Yve-Alain Bois defended his formalism in *The Art Bulletin* in 1995, he assailed the assumption that he was a Greenbergian, with a naïve belief in the isolability of art from politics.[96] When Bois, together with Krauss, Benjamin Buchloh, and Hal Foster, published the highly influential textbook *Art since 1900* in 2004, the right formalism had a strong presence: neither a Wölfflinian morphology nor Greenbergian, but Brechtian, a structuralist, ideologically imbricated formalism.[97]

Principles as Scapegoat

In Eugene Kleinbauer's widely disseminated primer on historiography (1971), the first comprehensive and accessible account of the

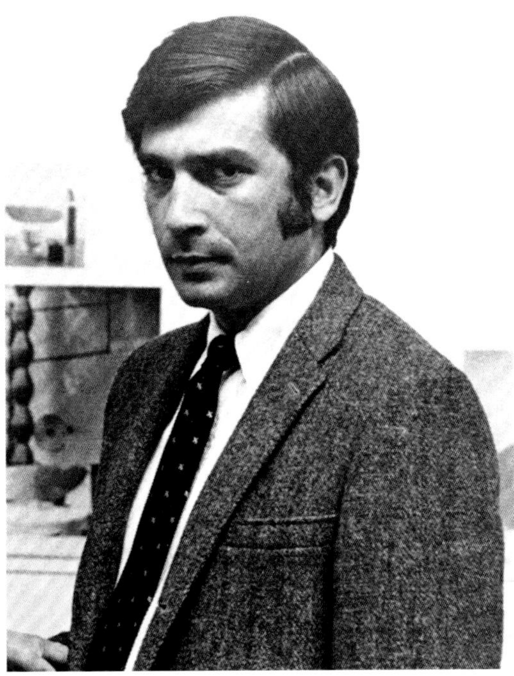

discipline published in the United States, the major critiques of Wölfflin's *Principles*—as a proponent of an art history without names that denies artistic agency; as an internal history of art impervious to social and other forces; as an immanent theory of change; and as disinterested in subject matter, cyclical in its view of history, unable to accommodate mannerism, and inapplicable to other historical moments—were all catalogued in one place.[98] Noting that in art history's largely untheoretical environment many found Wölfflin's framework untenable, Kleinbauer also observed that art historians continued to "refine and apply his terminology" in studies of style, iconography, and context alike.[99] Kleinbauer's text must have sounded like music to the ears of a new generation that took note of the consequences of a debilitating practical application of Wölfflin's formalism. At this time of radical disciplinary renewal, of a definitive move of mainstream art history to the left starting in the late 1960s, Wölfflin's formalism was often referred to in shorthand as one of the exhausted methods, a "mechanical" application of methods lamented repeatedly.[100]

The British-born art historian T. J. Clark made Wölfflin's formalism a symptom of art history's malaise in a signal article published in the *Times Literary Supplement* in 1974, the year he moved from England to UCLA. Art history's golden age, including "beautiful Wölfflin," as Clark called him, had slipped from view; the "mechanical formalism" of today could not continue.[101] Clark called for formalism to be wed to a critical social art history—and Wölfflin had nothing to offer this project.

Svetlana Alpers commented several times on Wölfflin in the late 1970s and early 1980s in probing interventions on the general question of style as practiced in art history. In *The Concept of Style*, essays from a conference organized by the philosopher Berel Lang in 1977, it was the two art historians, Alpers and George Kubler, who disputed the value of style in a volume that aspired to provide a long-needed theory of style across disciplines.[102] Here and in "Is Art History?" Alpers saw Wölfflin and Panofsky as the "dominant modes" of art history against which the new social art historians were working. One of the charges leveled at both these figures was that of Italian Renaissance-centrism.[103] This is untrue of Wölfflin (*Principles* is very preoccupied with northern European art), but it was a productive mischaracterization for Alpers, for it pushed her to develop her principal line of argument in *The Art of Describing* (1983). In the introduction she noted that "the definitive place of Italian art...means that it had proved difficult to find appropriate language to deal with images that do not fit this model."[104] Like Clark, Alpers rejected Wölfflin's language and marginalized him while very much keeping him in view.

Throughout the 1980s art historians in the United States articulated a "crisis in the discipline." A 1982 issue of *Art Journal*, the more progressive of the two journals published by the College Art Association, was dedicated to this theme and included the first serious work of historiography on Wölfflin by the American scholar Joan Goldhammer Hart. In 1986 the more conservative *Art Bulletin* launched a series of articles on the "state of research" in various

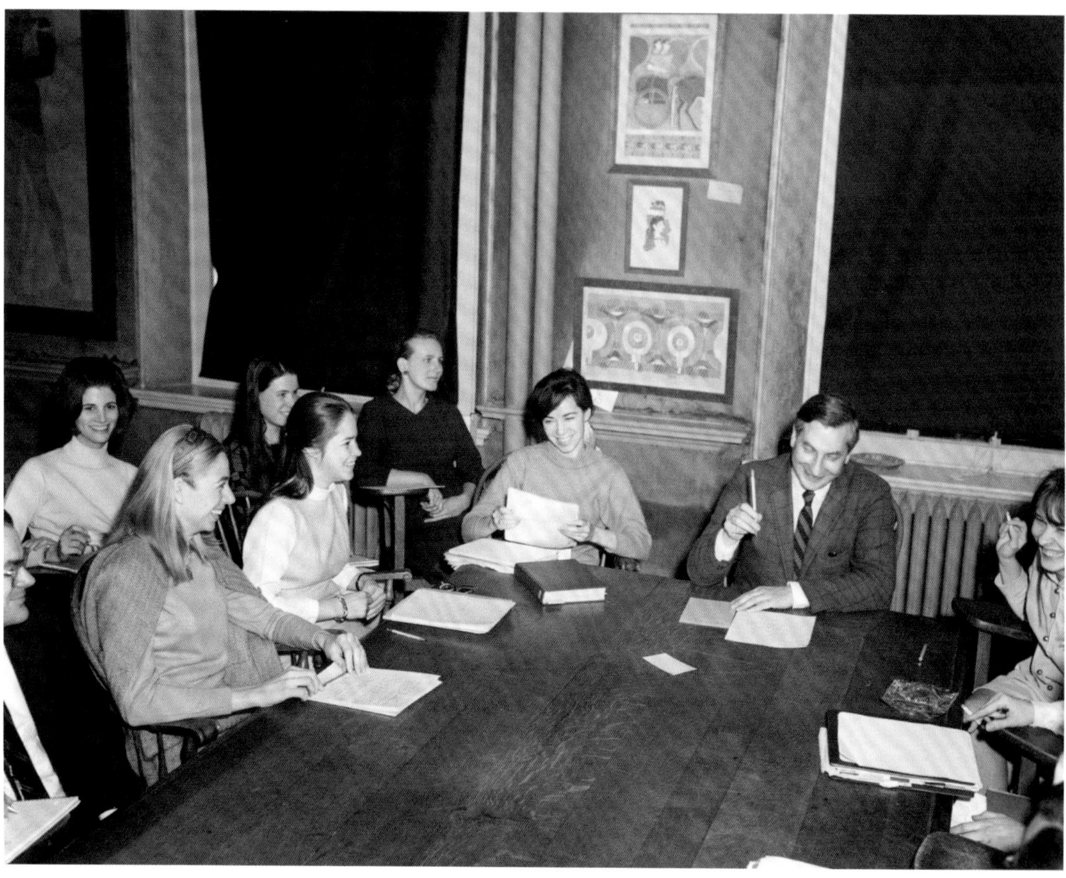

subfields, which provide a panorama of the state of formalism. *Principles* was a topic of several articles. Medieval art, as presented by Herbert Kessler, was unique among the subfields in sidestepping Wölfflinian formalism, as the internal history of style, with its "apparent consistency" typical of histories of Greek or Renaissance art, had always been resisted in art history of the Middle Ages.[105] The early modern subfields appeared the most embattled by debate about formalism and style history: William Hood pointed to a "formalist bias" in Italian Renaissance studies that had rejected psychoanalysis and semiotics and depoliticized social art history, while Charles Dempsey and Elizabeth Cropper, in their essay on Italian painting of the seventeenth century, lamented the inescapability of Wölfflin's syntheses in the absence of something better.[106] The tension between warring factions was most evident in Marvin Trachtenberg's essay on the "conservative" field of architectural history:

Previously, architectural historians were primarily concerned with the "horizontal" connections between formal events, that is, with the internal stylistic process; indeed, describing this process of formal change and evolution was all-consuming, albeit admitting the inclusion of a penumbra of historical and biographical data. We do not, to my mind, serve ourselves well to belittle this traditional enterprise.[107]

Using Wölfflin's terms, Trachtenberg admitted that most recent work was pushing into the "external" history of art, but he criticized theoretically progressive work as heavily as he did narrowly formalist studies, citing as an example of the latter a "competent, occasionally perceptive essay in the Wölfflinian tradition.'"[108] Trachtenberg's review of the literature cited further examples of a "solid," "vital," and "old-fashioned" but nonetheless inspired formalism. Here again, *Principles* functioned as scapegoat. In an essay on nineteenth-century studies in the same series, Richard Shiff carefully parsed an ideological deployment of formalism in which style is a battleground of social and political forces, a manifestation of tension and conflict that cannot resolve into the easy categorization of Wölfflinian *Sehformen*.[109] At the other extreme, "The Feminist Critique of Art History," by Thalia Gouma-Peterson and Patricia Mathews, noted that early feminist criticism was "always anti-formalist."[110]

Wölfflin's *Principles* is characterized as a scapegoat here in part because the theoretical turn in the United States also had a bite at the level of institutional politics, and the formalist was often the sacrificial victim. T. J. Clark's arrival at Harvard in 1980 hardened methodological positions, as became visible in his widely publicized dispute with his colleague Sydney Freedberg (fig. 10), whose work perpetuated the formalism of *Principles* perhaps more than that of anyone of his generation.[111] Around the same time, Kermit Champa positioned formalism as a bulwark against the new art history. In his "postformalist" *"Masterpiece" Studies: Manet, Zola, Van Gogh, and Monet*, a book that was very much a product of the 1980s, though published in 1994, he quoted from *Classic Art* to defend his position:

There is a conception of art history which sees nothing more in art than a "translation of life" (Taine) into pictorial terms, and which attempts to interpret every style as an expression of the prevailing mood of the age. Who would wish to deny that this is a fruitful way of looking at the matter? Yet it takes us only so far — as far, one might say, as the point at which art begins.[112]

This moment marked a definitive displacement by the new art history of the related traditions of formalism and connoisseurship.

The distancing from Wölfflin's text in the early 1980s also allowed it to become an object of study. The publication of an article by Martin Warnke that for the first time historicized *Principles* enabled art historians to freeze it in time and neutralize it. And Michael Ann Holly attempted to dissolve the oversimplification of the style-content polarity in *Panofsky and the Foundations of Art History*. At the same moment, Marshall Brown published his exhilarating deconstruction of *Principles*, showing that the classic and baroque were not successive phases but were mutually interdependent. Wölfflin's "classic," his "God term," did not in effect exist but was a regulatory principle, and the baroque was a morphological principle of existence, of expressivity.[113]

In spite of the publication in the United States of subtle, perceptive reinterpretations of *Principles* in the early 1980s, Joan Goldhammer Hart's excellent dissertation of 1981 on the entire body of Wölfflin's thought, informed by extensive research in his papers, never found a publisher.[114] The formalism of Wölfflin's generation would be kept alive through the awakening interest in Riegl — recast in the 1970s as a structuralist *avant la lettre* — though his work had some of the same problems as Wölfflin's.[115] That a Riegl renaissance began at the moment Wölfflin's *Principles* was scapegoated must be attributed to the book's emblematic status as reactionary style history.

The Return of the Repressed

Formalism and style analysis returned, to some extent, to art history in the United States in the 1990s, now tamed by a much greater interest in historiography. (Wölfflin is more benign as grandfather than as father.) Jaś Elsner noted the change in tide in his entry "Style," added to the second edition of *Critical Terms for Art History* (2003), pointing out that one of art history's fundamental operations had been overlooked in the first edition (1996).[116] And three of Panofsky's old essays on style were published in 1995, another sign of the collapse of the methodological antithesis that had sustained the discipline in art history's Cold War.[117] However, just in what form Wölfflinian formalism may have returned needs massive qualification. For the acknowledgment of the status of *Principles* as a foundational text does not mean that its basic propositions are considered valid, or worthy of imitation or of further theoretical refinement or redirection. After a century of criticism, Wölfflin's text has been largely eviscerated. Yet not only does it remain standing (Marshall Brown rightly remarked on its mysterious vitality), but scholars return to it to fuel new propositions, now heavily mediated by a growing body of literature on the historiography of art.

The "pictorial turn" heralded by W. J. T. Mitchell's essay of 1994 and the "visual turn" announced by Martin Jay were followed by a flood of textbooks for the emerging field of visual culture and visual studies. Foregrounding looking at images and the visual, or visuality, neither emergent field found a particular use for Wölfflinian formalism, especially since, in the expanded field of visual studies, objects often displaced works of art. Wölfflin himself would likely have been interested in Jonathan Crary's *Techniques of the Observer* (1992), though the project carries no trace of Wölfflin's notion of historically specific *Sehformen*. (Wölfflin's notebook meditations on visual praxis, what Baxandall later termed the "period eye," never made it into his books.)[118] And Wölfflin's text had been sufficiently undermined by previous generations that it was never subjected to critiques of gender and queer studies, or, more recently, postcolonialism, which could have made the text vitally problematic once again.[119] Nonetheless, *Principles* has remained on the edges of many of these discussions. Frederic Schwartz, who excavated the intertwinement of Frankfurt School theory with the work of Wölfflin and other art historians of his generation, was not alone in finding resonances with a body of theory that had so moved the field *away* from Wölfflin's work.[120] Such investigations gave the text some new credibility.

The productive theoretical engagement with Wölfflin's work in the past twenty years has often bypassed *Principles*, reaching back rather to Wölfflin's "Prolegomena to a Psychology of Architecture," with its interest in an embodied spectator.[121] Repeatedly, though, we find *Principles* brought into disciplinary discussions that need a historiographic grounding. So when John

Onians, a proponent of neural art history, wrote a series of biographies of neural art historians, he included Wölfflin.[122] And Whitney Davis's *A General Theory of Visual Culture* takes Wölfflin's statement that "vision itself has a history" for what should be a "founding proposition of visual-culture studies," an invitation to debate art's share in vision itself.[123]

In recent discussions of the prospects of a global art history, Wölfflin's *Principles* has been an irresistible point of departure. In the most ambitious undertaking by an American scholar to date to reconstitute art history as a world art history, David Summers originally conceived his project as an extension of Wölfflin's, calling attention to the relationship with his own provisional title, "Principles of World Art History."[124] *Principles* and its many translations were also discussed in James Elkins's Art Seminar, *Is Art History Global?* Summers found that students today read *Principles* with "a high degree of noncomprehension," and Elkins was taught as an undergraduate at Cornell that the text is "not proper art history" and does not "correspond to the discipline as we practice it." While noting that Marshall Brown's deconstruction of *Principles* served as a prism through which students now read the book, Elkins concluded: "We're perilously close to saying no one believes the text, and no one thinks it is pertinent to the current discipline: to me that would place it in the realm of historiographic inquiry, rather than methodological interest, and it would make me wonder about times and places where Wölfflin appears to retain methodological pertinence." [125] In spite of these pronouncements of the death of *Principles* by way of historiography, Elkins's volume returns to it repeatedly as a text around which the discussion of the issue of a global art history (and of Western methodological hegemony in particular) revolved, not least because it was so widely read among the international group of panelists that it could be meaningfully discussed.

Principles was and continues to be in the very substrate of American art history: in key concepts like modernism and as refashioned into a detheorized set of tools, Wölfflin's highly problematic but seductive concepts are part of the ground on which emerging art historians take their first steps. But more than that, *Principles* often stands at the discipline's fault line: of an even more complicated relationship to the German tradition of art history than has been understood; of crucial problems in global art studies; and between theory and however its opposite has been defined at a given moment. In this way *Principles* has repeatedly functioned as the crucible of the discipline in both senses of the word: it is a book that continually puts art history's assumptions to the test and one that possesses such force that opposition to it has been generative of disciplinary renewal.

NOTES

1. Heinrich Wölfflin, *Italian Renaissance Art: A Handbook for Students and Travellers*, with an introduction by Walter Armstrong (London and New York, 1903; later republished as *Classic Art: An Introduction to the Italian Renaissance*). A brief notice of the translation in preparation appeared in the *New York Times*, August 29, 1903, 593. A second printing in 1913 was copublished by the Knickerbocker Press in New York.

2. Heinrich Wölfflin, *Principles of Art History: The Problem of the Development of Style in Later Art* (London and New York, 1932).

3. *Exhibition of Contemporary German Art*, with an essay by Paul Clemen, trans. G. E. Maberly-Oppler (Berlin, 1908). There is a record in one of Wölfflin's notebooks of his refusal of the invitation together with a draft of a letter to the university rector Erich Schmidt (September 1, 1908). Heinrich Wölfflin, Notebook 47, fol. 24, Universitätsbibliothek Basel, Nachlass Heinrich Wölfflin.

4. Quoted (but undocumented) in Udo Kultermann, *The History of Art History* (Norwalk, CT, 1993), 180.

5. Edwin H. Zeydel, "The Teaching of German in the United States from Colonial Times to the Present," *The German Quarterly* 37 (1964): esp. 356–357, 361–362.

6. Paul Finkelman, "The War on German Language and Culture, 1917–1925," in *Confrontation and Cooperation: Germany and the United States in the Era of World War I, 1900–1924*, ed. Hans-Jürgen Schröder (Providence and Oxford, 1993), 184. Wölfflin observed with alarm the Germanization of foreign words in Munich during the war (and purged *Grundbegriffe* of them over two wartime editions). For Wölfflin's reaction to changing storefronts in Munich, see Martin Warnke, "On Heinrich Wölfflin," *Representations* 27 (1989): 175; for the Germanization of words in *Grundbegriffe*, see Heinrich Wölfflin, *Principles of Art History: The Problem of the Development of Style in Early Modern Art*, trans. Jonathan Blower, ed. Evonne Levy and Tristan Weddigen (Los Angeles, 2015), 22–23, 326n2.

7. E. Louise Lucas, "List of Books for a College Art Library," *The Art Bulletin* (1929): 242 (in "general literature"). Wölfflin's *Classic Art* and *Die Kunst Albrecht Dürers* appeared on the 1920 list, the revised edition of *Renaissance und Barock* (1926) on the 1929 list.

8. F. Bruckmann Verlag to G. Bell & Sons, February 3, 1930, Wölfflin, Heinrich (1930) ref–7225, Archive of George Bell & Sons Ltd, University of Reading Special Collections. See further Evonne Levy, "Wölfflin's *Principles of Art History* (1915–2015): A Prolegomenon for Its Second Century," in Wölfflin, *Principles* (2015), 30–32 and 44–45nn118–119.

9. On Diez and Riegl, see Matthew Rampley, *The Vienna School of Art History: Empire and the Politics of Scholarship, 1847–1918* (University Park, PA, 2013), 191.

10. Ernst Diez and Otto Demus, *Byzantine Mosaics in Greece, Hosios Lucas and Daphni* (Cambridge, MA, 1931).

11. See the essay by Hans Aurenhammer in this volume.

12. "In contradistinction to the abstract study of the aestheticians, the course in philosophy of art is based on the historical manifestations of art and searches for the laws of the historical way that art has taken.…this course will deal with the methods of looking at works of art and the explanation of the leading terms including the recent terminology in modern art. The second part will deal with the genesis of space by means of lines, planes, colours and chiaroscuro and the corresponding evolution of style in four grades, namely ornamental, plastic, tectonic and pictorial. This evolution occurred in accordance with the historical evolution of culture." *Bryn Mawr College Calendar 1932–1934*, 74.

13. Walter Heil's arrival was announced in *Bulletin of the Detroit Institute of Arts* 8, no. 4 (January 1927): 47–48.

14. "Kunstgeschichtliche Grundbegriffe. The Main Principles of the History of Art" (a summary based on the 6th edition of 1923), 1929, Paul Green Papers, #3693, Southern Historical Collection, The Wilson Library, University of North Carolina at Chapel Hill, folder 135.

15. See John Herbert Roper, *Paul Green: Playwright of the Real South* (Athens, GA, 2003), 118–119.

16. Wölfflin's *Grundbegriffe* is discussed in letters from Henry Herschel Brickell (Henry Holt and Company) to Paul Green, July 8, 1930, Paul Green Papers, #3693, folder 136; Paul Green to Richard Thornton (College Department, Henry Holt and Company), August 20, 1930: "Concerning our conversation recently about Wolfflin's [sic] book…I for one should like to see Wolfflin [sic] and his coterie of thought introduced to this country. It wouldn't do us any harm, don't you think?" Paul Green to Richard Thornton, August 20, 1931 (inquiring about the fate of the translation), Paul Green Papers, #3693, folder 147.

17. Review of *Principles of Art History* by Heinrich Wölfflin, *New York Times*, September 18, 1932.

18. E.O.C., review of *Principles of Art History* by Heinrich Wölfflin, *The American Magazine of Art* 25 (November 1932): 302.

19. Wilhelm Valentiner and R. H. Boothroyd, *Tino da Camaino: A Sienese Sculptor of the Fourteenth Century* (Paris, 1935), 96, 97, 141; Wilhelm Valentiner, *An Exhibition of Fifty Paintings by Frans Hals* (Detroit Institute of Arts, 1935); Ernst Scheyer, "Drawings by Correggio," *Bulletin of the Detroit Institute of Arts* 15 (1936): 103–109.

20. "And the ubiquitous adjective *malerisch* must be rendered, according to context, in seven or eight different ways: 'picturesque' as in 'picturesque disorder'; 'pictorial' (or, rather horribly, 'painterly') as opposed to 'plastic'; 'dissolved,' 'sfumato,' or 'non-linear' as opposed to 'linear' or 'clearly defined.'" Erwin Panofsky, "The History of Art," in *The Cultural Migration: The European Scholar in America*, ed. W. Rex Crawford (New York, 1961), 92.

21. Philip A. McMahon, review of *Principles of Art History* by Heinrich Wölfflin, *Parnassus* 4 (1932): 22, 27.

22. The German edition did not appear on the 1925 list. The English translation was listed under "aesthetics and technique" (not "Renaissance, 1500–1800") in the 1939 list. My thanks to Margaret English for this information.

23. "Catholic Book List Notes Moral Gain," *New York Times*, June 18, 1932. The quarterly list included books that were not necessarily written by Catholics but that combatted the "forces threatening civilization itself."

24. *A Short List of Books on the Fine Arts with Annotations* (New York, 1937), 43–44. Museum staff assembled the titles for "serious adult students" for the American Library Association convention.

25. Helen Gardner, *Art through the Ages*, 2nd rev. ed. (New York, 1936), xi. On Gardner's dominance of the market, see James Elkins, *Stories of Art* (New York, 2002), 65–74.

26. See especially Karin Michels, *Transplantierte Kunstwissenschaft: Deutschsprachige Kunstgeschichte im amerikanischen Exil* (Berlin, 1999), 145–163; Christopher S. Wood, "Art History's Normative Renaissance," in *The Italian Renaissance in the Twentieth Century, Acts of an International Conference, Florence, Villa I Tatti, 1999* (Florence, 2002), 65–92. For a broad-strokes account of forces of progress versus reaction, see Thomas Crow, "The Practice of Art History in America," *Daedalus* 135 (2006): 70–90.

27. Kevin Parker, "Art History and Exile: Erwin Panofsky and Richard Krautheimer," in *Exiles and Emigrés: The Flight of European Artists from Hitler*, ed. Stephanie Barron with Sabine Eckmann (New York, 1997), 318, 324 (where iconography is more ideologically chaste); Michels, *Transplantierte Kunstwissenschaft*, 145–148, 154–156 (where the dialectic between the two methods is more thoroughly discussed).

28. Michels, *Transplantierte Kunstwissenschaft*, 158–162.

29. See Michels, *Transplantierte Kunstwissenschaft*, 156n939, for references in letters from Panofsky to Alfred Neumeyer in 1955. On Panofsky's early work in Germany, in dialogue with Wölfflin's formalism, see Franco Bernabei, "Jan Białostocki, Formalism, and Iconology," *Artibus et Historiae* 11 (1990): 9–21; Whitney Davis, *General Theory of Visual Culture* (Princeton, 2011), 259.

30. Brendan Cassidy, "Introduction: Iconography, Tests, and Audiences," in *Iconography at the Crossroads: Papers from the Colloquium Sponsored by the Index of Christian Art, Princeton University, 23–24 March 1990*, ed. Brendan Cassidy (Princeton, 1993), 4.

31. For an overview, see Karen Michels, "Transfer and Transformation: The German Period in American Art History," in Barron and Eckmann, *Exiles and Emigrés*, 304–316.

32. Among the grand-*Schuler* are the pupils of A. E. Brinckmann: Gertrude Rosenthal, who worked at the Walters Art Gallery (1943–1956) and the Baltimore Museum of Art (1956–1968), and Ernst Scheyer, who taught at Wayne State University in Detroit (1938–1971), having been hired initially by Valentiner as a research associate at the Detroit Institute of Arts. Of the thirteen art historians who contributed to the sixtieth birthday festschrift for Wölfflin (various authors, *Festschrift Heinrich Wölfflin: Beiträge zur Kunst- und Geistesgeschichte zum 21. Juni 1924 überreicht von Freunden und Schuler* [Munich, 1924]), four (Hagen, Hans Swarzenski, Paul Frankl, and Martin Weinberger) emigrated to the United States. Concise biographies and bibliographies for all of these figures who left after 1933, with further references, can be found in Ulrike Wendland, *Biographisches Handbuch deutschsprachiger Kunsthistoriker im Exil: Leben und Werk unter dem Nationalsozialismus verfolgten und vertriebenen Wissenschaftler*, 2 vols. (Munich, 1998–1999).

33. For Hagen's role at Wisconsin, see Lee Sorensen, ed., "Hagen, Oskar," *Dictionary of Art Historians*, http://www.arthistorians.info/hageno.

34. Oskar Hagen, "Amerika" ("The Trip to America"), Uta Hagen and Herbert Berghof Papers 1889–2004 (T-Mss 2007–001), Series 1, Sub-series 2, b. 14 f.13 ("The Trip to America"), fols. 16–17, Billy Rose Theatre Division, The New York Public Library for the Performing Arts.

35. Hagen, "The Trip to America," fol. 14.

36. "Da ich in der Art Wölfflins und auf Grundlage seiner Grundbegriffe lese, ist es auch schwer die Studenten davon abzubringen, dass sie die Namen der Künstler auswendig lernen und begreifen, sie sollen eben einmal einen Überblick erhalten ohne Namen zu memorieren." Hagen, "The Trip to America," fol. 21.

37. Oskar Hagen, *Deutsches Sehen: Gestaltungsfragen der deutschen Kunst* (Munich, 1920); *Patterns and Principles of Spanish Art* (Madison, 1936).

38. Alfred Neumeyer, review of *Patterns and Principles of Spanish Art* by Oskar Hagen, *Journal of Aesthetics and Art Criticism* 2 (1943): 99.

39. That Wölfflin's own students saw his work as lacking in cultural perspective was put in evidence in the long chapter added to the 1926 edition of Wölfflin's *Renaissance und Barock* by Wölfflin's student Hans Rose.

40. See the account of the persistence of the Hegelian pursuit of national essence established by the German émigrés in Jochen Wierich, "Mutual Seduction: German Art History and American Art," in *Internationalizing the History of American Art*, ed. Barbara Groseclose and Jochen Wierich (University Park, PA, 2009), 41–79; and, in the same volume, Rebecca Zurier, "Newness, Flatness, and Other Myths: Looking for National Identity in European (and a Few British) Histories of American Art," esp. 25–29.

41. Oskar Hagen, *The Birth of the American Tradition* (New York, 1940), 148.

42. Wolfgang Born, *American Landscape Painting: An Interpretation* (New Haven, 1948), chapter 3.

43. Barbara Novak, *American Painting of the Nineteenth Century: Realism, Idealism* (New York, 1969). On Novak, see Wierich, "Mutual Seduction," 54–57. Novak continued to show her indebtedness to Wölfflin's *Principles* in *Nature and Culture: American Landscape and Painting, 1825–1875* (Oxford, 1980). Novak's scheme is as indebted to Wölfflin as it is to Alfred Barr, for which see below.

44. Alfred Neumeyer, *Geschichte der amerikanischen Malerei: Von der kolonialen Frühzeit bis zur naiven Malerei im 18. und 19. Jahrhundert* (Munich, 1974).

45. Wanda Corn, "Coming of Age: Historical Scholarship in American Art," *The Art Bulletin* 70 (1988): 190–191.

46. The Wölfflinian legacy in Chinese art history is described in Wen C. Fong, "The Study of Chinese Bronze Age Arts: Methods and Approaches," in *The Great Bronze Age of China: An Exhibition from the People's Republic of China*, ed. Wen C. Fong (New York, 1980), 23–33.

47. Harrie Vanderstappen and Diane M. Nelson, "Ludwig Bachhofer (1894–1976)," *Archives of Asian Art* 31 (1977/1978): 110–112.

48. Ludwig Bachhofer, *Die Kunst der japanischen Holzschnittmeister* (Munich, 1922), 10; *Chinesische Kunst* (Breslau, 1923), translated as *A Short History of Chinese Art* (New York, 1946); *Die frühindische Plastik* (Leipzig, 1929). In the late 1970s scholars again reacted negatively to Bachhofer's imposition of Western formalism on Indian art.

49. Bachhofer, *A Short History of Chinese Art*, 9.

50. Robert Bagley, *Max Loehr and the Study of Chinese Bronzes* (Ithaca, 2008), 49.

51. Wölfflin, *Principles* (2015), 84; Max Loehr, "The Bronze Styles of the Anyang Period," *Archives of the Chinese Art Society of America* 7 (1953): 42–53 (quotation on 41).

52. Otto Maenchen-Helfen, "Some Remarks on Ancient Chinese Bronzes," *The Art Bulletin* 27 (1945): 238–243.

53. Ludwig Bachhofer, "Some Remarks on Ancient Chinese Bronzes: Reply," *The Art Bulletin* 27 (1945): 243–246.

54. Benjamin Rowland, Jr., review of *A Short History of Chinese Art* by Ludwig Bachhofer, *The Art Bulletin* 29 (1947): 139–141. According to Wen C. Fong, the critique of Bachhofer turned many to archaeological and more focused problems.

55. Bagley (*Max Loehr and the Study of Chinese Bronzes*), for instance, passes over Loehr's substantial debts to Wölfflin.

56. Wen C. Fong "Why Chinese Painting Is History," *The Art Bulletin* 85 (2003): 258–280 (quotation on 271).

57. Fong, "Why Chinese Painting Is History," 272–273, figs. 17–19. First published in Wen C. Fong et al., *Images of the Mind: Selections from the Edward L. Elliott Family and John B. Elliott Collection of Chinese Calligraphy and Painting at the Art Museum, Princeton University* (Princeton, 1984), 27–45, 60–68.

58. See John M. Rosenfield, "Japanese Art Studies in America since 1945," in *The Postwar Developments of Japanese Studies in the United States*, ed. Helen Hardacre (Leiden, 1998), 161–94; Mimi Hall Yiengpruksawan, "Japanese Art History 2001: The State and Stakes of Research," *The Art Bulletin* 83 (2001): 105–122.

59. Walter Friedlaender, *Mannerism and Anti-Mannerism in Italian Painting* (New York, 1957). The translation was presented by his students on Friedlaender's eightieth birthday (1953), but he had taught the material in the United States since 1935. In course outlines from the 1940s he explicitly positioned his view of mannerism against Wölfflin's *Principles*: "If the sixteenth century is to be understood general comparisons such as Wölfflin's famous pairs of concepts of the Renaissance and Baroque are not sufficient. They are only justifiable in showing the difference of the two periods, but neglect all the transitions and ignore completely the period from 1520 to 1580." "Lecture—Florentine and Central Italian Painting of the Sixteenth Century 1940–1941," Walter Friedlaender Collection, AR 3393/MF 791, III.2, Leo Baeck Institute, New York. In 1971 Friedlaender's work was characterized as a "much refined application of Wölfflin's basic conceptual tools, though not his old-fashioned aesthetic psychology of vision." Eugene W. Kleinbauer, *Modern Perspectives in Western Art History: An Anthology of 20th-Century Writings on the Visual Arts* (New York, 1971), 49.

60. Leo Steinberg, "The Gestural Trace," interview by Richard Cándida Smith, 99; Art History Oral Documentation Project, compiled under the auspices of the Getty Research Institute for the History of Art and the Humanities.

61. An indicator is the early theoretical assessment of *Principles*, drawing upon the German reception, in Ernst C. Hassold, "The Baroque as a Basic Concept of Art," *College Art Journal* 6 (1946): 3–28. There were other reasons to find *Classic Art* of greater interest than *Principles*. Michael Baxandall and Svetlana Alpers stated their preference, perhaps following Kleinbauer, *Modern Perspectives in Western Art History*, 49, 155. "Michael Baxandall: Substance, Sensation, and Perception," interview of Michael Baxandall by Richard Cándida Smith (Getty Center for the History of Art and the Humanities, Oral History Documentation Project, 1998), 43–44; Svetlana Alpers, oral communication, Clark Art Institute Workshop on the reception of Wölfflin's *Principles* in the United States, 2012.

62. Michels, *Transplantierte Kunstwissenschaft*, 158.

63. Wolfgang Stechow, "Matter and Form," *Parnassus* 13 (1941): 104–106, 122.

64. Rudolf Wittkower, "Bernini und der römischer Barock," manuscript of a lecture given in Bonn, 1933. Rudolf Wittkower Papers, Columbia University, New York.

65. Interestingly, Panofsky is mentioned only once in the lecture, as having introduced the term *iconology* to symbolic studies. Wittkower characterizes symbolic studies as the heir to the Warburg school and as the dominant methodological shift after the war. Rudolf Wittkower, "Art History as a Discipline: With Some Thoughts on the Study of American Arts," *Winterthur Seminar on Museum Operation and Connoisseurship*, 1959 (Winterthur, DE, 1961): 55–69.

66. Mark Jarzombek, "De-scribing the Language of Looking: Wölfflin and the History of Aesthetic Experientialism," *Assemblage* 23 (1994): 43–44.

67. John Coolidge, "The Harvard Fine Arts Department," in *The Early Years of Art History in the United States*, ed. Craig Hugh Smyth and Peter M. Lukehart (Princeton, 1993), 53.

68. Wilibald Sauerländer suggested that the focus on the artist's monograph was precisely to counter Wölfflin's "art history without names," to secure the individual at a time when personal security was most important. See "Alterssicherung, Ortssicherung, und Individualsicherung," in *Kunstgeschichte: Eine Einführung*, ed. Hans Belting et al., 2nd ed. (Berlin, 1985), 134–141, as cited in Michels, *Transplantierte Kunstwissenschaft*, 145.

69. Seymour Slive, "Jakob Rosenberg," obituary, *The Burlington Magazine* 124, no. 946 (1982): 31.

70. James Ackerman, "The Nature of Art History," in James Ackerman and James Rhys, *Art and Archaeology* (Englewood Cliffs, NJ, 1963), 141, 142.

71. Interview of Julius S. Held, October 29, 1992, Art History—Oral Documentation Project, UCLA Library, Center for Oral History Research.

72. Erwin Panofsky, "The History of Art," in *The Cultural Migration: The European Scholar in America* (New York, 1953), 91.

73. Ackerman, *Art and Archaeology*, 194. Ackerman maintained that, among the outstanding figures who arrived in the 1930s, historical theory was not ignored but neither was it openly debated.

74. Irving Lavin, "The Crisis of 'Art History,'" *The Art Bulletin* 78 (1996): 13. Jarzombek ("De-scribing the Language of Looking," 59, 71) would characterize this as a "humanist" struggle against the inhumanity of inauthentic theory and totalitarianism, a corrective ideology, fully in swing in the 1950s.

75. James Ackerman, "On American Scholarship in the Arts," *College Art Journal* 17 (1958): 360–361.

76. James Ackerman, talk delivered at "Wölfflin's *Grundbegriffe* at 100: The North American Reception," Sterling and Francine Clark Art Institute, June 22–23, 2012.

77. Ackerman, "Style," in *Art and Archaeology*, 171.

78. Meyer Schapiro, "Style," in *Anthropology Today*, ed. Alfred L. Kroeber (Chicago, 1953), 287–312. See Alan Wallach, "Meyer Schapiro's Essay on Style: Falling into the Void," *The Journal of Aesthetics and Art Criticism* 55 (1997): 11–15.

79. Arnold Hauser, *The Philosophy of Art History* (New York, 1959).

80. George Kubler, *The Shape of Time: Remarks on the History of Things* (New Haven, 1962).

81. Max Loehr, "Some Fundamental Issues in the History of Chinese Art," *Journal of Asian Studies* 23 (1964): 185–193. See Bagley, *Max Loehr*, 125–126.

82. E. H. Gombrich, *Norm and Form: Studies in the Art of the Renaissance* (London, 1966).

83. Kleinbauer, *Modern Perspectives in Western Art History*, 35.

84. Barr was educated at Princeton and Harvard, where German art history was taught, and traveled in Germany in 1927–1929. Although Barr's biographer Sybil Gordon Kantor mentions Wölfflin's formalism as important to Barr, she does not attempt to tie the work to any particular aspect of Barr's formalism. Barr's abandoned dissertation on theory and criticism of modern painting, to have been supervised by Philip McMahon, is especially intriguing. Sybil Gordon Kantor, *Alfred H. Barr, Jr., and the Intellectual Origins of the Museum of Modern Art* (Cambridge, MA, 2002), esp. 21–26, 34, 38, 45–47, 189.

85. See Susan Noyes Platt, "Modernism, Formalism, and Politics: The 'Cubism and Abstract Art' Exhibition of 1936 at the Museum of Modern Art," *Art Journal* 47 (1988): 284–295. The recent exhibition about this exhibition did not bring Wölfflin to bear on Barr's thinking. See Glen Lowry, "Abstraction in 1936: Barr's Diagrams," and Leah Dickerman, "Abstraction in 1936: Cubism and Abstract Art at the Museum of Modern Art," in *Inventing Abstraction, 1910–1925: How a Radical Idea Changed Modern Art*, ed. Leah Dickerman (Museum of Modern Art, New York, 2013), 358–363 and 364–369, respectively. Griselda Pollock remarked on Barr's engagement with Germanophone art history in the exhibition, though not specifically with Wölfflin. Griselda Pollock, "Un-framing the Modern: Critical Space / Public Possibility" in Griselda Pollock and Joyce Zemans, *Museums after Modernism: Strategies of Engagement* (Malden, MA, 2007), 9–10.

86. *Italian Masters Lent by the Royal Italian Government*, preface, notes, and charts by Alfred H. Barr (Museum of Modern Art, New York, 1940). See also Kantor, *Alfred H. Barr*, 23–26, on the beginnings of Barr's chart-making following the example of Charles Rufus Morey.

87. Daniel Allan Adler, "Leaps of Faith: Formalist Notions of the Painterly" (PhD diss., City University of New York, 2002), chapter 2; Greenberg, "Crisis of the Easel Picture" and "Jackson Pollock: Inspiration, Vision, Intuitive Decision," in Greenberg, *The Collected Essays and Criticism*, 2:221–225 and 4:246–247, respectively.

88. See, for example, Greenberg, "The Venetian Line" (1950) and "Two Reconsiderations," in *The Collected Essays and Criticism*, 4 vols (Chicago, 1986–1993), 3: esp. 33–34 and 35–36, respectively.

89. Greenberg, "After Abstract Expressionism" (1962) in *The Collected Essays and Criticism*, 4:123. See also the opening of the exhibition catalog "Post Painterly Abstraction" (in *The Collected Essays and Criticism*, 4:192), where Wölfflin's terms are invoked as an aid to seeing things we might not see otherwise in the art of the present.

90. Arnold Hauser, *The Social History of Art*, 2 vols. (New York, 1951).

91. Meyer Schapiro, *Impressionism: Reflections and Perceptions* (New York, 1997). I owe this observation to Caroline Duffy.

92. Kermit S. Champa, *Studies in Early Impressionism* (New Haven, 1973).

93. See Corn, "Coming of Age: Historical Scholarship in American Art," 191, with reference to Winslow Homer and Albert Pinkham Ryder and the 1976 exhibition *The Natural Paradise: Painting in America, 1800–1950*, organized by MOMA.

94. Max Loehr, "Phases and Content of Chinese Painting," a conference paper (1970), as described in Fong, "Why Chinese Painting Is History," 271.

95. Fong, "Why Chinese Painting Is History," 274. See Jerome Silbergeld, "Commentary on James Cahill's 'Chinese Art and Authenticity,'" *American Academy of Arts and Sciences Bulletin* 55 (fall 2001): 31–35.

96. Yve-Alain Bois, "Whose Formalism?" *The Art Bulletin* 78 (1995): 9–12.

97. Hal Foster et al., *Art since 1900: Modernism, Antimodernism, Postmodernism* (London, 2004), 32–35.

98. Kleinbauer, *Modern Perspectives in Western Art History*, 27–29.

99. Kleinbauer, *Modern Perspectives in Western Art History*, 29.

100. When Wittkower accounted for art history's methods in 1959, Wölfflin had a prominent place among a large cast of characters. By the 1970s and 1980s art history's long and complex history came to be distilled into a very short list of names and what they stood for.

101. T. J. Clark, "The Conditions of Artistic Creation," *Times Literary Supplement*, May 24, 1974, 561–562. This essay and Ackerman's of 1963 in *Art and Archaeology* resonate strongly.

102. Svetlana Alpers, "Style Is What You Make It: The Visual Arts Once Again," and George Kubler, "Towards a Reductive Theory of Visual Style," in *The Concept of Style*, ed. Berel Lang (Ithaca, 1979).

103. Svetlana Alpers, "Is Art History?," *Daedalus* 106 (1977): 1–13.

104. Svetlana Alpers, *The Art of Describing: Dutch Art of the Seventeenth Century* (Chicago, 1983), xx.

105. Herbert Kessler, "On the State of Medieval Art History," *The Art Bulletin* 70 (1988): 177–179.

106. William Hood, "The State of Research in Italian Renaissance Art," *The Art Bulletin* 69 (1987): 175; Elizabeth Cropper and Charles Dempsey, "The State of Research in Italian Painting in the Seventeenth Century," *The Art Bulletin* 69 (1987): 494.

107. Marvin Trachtenberg, "Some Observations on Recent Architectural History," *The Art Bulletin* 70 (1988): 212.

108. Marvin Trachtenberg, "Some Observations," 212.

109. Richard Shiff, "Art History and the Nineteenth Century: Realism and Resistance," *The Art Bulletin* 70 (1988): 25–48.

110. Thalia Gouma-Peterson and Patricia Mathews, "The Feminist Critique of Art History," *The Art Bulletin* 69 (1987): 344.

111. Freedberg's debt to Wölfflin and *Principles* is most apparent in his *Painting of the High Renaissance in Florence and Rome* (Cambridge, 1961) and his *Painting in Italy, 1500–1600* (Middlesex, 1970), where *Principles* is cited in the general bibliography. His method is acknowledged as based in Wölfflin's in Paul Barolsky, "Sydney J. Freedberg, Historian and Critic: An Appreciation," *Artibus et Historiae* 1 (1980): 135–142. For Clark and Freedberg, see James Cuno, "Telling Stories: Rhetoric and Leadership, A Case Study," *Leadership* 1 (2005): 205–213; for Clark's Harvard appointment as an emblematic moment, see Hilton Kramer, "T. J. Clark and the Marxist Critique of Modern Painting," *New Criterion* 1 (March 1985): 1–8.

112. Heinrich Wölfflin, *Classic Art: An Introduction to the Italian Renaissance*, trans. Peter and Linda Murray (Oxford and New York, 1952), 287, quoted in Kermit S. Champa, *"Masterpiece" Studies: Manet, Zola, Van Gogh, and Monet* (University Park, PA, 1994), 14. See also James Panero, "Kermit Swiler Champa, 1939–2004," *New Criterion* 23 (September 2004): 78.

113. Marshall Brown, "The Classic Is the Baroque: On the Principle of Wölfflin's Art History," *Critical Inquiry* 9 (1982): 379–404.

114. Joan Goldhammer Hart, "Heinrich Wölfflin: An Intellectual Biography" (PhD diss., University of California, Berkeley, 1981).

115. See how Alpers gets around Riegl's Hegelianism in "Style Is What You Make It," 98. For Riegl as a structuralist see Sheldon Nodelman, "Structuralist Analysis in Art and Anthropology," in *Structuralism*, ed. Jacques Ehrmann (New York, 1970), 79–93. Riegl is favorably compared to Wölfflin and cast as a structuralist in Foster et al., *Art since 1900*, 34–35.

116. Jaś Elsner, "Style," in *Critical Terms in Art History*, ed. Robert S. Nelson and Richard Shiff, rev. ed. (Chicago, 2003), 98. See also Richard Neer, "Connoisseurship and the Stakes of Style," *Critical Inquiry* 32 (2005): 1–26, and T. J. Clark's journal of looking and autobiographical work, *The Sight of Death: An Experiment in Art Writing* (London and New Haven, 2006).

117. Erwin Panofsky, *Three Essays on Style*, ed. Irving Lavin (Cambridge, MA, 1995).

118. Jonathan Crary, *Techniques of the Observer: On Vision and Modernity in the Nineteenth Century* (Cambridge, MA, 1992). See Warnke ("On Heinrich Wölfflin," 177) for Wölfflin's musings on Velázquez's quick brushwork and rapid perception as linked to bullfights and dance theater.

119. A postcolonial critique of *Principles* has not, to my knowledge, been undertaken. For remarks on the implicit racial structure of *Principles*, see Claire Farago, "Vision Itself Has a History," in *Reframing the Renaissance* (London, 1995).

120. Frederic J. Schwartz, "Cathedrals and Shoes: Concepts of Style in Wölfflin and Adorno," *New German Critique* 76 (1999): 3–48. For Wölfflin and Merleau-Ponty, see Stephen Melville, "Division of the Gaze, or, Remarks on the Color and Tenor of Contemporary 'Theory,'" in *Vision in Context*, ed. Teresa Brennan (New York, 1996), 109, 110.

121. Mark Jarzombek's work has been fundamental in stimulating interest in this area.

122. John Onians, *Neuroarthistory: From Aristotle and Pliny to Baxandall and Zeki* (New Haven and London, 2007), 115–123.

123. Davis, *A General Theory of Visual Culture*, 5–7.

124. David Summers, *Real Spaces: World Art History and the Rise of Western Modernism* (London, 2003), 11–12.

125. James Elkins, *Is Art History Global?*, The Art Seminar, vol. 3 (New York, 2007).

MONICA JUNEJA

Universal Principles and Intransigent Contexts: Wölfflinian Aesthetics and the History of South Asian Art

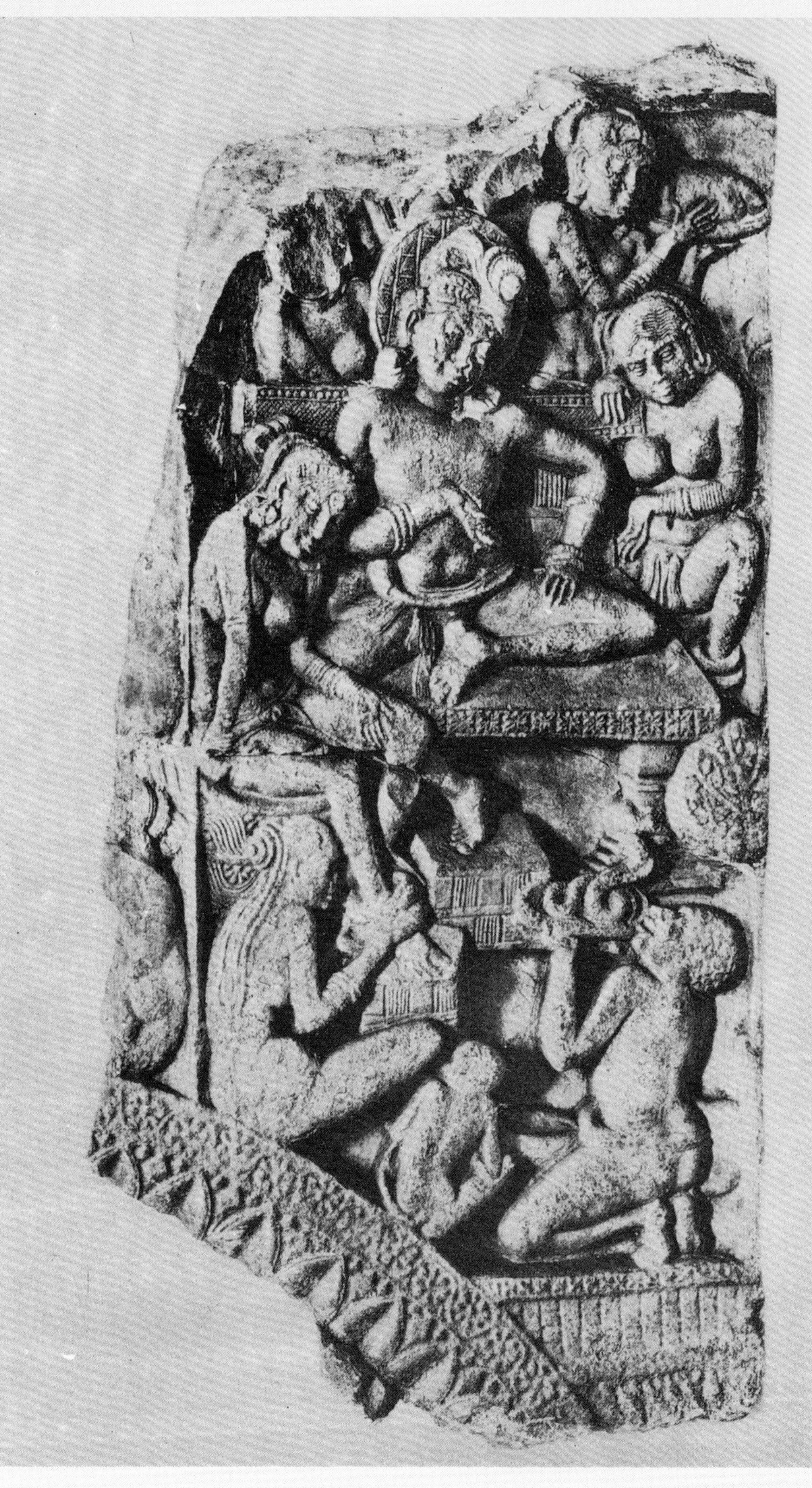

The essays collected in this volume are a testimony to the remarkably wide-spread transcultural reception of the work of Heinrich Wölfflin, in particular of *Kunstgeschichtliche Grundbegriffe (Principles of Art History*; 1915). In light of the book's history of translation, retranslation, and reissue, any discussion of the reception of Wölfflinian art history in South Asia must begin with the observation that to date there is no translation of the work in any of the numerous languages of the region. Readers of Wölfflin on the Indian subcontinent have relied on English-language translations and, more frequently, on the reception of *Principles* in English-language publications. Indeed, indirect channels have played a greater role than the book itself in transmitting Wölfflinian methods to scholarship on South Asian art. Uncovering these tracks and measuring their impact are more than an ordinary challenge to the project of investigating the global reception of Wölfflin's *Principles*. Despite the absence of an Indian translation of a text that has proved seminal to art-historical research and pedagogy in Europe and the Americas, Wölfflinian aesthetics is not without relevance for the art history of the Indian subcontinent. The story of its reception is, however, more diffused than one that focuses on a single text.

One of the central questions that has animated my engagement with Wölfflin's *Principles* and its connections to South Asian art is why the work has prompted a return to formalist principles as foundational for art history in general.[1] In particular, why has their exposition in Wölfflin's writings engaged art historians today? It is particularly striking that this project seeks to situate the various receptions that Wölfflin's work has found across the globe on a single, shared map, as if to use *Principles* to set in motion a conversation among art histories of different regions. How can we make such a conversation productive for the discipline a century after the work's initial publication, as it responds to the challenge of globality?

I start with the observation that, although Wölfflin's *Principles* was predicated on his study of Western civilization—more precisely, on the art of the Renaissance and the baroque in Western Europe—his concerns were in a certain sense also global; that is, *Principles* in its own way sought to offer an art-historical paradigm that could potentially serve as a universal history of form. In his preoccupation with finding a key to grappling with "world" as a category of art history, Wölfflin was not alone in his time. *Weltkunstgeschichte* was an important strain in German-language art-historical writing from the late nineteenth century, even though the term meant different things to different people.[2] Yet, unlike *Weltkunstgeschichte* and its present-day avatars in world art studies, bringing the world into the purview of the discipline was, for Wölfflin, not primarily about writing histories of the art produced in different world regions, plotted within a single narrative in units one next to the other and drawing on disciplines such as anthropology. Rather, his concern was to equip art history with a regime of looking that, if rigorously conducted, would bring forth categories to name formal qualities within a given place and especially at a given time. A new and ever-increasing diversity of objects had emanated in large quantities from contexts beyond Europe—in the wake of colonial collecting, archaeological

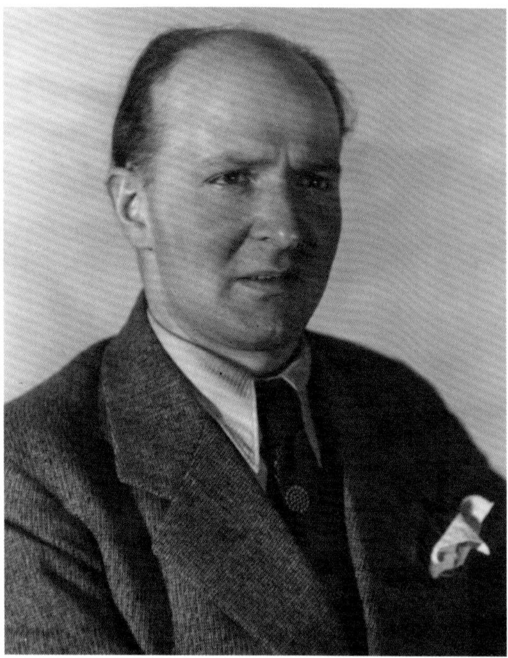

excavations, or diplomatic-cum-commercial exchange—and had brought with them a fresh set of challenges to museums, curators, publics, and not least to the discipline of art history. Wölfflin's paradigm promised to bring a scientific order to art history and to build a canon that was not uniquely applicable to the West, even though the focus of his writings rarely shifted beyond the frontiers of European art. Nonetheless, claims for the usefulness of the comparative method—the plotting of similarities and distinctiveness—went beyond the study of stylistic developments from classicism to the Renaissance and baroque: it could be made to function as a tool that would enable an entry point to study objects from alien cultural contexts. In the preface to the 1922 (sixth) German edition of *Principles*, Wölfflin wrote: "The scheme has proved useful even as far as the domains of Japanese and old Nordic art."[3] Recent research on Wölfflin has in addition drawn attention to the pedagogical mission of his art-historical enterprise. Daniel Adler, for instance, refers to the imperative need, in Wölfflin's view, of joining scholarship to a form of "universal cultivation."[4]

Fresh insights into Wölfflin's *Principles* made available by research, the results of which are assembled in this volume, have served as a useful lens through which to examine the intersections between Wölfflinian theory and South Asian art history. More nuanced accounts of his "founding principles" reveal them as transmitting more than a simplistic and narrowly defined formalism, even as their varied reception may have frequently flattened their import. Newer writings draw out the complexity of contexts and discussions surrounding the formalist concerns of which Wölfflin was an important spokesman, and the question of context remains significant for us today.

The intersection between a Wölfflinian aesthetic of form and South Asian art takes place on two registers. The first, more direct than the second, involves the reception of Wölfflin's *Principles* in South Asia mediated by the writings of his student Ludwig Bachhofer (1894–1976), a researcher who devoted his scholarly pursuits to the study of Asian art. The second aspect features what Evonne Levy and Tristan Weddigen, in their introduction to the symposium on which this volume is based, referred to as "indirect transmissions," a process involving several agents: theorists, exhibition curators, and art historians who responded to Wölfflin's *Principles*, again often through interlocutors and critics of the text.[5]

One of Wölfflin's rare direct references to the art of the Indian subcontinent can be found, not in *Kunstgeschichtliche Grundbegriffe*, but in his foreword, or *Geleitwort*, to *Indische Baukunst*, a multivolume work on Indian architecture edited by his friend and colleague from Basel, the architect Emanuel La Roche, and published in 1920–1921.[6] Wölfflin is said to have made plans to travel to Asia with La Roche, but for unknown reasons these did not materialize.[7] In his description of allegedly contrasting architectural idioms—the so-called Hindu and Indo-Islamic styles—encountered in South Asia, Wölfflin deployed a comparative method that parallels his treatment of Renaissance and baroque art in *Principles*. Taking the Taj Mahal to represent the pinnacle of Indian Islamic art, he

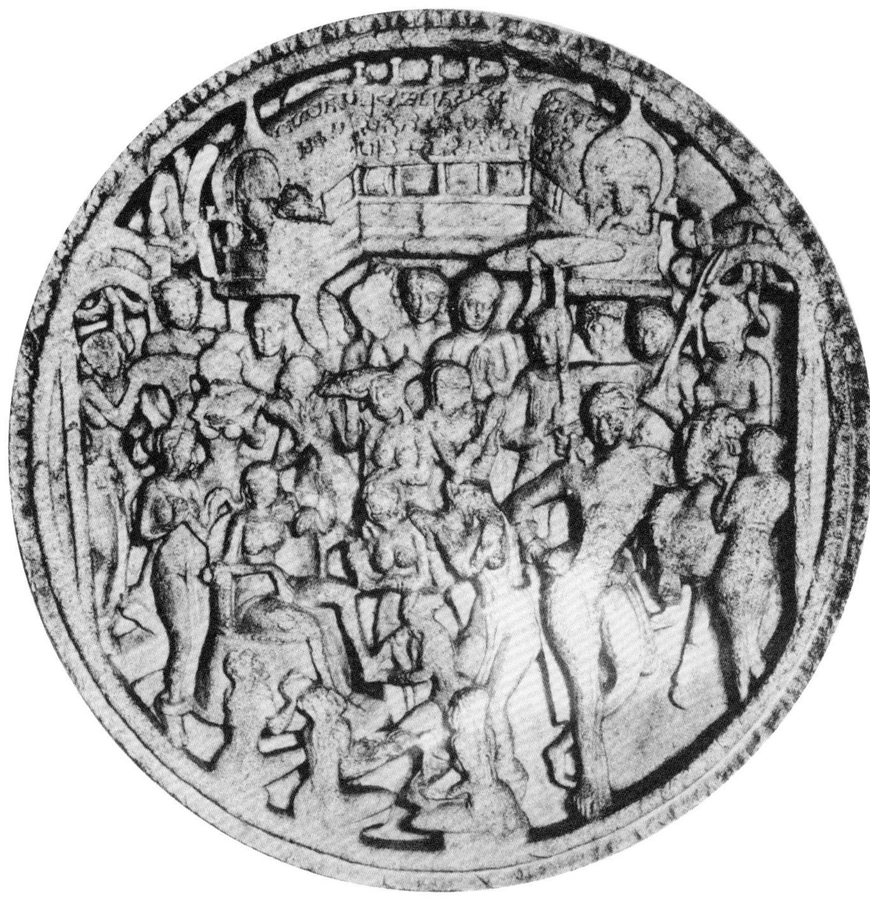

2. Tondo, post from a railing, Amaravati, mid-second century, reproduced from Ludwig Bachhofer, *Early Indian Sculpture* (New York, 1972), plate 116 and cover illustration

National Gallery of Art Library, Washington

contrasted its ethereal and graceful qualities together with its perfect proportions to the "disorderly," uncontrolled, and "suffocating" luxuriance of forms encountered in the architecture of the "Hindus," which he saw as akin to a "tropical jungle" and an unending source of creative energy, surpassing by far the powerful pathos of European baroque art.[8] In a discussion of the iconic motif of the four-armed dancing Shiva (Shiva Nataraja), Wölfflin drew an interesting parallel to the art of expressionism, for both, according to him, rely on a departure from naturalism and "bodily reality" to augment the expressive power of form.[9] His foreword to *Indische Baukunst* struggles with the intransigency of its object, with the paradox that renders "monstrosity" a necessary condition of forceful aesthetic expression.[10] While he regarded such a reading as affirming the applicability of his method to the art of different regions of the world, this

was a path of enquiry that he did not further pursue in his writings.

It was thus left to one of Wölfflin's students at the University of Munich, Ludwig Bachhofer (fig. 1), to carry forward the challenge of using *Principles* to come to grips with Asian artistic traditions and practices. Bachhofer, who completed his doctoral dissertation on Japanese woodblock prints in 1921 under Wölfflin's supervision, nurtured a lifetime interest in Asian art.[11] In addition to writing copiously on Chinese art, he dedicated several articles to the sculpture and bronzes from regions of Central and South Asia classified as the art of Gandhara. Interest in the latter brought forth a substantial book in two volumes on early Indian sculpture (c. 300 BCE–200 CE), *Die frühindische Plastik*, published and immediately translated into English in 1929.[12] Like Wölfflin, Bachhofer never traveled to Asia. His plans to do so were thwarted by political upheavals between the two world wars. Yet collections and exhibitions in Britain and the United States, to which he emigrated in 1935, gave him access to the objects of his study, much of which was undertaken on the basis of photographs.

Though Bachhofer does not directly transpose Wölfflin's comparative method based on polar opposites to South Asia, as he is believed to have done more explicitly in the case of Chinese painting, he does juggle with his mentor's founding principles and examines their usefulness as a tool to grapple with an alien—often resistant—cultural context. His method draws on the particular combination of the positivist and phenomenological methods that marked Wölfflin's conception of the painterly (*malerisch*). Bachhofer read this concept as a form of knowledge incorporating a relationship between the viewer and a work of art, wherein the former experiences the work sensually and psychically, an approach that indeed comes close to more recent ways of reading *Principles*. Such a reading served him as an entry point into early Indian sculpture, as a mode of access to aesthetic concepts rooted in a foreign cultural context.

It provided a language with which to talk about traditions that, in Bachhofer's understanding, we need no longer view as closed or incommensurable.

In his study of early Indian sculpture Bachhofer deployed Wölfflin's sequential scheme: more specifically, the combination of synchronic comparison and diachronic succession that characterizes Wölfflin's three-part narrative structure of the linear, classic, and painterly proved to be a useful tool with which to organize a study of a largely unfamiliar tradition of Indian sculpture and its alien iconography (fig. 2 and essay frontispiece). Bachhofer distinguished three phases within the evolution of Indian sculpture: "an early period full of confusion and contradiction; a middle or golden period, full of order and strength; and a late period, full of exuberance, both in form and outlook,"[13] characterized by "free and dissolved forms."[14] The description of the early period draws on the Sanskrit aesthetic notion of *rupa bheda* (separation of forms) as an explanatory tool. The structure of the individual image is elaborated in the minutest of details, with almost painful rigor and exactness; the human body appears as a composite of single members, carefully separated from one another.[15] The idea of proportion, which would play an important role in the following phase of Indian sculpture, is secondary here. The subsequent "golden age" is described in Bachhofer's account as exuding a calm grandeur and healthy joy in life,[16] while the third phase is marked by a new capacity for psychological differentiation. Art now reveals an understanding of powerful emotions, wherein form embodies an expression of passionate outburst or ecstatic devotion or maternal solicitude, emotions transmitted through the image in its totality.[17] In the Buddhist sculptures of Amaravati, "forms overlap, are welded together, and all the trammels are dissolved. Like a roaring mountain torrent, wild and irresistible, the baroque ornament flows forth" (fig. 3).[18] Bachhofer's use of the term "Indian baroque" to designate art of the Indian subcontinent during the second

and third centuries CE might be critiqued as a Eurocentric anachronism; it does, however, suggest that Wölfflinian categories lent themselves to a morphological rather than taxonomic usage, to designate a "period no longer satisfied with parallel echelons of planes," one in which "a universal reaching after depth-effect is felt."[19]

Bachhofer posited his model of evolving form as a counterscheme to writings such as those of Albert Grünwedel and Alfred Foucher, who studied the sculptures of Gandhara exclusively from the point of view of iconography.[20] He nonetheless recognized the informative value of iconography, in particular for those to whom the cultural context was alien, thereby following Wölfflin's postulate of the "twin roots of style" (*die doppelte Wurzel des Stils*), combining specific cultural content with form as a purely optical attribute.[21] In an article devoted to the iconic figure of Shiva Nataraja, before unraveling the sculpture's iconic meaning, Bachhofer, like Wölfflin before him, started with a plastic description of the "dense expression" that, according to him, distinguished Indian art from other traditions (fig. 4).[22] Bachhofer too argued that in the final analysis, the study of form—its dynamics and "inner (immanent) laws," "to which every visual perception is subjected"—comprises a universal principle, and such a study lies at the heart of art-historical investigation.[23]

At the end of the book the reader encounters a significant observation that identifies a source of fracture at the heart of South Asian art and art history, one that scholarship and exhibition practice continue to grapple with today: the distinction between a "religious" and an "aesthetic" object.[24] Indian art, in Bachhofer's words, is "religious only in name, showing an irresistible inclination for the profane.... [I]t escapes the enclosures of faith and moves about in open nature; it is everywhere at home, in fields and in the woods, in the hermit's hut as in the prince's palace, upon the battlefields as in the woman's apartments."[25] Coming in 1929, this observation signaled

an important taxonomic shift from cult
object to work of art, which, however, did
not occur at a formal level in institutional
practice until 1947.

Tracing the course of this shift brings me
to the second register of my investigation of

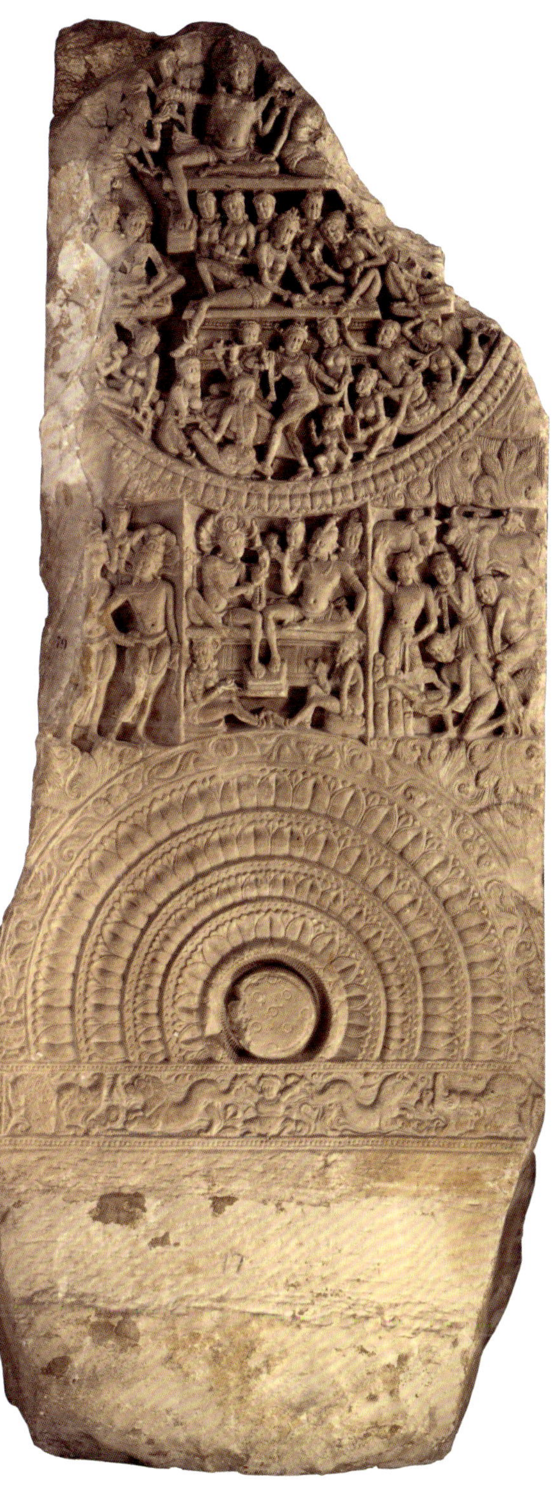

the Wölfflinian paradigm and South Asian
art. The first half of the twentieth century
saw the involvement with Indian objects
of a large number of actors from diverse
professional groups: archaeologists, anthro-
pologists, photographers, and makers of
plaster casts on the one hand, and collec-
tors, officials, and keepers of antiquities in
museums on the other. The status accorded
to these objects, however, remained a subject of controversy. Discussions took place
primarily within a colonial context of collection, administration, and knowledge
production; the terms used to designate
the objects ranged from "idol" to "artifact"
to "antiquity" to "curiosity," depending
on their provenance and their individual
trajectories.[26] The category of art, or fine
art, belonged to a securely guarded domain,
whose keepers were not yet ready to accord
Indian objects an entry.[27] A discipline fixated on classical Greek civilization continued to provide the normative framework
within which aesthetic quality was evaluated. The contestations surrounding the concepts deployed to write about Indian objects
and images can be illustrated through a
frequently cited incident that took place at
a meeting of January 13, 1910, at the Royal
Society of the Arts in London. E. B. Havell,
the principal of the Calcutta Art School
and passionate spokesman for the aesthetic
value of Indian objects, which he ascribed to
their "spiritual qualities," set out to counter
widespread prejudices of British observers in
relation to these objects (which they nonetheless collected avidly). He was countered
by George Birdwood, a referee of the Indian
section of the South Kensington Museum
(later the Victoria and Albert Museum), who
pointed to a Buddha image and derogatively
compared it to a "boiled suet pudding," an
"uninspired brazen image, vacuously squint-
ing down its nose to its thumbs, and knees,
and toes."[28]

A clear shift within this normative constellation can be discerned some three and
a half decades later, in 1947, soon after the
Indian subcontinent achieved independence
and was partitioned into the nation states

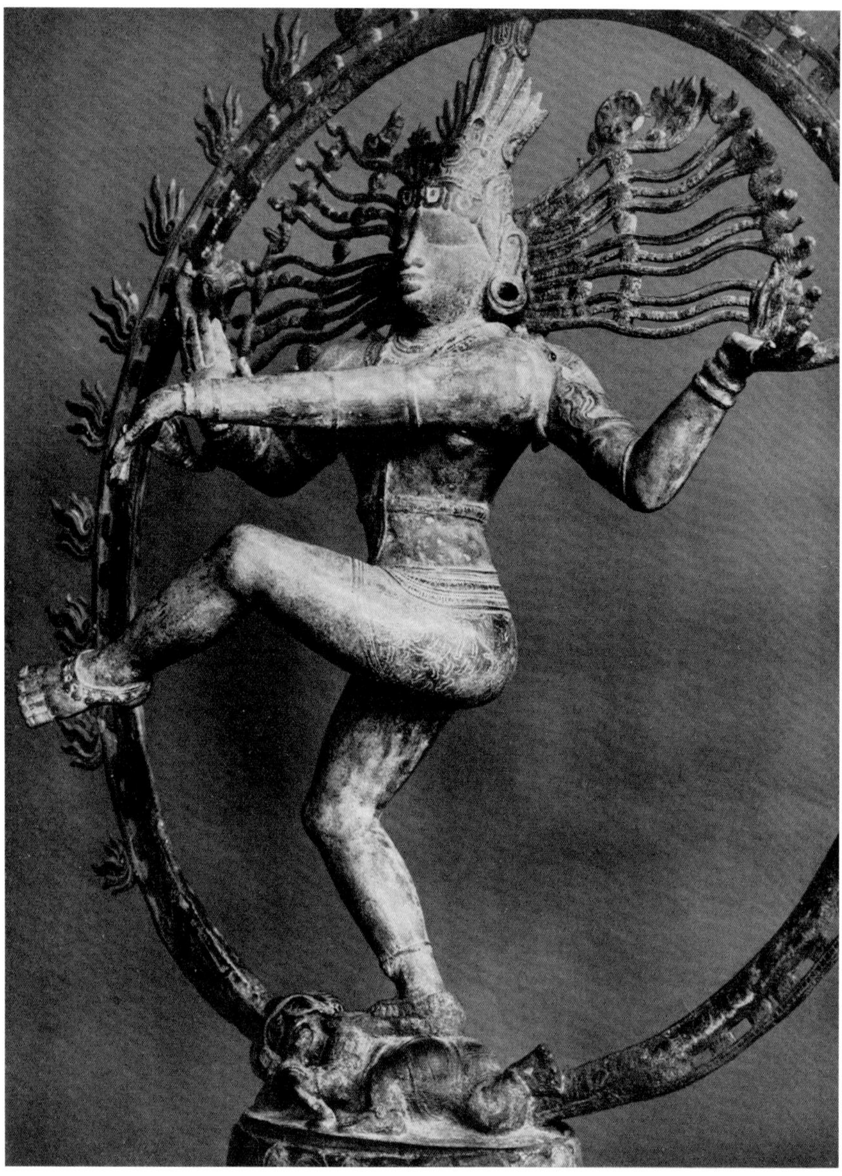

4. Shiva Nataraja, c. 990, bronze, from Ludwig Bachhofer, "Der tanzende Schiwa," *Die Kunst für Alle* 46 (1931): 369

approaches to Indian sculpture that read Indian art through the lenses of religion and metaphysics and, in his view, allowed iconography "too much weight." He urged viewers to concentrate on "the sculptures themselves," to attend to "significant form," thereby deploying a concept coined by Clive Bell, to whom he explicitly referred.[29] Bell, in turn, was a close friend and associate of Roger Fry, who had reviewed *Kunstgeschichtliche Grundbegriffe* in 1921 and later institutionally supported its translation into English.[30] Form, then, was the key to viewing Indian sculpture, one that visitors were urged to use with the same visual attentiveness, resonant of a Wölfflinian "gebildetes Sehen," that they would devote to any work of sculpture from another cultural tradition. Basil Gray, another member of the core committee responsible for the exhibition, underlined that the objects on view were chosen for their aesthetic value (as "objects of art and not documents of archaeology, history or ethnology") and insisted that all Indian objects would "speak directly by their formal qualities."[31] In doing so he, as did Codrington in his introductory essay, distanced himself from the position taken by Havell and, more important, the influential scholar Ananda Coomaraswamy, who had insisted that aesthetic quality derived from "spiritual" or "mystical" content and that a viewer needed to be steeped in the religions or philosophy of India to be able to appreciate its art.

of India and Pakistan. In an ambitious exhibition organized by the prestigious Royal Academy of Arts in London, titled *Art of India and Pakistan*, comprising some fifteen hundred objects from British, European, and Indian collections, artifacts were for the first time treated as "art"—a designation carried by the exhibition's title. Architectural fragments were presented as "sculpture," single manuscript folios became "painting," and "aesthetic" value became the criterion governing the choice of objects displayed at this canon-making institution.

In the exhibition catalog, one of the curators, K. de B. Codrington, criticized existing

Echoes of Wölfflin and Bachhofer are present in this valorization of formal characteristics that congeal into a style. This was indeed the organizing principle by which the exhibition objects were grouped into "styles" and "schools" determined by their formal qualities. Gray, who curated the section on painting, grouped the works into Mughal, Deccani, Gujarati, Rajasthani, and Pahari schools, each further subdivided into "styles" distinguished by their painterly characteristics.[32] In the decades to come, this approach to classification, marking a shift from iconography to form, became the backbone of Indian art history, even though the former was not entirely sidelined. Important art histories of the Indian subcontinent were authored by the organizers of the Royal Academy show—for instance, Douglas Barrett, who subsequently became keeper of Oriental antiquities at the British Museum (1969–1977), and Gray, who was keeper of the museum's department of Oriental prints and drawings at the time of the exhibition.[33]

The reception of a formalist approach in postcolonial India took two opposing directions. In an immediate sense, following 1947 it proved useful in taking the art of the "colony" out of the zone of "otherness." Dignifying an object as art meant discarding anthropology in favor of formalism. At the same time, however, art history in independent India was clearly implicated in the process of nation building, and this meant, to start with, creating a canon for Indian art that valorized aesthetic rather than iconographic criteria while generating a discourse of difference. Formalist-evolutionary methods that built on notions of styles and schools served the ends of a nationalist art history in that they argued—in the same way as Wölfflin—that formal criteria could be deployed to study any canon of great art, from any location in the world. This is not to draw a direct line connecting Wölfflinian methods to Indian art history of the 1950s and 1960s, but more to suggest a form of indirect resonance, or "trace,"[34] to writings that were clearly connected to the Wölfflinian paradigm, such as those of John Wilkinson, or of Gray and Barrett, mentioned above. In addition, nationalist scholars were anxious to situate works of art within an indigenous intellectual context, to identify texts in Sanskrit, for instance, that could be read as manuals for art production or as repositories of aesthetic philosophy. In their eagerness to fashion an indigenous genealogy of art-historical knowledge and practice, scholars tended to overlook the fact that many of the "texts" they drew upon were fragmentary and had undergone a process of selection and translation through the aegis of Orientalist scholarship of the nineteenth century. More important, the Indian textual tradition surrounding art chiefly consists of normative writings, in themselves inchoate, whose reception over the length and breadth of the Indian subcontinent has undergone interpretive shifts over centuries, making it difficult to single these out as standing for an undifferentiated canonical "tradition" or a uniform language of form. I will return to this aspect later, for it has become one of the argumentative planks of a specific strain of art history that strives to be global in its search for "indigenous" categories for studying artistic production in non-European cultures.

More recently, since the 1980s and 1990s, art-historical writing in South Asia has responded to theoretical perspectives of postmodernism and the linguistic turn, in a move to make art history a subject of postcolonial critique. Taking their cue from Dipesh Chakrabarty's call to "provincialize Europe," art historians have critiqued the formalist-evolutionary method for universalizing claims that create hierarchies between Western art and traditions from "elsewhere." Such a critique, however, cuts both ways. It seeks on the one hand to open the canon to include genres such as textiles, enamel work, ivory, lacquer, woodcarving, and so on, by transcending distinctions between "art" and "craft" and by including "technical education" within the framework of art education—all with the intent of arguing for an "alternative cultural modernity."[35] At the same time, the framework within which objects all over the world continue to be dignified as "art"—an agenda crucial to the art history of young postcolonial nations—has remained indebted to an Enlightenment dyad that construed art as the opposite of all that was "the uncivilized anterior to the imaginary 'disinterestedness' of European aestheticism." Such a "dyadic complementarity," as Donald Preziosi terms it, can have a flattening effect in that it rules out other possibilities and meanings that objects carry.[36] It was, however, built into a logic of nation building that required the discipline of art history to make works of art legible by harnessing them to the fabrication of a national past. Within such a framework, artistic form—and changes in form—are read as indicating a path of development that may be materially charted through stylistic changes over time and space.

I now return to the question I posed at the beginning of this essay: What is to be learned through our engagement with Wölfflin's *Principles* today? Where can this interest and the new research it has brought forth take us? Can it provide us with fresh impulses to engage with formalism and aesthetic concepts in different cultures, to draw these out of closed regional compartments and show the way to creating a global or transcultural frame within which regional art histories can be brought together? Can a nuanced and sensitive formalism respond to the challenge of globality, in the way Wölfflin hoped his morphology of forms would? While I cannot claim to have all the answers to these questions, here are some thoughts that seek to apply a notion of critical globality to art history and ask how a Wölfflinian formalism that has itself become transcultural through its widespread global reception could be made productive within the framework of a globally framed art history.[37]

In her contribution to this volume, Evonne Levy observes that Wölfflin's *Principles* has "functioned as the crucible of the discipline" and been "generative of disciplinary renewal."[38] Tracking the (potential) path of such renewal requires, to start with, a critical take on specific aspects of the Wölfflinian legacy to make it productive in new ways. I will briefly bring up a few of these from the perspective of a global or transculturally framed art history.

One of the legacies of an art history that sought to become a systematic, "scientific [*wissenschaftlich*] discipline" at the turn of the twentieth century was the fixing of criteria that would make individual works of art legible as part of an evolving stylistic system manifested either by the work of an individual artist or by a broader aesthetic movement. The unfolding of an individual artist's biography was now embedded in a set of relationships shaped primarily though not exclusively by the development of artistic form. Corresponding to this was a temporal notion of an art-historical "period" or "school" marked by similarities of style, thematic preoccupation, or technical approaches to formal construction or composition. The notion of style came to function as a key concept, a narrative anchor for art history. Jaś Elsner refers to style as a "crucial reminder of our discipline's depths," as its "lineage," without, however, drawing attention to the elisions built into that lineage.[39] In other words, the notion of style, whose genealogy Elsner traces to the sixteenth century and whose extraordinary subtlety and refinement he ascribes to Wölfflin's *Principles*, has indeed served as a convenient tool to coordinate and stabilize the mobility of objects and metamorphoses of forms.[40] In the case of postcolonial India, it enabled a self-fashioning that could reject the worst of colonial stereotypes and racist explanatory paradigms and assiduously cultivate its own narrative of cultural uniqueness, one that subsumes experiences of cultural braidedness under the taxonomic categories of influence, borrowing, and transfer. The idea of stylistic development, now firmly anchored within art history both in South Asia and elsewhere, implies a scheme that is artificially maintained by assuming that a geographic location is self-contained and by suppressing the plurality of agency and the circulation of objects, forms, and practices. The idea of style applied to South Asian art soon congealed into a notion of schools that does not take account of processes of migration and entanglement. More than that, the idea itself rehearses the logic of a biological, evolutionary construct applied to culture, where it hardly belongs and where it operates by suppressing human agency and the circulation of material objects. Grafting the study of style to a narrative of circulation could be a way to take forward and dynamize the notion, shifting the focus from the fixity of origins to an analysis of recontextualization.

In a discussion of the possibilities and potential of a global art history, James

Elkins locates Wölfflin's *Principles* and its many translations squarely within the historiography of a Euro-American art history and advocates at the same time, in a stance of extreme relativism, a global approach based on the use of each cultural tradition's core concepts of visuality and the image, whose incommensurability and fixity are assumed.[41] Yet, thinking through Wölfflin's statement that "vision itself has a history" would call for making vision and visuality a subject of historical investigation at a global level. [42] This includes studying both the distinctive cultural possibilities that are built into the act of seeing and the formative shifts within its practices as new relationalities are negotiated in the wake of cultural encounters. Historicizing vision means arguing that seeing and the representation of the seen on the two-dimensional surface of a painted page are processes that need to be unpacked beyond simple cultural relativism. This in turn implies a deconstruction of those systems of representation that art history has canonized as modern and scientific in a universalist sense; in other words, it calls for a reflexive engagement with the ways in which the disciplines, interpretive molds, and languages that have evolved to explain and theorize these practices are themselves a product of modern concerns.

More specifically, in a critical global perspective, the values transported within art-historical writing or by "art history's assumptions,"[43] to cite Levy again, would need to be put to the test: for instance, the assumption that the naturalist-perspectival mode of illusionism based on certain forms of recession and organization of space around a single vanishing point, together with the use of techniques like trompe l'oeil and sfumato, developed as a modern, rational form of sight and of plotting the world in Europe, where a "medieval way of seeing" was being repudiated. Following a linear logic, modern vision, then, is believed to have traveled to other regions of the world as a fully formed and self-confident mode. Even as Wölfflin sensitized his readers to changing ways of seeing from period to

period, these shifts were confined to a European context. The afterlife of Wölfflinian formalism also brought about the canonization of "rational" ways of seeing and representing that served as a criterion with which art from beyond the West was studied. The encounter with local regimes of visuality is frequently characterized in terms of partial absorption or of a failure to attain the full technical mastery required by illusionist forms. A number of writings in South Asian art history of the early modern period, for instance, are animated by a historical discourse about the "difficulties" experienced by North Indian artists in creating figures in space that would make for spatial coherence. Such a historiography is marked by a consensus around the idea of failure or partial success in attaining a perfect pictorial vision, rather than by examination of the field of opposing forces—philosophical, theological, and artistic—within which vision itself was implicated.[44] Tracking the history of vision at a global level would then take the discussion of the engagement with illusionist art to a different level, beyond thinking of it as purely a matter of acquiring expertise in a set of techniques and a form of coded information in order to enhance the narrative performance of an image.[45]

Art-historical inquiries that focus on the transcontinental journeys of objects and forms—especially in the wake of European expansion during the early modern period—suggest that such encounters brought with them a privileging of "optical authority" as a way of registering and controlling an unprecedented gamut of new experiences, desires, and knowledge.[46] Yet addressing the dynamics of such processes also urges us to expand and complicate our conceptions of the visual, to question whether seeing can be confined to being a purely optical category. While investigating the act of seeing as a participant in innumerable transactions across the divide of the familiar and the alien, a globally framed art history investigates the multiple valences it acquires as it resonates on new sites and is reconfigured in new contexts. Seeing in such encounters is frequently mediated by material objects that are both the media and the agents of transculturation, making their "thingness" a formative component of the encounter. This interaction both relates to and constitutes synaesthetic notions of sight in cultural settings beyond Europe.

When investigating cultural constructs of vision, the interactive moments are also about the encounter between the material and the visual. In the South Asian context, more specifically, the notion of art was more than primarily visual: seeing has been described as one element of a "corpothetic" sensibility.[47] For instance, a genre of paintings known as *ragamala* (musical modes) created an emotional mood that connected the visual and the aural. Motifs such as floral blooms and fruit-laden trees draw on memory to evoke the olfactory sense. The visual in many ways functioned as a crucible of multisensorial experience although confined to the two-dimensional space of the painted page.[48]

No straight line connects these thoughts to *Principles of Art History*. Yet one aspect of the intellectual gains of studying the global reception of Heinrich Wölfflin's seminal text, I suggest, is the mining of fresh impulses to reinterpret and apply formalism and aesthetic concepts in transcultural settings; another is bringing regional art histories into the mainstream without freezing them in their alterity. Perhaps the most productive way to engage with Wölfflinian thought is to consider it a form of living historiography that can serve as both a prism and a source of fresh propositions.

For my esteemed colleague Axel Michaels

1. This engagement was triggered by the kind invitation extended by the University of Zurich and Tristan Weddigen to deliver the Heinrich Wölfflin Lectures in Global Art History in 2014. Though these lectures did not focus directly on Wölfflin's work, they did engage from time to time with some of his key ideas from the perspective of a historian of South Asian art.

2. On *Weltkunstgeschichte*, see Ulrich Pfisterer, "Origins and Principles of World Art History: 1900 (and 2000)," in *World Art Studies: Exploring Concepts and Approaches*, ed. Kitty Zijlmans and Wilfried van Damme (Amsterdam, 2008), 69–89. For a critical take on Pfisterer, see Monica Juneja, "'A Very Civil Idea…': Art History, Transculturation and World Making—with and beyond the Nation," *Zeitschrift für Kunstgeschichte* 81 (2018): 461–485, here 464–466.

3. "Doch hat das Schema sich bis in die Gebiete der japanischen und der altnordischen Kunst hinein als brauchbar erwiesen." Heinrich Wölfflin, *Kunstgeschichtliche Grundbegriffe: Das Problem der Stilentwicklung in der neueren Kunst* (Basel, 1948), 6. For Wölfflin, India could be a channel to better understand Europe ("um neue Maßstäbe für die Beurteilung europäischer Kunst zu gewinnen"), an observation of 1922 that he made on the basis of his student Ludwig Bachhofer's dissertation on Japanese art, cited in Udo Kultermann, *Geschichte der Kunstgeschichte: Der Weg einer Wissenschaft* (Vienna, 1966), 320. In a lecture delivered at the University of Munich in winter 1914–1915, Wölfflin referred to the importance of *Weltkunstgeschichte* to *Principles*; see Hans Körner, "'Grundbegriffe der Kunstgeschichte': Heinrich Wölfflins Münchener Vorlesung im Wintersemester 1914/15," *Kritische Berichte* 4 (1988): 65–73, here 67.

4. The German word is *Bildung*, a notion opposed to a dilettantism that values a contextual approach as the primary source of art-historical knowledge. Daniel Adler, "Painterly Politics: Wölfflin, Formalism and German Academic Culture, 1885–1915," *Art History* 27, no. 3 (2004): 431–456, here 440, 445.

5. Evonne Levy and Tristan Weddigen, "Problems and Approaches to the Global Response of Heinrich Wölfflin's *Kunstgeschichtliche Grundbegriffe* (1915–2015)," internal paper, 6.

6. Emanuel La Roche, ed., *Indische Baukunst*, 3 vols. (Munich 1920–1921), I:xiii–xiv.

7. Ella Beaucamp, "Heinrich Wölfflin," in *Kunstgeschichten 1915: 100 Jahre Heinrich Wölfflin, Kunstgeschichtliche Grundbegriffe*, ed. Matteo Burioni, Burcu Dogramaci, and Ulrich Pfisterer (Zentralinstitut für Kunstgeschichte, Munich, 2015), 212.

8. "[A]ls ob wir in den tropischen Urwald kämen. Ein atembeklemmender Reichtum der Form, maßlos, ungeordnet…ein unendliches Quellen von Formen, das dumpfe Erlebnis eines ungeheuren, unstillbaren Ausdrucksdranges." La Roche, *Indische Baukunst*, xiii.

9. "Da haben wir also den Fall, daß die Gestalt nach ihrer körperlichen Wirklichkeit für uns zurückbleibt hinter der bloßen Ausdruckserscheinung. Das ist aber schon 'Expressionismus.'" La Roche, *Indische Baukunst*, xiv.

10. "Man kann nicht nur hinwegsehen über das Monströse, sondern man findet die Abweichung von der Natur geradezu notwendig, um jenen hohen Grad von Lebensfülle zu erreichen, den diese Tanzfigur besitzt." La Roche, *Indische Baukunst*, xiv.

11. Ludwig Bachhofer, *Die Kunst der japanischen Holzmeister* (Munich, 1922). See Lillian Lan-ying Tseng, "Traditional Chinese Painting through the Modern European Eye: The Case of Ludwig Bachhofer," in *Tradition and Modernity: Comparative Perspectives*, Yale–Beijing University Conference (Beijing, 2006), 508–533.

12. Ludwig Bachhofer, *Die frühindische Plastik*, 2 vols. (Florence, 1929). English editions: *Early Indian Sculpture* (Paris, 1929); *Early Indian Sculpture*, 2 vols. (New York, 1972). An Indian edition was published in 1973. All quotations are from the New York edition of 1972. See also Ludwig Bachhofer, *Zur Datierung der Gandhara-Plastik* (Munich, 1925).

13. Bachhofer, *Early Indian Sculpture*, 1:vii

14. Bachhofer, *Early Indian Sculpture*, 1:118

15. Bachhofer, *Early Indian Sculpture*, 1:18.

16. Bachhofer, *Early Indian Sculpture*, 1:vii, 118.

17. Bachhofer, *Early Indian Sculpture*, 54–55.

18. Bachhofer, *Early Indian Sculpture*, 57.

19. Bachhofer, *Early Indian Sculpture*, 57.

20. Albert Grünwedel, *Buddhistische Kunst in Indien* (Berlin, 1932); Alfred Foucher, *L'Art greco-bouddhique du Gandhara* (Paris, 1912); Bachhofer, *Early Indian Sculpture*, 1:vii–viii, 69–73.

21. One root comprised "der Stil, der Schule des Landes, der Rasse," which determined the concrete appearance of a given thematic content; the other was "die allgemeine optische Form, die Seh- und Darstellungsweise." Cited in Ulrich Pfisterer, "1915: Kunstgeschichte und Grundbegriffe," in Burioni, Dogramaci, and Pfisterer, *Kunstgeschichten 1915*, 5. See also Ludwig Bachhofer, "Der tanzende Schiwa," *Die Kunst für Alle* 46 (1930–1931): 368–371.

22. "…Das starke, übermächtige Bedürfnis nach gehäuftem Ausdruck,…das die indische Kunst von jeder anderen auszeichnet." Ludwig Bachhofer, "Der Tanzende Schiwa," *Die Kunst für Alle* 46 (1930–1931): 368–371, here 368.

23. Bachhofer, *Early Indian Sculpture*, 1:118.

24. For a study of a recent controversy surrounding this contentious distinction, see Monica Juneja, "From the Religious to the Aesthetic Image—Or the Struggle over Art That Offends," in *Taking Offense: Religion, Art and Visual Culture in Plural Configurations*, ed. Christiane Kruse, Birgit Meyer, and Anne-Marie Korte (Munich, 2018), 161–189.

25. Bachhofer, *Early Indian Sculpture*, 1:119.

26. See Richard H. Davis, *Lives of Indian Images* (Princeton, 1997), esp. chap. 3.

27. The project of colonial scholars in India was overwhelmingly antiquarian rather than art historical. See Monica Juneja, ed., *Architecture in Medieval India: Form, Contexts, Histories* (New Delhi, 2001); Tapati Guha Thakurta, *Monuments, Objects, Histories: Institutions of Art in Colonial and Postcolonial India* (New Delhi, 2004). Painting too was generally read as a mirror of society that "gives you a perfect idea of the customs, manners and the dress of men and women…also of their birds, trees and plants": William Watson, cited in Bernard Cohn, *Colonialism and Its Forms of Knowledge: The British in India* (Princeton, 1996), 99.

28. Cited in Davis, *Lives of Indian Images*, 177–178. As late as 1935, George Birdwood, who emerged as an ardent spokesman for the "decorative arts" of India, remarked on the absence of "sculpture" and the "fine arts" in India, a deficiency that he attributed to the "monstrous shapes of the Puranic deities," which rendered them "unsuitable for the higher forms of artistic representation." George C. M. Birdwood, *The Industrial Arts of India*, 2 vols. (London, 1880), 1:125. For a systematic history of these attitudes, see Partha Mitter, *Much Maligned Monsters: History of European Reactions to Indian Art* (Oxford, 1977); Cohn, *Colonialism*, chap. 4.

29. *The Art of India and Pakistan: A Commemorative Catalogue of the Exhibition Held at the Royal Academy of Arts, London, 1947–8*, ed. Leigh Ashton (London, 1950), 3–15, quotations 15, 5.

30. See Paul Binski's essay in this volume.

31. Basil Gray, "The Art of India and Pakistan with Special Reference to the Exhibition at the Royal Academy," *Journal of the Royal Society of Arts* 94, no. 4758 (1947): 75–81, 69–72 (plates), here 76.

32. *The Art of India and Pakistan*, 87–103.

33. Douglas E. Barrett, *Painting of the Deccan, XVI–XVII Century* (London, 1958); Douglas E. Barrett and Basil Gray, *Painting of India* (Lausanne, 1963); Douglas E. Barrett, *Studies in Indian Sculpture and Painting* (London, 1990). See also Benjamin Rowland, *The Art and Architecture of India: Hindu, Buddhist, Jain* (Harmondsworth, Middlesex, 1963); J. V. S. Wilkinson, "Indian Painting," in *Indian Art*, ed. Richard Winstedt (London, 1947), 103–150; and Mortimer Wheeler, *Splendors of the East: Temples, Tombs, Palaces and Fortresses of Asia* (New York, 1965), who reuses Wölfflin's analogy of the luxuriance of the "jungle" to describe Hindu art in contrast to the "desert," that is, the regions of Islam.

34. Levy and Weddigen, "Problems and Approaches" (see note 5 above).

35. Priya Maholay-Jaradi, *Fashioning a National Art: Baroda's Royal Collection and Art Institutions (1875–1924)* (New Delhi, 2016), 129 and following pages.

36. Donald Preziosi, "Epilogue: The Art of Art History," in *The Art of Art History: A Critical Anthology*, ed. Donald Preziosi (Oxford, 1998), 496.

37. The designation "global art history" has been used in a number of diverging ways to characterize recent perspectives within the discipline of art history. See, for example, James Elkins, ed., *Is Art History Global?* (London, 2007); Hans Belting, "Contemporary Art as Global Art: A Critical Estimate," in *The Global Art World: Audiences, Markets and Museums*, ed. Hans Belting, Andrea Buddensieg, and Peter Weibel (Ostfildern, 2008), 38–73. For an extensive critical discussions of these positions, see Monica Juneja, "Global Art History and the 'Burden of Representation,'" in *Global Studies: Mapping Contemporary Art and Culture*, ed. Hans Belting, Jacob Birken, Andrea Buddensieg, and Peter Weibel (Ostfildern, 2011), 274–297; Juneja, "'A Very Civil Idea…'" (see note 2 above). In both these programmatic essays, as also in my other writings, I have defined "global" as standing for a transcultural perspective, one that studies the transformations that ensue following long-term relationships between cultures. This definition in turn calls for an epistemic critique of the foundations of the discipline of art history. This was the perspective that informed the series of six Heinrich Wölfflin Lectures, "Can Art History Be Made Global? A Discipline in Transition," which I delivered at the University of Zurich in 2014. I discuss these issues in detail in "'A Very Civil Idea…,'" in which I coined and defined the notion of "critical globality" as an explanatory concept to theorize a globally framed art history (464).

38. See Levy, "Wölfflin's *Principles* in the United States: A Love-Hate Relationship," in this volume.

39. Jaś Elsner, "Style," in *Critical Terms for Art History*, ed. Robert S. Nelson and Richard Shiff, rev. ed. (Chicago, 2003), 98–109, here 108.

40. Elsner describes this as Wölfflin's "monumental contribution"; Elsner, "Style," 104.

41. Elkins, *Is Art History Global?*; James Elkins, "Different Horizons for a Concept of the Image," in *On Pictures and the Words That Fail Them* (Cambridge, 1998), 188–209, here 200–208. For a critical take on Elkins, see Juneja, "Global Art History," 279–280.

42. Cited in Whitney Davis, *A General Theory of Visual Culture* (Princeton, 2011), 5.

43. Levy, "Wölfflin's *Principles* in the United States."

44. I have discussed this issue and the historiography at length elsewhere; for references see Monica Juneja, "Tracking the Routes of Vision in Early Modern Eurasia," in *The Itineraries of Art: Topographies of Artistic Mobility in Europe and Asia, 1500–1900*, ed. Karin Gludovatz, Juliane Noth, and Joachim Rees (Berlin, 2015), 57–83.

45. Juneja, "Tracking the Routes of Vision in Early Modern Eurasia."

46. Dana Leibsohn, "Introduction: Geographies of Sight," in *Seeing across Cultures in Early Modern Europe*, ed. Dana Leibsohn and Jeanette F. Peterson (Farnham, Surrey, 2012), 1. Although neither Leibsohn nor other contributors to this collection cite Wölfflin, many of their arguments build on his assumptions.

47. The term has been used by Christopher Pinney, "Piercing the Skin of the Idol," in *Beyond Aesthetics: Art and the Technologies of Enchantment*, ed. Christopher Pinney and Nicholas Thomas (Oxford, 2001): 157–178; see also Diana Eck, *Darśan: Seeing the Divine Image in India* (New York, 1996), 9 and chap. 2, where seeing in the Indian devotional context is described as "a kind of touching."

48. For an extensive discussion, see Juneja, "Tracking the Routes of Vision in Early Modern Eurasia," 71–77.

SHIRAHARA YUKIKO

The 1936 Japanese Version of Kunstgeschichtliche Grundbegriffe *and the Study of Japanese Art*

的對照を爲して相互に作用するやうな圖式に持ち來たされてゐる。又、圖全體は構築的な力によつて支配されてゐる。圖の軸線と人物の軸線とは雙方から力を合はせあつてゐる。又、圖中、女像は片方の腕を舉げ、貝殻の中に己が姿を寫して

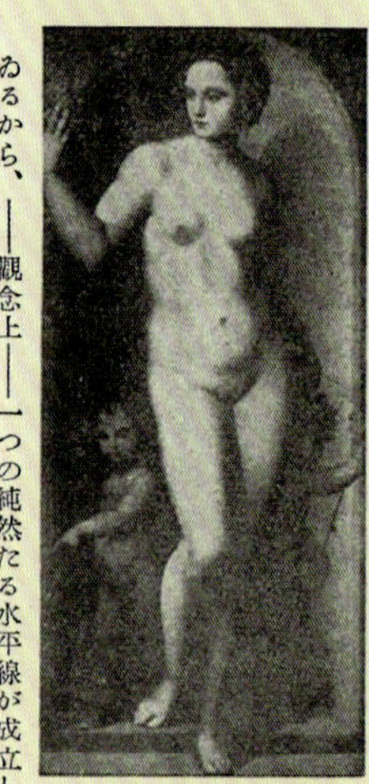

挿圖　三八　フランチァビデ■

ゐるから、――觀念上――一つの純然たる水平線が成立し、このものが再び垂直線の効果を強力に支持してゐる。かゝる人體構想の場合に於ては、建築的背景（階段のある壁龕）が常に全く相應しいものと思はれることであらう。――同じやうな仕上げの嚴密さは伴はないにしても、動機はこれを同じうして、北歐に於てその當時デューレルやクラーナハやオルライはヴェーヌス圖やルクレーティア圖を描いたのである。從つて、これらの諸圖の發展史的意義は就中畫面把捉の構築法に依つて評價されるのを至當とするのである。

後世になりリューベンスがこの主題を取り上げると、如何に忽ちに又自明のこととして彼の圖は構築的性質から脫却してゐることか、それは喫驚すべきものである。大作「アンドローメダー」（挿三九）

はその兩腕が高く緊縛されてゐて、到底垂直狀態を免れ得ないが、併しもはや構築的の効果を持つてゐない。圖面の矩形はその線中に人物との類線性をもはや保つてゐないやうに思はれる。人物と枠との距離はもはや構成上の畫面價値として數へ上げられない。肉體は正面向きであつても、その正面性を畫面から斜りてゐない。純粹なる方向の對立は廢棄され、又、肉體に於てその構築的の要素はたゞ內密に、恰も深所からするやうに現はれてゐるに過ぎない。効果の強調點が反對の側に移つて行つたのである。

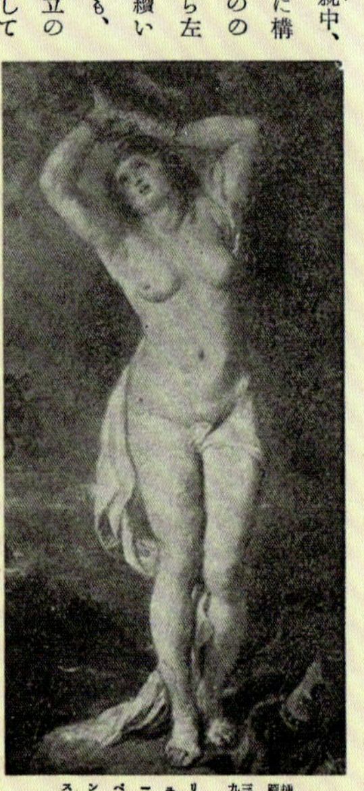

挿圖　三九　リューベンス

レンブラント

莊重な儀容の圖、就中、教會に於ける聖者圖は常に構築的姿勢を賴りにするものやうに思はれる。併し乍ら左右相稱が十七世紀に於て續いて採用されてゐるにしても、この種の構圖は畫面の組立の爲めにもはや拘束力を有して

Heinrich Wölfflin's *Kunstgeschich-tliche Grundbegriffe* (*Principles of Art History*, hereafter referred to as *Principles*) was translated into Japanese twice, first by Moriya Kenji (1898–1972), published in 1936, and then by Kaizu Tadao (1930–2009), published in 2000.[1] Although at the time of the first translation Japanese scholarship was geographically, ideologically, and philosophically a world away from the West, the relationship between Wölfflin and Japanese art history has noteworthy features. One Japanese scholar, Sawaki Yomokichi (1886–1930), had an opportunity to study Wölfflin's stylistic theory directly from Wölfflin before the publication of *Principles*, and there were plans as early as the 1920s to publish a Japanese version in order to establish a scientific methodology for the traditional study of Japanese art.

In this essay I examine who was behind this movement in Japan as well as the cultural setting around 1900 and after. Next I consider how Wölfflin's theory was introduced and translated and how it was used in early art-historical research and discourse in Japan. Exploring the application of Moriya Kenji's translation of *Principles* in the study of art history in Japan and referring to Kaizu Tadao's new Japanese version as a different approach to the text, in conclusion I discuss the meaning and function of *Principles* in the study of Japanese art.

Before Wölfflin

The Meiji Period (1868–1912)
In 1854 Japan's more than two centuries of seclusion ended, and the country changed direction almost overnight as it adopted Western thought and industrialization wholesale. These were the first steps to creating a modern Japanese nation that could stand as an equal to the nations of the West. The government also sought to promote Japan's unique culture and history to audiences both in and outside Japan. Thus the Meiji government set about encouraging as national policy the creation of paintings, sculpture, and decorative arts that represented the elegance and technical skill of traditional Japanese techniques, with these products serving as one element of the nation's budding export economy. The establishment of the academic study of art history also began in the Meiji period. This section explores the cultural and political background of the introduction and adoption of Wölfflin's method of stylistic analysis.

Before the Meiji period, Japanese art history consisted of artist biographies. *Shūko jisshu* (Ten types of antiquities), Japan's first catalog of a survey of cultural properties, with an introduction, was published in 1800. It divided Japan's tangible arts into ten types by medium and use.[2] Later editions were still in distribution through the Meiji period.

The Japanese government made its first official appearance at a world exposition in Vienna in 1873, and this year is regarded as a turning point in various fields. The German term *Kunstgewerbe*, used to refer to the works displayed in the exposition, was translated, and possibly intentionally mistranslated, into Japanese as *bijutsu* 美術 (fine arts).[3] The concept of the history of art, translated into Japanese as *bijutsushi* 美術史, combining the words for art and history, was explained to Japanese audiences as considering works of art from a historical perspective. Japan's first museum, the Tokyo National Museum, had its beginnings

Heinrich Wölfflin, *Bijutsushi no kiso-gainen: Kinsei bijutsu ni okeru yoshiki hatten no mondai* (*Principles of Art History: The Problem of the Development of Style in Later Art*), trans. Moriya Kenji (Tokyo, 1936), 242–243

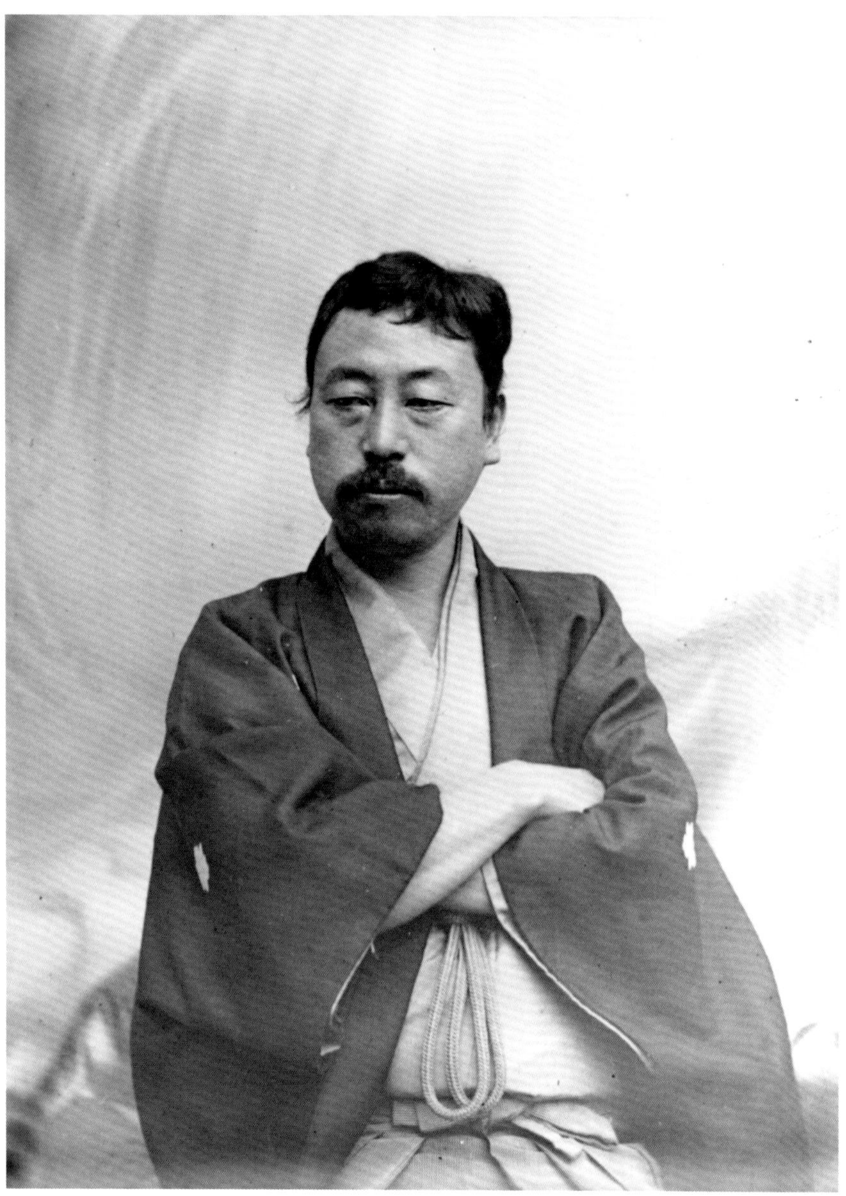

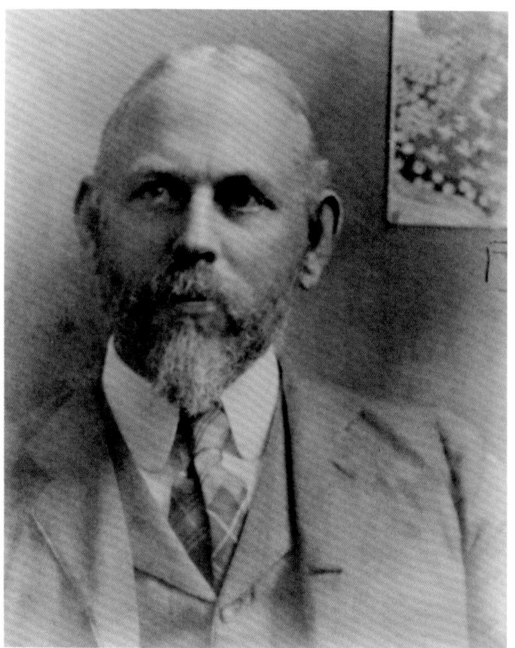

1. Okakura Kakuzō, c. 1898
Photograph Tenshin Memorial Museum of Art, Ibaraki

2. Ernest F. Fenollosa at the Museum of Fine Arts, Boston, c. 1890–1896
Photograph Museum of Fine Arts, Boston. All rights reserved.
© DNP *Partcom*

in a preview exhibition *(hakurankai)* held in 1872 in the Yushima district of Tokyo, preceding the event in Vienna.[4]

The movement to formulate a Japanese art history began in the late 1880s and early 1890s. Two events can be seen as emblematic of this era. In February 1889 the constitution of the Empire of Japan was adopted on the basis of modern constitutionalism, and in October of that year a deluxe monthly art journal titled *Kokka* (National treasures), in Japanese with English article summaries, was launched. The publication of an art journal that would introduce the highest

achievements of Japanese art to audiences in and outside Japan can be understood both as advancing the modernization of Japan's social structure and as a paean to the traditional arts.[5]

Ernest F. Fenollosa and Okakura Kakuzō

Among the contributors to the inaugural issue of *Kokka* were Okakura Kakuzō (1863–1913, also known as Okakura Tenshin; fig. 1), who wrote the prefatory essay for the issue, and the American Ernest Francisco Fenollosa (1853–1908; fig. 2). They are both renowned for their wide dissemination of the framework and value system of Japanese art history.[6]

Fenollosa studied Hegelian philosophy and Spencerian sociology at Harvard University and graduated with top honors. Later he sought to position himself in the fields of art education and art criticism and so in graduate school specialized in art history. He also studied painting technique at the art school of the Museum of Fine Arts, Boston. In 1878, on the recommendation of his Harvard history professor, Charles Eliot Norton, he was invited to Japan as a professor of political studies at Tokyo Imperial University (present-day University of Tokyo). There he taught political philosophy, philosophy

of economics, and history of philosophy, a
choice of subjects perhaps related to the fact
that many of Herbert Spencer's books had
been translated into Japanese, and social
Darwinism was welcomed in Japan at the
time as a pillar of modernization.

Fenollosa, however, quickly developed a
passionate interest in Japanese art.[7] He hired
Okakura Kakuzō, then one of his political
studies students who was fluent in English,
as his assistant and devoted himself to the
collection of antique Japanese paintings. By
1881 he had already established himself as
a collector and connoisseur. It seems that
Fenollosa's pursuit of the classification of
paintings by period and stylistic lineage was
influenced by Spencer's social Darwinism.
Later Fenollosa transferred to the arts administration bureau of the ministry of education (combined with the Imperial Household
ministry), and Okakura was named as a
ministry of education technical officer. The
official investigation team, including these
two, surveyed antique works of art and was
active in cultural properties conservation
efforts. Fenollosa and Okakura were also
involved in the founding of Tokyo Bijutsu
Gakkō (Tokyo School of Fine Arts, present-
day Tokyo University of the Arts), which
aimed to foster both artists and art educators.

Records indicate that before his departure
from Japan in July of 1890, Fenollosa gave
more than a dozen lectures on art. He highly
valued Japanese Buddhism and antique arts
and encouraged Japanese traditional painting. These concepts were welcomed as a
source of pride for the Japanese public and
of enthusiasm for the bureaucrats and intelligentsia of the day.[8] This American's praise
of Japanese art was favorable publicity for
the Japanese government policy of linking
the creation of a modern Japanese art to
national prosperity.

Okakura was active as an advisor in the
art world during this stimulating period
and is also known for his tumultuous career.
He worked closely with Fenollosa during
the latter's time in Japan, and they formed
a relationship of mutual influence in terms
of their views of art history. Following

his appointment as president of the Tokyo
School of Fine Arts in 1890, Okakura presented three years of lectures on Japanese
art history, the first on the subject given
by a Japanese scholar. Students shared and
copied notes from these lectures as the only
history of Japanese art they knew. The
notes became available to the public in 1922,
when they were published under the title
Nihon bijutsushi (Japanese art history).[9]

The year 1901 saw the publication of
Kōhon teikoku Nihon bijutsu ryakushi
(Draft version of the short history of impe-
rial Japanese art), the first systematic his-
tory of Japanese art. As indicated by the
term *kōhon*, this was the draft (edited by
Okakura, later by Fukuchi Mataichi) trans-
lated into French and published in 1900 as
Histoire de l'art du Japon for the Exposition
Universelle in Paris.[10]

In the larger realm, this was the period
between the Sino-Japanese War (1894–1895)
and the Russo-Japanese War (1904–1905).
The history of Japanese art established during these years clearly set out the importance
of Japan as separate from the nations of the
West and served the function of advertising
the superiority of Japanese culture and tradition, surpassing even those of China. The
establishment of a Japanese art history that
was the product of connoisseurship based
on Japanese government fieldwork, in which
Fenollosa and Okakura participated, was
seen as a political step that heralded Japan's
cultural superiority and was thus incorpo
rated into the education system.

The Creation of Okakura's Japanese Art History
The most noteworthy element of Okakura's
treatment of Japanese art in his *Nihon
bijutsushi* is that he wrote extensively about
antiquity (*kodai*), one of the periods he
discussed along with the medieval (*chūko*)
and the modern (*kindai*). He maintained
that Japanese art had already attained a
high standard in the antique period, and
he sought not only to compare it to the
art of Europe but indeed to emphasize
it. Okakura divided the *kodai* period into
three eras, each with its peak: the Suiko era

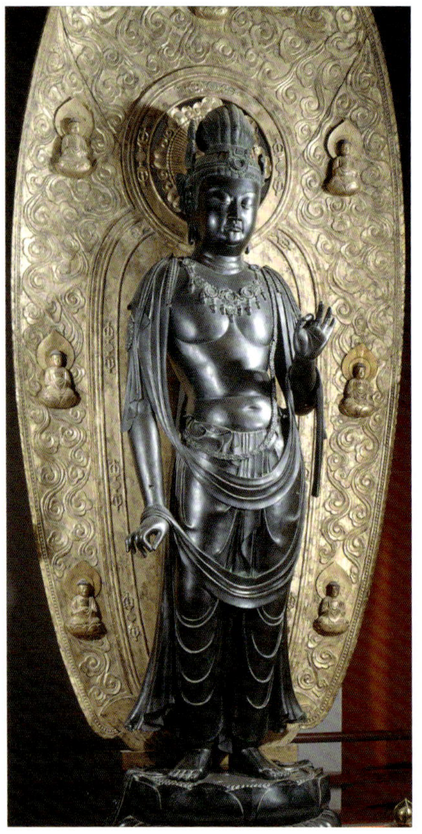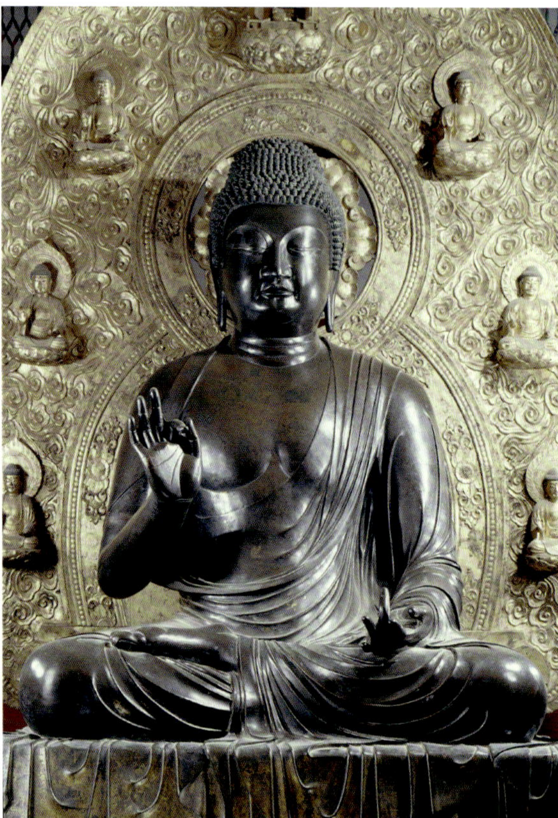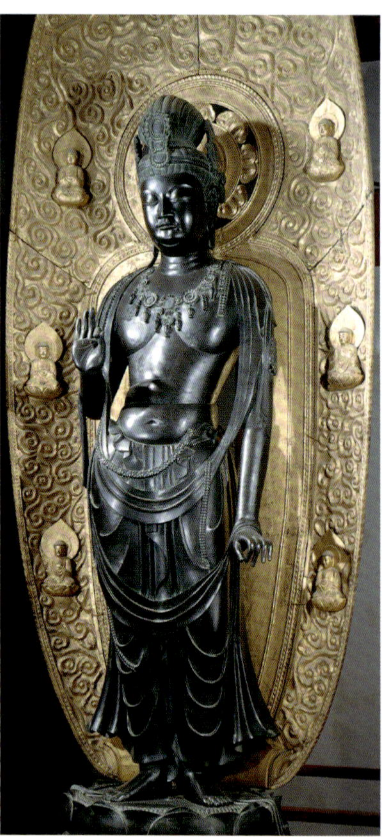

3. Yakushi Triad, gilded bronze, Kondō Hall, Yakushiji, Nara, beginning of the eighth century, National Treasure

Photographs provided by Asukaen and reproduced courtesy of Yakushiji

(early seventh century), named for Emperor Suiko (592–628); the Tenji era (late seventh century to 710), named for Emperor Tenji (662–671); and the Tenpyō era, when the capital was Heijo-kyō (now Nara, 710–794), with its peak in the reign of Emperor Shōmu (724–749). Okakura wrote that the artistic development of the Tenpyō era was the "pinnacle" of Japan's *kodai* period.

Of the arts of the Tenpyō period, he gave the greatest praise to the bronze Yakushi (Sk. Bhaishajyaguru) Triad in the Kondō Hall at Yakushiji, Nara, declaring it "Tenpyō daiichi," or first of the Tenpyō (fig. 3), noting the casting, balance between head and body, and refined features of the body and drapery pleats. He also singled out a group of molded clay figures, the Shitennō (Lokapala) at Kaidanin Hall and the Bonten and Taishakuten figures (today called the Nikkō and Gakkō or Suryaprabha and Chandraprabha) in the Sangatsudō Hall, both of Tōdaiji. "Even though Westerners acclaim the sculpture of ancient Greece," he

wrote, "if we compare that to the arts of the Nara (Tenpyō) period, I believe they are by no means second to Greek art," and "The pinnacle of Japanese sculpture was reached in the Nara period." Through such statements Okakura set the sculpture of the first half of the eighth century, exemplified by the Yakushiji Kondō figures mentioned above, as his standard of classical beauty, which he compared with the West's declaration of Greek art as its classical standard.

Fenollosa, who influenced Okakura, said that Nara was "Japan's Rome," thus also creating analogies between Western and Japanese art.[11] He extended such analogies to specific works, stating, in the case of the triad at Yakushiji, "The flow of the drapery…is as beautiful as the rhythms in a genuine Greek statue." Regarding the two figures in the Sangatsudō, Tōdaiji, he described "grand solid proportions that bring them into a sort of rivalry with the Parthenon torsos and the Venus de Milo."[12] While these comments are nothing other

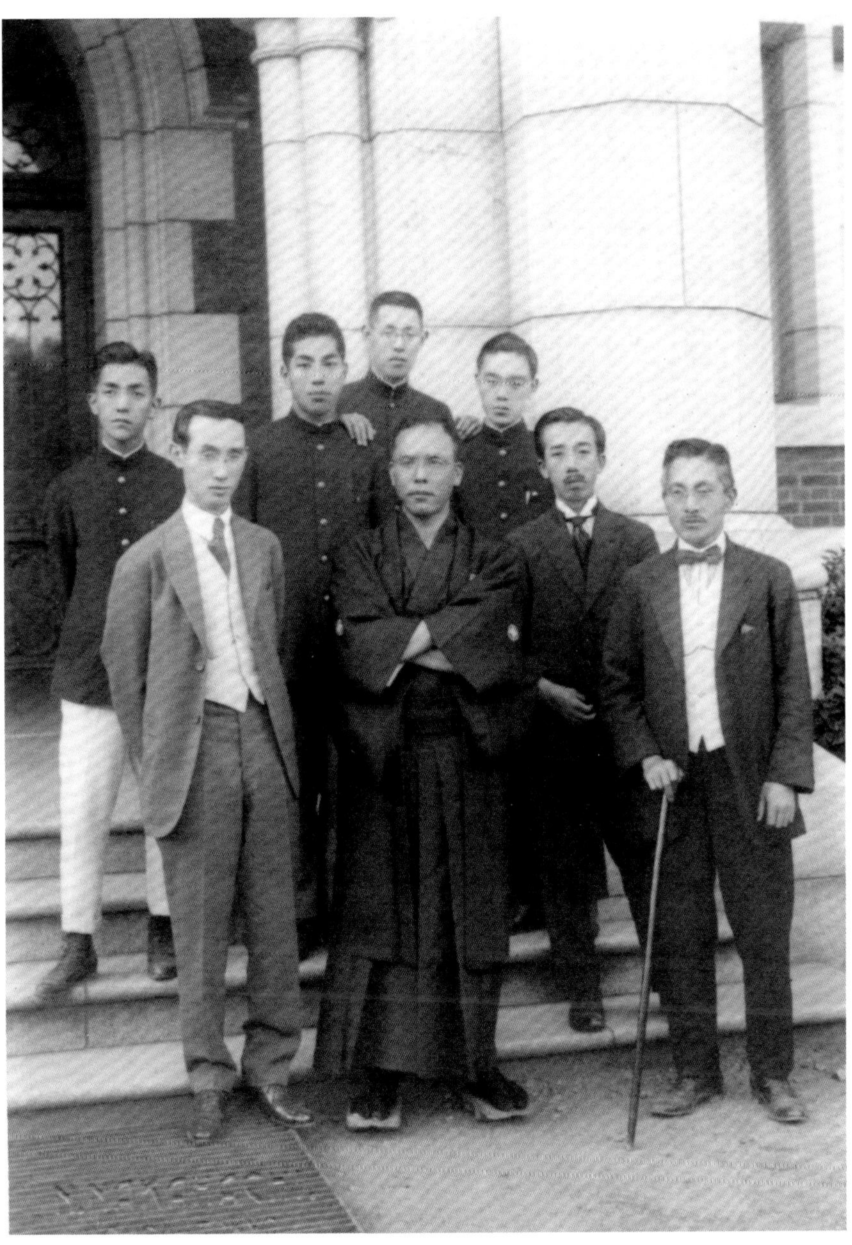

4. Professors and students of the art history department, Keio University; Sawaki Yomokichi at far left, front

Photograph provided by Mutō Haruta

than the Orientalism of a Westerner, by linking Japanese art history and Western art history Fenollosa sought to explain the high level of achievement in Japanese art and, more than anything else, to praise it. Through these efforts the seeds were planted for the Japanese to see the sculpture of the Tenpyō era as classical art. These beliefs are not only found among scholars of Japanese art but are also deeply rooted in the sentiments fostered by the commentary of scholars and critics. Indeed, they still underlie Japanese aesthetics.

As the final point in this section, I would note that the Japanese word for style, *yōshiki* 様式, was established in the early twentieth century as an art term.[13] Up to then, various other words were used in Japanese to describe the characteristics of a work of art—*yō* 様, *te* 手, *ryū* 流, *shiki* 式, *fū* 風, *tai* 体, *hō* 法, *kata* 型, *shumi* 趣味—with their use based on convention or the individual's preferences. In the first half of the 1890s, Okakura's writings, such as his travelogues for *Kokka* or the record of the lectures he gave at Tokyo School of Fine Arts, show him using terms such as *fū*, *hō*, and *yōshiki*. But by 1894, he had standardized these as *yōshiki*. The definitive adoption of *yōshiki* as the term for style (*Stil*) came in 1899–1902, when Mori Rintarō (1862–1922; also known as Mori Ōgai) translated German books on aesthetics.[14]

The Appearance of *Principles*

The Introduction of Principles *by Sawaki Yomokichi*
Sawaki Yomokichi (1886–1930; fig.4) was a scholar of Western art history, the fifth son of a wealthy industrialist in Akita.[15] In 1909 he followed his older brothers in graduating from Tokyo's Keio University. His interest at the time was Italian art. Lectures in aesthetics had begun at Keio University in 1892, but there was as yet no art history curriculum. Sawaki began as a German instructor in Keio's department of literature in April 1912. In July of the same year he went to Europe as an overseas student from Keio University and traveled in France, Germany, and England.[16]

At the time Heinrich Wölfflin, who had previously taught at universities in Basel and Berlin, had been appointed professor at the University of Munich and was reaching his major period of activity. Sawaki moved from Berlin to Munich in March 1913, attended Wölfflin's lectures, and enrolled in his summer course on Italian Renaissance art and a winter course on the history of prints. Sawaki, who was much influenced by Jacob Burckhardt's writing on Italian Renaissance art, highly esteemed Wölfflin

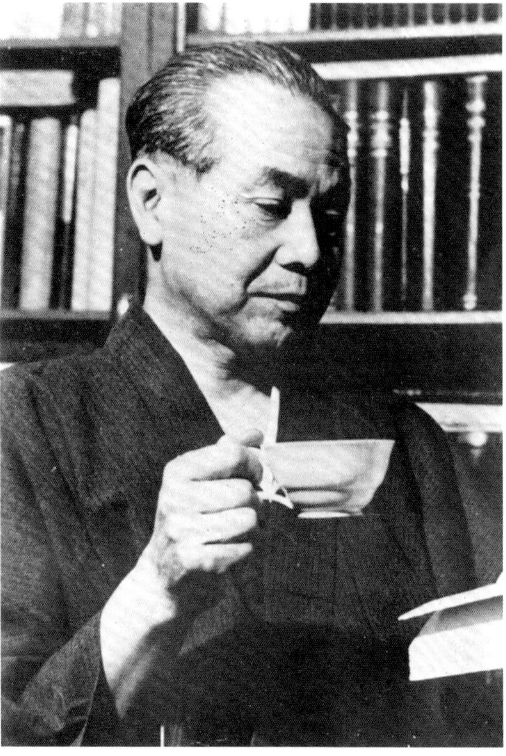

as Burckhardt's successor. In the preface to his *Bijutsu no miyako* (The capital of art), Sawaki noted: "I attended the lectures of Heinrich Wölfflin, the Renaissance art history authority acknowledged to be the greatest among contemporary German art historians."[17] Moriya Kenji, who studied under Sawaki, recalled that Sawaki was drawn to Wölfflin because of the latter's personality and tastes, from among "the American [Bernard] Berenson, who emphasized reference materials; [Max] Dvořák, who was of the Vienna School, which relied on a great deal of psychological study; and Wölfflin, with his strict principles."[18] Sawaki spent only a year in Munich because Japanese people were no longer allowed to live in Germany after the outbreak of World War I. He moved to Italy before returning to Japan in January 1916.

In 1920, at the age of thirty-three, Sawaki presented lectures on Western art history at both Keio University and Tokyo Imperial University, and, with his experience in Europe and new ways of thinking, would go on to exert a major influence on the study of art history in Japan (fig. 4). During

this period, and like many others fortunate enough to have had the opportunity to study overseas, he seems to have had a strong sense that his mission was to develop the study of art history. At the time there were plans for Sawaki to produce a Japanese translation of *Principles* as a volume in a series of translations of major German and French works on Western art history being published by Iwanami Shoten.[19] It was Sawaki's ill fortune to be infected with then untreatable tuberculosis. He fell ill while in Europe, and he was unable to lecture for two years after he began teaching following his return to Japan. He was still recovering when he published a series of articles in 1926 introducing *Principles*.[20]

Sawaki was not the only Japanese scholar to take note of Wölfflin's 1915 publication. The year he published his articles, the aesthetics specialist Fukada Yasukazu (1878–1928), who taught at Kyoto Imperial University, introduced the book from a perspective supporting its theories and stated that *Principles* was essential to the consideration of art history and deserved to be further enhanced and revised in the future.[21] The following year Ōnishi Yoshinori (1888–1959), an aesthetics scholar who was a professor at Tokyo Imperial University, criticized the discrepancy between Wölfflin's formal analysis and his psychology-based interpretation of art.[22] The notable difference between these scholars and Sawaki was that Sawaki not only understood *Principles* as a scholar of Western art history; he also valued Wölfflin's perspective and seriously sought to apply Wölfflin's scientific approach to the study of Japanese art history.

In Sawaki's words: "Today we are fed up with books on art history that describe a work of art on the basis of an artist's legendary biography as a means of explaining its historical aspects. What people need to know is what makes up the true character and value of the work."[23] His comment is nothing other than a criticism of Japanese art history as it had been practiced since Fenollosa and Okakura. For Sawaki, the approach of *Principles*, which seeks to explain the change in visual form from the Renaissance to the baroque through five sets of opposing principles, was not only a legitimate theory for Western art history; in contrast to Japanese art-historical studies of the day, which consisted solely of critical impressions and psychological theories, it indicated the importance of a research method based on observation and analysis.[24]

Sawaki died in November 1930, at the age of forty-three. The diaries from his final year indicate that his topics for future study were not only the arts of Greece and Italy but also stylistic observations of the ancient Buddhist wall paintings at Hōryūji in Nara. He sought to apply the stylistic analysis he had learned from *Principles* to the ancient paintings of Japan.

What Kojima Kikuo Considered Important about Principles

Kojima Kikuo (1887–1950; fig. 5) was known as a historian of Western art, art critic, and educator.[25] Even early on during his studies in the department of letters of Tokyo Imperial University, he was active as a Western-style painter of the Shirakaba school and remembered attending Okakura's lectures at the university.[26] The Shirakaba art movement, important at this time, focused on literary activities and art criticism, advocating humanism and idealism in its magazine *Shirakaba* (founded 1919, ceased 1923) and on introducing works of art and literature from overseas.

In 1921 Kojima, then professor at Gakushūin University, embarked on a five-year sojourn in Europe. He met a number of art historians and became known among European scholars for his study of Renaissance art, particularly that of Leonardo da Vinci. In 1924 he visited Wölfflin at his home in Zurich. During his European travels he was appointed assistant professor at Tohoku Imperial University (present-day Tohoku University) and began to teach at Tokyo Imperial University in 1935.

Upon his return to Japan in 1926, Kojima met Sawaki, and they talked about Wölfflin's writing and art historical methodology.

Sawaki died soon after, and Kojima wrote a newspaper obituary lamenting Sawaki's unfinished work.[27] Then on March 27, 1931, Kojima sent a telegram from Tohoku Imperial University, inviting Wölfflin to visit Japan and deliver a lecture.[28] Wölfflin's response, dated August 31 of that year, declined the invitation on the basis of his age (he was sixty-seven). He also noted that many in Germany seemed not to understand his ideas, and he wondered if they would be understood in Japan.[29] This was despite his statement in the preface to the sixth edition of *Principles*, published in 1922:

Our formulation of these concepts only corresponds with the development in the early modern era. They will have to be adapted and readapted time and again for other periods. Still, the schema has already proven to be of service as far afield as Japanese and old Nordic art.[30]

Albert Einstein visited Japan in 1922 and significantly influenced the development of physics research; we can but wonder what impact Wölfflin would have had on art-historical research in Japan if he had traveled there and spoken directly to Japanese art historians.

Kojima explained the importance of *Principles* in his university lectures and in his writing, stating that Wölfflin's stylistic analysis was the essential initial step toward an understanding of the artist's life and sentiments, which he viewed as the ultimate goal.[31] This belief differed from Sawaki's idea that by organizing works historically one could convey a set group of standards. Kojima felt that he must both be a scholar and, to no small degree, reflect the viewpoint and interests of the painter. Kojima's convictions naturally arose from his membership in the Shirakaba group. Art historian Ichijō Kazuhiko has noted that the artistic viewpoint of Shirakaba members was not concentrated on the works themselves but was rather a critique of the work on the basis of the personality and character of the artist. Conversely, Sawaki's articles focused on taking a work of art within a historical context and subjecting the form

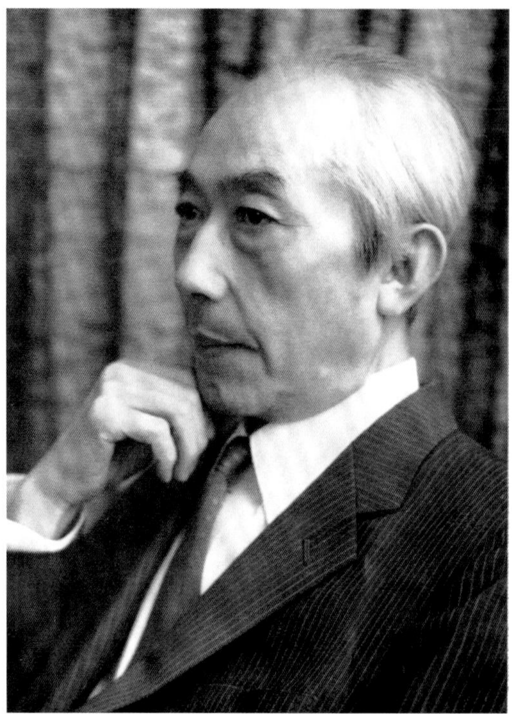

of the work to scientific observation and
analysis. I agree with Ichijō's statement that
Sawaki's articles on Wölfflin's theory can be
read as a critique of the Shirakaba school.[32]

Moriya Kenji's Translation

Moriya Kenji (1893–1972; fig. 6) started out
in Buddhist studies, then studied Western
philosophy and aesthetics and taught German at Keio University. In spite of that background he sought to become a scholar of
Japanese art history. His later achievements
as a historian of Western art were largely
based on the works of Sawaki.[33] After Sawaki's death, Moriya published two volumes
of his writings left in manuscript, and then,
with the assistance of Kojima Kikuo and the
German literature scholar Chino Shōshō,
in 1936 he published a Japanese version of
Principles, dedicated to Sawaki's memory.

The translation was based on Wölfflin's
first edition, published in 1915, as revised
up through the seventh edition, published in
1929, and it adds a translator's note at the
end of the volume explaining the changes
made to the text. Thus Moriya reflected
both Wölfflin's original intentions and the
latest revised version of his thought. In the
translator's preface, Moriya stated that he
had spent five years finalizing the translated
text in response to suggestions he received
from senior scholars, and he also noted that
he referred to Marie D. Hottinger's English
translation of the seventh edition in producing his Japanese translation of the text.

Written in the old-fashioned Japanese
of the early twentieth century, the text follows standard translation practice of the
day. Moriya represented names such as
ルネサンス (Renaissance), バロック (baroque),
and ラファエル (Raphael) in the katakana
transcriptions of their pronunciation, as is
usually done for Japanese renderings of foreign words. For vocabulary such as concepts
and descriptive terminology, he translated
the meaning into Japanese, with essential
terms also provided with the katakana pronunciation guide on first appearance. He
rendered the German *Manier* in kanji as
手法, normally pronounced *shuhō* in
Japanese, with the phonetic rendering
in katakana superscript (マニール). For
malerisch he used the translation 絵画的,
whose kanji are normally understood as
"pictorial," but Sawaki's katakana phonetic
transcription (マーレリツシユ) provides the
original term for readers. For chapter 3,
"Geschlossene Form und offene Form," he
appended an explanation in Japanese of
these terms, which were difficult for
Japanese readers to understand. However,
Wölfflin's use in chapter 3 of numerous illustrations—such as *Venus with Two Cupids*,
then attributed to Francesco Franciabigio,
as an example of a tectonic Renaissance
composition, and Peter Paul Rubens's
Andromeda as the removal of that tectonic
character in the baroque—provided visual
aids for the reader's understanding of the
terminology. Such comparisons most likely
evoked in Japanese readers an analytical
sense of stylistic differences also found in
Japanese art, for instance, painting compositions or sculptural poses from the late
Heian period (eleventh–twelfth century)
and the Kamakura period (thirteenth–early
fourteenth century). Thus we can say that
Moriya's version faithfully followed the

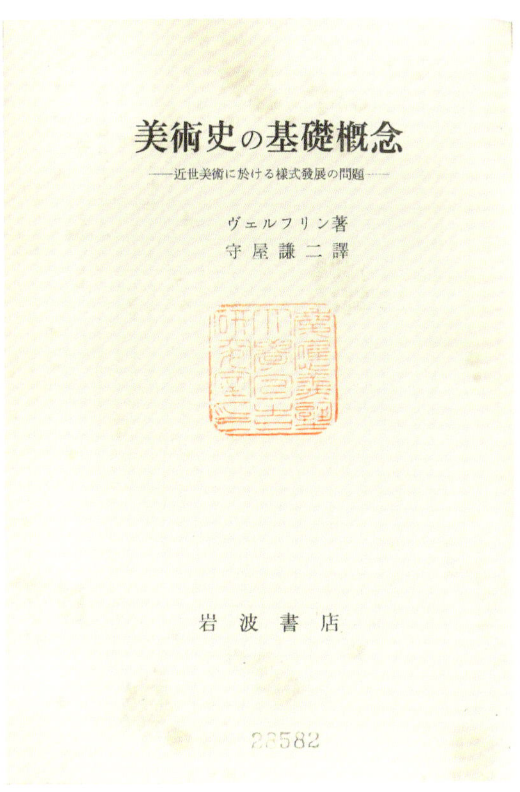

7. Heinrich Wölfflin, *Bijutsushi no kiso-gainen: Kinsei bijutsu ni okeru yūshiki hatten no mondai* (*Principles of Art History: The Problem of the Development of Style in Later Art*), trans. Moriya Kenji (Tokyo, 1936), title page

original, with the addition of thoughtfulness toward Japanese scholars.

The Japanese version (fig. 7 and essay frontispiece) was produced in a smaller format than the original book, so the plates were smaller than those in the original. Even so, it includes all 120 images published in the seventh edition. Moriya arranged 74 images in a layout similar to that of the original with the remaining images placed at the end of the book, all intended for comparative use. Further, by assigning plate numbers to the images and keying them to the text, Moriya paid more attention to the reader's convenience than had been apparent in the original book. Moriya's edition was deemed a faithful translation, and Japanese art historians and students have long read it as an essential text. Fourteen printings were issued up until 1982.

The connection between Moriya and Wölfflin's theory can be said to have deepened from 1936 on. Moriya studied in Germany starting in 1939, after he was named assistant professor at Keio University. The only way to study overseas in wartime was

to hold a scholarship from the host country, and Moriya received a Humboldt Foundation scholarship that allowed him to stay in Germany. His proposed study period was eighteen months, but the outbreak of hostilities between Germany and the Soviet Union in 1941 meant that he could not leave Germany, so he remained there until the end of the war as a lecturer in the Japanese studies department of Leipzig University.

In Munich Moriya met Hans Jantzen, a senior disciple of Wölfflin, and was accorded special treatment as the scholar who had produced the Japanese translation of *Principles*. Moriya's lectures on Japanese art were also well received. During this period he prepared a compilation of his lectures for publication in German as a book titled *Die japanische Malerei,* a chronological overview of Japanese painting from ancient times to the mid-nineteenth century, with eighty-five illustrations. Given Moriya's role as the person who introduced Wölfflin's theories to Japan, the book can be considered a history of Japanese painting for non-Japanese readers as seen from the vantage point of stylistic development.

Setbacks caused by the war and other factors meant that it was not until 1953, eight years after Moriya's return to Japan, that the book was published, with a jacket decorated with a screen painting of autumn grasses against a gold ground (fig. 8).[34] According to the jacket copy, the book was considered a good text for "vergleichende Kunstbetrachtung" (comparative examination of art) in more than seventy-five reviews that appeared in Europe and America. Moriya commented that he was particularly pleased by the review in the journal of the University of Vienna, which described him as one of Wölfflin's students. He noted: "While I regret never having had a chance to meet Professor Wölfflin, I have fulfilled my desires with this book."[35]

In November 1950 Moriya sent the second edition of the Japanese version of *Principles* to Wölfflin's brother Ernst (1873–1960), along with a request for gratis permission to make Japanese translations of *Die klassische*

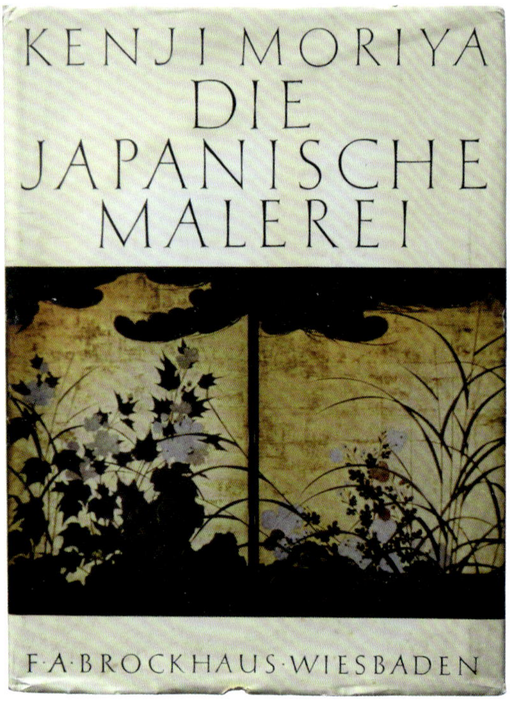

8. Moriya Kenji, *Die japanische Malerei* (Wiesbaden, 1953), cover
National Diet Library

Kunst and *Italien und das deutsche Form-gefühl*.[36] It appears that he received this permission, at least for the former; in 1962 he published a Japanese translation of *Die klassische Kunst* as *Koten bijutsu: Itaria-runesansu josetsu*.[37] Moriya's interests then shifted to the question of the classical in Japanese art.

Wölfflin's Theories Applied to Japanese Art History

From Kojima Kikuo to Machida Kōichi

How did scholars of Japanese art history take up *Principles* and Wölfflin's theories? This is linked to how Japanese art historians after World War II viewed and advanced prewar art-historical concepts. Whereas the first two generations after Moriya were aware of *Principles* and of Wölfflin's name, it seems that later historians up to the present have, unconsciously or as a matter of course, adopted Wölfflin's analytical viewpoint in discussions of issues of form and style. Whether this adoption was knowing or unknowing, Wölfflin's name can rarely be found either by mention or quotation in their articles.

Of special note among such scholars is Kojima's student Machida Kōichi (1916–1993; fig. 9), a specialist in the history of ancient Japanese sculpture. Machida's father was a Japanese-style painter, and Machida himself, as a high school student during the war, had experienced detention on suspicion of leftist activism. This experience led him to the field of art history, as far as possible from politics. He was inspired by his encounter with Kojima at the University of Tokyo and revered Kojima as the sole teacher of his life.[38] Machida's ideas survive in works published during his teaching career at the Tokyo University of Education, Nagoya University, and later Musashino Art University.

Hakuhō and Tenpyō: Debates on the History of Ancient Japanese Sculpture

It would not be an exaggeration to say that Machida's publications were produced under Kojima's influence and that his observations on the history of Japanese sculpture thus made use of the principles of Western art history that he had learned from Kojima. Throughout his writings was the undercurrent of Kojima's view of art history, which praised Tenpyō sculpture as "equivalent to the finest period of Greek sculpture."[39]

The so-called Hakuhō debate is one of the major debates in ancient Japanese art history and has continued since the beginning of the twentieth century. As noted above, Okakura Kakuzō had divided ancient art into the three periods Suiko, Tenji, and Tenpyō. Later the terms changged from Suiko to Asuka (from 538 to the mid-seventh century), from Tenji to Hakuhō (from the mid-seventh century to 710), and from Tenpyō to the Nara period (710–794). The problem is the definition of those terms and their periods, with scholars differing depending on their views of art history.[40]

Ancient Japanese sculpture has been examined in terms of developments in domestic political systems, the history of attitudes toward the adoption of Buddhism, and actual changes in artistic styles of China and the Korean Peninsula that were taken

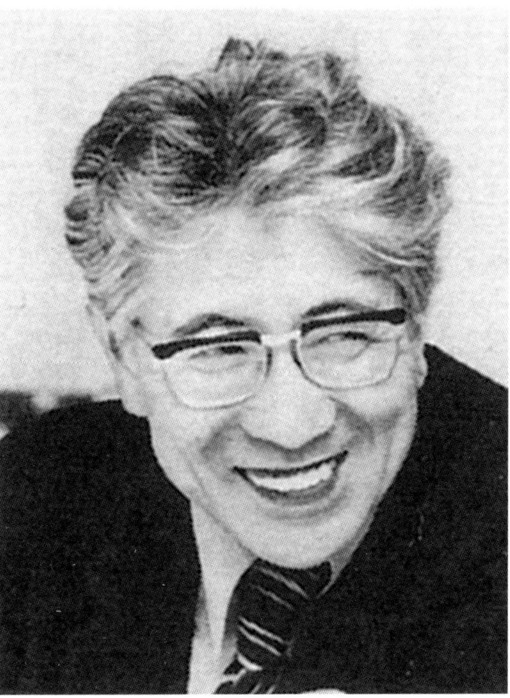

9. Machida Kōichi

Reproduced from Machida Kōichi, Bukkyō bijutsu ni omou (Thoughts on Buddhist art) (Tokyo, 1994)

as Japan's models. However, very few dated works or materials remain for the latter half of the seventh century, known as the Hakuhō period. Given that it was a time when a diverse array of Buddhist sculptural styles coexisted, it has been hard to arrive at a unified concept of the period.

In 1958 Andō Kōsei, a historian of Asian art, published his theory that the Hakuhō period was not necessary to this definition, and his assertion set off a major debate about the styles of this period.[41] Scholars who chose not to use the Hakuhō period as a basis believed that there was no clear definition of its extent or style, that it fell between the Asuka and Tenpyō periods and could be seen as a stage in development that maintained aspects of the Asuka style while showing the nascent Tenpyō style. Thus they asserted that the period lacked its own characteristics. Conversely, scholars who advocated the use of Hakuhō as a period name in art history believed that works from this period that contained elements of the preceding and following ones could not be included in either of these periods, but rather could be established as representing an independent cultural era, and that works

from this time that displayed a different sensibility indicated the need for a distinctive period name.

Amid this fierce debate, Machida, who supported the Hakuhō designation, published one article after another, citing the words and concepts of such Western art historians as Alois Riegl, Wilhelm Worringer, Johann Joachim Winckelmann, and Adolf von Hildebrand as well as Wölfflin.[42] He adopted Wölfflin's concept of formal development based on artistic vision (*künstlerisches Sehen*), in the context of the history and culture of the latter half of the seventh century in Japan. Then, following Hildebrand in his *Das Problem der Form in der bildenden Kunst*, he used the movement of the viewer's eyes (*Augentätigkeit*) to analyze a three-dimensional object to explain the differences between works of the Asuka and Hakuhō periods. In this manner, he indicated the change from the stationary view (*schauende Augentätigkeit*), used to observe the two-dimensional form of an object from a fixed vantage point (Asuka sculpture, fig. 10), to the moving view (*bewegende Augentätigkeit*), in which the vantage point changes, thus allowing the viewer to perceive the three-dimensional aspects of an object (Hakuhō sculpture; see fig. 3). After the capital was moved to Heijō-kyō, the three-dimensional fleshing out of figures reached a final stage in which every detail was expressed, in what came to be called the Tenpyō style. In this case, his discussion, using German terminology from the methodologies of Western art history, was a successful critique of the theories of those who said the Hakuhō designation was not necessary.

In 1990 the sculpture historian Mizuno Keisaburō brought an end to this perennial debate in a simple way. Setting the beginning of the Tenji reign in 662 as the stylistic boundary, he stated that the years before 662 were the early Asuka period, while the years from 662 to 710 were the Late Asuka period, thus avoiding the use of the Hakuhō (650–654) reign name, which indicated the era preceding 662.[43] After that publication,

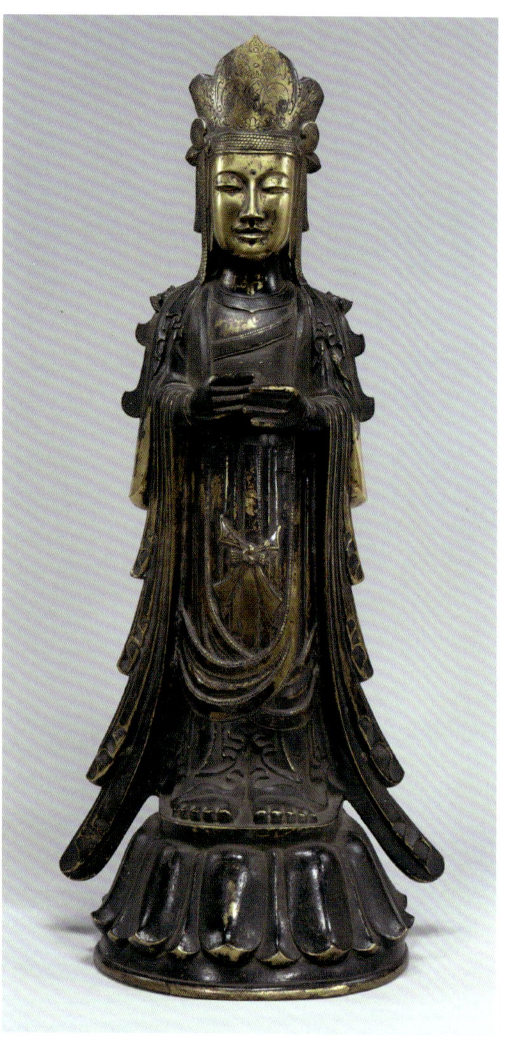

the term Hakuhō disappeared from the formal stylistic chronologies that appeared in object displays in museums as well as in textbooks.

The Hakuhō debate is complex, and one of its core issues is the dating of the Yakushi Triad in the Kondō at Yakushiji (see fig. 3), a masterpiece of Buddhist sculpture. This bronze group consists of a seated Yakushi figure more than eight feet tall and two bodhisattvas to right and left, standing taller than nine feet. The bodies of the figures in this splendid triad have a rich sense of volume and are wrapped in soft draperies. The surface is smooth, radiating a rich blackish-bronze glow. (The original gilding is thought to have been lost.) The naturalistic representation, much advanced beyond that of the Asuka period, presents a unified

form in three dimensions, reflecting China's early Tang dynasty (618–712) style. Scholars' opinions include the theory that the work was completed in 697 at the Moto-Yakushiji in Fujiwara-kyō, the capital before Heijō-kyō, and then transferred to Yakushiji in Heijō-kyō when the capital was shifted in 710 (shifted theory). Conversely, another theory states that the sculptures were not moved, that rather they were newly created soon after the establishment of Heijō-kyō as the capital (nonshifted theory). The former theory places the triad in the Hakuhō period, while the latter puts it in the Tenpyō period. This is then an important question regarding the definition of the relevant period styles.

Machida supported the nonshifted theory not only on the basis of a reading of historical materials and an understanding of remarkable advances from earlier examples; he also argued that early Tang influence from a stylistic point of view was possible only after the move to Heijō-kyō and thus maintained that the sculptures were made in the Tenpyō era.[44] Interestingly, he emphasized that these works must be considered the "father of Tenpyō style." The nonshifted theory has predominated among scholars, and accordingly, Machida's thoughts on Tenpyō style have also seemed to be accepted. However, his discussion contained a fatal contradiction between the scientific research and the concept that had been established by Fenollosa and Okakura and supported by Kojima.

In fact, some excavation reports of Moto-Yakushiji ruins in recent decades have led us to agree with the nonshifted theory in terms of the production location. Meanwhile, some scholars have reconsidered the diverse and transitional nature of late seventh-century style, the so-called late Asuka (or Hakuhō) period style, including the example of the Yakushi Triad. A century after the debate began, in the fall of 2015 an exhibition titled *Hakuhō*, held at the Nara National Museum, explored when the Yakushi Triad might have been created amid the various artistic styles present in the latter half of the seventh century, by using the Hakuhō-era designation.[45]

These debates can be seen as underscoring Machida Kōichi's achievements. Machida, as a Japanese art historian from the generation after Kojima Kikuo who worked in the direct line from the introduction of Wölfflin's theory, should be valued as a scholar who consciously and enthusiastically introduced Western theories to the study of Japanese art history. Indeed, his actions created quite a stir in the field. And yet today I wonder if his effort added a theoretical armament to deep-rooted Japanese conventional notions and aesthetics. In Machida's writing we cannot help but sense a strong belief in theories handed down from teacher to student. In this respect, although Machida seriously studied Wölfflin's methods, he unconsciously protected his position as a faithful student of his great predecessor Kojima. And indeed, such a stance is not only found in unconventional thinkers such as Machida but courses through the subconscious of Japanese scholars.

What Is the Classical in Japanese Art?
While Fenollosa and Okakura and their successors saw the group of Tenpyō sculpture extant in the old capital of Nara as classical, Moriya Kenji questioned another view. In 1962, after recovering from a serious illness, Moriya published a Japanese translation of Wölfflin's *Die klassische Kunst*, and in 1965 he published two short papers discussing the classical art of Japan.[46]

Moriya questioned whether what was truly Japanese in Japanese art could be compared to the sixteenth-century Renaissance art that Wölfflin deemed to be "classic." His subject was not the Tenpyō sculpture valued by the Westerner Fenollosa. Rather, Moriya believed that while Western art sought true beauty in the human figure, in Japan such truth should be sought in bird-and-flower paintings. He suggested that it could be found in the grasses-and-flowers paintings of the Momoyama period (from the late sixteenth to the early seventeenth

century), represented by a famous painting depicted on the *fusuma* (sliding door panels) at Chishaku-in in Kyoto. Moriya makes his statement on the cover of his *Die japanische Malerei*, which is adorned by a detail of this painting (see fig. 8).

Indeed, Tenpyō-era sculpture presents the human form, but as idealized Buddhist form. It was not until the introduction of Western artistic concepts in the nineteenth century and later that Japanese artists turned toward the idea and techniques of representing actual human figures.

The true meaning of Moriya's rebuttal was not an assertion of his own theory that Momoyama-period bird-and-flower paintings were classics. He sought to provoke discussion of the basic issue of Japanese art history, which had been formed with a political role in enhancing national prestige, and hence his ideas were met with criticism. Machida violently attacked Moriya's ideas when he presented them at an academic meeting.[47] There was also the opinion that Japanese art had no elements that could be called classical. This assertion should have shaken the foundations of the value system of Japanese art, but Moriya, then in his declining years, did not have the strength to continue the argument. Or the time may not have been ripe for carrying on such a debate.

Twenty-five years after Moriya's death, in December 1997, the Tokyo National Research Institute of Cultural Propertics held an international symposium titled "The Present and the Discipline of Art History in Japan." New waves of art history occur periodically, and it could be said that we are now in a period when it is important to recognize and discuss the political and ideological aspects of the Japanese art history formulated in the modern era. The symposium brought together scholars convinced of the need for such studies, and the resulting papers are meaningful for a consideration of the paradigms and discourse of the art historiography dependent on earlier research.[48] This discussion would indicate that the study of Japanese art history is ready to resume Moriya's argument.

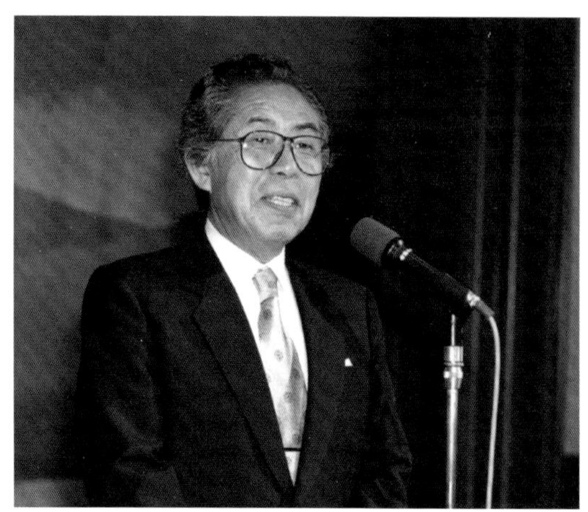

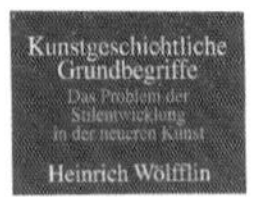

11. Kaizu Tadao, 1989
Photograph provided by Kaizu Yurie

12. Heinrich Wölfflin, *Bijutsushi no kiso-gainen: Kinsei bijutsu ni okeru yoshiki hatten no mondai* (*Principles of Art History: The Problem of the Development of Style in Later Art*), trans. Kaizu Tadao (Tokyo, 2000), title page

Moriya Kenji tried to be a faithful translator of Wölfflin's theories, to stay close to his concepts, and to apply his methodology to research on Japanese art. Moriya, from this point of view, should be remembered as a Japanese scholar sincerely dedicated to the Wölfflinian approach.

The Present State of Wölfflin's Methodology in the Study of Japanese Art and Kaizu Tadao's Translation

It was extremely fortunate for art history in Japan that a Japanese translation of *Principles* appeared in 1936, given the disruption of the war and postwar years.

Kawai Masatomo (1941–) is a historian of Japanese art who trained under Moriya at Keio University and studied in the United States, where he became aware of the importance of methodology as a scholar and an educator. In the 1990s, as a professor at Keio University, he included the reading and discussion of *Principles* and other methodologies in his Japanese art history courses. This attempt at practical application can be considered unusual in Japan because *Principles* has usually been discussed as a text for understanding historical development together with various forms of art-historical research methodology in aesthetics or art courses in universities. No matter what region or period they may be studying, students who specialize in art, whether or not they have actually read Wölfflin's writings, will have necessarily studied his research methodology. However, it is questionable whether these students are aware of what methodologies form the basis for their own research papers on Japanese art, or whether their way of formal analysis resulted from learning Wölfflin's thought. It was passed through their masters' papers, which can be traced back to those written by the postwar generation when basic scientific research concepts and methods as well as *Principles* were studied. It must be said that the approach of *Principles* has deeply and naturally permeated Japanese art history as practical theory.

In 2000 the historian of Western art Kaizu Tadao (1930–2009) published his Japanese translation of *Principles of Art History* (figs. 11 and 12). This translation of the eighteenth and final edition (1991) included the preface from the first (1915) edition. Kaizu studied under Moriya at Keio University and was later known for his solid research on Dürer and Holbein. He spent a year at the University of Basel beginning in July 1965, and there was taught by Wölfflin's senior disciple Joseph Gantner. Kaizu hoped to be considered a member of the Basel school, following Burckhardt, Wölfflin, and Gantner. He also felt responsibility as a scholar at Keio following Sawaki and Moriya, and he strove to reevaluate Sawaki's accomplishments in his later career. Whereas Moriya tried to be a faithful translator of Wölfflin's words as Sawaki's successor, Kaizu can be thought of as seeking to create his own scholarly contribution and as continuing the academic orthodoxy of the historically important predecessor he himself revered.

Published fifty-five years after Wölfflin's death, Kaizu's version of *Principles* was welcomed by Japanese readers as a new translation of a classic art-historical text, even though various new concepts of art history were popular at that time. Written in modern Japanese, it is particularly popular among students and keeps alive for Japanese art historians Wölfflin's name and his achievement.[49]

Conclusion: The Meaning of *Principles* in the Study of Japanese Art

Often the terms "to see" and "to read" are used in the study of Japanese art history to refer to the detailed study of a work of art. "Seeing" refers to observing and analyzing expressive style. "Reading" takes an iconographic stance, in which the work is "read" to explicate its symbolic meaning. It goes without saying that the former is a methodology reflecting Wölfflin's approach, while the latter expresses Erwin Panofsky's method. Generally speaking, these can be seen as the two axes of research methods that seek to understand the true nature of a work of art.

Erwin Panofsky's iconological theories were introduced to Japan from the late 1960s onward.[50] In Japanese art history this meant an increase in papers based on reading and interpreting the accumulation of symbolic elements and their relationship within a work. Indeed, such studies came to be the mainstream of presentations and publications. This "reading the work" tendency strengthened and diversified under the influence of the new art history. From the

latter half of the 1980s onward, books by Michael Baxandall and Svetlana Alpers were translated into Japanese. Norman Bryson presented his theories at Japanese academic meetings in 1995. The application of gender theory to Japanese art history has defined a new viewpoint in considering Japanese art.[51] "Reading" studies also expanded to material culture studies, and the approach of reading a work of art as a symbolic object in the field of phenomenology can also be said to have appeared in Japanese art studies. Interestingly, Erwin Panofsky's name and his iconological and later methods are sometimes seen even in research papers on Japanese art, written by authors who adopted these methods and insist upon their usefulness and relevance to their subjects.

Conversely, stylistic research on Japanese art naturally continued to be based on "seeing." In particular, the positioning within a historical context of objects without historical reference materials from the premodern and previous eras, the work of determining the style and composition of the work as form, can be considered only within the context of stylistic comparison. "Seeing"—examination based on a formal analytic point of view—is a stance required in various research realms in Japanese art, where every scholar attempts to set an effective framework for comparison in which to discuss the critical essence of historical development. Examples include transitions in ancient sculpture from the Asuka to the Nara era or those seen in architecture and painting from the Momoyama to the Edo period, at the dawn of the premodern age, and in the differentiation and development of works attributed to generations of Kanō-school painters whose family name spans four centuries. In Japan's art history, *Principles* was received as a practical model or book of useful approaches to thinking about a work's style and position, not as a text of Western art history whose details are to be criticized. In other words, a Wölfflin-style research stance is considered a natural attitude or silent undercurrent for studying Japanese art.

NOTES

Translated from the Japanese by Martha McClintock

Evonne Levy, University of Toronto, alerted me to the existence of the materials mentioned in notes 28, 29 and 36 and provided abridged English translations. I received additional materials from the department of manuscripts and rare books, Universitätsbibliothek Basel. Moriyama Midori, Keio University Art Center, made available articles, records, and images related to Sawaki. Ichijō Kazuhiko, Hokkaido University of Education, provided me with copies of his presentation manuscripts, mentioned in note 32. Kawai Masatomo, Keio University, provided information on Moriya's later years, such as that mentioned in note 47. I also thank Kanayama Hiromasa, Keio University, who studied under Kaizu Tadao as a graduate student in Western art history, for opportunities to discuss Kaizu's translation work and activities mentioned in note 49. Ishihara Aeka, University of Tokyo, also assisted me with the interpretation and complete Japanese translation of German materials in notes 28, 29, and 34 and the jacket flap copy and some chapters of *Die japanische Malerei*. I express my sincere gratitude to all involved for their assistance and cooperation.

1. Heinrich Wölfflin, *Bijutsushi no kiso-gainen: Kinsei bijutsu ni okeru yoshiki hatten no mondai* (*Principles of Art History: The Problem of the Development of Style in Later Art*), trans. Moriya Kenji (Tokyo, 1936); Heinrich Wölfflin, *Bijutsushi no kiso-gainen: Kinsei bijutsu ni okeru yōshiki hatten no mondai*, trans. Kaizu Tadao (Tokyo, 2000).

2. Matsudaira Sadanobu, ed., *Shūko jisshu* (Ten types of antiquities), 85 vols. The first edition is thought to have been published in 1800. The ten types were bell inscriptions, tomb inscriptions, weapons, bronze items, musical instruments, stationery, framed plaques, seals, Buddhist volumes, and ancient paintings.

3. The term *bijutsu* may have first been used in a January 1872 lecture manuscript by Nishi Amane (1829–1897), a pioneering scholar who introduced Western philosophy to Japan. See Kanbayashi Tsunemichi, "'Bijutsu' to 'bigaku'" ("Art" and "aesthetic"), *Lotus*, no. 31 (March 2011), and "'Bijutsu' to iu go no shoshutsu ni tsuite no gigi" (Doubts about the first appearance of the term 'bijutsu'), *Lotus*, no. 35 (April 2015).

4. Tokyo National Museum, ed., *Tokyo kokuritsu hakubutsukan hyakunenshi* (Centenary history of the Tokyo National Museum) (Tokyo, 1973), 42–60.

5. *Kokka* is a monthly art journal founded by Okakura Kakuzō and Takahashi Kenzō as principal editors, its first issue published in October 1889. Still in publication today, *Kokka* is considered the world's oldest ongoing art publication.

6. See Yamaguchi Seiichi's books regarding Fenollosa's biography and accomplishments, including Yamaguchi Seiichi, *Mii-dera ni nemuru fenorosa to bigerō no monogatari* (The tale of Fenollosa and Bigelow sleeping at Mii-dera) (Kyoto, 2012).

7. The French art critic Louis Gonse wrote a history of Japanese art before Fenollosa, as did the English physician William Anderson. Louis Gonse, *L'Art japonais*, 2 vols. (Paris, 1883); William Anderson, *Pictorial Arts of Japan* (London, 1886). It is thought that Fenollosa's interest in Japanese art was sparked by the work of Anderson, whom he knew personally. In fact, it can be said that the history of Japanese art compiled by Fenollosa and Okakura was created in reference to these two books. A Japanese translation of Gonse's book was published as a series of magazine articles in 1893–1894; Anderson's work was published in a two-volume Japanese translation in 1896. Mabuchi Akiko, "1900nen Pari bankoku hakurankai to *Histoire de l'art du Japon*" (The 1900 Paris World Exposition and *Histoire de l'art du Japon*), in *The Present and the Discipline of Art History in Japan: International Symposium on the Preservation of Cultural Property*, ed. Tokyo National Research Institute of Cultural Properties (Tokyo, 1999), 43–53.

8. Among these lectures, the one given in 1882, titled "Bijutsu shinsetsu" (The true theory of art), was published in Japanese and proved to be highly influential in Japan. See Yamaguchi Seiichi, ed., *Fenorosa bijutsu ronbunshū* (Collected essays of Ernest F. Fenollosa) (Tokyo, 2004), 7–36.

9. Okakura Tenshin, *Nihon bijutsushi* (Japanese art history), ed. *Nihon bijutsuin* (Tokyo, 1922).

10. Commission impériale du Japon à l'Exposition universelle de Paris, ed., *Histoire de l'art du Japon* (Paris, 1900); Nōshōmushō (Ministry of Agriculture and Commerce), ed., *Kōhon Nihon teikoku bijutsu ryakushi* (Draft version of the brief history of Japanese art) (Tokyo, 1901).

11. "Nara no shokun ni tsugu" (Ernest F. Fenollosa's speech: Dedicated to the citizens of Nara), *Hinode shimbun*, June 10, 1888.

12. Ernest F. Fenollosa, *Epochs of Chinese and Japanese Art*, 2 vols. (New York, 1921), 1:98, 102. Japanese translation: *Tōyō bijutsushi kō*, trans. Mori Tōgo (Tokyo, 1978); see 169–208.

13. Hashitera Tomoko and Kawamichi Rintarō, "Meiji • Seiyō kenchiku i'nyūki niokeru style no yakugo" (Japanese equivalents for style in architecture in the Meiji era), *Nihon kenchiku gakkai keikaku-kei ronbunshū*, no. 477 (November 1995): 181–188; Itō Hiroyuki et al., "Tōron: Geijutsu no yōshiki ni tsuite" (Discussion on style in art), in *Bijutsushi ronshū* (Collected essays on aesthetics and art history), no. 10 (Tokyo, 1995), 41–124.

14. Mori Rintarō was an army doctor, novelist, critic, and translator, known by his pen name, Mori Ōgai. He studied in Germany from 1884 to 1888. From 1917 until his death, Mori worked as the director of both the Imperial Museum (present-day Tokyo National Museum) and its affiliated library. In that role he changed the museum's displays from categorization by form to a historical arrangement by period. See Tokyo National Museum, *Tokyo kokuritsu hakubutsukan hyakunenshi*, 344–346. Mori published abridged Japanese translations of Eduard von Hartmann,

Philosophie des Schönen (1899); Johannes Volkelt, *Aesthetische der Wirklichkeit* (1900); and Otto Liebmann, *Zur Analysis der Wirklichkeit* (1902).

15. Regarding the career of Sawaki Yomokichi, see the detailed information assembled by Kaizu Tadao, whose translation of *Principles* is discussed in the last section of this essay. Kaizu Tadao and Katō Akiko, "Sawaki Yomokichi nenpu (Biography of Sawaki Yomokichi)," *Tetsugaku* (*Philosophy*), no. 94 (January 1993): 287–302.

16. Under the pen name Sawaki Kozue, he published books and articles in his university's journal about his numerous encounters with works of art and discussions with scholars and artists during his travels. See Sawaki Yomokichi [Sawaki Kozue], *Bijutsu no miyako* (The capital of art) (Tokyo, 1917).

17. Sawaki, *Bijutsu no miyako*, preface.

18. Moriya Kenji, "Sawaki sensei to Verufurin" (Professor Sawaki and Wölfflin), *Mita-hyōron*, no. 611 (January 1963): 18–19.

19. Moriya Kenji, "Nanajūnen no gen'ei" (Reminiscences of my seventy years), *Tetsugaku* (*Philosophy*), no. 53 (September 1968): 430.

20. Sawaki Yomokichi, "Bijutsushika Verufurin" (The art historian Wölfflin), *Shisō*, no. 51 (January 1926), and "Bijutsushika Verufurin (chū)" (The art historian Wölfflin [sequel]), *Shisō*, no. 54 (April 1926); Sawaki, "Verufurin no 'Bijutsushi no kiso-gainen' jō-ge" (Wölfflin's "Principles of Art History"), *Shisō*, nos. 73–74 (November–December, 1927).

21. Fukada Yasukazu established the foundations of Western art studies in Japan and was the first professor of aesthetics and art history appointed to Kyoto Imperial University (in 1910). Fukada Yasukazu, "Bijutsushijō no kiso-gainen toshite no runesansu to barokku" (The Renaissance and baroque as principles of art history), *Bi* (January 1926): 113–121.

22. A pioneer in comparative aesthetics in Japan, he published numerous books on what can be learned from Western aesthetics and how they can be applied to Japanese art. Ōnishi Yoshinori, *Gendai bigaku no shomondai* (Issues in contemporary aesthetics) (Tokyo, 1927).

23. Sawaki, "Bijutsushika Verufurin," 739–740.

24. Moriya, "Yakusha gen" (Translator's preface), in Wölfflin, *Bijutsushi no kiso-gainen*, 1.

25. "Source materials, including Tsuchiya Etsurō, ed., bibliography," in Kojima Kikuo, *Kojima Kikuo gashū* (Compendium of Kojima Kikuo's paintings) (Tokyo, 1987).

26. Yoshii Chōzō, ed., *Shirakaba-ha to sono shūhen* (The Shirakaba school and its associates) (Kiyoharu Shirakaba Museum, Yamanashi, 1994).

27. Kojima published his revised "Sawaki-kun wo omou" (Remembering Sawaki), first published in the newspaper *Tokyo asahi shimbun*, in *Mita Bungaku* magazine in March 1931.

28. Kojima Kikuo to Heinrich Wölfflin, telegram, Basel UB, NL 95, IV B 2, Universitätsbibliothek Basel, Nachlass Heinrich Wölfflin.

29. Wölfflin to Kojima, August 31, 1931. Joseph Gantner made a typed transcription of the letter, which he received from Sawayanagi Daigorō, a historian of Greek art trained by Kojima (Basel UB, NL 95, V A 3 1, Universitätsbibliothek Basel, Nachlass Heinrich Wölfflin).

30. Heinrich Wölfflin, *Principles of Art History: The Problem of the Development of Style in Early Modern Art*, trans. Jonathan Blower, ed. Evonne Levy and Tristan Weddigen (Los Angeles, 2015), 79.

31. Kojima Kikuo, "Tenpyō chōkoku to yōshiki mondai" (Tenpyō sculpture and issues of style), in *Tenpyō chōkoku* (Tenpyō sculpture), ed. Kojima Kikuo et al. (Tokyo, 1948), 160–173.

32. Ichijō Kazuhiko, "Sawaski Yomokichi no Verufurin: 'Bijutsushi no kiso-gainen' no hōyaku to Nihon ni okeru juyō" (Sawaki Yomokichi's Wölfflin: The Japanese translation of "Principles of Art History" and its reception in Japan), paper presented at Japan Art Society Eastern Division International Conference, Keio University (Mita), Tokyo, October 25, 2014.

33. Moriya, "Nanajūnen no gen'ei," 426–428.

34. Moriya Kenji, *Die japanische Malerei* (Wiesbaden, 1953).

35. Moriya, "Nanajūnen no gen'ei," 451–452.

36. Basel UB, NL 299, 158, Universitätsbibliothek Basel, Nachlass Heinrich Wölfflin.

37. Heinrich Wölfflin, *Koten bijutsu* (*Classic Art*), trans. Moriya Kenji (Tokyo, 1962). Moriya did not produce a Japanese translation of *Italien und das deutsche Formgefühl*.

38. Machida expressed his admiration of Kojima in several of his essays. Machida Kōichi, *Butsuzō no utsukushisa ni tsukarete* (Obsessed by the beauty of Buddhist sculpture) (Kyoto, 1986).

39. Kojima, "Tenpyō chōkoku to yōshiki mondai," 173–178.

40. The names Suiko and Tenpyō were changed to the place names Asuka and Nara. The change from the emperor's name, Tenji, to the eulogistic name Hakuhō for the period 650–654 was first advocated by the architectural historian Sekino Tadashi (1868–1935) in "Yakushiji kondō oyobi kōdō no yakushi-sanzon no seisaku-nendai wo ronzu" (Discussion of the production periods of Yakushi triads in the Golden Hall and Lecture Hall of Yakushiji), *Shigaku zasshi*, no. 137.

41. Andō Kōsei, "Hakuhō jidai ha sonzai shinai" (Hakuhō does not exist as a period), and Kuno Ken, "Hakuhō jidai ha sonzai suru" (The Hakuhō period exists), *Geijutsu shinchō*, vol. 9–8 (August 1958): 93–126.

42. Machida Kōichi, "Jōdai chōkokushi-jō niokeru yōshiki-teki jidai kubun no mondai" (Divisions of styles in ancient history of sculpture), *Bukkyō geijutsu* (*Ars Buddhica*), nos. 38–39 (April and June 1959).

43. Mizuno Keizaburō, "Asuka jidai no chōkoku" (Asuka-period sculpture), in *Nihon bijutsu zenshū* (Japanese art: The complete works), ed. Mizuno Keizaburō, Sekiguchi Kin'ya, and Ōnishi Shūya (Tokyo, 1990), 2:146.

44. Machida wrote numerous books and articles on the Yakushiji sculpture. Major examples include "Tenpyō yōshiki to Yakushiji kondō sanzonzō" (On the sculptural style of the Tenpyō period and the Yakushi triad in the Golden Hall of Yakushiji), *Kokka*, no. 799 (October 1958); "Yakushiji kondō sanzon no Hakuhō iza-setsu wo sai-hihan suru" (Recriticizing the shifted theory of the Yakushi Triad in the Golden Hall of Yakushiji), *Bukkyo geijutsu* (*Ars Buddhica*), no. 101 (1975); and *Yakushiji* (Tokyo, 1984).

45. Naitō Sakae, "Sōron: Hakuhō no bijutsu" (General remarks: Hakuhō arts), in *Hakuhō: Hana hiraku bukkyō bijutsu* (Hakuhō, the first full flowering of Buddhist art in Japan) (Nara National Museum, 2015), 6–16.

46. Moriya Kenji, "Nihon bijutsu niokeru 'koten-teki na mono'" ('The classic' in Japanese art), *Tetsugaku* (*Philosophy*), no. 46 (February 1965), and "Nihon niokeru koten bijutsu no mondai" (The problem of classical art in Japan), *Bigaku* (*Aesthetics*), no. 63 (December 1965). Moriya himself wrote numerous works on Asian art. An example considers the portraits of members of one family by a single painter and addresses the question of production date based on historical materials and stylistic elements; see Moriya Kenji, "Kawahara Keiga hitsu Buronhofu kazokuzu nitsuite" (Portrait of the Blomhoff family by Kawahara Keiga), *Bijutsu kenkyū* (Journal of Art Studies), no. 65 (May 1937).

47. Interviews with Kawai Masatomo, who was in attendance as a student of Moriya, late 2014.

48. Tanaka Atsushi, "Sesshon 1 hōkoku: Kindai to bijutsu / kindai to bijutsushi" (Report on session 1: Modernity and art / Modernity and the history of art), in *The Present and the Discipline of Art History in Japan*, ed. Tokyo National Research Institute of Cultural Properties (Tokyo, 1999), 95–107.
As an example of a work by a scholar of Western art history that considers style in Japanese art history, see *Nihon bijutsu zenshi* (A history of Japanese art) by Tanaka Hidemichi, a historian of Italian art. Tanaka outlines Wölfflin's stylistic theory and then divides Japanese art of the ancient to the medieval period into a classical period, from the end of the seventh through the eighth century (the Hakuhō through the Tenpyō period); a mannerist period, from the ninth century through the eleventh century (early Heian period); and a baroque period, from the twelfth through the fourteenth century (late Heian through the Kamakura period). He is also known to have considered the figural expression of the seventh and eighth centuries to be classical. His book was valued as a history of art written from a unique viewpoint by a single scholar, albeit it one that is rather hard to understand and accept. See Tanaka Hidemichi, *Nihon bijutsu zenshi: Sekai kara mita meisaku no keifu* (Art history of Japan in the world) (Tokyo, 1995). Joe Earle published an English translation titled *A History of Japanese Art: Style of Japanese Art; A Comprehensive Perspective*, in 2008.

49. In a lecture at Keio University around the time of his translation work, Kaizu indicated that his work was informed by the study of Wölfflin in the United States in the 1980s. Japanese scholars of Western art history have identified pros and cons in Kaizu's translation of terminology that reflect his own understanding of Wölfflin.

50. Erwin Panofsky, *Iconorojī kenkyū* (*Studies in Iconology*), trans. Asano Tōru et al. (Tokyo, 1971); Tsuji Shigefumi, "Iconology—sonogo" (Iconology—thereafter), *Nihon bijutsu kōgei*, no. 647 (August 1992).

51. Chino Kaori, "Nihon no bijutsushi ni okeru jendā-kenkyū no jūyōsei" (The importance of gender study in Japanese art-historical discourse)," in *The Present and the Discipline of Art History in Japan*, ed. Tokyo National Research Institute of Cultural Properties (Tokyo, 1999), 279–291.

ERIC MICHAUD

Wölfflin in France: From Racialism to Structuralism

HEINRICH WÖLFFLIN

PRINCIPES FONDAMENTAUX
DE
L'HISTOIRE DE L'ART

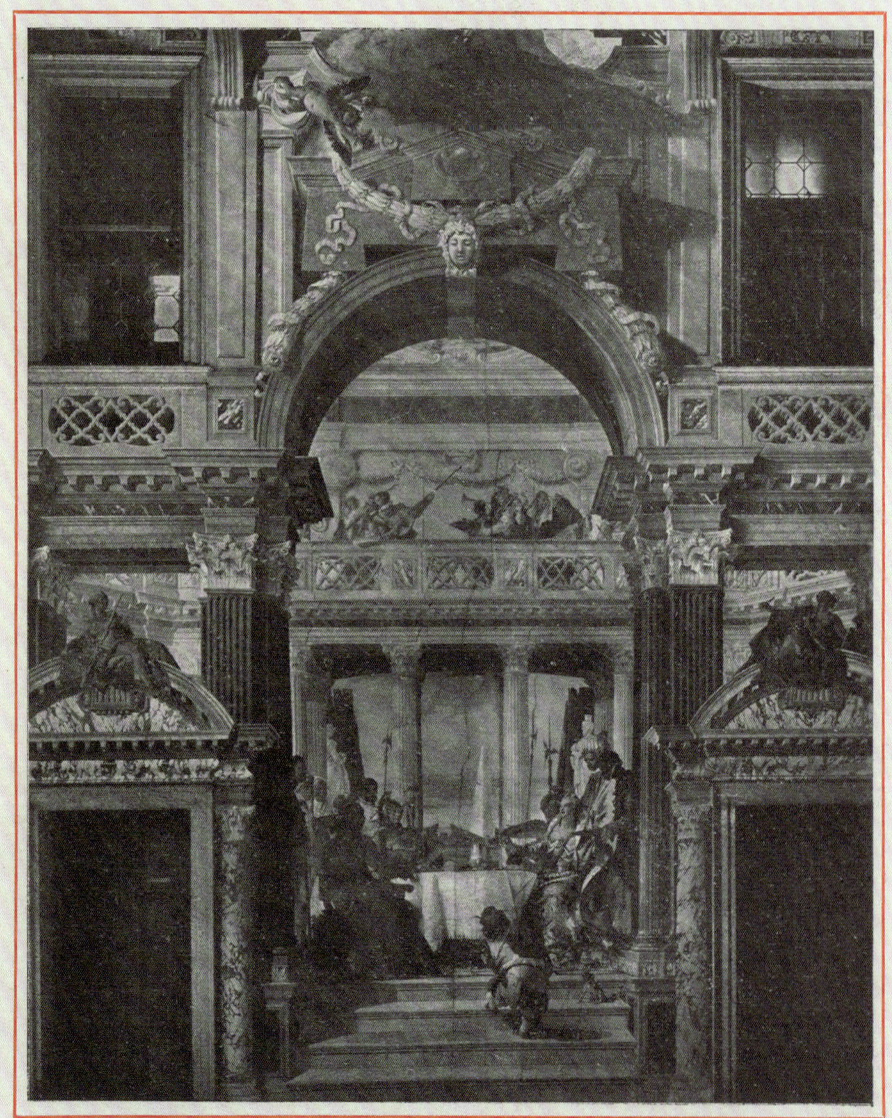

120 illustrations dans le texte

PLON

The French reception of *Kunstge-schichtliche Grundbegriffe* (*Principles of Art History*) has the singularity of having been divided by World War II into two quite distinct periods. Outside the small circle of art historians, the book remained virtually unknown until the publication in 1952 of a French translation (fig. 1).[1] From that point on, it gradually became—and remains today—an essential methodological reference for students of art history. Later, in the mid-1970s, at a time when French academia was still averse to structuralist theories, *Principles* achieved sudden and paradoxical fame for its protostructuralism. Although before the mid-1940s the work had been linked in France to ethnic and racialist theories, these were almost entirely ignored in its reception over the next half century.

But it was not the first book by Heinrich Wölfflin to appear in French. *Die klassische Kunst* (*Classic Art*) had been translated and introduced in 1911 by the art historian Conrad de Mandach (or von Mandach; 1870–1951), curator at the Kunstmuseum Bern and a professor at that city's university, under the title *L'Art classique: Initiation au génie de la Renaissance italienne*. It was hailed at the time as "one of the most fertile and evocative studies in the field of art history," and the same reviewer pointed out that whereas for a historian like Émile Mâle a work of art is of the spirit, "for Mr. Wölfflin it is above all a form."[2] As soon as Wölfflin's work became accessible in France, then, he was seen as an art critic who associated forms with emotions, rather than a historian.[3] But what appealed to so many French art historians of the period was the way in which *Classic Art* disconnected the Italian Renaissance entirely from

the legacy of classical antiquity. As Wölfflin saw it, neither archaeological discoveries nor antique monuments had played the slightest role in the emergence of classical art, which was simply the "natural continuation of the Quattrocento," a "purely national" art and a "completely free expression of the Italian people."[4] It was this nationalizing and ethnicizing of the "classic" that attracted French art historians: if classical Italian art could be defined in terms of its ethnic origins, it was perfectly legitimate to identify a classical *French* art that was of exclusively national provenance and genuinely hereditary in nature. Wölfflin himself had in fact intimated as much, for during his Paris sojourn in the winter of 1888–1889 he had been planning to write a book on the subject of Poussin and French classicism. His professor Jacob Burckhardt had discouraged the endeavor, however, prompting him rather to pursue his research on the Italian Renaissance.[5]

André Michel, a curator and professor at the École du Louvre, was one of the many French art historians who opted for an ethnic interpretation of art. A student of Louis Courajod and editor of a monumental multivolume history of Western art, Michel did not, it is true, entirely accept Wölfflin's vision of an Italian classicism that was absolutely unconnected to antique models: no one, he declared, would pretend that a living and expressive style could result from archaeological research and academic imitations, but it was nevertheless impossible that "the feeling for the beauty of lines" that emerged during the sixteenth century could be "independent of the Apollo Belvedere," as Wölfflin claimed. Still, Michel ultimately reconciled the Wölfflinian view of the Italian

Renaissance with his own by invoking "the genius loci, the Italian aesthetic sense that is entirely suffused, by nature and by heredity, with the spirit of antiquity."[6] Thus, he in turn asserted the hereditary nature of the transmission of style.

In the introduction to *Principles*, Wölfflin had written that while individual style is molded by "temperament" and period style by the zeitgeist, it is "racial character" (*Rassencharakter*) that shapes national style.[7] The term may have been new, but the ideology from which it arose was not. During the nineteenth century, the notion of race had been employed ever more widely in art-historical studies, and, however vaguely defined, had increasingly and with growing force been associated with the category of style (in France, by such authors as Eugène-Emmanuel Viollet-le-Duc, Hippolyte Taine, and Louis Courajod) until, between 1913 and 1915, Heinrich Wölfflin and his disciple Kurt Gerstenberg coined the term *Rassenstil*, or "racial style."[8] This development was no surprise: starting in the early nineteenth century the notion of race had gradually come to be seen as one of the most effective tools in understanding humanity and its history. It had, though, assumed a diversity of meanings since the mid-eighteenth century, continually changing according to which thinker was employing it and under what circumstances, and sometimes varying from one text to another in the work of a single author. A signifier of remarkable porosity, "race" was frequently assigned characteristics that were not just biological but also political, religious, social, linguistic, and, more broadly, cultural. Nor did it ever lose its connection to the notions of people, tribe, clan (the German *Stamm*), and later of ethnic group—but also of nation, since for so long it was "blood relationships" that defined the idea of nation and that still today often determine access to nationality. The assertion made by the nationalist Friedrich Ludwig Jahn in the early nineteenth century that a "nation results from the relationships that unite different families" was echoed in France during the 1870s by Émile Littré,

who defined race as "the family considered across time."[9] In both cases, the reference to family indicated that the vital link—horizontally and vertically, synchronically and diachronically—was blood. Regardless of semantic nuances, the common origins of a particular human group were clearly at the heart of virtually all uses of the term "race," but even more important was the idea of the genetic transmission of certain physical characteristics. In his effort to define race, Kant had distinguished between traits that were "invariably heritable" and those that were not.[10] To this somatic dimension was added during the final third of the nineteenth century the hereditary transmission of the psychological characteristics that were its consequence—a heredity elaborated by the new physiology and brilliantly explored in the novels of Émile Zola. As a result, thinkers such as Alois Riegl and Wilhelm Worringer, like all their contemporaries, identified these two elements—the somatic and the psychological—as indissolubly linked to each other.

It was clearly the notion of psychological heredity that had been the focus of Wölfflin's research since his doctoral dissertation of 1886, "Prolegomena zu einer Psychologie der Architecktur," where he had chosen to begin by exploring architectural proportions in the belief that they represent "what every nation presents as its very own."[11] Whereas Zola's novels were constructed around the psychological heredity of particular individuals, Wölfflin's theories were based on the hypothesis of a collective psychological heredity. The *coup de force* perpetrated by the author in this early text was the unexplained shift from what he called the "sense of form" (*Formgefühl*)—a form both produced and experienced by the body of an individual—to the "feeling of a people" (*Volksgefühl*), which he would later call the "national sense of form" (*nationales Formgefühl*). This presupposed the existence of national or racial bodies that collectively produce forms to which these same bodies, again collectively, in turn react emotionally. This conception of the "ethnic" definition of forms would be central to *Principles*, where each chapter includes a section devoted to the "national aspects" of the fundamental categories of paired opposing concepts. Undoubtedly much of the book's success in the interwar period, which saw a powerful surge in nationalist and racialist movements across Europe, can be attributed specifically to the ethnoracial dimension underlying it.

In *Renaissance und Barock* (*Renaissance and Baroque*) of 1888, Wölfflin had developed a number of simple formal categories, contrasting Renaissance classicism with the "painterliness" of the baroque, in order to account for a *historical change of style*—a change that he described as being *internal to Italy*. But twenty-seven years later, in *Principles*, the same categories were no longer used exclusively to divide historical periods but also to distinguish geographically between the northern and southern "races," each of which was said to possess its own "national sense of form." When Wölfflin stressed the "linearity of the Latin race," it was to contrast it with "the Germanic race [which] has always had the essence of the painterly *in its blood*"; it is in the northern countries, he maintained, that "the painterly sensibility seems *rooted in the soil*."[12] Similarly, he believed that Italy had "always been possessed of a stronger instinct for the plane than the Germanic north, which in turn has the agitation of depth *in its blood*."[13] (Emphasis in both passages is mine.) In the final section of *Principles* Wölfflin noted (as Riegl had before him) a shift in the gravitational center of European art: "In Italy it was the sixteenth century that produced the things that were most innovative and particular to that country alone; for the Germanic north it was the age of the baroque. In the former, a plastic talent that gave shape to classical art on the basis of linearism; in the latter, an aptitude for the painterly that first found its full authentic expression in the baroque."[14] A dictum from his introduction that has become famous—*Das Sehen an sich hat seine Geschichte*—is part of a sentence that reads: "Seeing as such has its own history, and uncovering these 'optical strata'

has to be considered the most elementary task of art history."[15] And in the "Revision" he added to *Principles* in 1933, Wölfflin again stressed that the history of vision involves processes that "have always been regulated by the dictates of time and race."[16] So while the forms of vision might evolve throughout history, they are determined at the outset by "race." This view was already discernible in *Classic Art*, which emphasized the continuity of Italian art over the long term—and it was this significant racial component to Wölfflin's thinking that attracted attention in France before World War II.

In the summer of 1931 a ten-day meeting—a "décade"—was held at Pontigny Abbey, in Burgundy, made famous by the account given of it by Eugenio d'Ors in his book *Du baroque*, published in 1935.[17] Since the gathering was devoted entirely to the subject of the baroque, it was hardly surprising that Wölfflin's name was mentioned by a number of the participants (who included Hans Tietze, Walter Friedlaender, Rudolf Wittkower, and Oskar Hagen). D'Ors described the meeting as a "debate on the baroque" and himself adopted a position fiercely opposed to the "Wölfflinians" Wittkower and Hagen, who advocated limiting the historical use of the concept to the seventeenth and eighteenth centuries. D'Ors proclaimed that the baroque was, on the contrary, a "constant," an "aeon" that spans the history of humanity, like classicism or Goethe's "eternal feminine." He added: "The races are also similar *constants*, aeons, not as anthropological entities, but as entities of culture" (d'Ors's emphasis).[18] While he may have been opposed to the Wölfflin of *Renaissance and Baroque*, d'Ors, in his insistence on this idea of "constants," was actually aligning himself (possibly without realizing it) with the Wölfflin of *Principles*, although he did not apply the notion to particular peoples or races.

In 1932, when *Principles* had still not been translated into French, the venerable *Gazette des Beaux-Arts*, founded by Charles Blanc in 1859, devoted a lengthy article to the book's author entitled "Un grand

2. Henri Focillon
*Dumbarton Oaks Research Library
and Collection, Washigton, DC*

3. Henri Focillon, *Vie des formes*,
Forme et style, Essais et mémoires
d'art et d'archéologie (Paris: Ernest
Leroux, 1934)

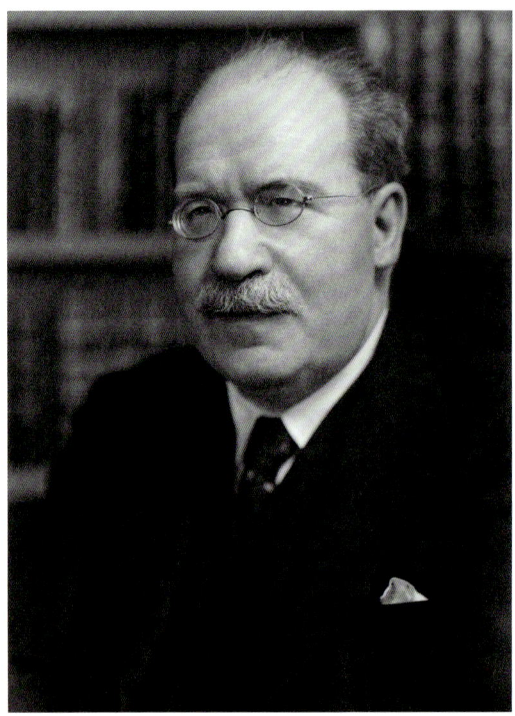

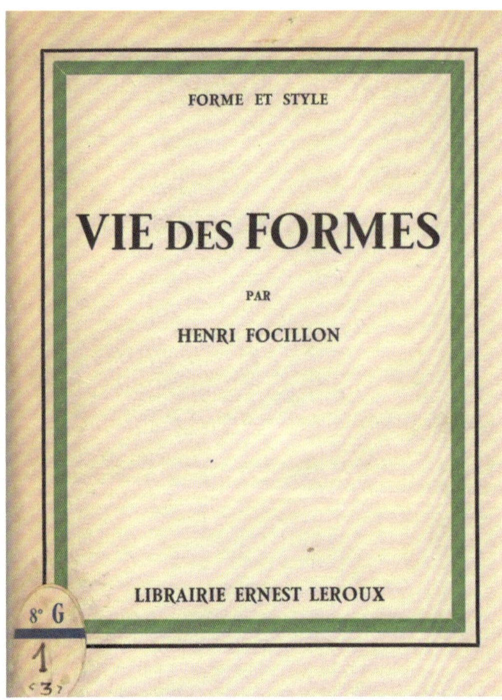

elements of our aesthetic emotion," had identified them in the correspondence between the forms of works of art and the psycho-physiological reactions these forms trigger in human beings.[19] With some justification, Malkiel-Jirmounsky saw the theories of *Einfühlung* on which "Prolegomena to a Psychology of Architecture" was based as the wellspring of Wölfflin's entire work. As he noted, "Prolegomena" maintained that a full understanding of the history of forms is contingent on a knowledge of "which fibers of human nature are affected by contact with the forms created by our imagination." Thus, wrote the author, did Wölfflin lay the groundwork for "his great theoretical construction, *Kunstgeschichtliche Grundbegriffe*, the brilliant conclusion of his aesthetic research."[20] Malkiel-Jirmounsky outlined the ten concepts, or principles, used in the formal analysis of two fundamentally different "forms of artistic expression," which "most historians of art and literature had hitherto referred to using the arbitrary and imprecise terms" *classicism* and *romanticism*.[21] Wölfflin had shown that these were in fact two dominant transhistorical principles determined by the opposing character of "psychic complexes." "Certain races," concluded Malkiel-Jirmounsky, "exhibit a predisposition for one or other of these two tendencies: the art of the northern countries leans toward the painterly, that of the Latin peoples toward the plastic."[22] Through this and various other articles and book reviews he published in the *Gazette des Beaux-Arts*, Malkiel-Jirmounsky worked diligently to help promote Wölfflin's thinking in France—particularly his ideas about "one of the most fascinating questions of art history, namely the contrast between plastic expression, typical of the Latin peoples, and the purely painterly or musical expression of what is called Germanic art in the broadest sense of the term (*linear-plastisch* as opposed to *malerisch*, *tektonisch* as opposed to *atektonisch*, in Wölfflin's terminology)."[23]

A number of writers, including André Chastel, Germain Bazin, and Udo Kultermann, have mentioned Wölfflin's

théoricien d'art: Heinrich Wölfflin." Written by the Russian-born historian Myron Malkiel-Jirmounsky, a consummate mediator among diverse European cultures who was then teaching at the Sorbonne, it hailed Wölfflin as he who, having striven harder than anyone to establish "the objective influence on Henri Focillon—the most important French art historian of the interwar period (fig. 2)—but without ever describing it precisely. In 1946 Chastel, who was from the 1950s to the 1990s the most powerful of Focillon's disciples, discerned in *Principles* an early version of "the 'life of forms' whose definition was adopted in France by Henri Focillon, and that each generation of cultivated men seems obliged to describe anew."[24] It is fascinating to look at the way in which Focillon actually assimilated Wölfflin's theories: he was evidently well aware of them in 1931, when, having achieved a degree of fame with the publication of *L'Art des sculpteurs romans*, he seems to have seen the Zurich historian as a rival. Discussing his work on "a more general treatise" (probably *Vie des formes*), Focillon wrote to a friend, the Romanian art historian Georges Opresco: "I must have Wölfflin's hide to decorate my study. Of course he's a royal tiger, and a great master. Perhaps, after all, I'll only succeed in giving him a few scratches, and it will be me who ends up adorning his lair, like a trophy."[25] But between the writing of this letter in 1931 and the publication of *Vie des formes* three years later (fig. 3), Focillon had clashed on several occasions during meetings of the Institut International de Coopération Intellectuelle with the Austrian Josef Strzygowski.[26] The latter's extreme racism drew regular criticism from the Frenchman, who saw himself as militantly antiracist. As a result, the positions Focillon adopted in *Vie des formes*, in opposition to Strzygowski, were actually quite similar to Wölfflin's.

Although sincere in his claim to be against all ideas of racial determination, Focillon made strikingly frequent references to what he called the "notion of race," assigning the term its most biological meaning. In fact, like so many of his antiracist contemporaries, Focillon believed in the reality of race. Nowhere, he wrote, are there "conservatories in which pure races may be found in flower," but it is still necessary to take account of the "age-old deposits" that manifest themselves in art, standing out

"like great rock-faults, tokens of the past, in a landscape now at peace."[27] In his view, "national groups tend to become families of the mind, and, because of this, they come to prefer certain forms."[28] So there exists "a kind of spiritual ethnography which cuts across the best-defined 'races.' It is composed of families of the mind—families whose unity is effected by secret ties, and who are faithfully in communication with one another, beyond all restrictions of time or place."[29] He surmised that "each style, each state of a style, even each technique seeks out by preference a certain state of man's nature, a certain spiritual family."[30] Since these "families of the mind" superimpose their network over racial networks, he speculated—exactly as Wölfflin had before him—about possible enduring affinities between races and forms: has it not been maintained, he wrote, that "certain formal systems are the authentic possession of certain races? That the interlace is the image and the symbol of a mode of thought characteristic of northern peoples?"[31] According to him, however,

the interlace, and…the entire vocabulary of geometry, are the common property of *all* primitive humanity, and when they reappear at the beginning of the high Middle Ages, masking and distorting the anthropomorphism of the Mediterranean world, they by no means represent the shock of impact between two races, but instead the meeting between two kinds of time, or, to put it more clearly, between two kinds of human society.[32]

Thus did Focillon relegate the "northern peoples" to a condition of primitive barbarism that he believed was their eternal destiny.

So unlike the evolutionism defended by Alois Riegl, Focillon's did not assign each race a particular place in history: his idea of a layering or stratification of time introduced into art history the equivalent of what Ernst Bloch was describing during the same period as the irruption of "non-contemporaneity" into the present.[33] But Focillon nonetheless practiced a racial essentialism or differentialism that revived a nineteenth-century idea regarding the limited perfectibility of certain races, according to which these races remained attached to the same forms throughout history.[34] (The American translation of *Vie des formes* by Charles Beecher Hogan and George Kubler [1942, revised 1948] eliminated the ambiguity of Focillon's French text on the question of race, adopting a more radically antiracist position and thereby substantially modifying the equivocality of an essay that had first appeared in 1934, before the disaster of Nazism.)

It was this ethnoracial approach to art and its history, central to Wölfflin's *Principles*, that was denounced by Hanna Levy (later Hanna Levy Deinhard), a friend of the Marxist art historian Max Raphael, who had studied under Wölfflin in Munich. After fleeing Nazi Germany, ousted from the University of Munich in 1933 because of her Jewish origins, Levy went to Paris, where she submitted a dissertation to the Sorbonne that was published in 1936 under the title *Henri Wölfflin: Sa théorie, ses prédécesseurs*.[35] At the age of only twenty-four, Levy had clearly discerned that "racial facts" were so closely linked to Wölfflin's categories that they determined "a priori and invariably the appearance of these categories among different peoples."[36] Although half of Levy's thesis was devoted to Burckhardt and it also included major sections on the theories of Konrad Fiedler and Adolf Hildebrand, the chapters on Wölfflin emphasized how the racial differences he claimed to observe represented for him the "ultimate criterion of style."[37] He used these pseudofacts about race as the basis for "two groups of types of representation or of intuitive vision that correspond[ed] to one or other of his series of concepts: the Latin group and the Germanic group."[38] As Levy pointed out, the Latin group corresponded *by its very nature* to the concepts of linearity, planarity, and so on, while the Germanic group corresponded just as naturally to the characteristics of the baroque: "This distinction according to race therefore constitutes—and herein lies its importance—the

only significant differentiation that Wölfflin acknowledges in the stylistic unity of a period."[39] From this she quite reasonably concluded that a "national sense of form" was the fundamental premise on which *Principles* was based. In support of her position, Levy ended by quoting a phrase from the preface to the sixth edition, published in 1923, which refers to "inherent differences in the basic visual sentiments of the various races" (die optische Grundstimmung von Natur aus eine verschiedene ist bei den verschiedenen Rassen).[40] But when, in her argument against Wölfflin's racialist position, she invoked the notion of "families of the mind," borrowed from Focillon, Levy failed to see it as another form of racialism, albeit less aggressive. Like Focillon, she believed in the reality of race. Ultimately, her principal complaint against Wölfflin was that his use of the notion of race as a determination of art was "too general" and too abstract,[41] and she recognized that "despite all his weaknesses [he had] revived and enriched contemporary scientific research in the field of art."[42] Wölfflin nevertheless reacted vehemently to the thesis, writing to his friend Joseph Gantner in April 1941: "It is terrible when, as an old man, one falls into the hands of a Hanna Levy, who with the acumen of a Jewish lawyer and the bravado of her youth criticizes my book to death, but has little sense of its essence."[43]

It is worth noting that during this period one of Wölfflin's disciples, Albert E. Brinckmann, was promoting his master's theories in France in a way that placed even greater emphasis on their racial dimension. Pierre Francastel described a lecture that Brinckmann gave in the spring of 1939 at the Centre Universitaire Méditerranéen in Nice and again at the University of Strasbourg: according to Brinckmann, the extraordinary liveliness characteristic of the finest examples of Romanesque sculpture in France had its source exclusively in regions once infused with the blood of the Germanic peoples.[44] He had just published *Geist der Nationen*, in which he had extrapolated at some length on his theory that forms and

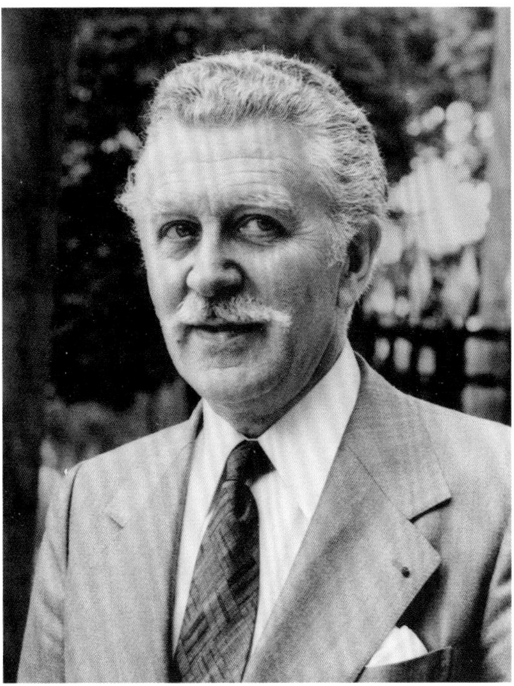

4. André Chastel
National Gallery of Art, Gallery Archives, Washington

styles are determined entirely by race and admonished Wölfflin for not having pushed this idea far enough: "More even than religion," he wrote, "artistic creation is the product of the particular racial tendencies of a people or a group of peoples." He was disappointed that Wölfflin, while recognizing these racial differences, "gladly described them as differences of vision."[45]

This was one of the last manifestations in prewar France of a critical reception of *Principles* that referred to its racial underpinnings. But although French commentators, with the notable exception of Pierre Francastel, were eager to ignore such unpleasant questions, a number of anglophone art historians, including Meyer Schapiro, did not hesitate to condemn the racial component of the Wölfflinian theory of "constants."[46]

André Chastel (fig. 4), who during his imprisonment in Germany in 1941–1942 had suggested to Wölfflin that he translate his book on Dürer, wrote a belated obituary in 1946 but did not really react to the French translation of *Principles* until two texts published in 1953 and 1954. In the first, he began by hailing the "magnificent construction" of the book that had at last been made available to French readers,

who were behind, he felt, "by at least a generation." He did wonder in concluding, however—without providing any answers—about the possibility of reconciling *Principles* "with the theory of 'national constants' to which Wölfflin had remained so attached."[47] In the second text Chastel issued a warning for which he offered no explanation: the appearance of a French version of Wölfflin's text, he wrote, "can no longer be considered an event, and it would even be dangerous to draw inspiration from it without caution."[48] It was, he felt, one of those great books—like Montesquieu's *L'Esprit des lois*—"whose defunct parts are perhaps the easiest to retain."[49] He nevertheless considered "the combination of the five 'a priori forms' as the most valuable content of the treatise."[50] He also recalled Wölfflin's debt to Burckhardt, for whom "art has its own life and history,"[51] although neglecting to attribute this principle of the autonomy of art to its original inventor, Karl Schnaase.[52] But on the subject of national and racial "constants," he said nothing. After World War II and the millions of deaths that had resulted from the idea that history is driven by race, it had become expedient to ignore any direct references to the concept, and in significantly attenuating the racial dimension of Wölfflin's theory, the French translation of *Principles* was very much of its time. Furthermore, the various prefaces accompanying the successive German editions were never translated into French, no doubt because several passages were considered too blunt. Much later, in 1982, the French version of Wölfflin's *Gedanken zur Kunstgeschichte*, translated by Rainer Rochlitz, again attempted to minimize the racialism of his approach by systematically translating the German term *Rasse* by the notion of ethnicity.[53]

As one of Focillon's most dedicated students, Chastel had been powerfully influenced by the Wölfflin polarities, and this influence was still discernible thirty-five years later. During the Twenty-Sixth International Congress of the History of Art in 1989, devoted to world art, Chastel, while

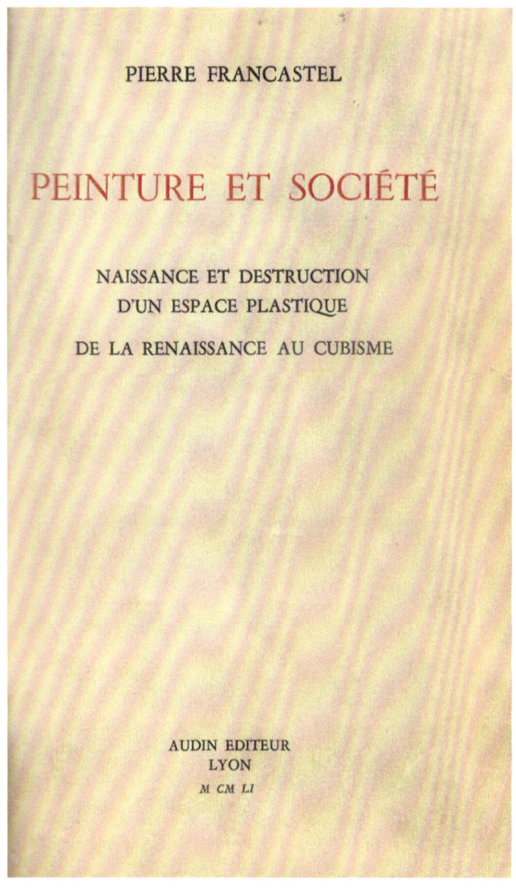

hardly suspected of sympathizing with racial or nationalist fanatics, nevertheless proposed "a model, possibly generalizable" based on "the polarity of north and south" identified by Wölfflin.[54] This enabled him, he claimed, to give a clear account of the artistic situation "in Western Europe around 1500."[55] The north, he recalled, had a reputation for being *industriosus* and the south *ingeniosus*, and the "anonymous activity" of the north could be similarly contrasted with the "concern for originality" characteristic of the south.[56] Based on his reading of historical texts, he had also identified a "division of skills…here, landscape; there, the figure," while, later, ideas about the *diligentia* of the north and the *ingenium* of the south persisted.[57] From all these north-south antitheses, which he saw as arising from "an interplay of propositions and responses that generated a constant interweaving, with alternating high and low points," Chastel believed it was possible to deduce "*a*

constant, which it would be worth exploring in other fields and which might even be postulated in areas where nothing is known about practices and conflicts."[58] Via Wölfflin's north-south polarity and its constants, Chastel was in fact reverting to a position very close to that of Karl Schnaase. Studying the art of different European nations some one hundred fifty years earlier, Schnaase had concluded that there was a "necessary *division of labor* between the Christian nations, each of which had its own particular field,"[59] and, as we have seen, this idea was echoed by Wölfflin in *Principles* when he compared the "plastic talent" of the Italians to the "aptitude for the painterly" of the Germanic north.

In contrast to Chastel, who fully embraced the idea of the autonomy of art and vision, Pierre Francastel, author of *Peinture et société: Naissance et destruction d'un espace plastique, de la Renaissance au cubisme* (fig. 5) was one of the very few art historians of the period who refused to accept that vision has its *own* history. Extremely critical of Wölfflin (but also of André Malraux and Benedetto Croce), Francastel saw his own work as a continuation of the historical psychology founded by Ignace Meyerson, which had affinities with Marcel Mauss's notions of the "total man" and the "total social fact."[60] In 1951 Francastel wrote: "Unlike Wölfflin, who tended to think of the visual function as independent of the intellectual functions, I believe it is necessary to study it in relation to the entirety of human activity at any given period."[61] Although in his polemical study entitled *L'Histoire de l'art, instrument de la propagande germanique*, written around 1940 but not published until 1945, he had simply noted that a major facet of "current art-historical theories in Germany is based on Wölfflin's teachings,"[62] a few years later his position had hardened. In a paper on the baroque presented at the fifth international congress of the International Federation for Modern Languages and Literatures (Florence, March 1951), he was far more critical of Wölfflin's conceptual system.

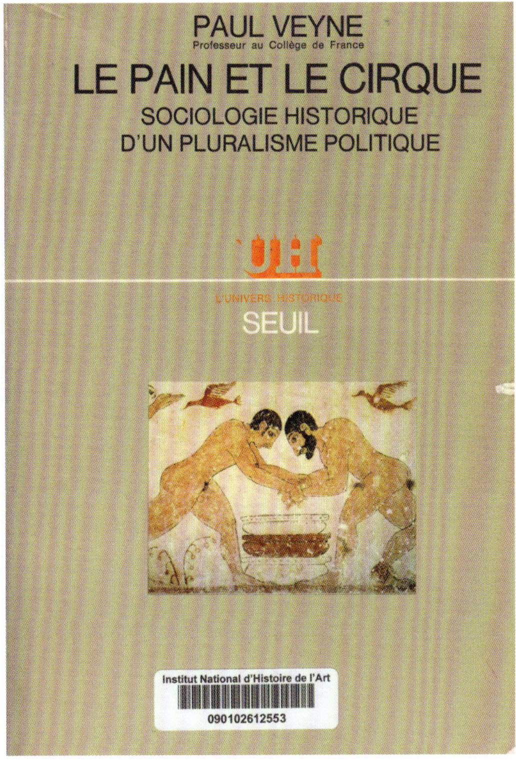

Borrowing Lionello Venturi's idea that there exists a sixth pair of concepts (life and death) that would justify the five others but that had not even been formulated, Francastel stated explicitly that "for Wölfflin, the only element that ultimately explains the material incarnation of these eternal forms of life—the baroque—and death—the classical—is the racial facts of history. The Germanic spirit, the Latin spirit—it is no longer a matter just of pseudo-thought, but of politics." And he added: "I would hope that when Marcel Raymond publishes a French translation of Wölfflin, as he plans to do, he is careful to mention the existence of scientific critiques like those of Lionello Venturi and Hanna Levy, or the one by Walter Passarge, who has so rightly condemned this 'anonymous history' of culture."[63] That the translators in fact made no reference to these critiques was hardly surprising since Marcel Raymond was among those who, like Jean Rousset and other members of the group that came to be known as the École de Genève, attempted to extrapolate Wölfflin's concepts to the field of literature.[64]

Francastel's historical psychology was obviously entirely at odds with the "psychology of art" of André Malraux, whose *Musée imaginaire* (*Museum without Walls*), first published in 1947, suggests that he was aware of Wölfflin's theories.[65] Although Malraux did not read German, he had been infused with German culture by his first wife, Clara Goldschmidt, and, as Rosalind Krauss has shown, had likely been introduced to Wölfflin's work by Daniel-Henry Kahnweiler.[66] Other possible links were his friend Bernard Groethuysen, who had studied under Wölfflin; Georg Simmel; and Wilhelm Dilthey in Berlin. But if the influence of Wölfflin can be detected in *Le Musée imaginaire*, it is essentially in the broad comparatism Malraux adopts in his appropriation of the idea of an "art history without names."[67] And this would seem to justify a remark made by Germain Bazin in 1986: "It is perhaps in France that the experimental value of the Wölfflinian method has been best understood, but in a sense more implicitly than explicitly."[68]

This assessment would be accurate if the impact of *Principles* on French thinking had stopped with Malraux. Some twenty or twenty-five years later, however, the work's influence broadened when, no longer simply the object of debates between art historians and specialists in aesthetics, it entered the far more general realm of the social sciences and philosophy.[69] This shift in the reputation of *Principles* in France can certainly be credited to the great historian of antiquity Paul Veyne. In 1976, the year he began teaching at the Collège de France—the prestigious institution where his friend Michel Foucault had been elected a fellow in 1970—Veyne extolled Wölfflin twice in writing: in the monument of scholarship entitled *Le Pain et le Cirque: Sociologie historique d'un pluralisme politique* (*Bread and Circuses: Historical Sociology and Political Pluralism*), which explores various irrational aspects of politics (fig. 6), and in *L'Inventaire des différences*, the short "inaugural lecture" presented to the Collège de France.[70] In the first, a section headed "Viscosité de la pensée: Wölfflin et

7. Paul Veyne, *Foucault: Sa pensée, sa personne* (Paris: Albin Michel, 2008)

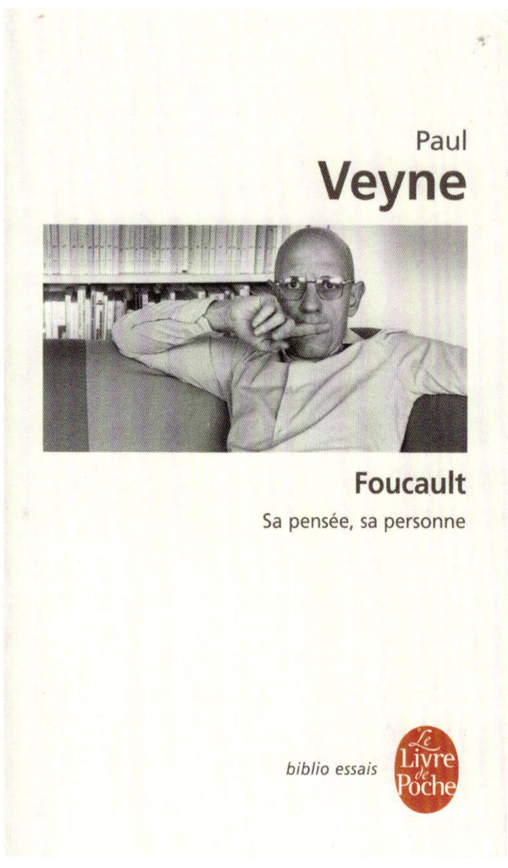

Foucault contre Panofsky" took Wölfflin's work as evidence that "all of history is composed of autonomous subsystems that are connected by purely contingent links and that each maintain their own history and their own speed."[71] Veyne maintained that the Swiss art historian had successfully shown that the choice of means cannot be attributed entirely to artists, since every painter is a product of his or her period, and "the open form, for example, however expressive it may be, expresses a century rather than an artist."[72] Further, if there was a connection between Foucault and Wölfflin, it was undoubtedly through the former's concept of episteme, which he employed in his *Les Mots et les Choses* (*The Order of Things*) of 1966, to define the "conditions of discourse" characteristic of each historical period—the episteme of the Renaissance (the age of similitudes) being distinct from that of the classical age (the age of representation) or of the modern era.[73]

L'Inventaire des différences identified Wölfflin even more specifically as the champion of the concept of the invariant, which Veyne saw as the sine qua non of the practice of history: "How is it possible to talk about anything in history without referring to a transhistorical invariant?"[74] In fact, he wrote, "invariant" could be replaced by "structure," if it is deemed "impossible to live without the word."[75] So what had been Wölfflin's achievement? "At the level of the concept," he formulated his five paired categories to be the "fundamental concepts of the history of art." "At the level of the real," by showing that "the evolution of pictorial vision is autonomous," he had demonstrated that it was "a subsystem with its own temporality, an inertia which is not that of the artists. In this way, artists are subject to the conventions, the pictorial 'discourse' of their epoch."[76] Panofsky had been shocked by Wölfflin, but he had not accused him of wishing to assassinate the artist in the way that Foucault was being accused of trying to obliterate human beings and humanity: "Wölfflin and Foucault have simply reminded us that man is not entirely active and that it befalls him to be subject."[77] The autonomy of subsystems, with their specific temporalities, merely reveals the passive component of human experience. Therein lies the power of the transhistorical invariant elevated to the conceptual level: "Without concepts we see nothing. Without concepts we do narrative history."[78] Thus, while taking a different route, did Paul Veyne arrive at a point very close to Wölfflin's "art history without names."

But of all French philosophers, the one who employed Wölfflin's concepts as the most direct source of inspiration in developing his own was not Foucault but Gilles Deleuze, who believed that it is the very object of philosophy to "create concepts."[79] Deleuze's original way of using Wölfflinian concepts as a box of tools for exploring the painting of Francis Bacon (*Francis Bacon: Logique de la sensation*, 1981), cinema (*Cinéma 1: L'Image-mouvement*, 1983, and *Cinéma 2: L'Image-temps*, 1985), and the relationship between Leibniz's writings and the baroque (*Le Pli: Leibniz et le baroque*, 1988, for which he drew not from *Principles* but from *Renaissance and Baroque*) resulted in some fascinating insights but also a few approximations.[80]

In 2008, in a short but brilliant book devoted to Foucault (fig. 7), Paul Veyne described the development of his friend's thinking up to the point—decisive, according to Veyne—when he was "ready to read Wölfflin": "There was once a structuralist who did not know he was one… Heinrich Wölfflin. 'You should read him, he's the Foucault of the history of art,' I suggested one evening to my interested student."[81] Once again, Veyne compared his two idols. Foucault had invented the notion of the "discourse" in seeking the tertium quid driving not only the natural history but also the grammar and the political economy of the eighteenth century. And Wölfflin, also, had discovered a new scientific object: the features of visual *language* associated with a particular period or a particular group. Quoting from "Pro Domo," the defense of *Principles* that Wölfflin wrote in 1920, Veyne stated: "In between works of art, on the one hand, and, on the other, the intentions and expressions of the artist…there is a tertium quid that is 'the general plastic form of an epoch' and that is to be found 'beneath any individual.'"[82]

As noted at the outset, Wölfflin had explained in the "Revision" he added to his masterwork in 1933 how the history of vision involves processes that "have always been regulated by the dictates of time and race" ("immer reguliert nach den Forderungen von Zeit und Rasse").[83] Before his death, the French reception of *Principles* had focused principally on the "dictates of race," but after World War II—after the millions of deaths and countless massacres committed in the name of race—this aspect of his theory was discounted or ignored, and all the attention was directed toward temporality and eras. Structuralism, then a growing force in the humanities at large, was less concerned with the origins of objects and forms than with their place and function within the structures that encompass them. The study of formal systems that characterizes synchrony of the late twentieth century was seen as more important than those systems' transformation over time. As a result, the formalist art history of the late twentieth-century in France, which revered a history "without names," referred to *Principles* in glowing terms. But the conservative and traditionalist art history of the same period, whose main mission was the establishment of catalogs and which was consequently obsessed with questions of attribution, also praised the work, admiring the "marvelous clarity" of formal analyses that enabled the discipline to classify and hierarchize its objects of study.[84]

NOTES

Translated from the French by Judith Terry

I thank Evonne Levy and Tristan Weddigen for their comments and suggestions.

1. Heinrich Wölfflin, *Principes fondamentaux d'histoire de l'art: Le Problème de l'évolution du style dans l'art moderne*, trans. Claire and Marcel Raymond (1952; Paris, 1966).

2. René Schneider, "Chronique d'histoire de l'art," *Revue des questions historiques* 47 (1912): 540.

3. René Doucet, "Problèmes et controverses: Dans quelle mesure les oeuvres historiques sont-elles condamnées à vieillir?," *Revue de synthèse historique* 25 (1912): 413.

4. Heinrich Wölfflin, *L'Art classique: Initiation au génie de la Renaissance italienne*, trans. and intro. by Conrad de Mandach (Paris, 1911), 13; English translation, *Classic Art: An Introduction to the Italian Renaissance*, trans. Peter and Linda Murray (London, 1994).

5. Joseph Gantner, "Présentation," *Réflexions sur l'histoire de l'art*, trans. Rainer Rochlitz (Paris, 1997), 9.

6. André Michel, *Histoire de l'art*, vol. 5, part 1, *La Renaissance dans les pays du Nord—Formation de l'art classique moderne* (Paris, 1912), 493–495.

7. Heinrich Wölfflin, *Kunstgeschichtliche Grund-begriffe: Das Problem der Stilentwicklung in der neueren Kunst* (Munich, 1915), 11; *Principles of Art History: The Problem of the Development of Style in Early Modern Art*, trans. Jonathan Blower (Los Angeles, 2015), 93. (These editions are henceforth cited as *Grundbegriffe* [1915] and *Principles of Art History* [2015]).

8 Kurt Gerstenberg, *Deutsche Sondergotik: Eine Untersuchung über das Wesen der deutschen Bau-kunst im späten Mittelalter* (Munich, 1913). See in particular the section entitled "Die Sondergotik als Ausdruck der germanischen Rasse," 108–116.

9 Friedrich Ludwig Jahn, *Essai historique sur les moeurs, la littérature, et la nationalité des peuples de l'Allemagne…*, trans. Pierre Lortet (Paris, 1832), § XLIV, 426; Émile Littré, *Dictionnaire de la langue française* (Paris, 1875), 4:1442.

10. Immanuel Kant, "Determination of the Concept of a Human Race" (1785), in *Kant and the Concept of Race: Late Eighteenth-Century Writings*, trans. and ed. Jon M. Mikkelsen (Albany, NY, 2013), 136.

11. Heinrich Wölfflin, "Prolegomena to a Psychology of Architecture," in *Empathy, Form, and Space: Prob-lems in German Aesthetics, 1873–1893*, trans. and intro. by Harry Francis Mallgrave and Eleftherios Ikonomou (Santa Monica, CA, 1994), 170; as published in German, *Prolegomena zu einer Psychologie der Architektur* (Munich, 1886), 30: "Die Proportionen sind das, was ein Volk als sein eigenstes gibt"; 49: "Daß weiterhin Stil-Formen nicht von Einzelnen nach Belieben gemacht werden, sondern aus dem Volks-gefühl erwachsen…."

12. Wölfflin, *Principles of Art History* (2015), 138 and 149; *Grundbegriffe* (1915), 61 and 73.

13. Wölfflin, *Principles of Art History* (2015), 187; *Grundbegriffe* (1915), 111: "Italien hat den Instinkt für Fläche immer stärken besessen als der germanischen Norden, dem das Aufwühlen der Tiefe im Blute steckt."

14. Wölfflin, *Principles of Art History* (2015), 316; *Grundbegriffe* (1915), 250.

15. Wölfflin, *Principles of Art History* (2015), 93; *Grundbegriffe* (1915), 11. See the excellent essay by Claire Farago, "'Vision Itself Has Its History': 'Race,' Nation, and Renaissance Art History," in *Reframing the Renaissance: Visual Culture in Europe and Latin America, 1450–1650*, ed. Claire Farago (New Haven, 1995), 67–88.

16. Wölfflin, *Principles of Art History* (2015), 324; "'Kunstgeschichtliche Grundbegriffe': Eine Revision (1933)," in *Gedanken zur Kunstgeschichte: Gedrucktes und Ungedrucktes* (Basel, 1941), 24, published origi-nally in *Logos: Internationale Zeitschrift für Philoso-phie der Kultur* 22 (1933): 210–218.

17. The Décades de Pontigny, held between 1910 and 1939 (with an interruption of some years following the outbreak of World War I), were annual summer gather-ings of intellectuals organized by Paul Desjardins. The session entitled "Sur 'le baroque' et sur l'irréductible diversité du goût, suivant les peuples et suivant les époques" took place August 6–16, 1931. See François Chaubet, "Les Décades de Pontigny (1910–1939)," *Vingtième siècle: Revue d'histoire* 57 (1998): 36–44. See also the essay by Tristan Weddigen in this volume, which discusses Eugenio d'Ors's important book in some detail.

18. Eugenio d'Ors, *Du baroque*, trans. Agathe Rouart-Valéry (Paris, 1935), 95 (emphasis is d'Ors's).

19. Myron Malkiel-Jirmounsky, "Un grand théoricien d'art: Heinrich Wölfflin," *Gazette des Beaux-Arts* 74 (1932): 236.

20. Malkiel-Jirmounsky, "Un grand théoricien d'art," 239–240.

21. Malkiel-Jirmounsky, "Un grand théoricien d'art," 241.

22. Malkiel-Jirmounsky, "Un grand théoricien d'art," 243.

23. Myron Malkiel-Jirmounsky, "Rembrandt en Amérique" (review), *Gazette des Beaux-Arts* 72 (1930): 62. See also Myron Malkiel-Jirmounsky, "Deux modes d'expression opposés dans l'histoire de l'art," *Gazette des Beaux-Arts* 79 (1937): 115–129.

24. André Chastel, "Henri Wölfflin, européen," *Le Monde*, January 3, 1946; reprinted in André Chastel, *L'Image dans le miroir* (Paris, 1980), 49.

25. Radu Ionesco, ed., *Lettres de Henri Focillon à Georges Opresco*, Revue roumaine d'histoire de l'art, vol. 29 (Bucharest, 1992), 71.

26. See Julio Arrechea Miguel, "Focillon y Strzy-gowski o la lejana raíz del arte occidental," *Revistas espacio, tiempo y forma*, ser. 1–7, no. 6 (1993): 559–606.

27. Henri Focillon, *Vie des formes*, Forme et style: Essais et mémoires d'art et d'archéologie (1934; 6th ed., Paris, 1970), 88. These and subsequent excerpts in English taken from Henri Focillon, *The Life of Forms in Art*, revised trans. Charles Beecher Hogan and George Kubler (New York, 1948); this quote, 56.

28. Focillon, *Vie des formes*, 90; *The Life of Forms in Art*, 58.

29. Focillon, *Vie des formes*, 25; *The Life of Forms in Art*, 15.

30. Focillon, *Vie des formes*, 25; *The Life of Forms in Art*, 15.

31. Focillon, *Vie des formes*, 89; *The Life of Forms in Art*, 57.

32. Focillon, *Vie des formes*, 89; *The Life of Forms in Art*, 57.

33. Ernst Bloch, *Héritage de ce temps*, trans.
J. Lacoste (Paris, 1978), 218; *Heritage of Our Times*,
trans. Neville and Stephen Plaice (Oxford, UK, 1991),
[37].

34. Focillon, *Vie des formes*, 88–90; *The Life of
Forms in Art*, 56–58.

35. Hanna Levy, *Henri Wölfflin: Sa théorie, ses prédécesseurs* (PhD diss., Université de Paris; Rottweil,
1936).

36. Levy, *Henri Wölfflin: Sa théorie, ses prédécesseurs*,
18.

37. Levy, *Henri Wölfflin: Sa théorie, ses prédécesseurs*,
18.

38. Levy, *Henri Wölfflin: Sa théorie, ses prédécesseurs*,
18.

39. Levy, *Henri Wölfflin: Sa théorie, ses prédécesseurs*,
18.

40. Levy, *Henri Wölfflin: Sa théorie, ses prédécesseurs*,
190; Wölfflin, *Principles of Art History* (2015), 80.

41. Levy, *Henri Wölfflin: Sa théorie, ses prédécesseurs*,
192.

42. Levy, *Henri Wölfflin: Sa théorie, ses prédécesseurs*,
214.

43. "Schrecklich, wenn man als alter Mann
einer Hanna Levy in die Hände fällt, die mit dem
Scharfsinn eines jüdischen Rechtsanwalts und dem
Draufgängertum ihrer Jugend mein Buch zu Tode kri-
tisiert, aber für das Wesentliche wenig Sensorium hat."
Quoted in Meinhold Lurz, *Heinrich Wölfflin: Biographie einer Kunsttheorie* (Worms, 1981), 261. See also
the more recent article by Daniela Kern, "Hanna Levy
e sua crítica aos *Conceitos Fundamentais* de Wölfflin"
(September 2015), accessed April 8, 2016: https://
www.academia.edu/16152251/2015_Hanna_Levy_e_
sua_cr%C3%ADtica_aos_Conceitos_Fundamentais_
de_W%C3%B6lfflin.

44. Pierre Francastel, *L'Histoire de l'art, instrument
de la propagande germanique* (Paris, 1945), 108–112.

45. "Stärker noch als Glaube…ist künstlerisches
Schaffen das Ausströmen der tiefsten rassenmäßigen
Triebkräfte eines Volkes, einer Völkergruppe. Wölfflin
selbst hat in seinem so klar geschliffenen wenn auch
wesentlich formalen Darlegungen jene rassengebun-
denen Underschiede—von ihm gern Unterschiede des
Sehens genannt—italienischer und deutscher Kunst
deutlich gemacht." Albert E. Brinckmann, *Geist der
Nationen: Italiener, Franzosen, Deutsche* (Hamburg,
1938), 20; *Esprit des nations: France, Italie, Allemagne*, trans. Paul de Man (Brussels, 1943), 14.

46. "The theory that the world view or mode of thinking and feeling is the source of long-term constants
in style is often formulated as a theory of racial or
national character. I have already referred to such
concepts in the work of Wölfflin and Riegl. They have
been common in European writing on art for over a
hundred years and have played a significant role in
promoting national consciousness and race feeling;
works of art are the chief concrete evidence of the
affective world of the ancestors. The persistent teaching that German art is by nature tense and irrational,
that its greatness depends on fidelity to the racial
character, has helped to produce an acceptance of
these traits as a destiny of the people." Meyer Schapiro,
"Style," in *Anthropology Today*, ed. Alfred L. Kroeber
(Chicago, 1953), 306.

47. André Chastel, review in *Bibliothèque
d'humanisme et Renaissance* 15, no. 1 (1953): 152–155.

48. André Chastel, "Situation de Wölfflin: Les
'Principes fondamentaux de l'histoire de l'art,'" *Revue
d'esthétique* 7 (1954): 277.

49. Chastel, "Situation de Wölfflin," 287.

50. Chastel, "Situation de Wölfflin," 282.

51. Chastel, "Situation de Wölfflin," 279.

52. Michael Podro, *The Critical Historians of Art*
(New Haven, 1982), 40–42.

53. Heinrich Wölfflin, *Réflexions sur l'histoire de l'art*,
intro. by Joseph Gantner, trans. Rainer Rochlitz (1982)
(Paris, 1997); see, for example, 53 (*ethnie*) and 57, 172
(*ethnique*).

54. André Chastel, "L'Art du monde: Le Problème des
'universaux,'" in *World Art: Themes of Unity in Diversity; Acts of the Twenty-Sixth International Congress
of the History of Art*, ed. Irving Lavin, 3 vols. (University Park, 1989), 1:15.

55. Chastel, "L'Art du monde: Le Problème des
'universaux,'" 15.

56. Chastel, "L'Art du monde: Le Problème des
'universaux,'" 18.

57. Chastel, "L'Art du monde: Le Problème des
'universaux,'" 17 (for quotation).

58. Chastel, "L'Art du monde: Le Problème des
'universaux,'" 18 (my emphasis).

59. Karl Schnaase, *Niederländische Briefe* (Stuttgart
and Tübingen, 1834), 442 ("eine nothwendige *Theilung
der Arbeit*"; Schnaase's emphasis).

60. Marcel Mauss, "Essai sur le don: Forme et raison
de l'échange dans les sociétés archaïques," *L'Année
sociologique*, n.s., 1 (1923–1924): 30–161.

61. Pierre Francastel, *Peinture et société: Naissance et
destruction d'un espace plastique, de la Renaissance
au cubisme* (Paris, 1951), 9.

62. Pierre Francastel, *L'Histoire de l'art, instrument
de la propagande germanique*, 26–27.

63. Pierre Francastel, "Le Baroque," in *Les langues et littératures modernes dans leurs relations avec les beaux-arts: Actes du cinquième congrès international des langues et littératures modernes, Florence, 27–31 mars 1951 (Le lingue e letterature moderne nei loro rapporti con le belle arti: Atti del Quinto Congresso internazionale di lingue e letterature moderne, Firenze, 27–31 marzo 1951)*, ed. Carlo Pellegrini (Florence, 1955), 165–177; this quotation, 169–170. He was referring to Hanna Levy's thesis (already cited); Lionello Venturi's essay "Gli schemi del Wölfflin," *L'esame: Rivista mensile di coltura e d'arte* (Milan) 1 (1922); and Walter Passarge, *Die Philosophie des Kunstgeschichte in der Gegenwart* (Berlin, 1930).

64. On Marcel Raymond see the work of Julien Zanetta (http://woelfflin.hypotheses.org).

65. André Malraux, *Le Musée imaginaire* (Geneva, 1947). Republished as the first part of *Les Voix du silence* (Paris, 1951); published in English in *The Voices of Silence*, trans. Stuart Gilbert (Garden City, NY, 1953).

66. Rosalind Krauss, "1959, 9 January: The Ministry of Fate," in *A New History of French Literature*, ed. Denis Hollier with R. Howard Block et al. (Cambridge, MA, 1989), 1000–1006.

67. The phrase "art history without names" (*Kunstgeschichte ohne Namen*) appears in the preface of the first edition (1915) of *Grundbegriffe* (p. v), which was not translated into French. See *Principles of Art History* (2015), 72.

68. Germain Bazin, *Histoire de l'histoire de l'art de Vasari à nos jours* (Paris, 1986), 178.

69. See, for example, Pierre Charpentrat, "Relecture de Wölfflin," *Baroque: Revue internationale* 4 (1969).

70. Paul Veyne, *Le Pain et le Cirque: Sociologie historique d'un pluralisme politique* (Paris, 1976), 64–67; Paul Veyne, *L'Inventaire des différences: Leçon inaugurale au Collège de France* (Paris, 1976).

71. Veyne, *Le Pain et le Cirque*, 59.

72. Veyne, *Le Pain et le Cirque*, 61.

73. Michel Foucault, *Les Mots et les Choses: Une archéologie des sciences humaines* (Paris, 1966); published in English as *The Order of Things: An Archaeology of the Human Sciences* (London, 1970).

74. Veyne, *L'Inventaire des différences*, 31. This and subsequent excerpts in English taken from "The Inventory of Differences," trans. Elizabeth Kingdom, *Economy and Society* 11 (1982): 173–199; this quote, 183. For more on Paul Veyne's method and his concept of "invariants," see François Hartog, "Paul Veyne naturaliste: L'Histoire est un herbier," *Annales: Économies, sociétés, civilisations* 33, no. 2 (1978): 326–330.

75. Veyne, *L'Inventaire des différences*, 30; "The Inventory of Differences," 183.

76. Veyne, *L'Inventaire des différences*, 32; "The Inventory of Differences," 184.

77. Veyne, *L'Inventaire des différences*, 33; "The Inventory of Differences," 184.

78. Veyne, *L'Inventaire des différences*, 34; "The Inventory of Differences," 185.

79. Gilles Deleuze and Félix Guattari, *Qu'est-ce que la philosophie?* (Paris, 1991), introduction; published in English as *What Is Philosophy?*, trans. Hugh Tomlinson and Graham Burchill (London, 1994).

80. See Susan Holden, "Finding the Architecture in Deleuze: Heinrich Wölfflin as a Source of Deleuze's Baroque," in *Panorama to Paradise: Proceedings of the 24th Annual Conference of the Society of Architectural Historians, Australia and New Zealand* (Adelaide, 2007), 1–12 (http://espace.library.uq.edu.au/view/UQ:136126, accessed October 29, 2015). Deleuze's sometimes approximate use of Wölfflin's concepts is particularly evident in *Francis Bacon: Logique de la sensation* (Paris, 1981) and in *Cinéma 1: L'Image-mouvement* (Paris, 1983).

81. Paul Veyne, *Foucault: Sa pensée, sa personne* (Paris, 2008), 169–170; English translation: *Foucault: His Thought, His Character*, trans. Janet Lloyd (Cambridge, UK, and Malden, MA, 2010), 101.

82. Veyne, *Foucault: Sa pensée, sa personne*, 170, 171; *Foucault: His Thought, His Character*, 102. See also Heinrich Wölfflin, "Pro Domo," in *Réflexions sur l'histoire de l'art*, 43–46.

83. Wölfflin, *Principles of Art History* (2015), 324; "'Kunstgeschichtliche Grundbegriffe': Eine Revision (1933)," in Wölfflin, *Gedanken zur Kunstgeschichte*, 24.

84. See "Wölfflin et la France," intro. by Jacques Thuillier to *Relire Wölfflin*, ed. Joan Goldhammer Hart, Roland Recht, and Martin Warnke (Paris, 1995), 13–29; this quotation, 27. Thuillier succeeded André Chastel at the Collège de France.

ANDREA PINOTTI

Who Is Afraid of Wölfflin's Schemas? *The Impact of* Kunstgeschichtliche Grundbegriffe *on Italian Art Historiography and Aesthetics*

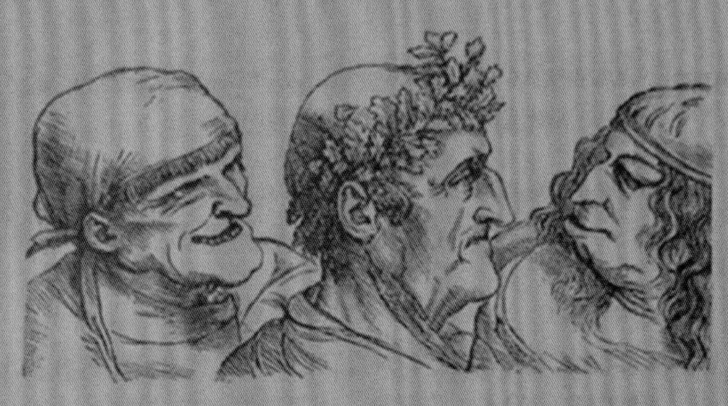

CONCETTI FONDAMENTALI DELLA STORIA DELL'ARTE

DI HEINRICH WÖLFFLIN

LA FORMAZIONE DELLO STILE NELL'ARTE MODERNA

LONGANESI & C.

Wölfflin's *Kunstgeschichtliche Grundbegriffe* exerted a significant impact on Italian culture, both in the area of art-historical discourse and in that of philosophical aesthetics. These were closely interconnected from a pedagogical point of view; the 1923 Fascist reform of the educational system, designed by the neo-idealist philosopher Giovanni Gentile, had introduced philosophy and art history as fundamental and compulsory disciplines (which they are still today) for elite education in the Italian secondary schools known as *licei classici*.

As we will see, the major critical issue raised by *Grundbegriffe* among its Italian readers was the status and legitimacy of Wölfflin's optical schemas (together with the corresponding separation of form and expression), which triggered serious concern among scholars preoccupied with the irreducible singularity of the individual work of art and of the individual artistic personality. In what follows, after a reconstruction of the history of the Italian editions—both integral and anthologized—of *Grundbegriffe*, I will examine the neo-idealist reception of Wölfflin's ideas (dominant in the first half of the twentieth century) and will subsequently take into consideration nonidealist approaches down to the present day.

History of the Editions

The history of Wölfflin's *Grundbegriffe* in Italian is the history of successive editions of the translation published by Longanesi in 1953 and subsequently reprinted by the publishers Tea and Neri Pozza (fig. 1).[1] This successful enterprise followed an attempt

by Rolf Hohenemser (also known as Rolf Tasna; 1920–1997), who in 1942 had completed a translation that was never published.[2] The Longanesi translator, who based his work on the sixth German edition of 1923, was Rodolfo Paoli (1905–1978), professor of German literature at the universities of Florence, Naples, and Bologna. The introduction was written by Giusta Nicco Fasola (1901–1960), a specialist in art treatises and professor of aesthetics and art theory on the faculty of architecture in Florence (1944–1947) and then in Genoa (from 1948). In her text she presented the overall evolution of Wölfflin's thought from psychological beginnings, closely related to the theories of empathy of Robert Vischer, to the more formalist approach inspired by Konrad Fiedler and Adolf von Hildebrand. She praised Wölfflin as an acknowledged master of method and reassured Italian readers that his schemas—introduced in *Renaissance und Barock* and *Die klassische Kunst* and then systematized in *Grundbegriffe*—were no longer to be feared and should be endlessly multiplied, adjusted to the infinite variety of works of art:

We must no longer be afraid of falling prey to his schematism.…Criticism is no longer based on concepts, types, schemas analogous to Wölfflin's.…Figurative concepts have to model themselves on works of art; they must therefore be innumerable and constantly renewed as is the reality of art itself.[3]

Nicco Fasola stressed that Wolfflin's categories were very general guidelines, on the one hand incapable of characterizing individual artistic personalities, on the other impossible to extend to any other artistic period. ("[E]very Western style, just as it has

1. Heinrich Wölfflin, *Concetti fondamentali della storia dell'arte: La formazione dello stile nell'arte moderna* (Milan: Longanesi & C., 1953), title page

works by Wölfflin, which appeared before 1953: *Renaissance und Barock*, published as *Rinascimento e barocco* (1928); *Die klassische Kunst*, published as *L'arte classica del Rinascimento* (1941); and *Das Erklären von Kunstwerken*, published as *Avvicinamento all'opera d'arte* (1948).[6] But as early as 1927, some parts of *Grundbegriffe* (passages from the introduction regarding the five pairs of concepts and the history of vision) had already been translated and published in an anthology (now quite a rare book) designed for teaching art history at the high school level (fig. 2).[7] The editors were the art historians Paolo D'Ancona (1878–1964) and Fernanda Wittgens (1903–1957). D'Ancona was the founder of the Istituto di Storia dell'Arte at the University of Milan.[8] Fernanda Wittgens, his pupil, was inspector of the Accademia di Belle Arti di Brera. An antifascist (she helped D'Ancona, who was Jewish, escape to Switzerland during Mussolini's regime), she became director of the Pinacoteca di Brera, where she organized the rescue and protection of works of art during World War II. She was responsible for the acquisition of Michelangelo's Rondanini Pietà by the city of Milan in 1952. Wittgens was the translator and the author of the introductions to the various sections of the anthology, which ranges from Roger de Piles to Croce. Significantly, Wölfflin is included in the last section, together with Fiedler, Hildebrand, Hans von Marées, Bernard Berenson, Max Dvořák, Lionello Venturi, and Benedetto Croce, under the title "Idealismo." In presenting this section, Wittgens recalls that Croce had interpreted Fiedler's arguments on the eye as a "metaphor" and relies on the interpretation of the schemas of pure visibility proposed by Venturi, to whom the anthology is dedicated. The last word is left to Croce's "lyrical" criticism of abstract formalism.

References to *Grundbegriffe* in Italy previous to the publication of the complete translation should include Matteo Marangoni (1876–1954). Professor of art history at the universities of Milan (1938–1946) and Pisa (1946–1951), Marangoni was also

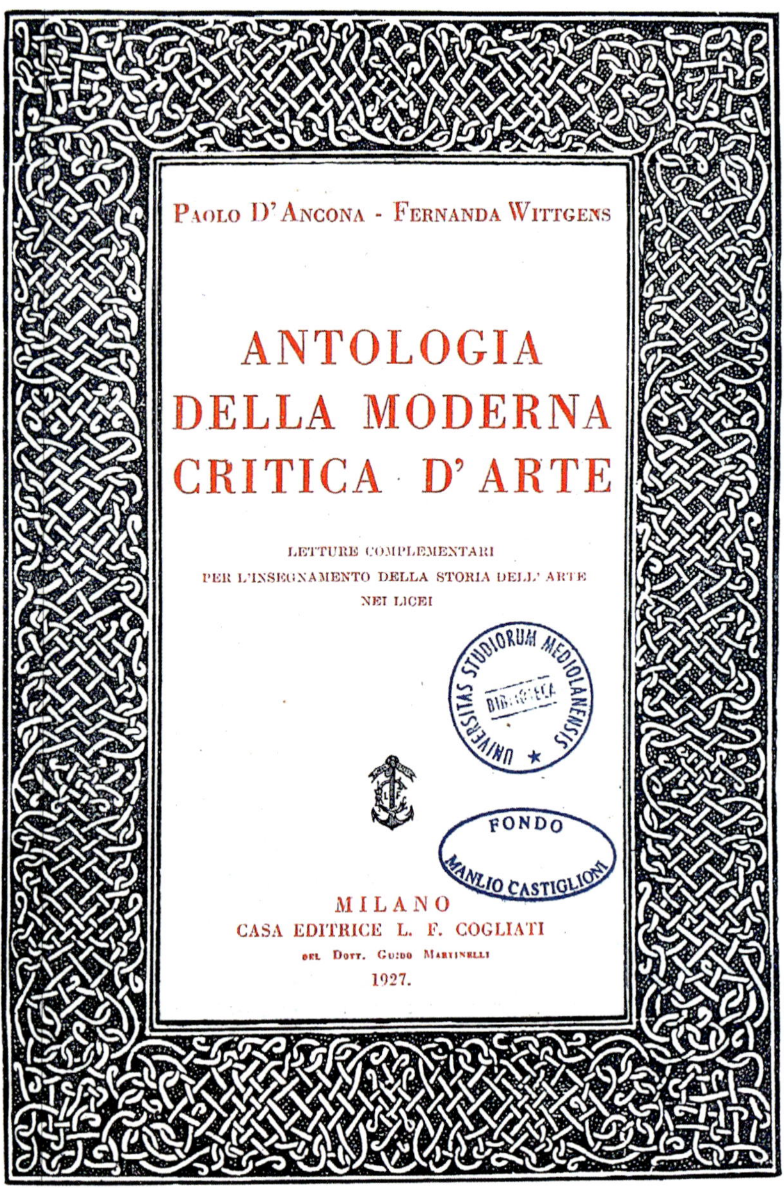

2. Paolo D'Ancona and Fernanda Wittgens, *Antologia della moderna critica d'arte: Letture complementari per l'insegnamento della storia dell'arte nei licei* (Milan: Casa Editrice L. F. Cogliati, 1927), title page

a classical epoch, will also have its baroque epoch, if only it is allowed to live out its time.")[4] Even the 1933 "Revision," published by Wölfflin in the journal *Logos* and translated as an appendix to the Italian edition, did not entirely persuade Nicco Fasola of a sufficient correction of his "schematisms," which was achieved in Italy only through the integration of Benedetto Croce's and Berenson's aesthetics.[5]

Grundbegriffe was offered to the Italian public following translations of three intensely active in popularizing the discipline for a larger cultivated but generalist public through nonspecialist volumes aimed at educating seeing and the appreciation of formal factors of the work of art. In his *Saper vedere* (knowing how to see, a title typical of von Marées's and Fiedler's theory), Wölfflin's *Grundbegriffe* in the 1918 edition and *Die klassische Kunst* were recruited for this pedagogical program.[9]

Another anthology, much more influential for the Italian (and later also French) reception of formalist methods, was published in 1949 under the editorship of Roberto Salvini (1912–1985; fig. 3). Director of the Galleria degli Uffizi in Florence (1950–1956) and professor of art history in Trieste and in Florence, Salvini himself translated many of the selected texts (from works by Fiedler, Hildebrand, Alois Riegl, August Schmarsow, A. E. Brinckmann, Berenson, Clive Bell, Roger Fry, Adrian Stokes, Jacques Mesnil, Henri Focillon, Roberto Longhi, and Venturi), including excerpts from four of Wölfflin's works ("'Kunstgeschichtliche Grundbegriffe': Eine Revision," 1933; *Über Formentwicklung*, 1940; *Albrecht Dürer, Handzeichnungen*, 1914; *Italien und das deutsche Formgefühl*, 1931).[10] In his introduction Salvini criticizes Wölfflin's dualism of form and content, vision and expression, as a typical difficulty in his approach. Moreover, Wölfflin is censured for not being interested in judgments of value ("the problem—so essential to us—of the judgment of value, namely of the distinction between art and nonart") or in supporting art criticism, and for focusing exclusively on the autonomous history of artistic vision.[11]

In Salvini's view the Swiss art historian was nevertheless unable to completely neglect the history of expression, but he never achieved a proper integration of the two views. The unidirectionality of the process from the first to the second stage of each of the famous five pairs claimed by Wölfflin as rational appears to Salvini highly problematic, since there are periods in art history when the direction of the process is clearly inverted (for example,

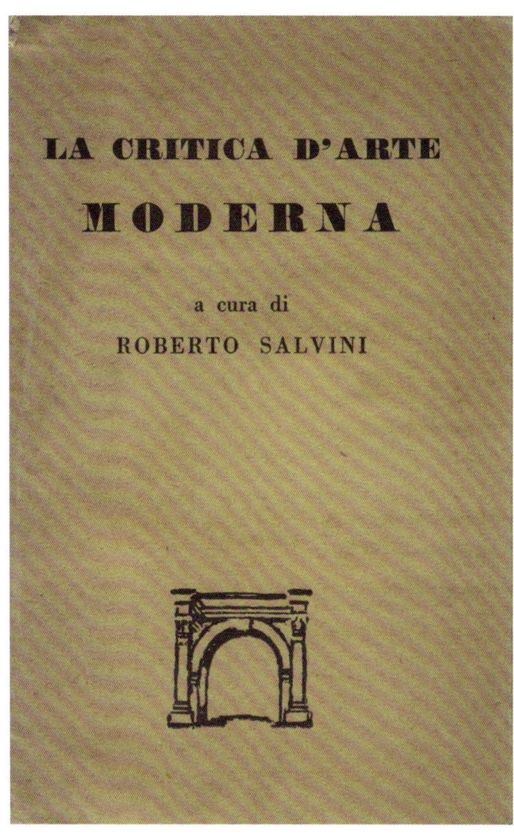

from Hellenistic and early Christian art to Byzantine art, or from impressionism to constructivism of the early twentieth century). Wölfflin's error consisted thus in an unjustified generalization of a process characteristic of the transition from Renaissance to baroque. Finally, Wölfflin is not clear when he talks of a "history of seeing": in *Renaissance und Barock* he seems to interpret this notion in a physiological way, whereas later on he tends to introduce references to imaginative and spiritual factors.

Salvini nevertheless acknowledged Wölfflin as a great master when he applied his abstract schemas to the analysis of an individual personality and of his corpus, as in the case of Dürer:

Line, painterliness, closed and open form, and so on, are schemas that can seem empty when theorized by Wölfflin as principles of the historical development of form. But they become alive and real when the author examines them in the specific work of art or when he follows them in their varied articulation through the work of an artist.[12]

Neo-Idealist Reception

After this presentation of the main publishing projects related to *Grundbegriffe* in Italy in the first half of the twentieth century (and we need to remember that some of those editions, which included *Grundbegriffe*, have been repeatedly reprinted in the second half), let us go back to the authors who, in the first decades of the century, read Wölfflin in the original German and had the major responsibility for the Italian reception of his ideas.

The foremost reader—a true cultural filter always up to date on European developments in the humanities and able to determine what could be imported and what had to be left out—was the neo-idealist philosopher Benedetto Croce (1866–1952), whose essays contributed key ideas to the theory of visual arts: "La teoria dell'arte come pura visibilità" (1911); "La critica e la storia delle arti figurative e le sue condizioni presenti" (1919); "Un tentativo eclettico nella storia delle arti figurative" (1919); "Nota per una migliore critica delle arti figurative" (1923).[13]

In his 1911 essay on von Marées, Hildebrand, and Fiedler, Croce coined the famous label "pura visibilità" (pure visibility), under which Wölfflin himself is frequently included) and many scholars nowadays still attribute to Fiedler. Actually there is no trace of "reine Sichtbarkeit" in Fiedler's texts: it was Croce's friend Julius von Schlosser who circulated the concept in the German-speaking world by translating Croce's essay into German.[14] Croce admired Fiedler because he represented the highest point in German art theory of his time, and he admitted to agreeing on many points with him, mainly the idea that art is a form of intuitive, nonlogical knowledge. But he criticized some aspects that are worth underlining here because they will help us understand Croce's criticism of Wölfflin. Fiedler lacked a solid theory of intuition, a general philosophical system, a clear separation of the beautiful and the artistic, of physiology and imagination, of life and art; moreover, the notions of "visibility" and of "the eye"

should be taken not in their literal sense, but as mere metaphors:

Upon closer consideration, the notions of "visibility" and "productive eye" reveal themselves as merely metaphors and symbols. They are rich in polemical efficacy, since they reject the idea that art can be reduced to conceptual knowledge, imitation of nature, or sentiment. But, as far as art is concerned, they lack positive determinations and prove overtly false when metaphors and symbols are taken for philosophical definitions. As concepts related to physiology and nature, the eye — a physiological organ — and vision — a physiological process — allow no passage to the philosophical concept of art, which is a spiritual activity.[15]

In 1919, reviewing the third (1904) edition of *Die klassische Kunst*, Croce added some specifics to his position on Wölfflin's approach. While insisting on the rejection of the physiological conception of vision, he introduced the criticism of the "dualistic" approach of the double root of style (*Ausdruck* versus *Sehen*, or expression versus seeing) that would become a leitmotiv in the subsequent Italian reception:

No particular demonstrative effort is required to show that such an idea of art history is more dualistic than formalistic. The author himself admits it in his theory of the "double root" and "expressive values," to which "merely formal" and "inexpressive" values should be added (values that however cannot be "deduced" from the first ones). This idea needs also no confutation, for it is an aesthetic stance that has already been surpassed and confuted in the history of Aesthetics, and that refers to a general philosophical position easily acknowledged as inconceivable and contradictory.[16]

In addressing Wölfflin's notion of *Sehen*, Croce raised an objection that seems very close to the argument developed by the young Erwin Panofsky five years earlier, in a severely critical article written in reaction to the seminal 1911 lecture and 1912 article that had constituted the foundation for Wölfflin's principles.[17] Panofsky had remarked:

The individual expressive effort, which leads the single artist to a configuration that is proper to him only and to a personal conception or determination of the object, certainly manifests in general forms, but these stem from an expressive effort as well: from the configurative will that is in a certain sense immanent to the entire epoch and is founded in a basically identical attitude of the *soul*, not of the eye.[18] [My emphasis]

Very similarly referring to the "soul," Croce asserted:

The eyes, which see differently, are actually the soul, which feels and dreams and imagines differently. This had to be investigated by establishing the unity of that new feeling and of that new motion of the line.[19]

In a note specifically devoted to *Grundbegriffe* in its third (1918) edition, Croce stressed what to his view appeared highly problematic for an autonomous history of art as a description of the immanent evolution of optical forms: Wölfflin neglected the beauty or ugliness of works, abstaining from any judgments of value; he was not able to explain the "cause" that determined the succession of styles because that cause must be sought outside the immanent history, in external circumstances. Thus in spite of all his schemas, Wölfflin ended up reconsidering the *Gesinnung* (temperamental disposition) as a foundation of *Darstellung* (representation), thus reintroducing the dualism—the double root of style—that he had programmatically tried to avoid. Yet there was still room for a positive appreciation: Wölfflin was to be praised for his nonmimetic conception of art and for his effort to aim at a purely artistic history of art:

When one wants to move from abstractions to reality, under those conceptual distinctions one finds no longer distinctions of pure, namely, aesthetic, form but rather distinctions between psychic content and ways of feeling. Thus one is brought back to considerations of the *Gesinnung*, of the temperamental disposition, from which one had thought to move away in order to follow the history of the artistic form, of the *Darstellung*. This is an ineluctable consequence because in abstraction we notoriously lose the dialectic nexus of form and content

and end up with this or that part of the abstract matter of art, rather than with art itself.[20]

The German philologist Karl Vossler, friend of both Wölfflin and Croce, tried to put the two scholars in contact, suggesting that the philosopher send the art historian a copy of the first (1920) edition of his collection of essays *Nuovi saggi di estetica*. But apparently, once he received the book, Wölfflin understood that there was no room for a productive encounter. Vossler wrote to Croce:

Now I must also thank you on Wölfflin's behalf. He was a little late in reading your criticism of his books and asked me to make his excuses to you. He believes that you would have neither time for discussions, nor pleasure in engaging in them, and thinks that reciprocal conversions are hopeless. He holds that you have no interest in his research perspectives. You have to do with aesthetic concepts, whereas he is focused only on the evolution of forms of vision. That he does not write personally is due to his clumsiness in such things, and not to lack of politeness or of good will. In brief, he thanks you and sends his greetings.[21]

Croce's aesthetics deeply influenced the Italian art historians and critics of the first half of the twentieth century.[22] Among the most prominent figures was Roberto Longhi (1870–1970), professor in Bologna in the 1930s and in Florence after the war.[23] Longhi was not deeply interested in theoretical and methodological issues, but in some of his early essays he nevertheless appears inspired by polarizations that might be traced back to the ideas of Wölfflin (and those of Fiedler and Hildebrand, which he had known through Croce's mediation).[24] For example, in his "short but truthful" history of Italian painting, a handbook for secondary schools published in 1914, Longhi emphasized the role of the practice of seeing for the visual artist:

While the poet transfigures through language the psychological essence of reality, the painter transfigures its visual essence: for the figurative artist feeling is nothing but seeing, and his style, namely, his own art,

is constructed entirely on the lyrical elements of
his vision.[25]

He also articulated the domain of seeing in
modes that recall Wölfflin's formal analysis, writing of a "linear style" (*stile lineare*)
as a "mode of vision" in which the artist
expresses visual reality as line and contour,
and of a "pure coloristic style" (*stile color-
istico puro*), that, compared to the linear,
appears "primordial."[26]

A more explicit reference to the Swiss
art historian is to be found in a review of a
monograph on Luca Giordano, written by
Longhi in 1920, in which he rejected the
critical method founded on biography and
on chronological evolution:

Criticism based in biography and chronology is…an
almost physical, and never intellectual, auxiliary to figurative criticism, which might be conceived — as, after all,
Wölfflin has recently posited it — as a "Kunstgeschichte
ohne Namen," an art history without names and, I would
add, without dates.[27]

"Art history without names" was the famous
formula Wölfflin introduced in the preface
to the first edition of *Grundbegriffe* and
defended in a short piece published in 1920.[28]

At the beginning of the 1940s, this basic
agreement between Wölfflin and Longhi
seemed to deteriorate when it came to the
national (and nationalistic) underpinnings of
art historiography, emblematically embodied in the "Italia-Germania" polarization,
which Wölfflin had addressed both in a
short essay, "Italien und das deutsche Formgefühl," and in the volume of the same title
(critically reviewed by the historian of architecture Giulio Carlo Argan).[29] In his reaction, openly quoting his adversary, Longhi
remarked:

[T]he binomial "clear-unclear," "bestimmtes-unbe-
stimmtes," created by Wölfflin to justify such a work,
seems a dilemma that can be resolved…only by rejecting the second term. In any case, the Germania-Italia
linguistic diversification…here becomes stronger and
stronger. Wölfflin offered the most famous exegesis of
such diversification. Nevertheless, as is always the case

when one pulls away from the artistic persona in favor
of formal schemas, this interpretation is far too peremptory. And, to be thoroughly peremptory, it must overlook
many other aspects of our art that are by no means
secondary, and that on the contrary, added to the previous ones, testify to a unique syntactic complexity.[30]

Croce reviewed this text, praising Longhi
for having objected to "turbid aesthetic-
nationalistic concepts" ("torbidi concetti
nazionalistico-estetici"), on the contrary
supported by "Wölfflin, a good connoisseur
of art, but a very weak builder of theories"
("buon conoscitore d'arte ma assai fiacco
costruttore di teorie.")[31]

Much more engaged than Longhi in
theoretical issues was Lionello Venturi
(1885–1961), professor of art history in
Turin and Rome; an antifascist, he was
exiled because he had been one of the few
to refuse to swear loyalty to Mussolini.[32]
Venturi wrote two theoretical and methodological essays in the early 1920s: the first is
devoted to Wölfflin's schemas in particular,
the second to pure visibility in general.[33] In
his reading of Wölfflin, Venturi agreed with
Croce on the danger of uncritical adoption
of abstract schemas, but he also acknowledged that nobody had ever written art
criticism without employing them. As a case
study, he chose *Grundbegriffe* in the third
(1918) edition. In addressing the five pairs of
categories, he stressed a series of difficulties,
some of which had already been emphasized
by Croce: lack of reference to artistic quality
and to content; the claim of logical progression, unjustified because the historical process can be inverted; incapability of reducing
the five pairs to a single dyad (tactile/optical),
when he should have brought them back to
the ancient opposition form/color. Nevertheless, Venturi admitted that after reading
Grundbegriffe one had a clearer comprehen-
sion of the passage from the Cinquecento to
the Seicento: the principles' utility is a preparatory, heuristic one, and they function as
practical tools for the orientation of the art
historian in the *mare magnum* of the history
of images:

Well, schemas are practical tools to orient oneself in the great sea of art, provisional classifications, ways to understand one another. As such, they accomplish their function precisely during the preparatory moment of the critical judgment, which corresponds to the interpretation of the work of art to be judged.[34]

But Venturi's main criterion for distinguishing between good and bad schemas is the origin of the schema itself in the creative moment of the individual artist. Schemas should not be superimposed on the history of art by the interpreter but rather should be found in authorship:

Schemas can be wrong because they are *invented* by the critic with no relation to the work of art for which they have been invented; or right because the artist had them in mind while creating and the critic *recovers* them in turn.[35]

Later, he devoted the tenth chapter of his influential *History of Art Criticism*, published first in English in 1936 and only in 1945 in an Italian version, to "art criticism and pure visibility." There he wrote that Wölfflin was "far more famous than Riegl, and he passes to-day as the greatest creator of schemes of pure visibility."[36]

By this time, Venturi could take into account the 1933 "Revision," but he nonetheless restated his former skeptical observations: the concepts should be varied to adapt perfectly to the single work of art (making the paradoxical ideal a schema for each individual work), and a history of art without names neglects the individual personality, which is the true foundation of the artistic creation. It is evident thus that the notion of "individual"—in the sense of both the object (the individual work of art) and of the subject (the individual artist)—is at the core of Venturi's criticism.

Longhi and Venturi are the better-known names, but they are not the entire Crocean party among art historians and theorists. Carlo Antoni (1896–1959), professor of philosophy of history at the University of Rome-La Sapienza and direct pupil of Croce, substantially repeated Venturi's remarks

concerning the impossibility of carrying the schemas to the level of individuality. In aiming at a "natural history of art,"[37] Wölfflin's approach resembled that of a scientist:

When Wölfflin declares that he hopes to offer us a natural history, he has quite correctly stated his aim. His procedure is that of the natural scientist insofar as he seeks to subsume art objects under general, abstract concepts. Art history, thus conceived, can never produce anything but abstract patterns, just as biology and mineralogy can never produce anything but abstract patterns. It is obvious that such schematizations can never be a priori, absolute, or universal, even though they may be useful in bringing some order out of chaos — at least when one is confronted, not by the work or art itself, but by the artistic production of an epoch, nation or the human race as a whole. And, in fact, this is Wölfflin's concern: he is not interested in the individual work of art, but in style, that is, in the common mean, the mediocre uniformity and generality of an epoch.[38]

In 1952, similarly inspired by Croce's aesthetics, Michele Guerrisi (1893–1963)—sculptor and theorist, professor of art history at the Accademia Albertina di Belle Arti in Turin and the Accademia di Belle Arti in Rome—published his *L'idea figurativa*, in which he devoted a chapter to Wölfflin's schemas (following a section on Riegl and preceding one on Berenson). He lamented the form / content duality; a fundamental ambiguity in oscillating between immanent and external causes of stylistic evolution; the contradiction between a process from the first to the second member of each of the paired concepts deemed by Wölfflin to be unidirectional and the inversions of such direction that historically took place; and a confusion of epistemologically different planes, merging physiology, philosophy, historiography, artistic practices, and art criticism in an overall disorder:

Not entirely clear ideas, in which there is a confusion of purely physiological concepts (*touch, the eye*) and philosophical concepts (*things in themselves*), historical qualifications (*the classical*) and geometric spatial conceptions (*space and surface*), elements of figurative representation (*the profile*) and of critical qualifications (*the emphasis on the limits of the thing*).[39]

Professor of art history at the universities of Messina, Catania, and Bologna, Stefano Bottari (1907–1967) published a number of works dedicated to art theory and criticism.[40] He was also the author of the introduction to the second Italian edition of *Die klassische Kunst*, published in 1953. Given his proximity to the Crocean environment, it is not surprising that he wanted to distance himself from the anonymous horizon of Wölfflin's approach, once again pleading the cause of individuality:

[T]he history of art is made of "persons" and not of "things," or rather of things that are at the same time persons. This is the limit of Wölfflin's procedure: a limit that affects any naturalistic approach, for which every characterization assumes a classificatory value, and historical development fades in the anonymous impassibility of a necessary evolution.[41]

But in the context of this younger generation of scholars inspired by Croce's aesthetics, the most prominent figure is certainly Carlo Ludovico Ragghianti (1910–1987).[42] Art and architectural historian and critic, pioneer in the use of film as an effective tool of art-historiographical research and popularization, he had attended the Scuola Normale Superiore in Pisa from 1928 to 1931.[43] Following the arrival of the fascist philosopher Giovanni Gentile as director, the antifascist Ragghianti was expelled from the school; he continued his studies at the University of Pisa under Matteo Marangoni. Strongly engaged by theoretical and epistemological issues in the foundations of art criticism, Ragghianti was particularly sensitive to the German formalist tradition: he encouraged his wife, Licia Collobi, to translate Riegl's *Spätrömische Kunstindustrie* and introduced a collection of essays by Konrad Fiedler.[44] He was nonetheless highly suspicious of the risks of excessive theorization: in a methodological article published in 1940–1941 he bemoaned the "aggressive superabundance of schemas in

Kunstwissenschaft" (sovrabbondanza truculenta di schemi della *Kunstwissenschaft*).[45] After a few years he made his criticism more specific. In reviewing the published correspondence of Burckhardt and Wölfflin (1882–1897), edited by Joseph Gantner,[46] Ragghianti stressed the difference between the two personalities, underlining Wölfflin's tendency to positivism, naturalism, and metaphysics. In this way,

art criticism aligned itself with the culture of the naturalistic and psychological positivism, the questions of personality and of art as an autonomous spiritual activity went more and more out of focus, and the analysis of the work of art consisted more and more in a reduction of particular languages to general schemas and classifications.[47]

In an essay specifically devoted to Wölfflin's schemas, Ragghianti insisted on a criticism with which we are now very familiar: the neglect of the personal and individual style, which falls victim to the impersonal laws of the evolution of form. Comparing "Prolegomena to a Psychology of Architecture," *Grundbegriffe*, and "Revision," Ragghianti found a common flaw:

His "history of form" neglected the existence of "personal styles" and also of what still appeared to him as "local (or national) styles," which we can interpret as pictorial traditions in the sense that we give to the notion of literary tradition.[48]

Again in 1986, at the end of his life, Ragghianti would go back to Wölfflin's doctrines, evoking Georg Wilhelm Friedrich Hegel and Auguste Comte (names that Arnold Hauser had already mentioned as references for "the phantom of a collective soul"[49] as his conceptual background for the project of an art history without names):

It is almost impossible to understand how Wölfflin could make radical claims such as those made by Comte.… It was right to claim that seeing as such had its history,… but when predetermined by an irreversible evolution, seeing was not a history but rather a fate.... Wölfflin never fully realized the authoritarian and fideistic implication presupposed by his system.[50]

Nonidealist Perspectives

In spite of the pervasive influence exerted by Croce's aesthetics on the principal representatives of Italian art history and theory in the first half of the twentieth century, Wölfflin's work did elicit alternative positions and readings.

In an article published in 1942, which provoked an irritated reaction from Croce,[51] Barna Occhini (1905–1978), writer and art historian, dared to take a passionate stand for the methodological legitimacy and epistemological validity of schemas and typologies in art historiography, praising Wölfflin for his paradigmatic approach. In Occhini's view, abstractions were not dead conceptualizations but instruments that allow the art historian to avoid empirical fragmentation:

I repeat that there are lively and vital abstractions, and some of the most illuminating were formulated by Wölfflin in his books *Renaissance and Baroque, Classic Art*, and *Principles of Art History*. It seems to me that, now that the premises have been restored for this important work, in art criticism and in other fields we can and must return with a renewed commitment to the difficult "general ideas," to the daring synthesis, to the typical constructions: these invite us to go beyond the minutiae of the particular, the fragmentary, the sensations and reflections of the moment; beyond the dust in which the mental and moral infantilism of a large part of our culture and civilization overindulges.[52]

On the anti-idealist side, an eminent and authoritative figure was the philosopher Antonio Banfi (1886–1957), the founder of the Milan school of phenomenology. Close to Edmund Husserl, Georg Simmel, and Max Dessoir, elected senator for the Italian Communist Party in 1948 and in 1953, Banfi promoted a series of translations for the Milanese publishing company Minuziano, among them Konrad Fiedler's *Aphorismen* (*Aforismi sull'arte*; 1945) and Wölfflin's *Das Erklären von Kunstwerken* (*Avvicinamento all'opera d'arte*; 1948). In the introduction to *Aforismi sull'arte*, Banfi defends the impurity of the schemas, judged not as sterilely abstract but rather capable of concreteness, and recommends integration of Wölfflin's and Fiedler's perspectives:

The theory of pure visibility is far from being capable of accounting for the integral structure of art, for its complex tension and its various lines of development; its visual schemas are actually all but pure, they are on the contrary saturated with meaning. Wölfflin did realize this, as everyone knows, but the revision of his position can instead be completed through a return to Fiedler's conception of art.[53]

Also influenced by a phenomenological orientation was Guido Morpurgo Tagliabue (1907–1997), a specialist of German literature, a philosopher, and professor of aesthetics at the universities of Milan (1951–1961) and Trieste (1964–1982). His influential overview of contemporary aesthetics, written in French and published in 1960, includes a chapter dedicated to "formalisme figuratif," in which Wölfflin is presented together with Hildebrand, Berenson, Venturi, Longhi, Ragghianti, Croce, Fry, Bell, and Focillon. Referring in particular to Wölfflin, Morpurgo rejects the allegation of abstraction, claiming that in his approach, so-called pure visibility is actually realized by acknowledging the role of physiological factors related to vital feelings (in accordance with the theory of empathy) and even by spiritual and moral elements:

In Wölfflin, even more patently than in Hildebrand, we can observe the manifestation of a double or triple level of critical values. For the analysis of formal values according to more and more specific categories of visibility there is a corresponding acknowledgment of physiological values, of vital feelings, according to the principle of *Einfühlung*; and these finally lead to moral values, to spiritual dispositions.[54]

Gillo Dorfles (1910–2018), philosopher, art critic, and painter, professor of aesthetics at the universities of Milan, Cagliari, and Trieste, looked at Wölfflin's categories as tools for identifying structural factors shared in a given epoch not only by the visual arts but also by any cultural product, determining thus a sort of "community of languages":

It seems important to me to acknowledge a structural factor underlying any work of art in itself, but also any product of a particular historical period, and thus the "style of an epoch." This allows us to explain what might be called a community of languages within the style of that epoch. This seems obvious for historical epochs but less evident for our times. Further, we must consider that without the appropriate historical perspective it is very difficult to determine the structural constants of an epoch, their number, and where they are to be found.[55]

Wölfflin actually suggested the possibility of identifying a structure common to heterogeneous cultural manifestations long before *Grundbegriffe*, as early as 1886, at the time of the publication of his dissertation on the psychology of architecture, where he underlined the analogy between Gothic architectural forms and contemporaneous items of fashion with pointed shapes (such as hats and shoes).[56] And the attempt to extend Wölfflin's schemas from the visual to the literary domain, made by Oskar Walzel as early as 1917, found sympathizers in Italy.[57]

Similarly interested in the problems of a common cultural language or grammar is Renato Barilli (1935–), professor (now emeritus) of aesthetics, history of contemporary art, and phenomenology of styles at the University of Bologna. A pupil of Luciano Anceschi (who was in turn a pupil of Antonio Banfi), Barilli started as a critic responsible for the visual arts section of the influential journal *Il verri*. In its first issue in 1956 he published a review of the XXVIII Venice Biennale that made reference to the Wölfflinian pair of closed and open form.[58] In his subsequent project of a "culturological"[59] phenomenology of styles, presented in a 1982 issue, Barilli devoted an entire chapter to Wölfflin, in which he also emphasized the Kantian stance of the Swiss art historian and the need to go beyond Kant's transcendentalism.[60] Wölfflin is Kantian, he wrote, in that he aims at seizing

universals in phenomena themselves, and he goes beyond Kant in that he does not limit himself to the identification of general structures but wants to seize them in their historical moment:

In short, it is a matter of relating the individual phenomenon to the type (the style or language) and then examining how these types succeed one another or how they change in the flow of history. This obliges us to formulate a law of variation or a typology of changes, in other words, a phenomenology of styles.[61]

It would therefore be wrong to state that Wölfflin neglected the role of the individual personality; like Ferdinand de Saussure, he was interested in the relationship between *parole* and *langue*, between individual linguistic acts and their possibilities as determined by the general social code. Moreover, he remarked that the categorical pairs are not rigid definitions but rather relational characterizations, gradients: there is no typical linear or painterly artist per se but an artist who is more linear or more painterly than another.

Given his culturological interests, Barilli had necessarily to confront the controversial issue of "autonomy" and "heteronomy" of stylistic development in Wölfflin's doctrine: significantly, he denied the predominance of "internal" factors and the self-sufficiency of artistic evolution and stressed Wölfflin's attention to the interference of "external" factors, which condition the style of an epoch not only in its artistic manifestations but also in the general style of the bodily and sensory habits. Through his culturological approach Barilli reintroduced Wölfflin's formalism into a wider *geisteswissenschaftlich* context, which was by no means foreign to the Swiss scholar: let us remember that he had been a pupil of Wilhelm Dilthey at the University of Berlin in 1885–1886. However, Barilli was not primarily interested in assessing a philological reading of Wölfflin's theories; rather, he took on Wölfflin's legacy in order to continue his work toward farther horizons from the perspective of a culturological and interdisciplinary approach in which his views were integrated with the approach to study of media developed by Marshall McLuhan. (McLuhan had similarly analyzed the structures shared in the Renaissance by movable-type printing and the method of perspective representation.)[62] Barilli wrote:

It appears to me entirely legitimate for those of us who follow Wölfflin's teachings to continue along the path he blazed and to attempt to carry out these expansions and go beyond both historical limits — if for no other reason than the fact that the history of styles has proceeded and new material on which to shine the interpretative light has accumulated — and interdisciplinary limits since we have greater awareness and more precise instruments at our disposal.[63]

Although from a different background (history of language and semiotics), Omar Calabrese (1949–2012), professor at the universities of Bologna and Siena, similarly looked at Wölfflin in the frame of a culturological project, aiming at integrating visual products within a more general domain, underpinned by a sort of isomorphism or homology of heterogeneous manifestations throughout an epoch. (As we know, the relation between the immanent sphere of art and external reality and life was very controversial in Wölfflin's thinking and even in that of his master Jacob Burckhardt). As early as 1951 Gillo Dorfles had hinted at baroque tendencies in modern art, explicitly speaking of a "neobaroque."[64] In 1987 Calabrese picked up this label and openly admitted his debt to Wölfflin's approach:

I have in a sense "rewritten" Wölfflin's basic idea, which in the course of time has been variously refuted in the name of a presumed "metaphysicism" or "metahistoricism." Perhaps it is time we treated it with the justice it deserves. Other formalists have probably run this risk, but not Wölfflin. On the contrary, if he is to be accused of anything, it would have to be an over-attachment to the idea of the historicity of style. Or rather, to an evolutionary continuity between styles so that, for example, the classical-baroque opposition of "linear"/"pictorial," "surface"/"depth," "open form"/"closed form,"

"multiplicity"/"unity," "absolute clarity"/"relative clarity," is conceived as a kind of historical rhythm or cadence.[65]

Such culturological readings of Wölfflin inevitably intersect the highly controversial question of the historicity of perception and of the permeability of the perceptual system by cultural conditioning: a question that in the writings of the Swiss art historian remained open, suffering, particularly in *Grundbegriffe* and in the 1933 "Revision," from a peculiar oscillation between the historicity of forms of vision (*Sehen*) and that of forms of representation (*Darstellung*).[66] This oscillation was resolved in an antipodal way by Panofsky[67] and by Walter Benjamin (who had been a pupil of Wölfflin in Munich in 1915).[68] In subsequent decades it has assumed various inflections: Michael Baxandall's notion of the "period eye," Marx Wartofsky's historical epistemology, Martin Jay's "scopic regimes," Jonathan Crary's attempt to discuss the historicity of vision in the context of the history of optical devices.[69] In recent years the question has also been addressed from the perspective of analytical philosophy and inspired a debate published in 2001 in the *Journal of Aesthetics and Art Criticism*.[70] The debate was translated into Italian by Michele di Monte, who is strongly critical of the possibility of a history of perception somehow correlated to a history of representational forms.[71]

I agree that it is a highly controversial issue, but at the same time — following Wölfflin and Riegl against Panofsky — I judge it quite naive to rigidly separate natural perception and cultural representation. I therefore prefer to speak of a historicity of "visibility" or of "the gaze" rather than of "vision." In my works I have tried to assess the hybrid character of Wölfflin's (and Riegl's) transcendental historicism — or historical transcendentalism — as a way to investigate at the same time the conditions of possibility of our sensible experience of images and their constitutively historical nature. This approach particularly stresses Wölfflin's and Riegl's phenomenological description of a pragmatics of the image, namely, an iconic agency that can invite beholders to a closer look or distance them from the picture: an apparently basic dialectics of near/far that can nevertheless assume complex syntactic, semantic, and symbolic implications.[72]

Notwithstanding the variety of the nonidealist approaches just examined, it is evident that Wölfflin's reception from the second half of the twentieth century to today is characterized by a reevaluation of the status and nature of his schemas. In the wake of a reformulation of the Kantian transcendental aesthetics promoted by phenomenology and other contemporary philosophical trends, the schemas no longer appear as abstract superimpositions threatening the irreducible singularity both of works of art and of artists but rather as modulations of the perceptual attitudes of the living body, as articulations of *aisthesis*, our sensible experience, which is always operating when we open our eyes to the world (and the art world).

NOTES

1. Heinrich Wölfflin, *Concetti fondamentali della storia dell'arte: La formazione dello stile nell'arte moderna*, trans. Rodolfo Paoli, introduction by Giusta Nicco Fasola (Milan, 1953, 1984, 1994; Vicenza, 1999).

2. Hohenemser had envisaged including in the volume a translation of the three essays collected in the chapter "Grundbegriffe" of Wölfflin's *Gedanken zur Kunstgeschichte: Gedrucktes und Ungedrucktes* (Basel, 1940), 7–24, together with the preface planned by Wölfflin for the new (eighth) edition of *Kunstgeschichtliche Grundbegriffe* (Munich, 1943). See Hohenemser to Wölfflin, February 11, September 28, and December 27, 1942; NL 95; IV, Briefe an Heinrich Wölfflin, Universitätsbibliothek Basel, Nachlass Heinrich Wölfflin, Handschriftenabteilung.

3. Giusta Nicco Fasola, "Presentazione," in Wölfflin, *Concetti fondamentali* (1984), 11–28, here 11: "Non c'è più da temere che si cada nei suoi schematismi.…Nessuna critica è più imperniata sopra *concetti, tipi, schemi* di analogia wölffliniana.…I concetti figurativi debbono modellarsi sulle opere, debbono cioè essere illimitati di numero e sempre rinnovati com'è della realtà dell'arte."

4. Heinrich Wölfflin, *Principles of Art History: The Problem of the Development of Style in Early Modern Art*, trans. Jonathan Blower, ed. Evonne Levy and Tristan Weddigen (Los Angeles, 2015), 311.

5. "'Kunstgeschichtliche Grundbegriffe': Eine Revision," *Logos: Internationale Zeitschrift für Philosophie der Kultur* 22 (1933): 210–218; published in Italian as Wölfflin, "Nota finale," in *Concetti fondamentali* (1984), 471–484. Another essay belonging to the section "Grundbegriffe" in Wölfflin's *Gedanken zur Kunstgeschichte* ("Über Formentwicklung," 8–15) has been translated by Andrea Pinotti under the title "Sullo sviluppo della forma," in *I percorsi delle forme*, ed. Maddalena Mazzocut-Mis (Milan, 1997), 102–114.

6. Heinrich Wölfflin, *Rinascimento e barocco: Ricerche intorno all'essenza e all'origine dello stile barocco in Italia*, trans. Luigi Filippi from the 1908 edition (Florence, 1928); *L'arte classica del Rinascimento*, trans. Rodolfo Paoli from the 1904 edition (Florence, 1941); *Avvicinamento all'opera d'arte*, trans. and ed. Umberto Barbaro (Milan, 1948). A new Italian edition of the last has recently been published under the title *Capire l'opera d'arte*, ed. Andrea Pinotti (Rome, 2015).

7. Paolo D'Ancona and Fernanda Wittgens, *Antologia della moderna critica d'arte: Letture complementari per l'insegnamento della storia dell'arte nei licei* (Milan, 1927).

8. See Francesca Pizzi, "Paolo D'Ancona e l'Istituto di Storia dell'Arte della Statale di Milano (1908–1957)," *Acme — Annali della Facoltà di Lettere e Filosofia dell'Università degli Studi di Milano* 63, no. 3 (2010): 243–292.

9. See Matteo Marangoni, *Saper vedere* (Milan and Rome, 1933), 113n1.

10. Roberto Salvini, ed., *La critica dell'arte moderna: La pura visibilità* (Florence, 1949), 181–212; reprinted under the title *La critica d'arte della pura visibilità e del formalismo* (Milan, 1977), 187–218. French edition: *Pure visibilité et formalisme dans la critique d'art du début du XXe siècle* (Paris, 1988).

11. Salvini, "Introduzione," in *La critica d'arte della pura visibilità e del formalismo*, 7–61, here 35: "il problema per noi così essenziale del giudizio di valore, ossia della distinzione fra arte e non-arte."

12. Salvini, "Introduzione," in *La critica d'arte della pura visibilità e del formalismo*, 7–61, here 50: "Linea, pittoricità, forma chiusa e forma aperta, e così via, sono schemi che possono apparire vuoti quando vengono teorizzati dal Wölfflin come principi dello svolgimento storico delle forme. Ma si fanno viva realtà quando l'autore li esamina nella singola opera d'arte o li segue nel loro diverso atteggiarsi attraverso l'opera di un artista."

13. These were subsequently collected in Croce's *Nuovi saggi di estetica* (Bari, 1920) and *La critica e la storia delle arti figurative: Questioni di metodo* (Bari, 1934) and are now in *Edizione nazionale delle opere*

di Benedetto Croce: Nuovi saggi di estetica, ed. Mario
Scotti (Naples, 1991), 215–261.

14. Benedetto Croce, *Kleine Schriften*, ed. Julius von
Schlosser (Tübingen, 1929), 2:191–212.

15. Croce, "La teoria dell'arte come pura visibilità" (1911), in *Nuovi saggi di estetica* (Naples, 1991),
215–230, here 223–224: "Il concetto di 'visibilità'
e quello di 'occhio produttore' si svelano, a chi ben
guardi, come nient'altro che metafore e simboli, ricchi
di efficacia polemica in quanto stanno a negare che
l'arte si risolva nella conoscenza concettuale, nella
imitazione della natura o nella emotività sentimen-
tale, ma poveri di determinazioni positive per ciò che
concerne l'arte, e grossamente falsi, se poi metafora e
simbolo vengano scambiati per definizioni filosofiche.
L'organo fisiologico, l'occhio, e il processo fisiologico
della visione, essendo concetti fisiologici e naturalistici,
non consentono alcun passaggio al concetto filosofico
dell'arte, che è attività spirituale."

16. Croce, "Un tentativo eclettico nella storia delle arti
figurative" (1919), in *Nuovi saggi di estetica*, 231–236,
here 233: "Ma che una siffatta idea della storia
dell'arte sia non tanto formalistica quanto *dualistica*,
non richiede sforzo di dimostrazione: è confessato
dall'autore stesso, con la sua 'doppia radice,' e coi suoi
'valori espressivi,' ai quali si aggiungerebbero (da essi
'indeducibili') valori 'meramente formali' e 'inespres-
sivi.' E non richiede nemmeno confutazione, perché
è una posizione estetica già sorpassata e confutata
nella storia dell'Estetica, e che rimanda a una generale
posizione filosofica, della quale si scorge ormai,
agevolmente, l'inconcepibilità e la contradizione."

17. Heinrich Wölfflin, "Das Problem des Stils in der
bildenden Kunst," *Sitzungsberichte der Königlich
Preussischen Akademie der Wissenschaften* 31 (1912):
572–578.

18. Erwin Panofsky, "Das Problem des Stils in der
bildenden Kunst," *Zeitschrift für Ästhetik und allgemeine Kunstwissenschaft* 10 (1915): 460–467, here
467: "Das individuelle Ausdrucksstreben, das den
einzelnen Künstler zu einer nur ihm eigentümlichen
Formgebung und zu einer persönlichen Auffassung
oder Bestimmung des Gegenstandes führt, äußert sich
zwar in allgemeinen Formen, aber diese selbst sind
ihrerseits nicht weniger aus einem Ausdrucksstreben
hervorgegangen: aus einem der ganzen Epoche
gewissermaßen immanenten Gestaltungs-Willen, der
in einer grundsätzlich gleichen Verhaltungsweise der
Seele, nicht des Auges, begründet ist."

19. Croce, "Un tentativo eclettico nella storia delle
arti figurative," 234–235: "Gli occhi che vedono
diversamente sono, invece, l'anima che sente e sogna e
vagheggia diversamente; e questo bisognava indagare,
e stabilire l'unità di quel nuovo sentire e di quel nuovo
moto della linea."

20. Croce, "Un tentativo eclettico nella storia delle
arti figurative," 236: "E, quando dalle astrazioni si
vuol passare alla realtà, sotto quelle distinzioni conc-
ettuali si ritrovano non più distinzioni di pura forma,
ossia estetica, ma distinzioni tra contenuti psichici, tra
diversi modi di sentire, cioè si ritorna a

quelle considerazioni sulla *Gesinnung*, sulla dispo-
sizione d'animo, dalle quali si era creduto di allon-
tanarsi per seguire la storia della forma artistica, della
Darstellung; vicenda ineluttabile, perché, com'è noto,
nell'astrazione va perduto il nesso dialettico di conte-
nuto e forma, e si finisce coll'avere sempre nelle mani,
invece dell'arte, questa o quella parte della sua astratta
materia."

21. Karl Vossler to Benedetto Croce, Munich, July 29,
1920, in *Carteggio Croce–Vossler: 1899–1949*, ed.
Emanuele Cutinelli Rèndina, *Edizione nazionale delle
opere di Benedetto Croce* (Naples, 1991), 275–276:
"Nun soll ich Dir auch noch im Namen von Wölfflin
danken. Er ist etwas spät dazu gekommen, Deine
Kritik seiner Bücher zu lesen, und bittet mich, ihn
bei Dir zu entschuldigen. Auf Diskussionen, meint
er, werdest Du wohl keine Zeit und Lust haben Dich
einzulassen, und halt gegenseitige Bekehrungen für
aussichtslos. Er glaubt, Du habest für seine besonderen
Forschungsabsichten kein Interesse; Dir sei es um
ästhetische Begriffe, ihm aber nur um die Abfolge der
Sehformen zu tun. Wenn er nicht selbst schreibt, so
liegt es an seiner Schwerfälligkeit in diesen Dingen,
nicht an einem Mangel der Höflichkeit oder des guten
Willens. Kurz, er läßt vielmals grüßen und danken."

22. For an exhaustive overview see Vittorio Stella, *Il
giudizio dell'arte: La critica storico-estetica in Croce e
nei crociani* (Macerata, 2005).

23. On Longhi, Wölfflin, and the Vienna School see
Ezio Raimondi, *Barocco moderno: Roberto Longhi e
Carlo Emilio Gadda* (Milan, 2003), in particular the
chapters "Il cerchio e l'ellisse" and "Le equivalenze
verbali." See also Giovanni Previtali, ed., *L'arte di
scrivere sull'arte: Roberto Longhi nella cultura del
nostro tempo* (Rome, 1982).

24. See Cesare Garboli, "Breve storia del giovane
Longhi" (1988), in Roberto Longhi, *Breve ma veridica
storia della pittura italiana* (Milan, 2001), V–XLVI,
here XII.

25. Longhi, *Breve ma veridica storia della pittura
italiana*, 9: "Mentre il poeta trasfigura per via di linguaggio l'essenza psicologica della realtà, il pittore ne
trasfigura l'essenza visiva: il sentire per l'artista figurativo non è altro che il vedere e il suo stile, cioè l'arte
sua, si costruisce tutto quanto sugli elementi lirici della
sua visione."

26. Longhi, *Breve ma veridica storia della pittura
italiana*, 10–12.

27. Roberto Longhi, review of Enzo Petraccone, *Luca
Giordano: Opera postuma* (Naples, 1919), *L'arte*
23 (1920): 92–93; reprinted in *Scritti giovanili:
1912–1922, Edizione delle opere complete*, 2 vols.
(Florence, 1961), 1:455–460, here 458: "La critica bio-
cronologica è dunque un sussidio quasi fisico, e mai
intellettuale, a quella critica figurativa che potrebbe
benissimo essere concepita — come del resto l'ha
recentemente preconizzata il Wölfflin — in forma di
'Kunstgeschichte ohne Namen,' di una storia dell'arte
senza nomi; ed io aggiungo senza date."

28. Heinrich Wölfflin, "Preface [1915]," in *Principles of Art History* (2015), 72; Wölfflin, "In eigener Sache: Zur Rechtfertigung meiner 'Kunstgeschichtlichen Grundbegriffe'" (1920), in *Gedanken zur Kunstgeschichte: Gedrucktes und Ungedrucktes*, 15–18, here 15.

29. Heinrich Wölfflin, "Italien und das deutsche Formgefühl," *Logos: Internationale Zeitschrift für Philosophie der Kultur* 10 (1921–1922): 251–260; *Italien und das deutsche Formgefühl* (Munich, 1931). The book has been published in Italian as *L'arte del Rinascimento: L'Italia e il sentimento tedesco della forma*, ed. Maurizio Ghelardi, trans. Bernardetta Carta (Livorno, 2001). Giulio Carlo Argan (1909–1992), professor of art history at the University of Rome–La Sapienza (1959–1976) had been a pupil of Giusta Nicco Fasola in Turin. For his review see *La cultura* 10, no. 8 (1931): 660–663.

30. Roberto Longhi, *Arte italiana e arte tedesca* (Florence, 1941); reprinted in *Arte italiana e arte tedesca con altre congiunture fra Italia ed Europa: 1939–1969*, vol. 9 of *Edizione delle opere complete* (Florence, 1979), 3–21, here 13: "[I]l binomio 'chiaro–non chiaro,' 'bestimmtes–unbestimmtes,' trovato dal Wölfflin per giustificare opere di questa fatta, a noi sembra piuttosto dilemma da non risolvere, in quei punti, altro che con un giudizio negativo per il secondo termine. In ogni caso la diversificazione linguistica Germania-Italia…si fa qui sempre più forte; di essa proprio il Wölfflin ha dato la più famosa esegesi. Come sempre però, quando si astrae dalle persone artistiche a favore degli schemi formali, essa è troppo apodittica. E, per esserlo più a fondo, è tenuta a dimenticare molt'altri aspetti dell'arte nostra, nulla affatto secondari e che anzi, aggiungendosi ai precedenti, stanno a riprova di una complessità sintattica senz'altri esempi."

31. Benedetto Croce, review of Roberto Longhi, *Arte italiana e arte tedesca* (Florence, 1941), *La critica* 40 (1942): 161–162.

32. Helmut Goetz, *Intellektuelle im faschistischen Italien: Denk- und Verhaltensweisen* (Hamburg, 1997); Giorgio Boatti, *Preferirei di no: Le storie dei dodici professori che si opposero a Mussolini* (Turin, 2001).

33. Lionello Venturi, "Gli schemi del Wölfflin," *L'esame* 1, no. 1 (1922): 3–10; reprinted in Lionello Venturi, *Pretesti di critica* (Milan, 1929), 25–35; Venturi, "La pura visibilità e l'estetica moderna," *L'esame* 2, no. 2 (1923): 73–88; reprinted in *Pretesti di critica*, 3–23.

34. Venturi, "Gli schemi del Woelfflin," 82: "Ebbene, gli schemi sono mezzi pratici per orientarci nel gran mare dell'arte, classificazioni provvisorie, modi di intendersi. E come tali esercitano la loro funzione precisamente in quel periodo preparatorio del giudizio critico, che corrisponde alla interpretazione dell'opera d'arte giudicanda."

35. Venturi, "Gli schemi del Woelfflin," 83: "Ci possono dunque essere schemi sbagliati, perché *inventati* dal critico senza rapporto con l'opera d'arte per cui sono stati inventati; e schemi giusti, perché tenuti presenti dall'artista nel momento della creazione e *ritrovati* dal critico."

36. Lionello Venturi, *History of Art Criticism* (New York, 1936), 290. For the first Italian edition see *Storia della critica d'arte* (Rome, Florence, Milan, 1945).

37. Wölfflin, "Preface [1915]," in *Principles of Art History* (2015), 75.

38. Carlo Antoni, "Heinrich Wölfflin" (1935), in *From History to Sociology: The Transition in German Historical Thinking*, with a foreword by Benedetto Croce, trans. Hayden V. White (Westport, CT, 1959), 207–228, here 222–223.

39. Michele Guerrisi, *L'idea figurativa* (Milan, 1952), 246: "Idee non interamente chiare, in cui si ritrovano insieme confusi concetti puramente fisiologici (*il tatto, l'occhio*), e concetti filosofici (*le cose prese per sé*), qualificazioni storiche (*il classico*), e concezioni spaziali geometriche (*lo spazio e la superficie*), elementi di rappresentazione figurativa (*il profilo*) e di qualificazioni critiche (*l'accento sui limiti della cosa*)." On Guerrisi see Walter Canavesio, "Michele Guerrisi e i *Discorsi*: Il punto di vista crociano sulla scultura," *Annali di critica d'arte* 11 (2015): 203–251.

40. Stefano Bottari, *La critica figurativa e l'estetica moderna* (Bari, 1935); *I miti della critica figurativa: Introduzione alla critica e alla storia dell'arte* (Messina and Milan, 1936); *Il linguaggio figurativo* (Messina, 1940); *Momento della critica d'arte contemporanea* (Messina and Florence, 1968).

41. The introduction to *L'arte classica* was reprinted under the title "Heinrich Wölfflin," in Bottari, *Momento della critica d'arte contemporanea*, 210–227, here 223: "Ma la storia dell'arte è fatta di 'persone' e non già di 'cose,' o di cose che sono tutt'insieme persone. Questo è il limite del procedere wölffliano, ed è limite che s'accompagna ad ogni procedimento naturalistico, per cui ogni caratterizzazione viene ad assumere valore classificatorio e lo svolgimento storico si scolora nell'anonima impassibilità di un'evoluzione necessaria."

42. See Raffaele Bruno, ed., *Ragghianti critico e politico* (Milan, 2004) and the contributions on Ragghianti collected in *Predella* 28 (2010), http://www.predella.it/index.php/cerca/2001–2012-new.html.

43. Valentina La Salvia, ed., *I critofilm di Carlo L. Ragghianti: Tutte le sceneggiature* (Lucca, 2006).

44. Alois Riegl, *Arte tardoromana*, trans. and ed. Licia Collobi Ragghianti (Turin, 1959). See Gianni Carlo Sciolla, "Carlo Ludovico Ragghianti e la Scuola di Vienna," *teCLa: Rivista di temi di critica e letteratura artistica* 1 (2010): 8–28. Carlo Ludovico Ragghianti, "Il significato dell'opera di Konrad Fiedler," in Konrad Fiedler, *L'attività artistica: Tre saggi di estetica e teoria della "pura visibilità,"* trans. Carlo Sgorlon, preface by Carlo Ludovico Ragghianti (Vicenza, 1963), 7–43.

45. Carlo Ludovico Ragghianti, "Sul metodo nello studio dei disegni," *Le arti* 3 (1940–1941): 9–19; reprinted in Ragghianti, *Commenti di critica d'arte* (1946), 203–241, here 217.

46. Joseph Gantner, ed., *Jacob Burckhardt und Heinrich Wölfflin: Briefwechsel und andere Dokumente ihrer Begegnung, 1882–1897* (Basel, 1948).

47. Carlo Ludovico Ragghianti, "Burckhardt e Woelfflin" (1952), in *Diario critico: Capitoli e incontri di estetica critica linguistica* (Vicenza, 1957), 33–38, here 38: "La critica d'arte si allineava sulla cultura del positivismo naturalistico e psicologico, si disperdeva sempre più l'attenzione al problema della personalità e dell'arte come autonoma attività spirituale e l'analisi delle opere d'arte diveniva sempre più riduzione dei linguaggi particolari a schemi generali, classificazioni."

48. Carlo Ludovico Ragghianti, "Schemi woelffliniani e leggi fonetiche" (1954), in *Diario critico*, 174–179, here 176: "La sua 'storia delle forme' lasciava fuori l'esistenza degli 'stili personali' ed anche di quelli che gli apparivano ancora come 'stili locali' (o nazionali), e che noi possiamo interpretare come tradizioni pittoriche col senso che diamo al concetto di tradizione letteraria."

49. Arnold Hauser, *The Philosophy of Art History* (New York, 1959), 123, 124.

50. Carlo Ludovico Ragghianti, "Woelfflin," in *La critica della forma* (Florence, 1986), 86–98, here 87 and 90: "Riesce quasi impossibile capire come il Woelfflin poesse fare affermazioni radicali come quelle di Comte. . . . Era giusto rivendicare che il vedere come tale aveva la sua storia, . . . ma predeterminato da un'evoluzione irreversibile il vedere non era una storia, bensì una fatalità. . . . Il Woelfflin non si rese mai pieno conto di questa implicazione autoritaria e fideistica comportata dal suo sistema."

51. Benedetto Croce, review of Barna Occhini, *La critica* 41 (1943): 49–51.

52. Barna Occhini, "A proposito del Woelfflin (note polemiche sulla critica delle arti figurative)," *La rinascita* 5, no. 26 (1942): 407–424: "Restano, torno a dire, le astrazioni vive, vitali, e di esse ne ha formulate alcune delle più illuminanti il Woelfflin nei suoi libri *Rinascimento e Barocco*, *L'arte classica del Rinascimento* e *Concetti fondamentali della storiografia artistica*. E a me sembra che ora che si sono recuperate le premesse per un lavoro importante, si possa e si debba tornare con nuovo impegno, nella critica d'arte e nel resto, alle difficili 'idee generali,' alle ardite sintesi, alle costruzioni tipiche. Quelle che invitano a sollevarsi sopra il tritume del particolare, del momentaneo, del frammentario, delle sensazioni e riflessioni di un attimo. Sopra il pulviscolo atomico nel quale si compiace l'infantilismo mentale e morale di tanta parte della nostra cultura e civiltà."

53. Antonio Banfi, "Introduzione," in Konrad Fiedler, *Aforismi sull'arte*, trans. Rossana Rossanda (Milan, 1945), 7–67; reprinted in Antonio Banfi, *Vita dell'arte: Scritti di estetica e di filosofia dell'arte*, ed. Emilio Mattioli and Gabriele Scaramuzza (Reggio Emilia, 1988), 341–376, here 374: "La teoria della visibilità pura è ben lungi dal rendere conto dell'integrale struttura, della complessa tensione dell'arte e delle varie linee del suo sviluppo; i suoi schemi visivi sono, in realtà, tutt'altro che puri; pregni anzi di significati. Di ciò il Wölfflin s'è reso, come ognuno sa, ben conto, ma la revisione della sua posizione può completarsi piuttosto con un ritorno alla teoria fiedleriana dell'arte." See Andrea Pinotti, "Forma e intuizione: Banfi e Fiedler," in *Banfi e l'arte contemporanea*, ed. Sileno Salvagnini (Naples, 2012), 103–115.

54. Guido Morpurgo Tagliabue, *L'Esthétique contemporaine: Une enquête* (Milan, 1960), § 45 "E. Woelfflin," 133–137, here 136: "Avec Woelfflin, plus ouvertement encore qu'avec Hildebrand, nous assistons à l'apparition d'un double ou d'un triple plan de valeurs critiques. À une analyse de valeurs formelles, selon des catégories de visibilité toujours plus précisées, correspond une reconnaissance de valeurs physiologiques, de sentiments vitaux, selon le principe de la *Einfühlung*, qui mènent enfin à des valeurs morales, à des dispositions spirituelles."

55. Gillo Dorfles, *Artificio e natura* (Turin, 1968), 225–226: "Ammettere un fattore strutturale sotteso a ogni opera d'arte, considerata a sé stante, ma anche ad ogni prodotto d'un determinato periodo storico, dunque allo 'stile d'un'epoca,' mi sembra molto importante, in quanto ci permette di giustificare il perché d'una certa qual comunità di linguaggi entro lo stile di una stessa epoca. Questo fatto appare ovvio per le epoche storiche mentre appare meno evidente per la nostra. Bisogna peraltro tener conto che senza la dovuta prospettiva storica è assai arduo valutare quali e quanti siano e dove si possano individuare tali costanti strutturali d'un'epoca."

56. Heinrich Wölfflin, "Prolegomena to a Psychology of Architecture" (1886), in *Empathy, Form, and Space: Problems in German Aesthetics, 1873–1893*, ed. Harry F. Mallgrave and Eleftherios Ikonomou (Santa Monica, CA, 1994), 149–190, here 183. On this question see Frederic J. Schwartz, "Cathedrals and Shoes: Concepts of Style in Wölfflin and Adorno," *New German Critique* 76 (1999): 3–48.

57. Oskar Walzel, *Wechselseitige Erhellung der Künste* (Berlin, 1917); Paolo Paolini, "Le teorie critico-figurative di Heinrich Woelfflin e la storiografia letteraria italiana," *Aevum* 40, nos. 1–2 (1966): 75–101.

58. Renato Barilli, "XXVIII Biennale di Venezia," *Il verri* 1 (1956): 146–155.

59. The term "culturology" was coined by the American anthropologist Leslie A. White: see his *The Science of Culture* (New York, 1949), 115–117 and 409–415; Italian edition, *La scienza della cultura*, trans. Danila M. Cannella Visca (Florence, 1969). Culturology became a relevant methodological approach in post-Marxist Russia: see Jutta Scherrer, *Kulturologie: Russland auf der Suche nach einer zivilisatorischen Identität* (Göttingen, 2003). For the Italian context see Pietro Scotti, "Considerazioni epistemologiche sulla culturologia," *Accademia Ligure di Scienze e Lettere* 32 (1975); Nicola Siciliani de Cumis, *Italia-Urss/Russia-Italia: Tra culturologia ed educazione 1984–2001* (Rome, 2001).

60. Similarly, Gianni Carchia (1947–2000), professor of aesthetics at the universities of Viterbo and Rome 3, underlines Wölfflin's peculiar Kantianism: "This is not pure transcendentalism, but as it were a sort of 'transcendental empiricism,' since the material of intuition is the evidence of historically constituted horizons." ("Non è trascendentalismo puro, ma per così dire una sorta di 'empirismo trascendentale,' dal momento che il materiale dell'intuizione è l'evidenza degli orizzonti storici costituiti.") Gianni Carchia, "Fiedler e Wölfflin: Il problema della forma classica," *Rivista di estetica* 18 (1984): 55–73, here 70. See also a similar argument in Carchia, *Arte e bellezza: Saggio sull'estetica della pittura* (Bologna, 1995), 76.

61. Renato Barilli, *The Science of Culture and the Phenomenology of Styles*, trans. Corrado Federici (Montreal, 2012), 139. Published in Italian as *Culturologia e fenomenologia degli stili* (Bologna, 1982); 2nd ed., *Scienza della cultura e fenomenologia degli stili* (Bologna, 1991).

62. Marshall McLuhan quotes Wölfflin's *Principles* in *The Gutenberg Galaxy: The Making of Typographic Man* (Toronto, 1962), 41, 81, 117.

63. Barilli, *The Science of Culture and the Phenomenology of Styles*, 146.

64. Gillo Dorfles, *Architetture ambigue: Dal neobarocco al postmoderno* (Bari, 1984).

65. Omar Calabrese, *Neo-Baroque: A Sign of the Times* (1987), trans. Charles Lambert, with a foreword by Umberto Eco (Princeton, 1992), 18. According to Barilli, "several traces of Wölfflin's approach recur in the classic postwar text by Umberto Eco *The Open Work*"; see Renato Barilli, *A Course on Aesthetics* (1983), trans. Karen E. Pinkus (Minneapolis and London, 1993), 166.

66. See Bence Nanay, "The History of Vision," *Journal of Aesthetics and Art Criticism* 73, no. 3 (2015): 259–271.

67. Panofsky, "Das Problem des Stils in der bildenden Kunst," 464: "Wölfflin takes as it were literally a figurative expression: an art that interprets what is seen in the sense of the painterly or of the linear is an art which sees in a painterly or linear way. Since he does not realize that the concept, employed in this sense, no longer refers to the merely optical process, but rather to a psychic process, he has assigned to artistic-productive seeing the position reserved for natural-receptive seeing: a position which is underneath the expressive faculty." ("…die übertragene Ausdrucksweise: von einer Kunst, die Gesehenes im Sinne des Malerischen oder Linearen ausdeutet, zu sagen, daß sie linear oder malerisch sieht, nimmt Wölfflin sozusagen beim Wort, und hat — indem er nicht berücksichtigt, daß, so gebraucht, der Begriff gar nicht mehr den eigentlich optischen, sondern einen seelischen Vorgang bezeichnet — dem künstlerisch-produktiven Sehen diejenige Stellung angewiesen, die dem natürlich-rezeptiven gebührt: die Stellung unterhalb des Ausdrucksvermögens.")

68. Walter Benjamin, "The Work of Art in the Age of Its Technological Reproducibility" (1935–1936), in *The Work of Art in the Age of Its Technological Reproducibility, and Other Writings on Media*, ed. Michael Jennings, Brigid Doherty, and Thomas Y. Levin (Cambridge, MA, 2008), 23: "Just as the entire mode of existence of human collectives changes over long historical periods, so too does their mode of perception. The way in which human perception is organized — the medium in which it occurs — is conditioned not only by nature but by history. The era of the migration of peoples, an era which saw the rise of the late-Roman art industry and the Vienna Genesis, developed not only an art different from that of antiquity but also a different perception."

69. Michael Baxandall, *Painting and Experience in Fifteenth Century Italy: A Primer in the Social History of Pictorial Style* (Oxford, 1972); Marx W. Wartofsky, "Art History and Perception," in *Perceiving Artworks*, ed. John Fisher (Philadelphia, 1980), 23–41; Martin Jay, "Scopic Regimes of Modernity," in *Vision and Visuality*, ed. Hal Foster (New York, 1988), 3–23; Jonathan Crary, *Techniques of the Observer: On Vision and Modernity* (Cambridge, MA, 1990).

70. *The Journal of Aesthetics and Art Criticism* 59, no. 1 (2001). See the contributions by Arthur C. Danto ("Seeing and Showing," 1–9); Noël Carroll ("Modernity and the Plasticity of Perception," 11–17); Mark Rollins ("The Invisible Content of Visual Art," 19–27); and Whitney Davis ("When Pictures Are Present: Arthur Danto and the Historicity of the Eye," 29–38).

71. Michele Di Monte, "Se fossi nei tuoi occhi…," introduction to Arthur C. Danto, *La storicità dell'occhio: Un dibattito con Noël Carroll e Mark Rollins* (Rome, 2007), 7–25.

72. Andrea Pinotti, *Il corpo dello stile: Storia dell'arte come storia dell'estetica a partire da Semper, Riegl, Wölfflin* (Palermo, 1998; 2nd ed., Milan, 1991); "'Un altro sole': Storia delle immagini e storia della percezione," *Reti, saperi, linguaggi: Italian Journal of Cognitive Sciences* 1 (2015): 67–88; "Why Anonymizing the History of Images?," in *A History of Cinema without Names: A Research Project*, ed. Diego Cavallotti, Federico Giordano, and Leonardo Quaresima (Milan, 2016), 31–39; Andrea Pinotti, "Introduzione," in Heinrich Wölfflin, *Capire l'opera d'arte*, 5–23.

ADI EFAL-LAUTENSCHLÄGER

Latent Wölfflinian Stylistics in the Israeli Artistic Formation

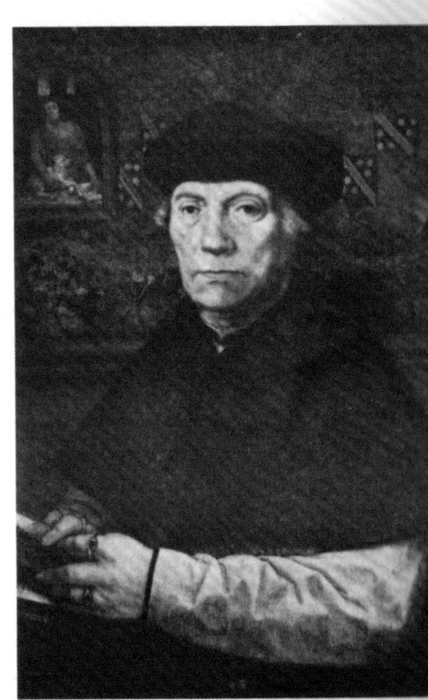

ירלי. דיוקנו של קאראנדולֶט

ג. התבוננות לפי עניינים

מי שרגיל אצל המאה הט״ו מרגיש כדבר חדש שעה שהוא רואה, כיצד נתחז־
קה עמידתו של המראה בדיוקנאותיהם של האמנים הקלאסיים. פיתוחם של
ניגודי־צורה חורצים, העמדת הראש בקו ניצב, צירופן של צורות־לוואי שנות־
נות סעד טקטוני, כגון אילנות קטנים סימטריים וכיוצא באלה — הכול עולה
בכוונה אחת. המתבונן, למשל, בדיוקנו של 'קאראנדולֶט' של בַּאר_ֶנְד וַאן־אוֹרְלִי,
יראה על־נקלה, כמה תפיסה זו תלויה באידיאל של מערכה טקטונית מוצקה,

[194]

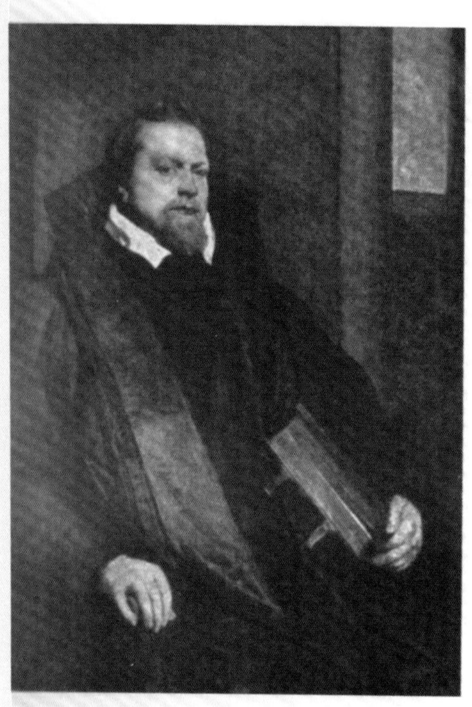

רובנס. דיוקנו

כמה מודגשת תקבולתם של הפה והעיניים והסנטר ועצם־הבריח, וכמה היא
מופרשת מן הכיוון הברור האנכי שכנגדה. הקו האופקי משוך על־ידי הכומתה
וחוזר ונשנה במוטיב של הזרוֹע המונחת ושל מעקה־הקיר ; הצורות הזקופות
נסמכות על קווי־הגובה של המלבֵּן. בכול אנו חשים את סמיכותם של הדמות
ושל הבסיס הטקטוני זו־לזה. הכל רצוף בתוך החלל בדרך, שהוא נראה קבוע
ולא בהיתק. רושם זה מתקיים גם במקום שהראש לא ניתן מפָנים, העמידה
הזקופה אינה פוסקת מלהיות הנורמה ; ולפי בחינה זו יובן, שאף חזיתיות־

[195]

1. Heinrich Wölfflin, *Musagei yesod be toldot haomanut*, trans. Nachman Ben-Ami, ed. and introduction by Moshe Barasch (Jerusalem: Mossad Bialik, 2003 (1962)

Courtesy Bialik Institute, Jerusalem

Working out a theme within the historiography of the Israeli humanities is not an easy matter: although the beginning of this history is relatively recent, a large part of it is either undocumented or inaccessible outside state archives. Moreover, one may say that in general the humanities are still in their initial stage of development in Israel, and this would be even truer for the discipline of art history, instituted in the country only in the last quarter of the twentieth century. Naturally, the use of Hebrew is central to the complexity of the situation, necessitating ample translation initiatives for an extremely limited circulation. An examination of the Hebrew translation of Heinrich Wölfflin's *Kunstgeschichtliche Grundbegriffe* in Israel must take this problematic platform into account. During the second half of the twentieth century one can detect in the teaching of the humanities in Israel an ambivalence toward incoming influences, an ambivalence whose roots are to be found in the continuity as well as the break of Zionism with the European legacy. There is no doubt that the corpus of German "Geisteswissenschaft" was primary and inevitable to the establishment and development of Israeli humanities curricula notwithstanding the recent horrific history of Germany. As for the discipline of art history, one can see almost no influence in the first generations of its development other than the German one, and within this canonical corpus, Wölfflin's *Grundbegriffe* was a cornerstone. Moreover, it was around the establishment and development of the Hebrew University of Jerusalem, instituted as early as 1925 and very much characterized by a German-speaking orientation, that the organization and consolidation of the Israeli academic system developed.[1]

The World Literature Masterpieces Project

In one of Jerusalem's industrial areas, among carpentry shops, garages, and furniture and electronics stores, are the offices of Mossad Bialik (Bialik Institute), one of Israel's distinguished academic publishers. The archive of the institute contains a letter dated October 28, 1957, to the prime minister of Israel, David Ben Gurion. The document, in eleven numbered paragraphs, attests to an enterprise taking shape between the U.S. secretary of state and the directors of the Bialik publishing house: a comprehensive translation initiative intended to create a Hebrew-language library of universal classics, an enterprise intended to serve general education by establishing a humanist canon for the Israeli public. The endeavor was rooted in cultural Zionism, which influenced deeply the philosophy of Martin Buber, the head of the committee directing the proposed project.[2] The conception of cultural Zionism, developed by the thinker Ahad Ha'am, viewed the movement as in essence a cultural undertaking, based on the synthesis of universal culture, the Jewish tradition, and, in Buber's later version, the Hebrew language. Viewed from that perspective, the world masterpieces series epitomized the ideal of cultural Zionism. Education from this orientation is conceived as a kind of a spiritual *Bildung*.[3] It must be universal, comprehensive, and comparative, providing insight into the treasures of human achievement. The letter was signed by Buber and two other members of the committee, Ben-Zion Dinur and Shimon Helkin.[4]

The Bialik publishing house was established in 1935 by the World Zionist Organization, the Histadrut, to promote the publication of distinguished prose and other literary forms.[5] Named after Haim Nachman Bialik, then the national poet of Israel, it was from early on associated with the Hebrew University of Jerusalem and, alongside the Magnes Press, has been considered the leading academic publisher in the country.

The letter noted a growing acknowledgment of the need to gather the best examples of thought and writing in world literature.[6] The signers acknowledged the work already accomplished in translating world masterpieces in the sciences and philosophy into Hebrew. Nevertheless, they wrote, these translations were produced without a preconceived plan, and the translated works were almost always chosen on the basis of commercial considerations rather than for their cultural or intellectual value. The directors of Mossad Bialik declared the necessity of instituting a generalized, state-supported translation enterprise, to be methodically planned and based exclusively on the intellectual merit of canonized masterpieces. The directorial committee, under Buber's leadership, furnished the scholarly standards for the enterprise, proclaiming the necessity not only of maintaining a high level of translation but also of supplying accompanying introductions and commentaries. In addition to being an educator and one of the central twentieth-century existential philosophers, Buber was active in political life in Israel, trying to realize the utopian ideal of an organic unity of society, of cultural, religious, and geopolitical cohesiveness.[7]

The Bialik committee determined that the translation enterprise should include creative and philosophical works that had made their mark on culture through the ages, books in which a turning point in the development of the human spirit could be identified because of the "truth" to be found in them, the emotional commitment and conceptual rigor invested in them, and their linguistically

expressive character, endowing them with special significance.[8] The universalist creed that directed the enterprise may be understood as a clear expression of the wish not only to connect the Hebrew reader to the history of world literature (as Erich Auerbach called it) but also to enable the Hebrew language itself to absorb the most carefully selected canonical expressions of intellect.[9] To this end, and with the intention of enriching the capacities of the Hebrew language, the letter continued, all translations were to be made from the original versions of the texts. Among the published or projected titles in the series were the *Bhagavad Gita;* works of Homer, Hesiod, Aeschylus, and Plutarch; Jacob Burckhardt (on Renaissance Italy) and Benedetto Croce (on European history); William James; Ignác Goldziher's *Vorlesungen über den Islam*; Immanuel Kant, Erich Auerbach, Montesquieu, John Dewey, Alexander von Humboldt, and Karl Mannheim; and Wölfflin's *Grundbegriffe,* the only representative of the domain of the visual arts. A contract between the Schwabe publishing house in Basel and Mossad Bialik, representing the World Zionist Organization, was signed in 1959, and the translation of Wölfflin's work (1962) took about three years to accomplish. The Bialik edition includes all images and is similar in design to the original (fig. 1).[10]

The Central Wölfflin Commentator: Moshe Barasch

The translator of the book, Nachman Ben-Ami, was a prolific translator of works not only in German but also in Czech and English, fiction and nonfiction.[11] He was, however, a freelance rather than a scholar of art history, so the academic aspect of the Wölfflin translation should be attributed not to him but rather to the scholarly editor of the volume, Moshe Barasch, who annotated the translation and added a methodological introduction.

Barasch was effectively the founder of the discipline of art history in Israel. He established the art history department at the Hebrew University of Jerusalem and became its first head in 1964, just after the translation of *Grundbegriffe* was published. Barasch, who was himself an autodidact, was responsible for the education of the first generations of art historians in the country, and among his many activities he was a regular contributor, board member, and advisor of the Bialik publishing house. Barasch was in his own right an intriguing, internationally acclaimed art historian and art theorist who produced widely known volumes on theory.[12] He also published a general introduction to art historiography in Hebrew, *Machshevet haomanut ba dorot haacharonim*, titled in English *Approaches to Art (1750–1959)* (1977), which is the first systematic and historical introduction to art historiography, preceding Michael Podro's *The Critical Historians of Art* by five years.[13] Barasch dedicated chapters to Johann Joachim Winckelmann, Johann Gottfried Herder, Jacob Burckhardt, Alois Riegl, Aby Warburg, Erwin Panofsky, Max Dvořák, and, naturally, Wölfflin. As the dominant figure in the history of art as a humanistic discipline in Israel, Barasch made historiography and questions of method central themes in his art-historical engagement. His relation to Wölfflin's work seems the most promising thread to follow in a historiographic look at the Hebrew Wölfflin translation.

Barasch's Understanding of Wölfflin

Barasch's general views of Wölfflin's art-historical method can be deduced both from the introduction to the translation of *Grundbegriffe* and from the chapter dedicated to Wölfflin in *Approaches to Art*.[14] As usual with Wölfflin's secondary reception, Barasch naturally underlines Wölfflin's alleged formalism and attributes it to a double tendency: on the one hand, to identify general laws in the development of styles and schemes of optical possibilities and, on the other, to lean on a descriptive, even impressionist approach to the examination of works of art. Wölfflin's formalism, indeed,

will lead us to the concluding parts of this essay.

Barasch observes in the introduction to the translation that, while assuming the role of a nonjudgmental kind of art history, Wölfflin's art history nevertheless retains a self-inflicted "undecideability" regarding the movement from classical to baroque art. As a follower of Winckelmann on this point, Wölfflin implicitly retains the classical Renaissance model as the primary given, from which the baroque derives as a reaction.[15] For Wölfflin as a follower of Goethe, notes Barasch, classical art expresses essential, "godly" necessity against the playful arbitrariness of the baroque style.[16]

Barasch's reception of Wölfflin takes the latter to be a thinker on classical form rather than the baroque per se. From a historiographic point of view, according to Barasch, the search for necessity in art-historical stylistic description and analysis stands at the heart of Wölfflin's endeavor, and therefore a special kind of rigid historicism issues from his system.[17] Wölfflin had a concept of history in which necessity precedes nominalist sensitivities to nuances and nonregularities of historical manifestations.[18] In this sense, one can consider *Grundbegriffe* as pertaining to the later generation of historicism, that of Ernst Troeltsch, in which the raw nominalist earlier version of historicism, which considered the singular contingent concreteness of historical reality as preceding any regularities or historical models and laws, was exchanged for a model of historical method ordered by a system of values (*Werte*), which are deduced a posteriori from the raw material of historical happening.[19]

Barasch identifies the philosophical influences and orientations of Wölfflin's method in Goethe, Burckhardt, Konrad Fiedler, and Croce, yet he also mentions the parallels one can establish between Wölfflin's method and the phenomenology of Edmund Husserl.[20] Barasch brings up widely discussed themes regarding Wölfflin's method. He concentrates on the "visual guidance" that Wölfflin's art history takes upon itself to provide for the history of art, being interested in the visibility of the work (*Sichtbarkeit*) while formulating the eye spirit (*Augengeist*) and the form spirit (*Formgeist*), serving as the basis for classifying individual works of art.[21] Barasch furthermore pays attention to what he views as a Kantian ingredient in Wölfflin's method, looking for the "optical possibilities" that the visual types carry with them and that serve as a transcendental basis for the history of art. The term "transcendental" is taken from Kantian philosophy, standing for an a priori infrastructure of phenomena, containing all possible patterns of appearance. In the context of art history, one can talk about "universal categories of art."[22] These optical universal, transcendental possibilities are genuinely expressed in works of art, and therefore Barasch suggests that, at least in its methodological aspiration, Wölfflin's model of art history could be secondarily characterized as an expressionist one.[23] Wölfflin's expressionism leans on intuition. Perceived images, *Anschauungsbilder*, are in fact what Wölfflin's art history distills from the demonstrative discussion of works of art, according to Barasch.[24]

Barasch allowed himself to treat Wölfflin's *Grundbegriffe* as something of an anachronistic art-historical method, and at the conclusion of the introduction, trying to sum up Wölfflin's place in the charts of art historiography, he quotes what Wölfflin himself wrote regarding his teacher, Burckhardt: "As the sun sets, so the brightness issuing from its rays is greater."[25] Therefore Barasch canonizes Wölfflin while pointing to the limitations of his method and to the fact that his suggestions are in decline rather than ascent in the current state of the discipline of the history of art. On the other hand, Barasch notes that many of the guidelines and principles that Wölfflin prescribed for the art-historical method still pose the greatest challenge to that method, as reflected in a coinage that may still be fitting today: "the Wölfflin problem."[26] As this volume demonstrates, Wölfflin's art history can, in fact, be viewed as an art-historiographical challenge, as it incubates our art-historical subconscious, informing our judgments and classifications of works even now.

The Barasch/Wölfflin Axis: Formalism and/or Iconology

Barasch's work as an art historian, far from being a formalist or purely stylistic analysis of works, was if anything iconological in its orientation. Moreover, according to his students, his teaching was not based on the image-to-image comparative method that *Grundbegriffe* has handed down to generations of art historians.[27] Most of his monographs fit well into an iconography-iconology framework. It seems that he developed some of his research in a direct dialogue with the work of Erwin Panofsky. For example, one can view Barasch's last book in art theory, *Icon: Studies in the History of an Idea*, which lays out the history of the apologetic theory of the icon, as a complementary volume to Panofsky's art-theoretical masterpiece, *Idea: Ein Beitrag zur Begriffsgeschichte der älteren Kunsttheorie*, which presented the history of the development of Western art theory as an apologetic response to Platonic iconoclasm.[28] And Barasch's thematic art-historical investigations, like the ones on blindness, despair, or the expression of emotion in Giotto, are rather iconologically oriented: they all deal with meanings to be found in recurring themes and motifs in the history of art.[29] Notwithstanding, Barasch's iconological orientation has its own peculiarities, which are not entirely free from Wölfflinian connotations. For example, unlike his art-theoretical works, Barasch's iconological works are more descriptive than textual: in most cases he does not attempt a detailed philological uncovering of the textual parallels of visual imagery but meticulously describes figures and compositional arrangements. Moreover, the motifs and themes that interested Barasch are expressive in their nature (despair, gesture, physiognomy), always reflecting some state of mind or affect.[30] In this sense, his iconology can be characterized as Warburgian in orientation, interested in some "pathetic," or, rather, empathic content to be found in works of art. The way in which forms are expressive of moods and states of mind is closer to the art-historical method Wölfflin was suggesting than to a rationally oriented Panofskyan iconology,[31] and perhaps even closer to Wölfflin's earlier studies on empathy in architecture.[32] Also like Wölfflin, Barasch was less interested in artists as individuals than in impersonal universal values in works of art.

In sum, I do not believe that Barasch's scholarly orientation and works supply us with the substance of a strong Wölfflinian influence in his art history. Nevertheless, the legacy of *Grundbegriffe* was obviously not absent from Barasch's oeuvre and teaching, and when one looks for direct textual evidence of reference to Wölfflin's historiography in Israel, Barasch's writings are the only available source. Even if there is no written evidence that Barasch was responsible for the decision to translate *Grundbegriffe*, he was undoubtedly actively engaged in the project.[33] Though he was not responsible for the overall organization of the world classics series and therefore was not the one to choose the art-historical masterpiece to be included, he was the only art historian in Israel who was competent enough in historiographical matters to take on its scholarly editing. One should remember that the head of the organizational committee, Martin Buber, himself had an art-historical education and aesthetic interests. According to Moshe Schwarz, Buber's aesthetics was influenced by the theories of Konrad Fiedler, which were also a source of Wölfflin's formalism of the seen, or "visibility of an appearance" (*Sichtbarkeit einer Erscheinung*).[34] Therefore, even if we do not know who selected Wölfflin's book for the Bialik series, surely we can determine that the orientation of Wölfflin's art history was woven into the interests of both Barasch and Buber.

A further possible reason for choosing to bring to the Hebrew reader the rather radical version of formalist art history is the existing translation of Ernst Gombrich's more concrete, historically oriented *The Story of Art*, which was translated into Hebrew as early as 1956 (by Am Oved, a leftist-oriented publishing house based near Tel Aviv, not in Jerusalem).[35] It may have seemed to the Bialik editors that a kind of a formalist balance was required.

For the moment one can suggest that Wölfflin's *Grundbegriffe* seemed an adequate text to promote the acknowledgment of the history of art among the humanities to a wider educated public. Moreover, given that the world masterpieces series was meant to reach the quasi-scholarly reader, it may well have been that *Grundbegriffe*, being composed almost without scholarly apparatus in a lively, fluent, demonstrative style and leaning on immediate visual observation and description, may have served as a good pioneer, being useful of course also to undergraduate courses in the universities and art academies.

Art Historians in Israel and the Subtle Diffusion of *Grundbegriffe*

It would take a wider frame of discussion to cover the entire map of second-generation art historians in Israel in order to determine what is Wölfflinian and what is not. Indeed, not every formalist method should be automatically counted as Wölfflinian: well-developed alternative formalist methods (for example, those of Alois Riegl or Clement Greenberg) for stylistic art history were and still are available and in use in art-historical practice. Yet I believe two central characteristics of Wölfflin's formalism make it a fitting prototype of formalist discourse, an incubator of many other versions of formalism: on the one hand, its direct applicative character, and, on the other, its meta-historiographical perspective. Unlike Riegl's formalism, for example, which is very elastic in its principles, always changing according to the subject in question and the historical reality discussed, Wölfflin's stays relatively constant and systematic throughout his writings. This makes Wölfflin's formalism more

2. Yehezkel Streichman, *Untitled*, c. 1968, oil on canvas

Tel Aviv Museum of Art, acquisition through a contribution from Joseph and Rebecca Meyerhoff, Baltimore, Maryland, 1975; photograph Elad Sarig. Courtesy Bialik Institute, Jerusalem

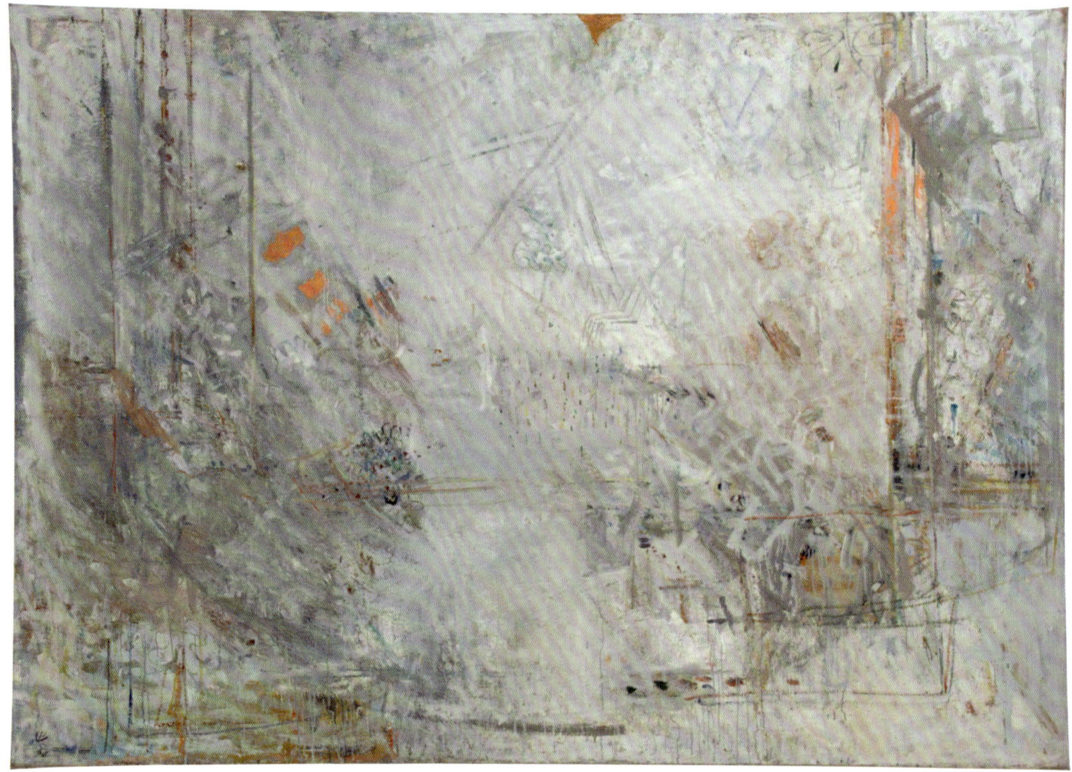

available to application, like a formula that can be implemented in different cases. Moreover, Wölfflin's formalism is not furnished specifically to give an account of modern art (unlike those of Greenberg or of Alfred Barr) but is rather conceived as a metaprinciple for the history of art at large. These two characteristics make Wölfflin's formalism what one may call art-historical formalism par excellence.

Returning to Israel, I look at a few examples that demonstrate the ambivalence of Wölfflin's presence in Israeli art history: the first entailing what can be seen as a direct influence through the Basel school, the second an indirect influence through the teachings of Barasch and the demands of formalist discourse on modern and Israeli art. This selection does not intend or pretend to be conclusive but is meant to serve as a historical sample that brings into view the latent presence of Wölfflin in Israeli art history.

Nurith Kenaan-Kedar, who was very influential in designating the orientation of the art history department at the University of Tel Aviv and whose legacy is still evident, wrote her doctoral dissertation at the University of Basel (1958–1964) under Joseph Gantner, Wölfflin's successor and follower. In her university teachings, stylistic formal analysis was the basis for any art-historical investigation. Kenaan-Kedar made Wölfflinian formal analysis historically meaningful, as style functioned for her as a first-order historical instrument. In this sense, from a methodological, art-historiographical point of view, Kenaan-Kedar's work remains faithful to the stylistic historicism found in Wölfflin's *Grundbegriffe*, which, as noted above, endows style with historical explanatory capacity. As a historian, Kenaan-Kedar worked mostly on medieval monumental sculpture and Christian art in general, from early to modern times.[36] If Wölfflin's formalist foundation was present in her lectures, in her writings one finds a more nuanced and complex picture: her works deal in many cases with historiographical questions, that is to say, questions of periodization and definitions of stylistic classifications of certain historical periods.[37]

Not only is historical periodization central in Kenaan-Kedar's works; so are questions of reading a work of art, referring explicitly to questions of the language of art, from a point of view based on methodological sources different from the Wölfflinian ones.[38] Many of the descriptions in her works begin with an identification of theme and then proceed to a detailed analysis of poses and gestures of figures, in a manner that is close to Barasch's physiological analysis of figures. Yet to my best observation, explicit use of Wölfflin's dual stylistic categories is not to be found in her books.

Considering the links of the Basel Gantner school to Israeli art history, it should be mentioned that Barasch himself was more than aware of the work of Joseph Gantner. In fact, in 1963, that is to say around the time the Hebrew translation of *Grundbegriffe* was published, Barasch devoted an essay to Gantner's concept of prefiguration, in which Barasch observed that "this theory is linked to the Wölfflin tradition, but raises its teachings to a higher plane than was reached in the original exposition."[39] He further observes that what Wölfflin conceived as "forms of representation" were developed by Gantner into the concept of "immaterial prefiguration," which Barasch conceived as a highly original and fruitful methodological tool in the history of art. What Gantner added and improved in the Wölfflinian model, according to Barasch, is the attention given to the formative, germinal stages of the work of art, making Wölfflinian formalism applicable to particular cases and to minute description of style formation.

In general, one should note that art theory and art historiography are still not accepted, either as integral and organic aspects of the Israeli consciousness in the history of art or in academic curricula. Art historians in Israel have tended to be suspicious of theoretical or methodological considerations in the discipline, or to make historiographical considerations in their works implicit rather than declared, notwithstanding the availability of influential historiographic works in translation. In this context, *Grundbegriffe* was taken as a pedagogical introduction to the history of art rather than as a theoretical piece in the full sense of the word. As such, it made sense to use it in art-historical pedagogy and heuristics.

One of the few examples of an Israeli art historian who deals explicitly with art-theoretical problems is one of Barasch's students at the Hebrew University of Jerusalem, Gila Ballas. Ballas's works encompass modern art theory and the history of modern art and Israeli art; she taught for many years at the University of Tel Aviv, and her work exhibits a latent character of Wölfflinian formal stylistics but in a different manner from the work of Kenaan-Kedar. Ballas's method is an interesting mixture of French morphology, which she absorbed during her doctoral and postdoctoral studies in Paris, and language that has its sources in Wölfflin's and in Barasch's reading of Wölfflin. In her book on the theory of color in modern painting, Ballas refers to Wölfflin's differentiation between classical and baroque as helpful in defining abstract art, in this case that of Piet Mondrian. Though Ballas herself came not from a Wölfflinian dynasty but rather from a French tradition of criticism, her written work is infused with detailed formalist description and analysis of composition, line, color, and so on.[40] Thus art-historical practice can combine competing and seemingly mutually exclusive methodological orientations.

Painterly Values: Ofakim Hadashim

In conclusion I propose another historical conjecture: why the publication of Wölfflin's *Grundbegriffe* was timely for its Israeli readership, or rather, why *Grundbegriffe* became relevant as an art-theoretical instrument at the beginning of the 1960s. This may have to do with the circumstances of the Israeli art scene at that time. The short history of Israeli visual arts exhibits an ongoing debate regarding the place of abstraction in art, a debate that in Israel assumes a special character deriving from the iconophobia implied in the Hebrew and Jewish sources.

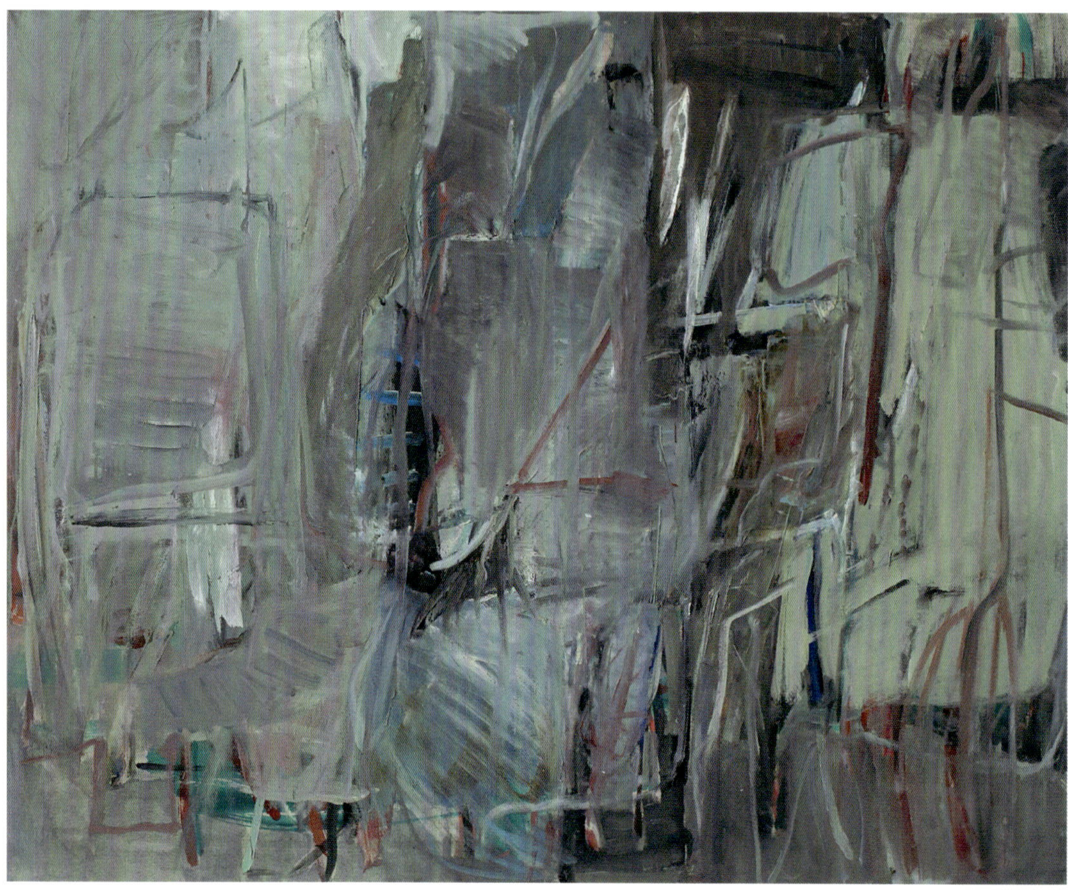

Between 1949 and 1963, the artists' group Ofakim Hadashim (New Horizons), led by Joseph Zaritsky and Yehezkel Streichman, dominated the field of Israeli art, orienting the development of formalist and abstract art and artistic discourse in Israel.[41] Its members promoted the values of a universal and abstract rather than a local and figurative language of art. Although one should be careful not to ascribe too much meaning to analogies between a book on the theory of art history and artistic practice, it seems that the theoretical duality of pure and passionate painterly values and classical tectonic order is often to be found in works by members of this group (fig. 2).

As the translation of *Grundbegriffe* appeared the year Ofakim Hadashim fell apart, there is no basis for assuming direct influence of the book on its artistic discourse. Notwithstanding, the vocabulary of the group was oriented toward finding a universal formalist visual grammar associated with the expression of sentiment.[42] And though the dominant impulse toward abstraction came from French art, and its most important art critic, Haim Gamzu, developed his vocabulary out of the tradition of French criticism,[43] one can see the translation of *Grundbegriffe* as accompanying the reception of abstraction in art. One of the group's members, Aharon Kahana, said in 1951: "It is no accident that in Hebrew the words 'simplicity' (*pashtut*) and 'abstraction' (*haphshatah*) share a common root."[44] This corresponds in a general way to Wölfflin's statement in *Grundbegriffe* that classical tectonics is rooted in the search for unity and simplicity, as opposed to the baroque tendency toward complexity and unclearness.[45]

The binding of classical art with simplicity did not begin with Wölfflin; certainly Winckelmann was the earlier and more prominent promoter of this view. Therefore, without in any way suggesting that Ofakim

Hadashim was influenced by Wölfflin, I would understand the publication of *Grundbegriffe* against the background of the development of abstract art in Israel. Israeli abstraction, as the paintings of Moshe Kupferman demonstrate, hands down to the scholar and to the critic a plethora of formal data calling for description, criticism, and interpretation. And the Wölfflinian vocabulary has had a part in the development of exchanges between artistic and scholarly practices (fig. 3). Ofakim Hadashim had its last official show in 1963, the year after the translation of *Grundbegriffe* was published. [46] Therefore one may suggest that the publication of *Grundbegriffe* announced the end, the sunset, of the era in which the Israeli mental habit conceived of itself as capable of maintaining a universal, modernist, and formal artistic creed. In this sense, *Grundbegriffe* came to Israel not as a precedent, a generator, or an influence on the development of abstract art but rather after abstract art had reached its apex and begun its decline, giving its place to a more American-influenced Pop Art. Wölfflin's text could have served as an a posteriori manifesto for pure painterly and stylistically oriented discussion of art, accommodating the development of art-historical research on artistic abstraction.

Wölfflinian Art Criticism and Stylistics: Oygen Kolb and Fritz Schiff

One voice directly connected to Wölfflin in Israeli art history is that of Oygen (Eugen) Kolb, an art critic and the director of the Tel Aviv Museum of Art from 1952 to 1959. [47] Kolb studied art history in Munich in 1919–1920, at the time Wölfflin was teaching there. [48] According to Galia Bar Or, Kolb's art criticism is permeated by Wölfflinian principles and observations, guided by the primacy of form and especially form as it is optically conceived, in both artistic and art-critical practice. [49] Moreover, Bar Or observes that Kolb was following Wölfflin's lead not only in the consideration of form and style but also

from the ideological point of view of finding a balance between a local or national character of art and the universality of visual form. [50] This ambivalence between local and universal also characterizes the creed of Ofakim Hadashim, the artistic movement to which Kolb dedicated most of his attention. Moreover, in an essay from 1955, whose title can be translated as "On the Problems of Explaining Works of Art," echoing Wölfflin's *Das Erklären von Kunstwerken*, Kolb asserted an intuitive, empathic understanding of a work of art as a precondition for any textual, historical grounding of its circumstances. [51] This comes close to the Wölfflinian attitude, making history not redundant, but rather dependent on the affect of the work of art. [52]

An example of less explicitly Wölfflin-related art criticism is Fritz Schiff's introduction to the catalog of an exhibition under his curatorship, from 1965 (just after the publication of the translation of *Grundbegriffe* and again, just after the dawn of Ofakim Hadashim abstraction and the opening of Israeli art to American influences and Pop Art). [53] Schiff had arrived in Palestine in 1936, having studied in Berlin and Munich from 1919 to 1921, when Wölfflin's influence was at its peak. The essay deals with the "possibility of an Israeli style," and most originally, in a manner that synthesizes Wölfflinian and later modernist-universalist formalisms, Schiff argues that there is no possibility of developing a genuinely Israeli formalism because modern art in general is based on the subjectivity of the artist, a globalized diffusion of ways of life, and secularization that dismantles the organic sacred place of art in society. This interesting critical constellation seems to set Wölfflinian formalism against its own premises. [54]

Conclusion

I suggest examining the Israeli reception of Wölfflin on two overlapping yet different levels: the organization and canonization of the Israeli humanities and the stylistic development of Israeli art, especially

painting and the discourse related to it, in
which one sees during the 1950s and 1960s
a tendency toward developing a language
that promotes pure artistic, formal, visual
values. At neither level can one say that in
Israel Wölfflin's reception has been either an
evident or a prominent one. Evonne Levy
has used the term "detheorization" to refer
to a *state* of theory, one in which it becomes
gradually latent and fundamental, that is
to say less and less discussed or criticized
explicitly, but more and more fundamental
and taken for granted. This process may
also be understood as a *naturalization* of a
concept or a set of concepts, or *habituation*
in the field of theory.[55] I believe that a detheorization has been taking place in Israel
regarding the place of Wölfflin's *Grundbegriffe*. In general it seems that Wölfflin's
work was secondary in both levels of discussion, playing a latent role, participating
in, but following rather than leading, the
development of both art-historical vocabulary and artistic stylistics. The reception of
Wölfflin came rather late, and it was part
of a general formalist tendency, having its
sources in numerous other traditions of art
theory and criticism, motivated by the flourishing of modern abstract art. Wölfflin's
formalism, nevertheless, seems to have met
the need within the history of art in Israel
to apply the formalist perspective to periods
other than the modern one: In this sense,
Wölfflin's stylistics may be considered as a
mediator between developing visual culture
and scholarly activity in the country. The
Hebrew version of *Grundbegriffe* has been
reissued by Mossad Bialik five times, the last
in 2003; thus the book is undoubtedly present, and its readership remains in place. It is
still to be seen whether a more rigorous historiographical consciousness in the history
of art will lead to further reappropriation
and retheorization of Wölfflin's work.

NOTES

1. Shaul Katz, Michael Heyd, and Hagit Levsky,
Toldot Hauniversita ha-ivrit be Yerushalaim (The
history of the Hebrew University in Jerusalem), 3 vols.
(Jerusalem, 1997–2009).

2. Martina Urban, "Ahad Ha'am's Theory of Culture
Revised," in *Aesthetics of Renewal: Martin Buber's
Early Representation of Hasidism as* Kulturkritik
(Chicago, 2008), 70–75.

3. See Rebekka Horlacher, *The Educated Subject
and the German Concept of* Bildung: *A Comparative
Cultural History* (New York, 2016).

4. Martin Buber was professor of the sociology of
culture at the Hebrew University of Jerusalem, a philosopher, and an educator. Ben-Zion Dinur was one
of the founders of the Hebrew University of Jerusalem,
head of its institute for Jewish studies, and dean of the
faculty of the humanities and in 1951 was appointed
national minister of education. See Katz, Heyd, and
Levsky, *Toldot Hauniversita ha-ivrit be Yerushalaim*,
1:153–158. Shimon Halkin was a literature scholar, a
poet, and a translator. In 1949 he became head of the
department of Hebrew literature at the Hebrew University of Jerusalem.

5. Bat Sheva Barack, *The Mossad Bialik Institute Jubi-
lee Catalogue, 1935–1985* (Jerusalem, 1985), III–VII.

6. My paraphrase from the Hebrew source.

7. See Dan Avnon, "Dialogue as Politics: Zionism
and the (Mis)Meeting of Bible, History, Philosophy,
and Politics," in *Martin Buber: The Hidden Dialogue*
(Lanham, MD, 1998), 179–214.

8. My translation.

9. Erich Auerbach, "Philologie der Weltliteratur,"
in *Weltliteratur: Festgabe für Fritz Strich zum 70.
Geburtstag*, ed. Walter Muschg and Emil Staiger (Bern,
1952), 39–50.

10. Heinrich Wölfflin, *Musagei yesod be toldot
haomanut* (*Principles of Art History*) (Jerusalem, 1963).

11. His other translations include the works of
Heinrich Boel and Erich Fromm.

12. Moshe Barasch, *Theories of Art 1: From Plato
to Winckelmann* (New York, 2000); Moshe Barasch,
Theories of Art 2: From Winckelmann to Baudelaire
(New York, 2000); Moshe Barasch, *Theories of Art 3:
From Impressionism to Kandinsky* (New York, 2000).

13. Moshe Barasch, *Machshevet haomanut ba dorot
haacharonim* (titled in English, *Approaches to Art,
1750–1950*) (Jerusalem, 1977); Michael Podro, *The
Critical Historians of Art* (New Haven, 1982).

14. Moshe Barasch, "Koroteyhem shel Ofney-ha-Re-
ie-ya" (The history of modes of seeing: On Wölfflin's
method of viewing the history of art," in Wölfflin,
Musagei yesod, 11–37; Moshe Barasch, "Torat ha-
Signon shel Wölfflin" (Woelfflin's theory of style),
in *Machshevet haomanut ba dorot haacharonim*,
119–135.

15. Barasch, "Torat ha-Signon shel Wölfflin," 132–133.

16. Barasch, "Torat ha-Signon shel Wölfflin," 131.

17. Barasch, "Koroteyhem shel Ofney-ha-Re-ie-ya," 29.

18. Barasch, "Torat ha-Signon shel Wölfflin," 134–135. See also Heinrich Wölfflin, *Das Erklären von Kunstwerken, mit einem Nachwort des Verfassers* (Cologne, 1940), 48.

19. Ernst Troeltsch, *Der Historismus und seine Überwindung: Fünf Vorträge* (Berlin, 1924).

20. Barasch, "Torat ha-Signon shel Wölfflin," 126n24.

21. Barasch, "Torat ha-Signon shel Wölfflin," 123.

22. See, for example, Michael Ann Holly, *Panofsky and the Foundations of Art History* (Ithaca, 1984), 95–96.

23. Barasch, "Koroteyhem shel Ofney-ha-Re-ie-ya," 16.

24. Barasch, "Koroteyhem shel Ofney-ha-Re-ie-ya," 15.

25. Barasch, "Koroteyhem shel Ofney-ha-Re-ie-ya," 37.

26. Barasch, "Koroteyhem shel Ofney-ha-Re-ie-ya," 35.

27. I am most grateful to Professor Luba Freedman of the Hebrew University of Jerusalem, Barasch's personal assistant, who introduced me to the history of his teaching, thought, and research during an interview at the Hebrew University of Jerusalem, September 1, 2015. I am also most grateful for her comments and assistance in shaping this essay.

28. Moshe Barasch, "Character and Physiognomy: Bocchi on Donatello's St. George; A Renaissance Text on Expression in Art," *Journal of the History of Ideas* 36 (1975): 413–430; Moshe Barasch, *Icon: Studies in the History of an Idea* (New York, 1992); Erwin Panofsky, *Idea: Ein Beitrag zur Begriffsgeschichte der älteren Kunsttheorie* (Berlin, 1924), 1–16. (English translation, *Idea: A Concept in Art Theory*, 1968.)

29 Moshe Barasch, *Gestures of Despair in Medieval and Early Renaissance Art* (New York, 1976); Moshe Barasch, *Giotto and the Language of Gesture* (Cambridge, 1987); Moshe Barasch, *Imago Hominis: Studies in the Language of Art* (Vienna, 1991).

30. On Barasch's scholarly range and interests, see Luba Freedman, "Thinking in Images: In Memoriam Moshe Barasch," *Artibus et Historiae* 52 (2005): 10–11.

31. On Panofskyan iconology, see, for example Holly, *Panofsky and the Foundations of Art History*; Adi Efal-Lautenschläger, *Habitus as Method: Revisiting a Scholastic Theory of Art* (Leuven 2017), 3–72.

32. Heinrich Wölfflin, "Prolegomena zu einer Psychologie der Architektur" (PhD diss., Universität München, 1886); published in English as "Prolegomena to a Psychology of Architecture," in *Empathy, Form, and Space: Problems in German Aesthetics, 1873–1893*, ed. Robert Vischer et al., trans. and intro. Harry Francis Mallgrave and Eleftherios Ikonomou (Santa Monica, CA, 1994).

33. Barasch was a member of the executive committee, the committee for scholarly and research books, the committee for introductory series, and the board of directors of the Bialik Institute. See Barak, *Bialik Institute*, VIII–X.

34. Moshe Schwarz, "Buber's Esthetics," in *Language, Myth, Art: Studies in Modern Jewish Thought* (Tel Aviv, 1966), 311–315. On Wölfflin and Fiedler see Barasch, "Koroteyhem shel Ofney-ha-Re-ie-ya," 14–15; see also Gianni Carchia, "Fiedler e Wölfflin: Il problema della forma classica," *Rivista di estetica* 24, 18 (1984): 55–73.

35. Ernst Gombrich, *Korot ha-omanut*, trans. Arie Lerner and Hanoch Kalai (Tel Aviv, 1956).

36. Nurith Kenaan-Kedar, *Tehiyato shel Hapisul Hamunomentaly be-Eropa* (The revival of monumental sculpture in Europe (Tel Aviv, 2002).

37. Nurith Kenaan-Kedar, *Marginal Sculpture in Medieval France: Towards the Deciphering of an Enigmatic Pictorial Language* (Aldershot, UK, 1995).

38. Nurith Kenaan-Kedar, "Reading the Language and Texts of Marginal Romanesque Sculpture," in *Marginal Sculpture*, 53–76; also 106.

39. Moshe Barasch, "Gantner's Theory of Prefiguration," *British Journal of Aesthetics* 3/2 (1963): 150.

40. For example, her *Robert Baser: Painter and Sculptor, 1908–1998* (Tel Aviv Museum of Art, 2010). There one can find a description such as "[L]ight is transformed into patches of color, which even when partly overlapping remain individually discernible and well defined. Accordingly, and thanks to the exposed parts of the white paper, the colors are reinforced and give the composition an uncommon radiance and richness." Ballas, *Baser*, 263.

41. Gila Ballas, *New Horizons: The Birth of Abstraction in Israeli Art*, trans. Jonathan Orr-Stav (Moshav Ben Shemen, 2014).

42. Ballas, *New Horizons*, 9e–12e.

43. Ballas, *New Horizons*, 13e; Haim Gamzu, *Bikoret omanut* (Art criticism), ed. Gila Ballas (Tel Aviv, 2006), 16, 30–32, 72.

44. Quoted in Ballas, *New Horizons*, 13e.

45. Heinrich Wölfflin, *Principles of Art History: The Problem of the Development of Style in Early Modern Art*, trans. Jonathan Blower, ed. Evonne Levy and Tristan Weddigen (Los Angeles, 2015), chapters 4 and 5, 234–304.

46. Ballas, *New Horizons*, 63e.

47. Galia Bar Or, *Oygen Kolb: Benyan tarbut be'eretz Israel* (Oygen Kolb: Construction of culture in the land of Israel) (Tel Aviv, 2003).

48. Kolb took at least two courses with Wölfflin, according to the records of the University of Munich. Bar Or, *Kolb*, 14n10.

49. Bar Or, *Kolb*, 31–32.

50. Bar Or, *Kolb*, 32-34, 237–291.

51. Published in *Ofakim* 1–2 (January–March 1955). In Bar Or, *Kolb*, 190–206. English translation is mine.

52. See also Wölfflin, *Das Erklären von Kunstwerken*, 9–10, 19.

53. Fritz Schiff, *91 Omanim* (Association of Painters and Sculptors of Haifa and the North) (Haifa, 1965), introduction (unpaginated).

54. Gideon Ofrat, "Fritz Schiff: Al efsharuto shel signon leumi" (Fritz Schiff: On the possibility of a national style), *The Warehouse of Gideon Ofrat*, https://getpocket.com/a/read/1353075556 (last accessed July 16, 2016).

55. See Evonne Levy's essay in this volume. See also Adi Efal, "Naturalization: Habits, Bodies and Their Subjects," *Phenomenology and Mind*, no. 6, *Mind, Habits and Social Reality*, ed. Emanuele Caminada and Matt Bower (2014), http://www.phenomenolog-yandmind.eu/wp-content/uploads/2014/07/08_Efal.pdf (last accessed July 16.2016), and Adi Efal, *Habitus as Method*.

WOJCIECH BAŁUS

In the Glow of a Classic:
Remarks on the Reception of Heinrich Wölfflin in Polish Art History

HEINRICH WÖLFFLIN

Podstawowe pojęcia

historii sztuki

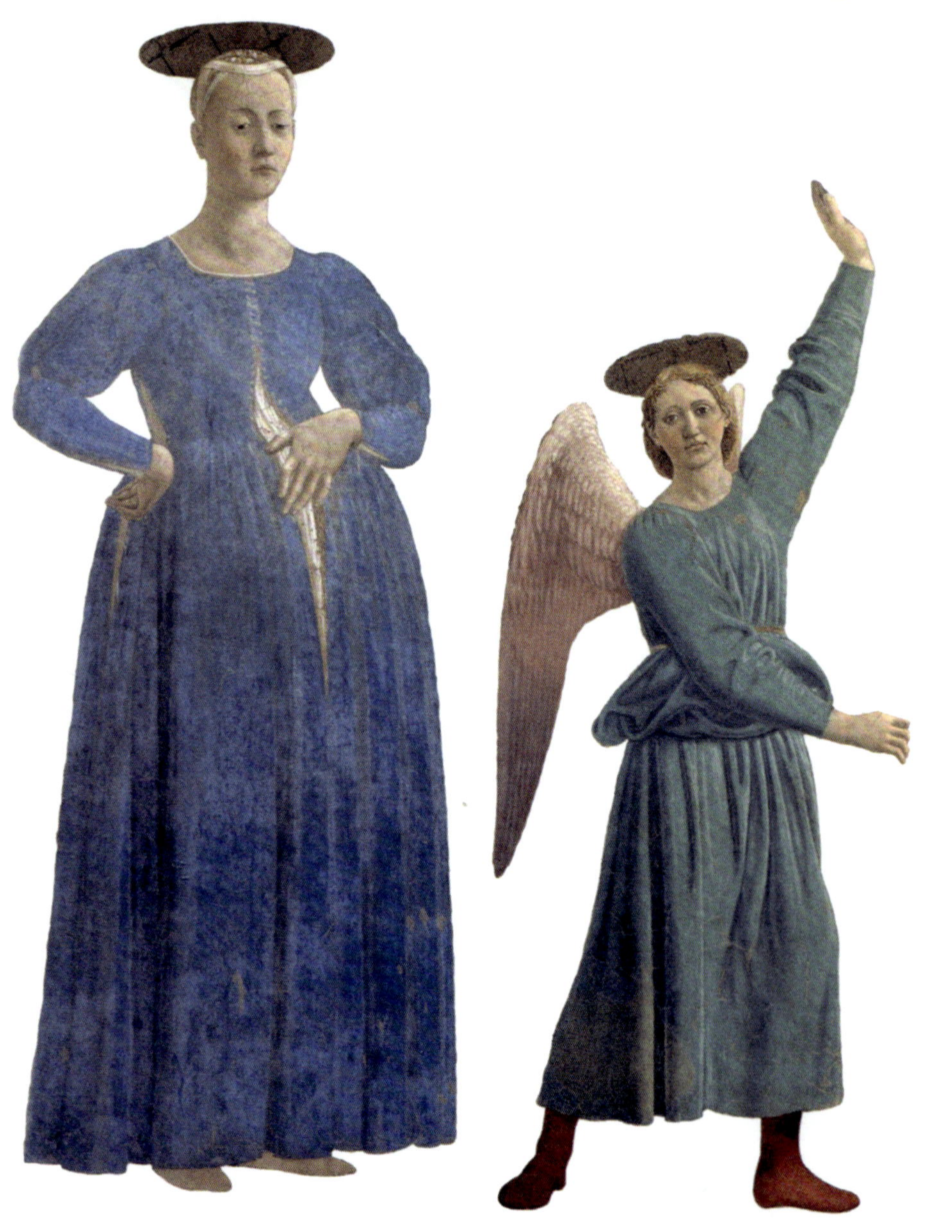

słowo/obraz terytoria

The Polish translation of *Principles of Art History* (*Podstawowe pojęcia historii sztuki*) appeared in 1962 (figs. 1 and 2).[1] It was based on the eleventh German edition, published in 1956 by Benno Schwabe & Co. in Basel.[2] The typographic layout draws on the original, particularly with regard to the illustrations, which are juxtaposed in accordance with the rule that works compared to each other in the text are reproduced on facing pages (fig. 3). The text is preceded by no fewer than three introductory pieces. The first, unsigned, is the publisher's; the second was written by Lech Kalinowski (1920–2004), at that time a forty-year-old professor of art history from Kraków; and the third is a reprint of an article on Wölfflin by Władysław Podlacha (1875–1951), professor of art history in Lvov and, after World War II, in Wrocław.[3]

The astounding inclusion of three introductions creates the impression of an attempt to take every possible precaution against potential attacks directed at the very decision to translate and publish this classic, nearly fifty-year-old publication on the methodology of art history. And indeed, each of the three texts approaches Wölfflin's book in a different way, either emphasizing its unquestionable value or, in at least two cases, developing problematic arguments. Each does so from the perspective of a different time: the publisher's introduction focuses on the present; Podlacha's article—because its author was of the prewar generation and wished to emphasize Wölfflin's topicality—belongs to the past; and Kalinowski's essay anticipates in its tone the declining popularity of *Principles of Art History* in the second half of the twentieth century.

The temporal nature of the introductions has an unquestionable value for my own essay: it allows me to treat them as a perfect "Ariadne's thread," providing a trail into the depths of the history and reception of Wölfflin's thought as well as the most significant of his books for Polish humanities.

During the Communist era, the process of book publication in Poland was very protracted. Thus one should assume that work on *Principles of Art History* was undertaken by the publisher, the National Ossoliński Institute (Ossolineum) toward the end of the 1950s. It was a special moment in the history of the Soviet bloc: the period of socialist realism, decreed in Poland in 1949, was followed by a thaw, which began shortly after the death of Stalin. In Poland, all attempts to propagate the type of art imposed by the authorities, as it were from above, were abandoned. *Art informel* became a specific sign of modernization; it was shown, in an atmosphere of scandal, as an official presentation of Polish artistic creativity at an art exhibition of the socialist states in Moscow in 1958.[4]

In art history, which was not as important to the Communist rulers as history or philosophy, ideological pressure had all but disappeared. Thus it became possible to publish the works of "bourgeois" and "formalist" authors, who—as was the case with Alois Riegl and Max Dvořák—had been condemned and criticized in previous years. Yet the memory of Stalinist terror was still very much alive; this was probably one of the reasons for the publisher's extreme caution. Wölfflin, however, was not prohibited in the Soviet Union (he was partly criticized, partly accepted), and that is why

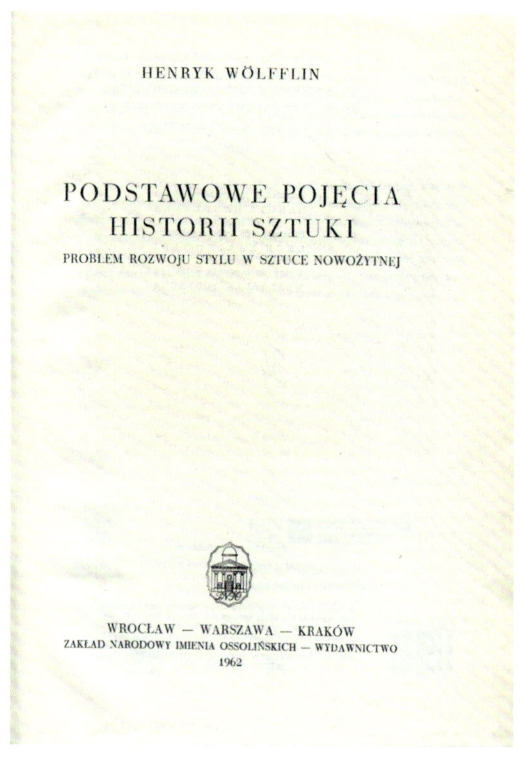

1. Heinrich Wölfflin, *Podstawowe pojęcia historii sztuki: Problem rozwoju stylu w sztuce nowożytnej*, trans. Danuta Hanulanka (Wrocław, 1962), title page

the publisher's introduction stated three reasons the book deserved to be published in Poland.[5] First, it emphasized the need to become acquainted with the specialist literature belonging to the theory of a given scientific discipline; second, it pointed out that such works were important from the point of view of further development of the discipline, even if some of their positions had already lost their validity; and third, it underlined that the author was a true master in conducting scientific discourse.[6] Yet this rationale both emphasized the value of *Principles of Art History* and established a distance between the publisher and the work. Wölfflin's book was being recommended not as ultimate "truth" but as a school of academic skills and a classic work with which the reader does not have to agree completely. Toward the end of the publisher's introduction, there also appeared a discussion of Wölfflin's "Revision" of 1933, according to which "comparing the creative labor of art to a reflection is not a good analogy."[7] For Soviet aesthetics the "theory of reflection" was the fundamental concept in describing the relation between art and reality. Lenin had argued that art is not a simple representation of the world but is always mediated by the dominant ideology of a particular historical period.[8] The author of the publisher's introduction criticized Wölfflin's negative attitude toward "reflection": "We are aware that the 'theory of reflection' is based on a different conception and that it contributes many positive research and interpretive propositions."[9] This bow to contemporary political correctness was in accord with the cautious tone of the entire text and, by satisfying the demands of censorship, allowed the publisher to introduce, in the last paragraph, some remarks about the topicality of Wölfflin's book in the eventuality of a departure from the doctrine of socialist realism. According to the writer, Wölfflin's discourse could play an important role in research on avant-garde art of the twentieth century. In the interpretation of contemporary works of art, one might take advantage of the "directive of depth perception," as modern-day paintings and sculptures should be viewed, above all, through the perspective of their formal character.[10]

In its line of reasoning as well as its entire manner of argumentation, the publisher's introduction has the character of an editorial peer review. This is best borne out by its closing: "The previously formulated remarks entitle one to conclude that the Polish edition of Heinrich Wölfflin's *Principles of Art History* should be regarded as necessary and expedient."[11] This origin cannot be confirmed because the archive of the Ossolineum publishing house was destroyed during the flood of 1997 in Wrocław. Yet one may hypothetically point to two likely authors.

The first possibility would be Ksawery Piwocki, a professor at the Academy of Fine Arts in Warsaw, pupil of Podlacha, and among other things a specialist of contemporary and folk art, associated with the scholarly establishment of the Stalinist period. These interests can be inferred from his bow to the official ideology ("reflection theory") and, above all, from his suggestion that Wölfflin's theory could be applied to

Frans Hals, *Portret mężczyzny*

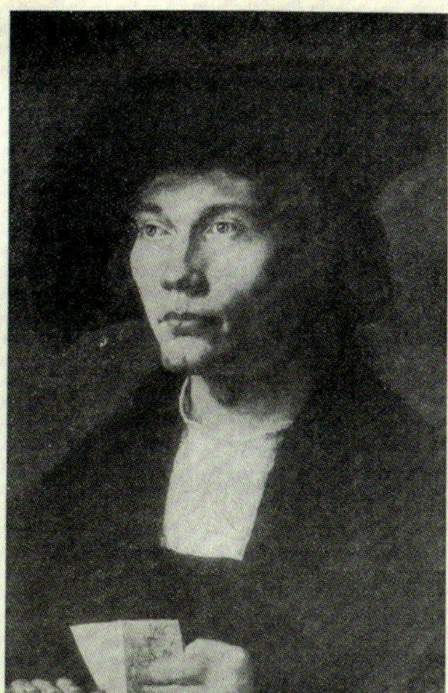

Albrecht Dürer, *Portret Berenda van Orleya*

Może jeszcze najbardziej przykonywająco oddziałuje sposób opracowania bielizny.

Jeżeli rozpatruje się różnice stylowe pod kątem widzenia wielkich kontrastów, różnice indywidualne tracą na znaczeniu. Widać wówczas, że to, co daje Frans Hals, istnieje w gruncie rzeczy także u van Dycka i Rembrandta. Zachodzą między nimi tylko różnice stopnia, wyodrębniające się w zamknięte grupy cech, jeżeli tylko grupie tych artystów przeciwstawić twórczość Dürera. Ale w miejsce Dürera można tu także podstawić Holbeina lub Massysa czy Rafaela. Z drugiej strony, oglądając w odosobnieniu dzieła danego malarza nie sposób uniknąć tego, by nie ogarniać jednakowymi pojęciami stylowymi wszystkich znamion jego warsztatu na kolejnych etapach rozwoju, od początku do końca.

A przecież portrety młodego Rembrandta są widziane (względnie) plastycznie i linearnie w porównaniu z portretami okresu dojrzałego.

Ale stwierdzenie, że późniejsze stopnie rozwojowe są zawsze równorzędne z optycznym pojmowaniem zjawiska, nie znaczy, że na początku każdego szeregu rozwojowego stoi koniecznie typ czysto plastyczny. Styl linijny Dürera jest nie tylko dalszym rozwijaniem istniejącej w tym zakresie tradycji, ale oznacza równocześnie eliminację wszystkich sprzecznych elementów w przekazie stylowym XV wieku.

Jak wygląda w szczegółach przechodzenie od czystego linearyzmu do malarskiego widzenia XVII wieku, można by wykazać wprost na portrecie. Tu jednak nie możemy się w to wdawać. Ogólnie można tylko stwierdzić, że narasta współgranie światła i cienia, torując drogę do zdecydowanego ujęcia malarskiego. Co to oznacza, zrozumie wyraź-

2. Heinrich Wölfflin, *Podstawowe pojęcia historii sztuki: Problem rozwoju stylu w sztuce nowożytnej*, trans. Danuta Hanulanka (Wrocław, 1962), 78–79

research on contemporary art. Piwocki was one of a few scholars who were studying twentieth-century art in Poland at that time and who tried to apply the classical methods of art history (for instance, the theory of Alois Riegl) to their work.[12]

Another possible author would be Marian Minich, director of the art museum in Łódź. He was a great admirer of Wölfflin. Already in 1929, during his studies in Lvov, he had written an essay for Podlacha's seminar, entitled "Koncepcja sztuki klasycznej u Wölfflina na tle rozwoju współczesnej nauki o sztuce" (The conception of classical art in Wölfflin against the background of contemporary art studies).[13] After the war he tried to combine the views of the author of *Principles* with Marxism and Leninism,

replacing the so-called idealist theory of an autonomous development of forms of artistic presentation with the conception of a development of "historical, economic, and social relations shaping the artist's way of thinking and feeling and influencing the developmental processes of his artistic constructs."[14] At the same time, he thought that Wölfflin's system could be applied to the art of the twentieth century, in which one could find certain optical patterns specific only to it. Minich's ultimate goal was to create a new type of museum in which displays would be grouped not by artists' life dates but in a way that would highlight certain developmental tendencies, such as transformations of "formal spatial structures from the baroque to Cézanne, cubism, suprematism, and neoplasticism" or the development of color "from the Venetians through the baroque and rococo, Delacroix, and the romantics to impressionism."[15]

Regardless of who wrote the publisher's foreword, it constitutes clear evidence that classical methodology clashed with the elements of Marxism in Polish art history of the 1950s. Wölfflin's book was among the canonical works with which one should be familiar as a mark of an all-round education but that one did not necessarily apply as methodological tools.

Władysław Podlacha was one of the few Polish art historians of the interwar period who systematically dealt with the theoretical and methodological issues of the discipline.[16] His article on Wölfflin appeared for the first time in 1949 as an homage to the Swiss scholar, who had died four years earlier.[17] Having combined conclusions drawn from *Principles of Art History* with Wölfflin's "Revision" of 1933, Podlacha concluded that their chief merit was that they distinguished between an external and an internal form of a work of art. Both aspects constituted integral parts of the concept of style and had their source in its dual root (*die doppelte Wurzel des Stils*): in Podlacha's words, the external form in the artist's "contemporary life" and the internal form "in the way of perceiving the surrounding world."[18] The external form, that is, "everything that constitutes the factual and psychological content of a work of art" was concentrated in the expression (*Ausdruck*) of a painting or sculpture; important to the internal form were the aspects of the purely artistic, autonomous development of art. Thanks to this distinction, besides the "historical method" Wölfflin was able to work out a "systematic method and, with its help, to gain access to those properties of art that the historical method is unable to reach": *Ausdrucksgeschichte* was supplemented by *interne Formgeschichte*.[19]

In discussing the "systematic method," Podlacha referred to a conception of three types of art studies that he had developed earlier. Following the views of Max Dessoir, he adopted the idea of a "general science of art" (*allgemeine Kunstwissenschaft*), which examined the philosophical foundations of art; a "historical science of art," that is, art history, focusing on stylistic transformations, the iconography of representations, and the biographies of artists; and a "systematic science of art," focusing on developing universal analytical categories for the needs of the discipline.[20] In this account, although art history had developed since the time of Johann Joachim Winckelmann, the general and systematic science of art began to take shape only in the first decades of the twentieth century.[21] For Podlacha, one of Wölfflin's chief achievements was that he had framed the systematic method within a "strictly scientific form."[22] This strictness consisted both in precise definitions of the concepts used in analysis of stylistic elements resulting from the method of perception that predominated in a given historical period and in the discovery of the mechanism of development in art, which always proceeds from the *Tastbild* (tactile image) and the linear style to the *Sehbild* (optical image) and the painterly style. The only supplement Podlacha added in presenting Wölfflin's views was a more precise definition of the mechanism of stylistic development. Indeed, he did not agree with the idea that development was stimulated exclusively by autonomous changes in human ways of perception. To a Polish scholar who had studied Max Dvořák's *Kunstgeschichte als Geistesgeschichte*, there could be no doubt that all changes in art must have a spiritual foundation.[23] Recalling Hermann Friedmann's book *Die Welt der Formen* of 1925, which recognizes the senses of sight and touch as the main sources of human cognition, leading to two different ways of presenting the world, he concluded that "one may not only come across art in which the element of sight (vision) predominates over that of touch, or conversely," but also that "the whole culture may in certain periods be pervaded with visual or tactile elements and that it consequently may create identical elements in various fields of man's activity, not excluding the world of science."[24]

Podlacha's article grew out of the conviction that, first, one may find certain rules and regularities in the development of art and that, second, these regularities find their expression in form. This way of thinking was characteristic of the methodology developed at the beginning of the twentieth century by Wölfflin and Alois Riegl. Podlacha complemented these formalist deliberations with Dvořák's views from the time of his *Kunstgeschichte als Geistesgeschichte*, expressing the opinion that the ways of thinking that contribute to the formulation of style characteristic of a given period were not autonomous but were determined by the "mental content" of the worldview that predominated in that period. This attitude was subjected to criticism already in the 1920s. German and Austrian scholars pointed out that, in looking for general laws of stylistic development and trying to examine the impact of the worldview on a given epoch, one tends to neglect the individual work of art, making it exclusively a symptom of style.[25] We do not find a reflection of these discussions in Podlacha's text. With all his intelligence and ability to analyze the views of other authors, the scholar represented a methodological awareness typical of the generation intellectually formed in the time of World War I and shortly after.[26]

The attitude combining formalism with *Kunstgeschichte als Geistesgeschichte* was quite typical of Polish art history in the interwar period. Tadeusz Szydłowski, professor of art history in Kraków, wrote in 1929 that the slogan "*Kunstgeschichte als Formengeschichte*, which once refreshed and deepened art analysis, no longer exerts such an influence today, although art history continues to absorb the main content of this trend as the most important part of its task…. Art history should focus on understanding not only the external shape but also the internal content of art phenomena; it should be preoccupied not only with, so to speak, the bodily beauty of works of art but also with the internal mental content,

which is perceivable through their form."[27] That is why Szydłowski had valued Dvořák more highly than Wölfflin, as the latter focused primarily on the "examination of artistic forms and trends (*Geschichte des künstlerischen Sehens*)," while the former, "without disregarding this important foundation, turned more toward the spiritual base, of which art is one of the expressions."[28]

In Polish art history of the interwar period, Wölfflin was present, above all, as the creator of the synthetic image of classical and baroque art. The translation of his *Classic Art,* already published in Kraków in 1931,[29] and his *Principles of Art History*—read in German before 1962—were widely used as teaching aids at university level.[30] References to his books appeared in articles chiefly in the context of general descriptions and analyses of individual stylistic periods. For example, in his monograph on the activity of Baldassare Fontana in Kraków, Julian Pagaczewski concluded: "Renaissance artists executed all parts of decoration meticulously and with equal devotion to detail; every minute element had its importance and value, as it were, its separate identity. [This was] [q]uite different from the baroque period. The latter style was to dazzle and impress; it strove to attain overall effect at all costs."[31]

In the detailed stylistic analyses of authors who wrote about the Renaissance and the baroque, Wölfflin's conclusions were interwoven with those of other scholars. Pure "visual" formal analysis had never really taken root in Polish art history, as from the very moment of birth of this discipline, stylistic analyses had been supplemented with historical research. That was precisely the method of Marian Sokołowski, the first professor of art history at Jagiellonian University, and of his students.[32] Feliks Kopera, who studied under Wölfflin in Basel in 1896–1897, wrote about him to Sokołowski, without much enthusiasm: "*Anschauung, Anschauung*—his favorite word"; and "I am disappointed. Wölfflin avoids the problem of source criticism: *Das ist gut, aber das ist Nebensache.* The main issue is the works, and one should be able to read and interpret them."[33] Wölfflin's concepts were also used by historians of literature, who followed mainly in the footsteps of Oscar Walzel. The philologists were particularly eager to apply them to analysis of newly discovered baroque poetry, to which they had had so far no other methodological key.[34]

At the level of the general science of art, a reference to Wölfflin had appeared but once. Ksawery Piwocki, mentioned earlier, tried to describe the phenomenon of folk art. While deliberating on the specificity of the representation of reality in folk painting and sculpture, he came to the conclusion that its particular features resulted from a way of perceiving the world that was different from that of modern societies. As "the country folk see a different reality than we do," in their art a specific style must arise.[35] This allowed him to formulate the hypothesis that only an art historian who follows Wölfflin is able to speak competently about the issue of folk art and define the specific features of "folk style."[36]

Lech Kalinowski consciously made his preface to the Polish translation of *Principles* a historical analysis that aimed to define the place of the book in the history of the discipline. For Kalinowski, Wölfflin's work was no longer a presentation of binding and acceptable scientific methods and results; it belonged to the "irretrievable past."[37] Referring to Podlacha's concept, the scholar saw *Principles* as belonging to the third phase of development of art history, when, after the period of collecting and ordering of historical material in the first half of the nineteenth century and after the shaping of a systematic science of art in the second half of the nineteenth century, a general science of art came into being at the beginning of the twentieth. According to Kalinowski, Wölfflin combined systematic study with research characteristic of the general science of art, focusing on the problems of artistic perception as an autonomous problem, independent of cultural background, artists' biographies, and historical events. He built a binary system, which,

though explicated with examples from the Renaissance and baroque periods, was to express a universal law of development in art. Thus, Kalinowski summed up: "In the existence of two forms of artistic perception Wölfflin saw the reflection of the absolute laws governing art."[38]

According to the Kraków scholar, the system had lost its binding force for three main reasons. First, "In 1955 *De Triomf van het Manerisme*, which was celebrated in Amsterdam [as] the first art exhibition initiated by the Council of Europe, had given a coup de grâce to the opposition between the Renaissance and the baroque. For it turned out then that what followed immediately after the Renaissance, in the years 1520–1590, was mannerism, not baroque. Thus, Wölfflin's Renaissance, extending from the beginning of the fifteenth century to the end of the sixteenth century, had shrunk to a hundred years, that is, 1430–1520, and, as a consequence of that chronology, it had lost its polarizing force in relation to the baroque."[39] Second, the art of the twentieth century had restored the significance of the material aspects of art. And third—Kalinowski argued—one could infer that a work of art, "as a material object, cannot be isolated from the entirety of life, and that is why, within the framework of social changes, it is always an expression of definite ideological content."[40]

The term "mannerism" was rarely used in the Polish art history of the interwar period. After World War II it was not accepted by Stalinist science or by some of the scholars of the previous generation.[41] In a textbook on the history of Italian architecture, reprinted as recently as 1972, we read that

the scope of ideological and developmental changes at the borderline between the Renaissance and the baroque have first been analyzed exhaustively by Wölfflin, an outstanding theoretician, who, after the peak period of the Renaissance in Rome, accepted not a decadent Renaissance in any form, but rather belated Renaissance artists. According to him, immediately after its culmination, the peak period of the Renaissance passes into the baroque.[42]

Yet the final acceptance of mannerism as a style of its own led to a situation, not only in Poland, in which—as Jacques Thuillier put it—"la pensée de Wölfflin se trouvait comme neutralisée" (Wölfflin's thought was in effect neutralized).[43] *Informel* painting, with which Kalinowski became acquainted both in Kraków and during the period he spent on a Ford Foundation fellowship in Paris (1958–1959), when he maintained close contact with the painter Tadeusz Kantor, was proof that in art one cannot separate form from material—in this case thick layers of pigment, sand, or other materials applied directly to the canvas.[44] Finally, the scholarly scientific views that evolved from the Christian iconology of Godefridus Johannes Hoogewerff toward Erwin Panofsky and the Warburg Institute assured him that there is no "pure seeing" independent of social reality, or a world of forms deprived of meaning.

Kalinowski's views reflect very well the transformations that art history in Poland underwent from the end of the 1950s. On the one hand, the early reception of iconology resulted in scholars' distancing themselves from formalist deliberations of the "general science of art"; on the other hand, the concept of style and the laws of formal development were seen more and more as problematic.[45] Young Jan Białostocki criticized attempts at finding a universal and simplified two- or three-element rhythm of transformation in art.[46] From the superior category ensuring the independence of art history, style had been gradually shrinking to a "technical" stock-taking tool. In the 1970s the widely discussed problem of stylistic pluralism, introduced in an essay by Joseph A. Schmoll genannt Eisenwerth, had ultimately deprived Wölfflin's conception of its binding status.[47] In Jan Białostocki's book *Historia sztuki wśród nauk humanistycznych* (Art history among the humanistic disciplines) of 1980, the chapter on style mentions Wölfflin only in passing, treating him as unimportant in the history of this discipline.[48] Zbigniew Beiersdorf, in introducing the concept of picturesque

eclecticism in 1973 in a debate on the oeuvre of Teodor Talowski, a late historicist architect in Kraków, mentioned five features of this style as it had been defined by Carroll L. V. Meeks; but he disregarded completely the fact that the American scholar had applied the term to the entirety of nineteenth-century architecture in an attempt to expand Wölfflin's dualistic model with a third element.[49]

Principles of Art History has kept its place in the teaching of art history as a useful tool for recognizing the fundamental stylistic features of a work of art. As Gerrit Willems has rightly observed, the five pairs of oppositional categories continue to be used today in describing Renaissance and baroque monuments.[50] Wölfflin's name is familiar to every Polish art historian, but *Principles* is known chiefly as a remote classic. The book (see essay frontispiece) was reissued in Poland in 2006 in a series of classics of world humanistic studies without any of the three introductory pieces.[51] Today one does not have to warn anyone against Wölfflin or persuade anyone to adopt his views.

It is difficult to say why *Principles* appeared in translation precisely in 1962. Before World War II nearly all Polish scholars were familiar with German, and the group who were interested in *Principles* was relatively small. Therefore, *Classic Art* was translated as a work that could find its way to a broader readership, while *Principles* was read by specialists in the original. It was not without significance either that both Podlacha and Szydłowski compared Wölfflin's book with *Kunstgeschichte als Geistesgeschichte.*

After the war, the situation changed. The German language had lost its popularity. At the same time, Wölfflin became something of a classic among art historians. Kalinowski wrote in the introduction to his book on Dvořák: "From the perspective of art history, Dvořák's method is one of classical research and explicatory methods, side by side with Heinrich Wölfflin's art history perceived as a history of forms and artistic perception, art history perceived as a history of overt and concealed cultural traditions of antiquity and the still unwritten psychology of human expression of Aby Warburg and his successors in the Institute, or art history understood as a history of symbolic forms, that is, cultural symptoms or documents related to *Weltanschauung*—in accordance with Erwin Panofsky's conception."[52] Translating the texts of the classics became suddenly necessary. In 1970 a book on Riegl containing fragments of his texts was published; a year later a selection of Panofsky's studies appeared in print; in 1974 an anthology of Dvořák's essays was published.[53] *Principles* was the first in this group. Maybe what determined its early publication was the influence exerted by a group of Podlacha's pupils, among others Minich and Piwocki. It is difficult to say precisely today. In any case, the Polish translation of Wölfflin's book did not bring about an increase in the popularity of its author but merely strengthened his position in the discipline. The republication of his work in 2006 only confirmed this assessment, which has been stressed in one of the very few reviews of *Principles*: "The book of the Swiss scholar, pupil of Jacob Burckhardt, belongs to the canonical titles of the European humanities."[54]

NOTES

1. Henryk [Heinrich] Wölfflin, *Podstawowe pojęcia historii sztuki: Problem rozwoju stylu w sztuce nowożytnej* (Principles of art history: The problem of the development of style in later art), trans. Danuta Hanulanka (Wrocław, 1962).

2. Wojciech Bałus, "Heinrich Wölfflin: *Podstawowe pojęcia historii sztuki; Problem rozwoju stylu w sztuce nowożytnej*," in *Kunstgeschichten 1915: 100 Jahre Heinrich Wölfflin*, Kunstgeschichtliche Grundbegriffe, ed. Matteo Burioni, Burcu Dogramaci, and Ulrich Pfisterer (Zentralinstitut für Kunstgeschichte, Munich, 2015), cat. VIII.9.

3. "Od wydawcy" (From the publisher), 7–9; Lech Kalinowski, "Przedmowa do wydania polskiego" (Preface to the Polish edition), 10–15; Władysław Podlacha, "Wstęp do wydania polskiego—Henryk Wölfflin i jego teoria sztuki" (Introduction to the Polish edition—Heinrich Wölfflin and his theory of art), 16–26.

4. Piotr Piotrowski, *In the Shadow of Yalta: Art and the Avant-Garde in Eastern Europe, 1945–1989* (London, 2009), 69–70.

5. Ekaterina Dmitrieva, "Heinrich Wölfflin en Russie: De la découverte de l'Italie et de l'art baroque russe à la conception de la méthode formaliste et structuraliste dans la critique littéraire," *Cahiers du monde russe* 51 (2010): 513–516.

6. "Od wydawcy," 7.

7. Heinrich Wölfflin, *Principles of Art History: The Problem of the Development of Style in Early Modern Art*, trans. Johnathan Blower, ed. Evonne Levy and Tristan Weddigen (Los Angeles, 2015), 319.

8. Boris Röhrl, *Kunsttheorie des Naturalismus und Realismus: Historische Entwicklung, Terminologie und Definitionen* (Hildesheim, 2014), 96.

9. "Od wydawcy," 9.

10. "Od wydawcy," 9.

11. "Od wydawcy," 9.

12. Wojciech Bałus, "Ksawery Piwocki and the Vienna and Lvov Schools of Art History," *Journal of Art Historiography* 8 (2013), http://arthistoriography.files.wordpress.com/2013/06/balus.pdf.

13. The paper is lost. Marian Minich mentions it in a document: Ankieta dla ubiegających się o tytuły naukowe samodzielnego pracownika nauki, 1954, family archive.

14. Marian Minich, "O nową organizację muzeów sztuki" (On the new organization of art museums), in *Sztuka współczesna: Studia i szkice* (Contemporary art: Studies and sketches), ed. Józef Dutkiewicz, vol. 2 (Kraków, 1966), 91.

15. Minich, "O nową organizację muzeów sztuki," 93.

16. Mieczysław Zlat, "Władysław Podlacha (1875–1951)," *Rocznik historii sztuki* 37 (2012): 21–37; Adam Małkiewicz, "'Szkoła krakowska' i 'szkoła lwowska' polskiej historii sztuki" (The "Kraków School" and the "Lvov School" of Polish art history), in *Z dziejów polskiej historii sztuki: Studia i szkice* (From the history of Polish art history: Studies and sketches), Ars vetus et nova, vol. 18 (Kraków, 2005), 52–53; Wojciech Bałus, "A Marginalized Tradition? Polish Art History," in *Art History and Visual Studies in Europe: Transitional Discourses and National Frameworks*, ed. Matthew Rampley et al. (Leiden and Boston, 2012), 441.

17. Władysław Podlacha, "Henryk Wölfflin i jego teoria sztuki" (Heinrich Wölfflin and his theory of art), *Sprawozdania Wrocławskiego Towarzystwa Naukowego* 3 (1948 [1949]): 221–233.

18. Podlacha, "Wstęp do wydania polskiego," 19. Besides Polish terminology, he quotes German equivalents, which I use here accordingly.

19. Podlacha, "Wstęp do wydania polskiego," 22.

20. Władysław Podlacha, "Niektóre zagadnienia nowoczesnej historyi sztuki" (Some problems of modern art history), *Kwartalnik historyczny* 29 (1916): 4–5; Lech Kalinowski, "Barok: Styl czy epoka?" (Baroque: Style or epoch?), *Biuletyn historii sztuki* 20 (1958): 106.

21. Podlacha, "Niektóre zagadnienia nowoczesnej historyi sztuki," 5–6.

22. Podlacha, "Henryk Wölfflin i jego teoria sztuki," 232.

23. Władysław Podlacha, "Historia sztuki, jej założenia i metody badawcze" (Art history, its principles and research methods), *Sprawozdania z posiedzeń wydziału II nauk historycznych, Społecznych i filozoficznych Towarzystwa Nnaukowego Warszawskiego* 42 (1949 [1950]): 78.

24. Hermann Friedmann, *Die Welt der Formen: System eines morphologischen Idealismus* (Berlin, 1925; 2nd edition, Munich, 1930); Podlacha, "Wstęp do wydania polskiego," 15.

25. Marlite Halbertsma, *Wilhelm Pinder und die deutsche Kunstgeschichte* (Worms, 1992), 90–103; Artur Rosenauer, "Zur neuen Wiener Schule der Kunstgeschichte," in *Révolution et évolution de l'histoire de l'art de Warburg à nos jours*, section 1–8, 5: *L'Art et les révolutions*, ed. Harald Olbrich (Strasbourg, 1992), 73–83.

26. In his deliberations on method, Podlacha reaches only as far back as the so-called older Vienna School (Riegl, Dvořák, Schlosser); see Podlacha, "Historia sztuki, jej założenia i metody badawcze," 75.

27. Tadeusz Szydłowski, "Spór o Giotta: Problem autorstwa fresków w Assyżu na tle rozwoju metody historji sztuki" (Debate over Giotto: The problem of the authorship of the frescoes in Assisi against the development of the method of art history), *Przegląd współczesny* 81 (1929): 22.

28. Szydłowski, "Spór o Giotta," 23.

29. Henryk [Heinrich] Wölfflin, *Sztuka klasyczna: Wstęp do włoskiego renesansu* (Classic art: An introduction to the Italian Renaissance), trans. Józef Muczkowski (Kraków, 1931).

30. Adam Małkiewicz, "Tradycja badań nad barokiem w krakowskim środowisku historii sztuki" (The tradition of research on the baroque period in the milieu of the Kraków art historians), in *Z dziejów polskiej historii sztuki*, 132; Lech Kalinowski, "Mój renesans" (My Renaissance), *Znak*, no. 504 (1997): 116.

31. Julian Pagaczewski, "Baltazar Fontana w Krakowie" (Baldassare Fontana in Kraków), *Rocznik krakowski* 11 (1909): 4.

32. Magdalena Kunińska, *Historia sztuki Mariana Sokołowskiego* (Marian Sokołowski's history of art) (Kraków, 2014); Adam Małkiewicz, "Storia dell'arte in Polonia rispetto alla 'scuola di Vienna,'" in *La scuola viennese di storia dell'arte*, ed. Marco Pozzetto (Gorizia, 1996), 143–149.

33. Quoted from Kunińska, *Historia sztuki Mariana Sokołowskiego*, 81, 153.

34. Wiktor Weintraub, "O niektórych problemach polskiego baroku" (Some problems of the Polish baroque), in *Od Reya do Boya* (From Rey to Boy) (Warsaw, 1977), 98–99.

35. Ksawery Piwocki, "Zagadnienie metody w badaniach nad sztuką ludową" (The problem of method in research on folk art; originally published 1931), in *Sztuka żywa: Szkice z teorii i metodyki historii sztuki* (Living art: Essays on the theory and methodology of art history) (Wrocław, 1970), 249.

36. Ksawery Piwocki, "Z badań nad powstaniem stylu ludowego" (Research on the origin of folk style; originally published in 1936), in *Sztuka żywa*, 131.

37. Kalinowski, "Przedmowa," 11.

38. Kalinowski, "Przedmowa," 12–13.

39. Kalinowski, "Mój renesans," 117.

40. Kalinowski, "Przedmowa," 14.

41. Wojciech Bałus, "Die Sigismundkapelle in Krakau oder die Renaissanceforschung zwischen dem wissenschaftlichen Diskurs der Stalinzeit und dem venezianischen Spiegel des Eisernen Vorhangs," *Ars* 48 (2015): 148.

42. Kazimierz Ulatowski, *Architektura włoskiego renesansu* (Architecture of the Italian Renaissance) (Warsaw and Poznan, 1972), 222 and 277.

43. Jacques Thuillier, "Wölfflin et la France," in *Relire Wölfflin*, ed. Joan Goldhammer Hart, Roland Recht, and Martin Warnke (Paris, 1995), 25.

44. For Kalinowski's Ford fellowship, see Jerzy Gadomski, "Lech Kalinowski 1920–2004," *Folia historiae artium* 10 (2005): 10.

45. Bałus, "A Marginalized Tradition?," 444–445.

46. Jan Białostocki, "W pogoni za schematem: Usiłowania systematycznej historii sztuki" (In pursuit of a paradigm: An attempt to present a systemic art history), *Biuletyn Historii Sztuki* 9 (1947): 225–239; Wojciech Bałus, "Jan Białostocki and George Kubler: In an Attempt to Catch Up with the System," *Ars* 43 (2010): 122.

47. Joseph A. Schmoll gennant Eisenwerth, "Stilpluralismus statt Einheitszwang: Zur Kritik der Stilepochen-Kunstgeschichte," in *Argo: Festschrift für Kurt Badt zu seinem 80. Geburtstag am 3. März 1970*, ed. Martin Gosebruch and Lorenz Dittmann (Cologne, 1970), 77–95.

48. Jan Białostocki, *Historia sztuki wśród nauk humanistycznych* (Art history among humanistic disciplines) (Wrocław, 1980), 36–55.

49. Zbigniew Beiersdorf: "Architekt Teodor M. Talowski," in *Sztuka 2 połowy XIX wieku: Materiały Sesji Stowarzyszenia Historyków Sztuki Łódź, listopad 1971* (Art of the second half of the nineteenth century: Proceedings of the Conference of the Society of Art Historians, Łódź, November 1971) (Warsaw, 1973), 208; Carroll L.V. Meeks, "Picturesque Eclecticism," *The Art Bulletin* 32 (1950): 226–228.

50. Gerrit Willems, "Erklären und Ordnen: Stilanalytische Ansätze in der Kunstgeschichte," in *Gesichtspunkte: Kunstgeschichte heute*, ed. Marlite Halbertsma and Kitty Zijlmans, trans. Thomas Guirten (Berlin, 1995), 89.

51. Heinrich Wölfflin, *Podstawowe pojęcia historii sztuki: Problem rozwoju stylu w sztuce nowożytnej* (Principles of art history: The problem of the development of style in later art), trans. Danuta Hanulanka (Gdańsk, 2006).

52. Lech Kalinowski, *Max Dvořák i jego metoda badań nad sztuką* (Max Dvořák and his method of art research) (Warsaw, 1974), 7–8.

53. Ksawery Piwocki, *Pierwsza nowoczesna teoria sztuki: Poglądy Aloisa Riegla* (First modern art theory: The views of Alois Riegl) (Warsaw, 1970); Erwin Panofsky, *Studia z historii sztuki* (Studies in art history), ed. Jan Białostocki (Warsaw, 1971); *Max Dvořák i jego teoria dziejów sztuki* (Max Dvořák and his theory of art history), ed. Lech Kalinowski (Warsaw, 1974).

54. Review in *Znak*, no. 622 (2007), http://www.miesiecznik.znak.com.pl/6222007paulina-korpal-jakubiecpowrot-formy/ (accessed November 16, 2016).

ROBERT BORN

The *Impact* of Principles of Art History on the *Historiography of Art in Hungary in the Twentieth Century*

Heinrich Wölfflin
Művészettörténeti alap-fogalmak

A stílus fejlődésének
problémája
az újkori művészetben

Corvina

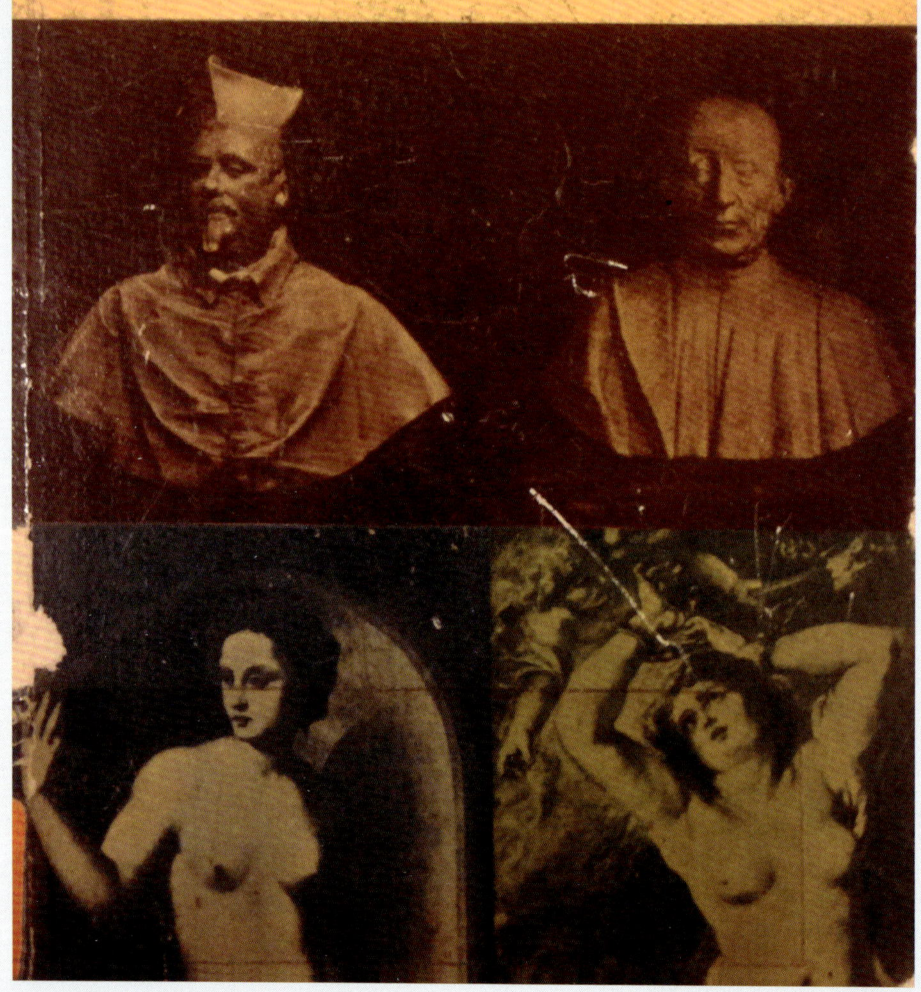

The first Hungarian translation of Heinrich Wölfflin's *Kunstgeschichtliche Grundbegriffe* (*Principles of Art History*) appeared in 1969 as the first volume in the new series Művészet és elmélet (Art and theory; fig. 1).[1] It proved to be the last translation of this classic work of art historiography to be published in the Eastern Bloc in the 1960s, following editions in Poland (1962) and Romania (1968).[2] The next edition was published in East Germany in 1984; a Bulgarian translation followed in 1985.[3] The lateness of the translations of *Principles* in Eastern Europe, half a century after the first edition of 1915, seems surprising, considering that a Russian-language version had been published in the Soviet Union in 1930.[4]

The lag in publishing a translation of *Principles*, however, did not in the slightest affect the spread of Wölfflin's concepts in Hungary. The reception of his ideas had peaked long before the Communist takeover in 1948. There were many reasons for the intensive study given to Wölfflin's work in various spheres of cultural life in Hungary. By the beginning of the twentieth century, Budapest, in its role as the second capital of the Austro-Hungarian monarchy, was a cultural and intellectual center where the latest European trends were adopted with almost no time lag. The early reception of *Principles* was facilitated also by the widespread use of the German language not only in scientific settings but also among the middle class in Hungary. This promoted scholarly cooperation with universities in the Germanophone realm.

As far as art history was concerned, apart from Vienna, the main centers were Berlin and Munich, two of Wölfflin's places of activity. Additionally, the Akademie der Bildenden Künste and the private painting schools of the Bavarian capital exerted a strong attraction for students from Hungary, Russia, and the young nations of southeastern Europe.[5] Wölfflin's lectures in these two cities were attended by Hungarians from different disciplines. They included the art critic Leó Popper (1886–1911); the art historians Máriusz Rabinovszky (1895–1953), Anna Zádor (1904–1995), Hugó Kenczler (1884–1922), Frederick (Frigyes) Antal (1887–1954) and András Péter (1903–1944); and the architect Virgil (Borbiró) Bierbauer (1893–1956) and the composer Zoltán Kodály (1882–1967).[6] Although Wölfflin was not a mentor to any of these, many helped to spread his ideas in Hungary. Bierbauer, who received his doctorate at the Technische Universität in Munich in 1920, became a member of the Hungarian delegation to the Congrès Internationaux d'Architecture Moderne (CIAM) and edited *Tér és forma* (Space and form), the leading architectural periodical of interwar Hungary.[7] Kodály later studied Wölfflin's *Renaissance and Baroque* as well as *Principles*, which influenced his formulations regarding artistic styles and national elements in Hungarian folk music.[8]

The impact of *Principles* in literary studies was farther reaching. Alongside Fritz Strich (1882–1963), one of Wölfflin's students, Oskar Walzel (1864–1944) detached the study of literature from cultural history, advocating the application of the dyadic categories and proclaiming the theory of the "mutual illumination" of various arts.[9] These new models developed in the German-speaking realm were instrumental in the dissemination of the concepts of *Principles* in the interwar period in Hungary as well as

1. Heinrich Wölfflin, *Művészettörténeti alapfogalmak: A stílus fejlődésének problémája az újkori művészetben* (*Principles of Art History: The Problem of the Development of Style in Later Art*), trans. Stefánia Mándy (Budapest: Corvina, 1969)

Early Influence of Wölfflin's Ideas in Hungary

In the decade before the outbreak of World War I, a number of art historians in Hungary were concerned with the formal qualities and problems of perception of works of art. Besides Wölfflin's earlier writings, the works of Konrad Fiedler, Adolf von Hildebrand, Alois Riegl, August Schmarsow, and Bernard Berenson drew intensive study. The focal point of work on these questions was the chair of art history at the University of Budapest, held by Gyula (Julius) Pasteiner (1846–1924) for almost three decades (1890–1916). Research by Ferenc Gosztonyi on graduates who studied under Pasteiner provides important evidence for the reception of Wölfflin's psychologizing history of style within academic art history in Hungary.[11] First, the dissertation by Olga Elefánt (1884–1951) should be mentioned for its conceptual parallels to Wölfflin's dissertation, "Prolegomena to a Psychology of Architecture" (1886).[12] Hugó Kenczler (1884–1922), who was awarded a doctorate in 1907 for his empirical analysis of the importance of form in the psychology of art, in particular with relation to the sculptures of Michelangelo, used Wölfflin's studies as a starting point in his attempt to redefine the formalist approach.[13] Several works by Pasteiner's students appeared in *Athenaeum*, the journal of the Hungarian Philosophical Society, in which the sole Hungarian review of the first edition of *Principles* was published in 1916.[14] László Éber (1871–1935), a pioneer of research on late Renaissance and baroque art,[15] pointed out the importance of the new work for the study of these periods and emphasized that Wölfflin achieved his results by "almost deliberately ignoring the pioneering role of the great personalities of art."[16]

Éber was referring to Wölfflin's project of writing an "art history without names."[17] This approach, informed by the positivist "histoire sans noms" of Auguste Comte (1798–1857), was viewed as an overdetermined stylistic model and drew criticism in Hungary already before the end of World War I.[18] It was Kenczler who pointed out the necessity of expanding Wölfflin's interpretations of stylistic change by considering sociohistorical factors such as the work of guilds.[19] This perspective may be understandable in light of Kenczler's participation in the meetings of the Galilei Circle (Hung. Galilei Kör) and the Bembék. Both groups were part of the leftist political spectrum, which encompassed bourgeois radical, social democratic, and socialist intellectuals.[20] The Galilei Circle also functioned as a platform for the exchange of ideas and concepts related to pressing social and ideological questions. Current developments in the arts were also discussed at meetings, in the presence of artists, such as the poet and later film theorist Béla Balázs (1884–1949), as well as representatives of sociology, which was forming itself as an autonomous discipline, among them Karl Mannheim (1893–1947).[21] Mannheim, who studied in Budapest, Paris, Heidelberg, and Berlin, where he attended the lectures of Georg Simmel (1858–1918), assumed a leading role in the dissemination of the *Geisteswissenschaften* (human sciences) direction of German sociology in Hungary.[22] Another regular participant was the young philosopher György Lukács (1885–1971), who, in his dissertation, "A dráma formája" (The form of drama) and the essay "Megjegyzések az irodalomtörténet elméletéhez" (Notes toward the theory of literary history; 1910), questioned the notion of style as a universal and normative form.[23] The new model he proposed saw style as a synthesis between the aesthetic perception of form and the sociological concept of development. This approach was significantly influenced by the ideas of Simmel, whose lectures Lukács had attended in Berlin in 1906.[24]

In 1915, the publication year of *Principles*, Lukács and Balász established the Sunday Circle (Hung. Vasárnapi Kör), following the model of the intellectual salon of Max Weber (1864–1920), which Lukács had come to know between 1912 and 1915 during his stay in Heidelberg, where he prepared his habilitation.[25] For about three years the Sunday Circle meetings, attended by poets, philosophers, musicians, and art historians, provided an important platform in Budapest for theoretical reflections on the relationship between artistic production and worldview. Preceding the formation of the group, individual members had already worked on the psychological aspects of artistic form. In 1910 Johannes (János) Wilde (1888–1954) had finished a Hungarian translation of Hildebrand's *Das Problem der Form in der bildenden Kunst*, a work that had strongly influenced *Principles*.[26] The aforementioned Frederick Antal initially studied under Wölfflin in Berlin before completing his doctorate in Vienna in 1914 under Max Dvořák.[27] Wilde and Charles de Tolnay (Karl von Tolnai; 1899–1981) also joined the circle of Dvořák's disciples after 1916 and 1918 respectively.[28]

The most intense examination of Wölfflin's works in the Sunday Circle came from Arnold Hauser (1892–1978), who had been introduced to the group by Mannheim in 1916. Previously he studied philosophy and German and French philology in Budapest and in Paris.[29] In his dissertation (1918), which was strongly influenced by Lukács's habilitation project in Heidelberg, Hauser distinguished between aesthetics and theory of art, while emphasizing the role of aesthetics as an autonomous system.[30]

Hauser's critical stance toward *Principles* had been influenced by the political radicalization of the Sunday Circle, which was set off in late 1918 when Lukács and Balázs joined the Communist Party and deepened with the declaration of the Hungarian Soviet Republic in March 1919.[31] Following Lukács's assignment as deputy commissioner for education, Hauser and Mannheim were appointed to leading positions in the education sector,[32] while Antal, Wilde, and Kenczler worked for the Committee for the Socialization of Works of Art (Hung. Műkincseket Társadalmasító Bizottság).[33] Most of the staff of the Budapest Museum of Fine Arts, which in the 1910s was the most important center of professional art history in Hungary, went through a similar process of political radicalization.[34]

The White Terror, initiated after the fall of the Soviet Republic by the new autocratic regime of Miklós (Nicholas) Horthy (1868–1957), as well as increasing anti-Semitism forced both leading figures of revolutionary institutions and many Hungarian intellectuals into exile. For most of them, it was a first stage of exile, to be followed by a second in 1933 (Germany) or 1938 (Austria). The effects of the short-lived Hungarian Soviet Republic (March–August 1919) reverberated in the intellectual life of Europe.[35] In the following decades Mannheim and the art historians from the Sunday Circle became pivotal figures in the discipline of art history.[36]

Hungarian Positions on *Principles* in the Interwar Period in Exile

The Sunday Circle reassembled in Vienna and attempted to reposition itself within the Hungarian émigré community. As not all members were actively serving the Communist cause, conflicts within the group increased and led to Hauser's exclusion. The tensions eventually led to the disbanding of the circle in 1921.[37] The dispersal of the Budapest group coincided with initiatives in Germanophone academe to establish art history as a rigorous and exact science.[38] The Viennese Kunsthistorisches Institut, where Dvořák's seminar had become a haven for many art historians from the Sunday Circle, played an important role in this process. Prominent figures of the so-called Second (New) Vienna School, like Julius von Schlosser (1866–1938) and Hans Sedlmayr (1896–1984), aimed to transform Alois Riegl's concept of *Kunstwollen* into a rigorous approach to formal problems. At the same time this group took up Benedetto Croce's (1866–1952) critique of Wölfflin's "pure visibility" approach.[39]

An important platform for these methodological debates was the periodical

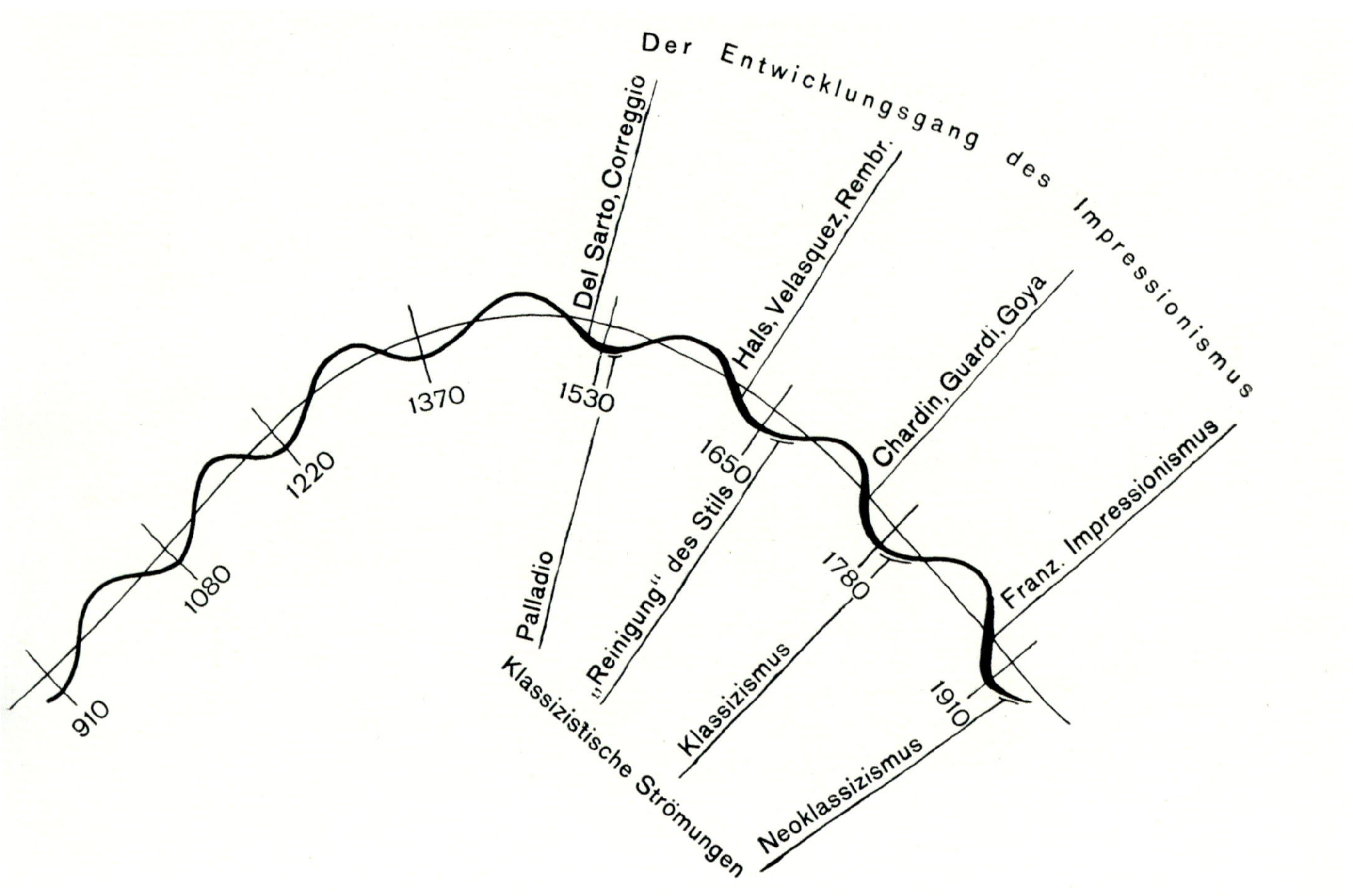

2. Impressionism and classicism, from Paul (Pál) Ligeti, *Der Weg aus dem Chaos: Eine Deutung des Weltgeschehens aus dem Rhythmus der Kunstentwicklung* (Munich, 1931)

Kritische Berichte zur kunstgeschichtlichen Literatur.[40] Antal, who had moved to Berlin, worked from 1926 until 1931 as its coeditor. His years in the German capital marked a period of intensive examination of Wölfflin's concepts. On the one hand, this concerned Antal's turn toward the concept of mannerism, passed over by Wölfflin in *Principles* but embraced by his second teacher, Dvořák. At the same time Antal tried to supplement analysis of form and style with reference to sociohistorical factors.[41] This new perspective on art production was furthered by his intensified contacts with Marxist groups and a trip to the Soviet Union in 1932.[42] There he was impressed by novel exhibition strategies in museums and art galleries.[43] An essential element of the new displays was the addition of historical objects or reproductions. These comparative exhibitions served to illustrate the economic and political contexts in which the works were created. The development of styles appeared as a reflex of class struggles. The theoretical justification for this novel presentation had been formulated by Aleksey Fyodorov-Davydov (1900–1969) and Fyodor Shmit (1877–1937) only a few years earlier.[44] Fyodorov-Davydov explained that these juxtapositions had been developed by merging Marxist theory with the art-historical approaches of Wölfflin and some of the key figures of the Vienna School.[45] Wölfflin's ideas also strongly influenced the works of Shmit, who for almost a decade directed the State Institute of Art History in Leningrad.[46] This institution, inaugurated in 1912, had been initially structured on the model of the Kunsthistorisches Seminar at the University of Berlin, where its founder, Count Valentin Zubov (1884–1969), had studied under Wölfflin.[47] In 1924 Zubov resigned as

director and emigrated to Paris. Shmit, who
was appointed as successor, had to accept
the implementation of a "sociological committee," which coordinated the activities
of the departments of the institute in the
field of sociology of art.[48] Shmit's displacement from this office in 1934 corresponded
with the wholesale dismissal from Soviet
museums in the mid-1930s of the new presentation strategies as strongly influenced by
"vulgar Marxism," a model that explained
the formation of the ideological superstructure as exclusively determined by economic
infrastructure.

Antal's shift of perspective coincided with
Hanna Levy's (1912–1984) Marxist critique
of *Principles*.[49] But Antal, who emigrated
to England in 1933, was able to finish and
publish his study on painting in Renaissance Florence only after the war. In the
monograph Antal identified the coexistence
of different styles, which he interpreted as
reflections of the diverging worldviews of
particular social strata, a model opposed to
the one presented in *Principles*.[50]

We encounter a similar constellation
with Arnold Hauser, who, after his dismissal from the Sunday Circle, studied art
history with Wölfflin's successor Adolph
Goldschmidt (1863–1944) and sociology
with Ernst Troeltsch (1865–1923) at the
University of Berlin until 1924. Upon returning to Vienna, while working for a film
company, he collected material for a survey
on the aesthetics and sociology of film and
studied the works of Wölfflin.[51] In 1938 he
had to leave Austria for England, where he
came into close contact with Mannheim,
who had fled earlier from Germany. During
the war years Hauser penned his *Social History of Art*, which was informed by categories such as social class, ideologies, and the
relevance of economic production methods.
This broad panorama of cultural production, which was published only in 1951, also
contained an extensive critique of the model
introduced by Wölfflin. In Hauser's view the
"self-contained…course of the history of art"
presented in *Principles* simplified complex
developments that in reality represented

dialectical processes with dynamic elements
in a constant change of meaning.[52]

Positions on *Principles* in Interwar Hungary

Against the backdrop of the general crisis
in the 1920s, publications that tried to
uncover an immanent rhythmic-periodic
structure of human culture became popular.[53] The most influential work from this
group was Oswald Spengler's (1880–1936)
Der Untergang des Abendlandes.[54] The
close connections between this publication
and formalist art history were addressed
even before the publication of its second
volume in 1923.[55] Although Wölfflin's name
was not mentioned, his "art history without names" remained central to Spengler's
rhythmic sequence of periods in the history
of mankind. Similar publications synthe-
sizing formalistic categories and models
became popular.

Hungary was no exception to this trend.
Crisis theories, labeled "krizeológia" (cris-
eology) by the philosopher and social critic
Béla Hamvas (1897–1968), gained considerable momentum in the country's intellectual
life. Spengler's book was received early in
Hungary, where it was criticized for its pes-
simistic outlook.[56] Nevertheless, it was a
landmark also in the field of artistic theory
and stimulated further reflections on the
interrelations between style and historical processes, for instance, in the works of
Ferenc (Franz) Lehel (1885–1975) and Pál
(Paul) Ligeti (1885–1941). Lehel, a painter
and art critic, presented a draft of a novel
morphology of style in his book, published
simultaneously in Hungary and Germany in
1929. In it Wölfflin is introduced as a "demi-
god of our heroic age," while his polarities
are characterized as obsolete.[57] The three-
layered system Lehel proposed as an alternative and his newly introduced style types
(primitive, classical, and baroque) were
rejected by the specialists.[58]

Ligeti's publications proved far more
influential. He started as a painter and then
studied architecture in Budapest, Berlin, and
Munich, where he presumably also attended

Wölfflin's lectures. After his return to Hungary he proclaimed the dawn of a new, internationalized architectural style, which would be shaped by the power of economics. Through his activities in the Hungarian section of CIAM-Ost, Ligeti got in contact with several leading modernist architects.[59] This close relationship is reflected in the title of his volume *Új Pantheon felé* (Towards a new Pantheon; 1926), which alludes to Le Corbusier's *Vers une architecture* (1923).[60] At the same time, Ligeti's ideas were strongly anchored in the German tradition, which "equated *Zeitgeist* and art history."[61] In his book he took up arguments from pre–World War I art-historical discourse and from the cultural-morphological works of Spengler and Kurt Breysig (1867–1940), whose *Stufenbau und die Gesetze der Weltgeschichte* (1905) shows similarities with the morphological development model of *Principles*.[62]

Ligeti developed arguments on the connection between architecture and society and presented a substantially extended German version of his work in 1931. In *Der Weg aus dem Chaos*, he charted the course of the history of mankind and human culture in large undulations with a nod to Marx and Spengler, albeit without adopting the latter's cultural pessimism.[63] Using examples from all branches of art and based on categories and combinations, relying on the concepts developed in Wölfflin's *Principles*, he asserted the existence of regular sequences or patterns. Ligeti divided the history of art into three major phases, each dominated by a certain genre: architecture stood for the Middle Ages, in which centripetal forces operated; sculpture represented consolidation during the Renaissance; and painting was the main genre in the baroque era—a period that was characterized by an easiness of life but also impeded progress. The main phases were split into subphases, which could be identified not only in art but also in all other areas of life, such as economics, religion, and politics. Ligeti used a variety of diagrams to visualize his main thesis of a society that had lost its unity

(fig. 2). Modern architecture, staged as a contrast to a contemptible past through images of the buildings of Le Corbusier, Walter Gropius, and J. J. P. Oud, appeared as a cohesive force enabling a new community.[64]

Principles and Academic Art History in Interwar Hungary

Wölfflin's writings and *Principles* in particular met with an ambivalent reception within institutional art history in Hungary. In the interwar period, debates on the applicability of formalistic and intellectual history (Hung. *szellemtörténet*) dominated art history and literary studies equally. Both fields were also engaged in a lively exchange with history as the leading discipline, in a period that witnessed the rise of cultural history and a series of initiatives to rewrite the national history after the fall of the monarchy and the territorial disintegration of Hungary after 1920. This is illustrated by the volume *A magyar történetírás új útjai* (New paths of Hungarian historiography), edited by Bálint Hóman (1885–1951). In his presentation of the discipline of art history in this collection, Tibor Gerevich (1882–1954), a follower of the positions of Benedetto Croce, acknowledged the extraordinary impact of *Principles* in the field but expressed reservations about the potential of Wölfflin's "optical art history."[65] In 1915 Gerevich had characterized the formalistic approach ironically as "optic-subjective."[66] He nonetheless used stylistic analysis to define national characteristics in art.[67] In this context he derived his interpretations of national artistic forms from Wölfflin's *The Sense of Form in Art* (*Italien und das deutsche Formgefühl*).[68]

Gerevich's approach, which associated the characteristically Hungarian with a certain psychic habitus, was criticized in 1936 by József Bodonyi (1908–1944) in a programmatic essay.[69] Bodonyi, who had studied in Vienna under Julius von Schlosser, combined his criticism with an introduction of his ideas of a rigorous scientific method. With his positive appraisal of the formalist method and theories of Wölfflin and Riegl that asserted an immanent stylistic development, he positioned himself against cultural historical approaches and the model of historical materialism.[70]

The application of *Principles* to the Hungarian artistic heritage also proved problematic in terms of chronology. Gerevich and other researchers increasingly based their interpretation of the Renaissance in Hungary on the periodization followed in the multivolume history of Hungary edited by Hóman and Gyula Szekfű (1883–1955) in the 1930s. There, the Renaissance had been defined as the period between Matthias Corvinus's accession to power in 1448 and the Battle of Mohács in 1526. In Wölfflin's chronology the initial phase of the baroque started in the mid-sixteenth century, while Szekfű, the influential Catholic ideologist of the Horthy regime, placed the baroque in the eighteenth century and associated it with the establishment of Habsburg rule in Hungary.

Against the background of these chronological differences it is not surprising that *Principles* at first played only a marginal role in the study of Hungarian baroque art and that one of the few affirmative references to Wölfflin's work in the Hungarian interwar historiography of art appears in György Gombosi's (1904–1945) investigations of Trecento painting.[71] Gombosi's studies are among the outstanding works on Italian Renaissance art, Hungarian research on which went almost unnoticed outside the country in the interwar period.[72] Further references to Wölfflin's approach can be found in Henrik Horváth's (1888–1940) monograph on the stonemasons of Buda, where morphological criteria as well as "art history without names" played an important role.[73]

In literary studies, Hungarian specialists took up the idea of a transfer of style categories across the genre boundaries introduced by Strich and Walzel. The forum for the discussion of these concepts was the Minerva Society, founded in 1921.[74] The journal *Minerva* published in the following two decades important studies on the history of ideas like Tivadar Thienemann's (1890–1985) work on basic concepts of literary history.[75] The most illustrious figure associated with the Minerva Society was the writer Antal Szerb (1901–1945), who partially followed Wölfflin's stylistic criteria of periodization but also integrated aspects of intellectual history, especially with a view to the Renaissance, in his history of world literature (1941).[76]

Wölfflin's works were also used by other members of the young generation of intellectual historians like the social philosopher Tibor Joó (1901–1945), who, in his debate with Szekfű, presented *Principles* as a balanced approach to research on the baroque. In contrast to the latter's one-sided emphasis on the Catholic component, Joó pointed out, Wölfflin deliberately considered works of art from Protestant as well as Catholic contexts.[77] Later Joó applied the concepts introduced in *Principles* in his reconstruction of the worldview of the poet Nicholas Zrínyi (1620–1664).[78] Finally, the analysis by the literary historian László Baránszky-Jób (1897–1987) of the new medium of film, using Wölfflin's concepts, should be mentioned.[79]

The period 1944–1948 marked a caesura for both art history and literary history in Hungary. A number of leading scholars who had also played an important role in the reception, transmittal, and critique of *Principles*, such as András Péter, György Gombosi, Antal Szerb, and Tibor Joó, fell victim to the terror of the Arrow Cross, the German occupation, or the fighting during the last months of the war.[80] From 1948, as the Hungarian Communists gradually took power, cultural and scientific institutions and organizations adapted to Stalinist imperatives issuing from Moscow. Accordingly, the interpretation of Wölfflin's works established in the Soviet Union dominated in Hungary for almost a decade.

Principles under Communist Auspices in the Soviet Union and Hungary

The reception of Wölfflin's writings in Russia dates from two decades before *Principles* was published in Russian. Russian versions of *Classic Art* (1912) and *Renaissance and Baroque* (1913) appeared at the moment in which art history was emerging as an academic discipline.[81]

After the revolution, *Principles* was first studied by pioneers of literary theory such as Boris Eikhenbaum (1886–1959), a member of the Society for the Study of Poetic Language (OPOJAZ), founded in 1916. Eikhenbaum read *Principles* in 1919 and highlighted it in his *Theory of the Formal Method* (1927) as a successful example of Western formalism, which, however, ignored the ideological significance of the work of art. Accordingly, *Principles* functioned as an important reference for the new formalist method.[82] As with contemporary developments in Hungary, the studies of Walzel and Strich were instrumental for the diffusion of the concepts of *Principles*. Here the Leningrad Germanist and pioneer of comparative literature Viktor Žirmunskij (1891–1971) played a key role.[83]

The Russian formalists were not a homogeneous group, and factional rivalry surfaced as early as the 1920s. Disputes between the groups were often linked to efforts to adapt a method to prevailing political or ideological conditions.[84] For example, *The Formal Method in Literary Scholarship*, published in 1928 by Pavel Medvedev (1891–1938) and influenced by Mikhail Bakhtin (1895–1975), accused the formalists around Eikhenbaum of incorrectly interpreting the Western formalist method. At the end of the volume Medvedev emphasized the importance of Wölfflin's "art history without names" as a way of developing an objective history of art. In contrast to Eikhenbaum, however, Medvedev saw the alternation of styles as determined by ideological factors.[85] Bakhtin was himself interested in Wölfflin's works and, despite his enthusiasm for writers like Dostoevsky and Rabelais, planned to write a history of literature "without names."[86]

Principles in the original German played an equally important role in the young Soviet academic art history. It was read along with works of other Western formalists in the Seminar for Theory of Art History and Museum Studies at the Rumyantsev Museum in Moscow, founded in 1921.[87] Another focal point was the Section of Spatial Arts of the State Academy of Artistic Sciences, under whose aegis a collective volume on the baroque in was published in 1926. Using Wölfflin's categories, its authors demonstrated that the Russian monuments were an integral part of the universal baroque phenomenon.[88]

The publication of the Russian translation of *Principles* in 1930 coincided with the project to develop a new Marxist theory of artistic creation. In these debates the Hungarian exiles to the Soviet Union György Lukács and Ivan Matsa (János Mácza; 1893–1974) assumed leading roles. Lukács finalized his theory of realism, which became the basis for the socialist realist doctrine of literature and visual art. He also collaborated with Mikhail Lifshitz (1905–1983) on an edition of the newly discovered early writings of Karl Marx. A related project was an anthology of texts of Marx and Engels on art edited by Lifshitz in 1933. The book, which was intended to provide the theoretical framework for socialist discourse on art, was disseminated worldwide in translations up until the collapse of the Soviet bloc in 1989.[89] Although in this publication Wölfflin's writings were classified as "vulgar sociology," they were not banned in principle in the Soviet Union.[90]

In this context, it is hardly surprising that the Russian translations of *Principles* and of *Italien und das deutsche Formgefühl*, published in 1934 as *Iskusstvo Italii i Germanii epohi Renessansa* (Art in Italy and Germany in the age of the Renaissance), were supplemented by introductory essays that positioned the publications dogmatically. The introduction to *Principles*, by Robert Pel'še (1880–1955), presented Wölfflin as a formalist and used his method as a pretext for a polemic against the sociological approach, opposed by Lenin. That these references were a rhetorical maneuver to evade censorship becomes clear if we consider that Pel'še also stressed the significance of Wölfflin's works.[91]

A less conciliatory interpretation was presented by Lazar' I. Rempel (1907–1992), one of Matsa's collaborators, who in 1934, in the light of contemporary political developments in Germany, introduced Wölfflin as a forerunner of bourgeois fascist science. He further accused Wölfflin not only of promoting irrational tendencies by emphasizing the national spirit in art but also of transforming the opposition between baroque and Renaissance into a German-Italian antinomy. In addition Rempel presented the defense of the "materialistic" perspective on Italian Renaissance art as an important task.[92] Rempel's attitude reflects the special place assigned to the Renaissance as a "healthy stage" in the development of art during the Stalinist period.[93] This assumption was based on Friedrich Engels's (1820–1895) introduction to *Dialectics of Nature* (1883), where he praised the Renaissance as the greatest progressive movement in the history of mankind. Accordingly, the Italian Renaissance formed a basis for the new Stalinist architecture and social realist painting.

The claim for a defense of the Renaissance against capitalist Western falsifications was voiced again in the anticosmopolitan campaign initiated by the All-Soviet Communist Party in February 1948. These new ideological paradigms are vividly illustrated in the volume published in 1951 by the Academy of Sciences of the USSR. There, leading art historians like Vladimir Kemenov (1908–1988), Viktor Lazarev (1897–1976), Boris Vipper (1888–1967), and Mikhail Alpatov (1902–1986) criticized the "formalist tendencies" of contemporary Western art (that is, surrealism) and the "bourgeois" historiography of Renaissance art.[94]

This collection of essays, in which the Soviet Union appears as the true heir of the humanistic ideals of the Renaissance, introduced to Moscow's satellites a model for a historical-materialist understanding of this epoch.[95] A Hungarian translation was published in 1953, followed by a German edition in 1954.[96] Although Wölfflin's name was not mentioned, his *Principles* was presumably the focus of Alpatov's criticism, presented in the tone of a war correspondent.[97] In his view, one of the main objectives of the "attacks of the bourgeois art historians" was the High Renaissance. With its associated vision of harmony, the High Renaissance appeared as a period without social struggle, which stood in contrast to the Marxist perspective. Alpatov's next indictment revolves around the phenomenon of mannerism, which in Wölfflin's cyclical model was symptomatic of the downswing. Here Alpatov's critique targeted German scholars' antihumanistic outlook on this period, which had been advanced in close interdependence with contemporary avant-garde currents.[98]

Additionally, Wölfflin was associated with an aggressive stance that presented the baroque as a manifestation of a "Germanic spirit." In the entry on the baroque (1950) for the *Bolshaya sovetskaya entsiklopediya* (Great Soviet encyclopedia), Viktor Lazarev and Mikhail Il'in (1903–1981) criticized the bourgeois interpretation of the baroque as an epochal style relying exclusively on formal aspects, a perspective diametrically opposed to the materialistic-dialectical approach, which associated the baroque with the heyday of absolutism and the culture of nobility.[99] That Lazarev's and Il'in's model was intended as a blueprint for studies on the baroque in the countries of the newly established Eastern Bloc is indicated by the translations of this article.[100] The Hungarian version appeared in the series Szovjet Művészettörténet (Soviet art history), which from 1951 to 1969 presented summaries of monographs and digests of ideologically relevant debates in the Soviet Union.[101] Among these, Anatoly Shtambok's article "A művészet fejlődésének idealista magyarázata" (Against the idealistic interpretation of the development of Art) deserves special attention, as its author located art history and other humanities in "the sphere of social ideology" and assigned them an important role in the education of the masses.[102] At the same time, Shtambok presented fundamental reflections on the development of styles in accordance with the Stalinist reading of the Marxist model of base and superstructure.[103] In an article on "tasks" following the Nineteenth Congress of the Communist Party of the Soviet Union in 1952 (the last public speech of Stalin), Wölfflin's *Principles* was branded as dangerous because of its denial of the events that shaped historical development.[104]

Frederick Antal and Arnold Hauser's critique of *Principles* in the Climate of the Cold War

At the height of the Cold War, the publications of Antal and Hauser faced criticism, primarily of their dialectical-materialistic perspective, associated in the West with Marxism.[105] In response, both tried to position their approaches within a wider art-historiographical framework. Antal criticized Wölfflin's formalist isolation of the work of art while lamenting the success of his followers in the United States. As a reaction to these trends Antal advocated a stronger consideration of sociohistorical factors.[106]

Hauser's *Philosophy of Art History* was a reaction to the reservations expressed about his *Social History*, and especially Ernst Gombrich's highly polemical review of this work.[107] Gombrich (1909–2001) saw Hauser "caught…in the intellectual mousetrap of dialectical materialism."[108] On the other hand, Gombrich's polemic against Hauser's model of stylistic development represents a stage in his criticism of studies of cultural wholes, which he associated with Hegelianism. According to his view these concepts paved the way for totalitarian ideas and therefore presented an imminent danger to art history as an independent field of inquiry.[109] Gombrich's perspective had been shaped by his personal experiences of exile and, above all, intellectual exchange with the philosopher Karl Popper (1902–1994), who criticized Karl Mannheim on several occasions. In his *The Open Society and Its Enemies* (1945), Popper situated Hegel as one of the spiritual fathers of modern totalitarianism.[110]

Hauser's critical stance against Wölfflin's immanent model of development had been influenced by cooperation with Theodor W. Adorno (1903–1969), the leading figure of the Frankfurt School of critical theory, on problems of ideology. Already in 1954 in a panel jointly organized with Adorno at the sociologists' meeting in Heidelberg, Hauser had criticized Wölfflin's adherence to an abstract concept of history as a major error.[111] This line of argumentation was broadened in *The Philosophy of Art History*, where the main point of critique was Wölfflin's "art history without names," which ignored individuals and rejected the notion of progress, advocating an aesthetic of anonymity and the existence of a collective in the tradition of Hegel.[112] The organismic principle used to describe the development of style emphasized constant contact with the past and was therefore compared by Hauser with the strategies previously used by reactionary powers as a "spiritual weapon" to deprive reform movements of their credit. The "organismic doctrine" was also held responsible for the rise of a conservative concept of the spirit of the nation (*Volksgeist*). From the angle of a critique of ideology, Hauser branded Wölfflin's organicist historicism as a conservative reactionary theory in the tradition of Hegel.[113] This perspective was certainly influenced by the later transformation of the organismic model of *Principles* in the works of Wilhelm Pinder (1878–1947) and Oswald Spengler.[114]

The Reevaluation of Principles between Thaw and Détente

Wölfflin's rehabilitation started during the de-Stalinization initiated by Nikita Khrushchev's so-called Secret Speech at the Twentieth Congress of the Communist Party in February 1956. In the same year an article on publishing practice in newly established Hungarian art history journals pointed out the impossibility of isolating the aesthetic component from the historical basis of art history. Wölfflin, Riegl, and Dvořák appeared together as models for a fruitful combination of both levels in research.[115]

During the thaw period, debates on realist dogma began in the Eastern Bloc, leading to a change in the assessment of Wölfflin's works. While artistic preferences were increasingly connected with humanistic values in general, Gerhard Strauss (1908–1984) presented Wölfflin in 1960, on the occasion of the 150th anniversary of the Humboldt University of Berlin, as an important part of the tradition of the Berlin institution and of the history of the discipline. This heritage formed a starting point for setting up a decidedly Marxist history of art. Strauss employed the customary rhetoric and, referencing Soviet specialists, introduced Wölfflin as a representative of a late bourgeois art history, which turned away from reality because of its idealistic outlook. At the same time he praised the critique of mannerism voiced by Wölfflin in his *Classic Art*. He saw Wölfflin's interpretation of individualization as a diagnosis of the alienation of the artist from the people. According to Strauss the recent developments of "bourgeois art" were a continuation of this direction, which Wölfflin criticized. Thus *Principles* appeared as a positive attempt to explore the dialectics on which artistic phenomena were based.[116] Strauss's initiative to position Wölfflin in a Marxist context was welcomed in Hungary as a "timely" approach.[117] In an anthology published concomitantly in Moscow, Natalija Geršenzon-Čegodaeva (1907–1977) praised Wölfflin's model for the development of Renaissance art while criticizing the ethnic connotation of certain aesthetic preferences in his works. The volume is of further interest because it mentions Antal and Hauser as Wölfflin's critics. The author advocates their sociohistorical approach in principle but characterizes both as followers of a "bourgeois sociology."[118] Similar associations with a "vulgar Marxism" were voiced in the afterword by Jaromír Neumann (1924–2001) to the Czech edition (1954) of Antal's monograph on Florentine painting as well as in contemporary publications of left-wing groups in Western Europe.[119]

Following the suppression of the 1956 uprising, historiography in Hungary witnessed a return of national momentum. At the same time, historical processes in Hungary were examined, taking into account both Eastern and Western Europe. In the course of this reorientation, contacts of Hungarian historical research with foreign countries intensified. Studies by the literary historian Tibor Klaniczay (1923–1992) are exemplary of the liberalization during the "new course" initiated by János Kádár (1912–1989) in 1961. Klaniczay addressed methodological issues of art historiography and integrated the approaches developed in this area into literary historical studies. The new approach required the establishment of a new system of periodization, a step that implied a return to the category of styles. Notwithstanding, Klaniczay criticized the positions of formalist art history, including Wölfflin. He praised Hauser's studies and thus contributed to popularizing his positions in Hungary.[120] Against this background, it is an irony of history that *Principles* was translated into Hungarian before Hauser's works. In the context of Hungarian academia, there have been few attempts since 1961 to apply *Principles*. These include a series of studies in architectural history by Zoltán Szentkirályi (1927–1999) and the literary-historical works of Iván Sándor Kovács (1937–) on mannerism.[121]

A special event was the Congress of the Comité International d'Histoire de l'Art (CIHA) in Budapest in 1969, organized by Lajos Vayer (1913–2001), which for the first time addressed artistic developments in East Central Europe and aimed at restoring contacts with the Eastern Bloc. The meeting was also the visible result of rapprochement between the representatives of the discipline on both sides of the Iron Curtain. One indicator of this new climate was readiness to discuss methodological issues, exemplified by the publication of articles by Alpatov in Western journals in the early 1960s.[122] At the CIHA meeting in Budapest, special attention was devoted to the social history of art and the positions developed in the context of the Sunday Circle as a methodological bridge between East and West. Interestingly,

Wölfflin's approach was discussed together with the positions of his staunch critic Arnold Hauser and Erwin Panofsky's iconological studies.[123]

A review of the Hungarian translation of *Principles* published shortly after the CIHA Congress emphasized that this work had not been "modern" at the moment of its publication, when compared to Lukács's *The Theory of the Novel*.[124] Nevertheless, Wölfflin's work, as presented in the review, provided important impulses for study in the most diverse areas of Hungarian culture, even without translation from Hungarian. The 1969 translation of Wölfflin's book proved to be far less influential, but its publication as the first volume in a newly created series nevertheless makes it an important document for the special climate in Hungary at the end of the 1960s. This liberal climate persisted in Hungary longer than in the other countries of the Eastern Bloc.

NOTES

1. Heinrich Wölfflin, *Művészettörténeti alapfogalmak: A stílus fejlődésének problémája az újkori művészetben* (*Principles of Art History: The Problem of the Development of Style in Later Art*), trans. Stefánia Mándy, with an introduction by Anna Zádor, Művészet és elmélet, vol. 1 (Budapest, 1969). A new edition (without the introductory essay) was published in Budapest in 2001.

2. See http://thewolfflinproject.utoronto.ca/editions-translations (accessed May 2, 2019), and, on Poland, the essay by Wojciech Bałus in this volume.

3. Heinrich Wölfflin, *Kunstgeschichtliche Grundbegriffe: Das Problem der Stilentwicklung in der neueren Kunst*, ed. and afterword by Hubert Faensen, Fundus-Bücher, vols. 87/88 (Dresden, 1984). See also Oliver Sukrow, in *Kunstgeschichten 1915: 100 Jahre Heinrich Wölfflin*, Kunstgeschichtliche Grundbegriffe, ed. Matteo Burioni, Burcu Dogramaci, and Ulrich Pfisterer (Zentralinstitut für Kunstgeschichte, Munich, 2015), cat. VIII.10. For an updated list of the translations see http://thewolfflinproject.utoronto.ca/editions-translations (accessed May 2, 2019).

4. Genrich Vel'flin [Heinrich Wölfflin], *Osnovnye ponjatija istorii iskusstv: Problema evoljucii stilja v novom iskusstve* (*Principles of Art History: The Problem of the Development of Style in Later Art*), trans. A. A. Frankovskij, introductory essay by Robert Pel'še (Moscow and Leningrad, 1930).

5. Petra Kárai and Nóra Veszprémi, eds., *München magyarul: Magyar művészek Münchenben 1850–1914* (Munich in Hungarian: Hungarian artists in Munich 1850–1914) (Magyar Nemzeti Galéria [Hungarian National Gallery], Budapest, 2009), A Magyar Nemzeti Galéria kiadványai; 2009, 6; Luka Skansi, "What Is Artistic Form? Munich–Moscow 1900–1925," in *Russian Émigré Culture: Conservatism or Evolution*, ed. Christoph Flamm, Henry Keazor, and Roland Marti (Cambridge, 2013), 69–71.

6. Leó Popper to György Lukács, February 17, 1910, in *Lukács György levelezése (1902–1917)* (The correspondence of György Lukács, 1902–1917), ed. Éva Fekete and Éva Karádi (Budapest, 1981), 176; Gábor Pataki, "Rabinovszky Máriusz (1895–1953)," in *"Emberek, és nem frakkok": A magyar művészettörténet-írás nagy alakjai* ("Humans, not tailcoats": Significant figures of Hungarian art historiography), ed. István Bardoly and Csilla Markója (Budapest, 2007), 387; Csilla Markója, "'Ellentétek keresztezési pontja vagy magad is'—Zádor Anna kapcsolatai és a magyar művészettörténet-írás a két háború között" ("The crossroads of contradictions or also yourself"—Anna Zádor's connections and Hungarian historiography of art between the two wars), *Enigma* 15, no. 54 (2008): 53; Anna Wessely, "Die Aufhebung des Stilbegriffs: Frederick Antals Rekonstruktion künstlerischer Entwicklungen auf marxistischer Grundlage," *Kritische Berichte* 4, nos. 2–3 (1976): 17; Mária Prokopp, "Péter András (1903–1944)—A művészettörténész példaképe" (Péter András [1903–1944]—The art historian's role model), *Enigma* 21, no. 80 (2014): 81.

7. Júlia Tészabó, "A tér és forma" (Space and form [journal]), *Kritika* 10, no. 11 (1981): 16–18.

8. Anna Dalos, "Kodály Zoltán: A fúga művészete; a concerto neoklasszicizmusáról" (Kodály Zoltán: The art of fugue; on the neoclassicism of the concerto), *Magyar zene* 42, nos. 3–4 (2004): 381–385.

9. Oskar Walzel, *Wechselseitige Erhellung der Künste: Ein Beitrag zur Würdigung kunstgeschichtlicher Begriffe* (Berlin, 1917); Fritz Strich, *Deutsche Klassik und Romantik oder Vollendung und Unendlichkeit: Ein Vergleich* (Munich, 1922). See also Jost Hermand, *Literaturwissenschaft und Kunstwissenschaft: Methodische Wechselbeziehungen seit 1900* (Stuttgart, 1965), 17–18, and Heinrich Dilly, "Heinrich Wölfflin und Fritz Strich," in *Literaturwissenschaft und Geistesgeschichte 1910 bis 1925*, ed. Christoph König and Eberhard Lämmert (Frankfurt am Main, 1993), 265–285.

10. Sándor Galamb, "Irodalomtörténetírás és művészettörténet" (Literary history writing and art history), *Budapesti szemle* 171, no. 487 (1917): 41–42.

11. Ferenc Gosztonyi, "A Pasteiner-tanítványok" (The Pasteiner disciples), *Ars Hungarica* 38, no. 1 (2012): 11–71.

12. Olga Elefánt, "A tér és a testtömeg az építészetben" (Space and body volume in architecture), *Athenaeum* 16, nos. 3 and 4 (1907): 339–355, 470–479. See also Gosztonyi, "A Pasteiner-tanítványok," 32.

13. Hugó Kenczler, "A forma jelentőségének empirikus vizsgálata a művészeti alkotás psychologiájában, különös tekintettel Michelangelo szobrászatára" (An empirical study of the significance of form in the psychology of art, with special regard to Michelangelo's sculpture), *Athenaeum* 16, nos. 3 and 4 (1907): 310–326, 456–469; 17, no. 1 (1908): 29–38. On Kenczler's biography see István Bardoly, "'Tévedéseiben is becsületes idealista': Apró adalékok Kenczler Hugó életéhez" ("He is also an honest idealist in his mistakes": Small additions to the biography of Hugó Kenczler), in *Etűdök: Tanulmányok Granasztóiné Györffy Katalin tiszteletére* (Etudes: Studies in honor of Katalin Granasztóiné Györffy), ed. István Bardoly (Budapest, 2004), 373–385.

14. László Éber, "Heinrich Wölfflin: *Kunstgeschichtliche Grundbegriffe*," *Athenaeum*, n.s. 2, no. 3 (1916): 233–235.

15. See Ernő Marosi, "Éber László: A normális művészettörténész" (László Éber: The normal art historian), in Bardoly and Markója, *"Emberek, és nem frakkok"*, 143–160.

16. Éber, "Heinrich Wölfflin," 235 (my translation).

17. Heinrich Wölfflin, *Kunstgeschichtliche Grundbegriffe: Das Problem der Stilentwickelung in der neueren Kunst* (Munich, 1915), v.

18. Daniel Adler, "The Formalist's Compromise: Wölfflin and Psychology," in *German Art History and Scientific Thought: Beyond Formalism*, ed. Mitchell Benjamin Frank and Dan Adler (Burlington, VT, 2012), 85; Gosztonyi, "A Pasteiner-tanítványok," 39.

19. See Gábor Endrődi, "A 'szentek fuvarosa': Divald Kornél felső-magyarországi topográfiája és fényképei 1900–1919" (The "Saint's Carriage": Kornél Divald's topography and photographs of Upper Hungary 1900–1919), *Ars Hungarica* 29, nos. 1–2 (2001): 379–380.

20. Zoltán Novák, *A Vasárnap Társaság: Lukács Györgynek és csoportosulásának eszmei válsága, kiútkeresésük az első világháború időszakában* (The Sunday Society: The ideological crisis during the First World War and the search for a solution by György Lukács and his group) (Budapest, 1979), 71 and 176 (on the Bembék Group) and 181–184 (on the Galilei Circle).

21. Péter Csunderlik, *Radikálisok, szabadgondolkodók, ateisták: A Galilei Kör (1908–1919) története* (Radicals, free thinkers, atheists: A history of the Galilei Circle [1908–1919]) (Budapest, 2017), 193.

22. Andrew Hemingway, "Arnold Hauser: Between Marxism and Romantic Anti-Capitalism," *Kunst und Politik* 20 (2018): 97.

23. An enlarged version of the dissertation was published in 1911 as György Lukács, *A modern dráma fejlödésének története* (The history of the evolution of the modern drama), 2 vols. (Budapest, 1911).

24. Tamás Demeter, "The Sociological Tradition of Hungarian Philosophy," *Studies in East European Thought* 60, nos. 1–2 (2008): 5; see also György Lukács, *Notes on Georg Simmel's Lessons, 1906/07, and on a "Sociology of Art," c. 1909*, introduction by Lívia Páldi (Ostfildern, 2011).

25. Gerhard Sauder, "Von Formalitäten zur Politik: Georg Lukács' Heidelberger Habilitationsversuch," *Zeitschrift für Literaturwissenschaft und Linguistik* 14 (1984): 80–85.

26. Ernő Marosi, "A bécsi művészettörténeti iskola magyar kapcsolataihoz" (On the Hungarian connections of the Vienna School of art history), *Enigma* 21, no. 84 (2015): 16. On *Principles* and Hildebrand's *Das Problem der Form* see David Summers, "Heinrich Wölfflin's 'Kunstgeschichtliche Grundbegriffe,' 1915," *The Burlington Magazine* 151, no. 1276 (July 2009): 478.

27. Wessely, "Die Aufhebung des Stilbegriffs," 17.

28. Paul Stirton, "The Vienna School in Hungary: Antal, Wilde and Fülep," *Journal of Art Historiography* 8 (June 2013).

29. See "Hauser Arnold két önéletrajza" (Two autobiographies of Arnold Hauser), *Enigma* 24, no. 91 (2017): 46–51.

30. Arnold Hauser: "Az esztétikai rendszerezés problémája" (The problems of aesthetic systematization, *Athenaeum* 4 (1918): 331–357. See also Sándor Radnóti, "Autonómia — heteronómia (Hauser Arnold életművéről)" (Autonomy—heteronomy [On the life of Arnold Hauser]), *Holmi* 4 (1992): 1891.

31. David Kettler, *Marxismus und Kultur: Mannheim und Lukács in den ungarischen Revolutionen 1918/19* (Neuwied–Berlin, 1967), 43–53.

32. Lee Congdon, *Exile and Social Thought: Hungarian Intellectuals in Germany and Austria, 1919–1933* (Princeton, NJ, 1991), 36–38.

33. See Ernő Margitay, "Vörös művészeti politika" (Red art policy), *Magyar Iparművészet* 22 (1919): 51–52.

34. Ernő Marosi, "Henszlmann, avagy: A művészettörténész helye a magyar társadalomban" (Henszlmann, or: The place of the art historian in Hungarian society), *Ars Hungarica* 26, no. 2 (1998): 33–34.

35. Peter Burke, "The Central European Moment in British Cultural Studies," in *Literary History—Cultural History: Force Fields and Tensions*, ed. Herbert Grabes (Tübingen, 2001), 281; Gail Day, *Dialectical Passions: Negation in Postwar Art Theory* (New York, 2011), 10–11.

36. See Csilla Markója, "János (Johannes) Wilde and Max Dvořák, or Can We Speak of a Budapest School of Art History?," *Journal of Art Historiography* 17 (December 2017); Marosi, "Henszlmann," 34.

37. Mary Gluck, *Georg Lukács and His Generation 1900–1918* (Cambridge, MA, 1985), 211–222.

38. Christian Fuhrmeister, "*Reine Wissenschaft*: Art History in Germany and the Notion of 'Pure Science' and 'Objective Scholarship,' 1920–1950," in Frank and Adler, *German Art History and Scientific Thought*, 166–168.

39. See Evonne Levy's introduction to this volume.

40. Heinrich Dilly, *Deutsche Kunsthistoriker 1933–1945* (Berlin, 1988), 17–22.

41. Wessely, "Die Aufhebung des Stilbegriffs," 26–27.

42. Nicos Hadjinicolaou and Yannis Hadjinicolaou, "Form als Ausdruck von Geschmack," in Frederick Antal, *Klassizismus, Romantik, Realismus: Vorgestellt von Nicos Hadjinicolaou und Yannis Hadjinicolaou* (Zurich, 2014), 223.

43. Frederick Antal, "Über Museen in der Sowjetunion" (1932), *Kritische Berichte* 4, nos. 2–3 (1976): 5–13.

44. Masha Chlenova, "Soviet Museology during the Cultural Revolution: An Educational Turn, 1928–1933," *Histoire@Politique*, no. 33 (September–December 2017), https://www.histoire-politique.fr/index.php?numero=33&rub=dossier&item=311 (accessed May 2, 2019); Vitaly Ananiev, "Fyodor Shmit's 'Social Museum': On the Theorization of the Form and Purposes of Museums in Early Soviet Russia," *Muzeológia a kultúrne dedičstvo* 6, no. 2 (2018): 33–41.

45. Konstantin Akinsha and Adam Jolles, "On the Third Front: The Soviet Museum and Its Public during the Cultural Revolution," *Canadian American Slavic Studies* 43, nos. 1–4 (2009): 205.

46. Marina Dmitrieva, "Formal′nyĭ metod v iskusstvoznanii i mezhdisstsiplinarnye granitsy: Genrikh Vel′flin—Ĭozef Strzhigovskiĭ—Fedor Shmit" (The formal method in art history and interdisciplinary boundaries: Heinrich Wölfflin—Josef Strzygowski—Fyodor Shmit), in *Epocha "Ostranenija": Russkij formalizm i sovremennoe gumanitarnoe znanie* (The era of "separation": Russian formalism and modern knowledge in the humanities), ed. Jan Levčenko and Igor Pil′ščikov, Novoe literaturnoe obozrenie, Naučnoe priloženie, vol. 164 (Moscow, 2017), 401–409.

47. Anna Troitskaya, "Actualization and Deactualization in Art Studies: The Experience of the Institute of Art History," *Rivista di estetica* 67 (2018): 117–118.

48. Vitaly Ananiev, "The Institute of Art History and the Problem of Aesthetic Education in Russia in the First Quarter of the Twentieth Century," *Muzeológia a kultúrne dedičstvo* 4, no. 2 (2016): 18–19.

49. Hanna Levy, *Henri Wölfflin: Sa théorie, ses prédécesseurs* (PhD diss., Université de Paris; Rottweil, 1936).

50. Frederick Antal, *Florentine Painting and Its Social Background: The Bourgeois Republic before Cosimo de' Medici's Advent to Power, XIV and Early XV Centuries* (London, 1947).

51. "Hauser Arnold két önéletrajza," 150.

52. Arnold Hauser, *The Social History of Art and Literature*, 2 vols. (London, 1951), 2:426–428. See also Axel Gelfert, "Art History, the Problem of Style, and Arnold Hauser's Contribution to the History and Sociology of Knowledge," *Studies in East European Thought* 64, nos. 1–2 (2012): 131–132.

53. See Paul Frankl, "Review of *Adama von Scheltema: Die Kunst unserer Vorzeit*, Leipzig 1936," *Kritische Berichte zur kunstgeschichtlichen Literatur* 6 (1937): 82–88.

54. Oswald Spengler, *Der Untergang des Abendlandes—Umrisse einer Morphologie der Weltgeschichte*, vol. 1, *Gestalt und Wirklichkeit* (Vienna, 1918); vol. 2, *Welthistorische Perspektiven* (Munich, 1923).

55. See Ludwig Curtius, "Morphologie der antiken Kunst," *Logos* 9 (1921): 195–221.

56. See Miklós Lackó, "Válságkorszak—válságelméletek: Három alapmű a 1920-as évek magyar szellemi élet éből" (Crisis age—crisis theories: Three fundamental works of Hungarian intellectual life of the 1920s), *Múltunk* 53, no. 3 (2007): 7.

57. Ferenc Lehel, *Haladó művészet: Újrendszerű stílusmorfológia vázlata* (Advancing art: Outline of a novel morphology of style) (Budapest, 1929); Franz Lehel, *Fortschreitende Entwicklung: Versuch einer reinen Kunstmorphologie* (Munich, 1929).

58. See Frederik Adama von Scheltema's review of Lehel in *Zeitschrift für Ästhetik und allgemeine Kunstwissenschaft* 25 (1931): 279–282.

59. Borbála Jász, *Modernizmus sátortetővel: Ligeti Pál művészetfilozófiája és építészetelmélete* (Modernism with a tent roof: Pál Ligeti's art philosophy and architectural theory), MMA Ösztöndíjas Tanulmányok, vol. 12 (Budapest, 2017), 35–54.

60. Pál Ligeti, *Új Pantheon felé: A kultúrák élete a művészet tükrében* (Towards a new Pantheon: The life of cultures reflected in art) (Budapest, 1926). See also Jász, *Modernizmus sátortetővel*, 61.

61. Rajesh Heynickx, "Obscure(d) Modernism: The Aesthetics of the Architect Pal Ligeti," *Modernist Cultures* 3, no. 2 (2008): 139–153.

62. Kurt Breysig, *Der Stufenbau und die Gesetze der Weltgeschichte* (Berlin, 1905). On the relationship between Wölfflin and Breysig at the University of Berlin, see Rudolf Pannwitz, *Das Werk des Menschen, Die vorhandene und die geschaffene Welt*, vol. 2 (Stuttgart, 1968), 267.

63. Paul Ligeti, *Der Weg aus dem Chaos: Eine Deutung des Weltgeschehens aus dem Rhythmus der Kunstentwicklung* (Munich, 1931).

64. Ligeti, *Der Weg aus dem Chaos*, 283–296. See also Jáz, *Modernizmus sátortetővel*, 61–62.

65. Tibor Gerevich, "Művészettörténet" (Art history), in *A magyar történetírás új útjai* (New paths in Hungarian historiography), ed. Bálint Hóman, A Magyar Szemle könyve, vol. 3 (Budapest, 1931), 134.

66. See Gosztonyi, "A Pasteiner-tanítványok," 33.

67. Ernő Marosi, "A magyar művészettörténet-írás tévútjai" (The aberrations of Hungarian art-historical writing), in *Magyar művészettörténészek, magyar művészettörténet a vészkorszakban* (Hungarian art historians, Hungarian art history in the Holocaust period), ed. Csilla Markója and István Bardoly (Budapest, 2014) (= *Enigma*, 21, no. 80), 9–14.

68. See Ernő Marosi, "Bevezetés" (Introduction), in *Magyarországi művészet 1300–1470 körül* (Hungarian art 1300–c. 1470), ed. Ernő Marosi, vol. 1 (Budapest, 1987), 23.

69. József Bodonyi, "A magyar művészettörténetírás új útjai?" (The new path of Hungarian historiography of art?), *Budapesti szemle* 64, no. 240 (1936): 226–245. On the author see Ferenc Gosztonyi, "A művészettörténet bécsi iskolájának százhatvannegyedik diplomása. Bodonyi József (1908–1942)" (The hundred fifty-fourth graduate of the Vienna School of art history: József Bodonyi [1908–1942]), in Markója and Bardoly, *Magyar művészettörténészek*, 32–43.

70. See also Árpád Tímár, "Bodonyi József művészettörténet-kritikája" (József Bodonyi's art-historical criticism), *Ars Hungarica* 22, nos. 1–2 (1994): 179–183.

71. György Gombosi, *Spinello Aretino: Eine stilgeschichtliche Studie über die Florentinische Malerei des ausgehenden XIV. Jahrhunderts* (Budapest, 1926). See also Vilmos Tátrai, "Gombosi György jelenléte kora és korunk szakirodalmában" (György Gombosi in the literature of his own time and our age), in Markója and Bardoly, *Magyar művészettörténészek*, 101–113.

72. Robert Born, "Die Renaissance in Ungarn und Italien aus marxistischer und nationaler Perspektive: Beobachtungen zur Situation in Ungarn vor und nach 1945," *Ars (Bratislava)* 48, no. 2 (2015): 167–168.

73. Henrik Horváth, *Budai kőfaragók és kőfaragójelek* (Buda stonemasons and stonemasons' marks) (Budapest, 1935). See also Ernő Marosi, "Kőfaragók, kőfaragójelek, Horváth Henrik" (Stonemasons, stonemasons' marks, Henrik Horváth), *Enigma* 25, no. 96 (2018): 60–71.

74. See Borbála Lukács H., *Szellemtörténet és irodalomtudomány* (The history of ideas and literary studies), Irodalomtörténeti füzetek 70 (Budapest, 1971).

75. Tivadar Thienemann, *Irodalomtörténeti alapfogalmak* (Basic concepts of literary history) (Budapest, 1931) (revised version of the series of articles published in *Minerva*).

76. See György Poszler, *Szerb Antal* (Budapest, 1973), 373–374.

77. Tibor Joó, "A barokk és az egyházak" (The baroque and the churches), *Protestáns szemle* 41 (1932): 625.

78. Tibor Joó, "Zrínyi történelemszemlélete és a barokk" (Zrínyi's view of history and the baroque), *Századok* 66 (1932): 261–305.

79. László Baránszky-Jób, "A film esztetikája" (The aesthetics of film), *Szépművészet* 2, no. 6 (1941): 151–154.

80. See the contributions in Markója and Bardoly, *Magyar művészettörténészek*.

81. See Irina Alter in Burioni, Dogramaci, and Pfisterer, *Kunstgeschichten 1915*, cat. VIII.6; Ekaterina Dmitrieva, "Heinrich Wölfflin en Russie: De la découverte de l'Italie et de l'art baroque russe à la conception de la méthode formaliste et structuraliste dans la critique littéraire," *Cahiers du monde russe* 51, no. 4 (2010): 507–508.

82. Dmitrieva, "Heinrich Wölfflin en Russie," 510–511. See also Evonne Levy's introduction to this volume.

83. Nina Žirmunskaja, "Viktor Žirmunskij: Zur Entwicklung einer marxistischen vergleichenden Literaturwissenschaft," in *Literaturtheorie und Literaturkritik in der frühsowjetischen Diskussion: Standorte-Programme-Schulen*, ed. Anton Hiersche and Edward Kowalski (Berlin, 1990), 251.

84. Galin Tikhanov, "Why Did Modern Literary Theory Originate in Central and Eastern Europe? (And Why Is It Now Dead?)," *Common Knowledge* 10, no. 1 (Winter 2004), 79.

85. Pavel N. Medvedev, *Die formale Methode in der Literaturwissenschaft*, ed. and trans. Helmut Glück, Studien zur allgemeinen und vergleichenden Literaturwissenschaft, vol. 8 (Stuttgart, 1976), 64–66.

86. See Katerina Clark and Galin Tihanov, "Soviet Literary Theory in the 1930s: Battles over Genre and the Boundaries of Modernity," in *A History of Russian Literary Theory and Criticism: The Soviet Age and Beyond*, ed. Galin Tihanov and Evgeny Dobrenko (Pittsburgh, 2011), 129.

87. Boris Mikhailov, "Coming of Age: Russian Art History as a Professional Discipline in the 1910s–1920s," *Experiment* 3, no. 1 (1997): 7–8.

88. Dmitrieva, "Heinrich Wölfflin en Russie," 510; Skansi, "What Is Artistic Form?," 75–77.

89. Stanley Mitchell, "Mikhail Alexandrovich Lifshits (1905–1983)," *The Oxford Art Journal* 20, no. 2 (1997): 23–41.

90. Mikhail Lifschitz, ed., *Karl Marx, Friedrich Engels über Kunst und Literatur: Eine Sammlung aus ihren Schriften* (Berlin, 1948), xi.

91. Vel'flin [Wölfflin], *Osnovnye ponjatija istorii iskusstv*; Dmitrieva, *Osnovnye ponjatija istorii iskusstv*, 513–514; Irina Alter, cat. VIII.6 in Burioni, Dogramaci, and Pfisterer, *Kunstgeschichten 1915*.

92. See Dmitrieva, *Osnovnye ponjatija istorii iskusstv*, 514, with references to the relevant publications of Rempel.

93. See Branko Mitrović, "Studying Renaissance Architectural Theory in the Age of Stalinism," *I Tatti Studies in the Italian Renaissance* 12 (2009): 233, epigraph (quotation from People's Commissar of Education Anatoly Lunacharsky, 1921).

94. Akademija Chudožestv SSSR, Institut Teorii i Istorii Izobrazitel'nych Iskusstv, *Protiv buržuaznogo iskusstva i iskusstvoznanija (*Against bourgeois art and art history), ed. Igor E. Grabar and Vladimir S. Kemenov (Moscow, 1951).

95. See Krista Kodres, "Stil und Bedeutung: Über konkurrierende Renaissancemodelle in der polarisierten Welt des Kalten Krieges," *Ars (Bratislava)* 48, no. 2 (2015): 120–121.

96. *Harc a burzsoá művészet és művészetelmélet ellen* (Budapest, 1953); *Gegen die bürgerliche Kunst und Kunstwissenschaft (*Berlin, 1954).

97. See Uwe Hartmann, "Die 'Verteidigung' der Renaissance: Zur Auseinandersetzung sowjetischer Kunsthistoriker mit der 'bürgerlichen' Kunstwissenschaft zu Beginn des Kalten Krieges," in *Kunst, Kontext, Geschichte: Festgabe für Hubert Faensen zum 75. Geburtstag*, ed. Tatjana Bartsch and Jörg Meiner (Berlin, 2003), 294–298.

98. Mikhail Alpatov, "Zur Verteidigung der Renaissance (Gegen die Theorien der bürgerlichen Kunstwissenschaft)," in *Gegen die bürgerliche Kunst und Kunstwissenschaft*, 161–170.

99. Viktor Lazarev and Mikhail Il'in, "Barokko," in *Bolshaya sovetskaya entsiklopediya*, vol. 4 (Moscow, 1950), 254–261; see also Krista Kodres, "Scientific Baroque—for Everyone: Constructing and Conveying an Art Epoch during the Stalinist Period in the Soviet Union and in Soviet Estonia," *Journal of Art Historiography* 15 (December 2016).

100. W. N. Lazarev and M. A. Iljin, *Der Barock*, Große Sowjet-Enzyklopädie, Reihe Kunst und Literatur 32 (Berlin, 1954).

101. "Barokk," *Szovjet Művészettörténet* 10 (1956): 93–107.

102. Anatoly Shtambok (Stámbok), "A művészet fejlődósének idealista magyarázata," *Szovjet művészettörténet* 2 (1951): 1–49. The Russian original appeared in *Isskustkovo* 5 (1950): 55–65.

103. See Kodres, "Scientific Baroque—for Everyone," 120–123.

104. Imre Trencsényi Waldapfel, "Nyelv- és irodalomtudományunk feladatai a Szovjet-unió Kommunista Pártiának XIX. kongresszusa után" (The tasks of linguistic and literary studies following the 19th Congress of the Communist Party of the Soviet Union), *A MTA Nyelv- és Irodalomtudományok Osztályának Közleményei* 3, no. 4 (1953): 338.

105. See Julian Gardner, "Painting in Florence and Siena after the Cold War," in *Medioevo: Arte e storia*, ed. Arturo C. Quintavalle (Milan, 2008), 662–668, and Jim Berryman, "Gombrich's Critique of Hauser's Social History of Art," *History of European Ideas* 43, no. 5 (2017): 494–506.

106. Frederick Antal, "Remarks on the Method of Art History: I," *The Burlington Magazine* 91 (1949): 49. See also Christine McCorkel, "Sense and Sensibility: An Epistemological Approach to the Philosophy of Art History," *Journal of Aesthetics and Art Criticism* 34, no. 1 (autumn 1975): 38.

107. Arnold Hauser, *Philosophie der Kunstgeschichte* (Munich, 1958); in English, *The Philosophy of Art History* (London and New York, 1959).

108. E. H. Gombrich, "Review of Arnold Hauser, *The Social History of Art*," *Art Bulletin* 35, no. 1 (1953): 80.

109. Peter Burke, "Gombrich's Search for Cultural History," *Meditations on a Heritage: Papers on the Work and Legacy of Sir Ernst Gombrich*, ed. Paul Taylor (London, 2014), 16–17; Hammam Aldouri, "Search for a Method: A Reassessment of Hegel's Dialectic in Art History," *Journal of Art Historiography* 20 (June 2019): 6–12.

110. Andrew Hemingway, "E. H. Gombrich in 1968: Methodological Individualism and the Contradictions of Conservatism," *Human Affairs* 19, no. 3 (2009): 297–303; Vardan Azatyan, "Ernst Gombrich's Politics of Art History: Exile, Cold War and 'The Story of Art,'" *Oxford Art Journal* 33, no. 2 (2010): 129–130.

111. Arnold Hauser, "Der Begriff der Ideologie in der Kunstgeschichte," *Kölner Zeitschrift für Soziologie* 6, no. 3 (1953–54): 381.

112. Arnold Hauser, *The Philosophy of Art History*, 130–132 and 137–139.

113. Hauser, *The Philosophy of Art History*, 134–138.

114. See Hans Heinz Holz, *Strukturen der Darstellung: Über Konstanten der ästhetischen Konfigurationen*, Philosophische Theorie und bildende Künste, vol. 2 (Bielefeld, 1997), 54–55.

115. "Vita művészeti folyóiratainkról" (Debate about our art journals), *Művészettörténeti értesítő* 5, nos. 2–3 (1956): 200.

116. Gerhard Strauss, "Heinrich Wölfflin: Über seine Bedingtheit und seine Bedeutung," in *Forschen und Wirken: Festschrift zur 150-Jahr-Feier der Humboldt-Universität zu Berlin*, 3 vols. (Berlin, 1960), 1: 417–451. See also Oliver Sukrow in Burioni, Dogramaci, and Pfisterer, *Kunstgeschichten 1915*, cat. IX.4.

117. Lajos Vayer, "A XXI. Nemzetközi Művészettörténeti Kongresszus" (The 21st International Congress of Art History), *A MTA Társadalmi-Történeti Tudományok Osztályának Közleményei* 14, no. 3 (1964–1965): 284.

118. Natalija Geršenzon-Čegodaeva, "Teorii razvitija iskusstva v zapadnoevropejskom iskusstvoznanii 1900–1940" (Theories of the development of art in the Western European historiography of art, 1900–1940), in *Sovremennoe iskusstvoznanie za rubezhom* (Contemporary art history abroad: Essays), ed. Boris R. Vipper and Tat'jana N. Livanova (Moscow, 1964), 44–45 and 48.

119. See Jaromír Neumann, "Das Werk Max Dvoráks und die Gegenwart," *Acta Historiae Artium* 83, nos. 3–4 (1962): 183–184; Born, "Die Renaissance in Ungarn und Italien aus marxistischer und nationaler Perspektive," 174.

120. Tibor Klaniczay, "A művészeti stílusok helye a marxista kutatásban" (The importance of artistic styles in Marxist research), in *Marxizmus és irodalomtudomány* (Marxism and literary studies) (Budapest, 1964), 66–109. See also Balázs Trencsényi, "Writing the Nation and Reframing Early Modern Intellectual History in Hungary," *Studies in East European Thought* 62, no. 2 (2010): 143–144.

121. Zoltán Szentkirályi, "A barokk forma objektivitásáról" (The objectivity of baroque form), *Építés és Közlekedéstudományi Közlemények* 7, nos. 1–2 (1963): 43–59. On Kovács see Pál Ács and Júlia Székely, "Kovács Sándor Iván és a manierizmus" (Iván Sándor Kovács and mannerism), *Irodalomtörténet* 36, no. 4 (2006): 515–522.

122. See Born, "Die Renaissance in Ungarn und Italien aus marxistischer und nationaler Perspektive," 175–177; Jennifer Cooke, "CIHA as the Subject of Art Theory: The Methodological Discourse in the International Congresses of Art History from Post-War Years to the 2000s," *RIHA Journal* 0199, September 30, 2018, https://www.riha-journal.org/articles/2018/0199-cooke (accessed May 2, 2019); Virve Sarapik, "CIHA Congresses and Soviet Internationalism," in *A Socialist Realist History? Writing Art History in the Post-War Decades*, ed. Krista Kodres, Kristina Jõekalda, and Michaela Marek (Vienna, 2019), 245–248.

123. Athanase Stojkov, "Aperçu sur trois conceptions de l'art: Wölfflin, Panofsky, Hauser," in *Évolution générale et développements régionaux en histoire de l'art: Actes du XXIIe Congrès International d'Histoire de l'Art; Budapest 1969*, vol. 2, Texte (Budapest, 1972), 485–491.

124. Lajos Csetri, "Heinrich Wölfflin, *Művészettörténeti alapfogalmak*," *Kritika* 8, no. 12 (1970): 47–49.

JENS BAUMGARTEN

Wölfflin in Brazil: Between Translation and Comparison

MINISTERIO DA EDUCAÇÃO E SAUDE

REVISTA DO SERVIÇO DO PATRIMONIO HISTORICO E ARTISTICO NACIONAL

N. 4

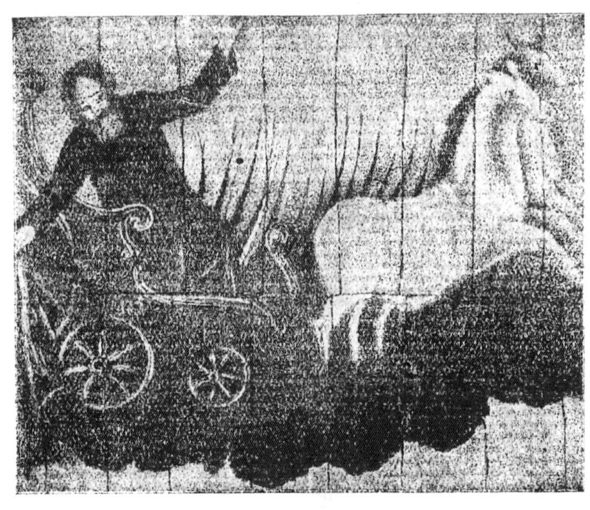

1940

RIO DE JANEIRO

his essay aims to outline the main aspects and moments of the discourse about Heinrich Wölfflin and his theoretical concepts in Brazil. To this end, I focus on the first author who brought a critical reading of his ideas to Brazil: Hanna Levy Deinhard (fig. 1).[1] This German émigré not only played a crucial role in introducing his work to art-historical discourse there; she helped institutionalize art history as a discipline and realized Wölfflin's objective of establishing it as a science. I then trace later developments, specifically the reappropriations of Wölfflin's concepts by authors like the art critic Mário Pedrosa and the transfer of Wölfflin's ideas into the area of historical cultural studies in the work of Janice Theodoro da Silva's work.

The first translation of Wölfflin's *Principles of Art History* into Portuguese was realized only in 1984; his *Renaissance and Baroque* had already been translated into Portuguese from the French version in the 1960s.[2] This in itself indicates an aspect of the reception of Wölfflin in Brazil. The Brazilian academic and university system followed the French model until the military dictatorship that began in 1964, and the intellectual elite read French. Claude Lévi-Strauss helped to establish the anthropology department at the main university in São Paulo (founded in the 1920s) during his stay in Brazil from 1935 to 1939, just one indicator of a general intellectual and artistic exchange that dated from the early nineteenth century and the so-called French Artistic Mission, which established the national art academy of Brazil.[3] Thus in the first decades after the French translation of *Principles* appeared (1952), it was not necessary to translate Wölfflin's work

into Portuguese, and it was not so much the translation itself as the introduction of his ideas by other scholars that was important. *Renaissance and Baroque* opened the debate on Wölfflin's ideas—and many scholars, especially of contemporary art, draw on both books.

Within this context, Hanna Levy's articles on Brazilian art constitute an important historiographical and analytical contribution. Her biography clearly shows the influence of her experience as an émigré on her intellectual development. A scholar of German Jewish origin, she emigrated in 1934 to Paris. With Henri Focillon as her advisor, in 1936 she completed her PhD at the Sorbonne; her dissertation constituted the first critical review of Wölfflin's *Principles* from the perspective of a sociology of art.[4] (The German leftist expatriate art historian Max Raphael marveled that a Marxist sociologist of art could defend her thesis in the Sorbonne.) After arriving in Brazil in 1937 she quickly learned to speak and write Portuguese and worked at the Institute for Historical and Artistic Patrimony (Instituto de Patrimônio Histórico e Artístico Nacional—IPHAN) in Rio de Janeiro. The institute had been founded in 1937 as a department of the ministry of education within the national project of Getúlio Vargas's Estado Novo.[5] Art history had existed as art criticism in the context of contemporary art production since the creation of the French Artistic Mission, but IPHAN was one of the first institutions in Brazil where it was taught in an academic sense. Only with the first general education reform in the late 1950s and 1960s were art history professorships established within departments of art education, architecture, and philosophy.

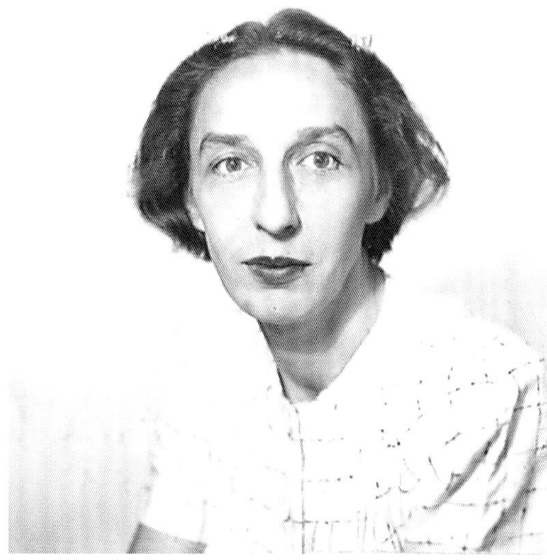

Besides teaching general art history (that is, excluding Asian art[6]) to staff members and professors, between 1940 and 1947 Levy published in the IPHAN journal a series of theoretical articles, equivalent to a German habilitation, that focus mainly on the Brazilian baroque.[7] On a superficial level she introduced the term "baroque" itself to the Brazilian discourse. The term that had usually been applied was "colonial." Even today the distinction between the two lacks a certain clarity and theoretical acuteness; they are used as synonyms in many publications.[8]

For a better understanding of Levy's role it is important to comprehend its cultural context. She had based the methodology of her dissertation on the dialectical Marxism of Max Raphael but also took into account the positions of Max Horkheimer, Walter Benjamin, Karl Mannheim, Erwin Panofsky, and Edgar Wind, as well as those of her teachers at the Sorbonne like Leo Balet and Henri Focillon. Despite her great respect for Wölfflin she strongly criticized some of his positions. According to Levy, he was not interested in the artistic process: "Wölfflin does not analyze the creative process of representation. In other words, we don't find…the concrete object…but only its essence."[9] This means that we ignore *how* the work of art was created and *why* it disappeared. She praised him principally for

having turned art history into a scientific field of study and for his case studies; her main criticism focused on his idealistic concept of history and on his idea of history as independent of observation and autonomous artistic development. Levy not only rejected the idea of a uniform and homogeneous style within a given epoch but suggested the influence of external factors such as nation and race.[10]

Levy's criticism focused on Wölfflin's concept of history as opposed to his description of the evolution of the visual arts.[11] She doubted that this kind of evolution existed and suggested a typology of the arts.[12] In her understanding, (art) history should be understood as a dialectical process in which different cultural spheres followed the principles of their "own dynamics" and connected with social history. Therefore, an analysis of a particular object had to include a consideration of the relation between art and society and bear in mind the constitution of an art-historical epoch by artistic and scientific institutions.

Her specific interest in the baroque must be seen against the background of its implicit politics insofar as she asks how the discourse about the baroque establishes a political discourse. Brazilian intellectuals were searching for a genuine and authentic style, and in the absence of a "precolonial monumental" architecture, Mário de Andrade and other founders of IPHAN traveled to Minas Gerais and believed they had found in the art of the hinterland an autochthonous "national style."[13] As an immigrant questioning essentialism, Levy could develop her theoretical and methodological approach by bringing her art-sociological questions addressed to Wölfflin together with colonial and/or baroque artifacts and architecture in Brazil. In her first two articles, "Valor artístico e valor histórico," on artistic and historic value, and "A propósito de três teorias sobre o barroco" (essay frontispiece and fig. 2), a comment on three theories of the baroque developed respectively by Heinrich Wölfflin, Max Dvořak, and Leo Balet, she delineated

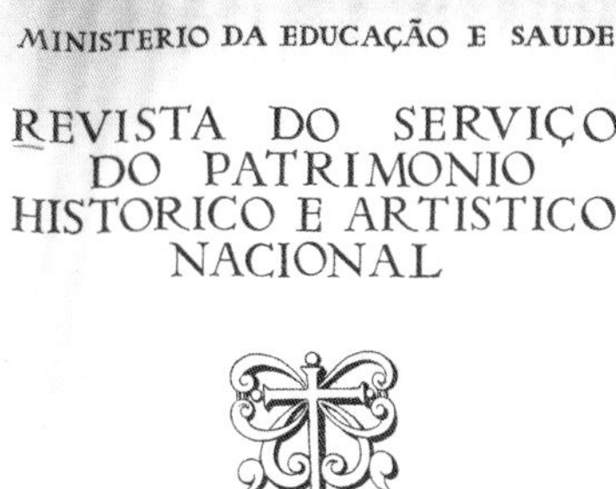

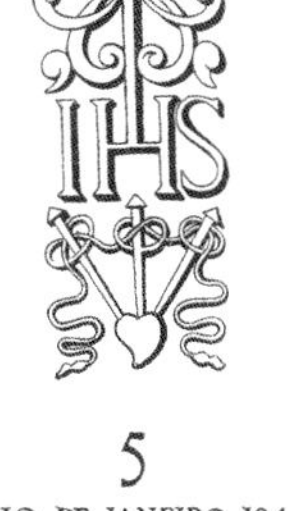

REVISTA DO SERVIÇO DO PATRIMONIO HISTORICO E ARTISTICO NACIONAL

5

RIO DE JANEIRO 1941

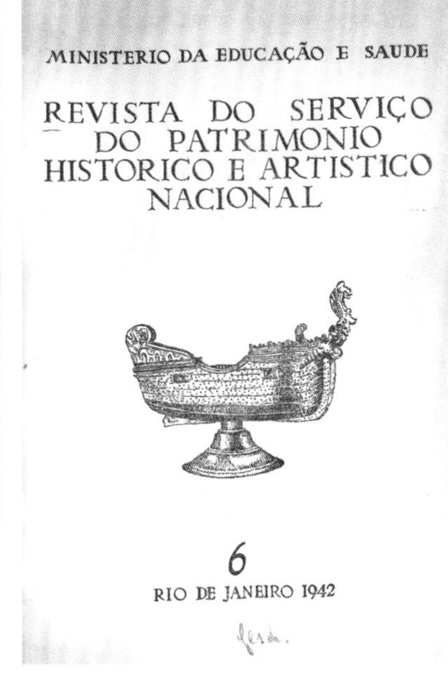

MINISTERIO DA EDUCAÇÃO E SAUDE

REVISTA DO SERVIÇO DO PATRIMONIO HISTORICO E ARTISTICO NACIONAL

6

RIO DE JANEIRO 1942

2, 3. *Revista do Serviço do Patrimônio Histórico e Artístico Nacional* 5 (1941) and 6 (1942), containing articles by Hanna Levy, "A propósito de três teorias sobre o barroco" and "A pintura colonial no Rio de Janeiro"

Bibliotheca Hertziana, Max-Planck-Institut für Kunstgeschichte, Rome

the general aspects of her theory, her epistemology, and her methodology.[14] In three articles that followed, she demonstrated her ideas by elaborating her research on Brazilian colonial art in Rio de Janeiro and Minas Gerais.[15]

In Levy's article on the three analytical approaches to the baroque, she discussed the problem of value judgments (in German, *wertendes Urteil*) of art-historical concepts. In her later book *Bedeutung und Ausdruck: Zur Soziologie der Malerei* (1967; published in English as *Meaning and Expresssion: Toward a Sociology of Art*), this focus is combined with her evaluation of the "timelessness" of works of art. In discussing the relation between meaning and expression, she reasoned that "artistic quality is provable by its potential content of expression."[16] With reference to Max Raphael, Lionello Venturi, and Henri Focillon, Levy established a distinction between historical and sociological approaches to works of art and applied them in her research at IPHAN.

In "Valor artístico e valor histórico," political questions are not explicit, but the discussion of value—in all its meanings—must be seen in light of them. In this context Levy argued that a work of art responsible for the formation of a

"school" in colonial Brazil had a historic value without necessarily being of great artistic value. A third value, that of documentation, applied to representations of important events in Brazilian history. This distinction was neither new nor progressive, but Levy's text made the relativism of evaluation perceivable: these values do not "constitute absolute values in history, they are completely relative."[17] This relativism reappeared later in a more detailed explanation of the criteria for evaluating a work of art as an intrinsic relationship of form that is represented in the "content of expression," as well as other criteria like historical iconographical importance, rarity, or curiosity, which are mutable and depend on their social functions.[18] In this context Levy also criticized Eurocentrism: "The relativity of values becomes evident if you consider (successively) a work of art in relation to the entire production of a single artist, a local school, the art history of a country, or world art history, etc."[19]

Levy's "Valor artístico e valor histórico" must be ascribed to her implicitly political thinking and her experience as an immigrant, but it also refers to positions already staked out in her French dissertation of 1938. In particular, her comments reveal her avoidance of nationalistic terms.[20] This contrasts strongly with the aforementioned national project, or search for "Brazilianness" (*brasilidade*) by modernist authors and critics like Mário de Andrade (1893–1945) and Lourival Gomes Machado (1917–1967), who established, in their desire to construct a national identity, the use of expressions like "our culture" (*nossa cultura*) with reference to the colonial art of Minas Gerais.[21] The architect and sculptor Aleijadinho (Antônio Francisco Lisboa) served as their main "evidence," even though his very existence is doubted by some critics.[22] Nonetheless, he was constructed as an autochthonous artist who worked in central Brazil, which served as a nucleus for the birth of the Brazilian nation and its artistic representation. In her writing Levy avoided open criticism of her hosts at IPHAN and made her political statements from a parallel theoretical platform.

In her articles on colonial painting from Minas and Rio (fig. 3), Levy approached Brazilian art without prejudice and distinguished among different categories of values. She questioned the primacy of European art history. She understood that the simple affirmation of the existence of a European influence had no special significance: "If tomorrow a historian brought irrefutable proof of a certain influence of a certain work of a given European artist on the statues of the prophets in Congonhas, this fact would certainly be of great interest from various standpoints. But the influence as such would say nothing about the historic value or artistic value of the work of [their sculptor,] Antônio Francisco Lisboa."[23] In her analysis she approached the objects with a genuine gaze. Her perspective directed her interest to the artistic relationship between center and periphery—a question that was equally fundamental in George Kubler's thinking.[24] Levy, in fact, demonstrated in her articles on colonial painting from Minas and Rio that it is possible to dismantle the hierarchy of European over non-European without losing focus on a particular work of art and its individual context.

In "A propósito de três teorias sobre o barroco," on the theories of the baroque developed by Wölfflin, Dvořak, and Balet, Levy equally considered the social, historical, and material conditions of a specific historical epoch. She combined Wölfflin's analysis of single and particular works of art with Balet's approach and included her interpretations of Brazilian colonial baroque. She argued that Brazilian baroque had solved the methodological problems of a colonial art made at a distance from the court in an environment whose social relations were dominated by slavery and whose treasure did not serve the representational needs of the local elite but was transferred to the metropole. According to Levy, the differences between the baroque produced in Brazil and the baroque produced in Portugal could therefore not be explained by the natural and necessary evolution of style, as Wölfflin outlined, since artistic changes were a result of human and material factors that were rejuvenated in the colony. In Levy's opinion, Dvořak's philosophical explanation was insufficient, since he understood the "spiritual world" as detached and independent from social circumstances. This kind of approach missed the socially determinative elements that come to bear on artistic reality.[25]

In "Modelos europeus na pintura colonial" (European models in colonial painting) of 1944, Levy affirmed without doubt that many colonial painters "used models of European art. Thence the eclectic character of colonial painting as a whole, and thence also the heterogeneous character that can frequently be noted in works by the same artist."[26] European prints of different origins, artistically as well as chronologically diverse, were both particularly and indifferently used as models for paintings.[27] Referring to her own research and observations on particular works of art, she concluded that the colonial painter copied the model faithfully in terms of composition and distribution of light and shadow as well as details of poses, minor objects, and clothing: "The panels translated perfectly the dramatic and agitated character of the engraved representations…or offered an even more dramatic effect than the originals.…On the other hand, the impression of agitation in the paintings results from the fact that the painter by simplifying the backgrounds concentrated…all his interest on the human figures."[28]

As I have shown, Levy applied Wölfflin's methodological approach to the individual art object. Therefore the results of her study could be useful for attribution and dating and could inform the work of restorers;[29] and it is notable that in her analysis of specific works of art she used Wölfflin's method by putting Brazilian examples in theoretical frameworks similar to his. But it is important to understand her implicit political discourse and her theoretical shift to include a sociological dimension in her approach. Furthermore, it is possible to identify a pattern of analysis that broke, for the first time in the context of art history, with a dichotomous view of productive and receptive culture.

Although her articles were harshly criticized by Lourival Gomes Machado, one of the most influential art historians and art critics at the University of São Paulo, as a simple "vulgarization" of earlier theories when they were published,[30] and were later almost forgotten, Levy clearly broke boundaries by expressing her preference for sociological methods in the colonial context of Brazil.[31] She developed a specific methodology for Brazilian art history within a global context. This methodology emancipates itself from European approaches without leading to a national or even nationalistic art history, as in the modernist projects of Machado and Andrade, who were searching for a national essence and constructing *brasilidade*.[32] Levy not only questioned the European canon; she also perceived the importance of a theoretical concept for a nonnationalist and non-Eurocentric art history. This focus is indeed remarkable because—despite her criticism of theoretical positions of some of art history's founding figures, like Wölfflin and Dvořak—she did not dismiss them wholesale. Especially in the case of Wölfflin, Levy praised his structural and formal analysis of works of art while revealing the implicit hierarchies and prejudgments and prejudices within his theories. Her articles from the 1940s can be considered the earliest attempts to integrate Brazilian colonial art into the concept of world art history.[33]

In the decades after World War II, two different, independent approaches to Wölfflin's concepts can be found in Brazil. In the 1950s and 1960s the debate on abstract art also drove the Brazilian discourse in art criticism. Mário Pedrosa, in reading Wölfflin's *Principles*, introduced Clement Greenberg's formalist ideas to Brazil and combined his ideas with some reflections on Wilhelm Worringer; but this is another topic. The postwar reception can be better discussed in terms of Pedrosa's understanding of the relationship of Greenberg's formalism to Wölfflin: "An evolution of form in art history follows historical development. But, he [Wölfflin] added, the development of the plastic imagination in its specificity [in contrast to other imaginations], as autonomous process, expressively imaginary, is a simple echo of the call of the world to external representation. In this way the sense [responsible for] the world of forms exists 'for itself' and continues to be rooted in the general spiritual culture."[34]

A surprising nonformalist reappropriation can be found in the development of Levy's interpretations and use of Wölfflin's ideas by the cultural historian Janice Theodoro da Silva. She has shown how Wölfflin, especially his *Renaissance and Baroque*, can be useful in spite of his formalist approach. She argued in her book *América barroca* (1992) that Wölfflin's concept of open form would allow Latin Americans to reflect on European and indigenous culture and their relation to each other as a way to understand the cultural matrix of this region.[35] She related to Wölfflin by affirming that his ideas, especially concerning the painterly style, monumentality, and massiveness of the baroque, constituted her interpretation of the cultural process in early modern Latin America. In her questions she often followed Wölfflin, transferring him to a cultural discourse. What would be the motives that led someone in the sixteenth century to devalue the linear and concentrate (here paraphrasing Wölfflin) "the essential mark of baroque architecture in its pictorial character"? She finished by transforming his formalist analysis into a cultural one, asking how it was possible that an enigmatic form was able to contain innumerable cognitive universes.

For Theodoro da Silva the contrast between closed and open form could be translated into a Latin American historical discourse that formed the nucleus of what later developed into the political and cultural discourse of *miscigenação* (hybridization). This hybridization in art can be seen and categorized as a specific Latin American baroque. In this sense the Wölfflinian concept of the baroque signified a theoretical cultural and historical approach that allowed a harmonization in historiography as well as in discursive practice: a softening of the initial violence of the Conquest through the construction of a new order. This new order, which could be considered Latin American, was governed by a basic principle that consolidates an image of a new world constructed in resemblance to the old. Therefore Theodoro da Silva declared that the baroque in Wölfflin's analysis served to explain how indigenous and European culture lived together in the same space by challenging the harmony between form and content: "[T]he baroque allowed a dissimulation, shifting form and content." [36]

I stress in conclusion that it is important to acknowledge Levy's theoretical attempts to balance Wölfflin's formal analysis, Dvořak's intellectual context, and Raphael's, Balet's, and Focillon's materialism. This balance enabled her to accept Wölfflin's analysis of the individual object and to combine it with her materialistic concept of a sociology of art that aimed to avoid generalization and the neglect of particularities. Wölfflin's "art history without names" served perfectly for Levy's approach to colonial art, with its lack of attributions, which were not important in artistic production in Brazil from the sixteenth to the nineteenth century. But there are some idiosyncratic contradictions, which might be understood as part of the Brazilian cultural discourse. Levy criticized Wölfflin because of his idealism and his racial ideas. But she participated through her affiliation with the IPHAN of Rodrigo Melo Franco de Andrade (1998–1969) and the other modernists in the nationalist movement of the 1930s and 1940s in Brazil. Perhaps this can be understood in the same way as the main intellectual protagonist of the Vargas era, the sociologist Gilberto Freyre, who used racialist theories in order to invert them and defend *miscigenação* as a national project against Nazi Germany but also against the isolationism of the United States. In so doing, he created the myth of the "racial democracy," for which the aforementioned artist Aleijadinho, a mulatto, served as founding representative.

Wölfflin's principles were translated into Portuguese very late, but his ideas served in many ways the purpose of comparative analysis—not only in the formalist way, but in many appropriations and reappropriations. As a future enterprise it would be interesting not only to analyze further the importance of comparison in relation to translation in a historiographical perspective but also to transform these discussions into a theoretical-methodological debate on recent attempts at a so-called world art history.

NOTES

1. Hanna Levy was born in 1912 in Osnabrück, Germany, and died in 1984 in Basel. She immigrated to Brazil in 1938 and in 1948 to the United States. From 1941 she published as Hannah Levy and, from 1948, following her marriage to Fritz Deinhard, as Hanna (Levy) Deinhard.

2. Heinrich Wölfflin, *Conceitos fundamentais da história da arte: O problema da evolucão dos estilos na arte mais recente*, trans. João Azenha (São Paulo, 1984); Heinrich Wölfflin, *Renascença e Barroco: Estudo sobre a essência do estilo barroco e a sua origem na Itália*, trans. Mary Amazonas L. de Barros e Antonio Steffen (São Paulo, 1989).

3. In contrast to Spanish-speaking countries, Brazil did not establish academies or universities during colonial times but founded them only after independence in 1822. Affonso d'Escragnolle Taunay, *A Missão Artística de 1816*, Publicação da Diretoria do Patrimônio Histórico e Artístico Nacional (Diretoria do Patrimônio Histórico e Artístico Nacional, Rio de Janeiro, 1957) and Elaine Dias, "Correspondências entre Joachim Le Breton e a Corte Portuguesa na Europa: O nascimento da Missão Artística de 1816," *Anais do Museu Paulista* (Impresso) 14 (2006): 301–316.

4. Hanna Levy, *Henri Wölfflin: Sa théorie, ses prédécesseurs* (PhD diss., Université de Paris; Rottweil, 1936).

5. On IPHAN see especially Silvana Rubino, "As fachadas da história: Os antecedentes, a criação e os trabalhos do Serviço do Patrimonio Historico e Artistico Nacional, 1937–1968" (master's thesis, Universidade Estadual de Campinas, Instituto de Filosofia e Ciencias Humanas, 1992), 106–157. Research remains to be done concerning Levy's relation with Brazilian politics during the Vargas era and her personal situation as emigrant compared to those of other Jewish refugees in the 1940s; for example, Claude Lévi-Strauss, one of the prominent founders of the University of São Paulo, was not allowed to enter Brazilian territory

after the occupation of France by Nazi Germany. Maria Luiza Tucci Carneiro, *Brasil um refúgio nos trópicos: A trajetória dos refugiados do nazi-fascismo* (São Paulo, 1996); *O veneno da serpente: Reflexões sobre o anti-semitismo no Brasil* (São Paulo, 2003); about the antisemitism in the Vargas era see also Jeff Lesser, *Negotiating National Identity: Immigrants, Minorities, and the Struggle for Ethnicity in Brazil* (Durham, NC, 1999), and *Welcoming the Undesirables: Brazil and the Jewish Question* (Berkeley, CA, 1995).

6. Hanna Levy, curriculum vitae, 1978, in Irene Below, "'Jene widersinnige Leichtigkeit der Innovation': Hanna Deinhards Wissenschaftskritik, Kunstsoziologie und Kunstvermittlung," in *Grenzen überschreiten: Frauen, Kunst und Exil*, ed. Ursula Wiedenmann and Beate Schmeichel-Falkenberg (Würzburg, 2005), 141–179, and, most recently, Irene Below and Burcu Dogramaci, eds., *Kunst und Gesellschaft zwischen den Kulturen: Hanna Levy-Deinhard im Exil und ihre Aktualität*, Frauen und Exil, vol. 9.1 (Munich, 2016).

7. Her articles were published in *Revista do Serviço do Patrimônio Histórico e Artístico Nacional* (SPHAN), later renamed *Revista do Instituto do Patrimônio Histórico e Artístico Nacional* (IPHAN).

8. On the historiography, see Jens Baumgarten and André Tavares, "O barroco colonizador: A produção históriográfico-artístico no Brasil e suas principais orientações teóricas," *Perspective* 2 (2013), http://journals.openedition.org/perspective/5538, posted September 30, 2014, consulted April 23, 2018.

9 Levy, *Henri Wölfflin: Sa théorie, ses prédécesseurs*, 206: "...Wölfflin n'analyse pas le processus de formation de représentation. En d'autres termes, nous ne trouvons pas advantage dans la forme de représentation intuitive la chose concrète que nous contemplons, mais seulement son essence."

10. Levy, *Henri Wölfflin: Sa théorie, ses prédécesseurs*, 185–214.

11. Levy, *Henri Wölfflin: Sa théorie, ses prédécesseurs*, 207, refers to Karl Mannheim's *Beiträge zur Theorie der Weltanschauungsinterpretation*: "Une histoire immanente du style est tout au plus capable de décrier et d'exposer d'une façon morphologique le développement des styles. Mais si elle prétend nous indiquer une cause plus profonde de ce développement, elle sera forcée de transgresser son propre domaine et d'avoir recours au concept du 'vouloir artistique'—pour employer un terme de Riegl—éternellement changeant et se trouvant en dehors du style pur et simple. Et si elle entend ensuite saisir les raisons profondes de ce changement permanent du 'vouloir artistique,' elle se heurtera à des entités encore plus générales telles que 'l'esprit de l'époque,' ou la 'conception du monde,' etc."

12. Levy, *Henri Wölfflin: Sa théorie, ses prédécesseurs*, 193.

13. See Myriam Andrade Ribeiro de Oliveira Andrade, *Aleijadinho: Passos e profetos* (Belo Horizonte, 2002); Guilherme Simões Gomes Júnior, *Palavra peregrine: O barroco e o pensamento sobre artes e letras no Brasil* (São Paulo, 1998), 50–63; and Tadeu Chiarelli, *Pintura não é só beleza* (Florianópolis, 2007), 69–96 and 247–248.

14. Hanna Levy, "Valor artístico e valor histórico," *Revista do Serviço do Patrimônio Histórico e Artístico Nacional* 4 (1940): 181–192, and "A propósito de três teorias sobre o barroco," 5 (1941): 250–284.

15. Levy, "A pintura colonial no Rio de Janeiro," *Revista do Serviço do Patrimônio Histórico e Artístico Nacional* 6 (1942): 7–79; "Modelos Europeus na pintura colonial," 8 (1944): 7–66; and "Retratos coloniais," 9 (1945): 251–290.

16. "[Die] künstlerische Qualität wird am potenzialen Ausdrucksgehalt...beweisbar": Hanna Levy Deinhard, *Bedeutung und Ausdruck: Zur Soziologie der Malerei* (Berlin, 1967), 80–81. In this work she also criticized professional art historians and art critics and praised authors who were pursuing synthesis instead of specialization (8).

17 "[Nenhum destes valores] constituem, na história concreta, valores absolutos, mas relativos": Levy, "Valor artístico e valor histórico," 188. Possibly incorrect phrasing in quotations from Levy's Portuguese text reflects the original.

18. Deinhard, *Bedeutung und Ausdruck*, 81.

19. "Esse sentido relativo dos valores evidencia-se se se seconsidear uma obra (sucessivamente) em relação à produção total de um só artista, a uma escola local, à história da arte de um país ou à história mundial da arte, etc.": Levy, "Valor artístico e valor histórico," 188.

20. Levy, *Henri Wölfflin: Sa théorie, ses prédécesseurs*, chapter 7 and p. 27.

21. For Mário de Andrade, see Gomes Júnior, *Palavra peregrina*, 50–63, and Chiarelli, *Pintura não é só beleza*, 173–175; for Lourival Gomes Machado, see Lourival Gomes Machado, *Barroco Mineiro* (São Paulo, 2010), 29–176, and Gomes Júnior, *Palavra peregrine*, 76–88. It is also important to mention that the foundation of Brazilian art history, or rather, art criticism, was connected to the membership of the communist and socialist parties in Brazil (for instance, Carlos Alberto Cerqueira Lemos, Caio da Silva Prado Júnior) and especially to artists, architects, and art critics such as Candido Portinari, Tarsila do Amaral, Emiliano Augusto Cavalcanti de Albuquerque Melo, known as Di Cavalcanti, Lúcio Marçal Ferreira Ribeiro de Lima Costa, and Oscar Niemeyer. Together they developed a national project of a specifically Brazilian art.

22. Chiarelli, *Pintura não é só beleza*, 173–175.

23. "Se amanhã um historiador trouxesse a prova irrefutável de que existe uma influencia certa de tal obra de determinado artista europeu sobre as estatuas dos profetas de Congonhas, este fato seria certamente de grande interesse sob muitos aspetos. Mas o fato dessa influencia em si não dirá jamais nada do valor histórico ou do valor artístico da obra de Antonio Francisco Lisboa." Levy, "Valor artístico e valor histórico," 191.

24. Thomas DaCosta Kaufmann, *Toward a Geography of Art* (Chicago, 2004), 219–225.

25. Levy, "A propósito de três teorias sobre o barroco," 250–284.

26. "[O artista colonial] utilizou de modelos da arte européia. Daí o caráter eclético da pintura colonial, vista em conjunto, e daí também o caráter hetergêneo que se nota freqüentemente nas obras de um mesmo artista." Levy, "Modelos europeus na pintura colonial," 46–47.

27. Levy stresses especially German and Flemish engravings as important for colonial artists.

28. '[Os] painéis traduziram perfeitamente o caráter dramático e agitado das representações gravadas…ou ainda ofereceram até um efeito mais dramático de que o das próprias gravuras originais.…Por outro lado, a impressão de agitação suscitada pelas pinturas resulta, também, da circunstância de haver o pintor, simplificando os fundos, concentrado…todo o interêsse sôbre as figuras humanas." Levy, "Modelos Europeus na pintura colonial," 48–49.

29. Levy, "Modelos Europeus na pintura colonial," 64. Because this article focuses not on specific problems of colonial Brazilian art but on aspects related to discussion of world art, it is not necessary to go into more depth about her observations. For the most recent discussion of stylistic questions, see Myriam Andrade Ribeiro de Oliveira, *O rococo religioso no Brasil e seus antecedentes europeus* (São Paulo, 2003).

30. Gomes Machado, *Barroco Mineiro*, 46. He did not consider other texts or further developments of Levy's theory, which culminated in *Bedeutung und Ausdruck*. He was connected to *Clima*, one of Brazil's most important journals of art and literary criticism; another famous contributor was the literary critic Antonio Candido.

31. "A teoria de Balet…explica os fenômenos artísticos pelas suas relaç[õ]es [c]om a totalidade das condições históricas existentes numa época determinada, [isto] nos parece ser, por isso mesmo, a [forma] mais apta a resolver também os problemas da historia da arte brasileira." Levy, "A propósito de três teorias sobre o barroco," 284.

32. Within a vast literature on *brasilidade*, most important is Aracy A. Amaral, *Textos do Trópico de Capricórnio: Artigos e ensaios (1980–2005)*, 3 vols., especially 1:241–330. See also Sônia Salzstein, "Transformações na esfera da crítica," *Ars* (Universidade de São Paulo) 1, no. 1 (2003): 221–226; concerning literature, Leyla Perrone-Moisés, *Vira e mexe, Nacionalismo: Paradoxos do nacionalismo literário* (São Paulo, 2007), 28–49; and, on the sociological context, Renato Ortiz, *A moderna tradição brasileira* (São Paulo, 1988), 182–205.

33. In this context it is possible to think of the discourse on the baroque in Brazil and Hanna Levy's analysis as a forerunner of debates about rethinking modernity, such as Regina Göckede, *Spätkoloniale Moderne: Le Corbusier, Ernst May, Frank Lloyd Wright, The Architects Collaborative und die Globalisierung der Architekturmoderne* (Basel, 2016).

34. Mário Pedrosa, *Arte, Ensaios* (São Paulo, 2015), 249.

35. Janice Theodoro da Silva, *América barroca: Tema e variações* (São Paulo, 1992), 139.

36. Janice Theodoro da Silva, *América barroca*, 143.

ZHANG PING

From Teng Gu to Fan Jingzhong: Principles of Art History *in China*

•李泽厚主编　美学译文丛书•

艺术风格学

【瑞士】H·沃尔夫林　著

潘耀昌　译

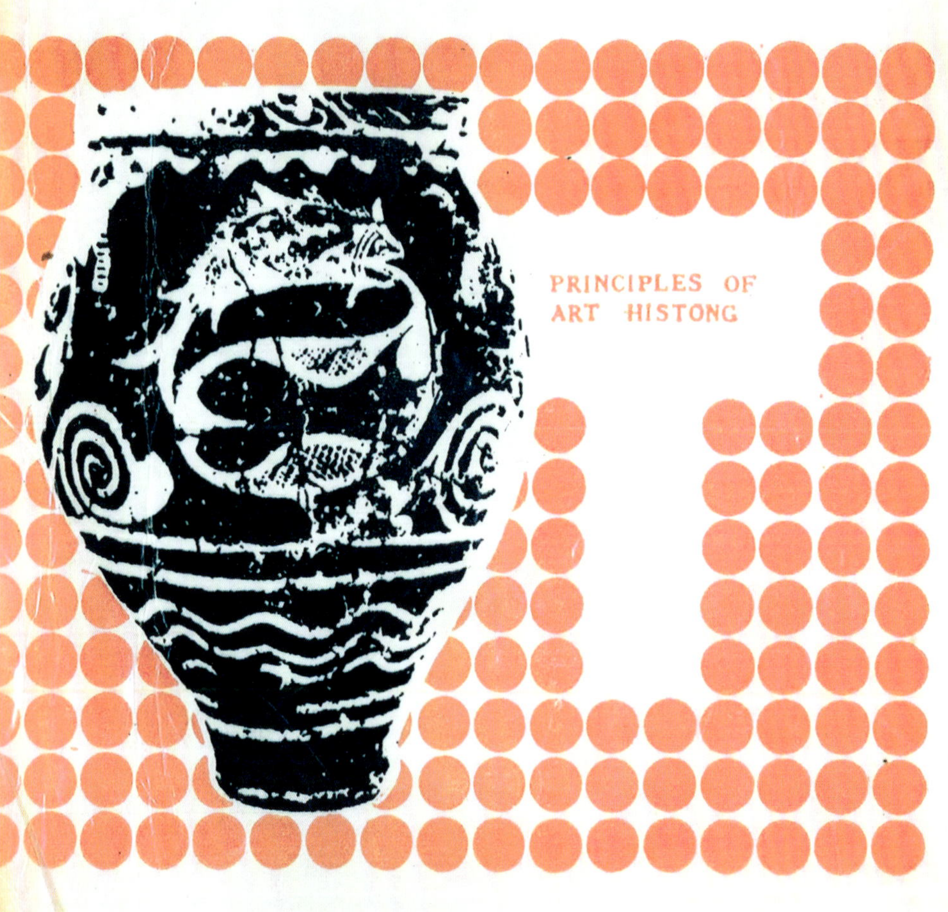

Until the beginning of the twentieth century, Chinese art historians practiced traditional art historiography as represented by Zhang Yanyuan (active ninth century), *Lidai minghua ji* (A record of famous painters of all the dynasties), and later attempts at the same subjects by those who tried to follow his example. Zhang's work incorporates biographies of painters and covers the history and theory of painting as well as collecting and connoisseurship. In reflecting the work of connoisseurs, critics, and academic art historians, it covers a somewhat broader territory than modern art history in the strict sense.

Beginning in 1872, the Manchu government sent students overseas, to the United States, Europe, and Japan. They brought back, among other things, aesthetic ideologies and art-historical theories then popular in those contexts. Heinrich Wölfflin (1864–1945) was among the first modern Western art historians to have an effect on the understanding of traditional Chinese art in China.[1] His influence was possible only because of the work of a few renowned Chinese scholars.

In 1912, following the end of the Qing dynasty, Cai Yuanpei (1868–1940), who had studied at Leipzig University for more than four years and was imbued with Western academic ideals, became minister of education in the newly established provisional government. He spared no effort in calling for public arts education. As a result, the first specialized art school in China, Shanghai College of Painting (renamed Shanghai Academy of Fine Arts in 1930) was established. One of its graduates was Teng Gu (1901–1941), the first art historian in modern China, who introduced *Principles of Art History* to Chinese readers (fig. 1).

Teng had received a traditional early education and was conversant with classical Chinese literature. After completing his studies in Shanghai, in 1920 he went to Japan and enrolled as a student in the department of philosophy of Toyo University. Having graduated in 1924 with a bachelor of arts, he returned to China and taught art theory and history at Shanghai Academy of Fine Arts and other institutions.

Along with the establishment of art schools, China in the 1920s and 1930s witnessed a boom in translations of Japanese scholarly publications. Textbooks on art, mostly based on Japanese examples, were compiled. Before Teng tried his hand at Chinese art history, he had an opportunity to read the works of Japanese scholars. We can assume that he read *Minzokuteki shikisai o shu to suru kindai bijutsu shichōron* (Trends in the history of modern art; 1927) by Itagaki Takaho (1894–1966), translated into Chinese by Lu Xun (1881–1936) and published in 1928. This work discussed Wölfflin's *Sehformen* and made his importance clear.[2] In 1931 Teng went to Germany and studied art history at the University of Berlin, where Heinrich Wölfflin had taught in 1901–1912 and, as a visiting professor, in summer 1930. Considering that the first Japanese version of *Principles* appeared in 1936, Teng must have read the book in Germany. He was quick to apply modern archaeological and art-historical paradigms, which he had studied there, to Chinese art. He published his doctoral thesis, on classical Chinese painting theories, under the title "Chinesische Malkunsttheorie in der T'ang- und Sungzeit" as well as three articles

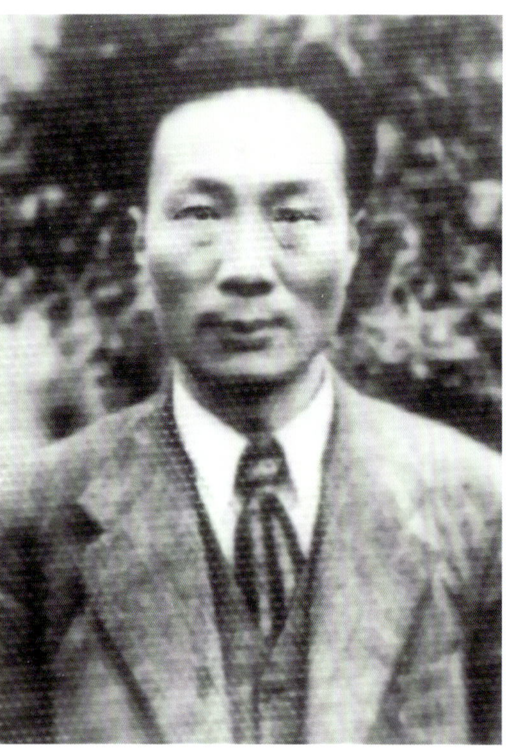

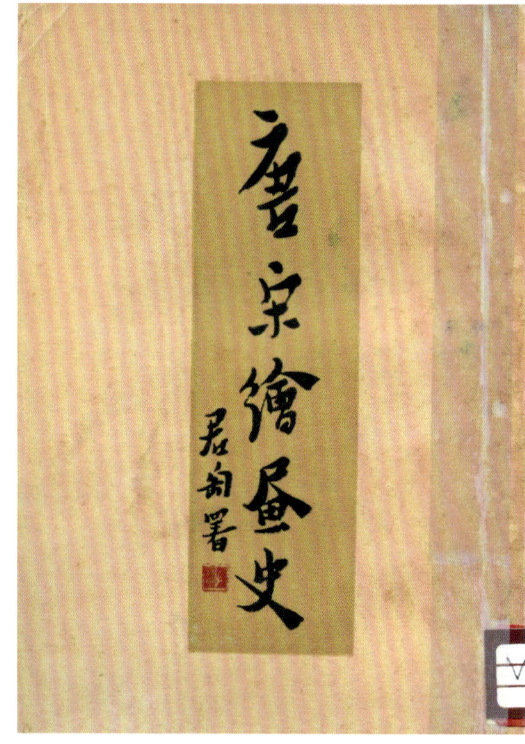

exhibiting scholarship of the highest level in contemporary studies of Chinese painting in Western languages.[3]

In his earliest attempt to introduce Wölfflin to Chinese readers, Teng quoted him to explain the concept of style. He noted that when a new artistic style appeared, its distinctness lay not only in the depiction of objects but also in the way the artist portrayed human gestures and movements. The new perception created by the latter was the essence of a new style.[4] He was confident in distinguishing styles of different groups of artists and various periods. His belief in the validity of Wölfflin's principles for explaining the development of style in Chinese art manifested itself in his interpretations.

A major contribution by Teng, *Tangsong huihuashi* (History of painting in the Tang and Song dynasties) was published in 1933 in Shanghai (fig. 2). It traced the history of styles, examined works of art and related literature, and studied artistic creation in cultural context. Teng stated at the beginning that art-historical studies should focus on *Stilentwicklung* (development of style) and that the genesis, growth, flourishing,

and transformation of a style were decided by intrinsic forces.[5] In an article published in 1935, he put forward a hypothesis mentioning Wölfflin's most widely applied concepts: "Dynamic and flexible lines in Chinese painting are the only essential constituent of beautiful forms, and the introduction of chiaroscuro could give impetus to the development of Chinese painting from 'linear' to 'painterly.'"[6] He borrowed this first pair of categories to explain differing styles in landscape painting. He believed that, as with the works of Dürer (1471–1528) and those of Rembrandt (1606–1669), landscape paintings by Wu Daozi (active 713–755) were "zeichnerisch" while those of Li Sixun (651–716) were "malerisch" because the former painted with concise and highly expressive lines, and the latter's works were marked by vigorous strokes and bright colors.[7] In addition, he saw in the heyday of the Tang dynasty a relaxed and spontaneous spirit, not only in painting and other art forms but also in religion, law, and politics.[8] It is unfortunate that Teng's lack of access during turbulent times to a large number of works of Chinese art prevented him from

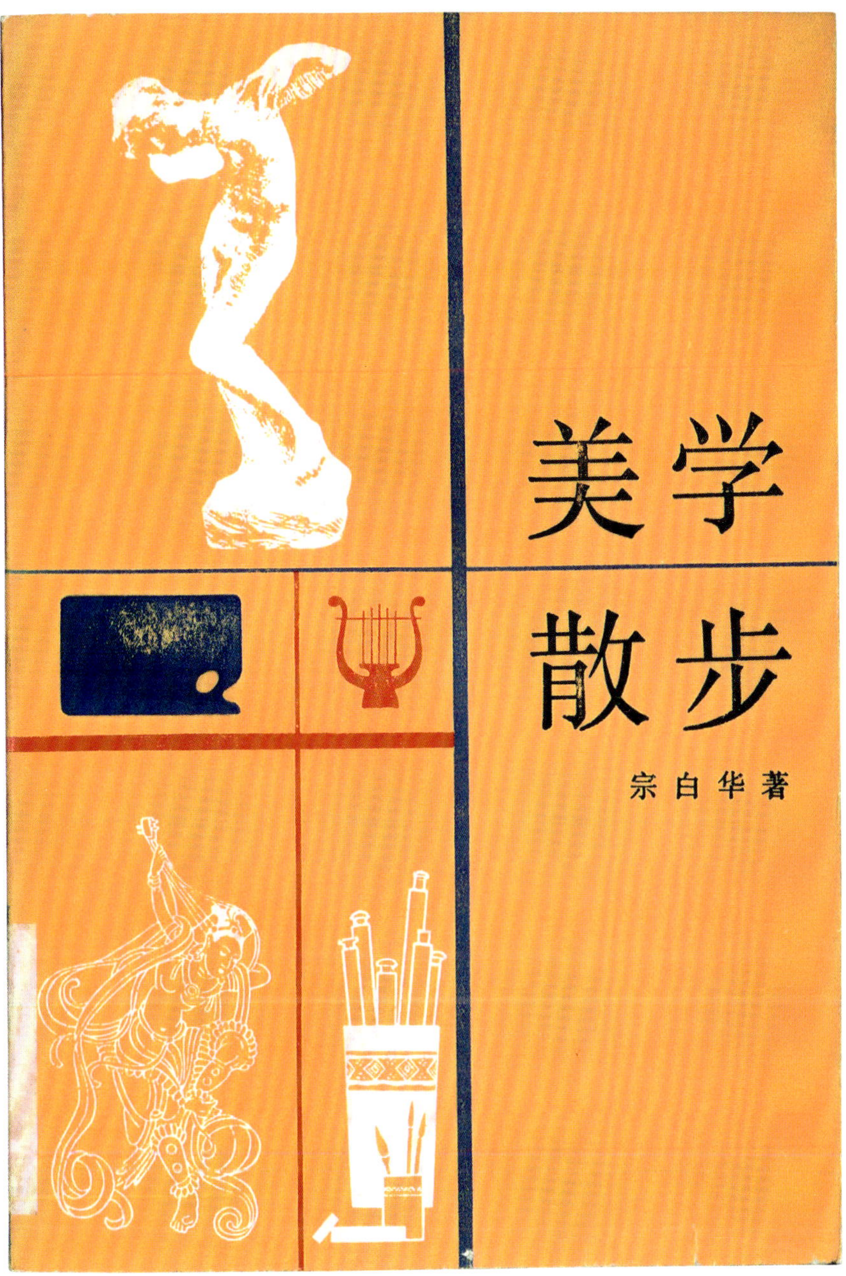

3. Zong Baihua, *Meixue sanbu* (Strolls in aesthetics) (Shanghai, 1981)

Courtesy of Shanghai People's Press, Shanghai

him.[11] Only in recent years have Teng and his exploration of Chinese art history been brought to scholars' attention again, partly because of a new consciousness of modern art historiography.[12] But Wölfflin's ideas and those of his German-speaking peers kept working their influence in a more subtle way. Zong Baihua (1897–1986), one of the influential figures of modern Chinese aesthetics, studied at the University of Berlin in 1922, majoring in aesthetics. He was impressed by the ideas of Max Dessoir (1867–1947), who taught there from 1897 to 1933, and whose course Teng also took in 1932.[13] The twenty-two essays on Chinese and Western art collected in *Meixue sanbu* (Strolls in aesthetics; 1981), Zong's most widely read work (fig. 3), manifest the influence of art-historical theories cultivated in the German-speaking world. He expressly valued Alois Riegl's (1858–1905) concept of *Kunstwollen* and, in an essay on the awareness of space in Chinese art, applied it to explain the absence of one-point perspective in Chinese painting.[14] Traces of Wölfflin's *Principles* are apparent in Zong's work even though he never declared his source. When describing artistic styles in the Renaissance and ancient Greece, he mentioned and explained "painterly style" as the successor to a classical "plastic style."[15] He also believed that imported techniques enhanced the effect of painterliness in Chinese painting.[16] Zong confidently singled out linearity as an important characteristic of traditional Chinese art, especially in comparison to its Western counterparts.[17]

Zong's writing is lyrical, knowledgeable, and full of reflection. *Strolls in Aesthetics* appeared in good times when the intellectuals of the 1980s, having been challenged by the influx of images and ideas from overseas during the reform and the opening-up period, tried to reevaluate the Chinese cultural heritage, and the book attracted a large number of readers who expected an inspiring interpretation of indigenous art. The preface was written by Li Zehou (1930–), an aesthetician of a younger generation. Li appears here as the third figure who promoted Wölfflin's influence

achieving his ambition to conduct a comprehensive stylistic analysis based on firsthand study.[9] Instead, he had to "tread the old paths taken by his predecessors from time to time, and count on lifeless documents for explanations."[10]

Teng Gu was one of the pioneers in the establishment of modern Chinese art history. His academic pursuits would have borne much more fruit had it not been for the war and his untimely death in 1941 at the age of forty. *Principles* fell into oblivion with

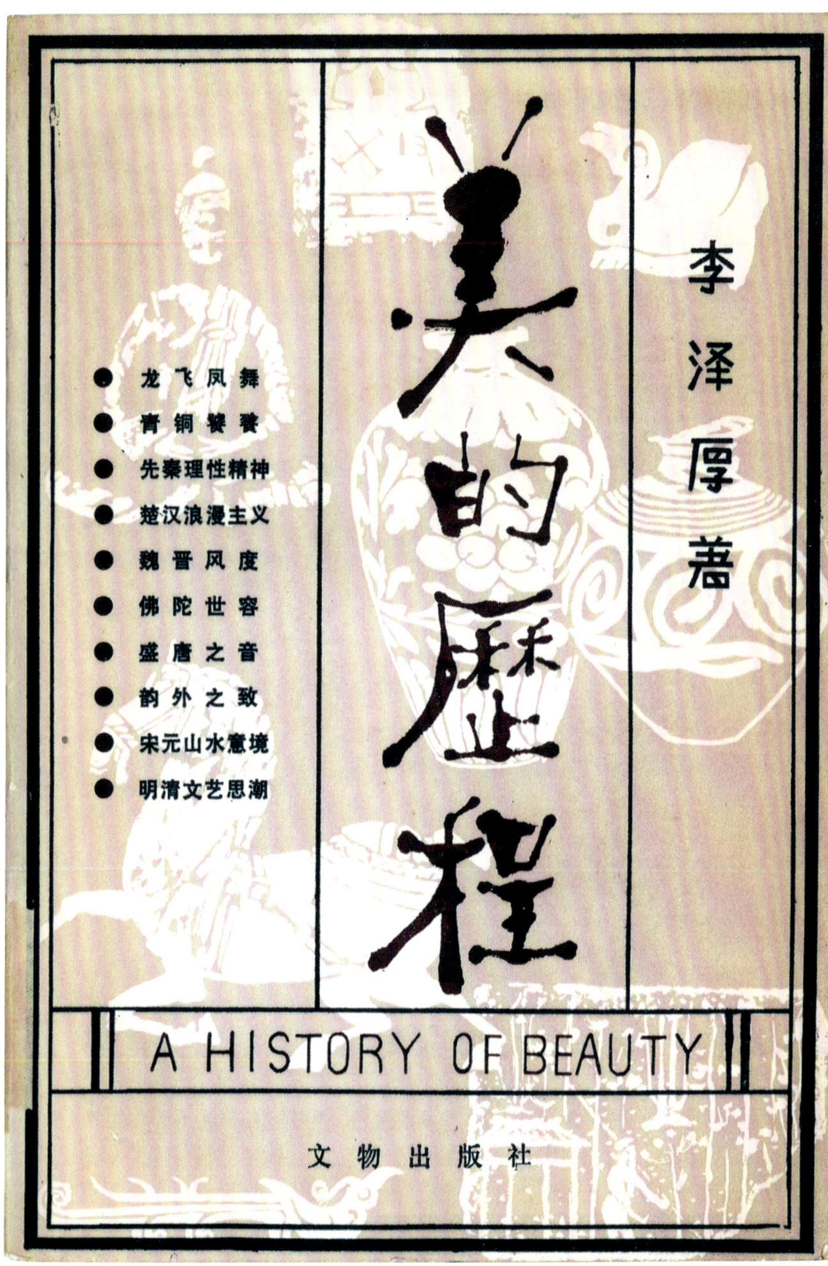

4. Li Zehou, *Mei de licheng* (*The Path of Beauty*) (Beijing, 1981) *Courtesy of Cultural Relics Press, Beijing*

on Chinese art history. His insightful and beautifully written *Mei de licheng* (1981; published in English in 1994 as *The Path of Beauty*) was also extensively praised (fig. 4). Li intended to help readers understand and experience the beauty embodied in Chinese art and, along with it, the identity of Chinese culture. He also read *Principles*. In his *Meixue si jiang* (Lectures on aesthetics) he referred to Wölfflin's definition of the Renaissance and baroque styles and cited *Principles* in the notes.[18] In *Mei*

de licheng, he quoted from Teng's *History of Painting in the Tang and Song Dynasties*, in which the latter explicitly introduced Wölfflin's theory.[19] Like Zong, Li attached great importance to linearity in Chinese art.[20] In addition, he stressed that change in artistic styles is the result of different collective psychologies in different times. He went as far as to identify a certain spirit of the time in ancient Chinese bronzes and stone reliefs, literature, and crafts.[21]

To art historians, the formulation of a collective psychological structure playing a vital role in artistic creation and reception and that of linearity as a distinguishing feature of Chinese art, though very appealing, are by no means satisfying. Wölfflin's ideas, generalized and propagated through Zong and Li, are less applicable when it comes to traditional Chinese painting and calligraphy. Besides, they leave the persistent question of artistic quality untouched, not to mention that their help in our understanding of the conception and execution of a work of art, the reading of a trained audience, the genesis of a style, or the cultivation of taste is limited. Since the study of art in the modern sense was still underdeveloped in China at the time when Wölfflin's ideas were introduced, such generalizations from the field of aesthetics could be misleading. As a result, they quickly became a cliché in art criticism, a relatively new domain much less burdened by legacy than art history is.[22] To some of the questions mentioned above, Wölfflin's *Principles* could have offered illuminating answers. But it took a long time before *Kunstgeschichte* was ready to break out of the soil of the older *Künstlergeschichte* in China. Wölfflin and his work gained little attention until the first Chinese translation in 1987. This publication has much to do with the art historian Fan Jingzhong (1951–) (fig. 5).

When Fan went to university in Beijing, *The Path of Beauty* and its author were so well received that it is not a total exaggeration to say that almost every college student then had a copy of the book. Fan kept a cautious distance from Li's ideas and the

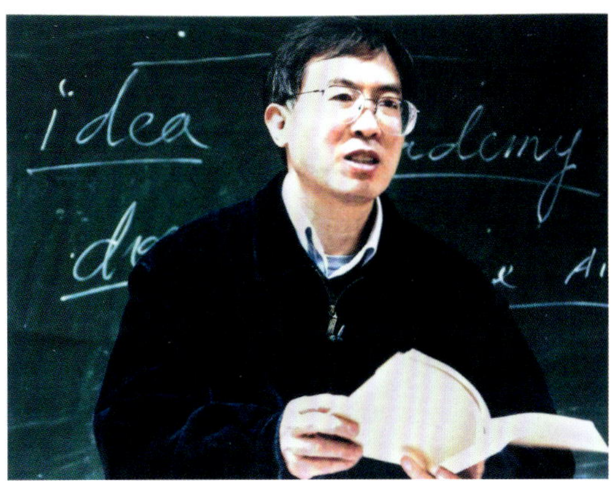

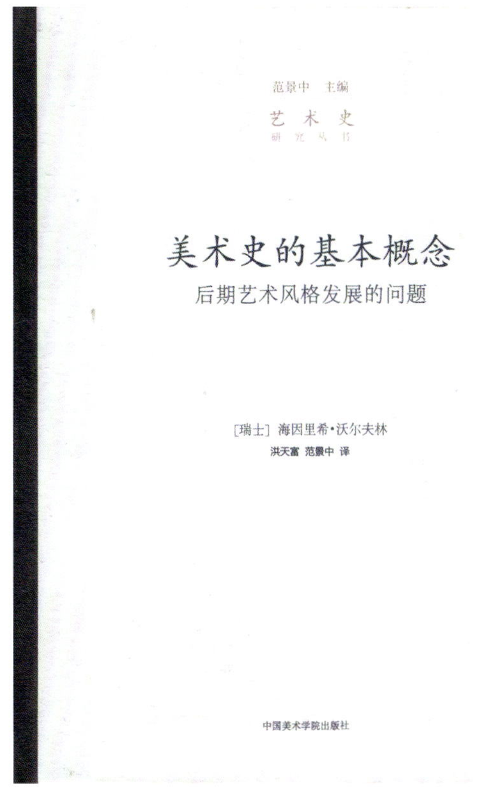

aesthetic ideologies prevalent in the 1980s. Instead, he turned to European and American art-historical methodologies for a reliable guide. In 1983, when he was appointed editor in chief of *Meishu yi cong*, an influential journal aimed at advancing Chinese art-historical studies through introduction of landmark theories and methodologies of Western art in translation, he was fully aware of the importance of Wölfflin's work.[23] In fact, Wölfflin's comparative stylistic analysis was one of the three schools of methodology highlighted in the journal, represented by Wölfflin himself, Erwin Panofsky, and Ernst Gombrich, respectively. Fan invited Pan Yaochang (1947–) to translate Wölfflin's *Principles* and published it in 1987 in a series titled Translations in Aesthetics (Meixue yiwen congshu), which included one hundred books in its original publishing plan, half of which reached completion (see essay frontispiece). What is noteworthy is that Li Zehou was the editor in chief of the series. In the preface to the Wölfflin translation, Li emphasized the urgent need to introduce key works in Western aesthetics to propel the growth of aesthetics in China.[24] Pan Yaochang's translation was well received, though the language seems somewhat stilted. It was followed by another rendering, also facilitated by Fan, aiming at a more intelligible version, but the project was not completed. In 2015, another translation, by Hong Tianfu (1934–) and Fan Jingzhong, appeared, with a revised subtitle (fig. 6). So far, *Principles* has had five Chinese translations including the unpublished one.

Besides the three mentioned there are those of Zeng Yayun (1987) and Yang Pengbo (2011).[25] Three of the five translations were endorsed by Fan, who clearly put a great deal of effort into disseminating the book and the ideas it conveys. But *Principles* was not the only work that attracted his attention. He also invited scholars to translate Wölfflin's *Classic Art* (*Gudian yishu*, 1992) and *Renaissance and Baroque* (*Wenyifuxing yu baluoke*, 2007). Since the 1980s Fan has worked with a few likeminded scholars to bring celebrated European and American art historians into public view in China. The first volume of *Meishushi de xingzhuang* (The shapes of art history; 2003), under his editorship, included Wölfflin's "Die antiken Triumphbogen in Italien." The projected work will represent different methodologies of Western art-historical studies in ten volumes, with eight volumes still in preparation. As it happens, Fan's project finds an echo in *The Books That Shaped Art History*, edited by Richard Shone and John-Paul Stonard, published more than twenty years after his initial volume.[26]

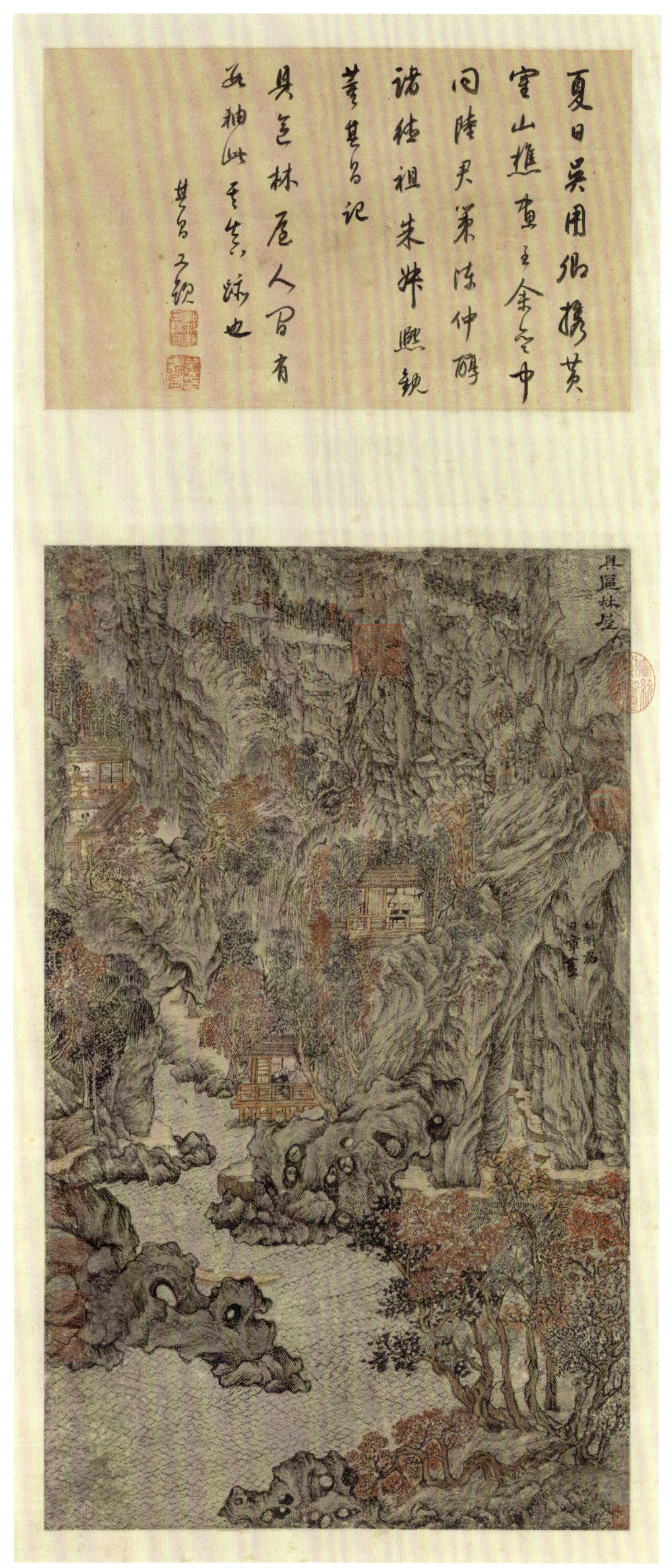

7. Wang Meng, *The Forest Grotto at Chü-ch'ü* (*Juqu lin wu tu*), Yuan dynasty (1271–1368), hanging scroll, ink and colors on paper

Courtesy of National Palace Museum, Taipei

Three of the published translations of *Principles* were based on the English version of the seventh German edition; the latest one, by Hong and Fan (2015) was directly based on the eighth German edition. According to Fan's preface, this translation offers a new dimension to the Chinese understanding of the text in more ways than one. First, a few minor adjustments to the "faithful and graceful" translation by Marie Hottinger (1893–1978) proved necessary when it was compared closely with the German version. Changes in more recent German editions, he points out, should also be noted. So this new translation reflects reconsideration of some renderings and includes one of Wölfflin's important notes and the postscript expounding the author's second thoughts about *Zeitgeist*, which were not included in the first English translation. In addition, it is a much freer translation and thus more accessible than Pan Yaochang's relatively literal one.[27]

Five translations attest to Chinese art historians' recognition of the importance of *Principles*. With the efforts of the translators, concepts like artistic style and its development, analysis of form, and comparative study of works of art have become familiar to Chinese scholars. Even before the first published translation, some of the ideas were tested in the study of Chinese painting, as we have seen with Teng Gu. And if we look beyond the border for those who studied Chinese art history with the help of Wölfflin's formalist methods, his student Ludwig Bachhofer (1894–1976) should be the first, followed by Bachhofer's disciple Max Loehr (1903–1988). Loehr's students James Cahill (1926–2014) and Wen C. Fong (1930–2018) in turn trained scholars in this field, many of whom became professors and taught in China and in the West, primarily the United States.

In the end, all the efforts to understand and master Wölfflin's formalist theories and methodologies encourage new research in more applicable methods born of local tradition. Teng Gu's experimental practice of applying Wölfflin's approach to Chinese art attracted no followers. Indeed, he was aware that those principles never fit traditional Chinese art as well as they did the art of the European Renaissance and baroque. He speculated about the development of Chinese style from "linear" to "painterly" but commented that it was "to be proved."[28] He emphasized that the revival of Chinese art lies in the cultural heritage of the nation rather than the cultivation of imported ideas.[29] Fan Jingzhong has also been thinking in this direction. In *Zhonghua zhu yun* (The book of bamboo; 2011), he cited two descriptions of *The Forest Grotto at Chü-ch'ü* (*Juqu lin wu tu*), by Wang Meng (c. 1309–1385), the great landscape painter of the Yuan dynasty (fig. 7). In the first, from 1982, James Cahill wrote,

The entire space of the picture is crowded with active, oppressive forms that overpower the ostensible subject: a traveler sitting by the stream in the foreground waiting for the ferry, which approaches from the left; the man to whom the picture is dedicated, seated in his house on the opposite bank; his wife, perhaps, in another building higher on the mountainside; a constricted view of the distant lake in the upper right.[30]

In the second, Dong Qichang (1555–1636), the famous painter and calligrapher of the Ming period, wrote:

Everything here is after Wang Wei [699–759]. The stones are hollowed and the tree branches are too meticulously painted. [The painter] still follows the manner of the Tang dynasty.[31]

Fan refers to the former description as linear and the latter as *malerisch*.[32] He is interested in the meaningful relationship between "schemas" of languages and inclinations in artistic creation and reception in different cultures. Through half seriously applying Wölfflinian concepts to languages, he draws a new angle from which we observe art. At the same time, he tries to derive from premodern Chinese language and aesthetic tastes a contribution to building a suitable model for modern Chinese art-historical studies.

How ancient Chinese employed this *malerisch* language in artistic creation and related aesthetic thought was not Wölfflin's concern. But it is one of the speculations inspired by his book. For Chinese art historians, it also offers an opportunity to revisit the work of Zhang Yanyuan, exploring the rich rhetoric of traditional Chinese art-historical literature. As Fan writes in *The Shapes of Art History*: "In a certain sense, the history of art history is the history of different ways of composing."[33]

That Wölfflin's paradigm has become a bit too familiar in our time does not discourage those who want to know more about his "way of composing" as an integral structure. One hundred years after its first publication, *Principles* is still read in various languages. And with the development of languages themselves, fresh attempts are being made to enrich our understanding of this important work. In 2015, a new English translation (by Jonathan Blower) and a new Chinese one appeared, saluting this milestone in the growing field of modern art history. It is still full of illuminating prospects that lure adventurers to set foot on different pathways.

NOTES

I am obliged to Evonne Levy and Tristan Weddigen, who kindly offered their very useful suggestions for revision of the text.

1. Cao Yiqiang, *Yishu yu lishi* (Art and history) (Hangzhou, 2001), 192.

2. Itagaki Takaho, *Jindai meishushi chao lun* (Trends in the history of modern art), trans. Xun Lu (Beijing, 2001), 3.

3. "Chinesische Malkunsttheorie in der T'ang- und Sungzeit" was published in *Ostasiatische Zeitschrift* in three parts: n.s. 10 (1934): 157–175, 236–251; n.s. 11 (1935): 28–57. It was also published as an offprint by De Gruyter in Berlin in the same year. The articles are "Zur Bedeutung der Südschule in der chinesischen Landschaftsmalerei," n.s. 7 (1931): 156–163; "Su Tung P'o als Kunstkritiker," n.s. 8 (1932): 104–110; and "Tuschespiele," n.s. 8 (1932): 249–255.

4. Teng Gu, *Tangsong huihuashi* (Shanghai, 1933), 144. Teng quoted from Wölfflin's *Die klassische Kunst* (7th ed., Munich, 1924), 227.

5. Teng, *Tangsong huihuashi*, 3. In his discussion of Guo Zhongshu (active tenth century), he found that the painter's personality was not consistent with the kind of painting at which he excelled. He went on to state that the appearance of a certain style was due to social customs much more than to the artist's personality. See Teng Gu, "Guanyu yuantihua he wenrenhua zhi shi de kaocha"(Study of the history of court painting and literati painting), in *Zhongguo meishu xiao shi, Tangsong huihuashi* (An introduction to Chinese art history: History of painting in the Tang and Song dynasties), ed. Shen Ning (Changchun, 2010), 334–356 (first published in *Fu ren xue zhi* 2 [1931]).

6. Teng, "Tangdai yishu de tezheng" (Characteristics of art in the Tang dynasty), in *Zhongguo meishu xiao shi*, 444–463 (first published in *Zhongyang daxue wenyi congkan* 2 [1935]).

7. Teng, "Guanyu yuantihua he wenrenhua zhi shi de kaocha."

8. Teng explained that this pair of categories was used here in a general sense. In his eyes, "zeichnerische" Chinese paintings emphasize lines and clarity, while "malerische" ones are rich in colors, and create space through chiaroscuro. Teng, "Tangdai yishu de tezheng."

9. According to Teng, an insufficient number of public museums, scattered private collections, and scarcity of printed images were among the main obstacles to serious study of Chinese art at his time. In addition, the problem of authenticity in Chinese art leaves the application of Wölfflin's principles on shaky ground. See Yizhe Deng, "Teng Gu zhu tangsong huihuashi jiao hou yu" (On the revision of history of painting in the Tang and Song dynasties by Teng Gu), in *Zhongguo meishu xiao shi*, 141–142 (first published in *Tangsong huihuashi*, 1958). According to Deng, Teng cited unreliable colophons in *Tang song huihuashi*.

10. Teng, *Tang song huihuashi*, 3.

11. Teng translated Adolph Goldschmidt's *Kunstgeschichte* (Berlin, 1930) and published it in 1937, introducing to China the development of art history in German-speaking countries. But with the outbreak of World War II, some theoretical monographs on art by authors in the Soviet Union attracted academic attention to a sociological perspective, and these became more influential starting in the 1950s.

12. Especially from 2000 on, dozens of articles have noted Teng Gu's role in the development of modern Chinese art history and his debt to Wölfflin in the realm of theory. See *Zhongguo meishu xiao shi*, 598–601 (bibliography).

13. Teng, "Shi shu hua san zhong yishu de liandai guanxi" (The relation among poetry, calligraphy, and painting), in *Zhongguo meishu xiao shi*, 357–361 (first published in *Jiaoyubu di er ci quanguo meishu zhanlanhui zhuankan* [1937]).

14. "It's not that a Chinese painter didn't know about perspective, but his 'will to form' was not willing to demonstrate it in his paintings." See Zong Baihua, "Zhongguo shi hua zhong suo biaoxian de kongjian yishi"(Spatial awareness in Chinese poetry and painting), in *Meixue sanbu* (Shanghai, 1981), 95–118. For an English translation of another essay from this work, "Zhongguo yishu yijing zhi dansheng," see "The Birth of Artistic Conception in China," *Art in Translation* 9, no. 3 (2017): 367–396.

15. Zong Baihua, "Lun zhongxi huafa de yuanyuan yu jichu" (The origin and foundation of Chinese and Western painting techniques), in *Meixue sanbu*, 119–135 (first published in *Wenyi congkan* 1 [1936]).

16. Zong, "Lun zhongxi huafa de yuanyuan yu jichu." Teng was impressed and inspired by this article. See Teng Gu, "Tangdai yishu de tezheng."

17. Zong, "Zhongguo meixueshi zhong zhongyao wenti de chubu tansuo (Preliminary study of some important questions in the history of Chinese aesthetics), in *Meixue sanbu*, 31–67 (first published in *Wenyi congkan* 6 [1979]). He points out that as opposed to Rembrandt and Rodin, whose works are compositions of light and shadow, Chinese paintings are created by the rhythm of lines.

18. Li Zehou, *Meixue si jiang*, in *Li Zehou shi nian ji 1979–1989 (Collected works by Li Zehou from ten years, 1979–1989)* (Hefei, 1994), 1:417–580; on Wölfflin, see 549.

19. Li Zehou, *Mei de licheng*, in *Li Zehou shi nian ji 1979–1989*, 1:159. English translation: *The Path of Beauty: A Study of Chinese Aesthetics*, trans. Gong Lizeng (New York, 1994).

20. Li, *Mei de licheng*, 101. Li stresses that the art of lines is the best developed and most characteristic in Chinese art. It is a manifestation of Chinese cultural and psychological structure.

21. Li, *Mei de licheng*, 83. About the bronzes of the Shang and Zhou dynasties, he says: "They are beautiful not because these images are decorative, as some art historians recently pointed out, but because these strange patterns, with forceful lines and cast protruding ornaments, perfectly embody an emotion, a perception, and an ideal of a primitive religion, which cannot be described with the language of concepts. Together with the grave, firm, and steady bodies of the bronzes, they successfully present a barbarian era of blood and fire." Li, *Mei de licheng*, 42–43. He believes that art forms of certain times experience similar conceptual development, reflecting the spirit of the time. Li, *Mei de licheng*, 197.

22. Fan Jingzhong, "Meishushi de xingzhuang: Sanshi nian lai wo de chuban jingli," *Shi shu hua* 15 (January 2015): 32–51.

23. Its predecessor was *Meishu lilun ziliao* (Materials on art theory), launched in 1956 and suspended in 1957. After resuming publication in 1978 as *Guowai meishu ziliao* (Materials on art abroad) at the Zhejiang Academy of Fine Arts, the journal was renamed *Meishu yi cong* (Translations of work on art) in 1980 and finally ceased publication in 1989.

24. Heinrich Wölfflin, *Yishu fengge xue (Principles of Art History* [A study on artistic style]), trans. Pan Yaochang (Shenyang, 1987), preface, 1. The Chinese title of this translation was changed to *Meishushi de jiben gainian* (Basic concepts in fine arts) in the new edition of Pan's translation (2011) as well as in the most recent translation by Hong Tianfu and Fan Jingzhong (2015).

25. Heinrich Wölfflin, *Yishushi de yuanze (Principles of Art History)*, trans. Zeng Yayun (Taipei, 1987), and *Yishushi de jiben yuanli*, trans. Yang Pengbo (Beijing, 2011), whose Chinese title translates as "basic principles of art history."

26. Richard Shone and John-Paul Stonard, eds., *The Books That Shaped Art History: From Gombrich and Greenberg to Alpers and Krauss* (London, 2013).

27. Heinrich Wölfflin, *Meishushi de jiben gainian*, trans. Hong Tianfu and Fan Jingzhong (Hangzhou, 2015), 1–3.

28. "This is nothing more than an aperçu, whose validity remains to be supported by future evidence." Teng, "Tangdai yishu de tezheng."

29. Teng, "Guomin yishu yundong" (National art movement), in *Zhongguo meishu xiao shi*, 294–295.

30. James Cahill, *The Compelling Image: Nature and Style in Seventeenth-Century Chinese Painting* (Cambridge MA, 1982), 53–54.

31. Dong Qichang, "Hua zhi" (On painting), in *Rongtai bie ji 4* (Rongtai anthology 4), vol. 2 of *Dong Qichang quanji* (Complete works of Dong Qichang), ed. Yan Wenru and Yin Jun (Shanghai, 2013), 595–627. The anthology, part of the Rongtai collection, was first published in 1630.

32. Fan Jingzhong, *Zhonghua zhu yun* (The book of bamboo) (Hangzhou, 2011), 390–391.

33. Fan Jingzhong, ed., *Meishushi de xingzhuang* (The shapes of art history), 2 vols. (Hangzhou, 2003), 1:8.

Contributors

HANS AURENHAMMER is professor of art history with a focus on Renaissance art at the Goethe-Universität Frankfurt am Main. He has also taught at the universities of Vienna, Venice, Berlin, and Dresden and at the École Pratique des Hautes Études, Paris. He is a corresponding member of the Österreichische Akademie der Wissenschaften. From 2009 to 2017 he was a member and, from 2013, also chairman of the scientific advisory board of the Centro Tedesco di Studi Veneziani in Venice. His areas of research are art and architecture of the Italian Renaissance, art theory in the early modern period, and the history of art history. He has written on the Vienna School of art history and coedited, with Regine Prange, *Das Problem der Form: Interferenzen zwischen moderner Kunst und Kunstwissenschaft* (2016).

WOJCIECH BAŁUS is a professor at the Institute of Art History of the Jagiellonian University in Kraków. His field of study includes the theory and history of art from the nineteenth century to today, as well as the relationship between art on the one hand and philosophy, cultural anthropology, and literary studies on the other. He is editor of the series Ars Vetus et Nova. He is president of the Polish National Committee of the Corpus Vitrearum and a member of the Polish Academy of Arts and Sciences, the Hessische Akademie der Forschung und Planung im Ländlichen Raum, and the International Association of Art Critics (AICA). His publications include *Gotik ohne Gott? Zur Symbolik des Kirchengebäudes im 19. Jahrhundert* (2016) and *Krakau zwischen Traditionen und Wegen in die Moderne: Zur Geschichte der Architektur und der öffentlichen Grünanlagen im 19. Jahrhundert* (2003).

OSKAR BÄTSCHMANN is professor emeritus and former chair of art history at Universität Bern, where he also served as dean of the faculty from 2001 to 2003. He was a Getty scholar at the Getty Center for the History of Art and the Humanities and a visiting professor at the École des Hautes Etudes en Sciences Sociales, Paris; the Institut National d'Histoire de l'Art (INHA), Paris; National Taiwan Normal University, Taipei; the Bibliotheca Hertziana, Max-Planck-Institut, Rome; and the Center for Advanced Study in the Visual Arts, National Gallery of Art, Washington. He has published widely on methodology and on Édouard Manet, Hans Holbein, Leon Battista Alberti, Ferdinand Hodler, Paul Klee, Ilya Kabakov, and Benedetto Varchi. His recent publications include *Ferdinand Hodler: Die Nacht, der Tag, die Wahrheit*, coauthored with Angelika Affentranger-Kirchrath (2019), and *Hodler und der Parallelismus* (2018).

JENS BAUMGARTEN is professor of art history at the Universidade Federal de Sao Paulo, Brazil. After studying art history and history in Hamburg and Florence and receiving postdoctoratal fellowships in Dresden, Mexico City, and Campinas (Brazil), he established one of the first autonomous departments of art history in Brazil. He was a visiting scholar at the Getty Research Institute (2010) and at the Kunsthistorisches Institut in Florence (2016–2017). He is a member of the Brazilian Committee of Art History (CBHA). He specializes in early modern art history of Latin America and Europe as well as in historiography of art and in visual culture and its theoretical and methodological contexts. He is the author of *Konfession, Bild und Macht: Visualisierung als katholisches Herrschafts- und Disziplinierungskonzept in Rom und im habsburgischen Schlesien (1560–1740)* (2004) and is preparing a book on visual systems in colonial Brazil and another on comparisons between Brazilian and Filipino art history.

PAUL BINSKI is professor of the history of medieval art at Cambridge University. He was Slade Professor, Oxford University, 2006–2007, and he also taught at Yale University and Manchester University. He is a fellow of the British Academy and a corresponding fellow of the Medieval Academy of America, and he delivered the Paul Mellon Lectures at the National Gallery, London, and at Yale University in 2002–2003 and the British Academy Aspects of Art Lecture in 2001. His publications include *Gothic Wonder: Art, Artifice and the Decorated Style, 1290–1350* (2014); *Becket's Crown: Art and Imagination in Gothic England, 1170–1300* (2004); and, most recently, *Gothic Sculpture* (2019). He now writes widely on general issues of aesthetics, rhetoric, and the visual arts.

ROBERT BORN is a research fellow at the Leibniz-Institut für Geschichte und Kultur des östlichen Europa (GWZO) in Leipzig. He was visiting professor of art and architectural history at the Humboldt-Universität zu Berlin in 2010–2011. In addition to his research and teaching, he curated (together with Guido Messling and Michał Dziewulski) the exhibition *The Sultan's World: The Ottoman Orient in Renaissance Art*, shown in 2015 at the Palais des Beaux-Arts, Brussels, and the Muzeum Narodowe, Kraków, for which he coauthored and edited the catalog. He is also coeditor of the volumes *Apologeten der Vernichtung oder "Kunstschützer"? Kunsthistoriker der Mittelmächte im Ersten Weltkrieg* (2017); *The Ottoman Orient in Renaissance Culture* (2015); and *Die Kunsthistoriographien in Ostmitteleuropa und der nationale Diskurs* (2004).

HORST BREDEKAMP is professor of art history at Humboldt-Universität zu Berlin. He founded the project The Technical Image at the Hermann von Helmholtz-Zentrum für Kulturtechnik, which developed a theory of pictorial knowledge in science and technology and medical visualization. His research ranges from antiquity to contemporary art, with a focus on iconoclastic fury, Romanesque sculpture, art of the Renaissance and mannerism, political iconography, and art and technology. His recent publications include *Warburg, Cassirer und Einstein im Gespräch: Kepler als Schlüssel der Moderne* (2015); *Galileis denkende Hand: Form und Forschung um 1600* (2015); *Der schwimmende Souverän: Karl der Große und die Bildpolitik des Körpers* (2014); and *Leibnitz und die Revolution der Gartenkunst: Herrenhausen, Versailles und die Philosophie der Blätter* (2012).

ADI EFAL-LAUTENSCHLÄGER is an independent scholar and lecturer who works in Germany, France, and Israel. Her publications include *Habitus as Method: Revisiting a Scholastic Theory of Art* (2017) and *Figural Philology: Panofsky and the Science of Things* (2016). Her current research involves the concept of method in seventeenth-century Cartesianism, art historiography, and psychotherapy and the concept of habitude in nineteenth-century French philosophy.

MONICA JUNEJA is professor of global art history at Universität Heidelberg. She has been a fellow of the Maison des Sciences de l'Homme, the German Academic Exchange Service, the Alexander von Humboldt Foundation, and the Volkswagen Foundation. Her areas of research span the fields of European and Indian studies and include practices of visual representation, the disciplinary trajectories of art history in South Asia, gender and political iconography in modern France, and the interface between Christianization, religious identities, and cultural practices in early modern South Asia. Her recent publications include *Architecture in Medieval India: Forms, Contexts, Histories* (2015), *Disaster as Image: Iconographies and Media Strategies across Europe and Asia*, coedited with Gerrit Jasper Schenk (2014); and *Die Universalität der Kunstgeschichte?*, coedited with Matthias Bruhn and Elke A. Werner (2012).

PETER KRIEGER is research professor at the Instituto de Investigaciones Estéticas and professor of art history and architecture at the Universidad Nacional Autónoma de México. He was the 2016 Aby Warburg Visiting Professor at the Warburg-Haus, Hamburg. His research work and publications encompass visual studies and history of citics and landscapes in the twentieth and twenty-first centuries, aesthetics and ecology of megacities, and political iconography of urban landscapes and architecture. His recent publications include *Epidemias visuales* (2017), *Megalópolis: La modernizacion de la cuidad de México en el siglo xx* (2007), and *El Nuevo Sueño de la Malinche: Reflexiones sobre globalidad, cultura e identidad de la megápolis* (2006).

EVONNE LEVY is professor of Renaissance and baroque art and architecture at the University of Toronto. Together with Tristan Weddigen, she spearheaded a decade-long project on Wölfflin's *Principles of Art History*, which included a website (http://thewolfflin-project.utoronto.ca); a student-directed documentary film, *Reading Wölfflin's* Principles: *Toronto Stories* (2015); a global webinar; and the coediting of a new English translation and the book's first critical edition: *Principles of Art History: The Problem of the Development of Style in Early Modern Art* (2015). She is the author of *Baroque and the Political Language of Formalism (1845–1945): Burckhardt, Wölfflin, Gurlitt, Brinckmann, Sedlmayr* (2016) and *Propaganda and the Jesuit Baroque* (2004) and coeditor of *Material Bernini* (2016), *The Lexikon of the Hispanic Baroque: Transatlantic Exchange and Transformation* (2014), and *Bernini's Biographies: Critical Essays* (2007).

ERIC MICHAUD is *directeur d'études* at the École des Hautes Etudes en Sciences Sociales, Paris. His research interests focus on the relationships among art, politics, propaganda, and the anthropological notion of race. He is the author of *Les Invasions barbares: Une généalogie de l'histoire de l'art* (2015; Spanish translation, 2017; English translation, 2019); *The Cult of Art in Nazi Germany* (English translation, 2004; Spanish translation, 2009); *Histoire de l'art: Une discipline à ses frontières* (2005); and *Fabriques de l'homme nouveau, de Léger à Mondrian* (1997).

ANDREA PINOTTI is professor of aesthetics, Piero Martinetti Department of Philosophy, Università degli Studi di Milano. His research focuses on image theory and visual culture studies, memorialization and monumentality, phenomenological aesthetics, empathy theory, and the morphological tradition from Goethe to the present day. His publications include *Cultura visual: Immagini sguardi media dispositivi*, coauthored with Antonio Somaini (2016); *Empathie: Histoire d'une idée de Platon au post-humain* (2016); *Memorie del neutro: Morfologia dell'immagine in Aby Warburg* (2001); and *Il corpo dello stile: Storia dell'arte come storia dell'estetica a partire da Semper, Riegl, Wölfflin* (1998). In 2018 he was awarded the Wissenschaftspreis der Aby-Warburg-Stiftung in Hamburg. He is currently directing a project under a European Research Council Advanced Grant titled An-iconology: History, Theory, and Practices of Environmental Images.

SHIRAHARA YUKIKO is chief curator of the Nezu Institute of Fine Arts in Toyko. She was previously John A. McCone Foundation Curator of Asian Art at the Seattle Art Museum, where she organized the ground-breaking 2007 exhibition *Japan Envisions the West: 16th–19th-Century Japanese Art from Kobe City Museum*. Other notable exhibitions include *Five Masterpieces of Asian Art: The Story of Their Conservation* (2007), *Elegant Earth: Photographs by Johsel Namkung* (2006), and *Mountain Dreams: Contemporary Ceramics* by Yoon Kwang-cho (2004). Her research has focused on relationships between Japanese and Chinese artists during the medieval period and between Japan and Korea through tumulus murals, Buddhist murals and paintings, portraits, and ink paintings. She recently published *The Fragrant Sublime: Koryŏ Buddhist Paintings* with Nezu Bijutsukan, Sen'oku Hakukokan, and Yōko Sanekata (2017).

TRISTAN WEDDIGEN has been director of the Bibliotheca Hertziana since 2017 and professor of the history of early modern art at the University of Zurich since 2009. His publications include the monograph *Raffaels Papageienzimmer* (2006) and the edited volumes Heinrich Wölfflin, *Principles of Art History: The Problem of the Development of Style in Early Modern Art* (2015); *Benedetto Varchi: Paragone* (2013); *Unfolding the Textile Medium* (2011); *Metatexile* (2010); *Functions and Decorations* (2003); *Federico Zuccaro* (2000); and *Barocke Inszenierung* (1999).

ZHANG PING is lecturer in art history in the College of Fine Arts, East China Normal University, Shanghai. In addition to teaching courses in Chinese art history, classical Chinese literature on art, and the history of European and American art, she has published articles on the study of Chinese art in German-speaking countries, art theory in the first half of the twentieth century in Vienna, and neuroarthistory. She also translated into Chinese Julius von Schlosser's *Die Wiener Schule der Kunstgeschichte* (2013) and Jessica Rawson's *Chinese Ornaments: The Lotus and the Dragon* (2019).

Barasch, Moshe, 4, 236–241; *Icon*, 238; *Machshevet haomanut ba dorot haacharonim* (*Approaches to Art*), 237

Bargellini, Clara, 118n26

Barilli, Renato, 226–227

baroque style: in Brazil, 282–284; characteristics of, 5; classical vs., 6, 30, 54, 75–76, 77, 78, 83–84, 86–87, 89, 93, 129, 153; in Cuba, 93; Dvořák's conception of, 54; in Eastern Bloc countries, 267–269; European conference devoted to, 85–87, 203; German art linked to, by Wölfflin, 205–206; Hispanic, 73, 75–77, 75, 85–91, 93–94, 113–116, 285–286; hybrid, 85, 91, 94; Levy on, 282–284; in Mexico, 113–114; modern art compared to, 52–53; Nietzsche's conception of, 114; origins of, 50, 51, 54; Riegl's conception of, 51–53; Wölfflin's conception of, 50–53, 75–76, 87, 89, 114, 143, 205–206, 242, 285–286

Bar Or, Galia, 243

Barr, Alfred H., 152–154, 163n84, 240; *Cubism and Abstract Art*, 152–153, 152; "Italian Sources of Three Great Traditions of European Painting," 153, 154

Barreiro, Plutarco, La Esperanza de María en la Resurrección del Señor, 116

Barrett, Douglas, 173

Basel school, 240–241

Basler Zeitung (newspaper), 32

Bauhaus, 37

Baxandall, Michael, 29, 131–134, 158, 195, 227

Baxter, Sylvester, *Spanish-Colonial Architecture in Mexico*, 91

Bazin, Germain, 96, 204, 209

Beiersdorf, Zbigniew, 255

Bell, Clive, 172, 219, 225

Belvedere (magazine), 58

Bembék, 262

Ben-Ami, Nachman, 236

Ben Gurion, David, 235

Benjamin, Walter, 38–39, 114, 227, 282

Berenson, Bernard, 121, 131, 186, 218, 219, 223, 225, 262

Bergson, Henri, 81, 89; *Italian Painters of the Renaissance*, 122

Berlin, Germany, Wölfflin in, 19–24

Bernini, Gianlorenzo, 51

Betjeman, John, 129–130

Białostocki, Jan, *Historia sztuki wśród nauk humanistycznych* (Art history among the humanistic disciplines), 255

Bialik (publisher), 235–237, 239, 244

Bialik, Haim Nachman, 236

Bier, Justus, 144

Bierbauer, Virgil (Borbiró), 261

Birdwood, George, 171

Birnbaum, Vojtěch, 3

Blanc, Charles, 203

Bloch, Ernst, 205

Bloomsbury group, 121

Blower, Jonathan, 298

Boase, T. S. R., 126

Bodonyi, József, 266–267

Bois, Yve-Alain, 154

Bonola, Roberto, 71

Borenius, Tancred, 123

Born, Max, 71

Born, Wolfgang, 144, 145–146

Bottari, Stefano, 224

Boughton, Alice, *Roger Fry*, 120

Bourdieu, Pierre, 2

Brauer, Heinrich, 86

Brazil: art history and criticism in, 5–6, 281–286, 287n21; reception of *Principles* in, 281–286

Bredekamp, Horst, 7

Breysig, Kurt, *Stufenbau und die Gesetze der Weltgeschichte*, 266

Brinckmann, A. E., 9, 144, 206–207, 219; *Geist der Nationen*, 206–207

British Broadcasting Corporation (BBC), 129

Brown, Marshall, 6, 157, 158

Bruckmann, Hugo and Elsa, viii

Bruckmann Verlag, viii, 142

Bryson, Norman, 195

Buber, Martin, 235, 236, 239, 244n4

Buchloh, Benjamin, 154

Buchtal, Hugo, 86

Bühler, Richard, 37

Burckhardt, Jacob, 51, 52, 54, 87, 123, 127, 129, 185–186, 195, 201, 206, 207, 224, 227, 236, 237, 256; *Die Kultur der Renaissance in Italien*, 121

Burlington Magazine, 121, 124

Buschiazzo, Mario J., 95

C

Cahill, James, 297

Cai Yuanpei, 291

Calabrese, Omar, 227

Camacho, Alberto, 92

Carnegie Corporation, 143

Carpentier, Alejo, 93–94

Carracci, 51

Cassou, Jean, 85; *Apologie de l'art baroque*, 87

Castedo, Leopoldo, *A History of Latin American Art from Pre-Columbian Times to the Present*, 85

Castiglione, Baldassare, *Il libro del cortegiano*, 53

Castro, Martha de, 93

Catholic Church, 143

Cecchi, Emilio, 114

Chakrabarty, Dipesh, 173

Champa, Kermit, 154, 155, 157; *"Masterpiece" Studies*, 157; *Studies in Early Impressionism*, 154

Charles Eliot Norton Lectures, Harvard University, 39

Chastel, André, 204–205, 207–208

China: art of, 146–147, 154, 297; reception of *Principles* in, 3, 9, 291–298

Chino Shōshō, 188

Chubinashvili, Giorgi, 3, 7

Clark, Kenneth, *122*, 123–124, 126, 133

Clark, T. J., *131*, *134*, *155*, 157

classical style: baroque vs., 6, 30, 54, 75–76, 77, 78, 83–84, 86–87, 89, 93, 129, 153; characteristics of, 5; Italian art linked to, by Wölfflin, 205–206; Japanese art and, 193; normative character of, 127, 237; Wölfflin's conception of, 201, 205–206, 242

Codrington, K. de B., 172

Cohn, William, 12n13

College Art Association (United States), 141

Collobi, Licia, 224

colonial art and architecture: in Brazil, 282–284, 286; in Cuba, 93; in India, 174; in Latin America, 8, 72–76, 78–79, 81, 83, 90; in Mexico, 91

comparative method: criticisms of, 6, 127, 131, 152; digital projection as disruption of, 5, 6, 131; double slide projection as tool for, 5, 21, 128; global extension of, 168–169; influence of *Principles* on, vii, 5, 37, 87, 127, 130–131, 249

Comte, Auguste, 224, 262

Concinnitas: Beiträge zum Problem des Klassischen (festschrift), 33

Condori, José, 95. *See also* San Lorenzo, Potosí

Congrès international d'architecture moderne (CIAM), 39, 261, 266

Congreso Panamericano de Arquitectos, 75, 76, 77

Congress of the Comité International d'Histoire de l'Art (CIHA), 271

content, in relation to form, 58, 83, 92, 132, 170, 204, 219, 223

Continental philosophy, 127

Coomaraswamy, Ananda, 172

Corn, Wanda, 146

Correggio, 50–52

Costa, Lúcio, 95

Coster, Howard: *Herbert Read*, 124; *Kenneth Clark*, 122

Courajod, Louis, 201, 202

Courtauld Institute of Art, 4, 123, 131

Crary, Jonathan, 158, 227

Cret, Paul, 143

Croatia, 7–8

Croce, Benedetto, 4, 5, 6, 58–59, 124, 208, 218, 220–225, 236, 237, 263, 266

Cropper, Elizabeth, 131, 156

Crossley, Paul, 131

Cuba: national character of art of, 92; reception of *Principles* in, 4, 92–94

Curtius, Ludwig, 85

Czechoslovakia, reception of *Principles* in, 3

D

D'Ancona, Paolo, 3; *Antologia della moderna critica d'arte* (with Fernanda Wittgens), 218, 218

Davis, Whitney, 158

Décades (summer academies), 85–87, 89, 203

Deinhard, Hanna Levy. *See* Levy, Hanna

Deleuze, Gilles, 210–211

Dempsey, Charles, 156

Demus, Otto, 142

Desjardins, Paul, 85–87

Dessoir, Max, 225, 252, 293

Detroit Institute of Arts, 143

Deutsche Gesellschaft für Anthropologie, Ethnologie und Urgeschichte, 35

Dewey, John, 93, 149, 236

Diez, Ernst, 142

Dilthey, Wilhelm, 81, 209, 226

Di Monte, Michele, 227

Dinur, Ben-Zion, 235, 244n4

Doménech, Rafael: *El nacionalismo en arte*, 85; *Tratado de técnica ornamental*, 72

Dong Qichang, 297

Dorfles, Gillo, 225–226, 227

D'Ors, Eugenio, 85–91, 93–94, 96, 114, 203; *Lo barroco*, 88; *Du baroque*, 86–89, 89

drawing, 21–22

Drummond de Andrade, Carlos, 95

Dürer, Albrecht, 96, 292

Dvořák, Max, 3, 4, 50, 53–55, 57, 63n56, 82–83, 123, 124, 186, 218, 237, 249, 256, 263–264, 270, 282, 284–286; *Kunstgeschichte als Geistesgeschichte*, 55, 252–253, 255

E

Ebbinghaus, Hermann, 20

Éber, László, 262

Echeverría, Bolívar, 112

École de Genève, 209

Eikhenbaum, Boris, 4, 268

Einfühlung (empathy), 81–82, 85, 91, 92, 134, 225

Einstein, Albert, 187

Einstein, Carl, *Negerplastik*, vii

Elefánt, Olga, 262

Elkins, James, 158, 174–175

Elsner, Jaś, 157, 174

Engels, Friedrich, 268, 269

England: art history as a discipline in, 125–127, 131–132, 134; reception of *Principles* in, 3–4, 121–135

epistemes, 210

Espasa Calpe, 111

ethnicity. *See* race/ethnicity

Ettlinger, Leopold D., 8, 10

evolution, 35, 88

F

Faensen, Hubert, 7, 17

Falke, Jakob von, *Geschichte des modernen Geschmacks*, 114

Falkenheim, Jacqueline, 122

Fan Jingzhong, 294–295, 295, 297; *Meishushi de xingzhuang* (The shapes of art history), 295, 298; *Zhonghua zhu yun* (The book of bamboo), 297

Fasola, Giusta Nicco, 217–218

Fenollosa, Ernest F., 182–185, *182*, 193, 196n7
Fernández, Justino, *Coatlicue*, 113
Ferriss, Hugh, *The Metropolis of Tomorrow*, 82
Fiedler, Konrad, 4, 81, 122, 206, 217–221, 224, 237, 239, 262; *Aphorismen*, 225
Fierens, Paul, 86
Finsler, Hans, 35, 36; *Drei Eier Negativ*, *35*
Fischer, Otto, 12n13
Focillon, Henri, 5, 85, 132, 151, 204, 205–206, 219, 225, 281–283, 286; *L'Art des sculpteurs romans*, 205; *La Vie des formes*, 6, 86, 204, 205–206
Fokker, Timon Henricus, 86
folk culture, 18, 32, 254, 261
Fong, Wen C., 147, 154, 297; *Images of the Mind*, 148
form, in relation to content, 58, 83, 92, 132, 157, 170, 204, 219, 223
formalism: Brazilian art and, 285; criticisms of, viii, 4–7, 17, 56, 79, 112, 113, 141; Fry and, 121; geometric, 72–75; Greenberg and, 153–154, 285; Guido and, 72–75, 77, 80, 82–83, 85; iconography/ iconology in relation to, 3, 112, 144, 148–149; contribution of *Principles* to, viii, 1, 3, 4–8, 17, 49–59, 77, 79, 82, 92, 112, 113, 147, 149–159, 167–168, 174, 211, 237, 239–240, 243–244, 268, 285; psychological, 74–75, 81; Russian, 268; South Asian art and, 167, 172–173; style analysis in relation to, 144; in US art history, 149, 152–158; Vienna School and, 49–59
Formgefühl (sense of form), 34, 96, 202
Formwille. See will to form
Foster, Hal, 154
Foucault, Michel, 209–211
Foucher, Alfred, 170
Francastel, Pierre, 206–209; *L'Histoire de l'art, instrument de la propagande germanique*, 208; *Peinture et société*, 208, *208*
France: national character of art of, 201; reception of *Principles* in, 29, 85, 201–211; Renaissance style in, *78*
Franco, Francisco, 87
Frank, Waldo, *The Re-Discovery of America*, 94
Frankfurt School, 7, 158, 270
Frankl, Paul, 6, 8, 79, 82, 92, 132, 144, 160n32; *Gothic Architecture*, 131
Freedberg, David, 134
Freedberg, Sydney J., *156*, 157
Frege, Gottlob, 127
Freud, Sigmund, 124
Frey, Dagobert, 53, 56, 130
Freyre, Gilberto, 286
Fried, Michael, 121, 154
Friedlaender, Walter, 86, 89, 144, 147, 162n59, 203
Friedmann, Hermann, *Die Welt der Formen*, 252
Friedrich-Wilhelms-Universität, Berlin, 20. *See also* University of Berlin
Fries, Willy, 32
Fry, Roger, *120*, 121–123, 126, 127, 129, 131, 133, 141, 153, 172, 219, 225; "The Artist's Vision," 122; "An Essay in Aesthetics," 122

Fukada Yasukazu, 186, 197n21
Fukuchi Mataichi, 183
Fyodorov-Davydov, Aleksey, 264

G

Galilei Circle, 262
Games, Stephen, 129
Gamzu, Haim, 242
Gantner, Joseph, 5, 8, 32, 36–37, 38, 39–41, 194–195, 206, 224, 240–241; *Revision der Kunstgeschichte*, 37, 38
Gardner, Helen, *Art through the Ages*, 142, 143
Gate of the Sun, Tiwanaku, Bolivia, 72, 73
Gazette des Beaux-Arts (journal), 203–204
Geistesgeschichte (cultural history), 4, 7, 54–55, 83, 145
genetics, 88
Gentile, Giovanni, 217, 224
Géo-Charles, 95
geography, as influence on style, 75–76, 80, 82, 128, 131, 174
geometric formalism, 72–75
George Bell and Sons, 142
Georgia, reception of *Principles* in, 3, 6–7, 8
Gerevich, Tibor, 266–267
German idealism, 82, 127
Germany, reception of *Principles* in, 3, 7, 17–18
germ plasm theory, 88
Geršenzon-Čegodaeva, Natalija, 271
Gerstenberg, Kurt, 141, 202
Gessner, Salomon, 31
Geymüller, Heinrich von, *Die Baukunst der Renaissance in Frankreich*, 78, 79
Ghyka, Matila C., 89
Giedion, Sigfried, 31, 32, 36–41, 38, 85, 144; *Bauen in Frankreich, bauen in Eisen, bauen in Eisenbeton*, 38, 39; *The Eternal Present*, 41, *41*; *Mechanization Take Command*, 40; *Space, Time and Architecture*, 39–40, *40*
Giedion-Welcker, Carola, 40; *Moderne Plastik* (*Modern Sculpture*), 36, 37
Giordano, Luca, 222
Glaser, Curt, 12n13
global art history, 158, 167, 174–176, 178n37, 285
Goethe, Johann Wolfgang von, 58, 237
Goldschmidt, Adolph, 21, 22, *22*, 265
Goldschmidt, Clara, 209
Goldziher, Ignác, 236
Göller, Adolf, 132
Gombosi, György, 267
Gombrich, E. H., 5, 6, 7, 21, *125*, 126–127, 131–132, 134, 270, 295; *Art and Illusion*, 128; *In Search of Cultural History*, 127; *Norm and Form*, 127, 132, 152; *The Sense of Order*, 128; *The Story of Art*, 239
Gomes Machado, Lourival, 283, 285
Gonçalves, Nuno, 90
Gonse, Louis, 196n7
Gosztonyi, Ferenc, 262
Gothic art, 8

Prinzhorn, Hans, 143
psychological formalism, 75, 81
pure visibility, 4, 5, 6, 218, 220, 222–223, 225, 263

R

Rabinovszky, Máriusz, 261
race/ethnicity: in art historical discourse, 202; European
    art historians on, 205–207; Latin American art/archi-
    tecture and, 80; Rojas's theories of, 73; Strzygowski's
    theory of art and, 55–56; theories of, viii, 130, 206;
    Wölfflin's theories of, viii, 8, 35–36, 56, 130, 151,
    202, 206–209. *See also* miscegenation; national
    character
radio, 129
Ragghianti, Carlo Ludovico, 224–225
Ramos, Samuel, 113
Raphael, 50–52, 84, 121, 132
Raphael, Max, 7, 86, 206, 281–283, 286
Rassenstil (racial style), 202
Rauschenberg, Robert, 154
Raymond, Marcel and Claire, 29, 209
Read, Herbert, ix, 124, *124*, 126, 127, 133; *Education
    through Art*, 124; *The Meaning of Art*, 124
Realismo mágico, 93
reception, concept of, 2, 29
reception of *Principles of Art History*: in Brazil,
    281–286; in China, 291–298; in Cuba, 4, 92–94;
    early, vii, 22; in England, 121–135; in France,
    201–211; Hispanic, 70–96; history of, viii, 1–3,
    10–11, 22–23; in Hungary, 261–272; international,
    5–9; in Israel, 235–244; in Italy, 217–228; in Japan,
    181, 190–195; in Latin America, 70–96; in Mexico,
    91–92, 111–114; negative/critical, viii, 1–2, 4–8,
    10, 17, 22, 54, 56, 58–59, 127, 132, 141, 147,
    149–152, 154–158, 207–209, 219–224, 263, 265,
    269–271, 282; obstacles to, 111–112; in other disci-
    plines, 22, 29, 132–133, 209, 254, 261–263,
    267–268; periods of decline in, 41; in Poland,
    249–256; politics and, 126–128; positive, 2, 18, 22,
    54, 143, 221, 225–227, 266, 271; readers' role in, 2;
    recent revival in, 41; reception of, 29–31; in South
    Asia, 167–176; in Soviet Union, 4, 6–7, 262,
    267–271; in Spain, 85–91, 111; in Switzerland,
    29–41; in United States, 141–159; by Vienna School,
    49–59. See also *Principles of Art History* (Wölfflin):
    publication and sales of
Rembrandt van Rijn, 50, 292
Rempel, Lazar' I., 269
Representations (journal), 18
Revista de occidente (journal), 71, 75, 93
*Revista do Serviço do Patrimônio Histórico e Artístico
    Nacional* (journal), 280, 283
Revue de Genève (journal), 86
Rewald, John, 154
Reynolds, Joshua, 121
Richards, I. A., 133
Rickert, Heinrich, 71

Riegl, Alois, 3, 8, 9, 10, 49, 51–57, 61n24, 71, 75, 77,
    82, 92–93, 121, 123–125, 127, 131, 132, 142, 149,
    151, 157, 191, 202, 205, 219, 223, 227, 237, 239,
    249, 251, 253, 256, 262, 263, 266, 270, 293; *Ent-
    stehung der Barockkunst in Rom (Origins of Baroque
    Art in Rome)*, 51–54; *Historische Grammatik der
    bildenden Künste*, 52; *Das holländische Gruppenpor-
    trät*, 52; *Spätrömische Kunstindustrie*, 224
Rintelen, Friedrich, 30
Rivera, Diego, 84
Rochlitz, Rainer, 207
Rodenwaldt, Gerhart, 8
Roh, Franz, 84, 93
Rojas, Ricardo, 71, 73, 75, 79, 93; *Eurindia*, 73–74
Rojkind Arquitectos, Liverpool Interlomas, Mexico City,
    110
Romania, 7
Rose, Hans, 4
Rose, Sam, 123
Rosenberg, Jakob, 144, 150
Rosenthal, Gertrude, 160n32
Rothacker, Erich, 22
Rouart-Valéry, Agathe, 86
Rousset, Jean, 209
Rowland, Benjamin, 147
Royal Academy of Arts, London, 172–173
Royal Society of the Arts, London, 171
Rubens, Peter Paul, 75
Ruskin, John, 123, 130, 133
Russell, Bertrand, 127

S

Sagrario, Catedral Metropolitana, Mexico City, 74
Salis, Arnold von, *Die Kunst der Griechen*, 29
Salvini, Roberto, *La critica dell'arte moderna*, 219
Sánchez Rivero, Ángel, 71, 74, 75
Sandau, Ernst, 96
San Lorenzo, Potosí, 73, *73*, 94, 95
San Sebastián Church, Cuzco, 74
Santa Clara, Querétaro, 114, *115*
Sauerländer, Wilibald, 162n68
Saussure, Ferdinand de, 226
Sawaki Yomokichi, 9, 10, 181, 185–188, *185*, 195,
    197n16
Schapiro, Meyer, 8, 149, 152, 154, 207; "Style," 151
Scharff, Edwin, 43n26; *Heinrich Wölfflin*, 30, 31
schemas, 217–219, 221–228
Scheyer, Ernst, 143, 160n32
Schiff, Fritz, 243
Schlink, Wilhelm, 35–36
Schlosser, Julius von, 5, 32, 36, 57–59, 127, 220, 263,
    266; "'Stilgeschichte' und 'Sprachgeschichte' der
    bildenden Kunst," 59; "Von Heinrich Wölfflins
    Sendung," 58
Schmarsow, August, 4, 10, 50, 52, 53, 82, 128, 132,
    219, 262
Schmidt, Georg, 30
Schmoll genannt Eisenwerth, Joseph A., 255
Schnaase, Karl, 207, 208

Schopenhauer, Arthur, 123

Schubert, Otto, 90; *Geschichte des Barock in Spanien*, 75

Schwabe (publisher), 236, 249

Schwartz, Frederic J., 7, 158

Schwarz, Hans, *Nikolaus Pevsner*, 126

Schwarz, Moshe, 239

Schweizerischer Werkbund, 37

science. *See* art history, concepts and methods: scientific foundation as Wölfflin's goal; *Kunstwissenschaft*

Scott, Geoffrey, 151

Second Vienna School. *See* New Vienna School

Sedlmayr, Hans, 5, 6, 56–59, 263; "Kunstwerk und Kunstgeschichte," 57; "Probleme der Interpretation," 57; "Die Quintessenz der Lehren Riegls," 56–57; *Zu einer strengen Kunstwissenschaft*, 57

seeing: art historical theories of, 227; in global art history, 175–176; in Japanese art history discipline, 195; race/ethnicity/national character and, 203; in Wölfflin's conception of art history, 4, 5, 17, 21, 23, 32, 87, 96, 129, 133, 145, 151, 158, 172, 175, 191, 203, 220–222, 227, 237–238, 263, 266

Segota, Durdica, 113

Semper, Gottfried, 37, 81, 132

Shiff, Richard, 156–157

Shirakaba group, 9, 187–188

Shiva Nataraja, 170, *172*

Shmit, Fyodor, 264–265

Shone, Richard, with John-Paul Stonard, *The Books That Shaped Art History*, 295

Shtambok, Anatoly, 267–269

Silbergeld, Jerome, 147

Simmel, Georg, 209, 225, 262

Siqueiros, David Alfaro, 84

Sitwell, Sacheverell, *Southern Baroque Art*, 91, 94

slide projection: art historical uses of, vii, 5, 20–21; double, vii, 5, 21; Wölfflin's use of, vii, 20–21

Smith, David, 153

Smith, Robert C., 85, 95

social Darwinism, 183

social history of art, 7, 112, 151–152, 155, 271

Society for the Study of Poetic Language, 268

sociology of art, 281, 286

Sokołowski, Marian, 253

Sommerfeld, Arnold, 145

Soto y Sagarra, Luis de, 4, 9, 92–93; *Filosofía de la historia del arte*, 92–93

South Asia: art of, 166–176; reception of *Principles* in, 167–171

Soviet Union: art historical practices in, 249–250, 264–265, 269; reception of *Principles* in, 4, 6–7, 262, 267–271

Spain: baroque style in, 85–89; national character of art of, 85–87; reception of *Principles* in, 85–91, 111

Spencer, Herbert, 183

Spengler, Oswald, 71, 75, 79, 80, 84, 88, 93, 265–266, 270; *Der Untergang des Abendlandes*, 71

Stadler, Hans Conrad, Haus Sihlgarten, Zurich, 32, 33

Staiger, Emil, 41; *Grundbegriffe der Poetik*, 30

Standing Bosatsu (bodhisattva), *192*

State Institute of Art History, Leningrad, 264–265

Stechow, Wolfgang, 147

Steinberg, Leo, 147, 154

Steiner, George, 135

Stettler, Michael, 32, 33

Stokes, Adrian, 123, 129, 219

Stonard, John-Paul, with Richard Shone, *The Books That Shaped Art History*, 295

Strauss, Gerhard, 271

Streichman, Yehezkel, 242; *Untitled*, *240*

Strich, Fritz, 261, 267, 268; *Deutsche Klassik und Romantik*, 29–30

Strossmayer Gallery, Zagreb, 9–10

structuralism, 201, 211

Strzygowski, Josef, 3, 4, 49–51, 54, 55–56, 142, 205; *Die Krisis der Geisteswissens*, 56; "Norden und Renaissance," 56; *Das Werden des Barock bei Raphael und Correggio*, 50

style: in Chinese art, 292–293; criticisms of concept of, 112, 147; double root of, 4, 58, 66n97, 132, 170, 177n21, 220–221, 252; formalism in relation to, 144; institutional role of, 174; in Japanese art history discipline, 185; Kubler on, 152; national character of, 78, 92, 130, 145, 202; Panofsky on, 23; psychology of, 124, 128; Schlosser on, 58–59; in US art history discipline, 151–152, 157–158; Wölfflin's concept of, 6, 7, 9, 58–59, 71, 78, 87, 129, 130, 132, 144, 147, 150, 151, 174, 202–203, 226, 240, 252, 292

Subieta Sagárnaga, Luis, 95

Summers, David, 158

Sunday Circle, 262–263, 271

Sur (journal), 94

Swarzenski, Hans, 160n32

Switzerland, reception of *Principles* in, 29–41

Swoboda, Karl Maria, 57, 59

Szekfű, Gyula, 267

Szentkirályi, Zoltán, 271

Szerb, Antal, 267

Szydłowski, Tadeusz, 253, 255

T

Tagliabue, Guido Morpurgo, 225

Taine, Hippolyte, 71, 75, 77, 80, 82, 83, 87, 93, 202

Talowski, Teodor, 255

Tanaka Hidemichi, *Nihon bijutsu zenshi* (A history of Japanese art), 198n48

Tapié, Victor Lucien, *Baroque et classicisme*, 89

Temple of Venus of Baalbek, 89

Teng Gu, 9, 291–294, 292, 297; *Tangsong huihuashi* (History of painting in the Tang and Song dynasties), 292, 292, 294

Tenpyō style, 9, 184–185, 190–193

Tér és forma (journal), 261

Theodoro da Silva, Janice, 281, 285–286

theory: and detheorization, 244; in US art history discipline, 149–152

Thienemann, Tivadar, 267

Thiersch, August, 72

Wölfflin, Heinrich: in Berlin, 19–23; birthday celebrations for, 31, 32, 33, 38, 58, 71; career of, 19, 31–32; character and personality of, 19, 33, 128; death of, 153; honors and awards received by, 38; house of, 32, 33; images of, *x*, *20*, *30*, *33*, *95*; influence of, viii, ix, 1–2, 8; influences on, 4, 20; as lecturer, 20–21, *20*, 127, 128; and national character, 35, 56, 96, 145, 202–209, 222, 266; as outsider, 58, 134; positive assessments of, 18; and psychology, 20, 22, 71, 82; racial theories of, viii, 8, 35–36, 56, 130, 151, 202, 206–209; relationships with women, 19; self-assessment of, 33; sketch of San Lorenzo, Florence, *21*, 22; students of, 3, 8, 9, 10, 11n11, 29–30, 32, 36–41, 85, 86, 128, 141, 144–149, 209, 227, 253, 261, 264; style concept of, 6, 7, 9, 58–59, 71, 78, 87, 129, 130, 132, 144, 147, 150, 151, 174, 202–203, 226, 240, 252, 292; in Zurich, 31–41

Wölfflin, Heinrich, writings and lectures: *Albrecht Dürer, Handzeichnungen*, 219; *Das Erklären von Kunstwerken*, 31, 34, 59, 218, 225, 243; foreword to La Roche's *Indische Baukunst*, 168–169; *Gedanken zur Kunstgeschichte*, 57; "Die geschichtliche Betrachtung der Kunst," 32; "Italien und das deutsche Formgefühl," 34, 56, 190, 222; *Die Jugendwerke des Michelangelo*, 49–50; *Die klassische Kunst (Classic Art)*, 29, 31, 49–50, 52–54, 71, 121, 124, 132, 133, 141, 145, 147, 157, 189–190, 193, 201, 203, 217, 218, 220, 224, 253, 255, 268, 271, 295; *Die Kunst Albrecht Dürers*, 59, 207; *Die Kunst der Renaissance: Italien und das deutsche Formgefühl (The Sense of Form in Art)*, 34–35, *34*, 58, 219, 266, 268; "'Kunstgeschichtliche Grundbegriffe': Eine Revision," 23, 32, 219; "Das Problem des Stils in der bildenden Kunst," 22; "Pro Domo," 211; "Prolegomena to a Psychology of Architecture," 22, 158, 202, 204, 224, 226, 262; *Renaissance und Barock*, 4, 49–51, 56, 71–72, 114, 203, 217–219, 261, 268, 281, 285, 295; "Revision," 20, 23, 32, 92, 203, 211, 218, 223, 224, 227, 250, 252; "Über das Erklären von Kunstwerken," 57; *Über Formentwicklung*, 219. See also *Principles of Art History* (Wölfflin)

Wollheim, Richard, 123, 132

world art history. *See* global art history

World Zionist Organization, 236

Worringer, Wilhelm, 8, 75, 79, 80–85, 87, 92–94, 96, 124, 125, 127, 131, 191, 202, 285; *Abstraktion und Einfühlung*, 55, 112–113; *Formprobleme der Gotik*, 55, 71, 87

Wu Daozi, 292

Wulf, Oskar, 22

Wundt, Wilhelm, 20

35 *The Architectural Historian in America,* edited by Elisabeth Blair MacDougall. Symposium Papers XIX, 1990

36 *The Pastoral Landscape,* edited by John Dixon Hunt. Symposium Papers XX, 1992

37 *American Art around 1900,* edited by Doreen Bolger and Nicolai Cikovsky Jr. Symposium Papers XXI, 1990

38 *The Artist's Workshop,* edited by Peter M. Lukehart. Symposium Papers XXII, 1993

39 *Stained Glass before 1700 in American Collections: Silver-Stained Roundels and Unipartite Panels (Corpus Vitrearum Checklist IV),* compiled by Timothy B. Husband. Monograph Series I, 1991

40 *The Feast of the Gods: Conservation, Examination, and Interpretation,* by David Bull and Joyce Plesters. Monograph Series II, 1990

41 *Conservation Research.* Monograph Series II, 1993

42 *Conservation Research: Studies of Fifteenth- to Nineteenth-Century Tapestry,* edited by Lotus Stack. Monograph Series II, 1993

43 Eius Virtutis Studiosi: *Classical and Postclassical Studies in Memory of Frank Edward Brown,* edited by Russell T. Scott and Ann Reynolds Scott. Symposium Papers XXIII, 1993

44 *Intellectual Life at the Court of Frederick II Hohenstaufen,* edited by William Tronzo. Symposium Papers XXIV, 1994

45 *Titian 500,* edited by Joseph Manca. Symposium Papers XXV, 1994

46 *Van Dyck 350,* edited by Susan J. Barnes and Arthur K. Wheelock Jr. Symposium Papers XXVI, 1994

47 *The Formation of National Collections of Art and Archaeology,* edited by Gwendolyn Wright. Symposium Papers XXVII, 1996

48 *Piero della Francesca and His Legacy,* edited by Marilyn Aronberg Lavin. Symposium Papers XXVIII, 1995

49 *The Interpretation of Architectural Sculpture in Greece and Rome,* edited by Diana Buitron-Oliver. Symposium Papers XXIX, 1997

50 *Federal Buildings in Context: The Role of Design Review,* edited by J. Carter Brown. Symposium Papers XXX, 1995

51 *Conservation Research 1995.* Monograph Series II, 1995

52 *Saint-Porchaire Ceramics,* edited by Daphne Barbour and Shelley Sturman. Monograph Series II, 1996

53 *Imagining Modern German Culture, 1889–1910,* edited by Françoise Forster-Hahn. Symposium Papers XXXI, 1996

54 *Engraved Gems: Survivals and Revivals,* edited by Clifford Malcolm Brown. Symposium Papers XXXII, 1997

55 *Vermeer Studies,* edited by Ivan Gaskell and Michiel Jonker. Symposium Papers XXXIII, 1998

56 *The Art of Ancient Spectacle,* edited by Bettina Bergmann and Christine Kondoleon. Symposium Papers XXXIV, 1999

57 *Conservation Research 1996/1997.* Monograph Series II, 1997

58 *Olmec Art and Archaeology in Mesoamerica,* edited by John E. Clark and Mary E. Pye. Symposium Papers XXXV, 2000, 2006

59 *The Treatise on Perspective: Published and Unpublished,* edited by Lyle Massey. Symposium Papers XXXVI, 2003

60 *Hans Holbein: Paintings, Prints, and Reception,* edited by Mark Roskill and John Oliver Hand. Symposium Papers XXXVII, 2001

61 *Italian Panel Painting of the Duecento and Trecento,* edited by Victor M. Schmidt. Symposium Papers XXXVIII, 2002

62 *Small Bronzes in the Renaissance,* edited by Debra Pincus. Symposium Papers XXXIX, 2001

63 *Moche Art and Archaeology in Ancient Peru,* edited by Joanne Pillsbury. Symposium Papers XL, 2001, 2005

64 *Large Bronzes in the Renaissance,* edited by Peta Motture. Symposium Papers XLI, 2003

65 *Tilman Riemenschneider, c. 1460–1531,* edited by Julien Chapuis. Symposium Papers XLII, 2004

66 *Circa 1700: Architecture in Europe and the Americas,* edited by Henry A. Millon. Symposium Papers XLIII, 2005

68 *Nationalism and French Visual Culture, 1870–1914,* edited by June Hargrove and Neil McWilliam. Symposium Papers XLV, 2005

69 *The Art of Natural History: Illustrated Treatises and Botanical Paintings, 1400–1850,* edited by Therese O'Malley and Amy R. W. Meyers. Symposium Papers XLVI, 2008

70 *Collecting Sculpture in Early Modern Europe*, edited by Nicholas Penny and Eike D. Schmidt. Symposium Papers XLVII, 2008

71 *Romare Bearden, American Modernist*, edited by Ruth Fine and Jacqueline Francis. Symposium Papers XLVIII, 2011

72 *French Genre Painting in the Eighteenth Century*, edited by Philip Conisbee. Symposium Papers XLIX, 2007

73 *A Modernist Museum in Perspective: The East Building, National Gallery of Art*, edited by Anthony Alofsin. Symposium Papers L, 2009

74 *Dialogues in Art History, from Mesopotamian to Modern: Readings for a New Century*, edited by Elizabeth Cropper. Symposium Papers LI, 2009

75 *The Woodcut in Fifteenth-Century Europe*, edited by Peter Parshall. Symposium Papers LII, 2009

76 *Orsanmichele and the History and Preservation of the Civic Monument*, edited by Carl Brandon Strehlke. Symposium Papers LIII, 2012

77 *Art and the Early Photographic Album*, edited by Stephen Bann. Symposium Papers LIV, 2011

78 *Modernism and Landscape Architecture*, edited by Therese O'Malley and Joachim Wolschke-Bulmahn. Symposium Papers LV, 2015

79 *Rediscovering the Ancient World on the Bay of Naples, 1710–1890*, edited by Carol C. Mattusch. Symposium Papers LVI, 2013

80 *The Artist in Edo*, edited by Yukio Lippit. Symposium Papers LVII, 2018

81 *The Civil War in Art and Memory*, edited by Kirk Savage. Symposium Papers LVIII, 2016

82 *The Global Reception of Heinrich Wölfflin's Principles of Art History*, edited by Evonne Levy and Tristan Weddigen. Symposium Papers LIX, 2020

Forthcoming

83 *The African American Art World in Twentieth-Century Washington, DC*, edited by Jeffrey C. Stewart. Symposium Papers LX

84 *Boundary Trouble: The Self-Taught Artist and American Avant-Gardes*, edited by Lynne Cooke. Symposium Papers LXI